Lecture Notes
in Business Information Processing 190

Series Editors

Wil van der Aalst
Eindhoven Technical University, Eindhoven, The Netherlands
John Mylopoulos
University of Trento, Povo, Italy
Michael Rosemann
Queensland University of Technology, Brisbane, QLD, Australia
Michael J. Shaw
University of Illinois, Urbana-Champaign, IL, USA
Clemens Szyperski
Microsoft Research, Redmond, WA, USA

T0183463

More information about this series at http://www.springer.com/series/7911

Hammoudi · José Cordeiro
A. Maciaszek · Joaquim Filipe (Eds.)

Enterprise Information Systems

15th International Conference, ICEIS 2013
Angers, France, July 4–7, 2013
Revised Selected Papers

 Springer

Editors
Slimane Hammoudi
Groupe ESEO
Angers
France

José Cordeiro
Joaquim Filipe
Polytechnic Institute of Setúbal
Setúbal
Portugal

and

INSTICC
Setúbal
Portugal

Leszek A. Maciaszek
Wroclaw University of Economics
Wroclaw
Poland

and

Macquarie University
Sydney, NSW
Australia

ISSN 1865-1348
ISBN 978-3-319-09491-5
DOI 10.1007/978-3-319-09492-2

ISSN 1865-1356 (electronic)
ISBN 978-3-319-09492-2 (eBook)

Library of Congress Control Number: 2014945219

Springer Cham Heidelberg New York Dordrecht London

Printed on acid-free paper

Springer is part of Springer Science+Business Media (www.springer.com)

Preface

The present book includes extended and revised versions of a set of selected papers from the 15th International Conference on Enterprise Information Systems (ICEIS 2013), held in Angers, France, during July 4–7, 2013, and co-organized by the ESEO Group. The conference was sponsored by the Institute for Systems and Technologies of Information, Control and Communication (INSTICC), held in cooperation with the Association for Advancement of Artificial Intelligence (AAAI), the IEICE Special Interest Group on Software Interprise Modelling (SWIM), the ACM Special Interest Group on Management Information Systems (SIGMIS), and the ACM Special Interest Group on Computer Human Interaction and in collaboration with the Informatics Research Center (IRC).

The conference was organized in six simultaneous tracks: Databases and Information Systems Integration, Artificial Intelligence and Decision Support Systems, Information Systems Analysis and Specification, Software Agents and Internet Computing, Human–Computer Interaction and Enterprise Architecture. The book is based on the same structure.

ICEIS 2013 received 321 paper submissions from 48 countries in all continents. From these, after a blind review process, 33 % were published and presented orally, from which 29 were selected for inclusion in this book, based on the classifications provided by the Program Committee. The selected papers reflect state-of-art research work that is often oriented toward real-world applications and highlight the benefits of information systems and technology for industry and services, thus making a bridge between the worlds of academia and enterprise. These high-quality standards will be maintained and reinforced at ICEIS 2014, to be held in Lisbon, Portugal, and in future editions of this conference.

Furthermore, ICEIS 2013 included four plenary keynote lectures given by Stephen Mellor (Freeter, UK), Fabien Gandon (Inria, France), Ulrich Frank (University of Duisburg-Essen, Germany) and Henderik A. Proper (Public Research Centre – Henri Tudor, Luxembourg). We would like to express our appreciation to all of them and in particular to those who took the time to contribute with a paper to this book.

On behalf of the conference Organizing Committee, we would like to thank all participants. First of all the authors, whose quality work is the essence of the conference, and the members of the Program Committee, who helped us with their expertise and diligence in reviewing the papers. As we all know, producing a conference requires the effort of many individuals. We wish to thank also all the members of our Organizing Committee, whose work and commitment were invaluable.

December 2013

Slimane Hammoudi
José Cordeiro
Leszek A. Maciaszek
Joaquim Filipe

Organization

Conference Co-chairs

Olivier Camp   IFI, Vietnam
Joaquim Filipe   Polytechnic Institute of Setúbal/INSTICC,
         Portugal

Program Co-chairs

Slimane Hammoudi   ESEO, MODESTE, France
Leszek A. Maciaszek   Wroclaw University of Economics, Poland
         and Macquarie University, Sydney, Australia
José Cordeiro   Polytechnic Institute of Setúbal/INSTICC,
         Portugal
Jan Dietz (Honorary)   Delft University of Technology, The Netherlands

Organizing Committee

Marina Carvalho   INSTICC, Portugal
Helder Coelhas   INSTICC, Portugal
Bruno Encarnação   INSTICC, Portugal
Ana Guerreiro   INSTICC, Portugal
André Lista   INSTICC, Portugal
Andreia Moita   INSTICC, Portugal
Carla Mota   INSTICC, Portugal
Raquel Pedrosa   INSTICC, Portugal
Vitor Pedrosa   INSTICC, Portugal
Cláudia Pinto   INSTICC, Portugal
Ana Ramalho   INSTICC, Portugal
Susana Ribeiro   INSTICC, Portugal
Sara Santiago   INSTICC, Portugal
Mara Silva   INSTICC, Portugal
José Varela   INSTICC, Portugal
Pedro Varela   INSTICC, Portugal

Senior Program Committee

Balbir Barn, UK   Albert Cheng, USA
Senén Barro, Spain   Jan Dietz, The Netherlands

Program Committee

Duminda Wijesekera, USA
Viacheslav Wolfengagen,
  Russian Federation
Ouri Wolfson, USA
Andreas Wombacher, The Netherlands
Robert Wrembel, Poland
Stanislaw Wrycza, Poland
Min Wu, USA
Wen-Yen Wu, Taiwan

Mudasser Wyne, USA
Haiping Xu, USA
Surya Yadav, USA
Hongji Yang, UK
Jasmine Yeap, Malaysia
Ping Yu, Australia
Eugenio Zimeo, Italy
Lin Zongkai, China

Additional Reviewers

Lerina Aversano, Italy
Vladimir Bartik, Czech Republic
Gabriele Bavota, Italy
Howard Hao-Chun Chuang, USA
Fernando William Cruz, Brazil
Emre Demirezen, USA
Necati Ertekin, USA
Fausto Fasano, Italy
Rodrigo Garcia-Carmona, Spain
Teresa García-Valverde, Spain
Carmine Gravino, Italy
Agnieszka Jastrzebska, Poland
Michael Kaisers, Germany
Kais Khrouf, Tunisia
Ronny Mans, The Netherlands
Paloma Cáceres García de Marina, Spain
Tomás Martínez-Ruiz, Spain
Andreas Metzger, Germany

Asmat Monaghan, UK
Rui Silva Moreira, Portugal
Luã Marcelo Muriana, Brazil
Álvaro Navas, Spain
Len Noriega, UK
Juan Luis Olmo, Spain
Annibale Panichella, Italy
Ignazio Passero, Italy
Hércules Antônio do Prado, Brazil
Abdallah Qusef, Italy
Deolinda Rasteiro, Portugal
Diego Seco, Chile
Yoshiyuki Shinkawa, Japan
Cleyton Slaviero, Brazil
Christian Stahl, The Netherlands Antilles
Panagiotis Symeonidis, Greece
Maria Tortorella, Italy
Thorsten Weyer, Germany

Invited Speakers

Stephen Mellor
Fabien Gandon
Ulrich Frank
Henderik A. Proper

Freeter, UK
Inria, France
University of Duisburg-Essen, Germany
Public Research Centre – Henri Tudor,
  Luxembourg

Contents

Information Systems Analysis and Specification

Software Agents and Internet Computing

Human-Computer Interaction

Enterprise Architecture

Invited Papers

Challenges in Bridging Social Semantics and Formal Semantics on the Web

Fabien Gandon[✉], Michel Buffa, Elena Cabrio, Olivier Corby,
Catherine Faron-Zucker, Alain Giboin, Nhan Le Thanh,
Isabelle Mirbel, Peter Sander, Andrea Tettamanzi, and Serena Villata

Inria, University of Nice Sophia Antipolis, CNRS, I3S, UMR 7271,
06900 Sophia Antipolis, France
fabien.gandon@inria.fr

Abstract. This paper describes several results of Wimmics, a research lab which names stands for: web-instrumented man-machine interactions, communities, and semantics. The approaches introduced here rely on graph-oriented knowledge representation, reasoning and operationalization to model and support actors, actions and interactions in web-based epistemic communities. The research results are applied to support and foster interactions in online communities and manage their resources.

Keywords: Semantic web · Social web · Knowledge representation · Ontologies · Typed graphs

1 Introduction: Toward Hybrid Societies on the Web

The Web is no longer perceived as a documentary system. Among its many evolutions, it became a virtual place where persons and software interact in mixed communities i.e. a hybrid space where humans and web robots interact and form new kinds of collectives that we will call here *hybrid societies*. These large scale interactions create many problems in particular the one of reconciling formal semantics of computer science (e.g. logics, ontologies, typing systems, etc.) on which the Web architecture is built, with soft semantics of people (e.g. posts, tags, status, etc.) on which the Web content is built.

Let us take a concrete and very common example. Many Web sites include forums, blogs, status feeds, wikis, etc. In other words, many Web sites include content management systems and rapidly build huge collections of information resources. As these collections grow, several tasks become harder to automate: search, notification, restructuring, navigation assistance, recommendation, trend analysis, etc. One of the main problems is the gap between the fairly informal way content is generated (e.g. plain text, short messages, free keywords) and the need for structured data and formal semantics to automate these functionalities (e.g. efficient indexes, domain thesauri). Mixed structures are starting to appear (e.g. structured folksonomies, hash tags, machine tags, etc.) but automating support in such collaboration spaces requires efficient and complete methods to fully bridge that gap.

© Springer International Publishing Switzerland 2014
S. Hammoudi et al. (Eds.): ICEIS 2013, LNBIP 190, pp. 3–15, 2014.
DOI: 10.1007/978-3-319-09492-2_1

As the Web becomes a ubiquitous infrastructure bathing all the objects of our world, this is just one example of the many frictions it will create between formal semantics and social semantics. This trend is also amplified by the growing number of datasets published and interlinked online by initiatives like Linking Open Data. This expanding web of data together with the schemas, ontologies and vocabularies used to structure and link it form a formal semantic web with which we have to design new interaction means to support the next generation of web applications.

This is why the Wimmics[1] research laboratory proposes to study methods, models and algorithms to bridge formal semantics and social semantics on the Web. This article provides a survey of the current research topics of the laboratory.

2 Challenges in Bridging Formal Semantics and Social Semantics

From a formal modeling point of view one of the consequences of the evolutions of the Web is that the initial graph of linked pages has been joined by a growing number of other graphs. This initial graph is now mixed with sociograms capturing the social networks structure, workflows specifying the decision paths to be followed, browsing logs capturing the trails of our navigation, automatas of service compositions specifying distributed processing, linked open data from distant datasets, etc.

Moreover, these graphs are not available in a single central repository but distributed over many different sources with very different characteristics. Some sub-graphs are public (e.g. dbpedia) while others are private (e.g. corporate data). Some sub-graphs are small and local (e.g. a users' profile on a device), some are huge and hosted on clusters (e.g. Wikipedia). Some are largely stable (e.g. thesaurus of Latin), some change several times per second (e.g. sensor data), etc.

And each type of network of the Web is not an isolated island. Networks interact with each other: the networks of communities influence the message flows, their subjects and types, the semantic links between terms interact with the links between sites and vice versa, the small changing graphs of sensors are joint to the large stable geographical graphs that position them, etc.

Not only do we need means to represent and analyze each kind of graphs, we also need the means to combine them and to perform multi-criteria analysis on their combination.

Wimmics proposes to address this problem focusing on the characterization of (a) typed graphs formalisms to model and capture these different pieces of knowledge and (b) hybrid operators to process them jointly. Our team especially considers the problems that occur in such structures when we blend formal stable semantic models and socially emergent and evolving semantics.

The two next sections detail this research program according to two main research directions combining two complementary types of contributions we target:

---

[1] Wimmics is a joint research laboratory between Inria Sophia Antipolis - Méditerranée and I3S (CNRS and Université Nice Sophia Antipolis). http://wimmics.inria.fr.

1. First research direction: to propose multidisciplinary approach to analyze and model the many aspects of these intertwined information systems, their communities of users and their interactions;
2. Second research direction: to propose formalizations of the previous models and reasoning algorithms on these models providing new analysis tools and indicators, and supporting new functionalities and better management.

In a nutshell, the first research direction looks at models of systems, users, communities and interactions while the second research direction considers formalisms and algorithms to represent them and reason on their representations.

In the short term we intend to survey, extend, formalize and provide reasoning means over models representing systems, resources, users and social links in the context of social semantic web applications.

In the longer term we intend to extend these models (e.g. dynamic aspects), unify their formalisms (dynamic typed graphs) and propose mixed operations (e.g. metrical and logical reasoning) and algorithms to scale them (e.g. random walks) to support the analysis of epistemic communities' structures, resources and dynamics.

Ultimately our goal is to provide better collective applications on the web of data and the semantic web addressing jointly two sides to the problem: (1) improve access and use of the linked data for epistemic communities and at the same time (2) use typed graph formalisms to represent the web resources, users and communities and reason on them to support their management.

3 Analyzing and Modeling Users, Communities and Their Interactions in a Social Semantic Web Context

The first challenge we identified in the introduction was to propose multidisciplinary approach to analyze and model intertwined information systems, communities of users and their interactions. Examples of research questions here include:

- How do we improve our interactions with an information system that keeps getting more and more complex?
- How do we reconcile and integrate the formalized stable semantics of computer science and the negotiable social interactions?
- How do we facilitate communication between systems and system developers using formal representations and between users and usage analysts using corresponding less formal or non-formal representations?
- How do we reconcile local contexts of users and global characteristics of the world-wide system?

The main goal of this first research direction is to improve the understanding the systems have of the communities of their users. To provide better collective applications on the web of data and the semantic web we need to adapt classical models to the specificities and variety of web systems (requirements, functionalities, specifications), users (profiles and context: location, devices, activities, etc.), and groups (communities and networks of interest, communities and networks of practice, social constructs, etc.). In Wimmics, these models are designed, integrated, and published according to web standards to support functionalities of web applications providing access and use of the linked data to epistemic communities.

We defend that such models necessarily call for multidisciplinary approaches to analyze and model the many aspects of the information systems. Our proposal relies:

– on extending requirement modeling to build models of the systems;
– on cognitive studies and user modeling results to build models of the users;
– on ergonomic studies and interaction design methods to model the interactions between users through the system and with the system, in order to support and improve these interactions.

We had several experiences in past projects with a user modeling technique known as Personas [1]. We are interested in these user models that are represented as specific, individual humans and we apply them to capture models of the members of web-based communities. Personas are derived from significant behavior patterns (i.e., sets of behavioral variables) elicited from interviews with and observations of users (and sometimes customers) of the future product. The main merit of the Personas method is to engage design team members more effectively in not only taking users into account but also having constantly in mind that they are designing for people. This effectiveness comes from several aspects, in particular:

1. by integrating concrete elements in the description of a user-type (name, photo, etc.)., it prevents that the user remains an abstraction for the designer (this abstraction leading the designer to lose sight of the user);
2. by connecting more strongly scenarios to the actors of these scenarios (i.e., the users), the Personas method avoids the problem often encountered in conventional methods of scenario-based design, namely to ignore users in the development of scenarios and thus "dehumanizing" these scenarios.

In the Personas method, the link between scenarios and users is established with the most important characteristic of personas: their goals. These goals form the basis for scenario development. Our user models specialize "Personas" approaches to include aspects appropriate to Web applications. The formalization of these models will rely on ontology-based modeling of users and communities starting with generalist schemas (e.g. FOAF).

Beyond the individual user models we propose to rely on social studies to build models of the communities, their vocabularies, activities and protocols in order to identify where and when formal semantics is useful. We already proposed an extension of the Persona approach to Collective Personas [2] and we now develop our method to encompass web-based communities. We compare this approach to the related "collaboration personas" method [3, 4] and to the group modeling methods [5] which are extensions to groups of the classical user modeling techniques dedicated to individuals. Both methods having been developed independently from one another, they differ along several dimensions, for example: whereas the Collaboration Personas method (CnP) focuses on forms of collaboration within a group, the Collective Personas method (CeP) focuses on the nature of the collective; whereas CeP refers to models or theories of collectives to define types of collectives, CnP uses pragmatic classifications; whereas CnP describes scenarios as stories, CeP describes them in a more structured way. We also propose to rely on and adapt participatory sketching and prototyping to support the design of interfaces for visualizing and manipulating representations of collectives.

Wimmics also has a background in requirement models and, in the short term, we want to consider their extension and specialization to web applications (in particular semantic web and linked data applications) and their representation in web-based formalisms in order to support mutual understanding and interoperability between requirements, resources and specifications of interconnected web applications and web datasets (e.g. [6]).

For all the models we identify we rely on and evaluate knowledge representation methodologies and theories, in particular ontology-based modeling.

In addition to the persona models identified previously, in a longer term we will consider a number of additional features to be captured in the user models.

We already added contexts, devices, processes and media descriptions that are formalized and used to support adaptation, proof and explanation and foster acceptation and trust from the users [46, 47]. We specifically target a unified formalization of these contextual aspects to be able to integrate them at any stage of the processing. This unified formalization already allows us to use the same model and data for very different functionalities such as access control [7] or presentation customization [8].

We extended current descriptions of relational and emotional aspects in existing variants of the personas technique. In particular we intend to exploit Olsen's characterization of a user's relationship to a product [9] since this characterization was made by analogy to human relationships. The elaboration of the characteristics to be included in a "relational-user" model will rely on work dealing with "relational agency" ("as a capacity to recognize others as resources, to elicit their interpretations and to negotiate aligned actions" [10]), and on "relational agents" (as "computational artifacts designed to build long-term social-emotional relationships with users" [11]). The elaboration of relational characteristics will be informed by empirical studies of relationship characterization, and of personality definition by users on the Web. These directions are a natural extension of our work on the use of affective ontologies in semantic web applications [12] and algebraic modeling of emotional states [13]. We also proposed algorithm to detect and classify the emotional states [14, 15] that can then be represented and exchanged together with their ontologies on the Web. Indeed, for each of these extensions we systematically consider additional extensions of the corresponding schemas to capture additional aspects and publish them as public ontologies on the semantic web.

Concerning the social dimension we now focus on studying and modeling mixed representations containing social semantic representations (e.g. folksonomies) and formal semantic representations (e.g. ontologies) and propose operations that allow us to couple them and exchange knowledge between them [16]. The very long term objective is to obtain a uniformed and integrated representation of social aspects (e.g., groups, networks, communities), social objects (web resources e.g. pictures, posts), social informal semantics (e.g. tags, folksonomies) and social formal semantics (e.g. ontologies, schemas).

In addition, to take into account social dynamics, we believe that argumentation theory can provide models (e.g. [17]) that must be adapted to open web constraints. Argumentation theory can be combined to requirement engineering to improve participant awareness and support decision-making (e.g. [18]). On the methodological side, we propose to adapt to the design of such systems the incremental formalization approach originally introduced by the CSCW and HCI communities [19, 20]. In incremental formalization users first express information informally and then the system helps them formalize it. The goal of such an approach is to get users to interact at least partially with formal representations, to make them contribute to a formalization closer to their needs [21].

Argumentation theory can also be combined with semantic web models and social web approaches to provide explicit formal representation of some social dynamics (e.g. opinions, agreements, debates, disagreements) more and more useful to understand the state and status of a resource and, for instance, decide on whether to trust it or not.

This kind of understanding and models allow scaling-up some very time-consuming tasks on the social web (e.g. managing and moderating Wikipedia) in particular when they are combined with natural language processing (NLP) to tackle the textual nature of these interactions as in [22–26]. In addition NLP approaches can also improve the design of interaction with the collections of models and data that are growing on the Web. For instance NLP allows us to support natural language querying of semantic web triple stores [27, 28].

And the linguistic knowledge useful for such processing can in turn be the subject of knowledge representation and data exchanged on the Web [29, 30].

Finally, on a very long term a much needed evolution of all our models is the temporal and dynamic dimension. We now plan to study and survey initiatives and contributions on dynamic graph representation and analysis and merge them with typed graph models of the Web of data to natively and uniformly support the time dimension in our representations.

4 Formalizing and Reasoning on Heterogeneous Semantic Graphs

The second challenge identified in the introduction is to propose formalizations of the previous models and reasoning algorithms on these models providing new analysis tools and indicators, and supporting new functionalities and better management. Examples of research questions include for instance:

– What kind of formalism is the best suited for the models of the previous section?
– How do we analyze graphs of different types and their interactions?
– How do we support different graph life-cycles, calculations and characteristics in a coherent and understandable way?

In this second research direction members of Wimmics focus on formalizing as typed graphs the models identified in the previous section in order for software to exploit them in their processing. The challenge is two-sided:

- To propose models and formalisms to capture and merge representations of both kinds of semantics (e.g. formal ontologies and social folksonomies). The important point is to allow us to capture those structures precisely and flexibly and yet create as many links as possible between these different objects.
- To propose algorithms (in particular graph-based reasoning) and approaches (e.g. human-computing methods) to process these mixed representations. In particular we are interested in allowing cross-enrichment between them and in exploiting the life cycle and specificities of each one to foster the life-cycles of the others.

While some of these problems are known, for instance in the field of knowledge representation and acquisition (e.g. disambiguation, fuzzy representations, and argumentation theory), the Web reopens them with exacerbated difficulties of scale, speed, heterogeneity, and an open-world assumption by default.

Many approaches emphasize the logical aspect of the problem especially because logics are close to computer languages. We defend that the graph nature of linked data on the Web and the large variety of types of links that compose them call for typed graphs models. We believe the relational dimension is of paramount importance in these representations and we propose to consider all these representations as fragments of a typed graph formalism directly built above the semantic Web formalisms. Our choice of a graph based programming approach for the semantic and social web and of a focus on one graph based formalism is also an efficient way to support interoperability, genericity, uniformity and reuse.

We targeted an abstract graph model close to the GRIWES model [31] and we evaluate it in merging social graphs (e.g. sociograms, folksonomies) and semantic Web graphs (e.g. RDF, schemas, linked data) in a unified typed graph formalism. This work on abstracting the knowledge representation models follows our experience with conceptual graphs and semantic networks approaches.

An example of such abstract structure is the ERGraph [31] defined relatively to a set of labels L as a 4-tuple $G = (E_G, R_G, n_G, l_G)$ where:

- E_G and R_G are two disjoint finite sets respectively, of nodes called entities and of hyperarcs called relations.
- $n_G : R_G \rightarrow E_G^*$ associates to each relation a finite tuple of entities called the arguments of the relation.
- $l_G : E_G \cup R_G \rightarrow L$ is a labelling function of entities and relations.

This type of oriented labelled multi-graph structure is at the core of most of our formalizations. New knowledge structures are regularly identified (e.g. folksonomies, named graphs) and old ones re-launched (e.g. thesauri and SKOS). This kind of abstract construct can be used and reused across graph representations such as RDF, Topic Maps, Social Networks, Knowledge Graphs, etc.

There exists now an extensive body of work in Graph-based Knowledge Representation [32] that we align with the ones needed for semantic web data structures (e.g. [31, 33, 34]) and in the short term we intend to continue specifying the required characteristics of such a language and systematically evaluate their effectiveness in implementing these abstract graph models in real applications [35, 36].

Likewise we extend our abstract graph machine not only to cover as many features as possible of new languages like SPARQL 1.1, RDF 1.1 and RIF, but also to extend them with experimental features (e.g. semantic distances) and a challenge is to integrate other operators with classical graph manipulation in particular: approximation, clustering, analysis operations, spreading algorithm, temporal reasoning and extend them to work on typed graphs. For instance, we considered the near linear time algorithm to detect community structures in large scale network RAK/LP [37] based on label propagation and changed the propagation algorithm to take semantics into account the algorithm SemTagP [38].

Currently, graph operators (joint, homomorphism, propagation, distances, etc.) allow us to perform a broad range of queries and reasoning operations. An example of abstract graph operation is an ERMapping [31]: Let G and H be two ERGraphs, an ERMapping$_{<x>}$ from H to G for a binary relation X over $L \times L$ is a partial function M from E_H to E_G such that:

- $\forall e \in M^{-1}(E_G), (l_G(M(e)), l_H(e)) \in X$
- $\forall r' \in R_{H'} \; \exists r \in R_G$ such that card$(n_{H'}(r'))=$ card$(n_G(r))$
- $\forall \; 1 \leq i \leq$ card$(n_G(r))$, $M(n_{H'}{}^i(r'))= n_G{}^i(r)$
- $\forall r' \in R_{H'} \; \exists \; r \in M(r')$ such that $(l_G(r), l_H(r')) \in X$ where H' is the sub-ERGraph of H induced by $M^{-1}(E_G)$.

This mapping operator can then be used and reused for many operations (searching, deriving, grouping, etc.) and across many graph formalisms compatible with the ERGraph structure. In particular when X is a preorder over L, it captures a hierarchy such as the taxonomical skeleton of an ontology, a thesaurus, a partonomy, etc.

Our implementations [35] and their applications (e.g. ISICIL [39], DATALIFT [40], DiscoveryHub [41]) show that type-based inference algorithms (e.g. conceptual graph projection, inference rules) and type-parameterized operators (e.g. parameterized betweeness centrality) provide declarative formalisms to flexibly define operations to monitor, filter, query, mine, validate, protect, etc. these imbricated graph structures taking into account constraints spanning several types of network at once.

In the longer term we intend to build on our experience with such formalisms to identify, propose and characterize fragments of typed graph formalisms best suited for each type of model identified before. We will restrain ourselves to specify the required characteristics of a limited number of formalisms (ideally one) and systematically evaluate their effectiveness in implementing these abstract graph models in real applications.

The mixed representations identified in the previous section really call for hybrid reasoning methods merging semantic Web inferences, social graph analysis and content mining in cross-dimensional indicators and operators. The key problem is to have integrated operators on these formalisms, able to perform at the same time exact reasoning and more approximate one to combine all aspects of the problem. For instance a centrality [42] can be computed on a social network taking into account only some relation types [43] or some topics of interest using an extension of regular expressions to graph paths [33]. This same centrality can also be computed by using a complete walk algorithm or approximated by using random walks but in both cases the ability to consider and reason on types of links and nodes will be a core problem. Another example is combining folksonomies and ontologies in the same application and using a combination of automated processing (e.g. a range of semantic similarities and inference rules) and human-based computing (e.g. analyzing the behaviors of users carrying out a search) to structure and maintain a thesaurus of tags and keywords used in a community [44].

Our final goal is to have both an abstract language dissociated from the concrete languages and an extensible abstract machine to process them. In particular this allows us to define parameterizable graph operators for instance to revisit classical structural metrics and adapt their definition to go beyond the pure structural calculation and take into account the types in the graphs. In the longer term, we intend to perform search (e.g. homomorphism) and logical derivation (e.g. homomorphism and merge) but also approximation (e.g. distances), clustering (e.g. propagation), analysis (e.g. centrality), etc. jointly on the same graphs. We target the design of an abstract graph machine [35] generalizing operations needed by and sometime shared across different languages (e.g. SPARQL, RIF, POWDER, RDF/S and OWL inferences) and operations. In addition we also believe it is interesting to study alternatives to OWL stack and the associated DL-reasoning. For instance a rule-based semantic web with an alternative stack (RDF/S + SPARQL + Rules) provides certain advantages: rules are often more natural for humans, they support event-based programming and web service integration, they are usable both for domain independent and domain dependent inferences, etc.

To adapt to web growth and dynamics, we also plan to evaluate other approaches (e.g. Random walk on graphs approaches) that do not naturally use labels but could be indirectly parameterized (e.g. making a correspondence between probabilistic distributions and the types of links) and to consider temporal reasoning approaches to include temporal context and change patterns to identify trends, mine temporal propagation to build oriented networks, track behavioral patterns to qualify actors and communities (e.g. detect a dying community) extending models from [45] for instance.

We believe that moving to graph languages with open-world logics, temporal aspects, distributed and loosely coupled algorithms and model-driven programming relying on higher abstractions (e.g. formal ontologies) provides an adequate theoretical and operational framework to allow not only the specification and operationalization of the models and algorithms, but also the opening of these black boxes to be able to explain, document, prove and trace query performances and results for the users, as in [46, 47].

As a last example, the same graph-based formalisms we propose to use in representing our models can be used to declaratively capture the landscape of the data distribution and the workflows of our operations [48], interpret them and execute them. This is the approach we would like to explore to support different operations on heterogeneous and distributed data (e.g. summarizing the content of distributed triple stores [49]) and automated explanation, trace and documentation of the processes.

5 Conclusion

Wimmics provides models and algorithms to bridge formal semantics and social semantics by formalizing and reasoning on heterogeneous semantic graphs.

The models we design include: users, their profiles, their requirements, their activities and their contexts; social links, social structures, social exchanges and processes; conceptual models including ontologies, thesauri, and folksonomies. Whenever possible these models are formalized and published according to standardized web formalisms and may motivate research and suggestions on extending these standards. The schemas and datasets produced are published as linked data following the web architecture principles.

The algorithms we study include: typed graphs indexing, reasoning and searching; hybrid processing merging logical inferences, rules and metrical inferences; approximation and propagation algorithms; distributed and scalable alternatives to classical reasoning. These algorithms are implemented and distributed as part of generic open source software.

Wimmics has indeed the culture of producing prototypes of applications and extensions of existing applications relying on web languages as demonstrators and proofs of concept. At the core of many of our prototypes is the abstract graph library we develop, maintain and publish as open-source software. This platform called Corese/KGRAM [35] currently implements W3C standards (in particular RDF/S 1.1 and SPARQL 1.1) and is both a research result and a library on top of which we test new ideas and algorithms. Currently this platform is extensively used in several applications such as: Isicil, Neurolog, DiscoveryHub, etc.

Finally we continuously participate to the extension, specifications, implementation, tests, deployment and teaching of W3C Web standards and our research results support, use and influence the evolution of these standards.

References

1. Cooper, A., Reinmann, R.: About Face 2.0: The Essentials of Interaction Design. Wiley Publishing Inc., Indianapolis (2003)
2. Giboin, A.: From individual to collective persona: modeling realistic groups and communities of users (and not only realistic individual users). In: Proceedings of the Fourth International Conference Advances in Human-Computer Interactions (ACHI 2011), Gosier, Guadeloupe, 23–28 February 2011
3. Matthews, T., Whittaker, S., Moran, T., Yang, M.: Collaboration personas: a framework for understanding & designing collaborative workplace tools. In: Workshop "Collective Intelligence In Organizations: Toward a Research Agenda" at Computer Supported Cooperative Work (CSCW) (2010)
4. Matthews, T., Whittaker, S., Moran, T., Yuen, S.: Collaboration personas: a new approach to designing workplace collaboration tools. In: Proceedings of the SIGCHI Conference on Human Factors in Computing Systems (CHI), pp. 2247–2256 (2011)

5. Gaudioso, E., Soller, A., Vassileva, J. (eds.): User Modeling to Support Groups, Communities and Collaboration. User Modeling and User-Adapted Interaction 16, Special Issue (2006)

6. Neveu, P., et al.: Using ontologies of software: example of R functions management. In: Lacroix, Z., Vidal, M.E. (eds.) RED 2010. LNCS, vol. 6799, pp. 43–56. Springer, Heidelberg (2012)

7. Costabello, L., Villata, S., Gandon, F.: Context-aware access control for RDF graph stores. In: 20th European Conference on Artificial Intelligence, ECAI 2012 (2012)

8. Costabello, L.: Error-tolerant RDF subgraph matching for adaptive presentation of linked data on mobile. In: Presutti, V., d'Amato, C., Gandon, F., d'Aquin, M., Staab, S., Tordai, A. (eds.) ESWC 2014. LNCS, vol. 8465, pp. 36–51. Springer, Heidelberg (2014)

9. Olsen, G.: Persona creation and usage toolkit. Information Architecture (IA) Summit, 15 p. (2004). http://www.asis.org/~iasummit/2004/finalpapers/Olsen_Handout_or__final __paper.pdf

10. Edwards, A.: Relational agency in professional practice: a CHAT analysis, action. Int. J. Hum. Act. 1, 1–17 (2007)

11. Bickmore, T.W., Picard, R.W.: ACM Trans. Comput.-Hum. Inter. 12(2), 293–327 (2005)

12. Giboin, A.: Motivating the use of affective ontologies in semantic web applications which mediate interactions between members of organizations or communities. In: COOP'2008 Workshop on Affective aspects of Cooperative Interactions, Carry-Le-Rouet, May 2008

13. Tayari, I., Le Thanh, N., Ben Amar, C.: Towards an algebraic modeling of emotional states. In: Proceedings of the the Fifth International Conference on Internet and Web Applications and Services (ICIW 2010), Barcelona, Spain, IARIA: Int. Academy, Research and Industry Association, pp. 513–518, CPS-IEEE CSDL, 9–15 May 2010

14. Berthelon, F., Sander, P.: Regression algorithm for emotion detection. In: IEEE International Conference on Cognitive Infocommunications, CogInfoCom, Budapest (2013)

15. Berthelon, F., Sander, P.: Emotion ontology for context awareness. In: IEEE International Conference on Cognitive Infocommunications, CogInfoCom, Budapest (2013)

16. Limpens, F., Monnin, A., Laniado, D., Gandon, F.: NiceTag ontology: tags as named graphs. In: International Workshop in Social Networks Interoperability, ASWC09 (2009)

17. Dung, P.M.: On the acceptability of arguments and its fundamental role in nonmonotonic reasoning, logic programming and n-person games. Artif. Intell. 77(2), 321–357 (1995)

18. Mirbel, I., Villata, S.: Enhancing goal-based requirements consistency: an argumentation-based approach. In: Fisher, M., van der Torre, L., Dastani, M., Governatori, G. (eds.) CLIMA XIII 2012. LNCS, vol. 7486, pp. 110–127. Springer, Heidelberg (2012)

19. Blythe, J., Gil, Y.: Incremental formalization of document annotations through ontology-based paraphrasing. In: Proceedings of WWW'04 Thirteenth International World Wide Web Conference, New York, NY, USA, 17–22 May 2004

20. Shipman III, F.M., McCall, R.: Supporting knowledge-base evolution with incremental formalization. In: Proceedings of CHI '94, Boston, Mass, USA, pp. 285–291, 24–28 April 1994

21. Giboin, A., Prié, Y.: Interagir avec des représentations formelles. In: Actes complémentaires de la Conférence IHM'2011, pp. 57–58 (2011)

22. Cabrio, E., Tonelli, S., Villata, S.: A natural language account for argumentation schemes. To appear in Proceedings of the XIII Conference of the Italian Association for Artificial Intelligence (AI*IA 2013), Turin, Italy, December 2013

23. Cabrio, E., Cojan, J., Villata, S., Gandon, F.: Hunting for Inconsistencies in Multilingual DBpedia with QAKiS. To appear in Proceedings of the 12th International Semantic Web Conference (ISWC 2013), Poster/Demo paper, Sydney, Australia, October 2013

24. Cabrio, E., Cojan, J., Villata, S., Gandon, F.: Argumentation-based inconsistencies detection for question-answering over DBpedia. To appear in Proceedings of the ISWC 2013 Workshop NLP & DBpedia, Sydney, Australia, October 2013

25. Cabrio, E., Tonelli, S., Villata, S.: From discourse analysis to argumentation schemes and back: relations and differences. In: Leite, J., Son, T.C., Torroni, P., van der Torre, L., Woltran, S. (eds.) CLIMA XIV 2013. LNCS, vol. 8143, pp. 1–17. Springer, Heidelberg (2013)

26. Cabrio, E., Villata, S., Gandon, F.: A support framework for argumentative discussions management in the web. In: Cimiano, P., Corcho, O., Presutti, V., Hollink, L., Rudolph, S. (eds.) ESWC 2013. LNCS, vol. 7882, pp. 412–426. Springer, Heidelberg (2013)

27. Cabrio, E., Cojan, J., Gandon, F., Hallili, A.: Querying multilingual DBpedia with QAKiS. In: Cimiano, P., Fernández, M., Lopez, V., Schlobach, S., Völker, J. (eds.) ESWC 2013. LNCS, vol. 7955, pp. 194–198. Springer, Heidelberg (2013)

28. Cojan, J., Cabrio, E., Gandon, F.: Filling the gaps among DBpedia multilingual chapters for question answering. In: Proceedings of ACM Web Science 2013, Paris, France, May 2013

29. Lefrançois, M., Gugert, R., Gandon, F., Giboin, A.: Application of the unit graphs framework to lexicographic definitions in the RELIEF project. To appear in Proceedings of the 6th International Conference on Meaning-Text Theory (MTT 2013), Prague, Czech Republic, August 2013

30. Lefrançois, M., Gandon, F.: Reasoning with dependency structures and lexicographic definitions. To appear in Proceedings of the 2nd International Conference on Dependency Linguistics (Depling 2013), Prague, Czech Republic, August 2013

31. Baget, J.-F., Corby, O., Dieng-Kuntz, R., Faron-Zucker, C., Gandon, F., Giboin, A., Gutierrez, A., Leclère, M., Mugnier, M.-L., Thomopoulos, R.: Griwes: generic model and preliminary specifications for a graph-based knowledge representation toolkit. In: Proceedings of the 16th International Conference on Conceptual Structures (ICCS'2008), Toulouse, July 2008

32. Chein, M., Mugnier, M.-L.: Graph-based Knowledge Representation: Computational Foundations of Conceptual Graphs. Advanced Information and Knowledge Processing. Springer, New York (2009). ISBN-13: 978–1849967693

33. Corby, O.: Web, Graphs & Semantics. In: Proceedings of the 16th International Conference on Conceptual Structures (ICCS'2008), Toulouse, July 2008

34. Gandon, F.: Graphes RDF et leur Manipulation pour la Gestion de Connaissances, Habilitation à Diriger les Recherches (HDR), soutenue le Mercredi 5 Novembre 2008

35. Corby, O., Faron-Zucker, C.: The KGRAM abstract machine for knowledge graph querying. In: IEEE/WIC/ACM International Conference, Toronto, Canada, September 2010

36. Corby, O., Faron-Zucker, C.: Implementation of SPARQL query language based on graph homomorphism. In: Priss, U., Polovina, S., Hill, R. (eds.) ICCS 2007. LNCS (LNAI), vol. 4604, pp. 472–475. Springer, Heidelberg (2007)

37. Raghavan, R.N., Albert, R., Kumara, S.: Near linear time algorithm to detect community structures in large scale network. Phys. Rev. E **76**, 036106 (2007)

38. Erétéo, G., Gandon, F., Buffa, M.: SemTagP: semantic community detection in folksonomies. In: IEEE/WIC/ACM International Conference on Web Intelligence, Lyon, August 2011

39. Buffa, M., Ereteo, G., Limpens, F., Gandon, F.: Folksonomies and social network analysis in a social semantic web. In: 39th International Conference on Current Trends in Theory and Practice of Computer Science, 26–31 January 2013

40. Scharffe, F., Atemezing, G., Troncy, R., Gandon, F., Villata, S., Bucher, B., Hamdi, F., Bihanic, L., Képéklian, G., Cotton, F., Euzenat, J., Fan, Z., Vandenbussche, P.-Y., Vatant, B.: Enabling linked data publication with the Datalift platform. In: Proceedings of the AAAI Workshop on Semantic Cities (2012)

41. Marie, N., Ribiere, M., Gandon, F., Rodio, F.: Discovery hub: on-the-fly linked data exploratory search. To appear in Proceedings of I-Semantics 2013 (2013)

42. Freeman, L.C.: Centrality in social networks: conceptual clarification. Soc. Netw. **1**, 215–239 (1979)

43. Erétéo, G., Buffa, M., Gandon, F., Corby, O.: Analysis of a real online social network using semantic web frameworks. In: Bernstein, A., Karger, D.R., Heath, T., Feigenbaum, L., Maynard, D., Motta, E., Thirunarayan, K. (eds.) ISWC 2009. LNCS, vol. 5823, pp. 180–195. Springer, Heidelberg (2009)

44. Limpens, F., Gandon, F., Buffa, M.: Helping online communities to semantically enrich folksonomies. In: Web Science Conference, Raleigh, NC, USA, April 2010

45. Angeletou, S., Rowe, M., Alani, H.: Modelling and analysis of user behaviour in online communities. In: Aroyo, L., Welty, C., Alani, H., Taylor, J., Bernstein, A., Kagal, L., Noy, N., Blomqvist, E. (eds.) ISWC 2011, Part I. LNCS, vol. 7031, pp. 35–50. Springer, Heidelberg (2011)

46. Hasan, R.: Generating and summarizing explanations for linked data. In: Presutti, V., d'Amato, C., Gandon, F., d'Aquin, M., Staab, S., Tordai, A. (eds.) ESWC 2014. LNCS, vol. 8465, pp. 473–487. Springer, Heidelberg (2014)

47. Hasan, R.: Predicting SPARQL query performance and explaining linked data. To appear in the Ph.D. Symposium of 11th Extended Semantic Web Conference (ESWC2014) (2014)

48. Lo, M., Gandon, F.: Semantic web services in corporate memories. In: International Conference on Internet and Web Applications and Services, ICIW 2007, Mauritius, 13–19 May 2007

49. Basse, A., Gandon, F., Mirbel, I., Lo, M.: Frequent graph pattern to advertise the content of RDF triple stores on the Web. In: Proceedings of the Web Science Conference, Raleigh, NC, USA, April 2010

Enterprise Architecture: Informed Steering of Enterprises in Motion

Henderik A. Proper[1,2](✉)

[1] CRP Henri Tudor, Luxembourg, Luxembourg
e.proper@acm.org
[2] EE-Team, Luxembourg, Luxembourg

Abstract. Enterprises are constantly in motion. Novel technologies, new markets opportunities, cost reduction, process improvement, service innovation, globalisation, mergers, acquisitions, etc., continuously trigger enterprises to change. This variety of change drivers also fuels the need for enterprises to seek the right balance between the many, quite often contradicting, drivers for change.

In this position paper, we aim to investigate the potential role of enterprise architecture as a means to support senior management in steering/influencing the direction in which an enterprise "moves" in response to, or in anticipation of, the many change drivers. In doing so, we aim to develop a fundamental understanding of the systemic playing field in which enterprise architecture is to play a role. To this end, we will start by exploring how enterprises can be seen as being continuously "in motion". We then turn to the *control paradigm* to reflect on the need to steer this motion. We will also argue that the resulting steering system is a second order information system. Using this understanding we then identify the ingredients needed for enterprise architecture.

Keywords: Enterprise architecture · Enterprise transformation · Enterprises in motion

1 Introduction

Modern day enterprises, be they businesses, government departments or organizations, are constantly in motion. Socio-economic challenges, such as the financial crisis, mergers, acquisitions, innovations, novel technologies, new business models, servitisation of the economy, reduced protectionism, de-monopolisation of markets, deregulation of international trade, privatisation of state owned companies, increased global competition, etc., provide key drivers for change.

This work has been partially sponsored by the *Fonds National de la Recherche Luxembourg* (www.fnr.lu)

The EE-Team is a collaboration between CRP Henri Tudor, the Radboud University Nijmegen, the HAN University of Applied Sciences, the Utrecht University of Applied Sciences, and the University of Luxembourg (www.ee-team.eu).

S. Hammoudi et al. (Eds.): ICEIS 2013, LNBIP 190, pp. 16–34, 2014.
DOI: 10.1007/978-3-319-09492-2_2

These challenges are fuelled even more by advances in technology, in particular the development of information technologies. As a result, enterprises need be continuously "on the move" to find the right balance between these many, sometimes contradicting, change drivers. The resulting changes can materialise in different forms. They might, for example, take shape as top-down and premeditated efforts, but might also occur as numerous small changes that emerge bottom-up in a seemingly spontaneous fashion.

Organizations increasingly turn to enterprise architecture as a means to steer the direction of the changes that occur in an enterprise [12,22,31,33,42,60]. Over the past decades, the domain of enterprise architecture has seen a tremendous growth, both in terms of its use and development in practise and as a subject of scientific research. The roots of the field of enterprise architecture can actually be traced back as far as the mid 1980s [46].

In this position paper, we aim to investigate the potential role of enterprise architecture as a means to support senior management in dealing with challenges brought forward by the continuous motion of modern day enterprises. In doing so, we aim to develop a fundamental understanding of the systemic playing field in which enterprise architecture is to play a role. We will therefore start by exploring what it means for an enterprise to be "in motion" (Sect. 2). We then turn to the *control paradigm* from management science [34,35], to reflect on ways to steer this motion (Sect. 3). This will also lead to the introduction of the notion of *second order information systems* being information systems that are not targeted at supporting the operational processes of an enterprise, but rather at supporting the change processes of an enterprise. Second order informations systems enable the enterprise, and senior management in particular, to steer the motion of an enterprise. Using this understanding we then zoom in on the potential role of enterprise architecture in steering an enterprise's motion (Sect. 4). In doing so, we also discuss what we regard as being the core ingredients of enterprise architecture.

2   Enterprises in Motion

In line with [17], we consider an enterprise to primarily be a social system, in particular a social system with a purpose. The social individuals, i.e. humans, making up the enterprise will typically use different technological artefacts to (better) achieve their purpose. As a result, enterprises are generally regarded as being socio-technical systems. In using the term enterprise we will therefore also refer to the used technological artefacts.

2.1   Challenges to Enterprises

In [23,42,46], we discussed several challenges facing an enterprise. Each of these challenges potentially drive an enterprise to change. Below we briefly summarize three of these challenges.

Keep Up or Perish. Enterprises face many changes, such as mergers, acquisitions, innovations, novel technologies, new business models, reduced protectionism, deregulation of international trade, privatisation of state owned companies, increased global competition, etc. These factors all contribute towards an increasingly dynamic environment in which enterprises want to thrive.

Shifting Powers in the Value Chain. Clients of enterprises have become more demanding. A shift of power in the value chain is occurring. Clients have grown more powerful and demand customized, integrated and full life-cycle products and services. Rather than asking for a "printer", they require a guaranteed "printing service". A shift from basic products to full services. Even more, websites and social media, where consumers can share pricing information, experiences, ratings, etc., creates a transparency on the market that provides even more control to the consumers.

The creation and delivery of such complex products and services requires additional capabilities which may not be readily available within a single (pre-existing) enterprise. In this pursuit they increasingly engage in complex product-offerings involving other parties, leading to cross selling and co-branding. To ensure the quality of such products and services, a high level of integration and orchestration between the processes involved in delivering them is required.

Comply or Bust. In the networked economy, governance of enterprises becomes increasingly complex. One sees a shift in governance from individual departments within an organization, to the entire organization, and lately to the organization's value web. Management does not only have to worry about the reputation of their own organization, but also about the other organizations in their value web.

How daunting the latter might be can be illustrated by real life examples, such as a large shoe manufacturer who outsourced the production of shoes to another company, to only discover at a later stage that the latter made use of child labour. Although the latter company was not part of the shoemaker's own organization, their reputation was still damaged, threatening their survival on the market-place.

Governance is not only an issue to an organization on its own, but also a major concern to society as a whole. As a result of undesired and uncontrollable effects of the increased socio-economical complexity and interdependency of organizations, services, products and financial instruments. Examples of such side-effects are the well-known Enron scandal, as well as the sub-prime mortgage crises. To control and/or prevent such effects, new legislation has been put in place to better regulate enterprise practises.

Excel or Outsource. Increasingly enterprises outsource business processes. Outsourcing of business processes requires organizations to precisely understand and describe what needs to be outsourced, as well as the implementation of measures to ensure the quality of the outsourced processes. In deciding on what to outsource and how to safeguard its quality, management needs insight into the extent to which processes can be outsourced, the risks that may need to be managed when doing so, as well as the interdependencies within the outsourced processes and between the outsourced processes and the retained organization.

Conversely, organizations with a strong tradition in a certain business process may decide to become industry leader for such processes. For example, processing of payments, management of IT infrastructure, and logistics.

IT as the Business Differentiator. In most enterprises, the role of IT started with the 'automation of administrative work'. While there continues to be a clear role for IT to automate administrative information processing, the actual use of IT has moved far beyond this. In numerous situations, IT has given rise to new social structures, and business models. Consider, for example, the development of social media, the (acclaimed) role of twitter in time of social unrest, the emergence of on-line music stores, app-stores, music streaming services, etc. The advent of 'big data' [27] is expected to drive such developments even further by allowing IT based systems to use statistical data to tune their behaviour to observed and learned trends.

At the same time, IT has become firmly embedded in existing technological artefacts. The cars in which we drive may contain more lines of code than typical banking applications do. The next generation of cars will even be able to (partially) do the driving for us. The so-called smart (power) grid, is likely to lead to the 'smartening' of household appliances. The military use of all sorts of drones also spearheads more peaceful applications of such self-reliant devices that can e.g. perform tasks on behalf of us in hostile or unpleasant environments.

The evolution of information technology brings an abundance of new opportunities to enterprises. Technology becomes part of almost everything and most processes have become IT reliant, if not fully automated. The technological evolutions confront enterprises with the question of which technologies are relevant to the enterprise? Which technology should be replaced and which technology could be of use for developing new products (or services) of to enter new markets [2]?

2.2 Continuous Motion as a Primary Business Process

As a result of a.o. the above discussed socio-economical and technical challenges, enterprises need to change continuously. Different kinds of, and views on, change in enterprise exist. Some examples include:

1. *Large scale technology migrations* [45] concerned with large scale migration of IT platforms.
2. *Enterprise transformation* [23,53], concerned with pre-meditated and fundamental changes to an enterprise's relationships with one or more key constituencies, e.g., customers, employees, suppliers, and investors.

3. *Business innovation* [18], dealing with continuous innovation of the business, its products and/or services.
4. *Continuous process improvement* and other forms of *business process reengineering* [14,50].
5. *Mergers & acquisitions* of new parts of an enterprise [1].
6. *Organisational splitting*, the "inverse" of mergers & acquisitions [41].
7. *Organisational drift*, dealing with gradual misalignment between an enterprise's original intent (strategy, business model, operating model, etc.), and the actual operational activities [36][1].
8. *Self-organisation* by self-steering teams [5,44].
9. *Bricolage & emergence* may, as argued by Ciborra [13], provide enterprises with strategic advantages in terms of the bottom-up evolution of socio -technical systems that will lead to outcomes that are deeply rooted in an enterprise's organizational culture, and hence much more difficult to imitate by others.

We suggest to generalize these different flavours of change in enterprises to *"enterprises in motion"*, where the word *motion* refers to *"an act, process, or instance of changing place"* [38].

It is important to note that enterprises do not just change by means of premeditated change programs. We even go as far as to argue that small changes actually make up the bulk of an enterprise's motion. As such, these seemingly small changes should be taken into due consideration as well (e.g. to identify organizational drift). For example, it is quite common that business processes are *not* executed as designed. People working in an enterprise are likely to make changes to the design of business processes just 'to make it work'. Either to make it work for the individual worker, or because the designers did not realize all the variety and complexity one has to deal with in the day to day operations of the enterprise. One might even argue that business processes only work, because people will *make* them work, even if they are not designed well enough. Should senior management be aware of such changes? We take the stance that, in view of challenges such as the 'Comply or bust' challenge, the answer is: *potentially* yes.

Another example would be the use of technologies such as social media (LinkedIn, Facebook, etc.), cloud storage (Dropbox, Google Drive, etc.), and privately owned mobile devices (Tablets, smart phones, etc.). The use of such technologies leads to several bottom up changes of the IT used in support of business processes. Co-workers may start sharing work files within, or beyond, the enterprise using cloud storage services, they may also start using their own mobile devices (BYOD[2]) in the office, etc. Once 'detected', enterprises may respond to such changes in different ways. It usually leads to a pre-meditated response, where one e.g. forbids the use of some forms of new technology, provides more controlled alternatives, or even fully embraces the developments. Underlying all of this, one can usually see a struggle between ease-of-use, and security and risk

---

[1] http://www.marchmenthill.com/qsi-online/2011-06-19/organizational-drift
[2] http://en.wikipedia.org/wiki/Bring_your_own_device

considerations. This trade-off, once again, illustrates the need for senior management to ultimately be aware (to a level relevant to them) of such developments.

Given the needs of modern day enterprises to be constantly in motion to meet ever changing challenges, we also argue that the continuous motion of an enterprise is actually one of its primary business processes, next to the 'normal' operational business processes. As such, the business process for continuous motion deserves careful design and management.

2.3 Motioning the Running Enterprise

Based on the view that enterprises are continuously in motion, we suggest to make a distinction between two aspect systems of an enterprise: the *running* aspect system and the *motioning* aspect system. Where the motioning aspect concerns the actions involved in changing the enterprise, the running aspect concerns its regular operational activities. This situation is illustrated in Fig. 1. Note that the motioning system can motion *both* aspect systems. In other words, the motioning system can change itself as well.

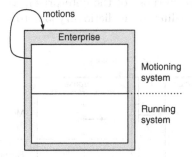

Fig. 1. Motioning and running aspect systems.

Being aspect systems, the actual social (and technological) actors in an enterprise can play roles (simultaneously) in both aspect systems. We argue that this is actually quite normal for us as human beings. While doing our day-to-day activities we also tend to reflect, depending on our personal goals, on how to make these activities more efficient, effective, pleasurable, etc., while consequently making the necessary changes. In the case of e.g. changes by self-steering teams, there is likely to be a larger overlap between the actors playing roles in both aspect systems, while in the case of pre-meditated and large scale change, this overlap will be less (but still essential and existent).

The authors of [4] suggest to distinguish between multiple levels of motioning: *improvement* to deal with minor optimizations, *transformation* to deal with structural changes, and *improvisation* covering 'out of bound' situations (e.g. when competitors introduce a game-changing product/technology, or unexpected socio-economical developments).

3   Steering the Motion of Enterprises

Given the potential impact which the challenges as discussed in Sect. 2 may have on an enterprise, and that as a consequence enterprise are continuously in motion, we argue that there is a need to steer this motion. It needs to be ensured that the motion is in line with the overall purpose and strategy of the enterprise, while also staying within the bounds of e.g. external regulations.

3.1   Steering

In terms of Fig. 1, this leads to the introduction of two additional aspects systems: the *producing* and *steering* aspect systems. This distinction runs orthogonal to the distinction between the running and motioning systems. The resulting situation is depicted in Fig. 2. The production aspect is concerned with the actual performance of activities of e.g. the motioning system (i.e. making changes) or the running system (e.g. producing products or delivering services). The steering aspect is concerned with the overall steering of the activities of the production system, such as ensuring their mutual alignment, efficiency and contribution to the overall goals (e.g. the purpose of the enterprise), as well as compliance to external regulations. According to the dictionary [38], to *steer* specifically means:

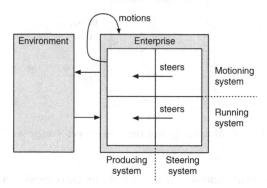

Fig. 2. Producing and steering aspect systems.

1. *to control the direction in which something (such as a ship, car, or airplane) moves;*
2. *to be moved or guided in a particular direction or along a particular course.*

We consider this to be applicable to the motion of an enterprise as well.

  Note again that Fig. 2 concerns *aspect systems*, so actual (human or technological) actors in the enterprise may play roles in all four aspect systems as identified in Fig. 2.

Depending on the enterprise, its purposes, context, and concerns, the steering system can use different styles of steering. For example, a restrictive top-down style of control approach, or a more laissez-faire based care-taking/stewarding approach. It may also apply different rhythms towards steering the activities in the producing system. For example, a regular planning-based approach or a more evolutionary/agile approach in line with e.g. the Deming cycle [15].

3.2 Control Paradigm

The role of the steering system can be illustrated more specifically in terms of the control paradigm (see Fig. 3) from management science [34, 35]. The essence of the control paradigm is that during the execution of a process there is some kind of interaction with the environment (input and output), and that this process is controlled by some authority which monitors, and if necessary adjusts, the process to make sure the intended objectives are reached. For the controlling system to operate effectively, it needs awareness of:

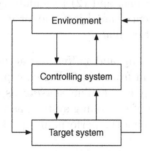

Fig. 3. The control paradigm, taken from [34, 35].

1. the current & anticipated steering goals, concerns and constraints,
2. the state & motion of the object's environment,
3. the state & motion of the object itself,
4. the impact of earlier interventions.

In addition, it requires the abilities to:

1. perform a SWOT analysis of the motion of the object and its environment, in relation to the coordinative goals and constraints, as well as earlier intervention actions,
2. formulate (when needed/desired) an intervention plan to influence the object and/or its environment,
3. perform an intervention plan.

3.3   The Sense-Think-Act Paradigm

From a theoretical point of view, the control paradigm is based on the more general notions of cybernetics [6] and feedback systems [7]. The field of robotics has developed a variation of the control paradigm in the form of the Sense-Think-Act paradigm [25,55]. In terms of Fig. 3, *sensing* corresponds to the two arrows leading into the control system, while *thinking* is internal to the control system, and *acting* corresponds to the two outgoing arrows. As a consequence of its origins in robotics, sensing, thinking and acting is inherently intended as a continuous process involving rapid revolutions of a Deming [15] alike cycle.

In terms of the requirements on a controlling system, we would have the following correspondence:

1. *Sense*: (1) the current & anticipated coordinative goals and constraints, (2) the state & motion of the object's environment, (3) the state & motion of the object itself and (4) the impact of earlier coordinative interventions.
2. *Think*: (1) perform a SWOT analysis of the motion of the object and its environment, in relation to the coordinative goals and constraints, as well as earlier intervention actions, and (2) formulate (when needed/desired) an intervention plan to influence the object and/or its environment.
3. *Act*: perform an intervention plan.

We argue that *sensing*, *thinking* and *acting* are actually more specific aspect systems of the *steering* system from Fig. 2. For enterprises in motion, this leads to the situation as shown in Fig. 4. The *sensing* aspect system observes the environment, the performing of motioning system, as well as the running system as a whole. It *acts* by influencing the performance part of the motioning system.

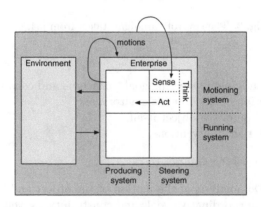

Fig. 4. Sense, Think and Act aspect systems added.

It should be noted that the sense-think-act paradigm, and associated aspect systems, can be applied to all four quadrants of Fig. 2. The steering aspect system only refers to the overall steering of activities, of both the motioning and running

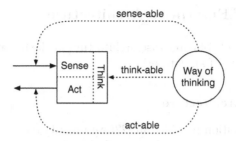

Fig. 5. Role of a way-of-thinking.

systems. In other words, the producing system certainly involves its own (local) steering/control systems, e.g. human actors planning/steering their own work activities. In Sect. 4.2 we will return to this issue.

3.4   Role of the Way-of-Thinking

In the context of designing and engineering of information systems and enterprises, several frameworks have been developed. These include, for example, Zachman [67], SEAM [65], and DEMO [51]. In [54], Seligmann et al. argue that system design and development methodologies are based on a *way of thinking* that verbalises the assumptions and viewpoints of the method on the kinds of problem domains, solutions and designs that can be developed. This notion is also referred to as *die Weltanschauung* [56], *underlying perspective* [37] and *philosophy* [8].

We argue that in the context of enterprises in motion, it is necessary to take the way of thinking explicitly into account. This is illustrated in Fig. 5. The way of thinking influences the sensing in the sense that it implicitly biases that what is *sense-able*, i.e. that what can be observed. Similarly, it influences/biases that what is considered to be *think-able*, and ultimately *act-able*. More specifically, it means e.g. that the used design and engineering framework, e.g. the above mentioned Zachman [67], SEAM [65], or DEMO [51] frameworks, influences what is *sense-able, think-able* and *act-able* upon by the steering system.

3.5   Second Order Information Systems

The motion-steering system can be regarded as a second order information system [26]. As such, it is actually to be regarded an information system in the broad sense, as it involves both human and computerised actors. Needless to say, that IT can play an important role in this information system [47].

In this vein, techniques such as process mining [3], software cartography [57,58] and enterprise cartography [58] are examples of IT based techniques that can support the sensing activities of the motion-steering system. Similarly, IT based techniques can be used to support the thinking and acting activities.

4   The Role of Enterprise Architecture

We now turn to the role of enterprise architecture in the context of the motion-steering aspect system of an enterprise.

4.1   Enterprise Architecture

In line with the definition provided in [22] we regard architecture as essentially being about: "*Those properties of an artefact that are necessary and sufficient to meet its essential requirements*". The focus on the properties *that matter*, is also what distinguishes it from design. Consequently, an enterprise architecture focuses on those properties of an enterprise that are necessary and sufficient to meet its essential requirements. This includes, in principle, all aspects of Fig. 2, in particular the running, motioning, producing, and steering aspect systems.

The reference to properties that are necessary and sufficient to meet its *essential requirements* introduces subjectivity to the scoping of architecture: *Who determines what the essential requirements are?* What is indeed to be regarded as essential, or not, is in the eyes of the beholder. It strongly depends on the purposes, goals and associated concerns, of the individual stakeholders. This, in particular, means that the essential requirements can be linked directly to the enterprise's (past/current) strategy, next to other core concerns of the key stakeholders [22]. As such, we argue that enterprise architecture should first and foremost be about *essential sense-making* in that it should primarily:

1. make sense of the past and future of the enterprise with regards to the way it has/will meet its *essential requirements* as put forward by its core stakeholders and captured in its strategy;
2. provide clear motivations/rationalisation, in terms of the above essential requirements, as well as e.g. constraints, of the trade-offs that underly the presence of the elements (e.g. building blocks or architecture principles) included in the architecture.

This will enable enterprise architects and senior management to take *informed* decisions about an enterprise's motion. In line with this, we argue that:

1. the *purpose* of an enterprise architecture is (i) to understand the current motion of the enterprise, including its past and its likely future motion and (ii) formulate, as well as motivate/rationalize, the desired future motion and the interventions needed to achieve this;
2. its *meaning* is that it expresses, in relation to the (current) essential requirements: (i) the understanding how the enterprise has evolved so-far, (ii) what the expected natural motion of the enterprise is and (iii) the desired future motion of the enterprise and actions needed to change/strengthen the current motion;
3. its *elements* should focus on the fundamental properties that have played a role in its past motion, as well as its expected/desired future motion.

It is important to note that while an enterprise is in motion, it is likely that the understanding of what the *essential requirements* are, will change. This means that the boundary between what was included in the architecture and what is considered design may also shift over time.

4.2   Levels of Steering

Given the fact that an enterprise architecture forms a bridge between strategy and design [16, 42], it follows that the motion-steering system actually involves (at least) three levels of steering. These are illustrated in Fig. 6.

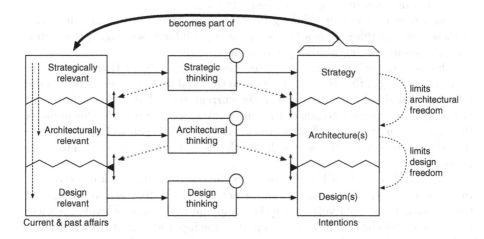

Fig. 6. Levels of steering.

At the top level we find the steering of strategically relevant issues. This concerns the definition and evolution of the enterprise's strategy. Depending on the goals and concerns that are involved in the strategic thinking level, the border between the strategic level and the architectural level would need to be adjusted. Needless to say, that this border cannot be fixed a priori. It will depend on the situations and concerns as they evolve.

At the next level, we find the architectural level. There the same applies. Depending on the essential requirements that follow from the strategic level, as well as the goals and concerns of the stakeholders, the border between the architectural level and design level can be adjusted. Again, this border cannot be fixed a priori as well. For example, a shifting societal focus towards e.g. the carbon footprint of the production of services and goods, may all of a suden trigger the architectural need to study the carbon impact of the enterprise's business processes. This would entail the need to, at an architectural level, now consider and design business processes at a finer level of detail then before.

As suggested in TOGAF [60], the architectural level might be subdivided into additional levels, e.g. a strategic, a segment, and a capability architecture level.

The last level of the steering system involves the design level. This design level is filled in by e.g. system development projects and/or decisions by self-steering teams on how they plan/organize their work.

Note that, Fig. 6 does *not* suggest that the decision makers involved in one level of thinking cannot be involved in another level. On the contrary. We argue that the decision makers at the strategic level (i.e. senior management) should also be involved in (some of) the decisions taken at the architectural level, and similarly, decision makers from the architectural level (i.e. architects) should be involved in decision making at the design level.

The circles on the four thinking boxes are a reminder of the fact that each of these levels of thinking has (its own) way of thinking (see Fig. 5) that influences/biases its sensing, thinking and acting abilities.

The left hand side of Fig. 6 shows the input, i.e. the abstraction (typically in terms of models) of the sensing activities, to the thinking activities. To stress the fact that this should not just involve the current state, but rather a historical perspective and current trends of the entire enterprise, we refer to this input as the *current & past affairs*[3]. The dotted arrows on the left side of Fig. 6 illustrate that the lower levels can take the higher levels of information as (contextual) input.

The right hand side of Fig. 6, represents the results of the thinking activities. In other words, the intentions/plans for action. The dotted arrows illustrated the fact that the lower levels need to be compliant to the higher levels. As such, the (higher level) intentions are also a part of the input for the at the lower level. This is signified by the fat arrow running across the top of the diagram.

It should be noted that, as also argued in [11,23], there is a potential correspondence between the different levels of steering and the Beer's viable systems model [9][4]. For more details, refer to e.g. [11,23]

4.3   Ingredients of Architecture

Given our current understanding of the role of architecture, and the related activities, we will now list what we regard as being the key ingredients of architecture. We have grouped these into five frameworks concerned with: stakeholder engagement, design motivation, structuring the design thinking, communication of architectures, and the architectural process, respectively.

Engagement Framework. Architectural decision making is not only the work of architects. It should involve several stakeholders within, and possibly beyond, the enterprise. Architecture methods/approaches such as SEAM [65], GEA [64] and CAEDA [39] focus on the involvement of stakeholders.

---

[3] http://en.wikipedia.org/wiki/Current_affairs_(news_format)
[4] http://en.wikipedia.org/wiki/Viable_System_Model

A distinction can be made between the identification of the groups of stake-holders that needs to be involved, e.g. in terms of GEA's dashboard [63], on one hand, and strategies to deal with their actual involvement in gathering require-ments, designing and decision making as provided in SEAM [65] and CAEDA [39] on the other hand. Together, they provide a framework for stakeholder engage-ment, clearly identifying which stakeholder groups to involve, when to involve them, what their interests/purposes are, and how to involve them in the archi-tectural thinking process.

Which stakeholders groups to involve depends highly on the strategy and focus of an enterprise, as well as its internal and external social-political con-stellation. Traditional approaches and frameworks, such as the Zachman [59] framework, provides a pre-defined grouping of stakeholders. As argued in [63], this grouping should be more organization and situational specific.

Motivation Framework. As argued in [49], several lines of reasoning can be used in architectural thinking, a very important one being the *design motivation* dimension. It bridges between needs and solutions. Building on the work reported in [61], we suggest to distinguish three levels:

1. **Why** − *Needs* of the stakeholders towards different elements of the enter-prise. In the case of architecture, the focus will be on the *essential* goals and needs of the stakeholders.

   The needs are to be formulated in terms of goals and activities of the stake-holders. For example, in terms of the affordance [21] (a property of an object, or an environment, which allows an individual to perform an action) towards the activities of the stakeholder, or the positive/negative value it may bring to the stakeholder in general. A linkage to the goal-oriented requirements engineering [32] is apparent.

2. **What** − *Requirements* towards the solution design space. Where the stake-holder needs are formulated in terms of the experience, value, or usage space of stakeholders, the requirements are formulated towards the actual design space of the enterprise and its constituting elements. At an architecture level, these requirements may take the form of so-called architecture principles [22].

3. **How** − *Designs* concerned with the composition/selection of actual building blocks of the enterprise. At an architecture level, this typically takes the form of e.g. models in terms of ArchiMate [33], BPMN [40] or DEMO [51] models.

The above three levels suggest a motivational flow from the needs of stakehold-ers, via requirements limiting the design space, to the actual design itself. The missing link, however, are the actual design motivations. The selection of design elements must be motivated in terms of requirements, while requirements must be motivated in terms of actual needs. The desire to bridge this gap, fuels work on the rationalisation of architectural design decisions [19,43].

Design Framework. Where the stakeholder engagement framework identifies the groups of stakeholders to involve in the architectural thinking processes, a design framework is needed to structure the actual architectural thinking. It embodies, and structures, the *way of thinking* about the enterprise as a designable artefact.

This is where existing frameworks/approaches for the architecting, design, or engineering, of enterprises, such as DEMO [51], Zachman [59], TOGAF's content framework [60], IAF [66], GERAM [29] or ArchiMate's [28,33] core framework, can play their main role. They provide (parts of) the way of thinking that can be used to structure the actual architectural thinking. Where necessary, existing frameworks and approaches can be combined. For example, combining the ontological focus of DEMO with the more implementation oriented focus of ArchiMate [30,52].

Depending on the concerns of stakeholders, more specific extensions of the design framework may be necessary. For example, extensions dealing with security and access control [20].

Both the design and motivation frameworks should have an underlying modelling landscape that integrates the different aspects of the enterprise that are considered relevant from the perspective of the design framework [10]. Standards such as ArchiMate [28] provide a good starting point. However, as argued in [10], more flexibility is needed to cater for organization/context specific language use and/or refinements. Furthermore, the design and motivation frameworks should be used as the way of thinking (see Fig. 5) towards the sensing, thinking and acting activities at the architectural steering level.

Communication Framework. Where the engagement framework provides a view on *who* to communicate with, and the motivation and design frameworks set the level and topics about *what* to communicate about, the communication framework should define *how* to communicate.

In [48] a detailed discussion is provided on how to create different communication strategies for architectures. This involves a tuning between the audience involved in the communication, the purpose of communication (e.g. informing or decision making), the characteristics of the information to be communicated, and the strategy used.

Process Framework. The final ingredient concerns the processes involved in 'doing architecture'. In other words, architecture process frameworks including e.g. TOGAF's ADM [60], GERAM's process framework [29] and DYA [62], while GEA [64] also provides explicit processes to include the identified stakeholder groups.

We argue that the chosen/composed processes framework should always involve activities pertaining to the continuous (e.g. PDCA [15] alike) *sensing, thinking* and *acting*, while using the engagement framework to engage the right stakeholder groups, and using the design framework to structure the architectural thinking. We find that existing architecture approaches tend to put a strong emphasis on the *thinking* aspect, quite often even without the use of an effective engagement framework.

5   Conclusions

In this position paper, we investigated the potential role of enterprise architecture as a means to support senior management in steering enterprises in motion. We presented our fundamental understanding of the playing field, in which enterprise architecture is to play a role, based on a.o. the *control paradigm*.

We also argued that the motion-steering system of an enterprise is essentially a second order information system, yielding several future challenges for the field of information systems [47].

Based on this, we also identified different levels of steering enterprises in motion, positioning architectural steering (and thinking) in between strategic level steering and design level steering. Finally, we suggested the key ingredients of enterprise architecture as being: an engagement framework, a motivation framework, a design framework, a communication framework, and a process framework.

References

1. Mergers and Acquisitions; Dangerous Liaisons – the integration game. Research and opinions; executive summary, Hay, Group (2007)
2. TechnoVision 2012 – Bringing business technology to life. Research report, Capgemini, Utrecht, The Netherlands (2009)
3. van der Aalst, W.M.P.: Process Mining: Discovery Conformance and Enhancement of Business Processes. Springer, Heidelberg (2011)
4. Abraham, R., Tribolet, J., Winter, R.: Transformation of multi-level systems – theoretical grounding and consequences for enterprise architecture management. In: Proper, H.A., Aveiro, D., Gaaloul, K. (eds.) EEWC 2013. LNBIP, vol. 146, pp. 73–87. Springer, Heidelberg (2013)
5. Achterbergh, J., Vriens, D.: Organisations: Social Systems Conducting Experiments. Springer, Heidelberg (2009)
6. Ashby, W.R.: An Introduction to Cybernetics. Chapman & Hall, London (1956)
7. Åström, K.J., Murray, R.M.: Feedback Systems: An Introduction for Scientists and Engineers. Princeton University Press, Princeton (2008)
8. Avison, D.E.: Information Systems Development: Methodologies Techniques and Tools, 2nd edn. McGraw-Hill, New York (1995)
9. Beer, S.: Diagnosing the System for Organizations. Wiley, New York (1985)
10. Bjekovic, M., Proper, H.A., Sottet, J.-S.: Towards a coherent enterprise modelling landscape. In: Sandkuhl, K., Seigerroth, U., Stirna, J. (eds.) Short Paper Proceedings of the 5th IFIP WG 8.1 Working Conference on the Practice of Enterprise Modeling, Rostock, Germany, 7–8 November 2012, vol. 933, CEUR Workshop Proceedings, CEUR-WS.org (2012). http://ceur-ws.org/Vol-933/pap3.pdf
11. Buckl, S., Matthes, F., Schweda, C.M.: A viable system perspective on enterprise architecture management. In: 2009 IEEE International Conference on Systems, Man and Cybernetics, SMC 2009. pp. 1483–1488, October 2009
12. Buckl, S., Matthes, F., Schweda, ChM: A method base for enterprise architecture management. In: Ralyté, J., Mirbel, I., Deneckère, R. (eds.) ME 2011. IFIP AICT, vol. 351, pp. 34–48. Springer, Heidelberg (2011)

13. Ciborra, C.U.: From thinking to tinkering: the grassroots of strategic information systems. Inf. Soc. **8**, 297–309 (1992)
14. Davenport, T.H.: Process Innovation: Reengineering Work Through Information Technology. Harvard Business School Press, Boston (1993)
15. Deming, W.E.: Out of the Crisis. MIT Center for Advanced Engineering Study, Cambridge (1986)
16. Dietz, J.L.G.: Architecture - building strategy into design. Netherlands Architecture Forum, Academic Service - SDU, The Hague, The Netherlands (2008). http://www.naf.nl
17. Dietz, J.L.G., Hoogervorst, J.A.P., Albani, A., Aveiro, D., Babkin, E., Barjis, J., Caetano, A., Huysmans, P., Iijima, J., van Kervel, S.J.H., Mulder, H., Op 't Land, M., Proper, H.A., Sanz, J., Terlouw, L., Tribolet, J., Verelst, J., Winter, R.: The discipline of enterprise engineering. Int. J. Organ. Des. Eng. **3**(1), 86–114 (2013)
18. Drucker, P.F.: Innovation and Entrepreneurship. Harper Collins, New York (2006)
19. Farenhorst, R., de Boer, R.: Architectural knowledge management: supporting architects and auditors. Ph.D. thesis, Free University of Amsterdam, Amsterdam, The Netherlands, December 2009
20. Feltus, C., Dubois, E., Proper, H.A., Band, I., Petit, M.: Enhancing the ArchiMate standard with a responsibility modeling language for access rights management. In: Singh Gaur, M., Elçi, A., Makarevich, O.B., Orgun, M.A., Singh, V. (eds.) 5th International Conference of Security of Information and Networks, SIN '12, Jaipur, India, 22–26 October 2012, pp. 12–19. ACM (2012)
21. Gibson, J.J.: The theory of affordances. In: Shaw, R., Bransford, J. (eds.) Perceiving, Acting, and Knowing, pp. 76–82. Erlbaum, Hillsdale (1977)
22. Greefhorst, D., Proper, H.A.: Architecture Principles - The Cornerstones of Enterprise Architecture. Enterprise Engineering Series. Springer, Heidelberg (2011)
23. Harmsen, F., Proper, H.A.E., Kok, N.: Informed governance of enterprise transformations. In: Proper, E., Harmsen, F., Dietz, J.L.G. (eds.) PRET 2009. LNBIP, vol. 28, pp. 155–180. Springer, Heidelberg (2009)
24. Harmsen, F., Proper, E., Schalkwijk, F., Barjis, J., Overbeek, S. (eds.): PRET 2010. LNBIP, vol. 69. Springer, Heidelberg (2010)
25. Hayles, N.K.: Computing the human. Theor. Cult. Soc. **22**(1), 131–151 (2005)
26. Hoppenbrouwers, S.J.B.A., Proper, H.A.: A communicative perspective on second order information systems. In: Lasker, G.E. (ed.) Proceedings of the 16th International Conference on System Research, Informatics and Cybernetics, Baden-Baden, Germany. IIAS (2004)
27. Hurwitz, J., Nugent, A., Halper, F., Kaufman, M.: Big Data For Dummies. Wiley, Hoboken (2013)
28. Iacob, M.-E., Jonkers, H., Lankhorst, M.M., Proper, H.A., Quartel, D.A.C.: ArchiMate 2.0 Specification. The Open Group (2012)
29. IFIP-IFAC Task Force. GERAM: Generalised Enterprise Reference Architecture and Methodology. March 1999. Version 1.6.3, Published as Annex to ISO WD15704
30. de Kinderen, S., Gaaloul, K., Proper, H.A.E.: On transforming DEMO models to ArchiMate. In: Bider, I., Halpin, T., Krogstie, J., Nurcan, S., Proper, E., Schmidt, R., Soffer, P., Wrycza, S. (eds.) EMMSAD 2012 and BPMDS 2012. LNBIP, vol. 113, pp. 270–284. Springer, Heidelberg (2012)
31. Lahrmann, G., Winter, R., Fischer, M.M.: Design and engineering for situational transformation. In: Harmsen et al. [24], pp. 1–16
32. van Lamsweerde, A.: Goal-oriented requirements engineering: a guided tour. In: Proceedings of RE'01: 5th International Symposium on Requirements Engineering (2001)

33. Lankhorst, M.M., et al.: Enterprise Architecture at Work: Modelling Communication and Analysis. Enterprise Engineering Series, 3rd edn. Springer, Heidelberg (2012)
34. de Leeuw, A.C.J.: Organisaties: Management, Analyse, Ontwikkeling en Verandering, een systeem visie. Van Gorcum, Assen (1982). In Dutch
35. de Leeuw, A.C.J., Volberda, H.W.: On the concept of flexibility: a dual control perspective. Omega Int. J. Manage. Sci. **24**(2), 121–139 (1996)
36. Mandis, S.G.: What Happened to Goldman Sachs: An Insider's Story of Organizational Drift and Its Unintended Consequences. Harvard Business Review Press, Boston (2013)
37. Mathiassen, L.: Systemudvikling og Systemudviklings-Metode. Ph.D. thesis, Aarhus University, Aarhus, Denmark (1981) (In Danish)
38. Meriam-Webster. Meriam-Webster Online, Collegiate Dictionary (2003)
39. Nakakawa, A., van Bommel, P., Proper, H.A.: Definition and validation of requirements for collaborative decision-making in enterprise architecture creation. Int. J. Coop. Inf. Syst. **20**(1), 83–136 (2011)
40. Object Management Group. Business process modeling notation, v1.1. OMG Available Specification OMG Document Number: formal/2008-01-17, January 2008
41. Liu, X., Pedrycz, W.: Fundamentals. In: Liu, X., Pedrycz, W. (eds.) Axiomatic Fuzzy Set Theory and Its Applications. STUDFUZZ, vol. 244, pp. 3–60. Springer, Heidelberg (2009)
42. Op 't Land, M., Proper, H.A., Waage, M., Cloo, J., Steghuis, C.: Enterprise Architecture - Creating Value by Informed Governance. Enterprise Engineering Series. Springer, Heidelberg (2008)
43. Plataniotis, G., de Kinderen, S., Proper, H.A.: EA anamnesis: towards an approach for enterprise architecture rationalization. In: Printing, S. (ed.) Proceedings of the 12th Workshop on Domain-Specific Modeling (DSM12). ACM DL (2012)
44. Prakken, B.: Information, Organization and Information Systems Design: An Integrated Approach to Information Problems. Springer, Heidelberg (2000)
45. Proper, H.A.: ISP for Large-scale Migrations. Information Services Procurement Library. Ten Hagen & Stam, Den Haag, The Netherlands (2001)
46. Proper, H.A.: Enterprise Architecture - Growing up to evidence-based management? Chapter 8.1, pp. 317–328. Netherlands Architecture Forum, The Netherlands (2012)
47. Proper, H.A.: Business informatics for enterprise transformations. In: 2013 IEEE 6th International Conference on Service-Oriented Computing and Applications (SOCA), pp. 251–251, December 2013
48. Proper, H.A., Hoppenbrouwers, S.J.B.A., Veldhuijzen van Zanten, G.E.: Communication of enterprise architectures. In: Enterprise Architecture at Work: Modelling, Communication and Analysis [33], pp. 67–82
49. Proper, H.A., Op 't Land, M.: Lines in the water - the line of reasoning in an enterprise engineering case study from the public sector. In: Harmsen et al. [24], pp. 193–216
50. Pyzdek, T.: The Six Sigma Handbook: The Complete Guide for Greenbelts, Blackbelts, and Managers at All Levels, 2nd edn. McGraw-Hill, New York (2003). Revised and Expanded Edition
51. van Reijswoud, V.E., Dietz, J.L.G.: DEMO Modelling Handbook, vol. 1, 2nd edn. Delft University of Technology, Delft (1999)
52. Ettema, R., Dietz, J.L.G.: ArchiMate and DEMO – mates to date? In: Albani, A., Barjis, J., Dietz, J.L.G. (eds.) CIAO! 2009. LNBIP, vol. 34, pp. 172–186. Springer, Heidelberg (2009)

53. Rouse, W.B.: A theory of enterprise transformation. Syst. Eng. **8**(4), 279–295 (2005)
54. Seligmann, P.S., Wijers, G.M., Sol, H.G.: Analyzing the Structure of I.S. Methodologies, an alternative approach. In: Maes, R. (ed.) Proceedings of the 1st Dutch Conferenceon Information Systems. Amersfoort, the Netherlands, 1-2 November 1989
55. Siegel, M.: The sense-think-act paradigm revisited. In: 2003 1st International Workshop on Robotic Sensing, ROSE' 03, pp. 5–10, June 2003
56. Sol, H.G.: A feature analysis of information systems design methodologies: methodological considerations. In: Olle, T.W., Sol, H.G., Tully, C.J. (eds.) Information Systems Design Methodologies: A Feature Analysis, Amsterdam, The Netherlands, pp. 1–7. North-Holland/IFIP WG8.1, Amsterdam (1983)
57. Sousa, P., Lima, J., Sampaio, A., Pereira, C.: An approach for creating and managing enterprise blueprints: a case for IT blueprints. In: Albani, A., Barjis, J., Dietz, J.L.G. (eds.) CIAO! 2009. LNBIP, vol. 34, pp. 70–84. Springer, Heidelberg (2009)
58. Sousa, P., Gabriel, R., Tadao, G., Carvalho, R., Sousa, P.M., Sampaio, A.: Enterprise transformation: the Serasa experian case. In: Harmsen, F., Grahlmann, K., Proper, E. (eds.) PRET 2011. LNBIP, vol. 89, pp. 134–145. Springer, Heidelberg (2011)
59. Sowa, J.F., Zachman, J.A.: Extending and formalizing the framework for information systems architecture. IBM Syst. J. **31**(3), 590–616 (1992)
60. The Open Group: TOGAF Version 9. Van Haren Publishing, Zaltbommel (2009)
61. Veldhuijzen van Zanten, G.E., Hoppenbrouwers, S.J.B.A., Proper, H.A.: System development as a rational communicative process. J. Syst. Cybern. Inf. **2**(4), 47–51 (2004). http://www.iiisci.org/Journal/sci/pdfs/P492036.pdf
62. Wagter, R., van der Berg, M., Luijpers, J., van Steenbergen, M.: Dynamic Enterprise Architecture: How to Make It Work. Wiley, New York (2005)
63. Wagter, R., Proper, H.A., Witte, D.: The extended enterprise coherence-governance assessment. In: Aier, S., Ekstedt, M., Matthes, F., Proper, E., Sanz, J.L. (eds.) PRET 2012 and TEAR 2012. LNBIP, vol. 131, pp. 218–235. Springer, Heidelberg (2012)
64. Wagter, R., Proper, H.A., Witte, D.: A theory for enterprise coherence governance. In: Saha, P. (ed.) A Systematic Perspective to Managing Complexity with EA. IGI Publishing (2013, To appear)
65. Wegmann, A.: On the systemic enterprise architecture methodology (SEAM). In: International Conference on Enterprise Information Systems (ICEIS 2003) (2003)
66. van't Wout, J., Waage, M., Hartman, H., Stahlecker, M., Hofman, A.: The Integrated Architecture Framework Explained. Springer, Heidelberg (2010)
67. Zachman, J.A.: A framework for information systems architecture. IBM Syst. J. **26**(3), 276–292 (1987)

Databases and Information
Systems Integration

An Evaluation of Multi-way Joins
for Relational Database Systems

Michael Henderson and Ramon Lawrence$^{(\boxtimes)}$

Department of Computer Science, University of British Columbia,
Kelowna, BC, Canada
mikecubed@gmail.com, ramon.lawrence@ubc.ca
https://people.ok.ubc.ca/rlawrenc/

Abstract. In database systems most join algorithms operate on only
two inputs at a time. Research into joins on more than two inputs, called
multi-way joins, has shown that the intermediate partitioning steps of a
traditional hash join based query plan can be avoided. This decreases the
amount of disk based input and output (I/Os) that the query requires.
This work studies the advantages and disadvantages of implementing and
using different multi-way join algorithms and their relative performance
compared to traditional hash joins. Specifically, this work compares hash
join with three multi-way join algorithms: hash teams, generalized hash
teams and SHARP. The results of the experiments show that in some
cases multi-way hash joins can provide a significant advantage over hash
join but not always. The cases where hash teams and generalized hash
teams have better performance is limited, and it does not make sense to
implement these algorithms in a production database management system. SHARP provides enough of a performance advantage that it makes
sense to implement it in a database system used for data warehousing.

Keywords: Multi-way join · Hybrid hash · Join ordering · Query
optimization · PostgreSQL

1 Introduction

Multi-way joins are capable of joining more than two relations at a time.
These algorithms have the potential for significant performance improvements
over multiple binary joins by avoiding intermediate partitioning and materialization steps. However, database systems are not using multi-way joins. This work
experimentally evaluates several multi-way join algorithms and compares their
performance to traditional binary join query plans.

The positive argument for multi-way joins is supported by a significant
amount of research literature that demonstrates performance benefits. Hash
teams [1] implemented in Microsoft SQL Server 7.0 and generalized hash teams [2]
improve I/O efficiency compared to binary plans by avoiding multiple partitioning steps. These algorithms can be used for joins of relations on the same join

© Springer International Publishing Switzerland 2014
S. Hammoudi et al. (Eds.): ICEIS 2013, LNBIP 190, pp. 37–50, 2014.
DOI: 10.1007/978-3-319-09492-2_3

attributes (hash teams) or join relations related by a chain of functional dependencies/foreign keys (generalized hash teams). It has been shown by the SHARP [3] query processing system that a multi-way operator adapts to estimation inaccuracies, has the ability to dynamically share memory easier than binary plans, and avoids redundant next() calls in the iterator model. Further, streaming multi-way joins such as MJoin [4] and slice join [5] compensate for network delays and blocking. A streaming multi-way join operator allows tuples to be processed from any input at any time which simplifies optimization issues such as join order selection and handles changing input arrival rates.

However, there are issues with robustness of multi-way operators. A multi-way operator still must select a probe ordering internally which has similar complexity as join order selection with the additional goal that it is adaptable to the data characteristics during join processing. The one known commercial implementation, hash teams in Microsoft SQL Server 7.0 [6], was later dropped in SQL Server 2000 SP1 [7] in order to improve stability and due to limited performance benefits. There are limitations on the types of joins possible using a multi-way operator. Hash teams are limited to joins of relations all on the same join attributes, generalized hash teams support chains of foreign key joins, and SHARP supports star queries. Finally, although it has been argued that the changes to the query optimizer to support multi-way joins are straightforward, in practice that is not the case. A typical query optimizer [8] is only capable of exploring binary plans. Without modifying the plan generator to cost multi-way plans simultaneously with binary plans, multi-way operators must be constructed after binary optimization is complete.

To gain insights on the capability of multi-way joins in a database system, we implemented three multi-way join algorithms: hash teams, generalized hash teams, and SHARP. The algorithms were evaluated both in PostgreSQL and in a stand-alone C++ implementation. In both experimental environments, multi-way join algorithms demonstrated some performance benefits, especially with regards to I/O, compared to binary plans. However, their CPU utilization was often higher resulting in mixed performance relative to binary plans. The contribution of this work is an experimental evaluation in two environments of the multi-way algorithms and a discussion on their general applicability in database systems. This paper is an extension to previously published work [9] that included the first set of results with PostgreSQL and an algorithm for converting binary to multi-way join plans. This work contains new experimental results with a second, independent implementation of the algorithms to verify the original results and related further discussion.

The organization of this paper is as follows. In Sect. 2, we overview existing work on multi-way hash joins. The algorithm implementations are briefly described in Sect. 3. Experimental results in Sect. 4 demonstrate benefits but also implementation challenges of multi-way joins. The paper closes with conclusions and future work.

2 Previous Work

2.1 Binary Hash Joins

A join combines two relations into a single relation. We refer to the smaller relation as the *build relation*, and the larger relation as the *probe relation*. A hash join first reads the tuples of the build relation, hashes them on the join attributes to determine a partition index, and then writes the tuples to disk based on the partition index. It then repeats the process for the probe relation. The partitioning is designed such that each build partition is now small enough to fit in a hash table in available memory. This hash table is then probed with tuples from the matching probe partition. Hybrid hash join (HHJ) [10] is a common hash join algorithm implemented in most database systems. Hybrid hash join selects one build partition to remain memory-resident before the join begins. Any available memory beyond what is needed for partitioning is used to reduce the number of I/O operations performed. Dynamic hash join (DHJ) [11,12] can adapt to memory changes by initially keeping all build partitions in memory and then flushing on demand as memory is required. Hash join optimizations [13] include bit vector filtering and role reversal.

2.2 Multi-way Joins

A multi-way join can join two or more relations at the same time. The common issues in all multi-way join implementations are the hash table structure, the probe ordering, and the join types supported.

The hash table structure must support the ability to partition the input relations such that only tuples at the same partition index can join together. Each input typically has its own hash table and associated partition file buffers. A multi-way operator that has multiple hash tables can use the memory available to buffer tuples from any input. Internally, the algorithm must select a probe ordering. The probe ordering specifies the order of inputs to probe given a tuple of one input. The probe ordering may differ based on the input tuple and may adapt as the join progresses.

Not all joins can be efficiently executed using multi-way hash joins. If all inputs cannot fit in memory, the only join plans that can be executed using one partitioning step are those where the inputs all have common hash attributes or joins where indirect partitioning is possible. One partitioning step is sufficient as the cleanup can be performed by loading all partitions at the same index in memory and then probing. Star joins can be processed using multi-dimensional partitioning. Multi-dimensional partitioning requires the build relations be read multiple times during the cleanup phase, but this still may be more efficient than the corresponding binary plans.

Hash Teams. Hash teams [1] was invented by Goetz Graefe, Ross Bunker, and Shaun Cooper at Microsoft and implemented in Microsoft SQL Server 7.0 in 1998. Performance gains of up to 40 % were reported. Hash teams perform a multi-way hash join where the inputs share common hash attributes. Hash teams can also include other types of operators that use hashing such as grouping. A hash team is split into two separate roles: the hash operators and a team manager. The hash operators are responsible for consuming input records and producing the output records. They manage their hash table and overflow files. They also write partitions to disk and remove them from memory as well as loading them back into memory on request of the team manager. The team manager is separate from the regular plan operators. Memory management and partition flushing are coordinated externally by the team manager. It also maps hash values to buckets and buckets to partitions. When the manager decides that a partition needs to be flushed, it asks all of the operators in the team to flush the chosen partition.

Generalized Hash Teams. Hash teams were extended to generalized hash teams [2] by Alfons Kemper, Donald Kossman and Christian Wiesner in 1999. Like hash teams, the tables are partitioned one time and the join occurs in one pass. However, generalized hash teams are not restricted to joins that hash on the exact same attributes as they allow tables to be joined using *indirect* partitioning. Indirect partitioning partitions a relation on an attribute that functionally determines the partitioning attribute. A TPC-H [14] query joining the relations *Customer, Orders*, and *LineItem* can be executed using a generalized hash team that partitions the first two relations on *custkey* and probes with the *LineItem* relation by using its *orderkey* attribute to indirectly determine a partition number using a mapping constructed when partitioning *Orders*. This mapping provides a partition number given an *orderkey*.

The major issue with indirect partitioning is that storing an exact representation of the mapping function is memory-intensive. In [2], bitmap approximations are used that consume less space but introduce the possibility of mapping errors. These errors do not affect algorithm correctness but do affect performance. The bitmap approximation works by associating a bitmap of a chosen size with each partition. A key to be stored or queried with the mapping function is hashed based on the bitmap size to get an index I in the bitmap. The bit at index I is set to 1 in the bitmap for the partition where the tuple belongs. Note that due to collisions in the hashing of the key to the bitmap size, it is possible for a bit at index I to be set in multiple partition bitmaps which results in *false drops*. A false drop is when a tuple gets put into a partition where it does not belong.

The generalized hash team algorithm does not have a "hybrid step" where it uses additional memory to buffer tuples beyond what is required for partitioning. Further, the bitmaps must be relatively large (multiples of the input relation size) to reduce the number of false drops. Consequently, even the bitmap approximation is memory intensive as the number of partitions increases.

SHARP. Another multi-way join algorithm is the Streaming, Highly Adaptive, Run-time Planner (SHARP) [3] that performs multi-dimensional partitioning. SHARP was invented by Pedro Bizarro and David DeWitt at the University of Wisconsin - Madison in 2006. An example TPC-H star query involves *Part*,

Orders and *LineItem*. In multi-dimensional partitioning, *Part* and *Orders* are the build tables and are partitioned on *partkey* and *orderkey* respectively. *LineItem* is the probe relation and is partitioned simultaneously on *(partkey,orderkey)* (in two dimensions). The number of partitions of the probe table is the product of the number of partitions in each build input. For example, if *Part* was partitioned into 3 partitions and *Orders* partitioned into 5 partitions, then *LineItem* would be partitioned into 5*3 = 15 partitions.

For a tuple to be generated in the memory phase, the tuple of *LineItem* must have both its matching *Part* and *Orders* partitions in memory. Otherwise, the probe tuple is written to disk. The cleanup pass involves iterating through all partition combinations. The algorithm loads on-disk partitions of the probe relation once and on-disk partitions of the build relation i a number of times equal to $\prod_{j=1}^{i-1} X_j$, where X_i is the number of partitions for build relation i. Reading build partitions multiple times may still be faster than materializing intermediate results, and the operator benefits from memory sharing during partitioning and the ability to adapt during its execution.

2.3 Other Join Algorithms

There are two other related but distinct areas of research on join algorithms. There is work on parallelizing main-memory joins based on hashing [15] and sorting [16]. The assumption in these algorithms is that there is sufficient memory for the join inputs such that the dominate factor is CPU time rather than I/O time. In this work, we are examining joins where I/O is still a major factor. The main-memory and cache-aware optimization techniques employed in these works could also be applied to I/O bound joins.

Another related area is performing multi-way joins on Map-Reduce systems such as in [17,18]. Map-Reduce systems are designed for very large-scale queries over a commodity cluster. The join algorithms used and how they apply to multi-way joins are distinct from traditional relational database systems.

3 Multi-way Join Implementation

Performance of the multi-way join algorithms depends on the implementation. Multiple implementations of the algorithms allow for testing in different conditions. Implementations were created in the open source database system PostgreSQL as well as a standalone C++ implementation.

3.1 Implementation in PostgreSQL

To test the effectiveness of the multi-way join algorithms in a real world setting, the algorithms were implemented in the open source database system PostgreSQL [19]. PostgreSQL is an advanced enterprise class database system. It includes a query planner and optimizer, memory manager, and a hybrid hash join implementation.

Adding the three multi-way join algorithms involved the addition of six source code files with more than 5000 lines of code. Each join had a file defining its hash table structure and operations and a file defining the operator in iterator form. Generalized hash teams (GHT) had two mapper implementations: exact mapper and bit mapper. The exact mapper assumed an integer join attribute and mapped its input to a partition number.

In comparison to implementing the join algorithms themselves, a much harder task was modifying the optimizer and execution system to use them. The basic issue is both of these systems assume a maximum of two inputs per operator, hence there are many changes required to basic data structures to support a node with more than two inputs. The changes can be summarized as follows:

- Create a multi-way hash node structure for use in logical query trees and join optimization planning.
- Create a multi-way execution node that stores the state necessary for iterator execution.
- Modify all routines associated with the planner that assume two children nodes including EXPLAIN feature, etc.
- Create multi-way hash and join clauses (*quals*) from binary clauses.
- Create cost functions for the multi-way joins that conform to PostgreSQL cost functions which include both I/O and CPU costs.
- Modify the mapping from logical query trees to execution plan to support creation of multi-way join plans.

The changes were made as general as possible. However, there are limitations on what queries can be successfully converted and executed with multi-way joins.

3.2 Standalone C++ Implementation

The algorithms were also implemented in C++ to isolate them from the complete database system (such as the buffer manager) of PostgreSQL. All the supporting data structures, algorithms, and memory management also were implemented. This includes all code that defines relations, tuples, attributes, and other basic relational database data structures. Each algorithm was implemented in a separate source file and extended the same base *Operator* class. All the algorithms were implemented using the same hashing algorithms and hash tables. The source contains 8400 lines of code across 46 files. The source code can be found online [20]. Source was built using Visual Studio 2012.

The hash tables used separate chaining. Each hash table is an array of linked lists. Hash collisions are handled by adding each tuple that hashes to a specific array index to the end of the linked list for that array index. The array length is set to the number of tuples that will be stored in it to obtain a load factor of 1. The load factor α of a table of size m with n tuples is calculated with $\alpha = n/m$. A low load factor as well as a good hash function is needed to keep the average cost of a hash lookup as small as possible. This is important since each probe tuple that is looking for its matches will need to be checked against every tuple stored in the hash table that hashes to the same array index as the probe tuple.

When in the probe phase of a join each tuple of the probe relation is read into memory, hashed and then probed against the existing in memory hash table. Each tuple in the hash table that matches the hash of the probe tuple must then be checked to see if its join attributes match the join attributes of the probe tuple. If the tuples have more than one attribute that they are joined on or they are joining on non-integer attributes this can be a very CPU intensive operation.

The C++ implementation does not include a query parser or optimizer. Each query was hand optimized and hard coded into the program. Multiple runs of the program were scripted using Windows PowerShell.

4 Experimental Results

4.1 PostgreSQL Results

The PostgreSQL experiments were executed on a dual processor AMD Opteron 2350 Quad Core at 2.0 GHz with 32 GB of RAM and two 7200 RPM, 1 TB hard drives running 64-bit Linux. Similar results were demonstrated when running the experiments on a Windows platform. PostgreSQL version 8.3.1 was used, and the source code modified as described. Since PostgreSQL includes a hybrid hash join (HHJ) algorithm by default, all the multi-way join algorithms were compared against it in order to see how they performed against an optimized and tested hash join algorithm.

Relation	Tuple Size	#Tuples	Relation Size
Customer	194 B	1.5 million	284 MB
Supplier	184 B	100,000	18 MB
Part	173 B	2 million	323 MB
Orders	147 B	15 million	2097 MB
PartSupp	182 B	8 million	1392 MB
LineItem	162 B	60 million	9270 MB

Fig. 1. TPC-H 10 GB relation sizes.

The data set was TPC-H benchmark [14] scale factor 10 GB[1] (see Fig. 1) generated using Microsoft's TPC-H generator [21], which supports generation of skewed data sets with a Zipfian distribution. The results are for a skewed data set with $z = 1$. Experiments tested different join memory sizes configured using the work_mem parameter. The memory size is given on a per join basis. Multi-way operators get a multiple of the join memory size. For instance, a three-way operator gets 2*work_mem for its three inputs.

---

[1] The TPC-H data set scale factor 100 GB was tested on the hardware but run times of many hours to days made it impractical for the tests.

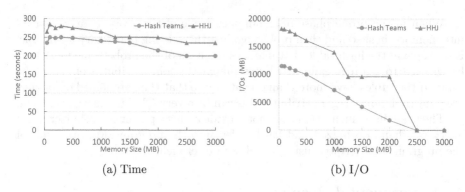

(a) Time   (b) I/O

Fig. 2. PostgreSQL: hash teams.

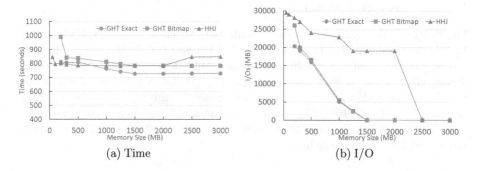

(a) Time   (b) I/O

Fig. 3. PostgreSQL: generalized hash teams.

Direct Partitioning with Hash Teams. One experiment was a three-way join of *Orders* relations. The join was on the *orderkey* and produced 15 million results. The results are in Fig. 2.

The results clearly show a benefit for a multi-way join with about a 60 % reduction in I/O bytes for the join and approximately 12–15 % improvement in overall time. The multi-way join performs fewer I/Os by saving one partitioning step. It also saves by not materializing intermediate tuples in memory and by reducing the number of probes performed. The multi-way join continues to be faster even for larger memory sizes and a completely in-memory join.

Indirect Partitioning with Generalized Hash Teams. Indirect partitioning was tested with a join of the *Customer*, *Orders*, and *LineItem* relations. Generalized hash teams was compared using both a bit and exact mapper. The bit mapper used 12 bytes * number of tuples in the *Orders* relation as its bit map size which is the same amount of space used by the exact mapper. The results are in Fig. 3.

For this join, GHT had fewer I/Os but that did not always translate to a time advantage unless the difference was large. HHJ had worse performance on a memory jump from 2000 MB to 2500 MB despite performing 20 GB fewer I/Os!

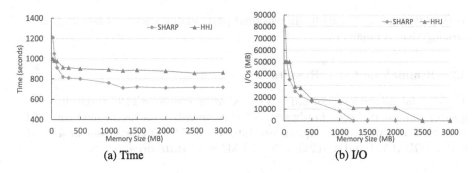

(a) Time   (b) I/O

Fig. 4. PostgreSQL: SHARP.

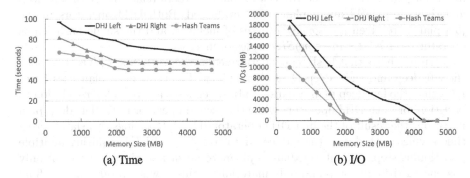

(a) Time   (b) I/O

Fig. 5. Stand-alone implementation: hash teams.

The difference was the optimizer changed the query plan to join *Orders* with *LineItem* then the result with *Customer* at 2500 MB where previously *Customer* and *Orders* were joined first. This new ordering produced double the number of probes and join clause evaluations and ended up being slower overall. These results show that CPU cost in probing hash tables is as significant factor as the number of I/Os performed.

The major limitation was the mapper size. The mappers did not produce results for the smaller memory sizes of 32 MB and 64 MB as the mapper could not be memory-resident. For 128 MB, the bit mapper performed significantly more I/Os and had larger time than the exact mapper due to the number of false drops. The number of false drops was greatly reduced as the memory increased. The CPU and memory cost of the mapper reduced the performance of generalized hash teams significantly.

Multi-dimensional Partitioning with SHARP. One of the star join tests combined *Part*, *Orders*, and *LineItem*. The performance of the SHARP algorithm versus hybrid hash join is in Fig. 4. SHARP performed 50–100 % fewer I/Os in bytes and was about 5–30 % faster. Only at very small memory sizes did the performance become slower than HHJ, and it was faster in the full memory case. SHARP had a performance advantage as the CPU time decreased as well as the I/O time as the multi-dimensional partitioning results in less hash table probing than a binary plan.

4.2   Standalone C++ Results

The standalone implementation was tested using the same TPC-H database and queries but on different hardware. All experiments were performed on a PC running Windows 8 with a quad core Intel Core i7 2600K processor at 4.4 GHz with 24 GB RAM and a 512 GB Crucial M4 solid state drive.

Direct Partitioning with Hash Teams. Hash teams was compared to dynamic hash join (DHJ) for the three-way join of *Orders* relations. Both left deep and right deep DHJ query plans were evaluated. Both DHJ operators in the join plan were given *memorySize* bytes of memory, and the single hash teams operator received $2 \times memorySize$ bytes of memory.

Figure 5 shows that hash teams performed significantly fewer I/Os than both the left deep and right deep DHJ query plans. The right deep plan uses fewer I/Os than the left deep plan because it always chooses a single *Orders* relation to partition for both DHJ operators while the second operator in the left deep plan partitions the result of the first DHJ operator. This I/O savings translates into a time savings both due to the reduced data transfer and DHJ requiring multiple partitioning steps and intermediate tuple materialization. Since hash teams only has one partitioning step and only materializes tuples when producing the final output it is able to gain a significant advantage over the widely used dynamic hash join.

Indirect Partitioning with Generalized Hash Teams. Generalized hash teams (GHT) were compared to DHJ using the three-way join of *Customer*, *Orders*, and *LineItem* relations. Both left deep and right deep DHJ query plans were evaluated. First, GHT was evaluated using a large amount of memory for the map in order to ensure that there were no false drops. This is to show the behaviour of GHT in its best possible conditions as the memory for the map is not counted against the memory for the join. Second, GHT was evaluated with the map memory counted against the join memory to show its behaviour in normal conditions.

Figure 6 shows that even though generalized hash teams performed 30 % to 100 % fewer I/Os than the left and right deep DHJ query plans, this did not always result in a time advantage. GHT is approximately 8 % slower than the right deep DHJ plan when performing zero I/Os and 25 % slower than the left deep DHJ plan. GHT is slower because of the extra hashing and probing of the map GHT needs to match tuples when joining relations. It is not until low memory sizes that GHT becomes faster than both the left and right deep DHJ plans.

Figure 7 shows the I/Os used for GHT when the memory used by the map is removed from the memory available to the join. GHT behaves reasonably until there is not enough memory to keep the number of false drops low. Once GHT

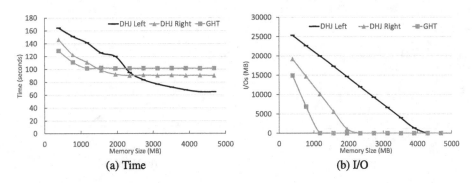

Fig. 6. Stand-alone implementation: generalized hash teams.

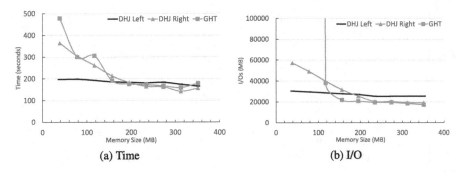

Fig. 7. Stand-alone implementation: generalized hash teams for small memory sizes.

has only a very small amount of memory the mapping places each *Lineitem* tuple in a large number of partitions causing the amount of file I/O to increase significantly. It also shows that once the I/Os increase for GHT it becomes the slowest join. GHT is not executable for smaller join memory sizes as its performance degrades significantly.

Figure 8 shows the effect of the number of bits per tuple that is used for the map. When there is a small amount of memory available for the map (approximately 1 bit for every 10 tuples) the number of false drops becomes very large. The bit map size should be at least 1/4 of the mapped relation size to avoid severe false drop penalties.

Multi-dimensional Partitioning with SHARP. SHARP was compared against DHJ using a query joining *Part*, *Orders*, and *LineItem*. In this star join, *Lineitem* is the fact table and *Orders* and *Part* are the dimension tables. As shown in Fig. 9 SHARP is able to make much more efficient use of the join memory to perform fewer I/Os in low memory conditions. This is because SHARP partitions each relation independently. Since SHARP performs fewer I/Os and does not need multiple partitioning steps, it is faster than DHJ at all memory sizes.

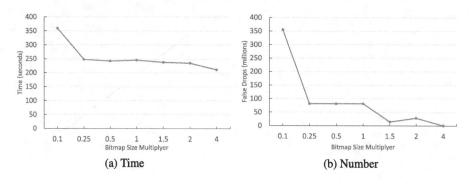

Fig. 8. Stand-alone implementation: false drops compared to bitmap size

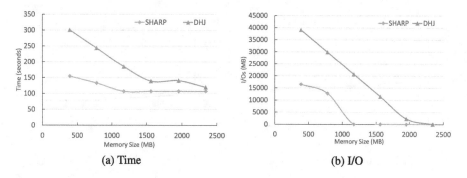

Fig. 9. Stand-alone implementation: SHARP.

5   Discussion and Conclusion

Implementing efficient, robust, and scalable multi-way joins is a non-trivial challenge. The experimental results clearly show that multi-way performance depends on the join type. Direct partitioning joins are efficient and are clearly superior when the hash attributes uniquely identify tuples in each input. However in that case, it is also likely that interesting orders based on sorting may apply (as the relations may be sorted on the primary/unique attribute) which would have even better performance.

Indirect partitioning has benefits, but the mapping functions consume both space and CPU time. Indirect partitioning is inapplicable if the mappers cannot be completely memory-resident during partitioning. Indirect partitioning without a hybrid step is not competitive with binary plans. Note that this does not contradict the results in [2] as the join algorithm was not used in conjunction with the space saving hash aggregation structure proposed. The results clearly show both a benefit and an issue with direct and indirect partitioning joins. The number of I/Os performed is less but that does not always translate into a time advantage. The I/O cost is often reduced by intelligent operating system buffering. Overall, indirect partitioning joins are not as robust as binary joins and the high CPU cost often outweighs any I/O advantages. Similar to main-memory optimized joins, optimizing algorithms for cache-awareness is very beneficial for performance. A cache-aware multi-way join may have better performance.

Multi-dimensional partitioning as implemented in SHARP is a much more consistent winner. The major bad case relates to the "curse of dimensionality" when build inputs are read multiple times and more I/Os are performed than the corresponding binary plan. This case can be identified by the cost functions and will be avoided by the optimizer. Like the one-to-one direct partitioning joins, multi-way partitioning is faster than binary plans for the fully in-memory case. This speed improvement occurs as it does not materialize intermediate results and performs the same (or fewer) number of probes than binary plans. Further, star queries are much more common than the types of queries that would be beneficial for direct or indirect partitioning. Multi-dimensional partitioning is a beneficial addition to the set of join operators and in its most basic implementation (without any adaptability) is fairly straightforward to implement.

6   Conclusions

The goal of this paper was to determine if multi-way joins are useful in a database system. The answer is yes, but primarily for star queries. Direct and indirect partitioning multi-way joins improve performance in some cases, especially for one-to-one joins. The two major issues are the relatively limited number of queries affected, and the care that must be taken to guarantee good performance. Multi-dimensional partitioning is beneficial for a larger number of queries, more efficient except for known cases, and more stable to implement. Multi-dimensional partitioning joins should be implemented in commercial database systems.

Future work includes allowing the optimizer to cost multi-way joins simultaneously with binary plans and conducting experiments to evaluate multi-way joins in conjunction with aggregation operators.

References

1. Graefe, G., Bunker, R., Cooper, S.: Hash joins and hash teams in Microsoft SQL Server. In: VLDB, pp. 86–97 (1998)
2. Kemper, A., Kossmann, D., Wiesner, C.: Generalised hash teams for join and group-by. In: VLDB, pp. 30–41 (1999)
3. Bizarro, P., DeWitt, D.J.: Adaptive and robust query processing with SHARP. Technical report 1562, University of Wisconsin (2006)
4. Viglas, S., Naughton, J., Burger, J.: Maximizing the output rate of multi-way join queries over streaming information sources. In: VLDB, pp. 285–296 (2003)
5. Lawrence, R.: Using slice join for efficient evaluation of multi-way joins. Data Knowl. Eng. **67**(1), 118–139 (2008)
6. Graefe, G., Ewel, J., Galindo-Legaria, C.: Microsoft SQL Server 7.0 query processor. Technical report, Microsoft Corporation. http://msdn.microsoft.com/en-us/library/aa226170(SQL.70).aspx, September 1998

7. Microsoft Corporation: Description of Service Pack 1 for SQL Server 2000. Technical report, Microsoft Corporation. http://support.microsoft.com/kb/889553, May 2001

8. Moerkotte, G., Neumann, T.: Dynamic programming strikes back. In: ACM SIGMOD, pp. 539–552 (2008)

9. Henderson, M., Lawrence, R.: Are multi-way joins actually useful? In: Proceedings of the 15th International Conference on Enterprise Information Systems, ICEIS 2013. SciTePress (2013)

10. DeWitt, D., Katz, R., Olken, F., Shapiro, L., Stonebraker, M., Wood, D.: Implementation techniques for main memory database systems. In: ACM SIGMOD, pp. 1–8 (1984)

11. DeWitt, D., Naughton, J.: Dynamic memory hybrid hash join. Technical report, University of Wisconsin (1995)

12. Kitsuregawa, M., Nakayama, M., Takagi, M.: The effect of bucket size tuning in the dynamic hybrid GRACE hash join method. In: VLDB, pp. 257–266 (1989)

13. Graefe, G.: Five performance enhancements for hybrid hash join. Technical report CU-CS-606-92, University of Colorado at Boulder (1992)

14. TPC: TPC-H benchmark. http://www.tpc.org/tpch/

15. Blanas, S., Li, Y., Patel, J.M.: Design and evaluation of main memory hash join algorithms for multi-core CPUs. In: SIGMOD Conference, pp. 37–48 (2011)

16. Albutiu, M.C., Kemper, A., Neumann, T.: Massively parallel sort-merge joins in main memory multi-core database systems. PVLDB 5(10), 1064–1075 (2012)

17. Zhang, X., Chen, L., Wang, M.: Efficient multi-way theta-join processing using mapreduce. PVLDB 5(11), 1184–1195 (2012)

18. Afrati, F.N., Ullman, J.D.: Optimizing multiway joins in a map-reduce environment. IEEE Trans. Knowl. Data Eng. 23(9), 1282–1298 (2011)

19. PostgreSQL: open source relational database management system. http://www.postgresql.org/

20. Henderson, M.: C++ source code for multi-way join algorithms. https://bitbucket.org/mikecubed/hashjoins

21. Chaudhuri, S., Narasayya, V.: TPC-D data generation with skew. Technical report, Microsoft Research. ftp://ftp.research.microsoft.com/users/viveknar/tpcdskew

What Do We Know About ERP Integration?

Tommi Kähkönen[✉], Andrey Maglyas, and Kari Smolander

Software Engineering and Information Management,
Lappeenranta University of Technology, Lappeenranta, Finland
{tommi.kahkonen,andrey.maglyas,kari.smolander}@lut.fi

Abstract. Enterprise Resource Planning (ERP) systems have been the major interest of companies to improve the business performance with integrated business systems during the last 15 years. As demands for collaborative business through supply chain increased, so did the integration requirements for ERPs that are today connected externally with customers, suppliers and business partners and internally with continuously changing system landscape of the enterprise. We conducted a systematic mapping study to investigate how ERP integration has been studied by the academia from 1998 to 2012. Studies about technological issues are mostly dealing with systems inside a company whereas studies on methodological issues focus on the integration of the supply chain management and e-business. However, these studies are often either carried out without a rigorous empirical research method or they are based on single cases only. Quantitative methods have been mainly used to investigate quality attributes of ERPs but issues related to ERP integration in terms of a network of stakeholders in an ERP project still need more research in the future.

Keywords: Enterprise resource planning · Integration · Systematic mapping study · Literature review

1 Introduction

ERP systems are integrated information systems that aim to integrate the core business processes in a company, previously automated by monolithic legacy applications [1, 2]. They are designed to automate the flow of information, material and financial resources of these processes to a single storage, which can be accessed to get the enterprise data whenever it is needed [3, 4]. The rationale for adopting an ERP system is that the enterprise can enhance its business performance, financial predictability, productivity and decision making by business process automation with timely access to management information [2, 5]. Adopting an ERP system is challenging and expensive project for a company, which usually chooses an ERP product from one or several vendors (e.g. SAP, Oracle or Microsoft) and either re-engineers its business processes to match those offered by the ERP product, or customizes the ERP product to match the existing processes [3, 6].

ERPs originate from inventory control systems, which later transformed into mainframe-based material requirements planning systems (MRP and later MRP2) first to convert production plans into raw material requirements and later to optimize the

© Springer International Publishing Switzerland 2014
S. Hammoudi et al. (Eds.): ICEIS 2013, LNBIP 190, pp. 51–67, 2014.
DOI: 10.1007/978-3-319-09492-2_4

production process of a plant [7, 8]. In 1990s more functions were included to the unified system that was renamed to ERP [7]. Originally designed to integrate only the internal business functions, it was soon realized that ERPs could not meet all integration requirements of the changing business environment. It became necessary to integrate operations across national borders and coordinate business processes with partners in strategic alliances [9].

Business collaboration has become a key strategy for companies and it needs cooperation among organizations, integration of business processes and enterprise systems [10]. In a modern business environment, a single organization is a part of the network of delivering and supporting organizations – a part of the supply chain [4]. Even though it is challenging to accomplish, integration is needed to interconnect customers, distributors and suppliers via integrated supply chains [9]. Implementing an ERP system is seen as the first step in the process of enterprise-wide supply chain integration [2, 11]. Indeed, the ERP system became just one, but important part of the complex IT-architecture of an organization [12]. The literature has noted this by renaming the ERP to *ERPII or Extended ERP,* in which the traditional ERP is seen as a backbone of the enterprise business suite, that is tightly integrated with other operational systems such as SCM (Supply Chain Management) and CRM (Customer Relationship Management) [13]. As these systems cross the boundaries of organizations, additional challenges are encountered in integration: customers need to access the system via web interfaces [13] and there is also a need to provide a mobile access to the enterprise data, regardless of the location [14, 15].

Even though significant amount or research has been conducted on ERP systems during the last 15 years and ERP vendors have constantly upgrade their products, we can still read from the news about ERP disasters[1].

The growing number of information systems dealing with products manufacturing and delivery leads to the key role of integration in ERP projects. Therefore this study maps systematically the existing knowledge in the field of ERP integration and investigates how it has been studied in the academia in order to provide a solid baseline for further ERP integration research.

The next section provides the definition for the concept *integration* and discusses other literature reviews performed on ERPs. Section 3 explains the process of this mapping study. Results are presented in Sect. 4. Section 5 discusses about the future directions of ERP integration research and Sect. 6 provides the conclusions.

2 Background

In the domain of information systems, integration is a multidimensional concept often represented with different perspectives. For example, Barki and Pinsonneault list three perspectives *technical, business,* and *strategic* [9].

---

[1] http://www.cio.com/article/721628/Air_Force_scraps_massive_ERP_project_after_racking_up_1_billionin_costs

Application integration is a strategic approach to bind information systems together [16]. According to Linthicum, application integration can be both internal (Enterprise Application Integration, EAI) and external (business-to-business, B2B) [16]. Internal integration deals with interrelationships and trade-offs within a firm while external integration refers to coordination with customers and/or suppliers [17]. From the integration point-of view, the focus of ERP has traditionally been internal system, but however, along with the evolution of ERPII, The Internet and web technologies have changed the focus of ERP integration to external, to consider also external stakeholders, to connect customers and suppliers through CRM and SCM to the ERP system [18, 19].

Seven systematic literature reviews to map all the conducted research on ERP systems have been done since the end of 1990s [20–26]. These literature reviews address the integration issues only partly. Moreover, the number of papers identified varies between studies. For example, Botta-Genoulaz et al. found only five articles that deal with integration of ERP and other systems (a survey on recent literature) while Esteves and Bohorquez identified 21 integration-related articles and categorized these articles as "Evolution" [22].

Rather than examining all the ERP related research we aim at finding out the ERP integration issues from the literature in order to provide a comprehensive view to this topic. Only Schlichter and Krammergaard had similar approach and identified the research methods of the studies, but they did not highlight what methods have been used to investigate integration issues [25].

For this study, we have set the following research questions: (1) How have the number of publications related to ERP integration been evolved between 1998 and 2012? (2) What aspects of integration have been investigated? (3) What research methods have been used in these studies? and (4) What topics need to be investigated further?

3   Research Method

A systematic literature review (SLR) is a secondary study which aims to gather and evaluate all the evidence on a selected research topic [27, 28]. It aims at identifying gaps in current research to point out the potential areas of further research and it can also provide background to position new research activities [29].

Systematic mapping study (SMS, sometimes called as scoping review) is a study complementary to SLR [29, 30]. Kitchenham and Charters highlight qualitative differences between SLR and SMS [29]. Petersen et al. provide more comprehensive comparison by stating that there are similarities and differences in goals and process as well as in breadth and depth of these studies [30]. Unlike SLR, SMS does not aim at establishing the state of evidence and identifying the best practices based on empirical evidence. Mapping studies do not study articles in detail but aim at classification and thematic analysis. The goal of both types of studies is to identify the research gaps with the aim to influence the future direction of primary research. An SMS aims to classify and structure a certain field of interest, often by analysing the categories and frequencies of publications [30]. An SMS analyses the literature to find out what kind

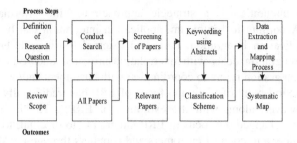

Fig. 1. A process of systematic mapping study.

of studies related to research question have been done, what is their publication forum and what kind of outcomes have been produced [31]. The process for SMS in software engineering has been defined by Petersen et al. [30]. Figure 1 presents this process.

First, the research questions are defined for the SMS. Search strings are selected and they are used to search articles from scientific databases to identify the primary studies, by manually browsing and handling the results of the search. Screening of papers for inclusion and exclusion is used to filter out the papers that do not answer the research questions. In keywording of abstracts, the context and contribution of research is identified. This can be done by identifying a set of keywords and combining them to form a high-level understanding of the research area. Based on the keywording, the population of related papers can be classified and categorized. Finally, the data is extracted from studies and presented in a form of a systematic map that visualizes the results with graphs and tables or other graphical representations [30].

In our study, keywords and databases were selected after defining the research questions. Searches were made by using the advanced search functionality offered by the databases. A set of related articles was identified from the search results by using inclusion and exclusion criteria. Categorization was made iteratively by handling the set of related articles that were not excluded. Finally, the results were presented, a systematic map was produced and the meaning of results was interpreted.

3.1 Selecting Keywords and Databases

First, a pilot search from different databases was made to estimate how feasible the chosen area of interest is for performing a systematic mapping study. It appeared that the number of search results varied from 20 to 260 depending on the database by using keywords *"ERP" AND "integration"*. We decided that this number of articles is possible for closer investigation.

Rather than choosing specific journals or conferences, we selected six databases for review: ACM, CiteSeer, IEEEXplore, Sciverse, SpringerLink and EBSCO. These databases target a wide range of the most important conferences and journals in computer science, software engineering, and information systems. Moreover, they all offer an advanced search functionality that allows searching from different parts of the article, like from titles, abstracts, and keywords.

We decided to search the terms *"ERP" AND "integration"* from the metadata (titles, keywords and abstracts) of articles. The time period was set from 1998 to 2012. From ACM, CiteSeer and EBSCO we had to perform two searches, because the search engines allowed only searching from titles or from abstracts instead of from all the metadata. Filtering was used in searching to crop the unrelated topics in Sciverse and EBSCO. Table 1 shows the results from actual search.

Table 1. Results from actual search.

Source	Search criteria and filtering	Selected/Total
ACM	(1) ERP and integration from abstracts, published in 1998–2012 (2) ERP and integration from titles, published in 1998–2012	5/21 1/1
CiteSeer	(1) ERP and integration from abstracts, published in 1998–2012 (2) ERP and integration from titles, published in 1998–2012	25/66 5/7
IEEEXplore	ERP and integration from metadata, published in 1998–2013	141/239
Sciverse	ERP and integration from titles, abstracts and keywords limiting to Computers in Industry, European Journal of Operational Research, Expert Systems with Applications, Information & Management, International Journal of Production Economics	18/26
SpringerLink	ERP and integration from titles and abstracts since 1.1.1998, no book chapters	12/42
EBSCO	(1) ERP and integration from abstracts, source type: academic journals, published in 1998–2012, filtering out evoked potentials from thesaurus terms (2) ERP and integration from titles, source type: academic journals	88/261 15/58
Total		**310/721**

3.2   Handling the Related Articles

Each of 721 papers was first reviewed by reading the title, keywords and abstract. This was done to decide if the article meets the criteria. At this point, articles focusing on completely different topics such as Event Related Potentials, or articles written in other language than English were dropped out. We also removed duplicate articles. In total 310 articles were identified as potentially interesting, and they were reviewed in more detail.

Exclusion Criteria. During the further analysis of the remaining 310 articles, filtering was performed to drop out unrelated articles. An article was excluded if it was not related to integration issues. For example, many articles mentioned the used keywords in the abstract, but focused on other issues than the integration with other systems. The term "Integration" usually appears in a definition of ERP, which is often presented in the abstract to introduce the research area. Also, if it occurred that the article just briefly mentioned ERP and mainly focused on some other subject, the article was left out. This filtering reduced the total number of articles from 310 to 140. Then, we made a decision to focus only on journal articles because they are often the extended versions of conference papers. It reduced the number of articles to be reported from 140 to 56. The full data is available in http://enact.lut.fi/erp_sms.

Categorization of Articles. The categorization was made by analysing the 56 selected journal articles. The data recorded from the related articles is shown in Table 2.

From each publication, publication name, publication type, name of the publication forum, year and country were recorded. The categorization was made by dividing articles to classes based on their scope of integration: *Internal* or *External*. *Internal* deals with the integration of applications, systems and devices inside a company with no involvement of business partners, or with no relation to business partners. *External* means that ERP integrates with information systems outside the organization or that the integration aims at collaboration of business partners or external stakeholders. Furthermore, the related sub-categories were identified. The sub-categories were created inductively by labeling conceptually the most essential topic of interest of the article. The list of sub-categories included *Technological issues*, *Methodological issues*, *Quality issues*, and *Extending ERP*.

The research method used in the article was recorded. It was not always clearly defined in the article. In these cases the method was set either to *literature study* in cases where article just presented some ideas by relying on literature or *constructive research* in cases where the article proposed a construct based on the literature. Table 3 lists the applied research methods used in these articles.

Table 2. Data collected from articles.

Article data	Categorization data
Publication name	*Scope of integration* (internal or external)
Publication type (journal, conference or other)	*Sub category* (technological issues, methodological issues, quality issues, or extension to ERP)
Publication forum (if available)	*Research method* (systems dynamics, literature study, focus group, survey, Delphi study, constructive research, case study, multiple case study)
Publication year (1998–2012)	
Keywords (if available)	
Author's home country	

4 Results

Figure 2 shows the number of ERP integration related journal publications yearly. ERP integration has become the interest of researchers after 2002. The year 2006 had the biggest number of publications. Since there are no published articles in years 1998 and 1999, it seems that the time period used as the search constraint is suitable.

It is notable that most of the articles are case studies, use constructive approach or are based on literature only (Table 3). In addition, a common qualitative approach such as ethnography is completely missing from this population of journal articles and grounded theory is applied only in one article.

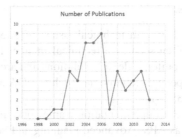

Fig. 2. The number of journal publications on ERP integration.

Table 3. Applied research methods.

Applied research method	Number of publications
Systems Dynamics (SD)	1
Literature Study (LS)	11
Focus Group (FG)	1
Survey (S)	7
Delphi Study (DS)	1
Constructive Research (CR)	16
Case Study (CS), Multiple-case study (MCS)	16, 2
Grounded Theory (GT)	1

About half (28) of the publications address *methodological issues*. These articles discuss about processes and approaches of how integration was carried out in a certain case. They also discuss about critical success factors, challenges, management and information sharing in ERP integration. Some of these articles proposed a conceptual research framework. The second biggest subset (12 articles) deals with *technological issues*. These articles propose a technological approach to integration typically by presenting an architectural solution or by discussing about certain technologies used in integration. 7 publications discuss about *extending ERP* by identifying additional functionality that could be provided by the ERP system, or by proposing a new architecture for the ERP system.

Quality issues was selected as a sub-category if the article addressed measureable characteristics of ERP systems or benefits provided by the ERP system related to integration. 9 articles addressed this sub-category.

The systematic map of ERP integration is presented in Table 4. The scope of integration, related sub-category and applied research methods of the articles are presented in the map. For research methods, abbreviations from Table 3 are used. The next chapters walk through the main findings from the found articles and interprets the systematic map of ERP integration.

4.1   Technological Issues

Twelve identified articles deal with technical issues of integration. This is not surprising, as integration is often seen as a technical matter. These articles addressing technological issues aim at building flexible solutions and architectures for integrating ERP with other systems. Specific technologies such as SOA and EAI are often used to aid the integration effort [38, 41].

Systems targeted by these implementation frameworks include other information management systems such as APS (Advanced Planning and Scheduling), DSS (Design Support Systems) or Product Data Management (PDM) [34–36]. The process of integrating ERP with APS is presented, problems encountered, best practices in integration as well as a functional architecture is presented [33]. Also, an architecture to integrate the DSS over SCMs and ERPs of multiple organizations is proposed [39]. In manufacturing companies, there is often a need to integrate ERP with robots on the

Table 4. A systematic map of ERP integration.

	Internal	External	ERP Characteristics
Technological Issues	[32] CR, [33] CS, [10] CR, [34] CR, [35] CR, [36] CR, [12] CR	[37] LS, [38] CS, [39] CR [40] CR, [41] CR	
Methodological Issues	*Processes and Approaches:* [42] GT, [1] CS, [43] CS, [44] CS, [45] CS, [46] CR, [47] LS, [48] CS *Challenges:* [49] CR, [2] CS, [50] S, [51] LS	*Processes and Approaches:* [52] LS, [53] CS, [18] CS, [6] CS, [54] CS, [55] LS, [56] LS, [13] FG, [57] LS, [58] LS, [59] S *Information sharing:* [60] LS, [17] MCS *Challenges:* [61] DS, [62] CS, [63] CS	
Quality Issues	*Benefits:* [64] S, [65] MCS, [66] S	*Benefits:* [67] CS, [68] CS, [69] LS, [8] S *Characteristics of ERP:* [19] CR, [70] S	
ERP Extension			*New Functionality to ERP:* [7] LS, [71] S, [72] SD *New Architecture for ERP:* [73] CR, [74] CR, [75] CR, [76] CR

execution level through a MES (Manufacturing Execution System). An approach to develop a distributed MES that integrates ERP with operational systems at the lower level is proposed [32]. A process and technology for ERP and MES integration is presented [12].

Sometimes ERP integration targets both manufacturing and planning systems. An approach where data exchange is made internally and externally between ERP, APS and MES is proposed in [40]. Enabling technologies for ERP and E-commerce technologies are briefly discussed [37]. Integration can also target legacy systems and other systems of business partners [38, 41]. Also, an approach for integrating distributed relational database systems with different enterprise systems is described [10].

The articles related to technological issues are often made with no systematic research approach. Instead, they are mostly relying on literature or they are based on specific cases. Because of this, they may not be fully applicable to other organizations. In addition, the studies related to implementation do not generally cover the systems accessed by external stakeholders, such as SCM and e-commerce systems. Moreover, mobile and web interfaces which are important in modern ERPs are not discussed in these articles at all.

4.2 Methodological Issues

Another group of studies addresses the integration challenges caused by ERP systems that are generally seen as difficulties in the integration with other applications. There are challenges when interconnecting specific ERP modules with other subsystems internally [50]. Also, implementing the interfaces between systems and connecting ERP with non-ERP systems can sometimes be a complex effort [51, 63]. Retrieving data from legacy systems by building temporal interfaces can be challenging [2]. It has also been identified that ERP systems sometimes prohibit the building of additional systems that communicate with it [49]. It is argued that ERP systems are not designed to cross organizational boundaries, and additional technologies, such as EAI are needed to cross-organizational integration [62]. Because of the non-modular and closed system architecture, insufficient for an extended enterprise functionality, the current ERP solutions cannot support SCM integration efficiently [61].

This group also includes studies that report processes and approaches to integrate ERP with different systems. The critical success factors when integrating ERP with computer-aided design and manufacturing (CAD/CAM) systems has been evaluated [42]. A process of building a decision support system by integrating carefully selected functions from SCM, GIS (Geographic Information System) and ERP is presented [43]. In a case study of an ERP project in healthcare, integration with various different internal systems such as non-ERP applications, web applications and mobile devices was needed [45]. Two literature-based studies discuss the integration of ERPs and Knowledge Management (KM) systems [46, 47]. An integration methodology for PDM and ERP integration by digital manufacturing is proposed [48].

EAI is sometimes used to integrate ERP with other systems and ERP modules. A case study of an EAI project where ERP was integrated with several other internal systems is made [44]. It is also suggested that processes can be easily integrated when combining ERP with EAI [6]. An approach to integrate ERP modules from different vendors by using EAI to minimize the need of customization of ERP packages is made [1]. A high-level comparison between ERP and EAI as means for enterprise integration is proposed [56].

ERP is strongly related to Supply Chain Management and e-business. Relationships of ERP and SCM have been studied [55, 59]. The integration methods and strategies of ERP and SCM are discussed [52, 54]. An approach for SMEs to extend their ERP system across the supply chain is also presented [18]. Requirements for an electronic supply chain are studied and it is pointed out that ERP should be first integrated with other internal applications before forming an e-supply chain [57]. ERP is also seen as a backend system for e-business and an inter-organizational ERP process model has been constructed [13]. Existing e-business frameworks and their relationships to enterprise applications such as ERP and CRM is made and a prediction of their future state and challenges is proposed [58]. A framework for E-business change is proposed by stating that there are other than technological matters, such as cultural and change management issues that affect the integration in E-business projects [53].

Two studies [17, 60] address information sharing and cooperation. Internal and external information sharing as an integrative practice to enable better collaboration in supply chain planning is examined [17]. Also, a framework of cooperation for supply chain partners is provided by analyzing both enablers and obstacles in ERP systems that facilitate supply chain information sharing and cooperation [60].

The studies addressing methodological issues mainly focus on external integration of SCM and e-business. Information sharing and collaboration practices are not studied broadly as well as the tools used to aid integration efforts. A major part of these studies is based on a single case study only. It would be beneficial to know more about general challenges and success factors that can be adopted in other situations as well. Therefore, besides qualitative studies, there is a need for industry-wide quantitative studies. Moreover, the use of tools to aid integration efforts is unrecognized by these studies.

4.3 Quality Issues

Nine studies that investigate certain quality attributes of ERP systems or evaluate the relationships between ERP benefits and integration were found. They include a framework to evaluate the potential of ERP to e-business by considering flexibility, modularity and integration of an ERP system [19]. In addition, a linkage between ERP and SCM is studied by developing a framework to evaluate ERPs capabilities to support SCM initiatives [69]. Also, benefits of integrating ERP with SCM is discussed [67, 68].

The effect of integration on performance is examined by Kang et al. who investigated how non-IS integration (people, standardization and centralization) affects performance [64]. A multi-level view of integration and its influence on ERP performance is studied in [8]. Also, the benefits of ERPs with a greater physical scope have been investigated in [66].

The ERP package selection criteria is studied with a conclusion that the system's fit with partners' systems, cross-module integration and compatibility between other systems are the top criteria when selecting ERP systems [70].

This category contains the most quantitative studies conducted on ERP integration issues in the population. Integration is generally considered as beneficial to enterprises. These studies also suggest the role of ERP as a backbone of an extended business system. The non-IS perspective of integration proposed by Kang et al. could be studied also with qualitative methods, such as grounded theory and case studies [64].

4.4 Extending ERP

This group of articles discusses the need for additional functionality for ERP systems and completely new approaches for ERP system architecture.

The similarities and differences of ERP and workflow management systems are identified and it is noted that ERP vendors have been starting to add workflow capabilities on their products [7]. The relationships between ERP and Strategic Enterprise Management (SEM) systems are investigated and their integration is proposed [71]. A knowledge-based system for production-scheduling as an ERP module is proposed in [73]. It has been suggested that an on-demand ERP could provide a sustainability benchmarking service and also other services based on the ERP data [72].

An ERP system architecture, based on re-configurable characteristics of material objects and financial objects, and having the advantage of workflow re-configurability and re-usability is proposed [75]. An architecture for integrating distributed ERP systems with e-commerce systems is presented [74]. Also, a prototype based on a multi-agent ERP to achieve enterprise wide integration is suggested [76].

These articles address diverse topics, but they all identify the need of extending the functionality of ERPs. New architectures for ERP systems are proposed because of the need for more flexible ERP system architecture where other systems can easily be integrated. ERP as an on-demand service is addressed by one article only [72]. The future studies could investigate how the requirement for on-demand ERP integration affects integration.

5 Discussion

The results of this study highlight the multidimensional nature of ERP integration [9]. We clearly identified internal and external technological issues of ERP integration related to technical perspective, but these studies do not often use a systematic research approach, which makes them difficult to generalize. Similar results were observed by Esteves and Pastor who found a set of articles dealing with connecting ERPs with other systems [23]. They identified that these articles were mainly technology-oriented and focus on the development of interfaces with other systems, web technologies and integration of CRM modules [23]. In their updated literature review, the authors highlighted the need for more research on ERP and SCM integration and saw mobile technologies, on-demand and open source ERPs as future trends [22].

The business process perspective of ERP integration is covered by methodological and quality issues. These studies are often based on single case studies and therefore other qualitative and quantitative approaches would be beneficial for investigating the phenomenon deeply from different viewpoints. When comparing our study with other literature reviews, e.g. [21], we observe that methodological issues have been increasingly targeted, even more than technical issues.

One group of studies on ERP integration that we called *ERP Extension* was in that sense different from technological, methodological, and quality issues that it could not be divided into external and internal issues. However, these studies discussed matters closely related to ERP integration and fitted well to the strategy perspective of ERP integration presented by Barki and Pinsonneault [9]. This group of studies mainly discussed possible ways to extend existing ERP systems in order to integrate them with other enterprise information systems. This trend was recognized by Moon, who identified a set of articles dealing with ERP extension and observed a further expansion of ERP's scope as a future trend [24]. According to Moon, companies are considering extensions to their ERP systems towards e-business, SCM, CRM, MES, supplier relationship management, and business intelligence systems. Our study brings out a more detailed viewpoint on how integration issues with these systems have been studied. Addo-Tenkorang and Helo also identified the extended nature of ERP and proposed that future ERPs are based on more advanced technologies, such as SOA, web services, Web 2.0 and they state that future ERPs will be delivered in SaaS (Software as a Service) model [20].

Probably the trend predicted by Moon takes place and ERP products will be enhanced with advanced technologies. However, the integration of ERP systems is not only a technical matter but mostly a socio-technical phenomenon dealing with both technologies and interactions between stakeholders. There is no doubt that ERP products will be enhanced with more advanced technologies. However, we believe that instead of technical issues, methods, tools, and coordination to manage the integration in future ERP systems will become more relevant than technological matters.

5.1   Limitations of Study

The study focuses only on journal articles. Conference articles and their contribution to this area have been left out due to space limitations. We have, however, also collected and analyzed all conferences articles that met the query criteria. The full data table is available in http://enact.lut.fi/erp_sms. It is also possible that we miss some studies if authors have used some other terms, such as "interconnecting systems." Another limitation is that the set of related articles may not be complete. Some databases such as Google Scholar were left out because of the limitations of their search functionality. However, we believe that the selected databases and their query results provide a representative view of previous research.

5.2   Future Research

As ERP systems are becoming more complex, there is also a more urgent need to solve the integration issues in ERP projects. The concept of an ERP community has been defined as a tactical group consisting of an ERP vendor, an ERP consultant and the implementing organization [77]. There is a need to study ERP projects from the ERP stakeholder network perspective to investigate how integration issues are effectively solved in this network; what kind of tools, methods, and processes are used to aid the integration and how are people collaborating. ERP adoption is often a long project with its own lifecycle and therefore the investigation of integration issues during ERP system lifecycle would be useful for understanding when and what kind of problems should be expected.

6   Conclusions

This paper mapped the existing literature of ERP integration by searching articles from scientific literature databases. We searched journal articles related to ERP integration issues. A total of 56 articles were analyzed further. The articles were categorized based on their scope of integration (internal, external) and also by using four sub-categories: technological issues, methodological issues, quality issues and extending ERP.

ERP integration is necessary due to ERP's role as a backbone of the enterprise business system. According to our analysis, the research that aims at solving techno-logical issues is often conducted with no rigorous and well-defined research method. Moreover, the observed research on technology deals mostly with internal manufac-turing and decision making systems, and lacks the focus on SCM and e-commerce that are accessed by external parties. The device aspect with mobility and Internet has not been widely considered either. The methodological issues that have been investigated focus mostly on e-business and SCM integration, but mainly with single cases only. The use of tools and collaboration practices are quite unrecognized by the current studies. The most comprehensive research on ERP integration has been done on quality issues by examining the ERP characteristics and benefits of integration.

Even though ERP products have improved over the years, there still seems to be significant issues with ERP projects. A fair amount of research has been conducted on ERP systems, so this makes us wonder why – with better products and a huge knowledge base – these projects still fail frequently. One reason for this could be the more complex environment and unrecognized area of research – the ERP stakeholder network. The future research should consider various stakeholders in the ERP development network and study how integration issues are solved within this network.

Acknowledgements.   This study was funded by Academy of Finland grant #259454.

References

1. Alshawi, S., Themistocleous, M., Almadani, R.: Integrating diverse ERP systems: a case study. J. Enterp. Inf. Manage. **17**(6), 454–462 (2004)
2. Yusuf, Y., Gunasekaran, A., Abthorpe, M.S.: Enterprise information systems project implementation: a Case Study of ERP in Rolls-Royce. Int. J. Prod. Econ. **87**(3), 251–266 (2004)

3. Somers, T.M., Nelson, K.G.: The impact of strategy and integration mechanisms on enterprise system value: empirical evidence from manufacturing firms. Eur. J. Oper. Res. **146**(2), 315–338 (2003)
4. Su, Y., Yang, C.: A structural equation model for analyzing the impact of ERP on SCM. Expert Syst. Appl. **37**(1), 456–469 (2010)
5. Berchet, C., Habchi, G.: The implementation and deployment of an ERP system: an industrial case study. Comput. Ind. **56**(6), 588–605 (2005)
6. Themistocleous, M., Corbitt, G.: Is business process integration feasible? J. Enterp. Inf. Manage. **19**(4), 434–449 (2006)
7. Cardoso, J., Bostrom, R.P., Sheth, A.: Workflow management systems and ERP systems: differences, commonalities, and applications. Inf. Technol. Manage. **5**(3/4), 319–338 (2004)
8. Hwang, Y., Grant, D.: Understanding the influence of integration on ERP performance. Inf. Technol. Manage. **12**(3), 229–240 (2011)
9. Barki, H., Pinsonneault, A.: Explaining ERP Implementation Effort and Benefits with Organizational Integration (2002)
10. Wang, C.-B., Chen, T.-Y., Chen, Y.-M., Chu, H.-C.: Design of a meta model for integrating enterprise systems. Comput. Ind. **56**(3), 305–322 (2005)
11. Downing, C.E.: Is web-based supply chain integration right for your company? Commun. ACM **53**(5), 134 (2010)
12. Oman, S.: Application of intermediate document message in the process of enterprise resource planning and manufacturing execution system integration, vol. 2, pp. 141–156. Problems of Management in the 21st Century (2011)
13. Vathanophas, V.: Business process approach towards an inter-organizational enterprise system. Bus. Process. Manage. J. **13**(3), 433–450 (2007)
14. Frank, L., Kumar, A.V.S.: Architecture for mobile control functions in supplier deliveries for distributed integrated ERP modules. In: Proceedings of the 6th International Conference on Ubiquitous Information Management and Communication, Article 84, 8 p. (2012)
15. Jankowska, A.M., Kurbel, K.: Service-oriented architecture supporting mobile access to an ERP system. In: Ferstl, O.K., Sinz, E.J., Eckert, S., Isselhorst, T. (eds.) Wirtschaftsinformatik 2005, pp. 371–390. Physica-Verlag, Heidelberg (2005)
16. Linthicum, D.S.: Next Generation Application Integration: from Simple Information to Web Services. Addison-Wesley, Boston (2004)
17. Welker, G.A., van der Vaart, T., van Donk, D.P.: The influence of business conditions on supply chain information-sharing mechanisms: a study among supply chain links of SMEs. Int. J. Prod. Econ. **113**(2), 706–720 (2008)
18. de Búrca, S., Fynes, B., Marshall, D.: Strategic technology adoption: extending ERP across the supply chain. J. Enterp. Inf. Manage. **18**(4), 427–440 (2005)
19. Turner, D., Chung, S.H.: Technological factors relevant to continuity on ERP for E-business platform: integration, modularity, and flexibility. J. Internet Commer. **4**(4), 119–132 (2005)
20. Addo-Tenkorang, R., Helo, P.: Enterprise Resource Planning (ERP): a review literature report. In: Proceedings of the World Congress on Engineering and Computer Science (2011)
21. Botta-Genoulaz, V., Millet, P.-A., Grabot, B.: A survey on the recent research literature on ERP systems. Comput. Ind. **56**(6), 510–522 (2005)
22. Esteves, J., Bohorquez, V.: An updated ERP systems annotated bibliography: 2001–2005. Commun. Assoc. Inf. Syst. **19**, Article 18 (2007)
23. Esteves, J., Pastor, J.: Enterprise resource planning systems research: an annotated bibliography. Commun. Assoc. Inf. Syst. **7**(8), 1–51 (2001)

24. Moon, Y.B.: Enterprise Resource Planning (ERP): a review of the literature. Int. J. Manage. Enterp. Dev. **4**(3), 235–264 (2007)
25. Schilichter, B.R., Kraemmergaard, P.: A comprehensive literature review of the ERP research field over a decade. J. Enterp. Inf. Manage. **23**(4), 486–520 (2010)
26. Shehab, E.M., Sharp, M.W., Supramaniam, L., Spedding, T.A.: Enterprise resource planning: an integrative review. Bus. Process Manage. J. **10**(4), 359–386 (2004)
27. de Almeida Biolchini, J.C., Mian, P.G., Natali, A.C.C., Conte, T.U., Travassos, G.H.: Scientific research ontology to support systematic review in software engineering. Adv. Eng. Inf. **21**(2), 133–151 (2007)
28. Kitchenham, B., Pearl Brereton, O., Budgen, D., Turner, M., Bailey, J., Linkman, S.: Systematic literature reviews in software engineering – a systematic literature review. Inf. Softw. Technol. **51**(1), 7–15 (2009)
29. Kitchenham, B., Charters, S.: Guidelines for performing systematic literature reviews in software engineering (2007)
30. Petersen, K., Feldt, R., Mujtaba, S., Mattson, M.: Systematic mapping studies in software engineering. In: EASE'08 Proceedings of the 12th International Conference on Evaluation and Assessment in Software Engineering, pp. 68–77 (2008)
31. Bailey, J., Budgen, D., Turner, M., Kitchenham, B., Brereton, P., Linkman, S.: Evidence relating to Object-Oriented software design: a survey. In: Proceedings of the First International Symposium on Empirical Software Engineering and Measurement, pp. 482–484 (2007)
32. Huang, C.-Y.: Distributed manufacturing execution systems: a workflow perspective. J. Intell. Manuf. **13**(6), 485–497 (2002)
33. Wiers, V.C.S.: A case study on the integration of APS and ERP in a steel processing plant. Prod. Plan. Control **13**(6), 552–560 (2002)
34. Ou-Yang, C., Hon, S.J.: Developing an agent-based APS and ERP collaboration framework. Int. J. Adv. Manufact. Technol. **35**(9–10), 943–967 (2006)
35. Hu, Y., Wang, R.: Research on collaborative design software integration based on SOA. J. Adv. Manufact. Syst. **07**(01), 91–94 (2008)
36. Wei, Z., Tan, J., Feng, Y.: Integration technology of ERP and PDM based on business remote function call. Int. J. Adv. Manuf. Technol. **40**, 1044–1052 (2008).
37. Siau, K., Messersmith, J.: Enabling technologies for E-commenrce and ERP Integration. Quart. J. Electron. **3**(1), 43–53 (2002)
38. Margaria, T., Steffen, B., Kubczak, C.: Evolution support in heterogeneous service-oriented landscapes. J. Braz. Comput. Soc. **16**(1), 35–47 (2010)
39. Shafiei, F., Sundaram, D., Piramuthu, S.: Multi-enterprise collaborative decision support system. Expert Syst. Appl. **39**(9), 7637–7651 (2012)
40. Tao, Y.-H., Hong, T.-P., Sun, S.-I.: An XML implementation process model for enterprise applications. Comput. Ind. **55**(2), 181–196 (2004)
41. Wang, M., Zhang, S.: Integrating EDI with an E-Scm system using Eai technology. Inf. Syst. Manage. **22**(3), 31–36 (2005)
42. Soliman, F., Clegg, S., Tantoush, T.: Critical success factors for integration of CAD/CAM systems with ERP systems. Int. J. Oper. Prod. Manage. **21**(5/6), 609–629 (2001)
43. Gayialis, S.P., Tatsiopoulos, I.P.: Design of an IT-driven decision support system for vehicle routing and scheduling. Eur. J. Oper. Res. **152**(2), 382–398 (2004)
44. Lam, W.: An Enterprise Application Integration (EAI) case-study: seamples mortage processing at Harmond Bank. J. Comput. Inf. Syst. **46**(1), 35–43 (2005)
45. Stefanou, C.J., Revanoglou, A.: ERP integration in a healthcare environment: a case study. J. Enterp. Inf. Manag. **19**(1), 115–130 (2006)

46. Xu, L., Wang, C., Luo, X., Shi, Z.: Integrating knowledge management and ERP in enterprise information systems. Syst. Res. Behav. Sci. **23**(2), 147–156 (2006)
47. Metaxiotis, K.: Exploring the rationales for ERP and knowledge management integration in SMEs. J. Enterp. Inf. Manage. **22**(1/2), 51–62 (2009)
48. Lee, C., Leem, C.S., Hwang, I.: PDM and ERP integration methodology using digital. manufacturing to support global manufacturing. Int. J. Adv. Manuf. Technol. **53**(1–4), 399–409 (2010)
49. Worley, J.H., Castillo, G.R., Geneste, L., Grabot, B.: Adding decision support to workflow systems by reusable standard software components. Comput. Ind. **49**(1), 123–140 (2002)
50. Zhu, Z.: A systems approach to developing and implementing an ERP financial subsystem. Syst. Res. Behav. Sci. **23**(2), 237–250 (2006)
51. Momoh, A., Roy, R., Shehab, E.: Challenges in enterprise resource planning implementation: state-of-the-art. Bus. Process Manage. J. **16**(4), 537–565 (2010)
52. Tarn, J.M., Yen, D.C., Beaumont, M.: Exploring the rationales for ERP and SCM integration. Ind. Manage. Data Syst. **102**(1), 26–34 (2002)
53. Ash, C., Burn, J.: A strategic framework for the management of ERP enabled e-business change. Eur. J. Oper. Res. **146**(2), 374–387 (2003)
54. Koh, S.C.L., Saad, S., Arunachalam, S.: Competing in the 21st century supply chain through supply chain management and enterprise resource planning integration. Int. J. Phys. Distrib. Logistics Manage. **36**(6), 455–465 (2006)
55. Toloie-Eshlaghi, A., Asadollahi, A., Poorebrahimi, A.: The Role of Enterprise Resources Planning (ERP) in the contribution and integration of the information in the supply chain. Eur. J. Soc. Sci. **20**(1), 16–27 (2011)
56. Lee, J., Siau, K., Hong, S.: Enterprise integration with ERP and EAI. Commun. ACM **46**(2), 54–60 (2003)
57. Akyuz, G.A., Rehan, M.: Requirements for forming an 'e-supply chain'. Int. J. Prod. Res. **47**(12), 3265–3287 (2009)
58. Hvolby, H.-H., Trienekens, J.H.: Challenges in business systems integration. Comput. Ind. **61**(9), 808–812 (2010)
59. Cagliano, R., Caniato, F., Spina, G.: The linkage between supply chain integration and manufacturing improvement programmes. Int. J. Oper. Prod. Manage. **26**(3), 282–299 (2006)
60. Kelle, P., Akbulut, A.: The role of ERP tools in supply chain information sharing, cooperation, and cost optimization. Int. J. Prod. Econ. **93–94**, 41–52 (2005)
61. Akkermans, H.A., Bogerd, P., Yücesan, E., van Wassenhove, L.N.: The impact of ERP on supply chain management: exploratory findings from a European Delphi study. Eur. J. Oper. Res. **146**(2), 284–301 (2003)
62. Themistocleous, M.: Justifying the decisions for EAI implementations: a validated proposition of influential factors. J. Enterp. Inf. Manage. **17**(2), 85–104 (2004)
63. Bose, I., Pal, R., Ye, A.: ERP and SCM systems integration: the case of a valve manufacturer in China. Inf. Manage. **45**(4), 233–241 (2008)
64. Kang, S., Jong-Hun, P., Hee-Dong, Y.: ERP alignment for positive business performance: evidence from Korea's ERP market. J. Comput. Inf. Syst. **48**(4), 25–38 (2008)
65. Uwizeyemungu, S., Raymond, L.: Impact of an ERP system's capabilities upon the realisation of its business value: a resource-based perspective. Inf. Technol. Manag. **13**, 69–90 (2012)
66. Ranganathan, C., Brown, C.V.: ERP investments and the market value of firms: toward an understanding of influential ERP project variables. Inf. Syst. Res. **17**(2), 145–161 (2006)

67. Zheng, S., Yen, D.C., Tarn, J.M.: The new spectrum of the cross-enterprise solution: the integration of supply chain management and enterprise resources planning systems. J. Comput. Inf. Syst. **41**(1), 84–94 (2000)
68. Ghani, K., Zainuddin, Y., Ghani, F.: Integration of supply chain management with internet and enterprise resource planning (ERP) systems: case study **1**(3/4), 97–104 (2009)
69. Chung, S.H., Tang, H.-L., Ahmad, I.: Modularity, integration and IT personnel skills factors in linking ERP to SCM systems. J. Technol. Manage. Innov. **6**(1), 1–3 (2011)
70. Baki, B., Çakar, K.: Determining the ERP package-selecting criteria: the case of Turkish manufacturing companies. Bus. Process Manage. J. **11**(1), 75–86 (2005)
71. Rom, A., Rohde, C.: Enterprise resource planning systems, strategic enterprise management systems and management accounting: a Danish study. J. Enterp. Inf. Manage. **19**(1), 50–66 (2006)
72. Koslowski, T., Strüker, J.: ERP on demand platform. Bus. Inf. Syst. Eng. **3**(6), 359–367 (2011)
73. Metaxiotis, K.S., Psarras, J.E., Ergazakis, K.A.: Production scheduling in ERP systems: an AI-based approach to face the gap. Bus. Process Manage. J. **9**(2), 221–247 (2003)
74. Frank, L.: Architecture for integration of distributed ERP systems and e-commerce systems. Ind. Manage. Data Syst. **104**(5), 418–429 (2004)
75. Ip, W.H., Chen, B., Lau, H., Sunjing, W.: An object-based relational data base system using re-configurable finance and material objects. J. Manuf. Technol. Manage. **15**(8), 779–786 (2004)
76. Lea, B.-R., Gupta, M.C., Yu, W.-B.: A prototype multi-agent ERP system: an integrated architecture and a conceptual framework. Technovation **25**(4), 433–441 (2005)
77. Sammon, D., Adam, F.: Decision making in the ERP community. In: ECIS 2002 Proceedings (2002)

Fairtrace: Applying Semantic Web Tools and Techniques to the Textile Traceability

Bruno Alves[1]([⊠]), Michael Schumacher[1], Fabian Cretton[1], Anne Le Calvé[1],
Gilles Cherix[2], David Werlen[2], Christian Gapany[2], Bertrand Baeryswil[3],
Doris Gerber[4], and Philippe Cloux[4]

[1] Institute of Information Systems, University of Applied Sciences Western
Switzerland, TechnoArk 3, Sierre, Switzerland
bruno.alves@hevs.ch
[2] Institut Icare, TechnoArk, Sierre, Switzerland
[3] Fairtrace, Technoark, Sierre, Swtizerland
[4] Importexa SA, 1095 Lutry, Switzerland

Abstract. This paper presents solutions that leverage Semantic Web
Technologies (SWT) to allow pragmatic traceability in supply-chains,
especially for the textile industry. Objectives are the identification of the
supply-chain, order management, tracking and problem reporting (such
as dangerous substance detection). It is intended to be a generic platform
supporting potentially any kind of industrial supply-chain, to be usable
in harsh environments (mobile appliances) without any kind of communications possibility and to be fully usable to non-IT people, including
for the modelling of the production processes. The developed solutions
also allow the consumer to benefit from the traceability through information pages available by scanning the QR codes available on the finished
products (clothes, clocks, etc.). This paper presents: (i) the methodology
applied to achieve those functionalities, (ii) the design and implementation choices, and (iii) the test results. The main value of this paper is the
usage of the Semantic Web in real-world industrial traceability solutions,
which were tested in real supply-chains in Switzerland and India. The
commercialization of the developed solutions has started.

Keywords: Traceability, Ontology · Semantic web · Textile industry

1 Introduction

In 2007, a new European regulation on chemicals called REACH[1] initiated the
creation of a catalogue of potentially dangerous substances actively used in every-
day consumer goods. Many of these have been identified as potential threats to
human health and are therefore forbidden on the European territory.

---

[1] REACH - Registration, Evaluation, Authorization and Restriction of Chemical Substances - http://ec.europa.eu/environment/chemicals/reach/reach_intro.htm.

© Springer International Publishing Switzerland 2014
S. Hammoudi et al. (Eds.): ICEIS 2013, LNBIP 190, pp. 68–84, 2014.
DOI: 10.1007/978-3-319-09492-2_5

REACH puts the responsibility on the industry for evaluating and managing the risks about chemicals they use or import. As a consequence, industrial actors henceforth have the duty of tracking all substances used in the products they manufacture or import in Europe. Unfortunately, in practise this is barely the case. As an example, during the EURO 2012 soccer championship, Europe's Consumer Watchdog revealed unusually high concentrations of dangerous chemical substances in several team shirts that could potentially be harmful to fans' health[2]. Independent tests highlighted high concentrations of lead, nickel and organotin, a chemical that can irreversibly damage the human nervous system. That's just one example among many others, but it shows a major failure of brands and the general clothing industry in their capacity of fully capturing or even understand their own manufacturing processes. When a problem is finally discovered, it is often already too late and the cost of any corrective measure is usually too high.

Such situation is unfortunately too common and stands as a motivation driver for the work described in this paper. Bringing supply-chain traceability to the end consumer and to the economic partners (resellers or brands) is a difficult task. Information related to the manufacturing process is usually not made available (obfuscated on purpose or by lack of sufficient means) or extremely opaque. However, in order to become REACH-compatible, industrial actors will have the difficult task of motivating each participant belonging to the process to commit to the gathering of the necessary information.

This paper describes an extension of the work previously published in the ICEIS'13 proceedings. The Fairtrace framework is currently undergoing the commercialization phase and intends to provide additional answers to the former research questions. In addition to what has already been done, we also provide an additional insight into the data models and the validation mechanisms that we are currently developing. Our goal is to continue supporting pragmatic solutions and also to continue using semantic technologies as the backbone for traceability.

The objectives of Fairtrace are primarily the identification of the supply-chain (activities), order management and monitoring, as well as problem reporting (such as dangerous substance detection). It is intended to be a highly generic platform supporting potentially any kind of industrial supply-chain (clock industry, cocoa, ...); to be usable in harsh environments (mobile appliances) without any kind of communication facilities and to be usable by non-IT people (including the modelling of their production processes). Our solution must also benefit the final consumer (buyer), allowing him/her to obtain information on the traceability with a simple scan of a QR code on finished products (clock, cloth, ...). To support our objectives, we decided to leverage Semantic Web Technologies (SWT) in the core of the Fairtrace software to assess potential advantages when applied to an industrial setting.

---

[2] http://news.stepbystep.com/euro-2012-football-fans-warned-against-buying
 - toxic-shirts-313/

A fully functional prototype has already been designed, implemented and described in [1]. Field tests have been realized in India in February 2012. We have collected real-time information triggered by an order for an organic fair tee-shirt. A startup company founded by our commercial partner Importexa is currently preparing the commercialization of a product based on Fairtrace applied to the textile industry. A part of the technology has already been patented (a dynamic formular creation system based on semantic data [2]).

This paper is structured in five parts: the first part discusses some aspects of research in specific areas of supply-chain management. In the second part, we detail in descriptive terms the methodology of our work. Then, in the third, we present the results of the project and various discussion issues in the fourth part. We then conclude with some future directions and challenges still to overcome.

2   Related Work

Fairtrace aims at achieving an agile traceability system that can help in the management and monitoring of supply-chains. Supply-chain management (SCM) is concerned with the coordination of activities for producing a product demanded by a customer [3,4]. Because thoughtful management of the supply-chain often results in substantial cost savings, the field has seen considerable industrial and research activity. It is no surprise then, the literature on the subject is so abundant that all aspects are well covered. References [5,6] describe issues and opportunities of SCM. Other works propose formal SCM frameworks [7], infrastructures [8,9] and models [10]. Logistics is a very active field where research focuses especially on optimization patterns [11]. Supply-chain monitoring (SCMo) is a sub-branch of SCM that operates on information, inventory management and cash-flow [5]. The monitoring strives to rapidly identify problems in the supply-chain and solve them with the help of established procedures.

The focus of this paper is on supply-chain traceability (SCMt), which primarily addresses the problem of tracing goods from raw materials to finished products. An identifiable trend on SCMt is the use of external technologies such as RFID to enable traceability [12,13], including in the textile industry [14]. Many publications also exist on SCMt processes and implications, such as [15]. An important research track has been also developed on the composition of Web services in the supply-chain in order to ensure traceability among the partners of the chain [16]. These works have been extended by enriching Web services with Semantic descriptions, in order to avoid ambiguity among the services and allowing an explicit meaning of the data interchange [17]. These Semantic Web Services [18] and their coordination [19] allowed to improve mutual sharing of information for business-to-business integration.

In order to define a common understanding of supply-chain models, several research works proposed the use of supply-chain ontologies [7]. For instance, [20] proposed quite a complex ontology that is not industry specific. Those work show that Semantic Technologies can have many advantages for the interoperability of the business partners in the chain. Research works also exist to use Semantics with RFID solutions [21]. Reference [22] also proposes semantics description to ensure traceability. Other interesting research papers describe the usage of autonomous agents to deal with the information in the supply-chain [8], including its combination with Semantic Web descriptions [23].

In relation to the research above, the work presented in this paper can be specified as follows: Fairtrace is meant to trace all activities of the entire manufacturing process, including documents and products. It is able to identify the raw materials which were used, certificates, waste, etc. It can also be used to identify roles and responsibilities and to keep track of who did what. It does not currently include optimization techniques for the logistics. Fairtrace can track many variables, which can be used as performance indicators. A customizable chain of validators also allows to track problems arising along the supply-chain, such as the detection of dangerous chemical substances. Businesses can thus react very quickly to any unexpected condition. From a technological perspective, Fairtrace was conceived with a focus on Semantic Web Technologies (SWT). Every piece of data in the system is related to a concept in a semantic data repository. All models use semantic descriptions and traceability information can be displayed to the user hierarchically.

The next sections explain thoroughly how Fairtrace was conceived, and its main results.

3   Methodology

The scoping phase of the project consisted in capturing and understanding the requirements of traceability. An analysis of a typical textile manufacturing chain was made to get a rough idea on the process. A consultant specialized in the textile industry was commissioned to analyze Importexa's own supply-chain in India. Her mission was to visit factories, identify and document all activities throughout the manufacturing process. She captured information about certificates, delivery challans, cotton lots, mixing lots and many other documents, but also took pictures of places and production machines. Our task was thereafter to analyze all those paper resources in order to sketch out a formal description of the longitudinal process. The very first model was a transcription of the complete, moderately detailed manufacturing process using the primitives of BPMN[3].

The process was complemented by several additional documents more accurately describing the information to be captured on the supply-chain. A critical path — a minimal path from the starting activity (order) to the end (ginning)— was defined. The method consisted in searching through pairs of documents such as orders, challans or bills for matching identifiers to find a complete and continuous traceability path up to the origin of the cotton. The base model was augmented with additional attributes (GSM, weight, ...) extracted from the documents that we analyzed. This extra information helps tracking quantities and waste.

---

[3] BPMN - Business Process Modeling and Notation - http://www.bpmn.org.

3.1 Requirements

Fairtrace objectives focus on usability, supply-chain data transparency, genericity and adaptability.

As a consequence of the first requirement, business partners in the supply-chain needed a simple way to enter data about their production directly into our system. Among all alternatives considered, a system of minimally constrained web formulars was retained. On one hand, it was important to give users the freedom to design themselves these formulars — possibly by drag-dropping GUI components — without having to resort to any particular IT knowledge or skills. On the other hand, formulars needed to the bound to the underlying data model. Web formulars coupled to a flexible data binding system offer the kind of usability that was required in this project. Web forms can be implemented in pure HTML and are supported natively by all kinds of devices. They can be adapted to any sort of display they are affected to, with relatively few lines of CSS code. They can be edited and pre-filled with data coming from the repository and customers can mark fields optional or required at wish.

The formular system was also designed to be adaptable. Each formular is dynamically linked to the underlying data model by a dynamic binding system that uses specific binding names to associate fields from the formulars to particular objects and properties in the model. Coupled to an instantiation engine that creates model instances based on the data acquired, the whole system provides a very generic framework that can adapt to almost any model or domain, without requiring recompilation.

To provide transparency on the data, it is important that information can be accessed without any technological barriers. A dashboard system providing supply-chain monitoring support and capable of providing easy data exploration was designed as a consequence. Furthermore, we wanted the information to be presented to the customer both horizontally (information for a specific time frame) and vertically (hierarchy of data). Such a system would allow anyone entitled to do so, to descend into any part of the traceability data chain providing them with a full transparent access to its contents.

3.2 Domain Modelling

The data model in Fairtrace was designed to capture many different aspects of the supply-chain, including details on the process itself and on the products deriving from it. We divided the modelling task into creating models for both.

To improve on usability, we wanted to empower the customers (or any one entitled to do so) to design graphically their supply-chains. We had to provide the necessary primitives (activity, flow) to allow it. For that reason, we did not hard-code the process into a model for each different customer, but decided instead to specify a language partly derived from BPMN describing business process concepts such as activities, flows, roles, users, partners, authorizations and collection points. Supply-chains would then be specified in terms of these primitives.

Our process model provides support for a small subset of BPMN-like constructs. We added a few more custom primitives (collection points) that are used by the security granting mecanism. Before resigning ourselves to model everything from scratch, we tried on different approaches. We had a look to the PSL[4] specification and ontogy, M3PO [24] and BPMNO[5]. Unfortunately, the complexity of the semantics and the verbosity of those models seemed a bit excessive for our needs.

The product model is strongly bound to the industrial domain it describes; in this case, the domain was the textile supply-chain. We searched on-line for existing ontologies describing domain knowledge on textile products, but unfortunately, we could not find any that more or less suited our needs. We decided thus to also model the product domain from scratch. To do so, We have literally analysed dozens of documents brought back from India by the consultant.

3.3   Semantic Technologies

Leveraging Semantic Web Technologies has been a strong requirement of this project from the very beginning. Throughout the first prototyping phase, we have learned a lot on the subject and gained much more confidence on how to properly model our domains. This insight led us to correct most of the mistakes we did.

The models we have designed do not require much expressiveness. As such, we do not use elaborated constructs like Restrictions, because decidability can be an important issue. We needed the language to be sound, complete (all logical consequences are drawn) and monotonic (i.e. all statements remain valid after inserting new knowledge). During the development of the prototype, we decided to translate our conceptual models (process, products) to RDFS instead of a more expressive OWL. First, it was easier to work with and the semantics of its constructs were also easier to grasp. Since our models were mainly based on subsumption hierarchies using sub-class and sub-property relations (`rdfs:subClassOf, rdfs:subPropertyOf`), RDFS was a sufficient choice.

In the current version, however, we shifted towards OWL2 RL. Supported natively by our semantic repository solution, OWL2 RL fits perfectly in rule-based systems. Our goal was to take our initial modelling further and take advantage on the new constructs available to us right out of the box, without having to resort to custom rule sets. The former models were intended to be merely "object-oriented style" specifications, without any "advanced feature". Current models leverage OWL constructs such as `owl:inverseOf` to link objects, so that the data they describe can easily be displayed in dashboard's object browser tree. This shift of trend was operated primarily to ease the modelling, more than a will to define the precise semantics of our domain objects.

The current process model hasn't changed dramatically compared to the former model. We opted out on reliance on the `owl:AnnotationProperty` to

---

[4] PSL - Process Specification Language - http://www.mel.nist.gov/psl/.

[5] BPMO - BPMN Ontology - https://dkm.fbk.eu/index.php/BPMN_Ontology.

annotate our model classes and properties (give them JSON-style names). We used the `owl:inverseOf` construct to express direct symmetrical links between objects. `owl:propertyChainAxiom` was used to infer missing links between somehow related nodes. We wanted to be able to process nodes quickly in the middleware. We focused thus on easing the translation between the RDF models and their JSON serialization that we use to exchange object data with the front-end. We wanted to simplify this step, since it was decided not to expose any RDF details to the front-end.

The product model however has required a bit more expressiveness to model sometimes complex relationships between objects of different classes, but also to compensate for potential gaps due to the lack of sufficient data. We took advantage of `owl:inverseOf`, `owl:subPropertyOf` and `owl:propertyChainAxiom` constructs to bring data to where it was needed. Since every order only represents a few thousands triples, we are far more concerned with the speed of the requests, than the size of the data. For this reason, it seemed a good compromise to design rules to migrate data to where it can be quickly collected and queried for.

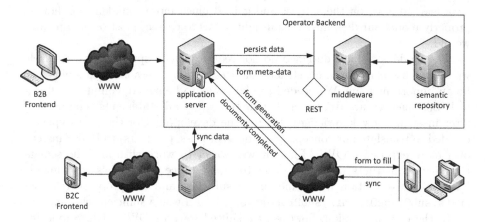

Fig. 1. Overview of the architecture.

3.4   Infrastructure

The prototype infrastructure was designed to meet requirements for the three types of customers we wanted to target: business partners, end users and supply-chain partners.

The business partners category is mostly composed of brands and resellers that will license the future Fairtrace solution for monitoring their own supply-chain. Their needs are primarily basic-management controls, extensive information and problem reporting. Those requirements were implemented into the prototype as a supply-chain designer, a graphical formular edition interface and a dashboard to control all operations, assign users, roles and authorizations.

To end users we wanted to provide them with traceability information about a product on scanning a QR code on the finished product. We had to design a system to map these codes to specific views on the information collected from the data store. That information is then formatted to target the particular device the user browses on.

Finally, we had to provide a way for the supply-chain partners to send data to the system. By partners, we mean any entity working in the supply-chain to create and finalize the product. These can be factories, transporters, single users... The dynamic formular system we designed was meant to be simple and functional. It supports simple common controls such as date pickers, file selectors, picture boxes, text fields, lists, combo boxes and other types of selectors. It is thus possible to integrate certificates (such as for biological production) as PDF/A files as well as other kind of documents. Those binary resources are stored on the cloud and a link is kept inside the RDF data store. The formular design and the dynamic binding systems were thought to be used by designers not especially proficient with technology. We favored simplicity and wanted to hide the technical details (URIs, JSON object, ...).

The data binding system uses formulas to define the proper binding to the data model. We have design an expression language that is evaluated at run-time and allows finding the correct binding dynamically. We resorted to this solution in order to overcome some limitations of the formular design language, that can cannot unfortunately be changed with the current funding.

Furthermore, we also considered both mobile and browser-enabled applications to display formulars. The mobile application was designed to manage and display the formulars in potentially non connected configurations. We had to take into account that wireless signal could be a problem in some places where the application was meant to be used (such as in cotton fields in India). We designed an offline mode, that would allow later synchronization with the Fairtrace server. The browser-enabled application was meant to be used directly in factories, where Internet is generally available. We considered this option too, because it was obviously easier and faster to input data from a keyboard rather than on a mobile.

3.5   Implementation

The actual implementation phase of the prototype went surprisingly well. We opted for an agile development process with a relatively short feature development cycle (<1 month). We were able to finish both on time and on budget. We spent extra resources on polishing important features, so that the prototype would be ready for a demonstration to potential customers. The last step of the development was testing the prototype in a real situation. We modeled Importexa's supply-chain and requested them to initiate the process. Importexa started an order for an organic fair cotton tee-shirt. When the actual manufacturing began, we had the consultant in India to teach the functioning of the system and to check that everything was going as planned. We wanted to show off that the prototype was able to trace all the manufacturing activities and capture all the products of it.

The current implementation is ongoing work and draws heavily to what has already been done. We tried to avoid as much heavy changes as possible. We just made sure to provide a better integration while designing slightly overhauled functionality. The core remains basically, ensuring data quality is where our efforts are now concentrated.

4   Results

The original project yielded three main results, which were a functional prototype, two ontologies created from the process and product models and the system and the modeling of a textile manufacturing chain. We also describe advances in the current implementation.

4.1   Prototype and Current Work

The current infrastructure shown on Fig. 1 is a three-tier infrastructure composed of a data, a business and a presentation layers and was developed in Java as a Spring MVC application running on a Tomcat 6 servlet container. It is quite similar to the former prototype, but uses different technologies. The data layer hosts the RDF store (semantic repository). The middleware is comprised of the business layer and acts as a message translator and rule enforcer between the application server and the RDF store. Finally, the presentation layer contains both the Business To Business (B2B) and front-end operators. A Business To Consumer (B2C) front-end solution maps QR codes that come on the final products with information views about the whole upstream chain to be presented to the final consumer.

The semantic functionality (i.e. semantic store) is provided by the OWLim SE 5.3 engine from OntoText[6] running as an extension of the OpenRDF[7] Sesame 2.6.0 runtime. A set of Data Transfer Object (DTO) classes provide seamless data access and querying functionality. The current backend exclusively relies SPARQL 1.1 for updating data. Indeed, SPARQL 1.1 UPDATE was not supported by the versions of OWLim and Sesame used in the prototype. Data had to be programmatically inserted, updated or removed; that was time consuming and error prone. Queries for traceability data are made against the implicit graph containing the inferred triples. Queries on the process itself are made against the explicit graph and returned to the API caller via the DTOs.

The business layer is comprised of a set of classes that receive requests through a series of REST Web service endpoints. The requests and responses are encoded as JSON objects. Payloads are translated, verified, business rules are enforced, security applied and then forwarded as a data access requests.

---

[6] http://www.ontotext.com
[7] http://www.openrdf.org

Data extraction is done with SPARQL SELECT and CONSTRUCT queries. Repository modifications are done in transactions and are rolled back in case of problem. Service endpoints that manage process resources (objects) use the CRUD paradigm (Create, Retrieve, Update, Delete) and produce JSON-encoded messages. Data requested for products is returned as a group of properties along with the identifier of the individual (Listing 1.1).

Listing 1.1. Product object encoded in JSON.

```
property_set: {
  properties: [
    {
      property: {
        name: "order_id",
        label: {
          "en": "original order number"
        },
        value: "CA16576"
      }
    },
    {
      property {
        name: "reference_id",
        label: {
          "en" : "internal order reference"
        },
        value: "FE00047"
      }
    },
    ...
  ],
  object_id: "order001"
}
```

The application server was built on the latest version of Ruby on Rails and coordinates all requests between the presentation layer components and the back-end storage. It also enforces a certain number of business rules, but its role is more to coordinate B2C and B2B actions, unlike the back-end, which role is to coordinate data requests. The B2B front-end is the Web-based control panel of the system. It is intended to be customizable to businesses willing to license the Fairtrace ecosystem. It allows to dynamically and graphically model the supply-chains, creating the formulars and binding them to any step of the associated process. It can monitor order progress by showing various indicators and track any upstream issue such dangerous chemical detection. Users can then navigate vertically through traced data (Fig. 2) or horizontally (Fig. 3) by querying the date inside a specific time span.

The Operator front-end is aimed at supply-chain partners working in coordination. It presents them formulars that were previously created in the B2B front-end for them. It allows them to send data related to their activities into

▷ 🏭 fabric	fabric001
▷ 🏭 fabric	processed_fabric001
▷ 🏭 yarn	yarn001
▷ 🏭 yarn	yarn013
▷ 🏭 color	color001
▢ order id	CA16576
▷ 🏭 batch	batch001
▷ 🏭 transaction	transaction001
▢ fairtrade id	18753
▢ reference id	2219
▢ buyer code	E 150
▷ 🏭 processed fabric	processed_fabric001

Fig. 2. Vertical navigation through data hierarchy.

⊘ QUERY

Order ID :	CA16576		is linked with order	order001
From :	yy-mm-dd		has certificate	GOTS
To :	yy-mm-dd		has certificate	FAIRTRADE
Collection point :			is linked with mixing lot	mixing lot001
○ Job Card			type of coton	Organic & Fairtr
○ Mixing Lot			yarn count	30/1 COMBED
● Yarn			quantity	128
○ Dyeing				
○ Manufacturing				
○ Packing List				
	Search			

Fig. 3. Horizontal navigation through data.

the system. The frontend is currently being modified to include enterprise-level General Performance Indicators (GPIs) that provide invaluable information on performance. On the mobile appliances, the frontend is an HTML5 container application that allows to download pending formulars created on the B2B frontend, fill them, update them and synchronize them back with the application server. It provides support for an offine mode, where data can be synchronized back later.

4.2 Ontologies

Implementing the models was a bit delicate in that a clear separation of concerns was necessary. Having a multi-disciplinary team, we needed a modularized design in order to allow parallel and effective development. In order to create the ontologies based on our models a RDF repository to store ontology data was required. The choice of OWLim as the semantic repository and reasoner is the result of an objective test, where different semantic repositories were compared based on a few metrics (size, simplicity, ..). The OWLim SE 5.3 engine works as an extension of a SAIL repository in Sesame. It is easy to setup, provides really fast inferences on vast amounts of data, supports geo-spatial and full-text search capabilities.

OWLIM Triple Reasoning and Rule Entailment Engine (BigTRREE) uses a total materialization reasoning strategy that computes inferences after insert/update/delete cycles. That kind of strategy has the disadvantage of making inferences a bit slower (especially on very large datasets), because it computes the complete closure (optimizations aside) on each transaction. Even so, it does allow extremely fast queries, almost on par with traditional DBMS systems. The Fairtrace prototype heavily relies on queries, so OWLim SE was certainly a righteous choice. An additional feature that also helped in our choice was that it was actually very easy to deploy and write entailment rules for.

Almost every object used by the web and mobile platforms is stored in the repository A-BOX as an individual from either the process ontology or the product ontologies. Each ontology is the implementation of a conceptual model in RDF Schema[8].

The process ontology defines the building blocks for modeling business processes. It is a straight mapping from an object model to RDF. It does not define any particular semantics, except the ones explicitly given in the RDF Schema specification (`?x rdfs:type rdf:Resource` for instance). It builds around concepts like steps (activities), flows (links), users, roles, authorizations, partners, collection points and formulars. Formulars are assigned to a particular collection point linked to a specific step. Authorizations are defined for collection points to state who and on what role can enter data and download the formulars. The intent of these primitives is not to fully map the BPMN specification, but to present a synthetic view of the supply-chain. Conditions, loops and other advanced primitives are not yet supported. We did not reuse existing ontologies, because we needed a simple and efficient ontology.

The product ontology models the domain objects. In contains definitions for textile industry objects, such as fabrics, parts, dyes, yarns, mixing lots. Concepts are linked together – in a critical path – so a customer can eventually navigate through individuals from the initial order down to the geographical place where the cotton was produced. Every step and every product of the supply-chain can thus be identified. Documents and special objects, such as certificates are also modeled and can be linked to binary data (pictures). They can be used to prove that cotton is really organic and fair and that all authorizations have been obtained by a partner for instance. Importexa can enforce that business partners insert them in the system. In terms of semantics, the model uses mostly subsumption hierarchies. We assert for example:

---

[8] http://www.w3.org/TR/rdf-schema/

```
fto:Certificate rdfs:subClassOf fto:Document.
fto:ProcessedFabric rdfs:subClassOf fto:Fabric.
fto:hasCertificateName rdfs:subPropertyOf rdfs:label.
```

Furthermore, to compensate for the lack of property-chains (only available in OWL 2), we defined custom rule-sets (see Sect. 3.3). These are necessary in order to bridge the gaps in the model that can occur due to the lack of sufficient data, causing thus an impossibility to descend in the hierarchy.

4.3   Validators

In order to take advantage of data analysis, it is important that we ensure the quality of the data is good. However, since most information entered in the system is not within direct control, we must provide a general framework to keep it under control. To tackle this problem, we designed a three layered validation system, composed of field, dataset and data validators.

Field Validation. Field validators ensure that data entered in the form fields are within bounds and are compliant to the specified data type. In general, field validators are implemented on the client side (Javascript), but we also offer the possibility to configure them on the server-side. Field validators can be configured dynamically with regular expressions and data type constraints. This kind of validators can interrupt submission.

Dataset Validation. Dataset validators check the data that is passed along with a form submission. Those validators are configured to react to the presence of specific objects. They generally operate on the data level, that is, once the submission data is transformed into RDF triples. They search for specific instances in the data, such as chemicals. This kind of validators can either interrupt the submission or just emit warnings.

The detection of dangerous substances of the prototype was not codified in the model ontologies themselves. We decided to develop that functionality with a fixed chain of Java classes that emulate rules. Each validator was created as a plug-in to analyze a subset of the dataset and generate messages on specific conditions. The current iteration of Fairtrace goes further and allows dataset validators to connect to external data sources and send triples directly into the repository along with the dataset. This allows the engine to infer certain conditions. For example if a particular substance is encountered within form submission data (an instance of fto:Substance that is part of REACH's forbidden list for instance), the validator can tag that instance with the `fto:DangerousSubstance` class, so that the system will know that this object represents a global threat.

Data Validation. Data validators can either be triggered manually or automatically. They run against the whole graph of data context of a single order. They can track things like inconsistencies and even correct them given a set of general rules. They can also track certain types of instances and produce warnings upon detection. This kind of validators also issue warnings.

4.4 Supply-Chain Modelling

We also modeled a simple textile supply-chain obtained from the analysis of the information taken in the supply-chains in India. According to our consultant, our process model, even simple matches almost 90 % of existing real chains. It models all upstream steps such as Mixing, Spinning, Dyeing, Processing, Transforming, Weaving, Sewing and Packaging. Ginning was purposely left aside, since information about the provenance of cotton was readily available at the Mixing step.

4.5 Testing

The infrastructure was deployed and tested in India. The objective was purely to assess its flexibility. We did not acquire quantitative indicators such as number of queries for each order, etc., because it was materially (i.e. financially) not possible to launch enough real orders to gather enough data for the results to turn out meaningful. We concentrated thus on a feasibility study following the project plan methodology:

- We selected the supply-chain partners in India that usually work with the textile company Importexa in Switzerland;
- A consultant from Importexa visited the partners on site in order to thoroughly document the supply-chains;
- The consultant described formally the supply-chains using a Business Process Modeling notation;
- On the basis of the consultant documentation (data description, business process model, etc.), we designed in our Web-based B2B Frontend the processes and formulars acquiring information inside those formulars;
- Those formulars were instantaneously deployed for data acquisition, both as HTLM5-enabled mobile and Web formulars;
- Importexa launched a real order for an organic fair cotton tee-shirt, whose production data should be acquired with our solutions;
- A consultant was then sent to India in order to teach working partners how to input data on the forms and send it for treatment;
- A final report described the results of the tests.

The tests ran for many days and a couple of formulars had to be re-adjusted to better match the partner's requirements. We were reactive and could almost immediately update the formulars and they were able to use it straight away. As the tests were made on a real Importexa order, we could monitor data incoming from all steps including all chemicals and certificates (GOTS, Fairtrade, GMO free, and so on) in realtime (Fig. 4).

5 Discussion

Fairtrace is regarded as a success on management, collaboration and technology support levels. It raised high commercial interest when it was presented

Fig. 4. Test data acquisition in India.

and demonstrated in a technical session to potential customers. One customer is ready to deploy the solution for his supply-chains. Although we had no quantitative metrics for the tests, we could assess on its success in a real scenario. We faced many unexpected real-world conditions that could not be foreseen. We were able to respond to problems and modification requests quickly (in a matter of minutes) and could attest of the flexibility of the prototype.

Importexa has now created the Fairtrace SA start-up that will commercialize the finished product. Fairtrace is currently being improved and adapted to market segments other than the textile industry. A survey on potential markets has already been done and first discussions have already taken place with interested brands and Swiss resellers, in order to adapt the tool to new markets (clock industry, controlled cheese production, cocoa, ...). Supply-chain traceability can be a strong selling argument, because it implies that companies master the entire production chain, can react quickly to potential problems (such as to follow the REACH regulation) and can prove their customers that they exactly know what they produce.

The difficulty will be however to convince partners to use the system on an daily basis. We have already encountered resistance in the textile domain with some suppliers. Although the problem was not directly bound to a misconception of the system, it shows that there's still much way to go to make such solution viable. This is the biggest challenge that will face the newly established start-up and for which we are still trying to find solutions. If we fail to show partners immediate return, they will never use it.

In this project we have set Semantic Web Technologies was a prerequisite, because the opportunity was good to explore its possibilities for future projects. Fairtrace helped us understanding that SWT are now mature enough to use in commercial projects. We were very pragmatic about there use, so we only had a glimpse at the full range of possibilities that it has to offer. However, the expressiveness of the languages coupled to the rule-based OWLIM reasoning engine was good enough to allow complex constructs. We still have directions for improvements: we can link geographical places to GeoNames[9] features for instance, redirect specific concepts to DBpedia[10] definitions or even automatically categorize items as dangerous by making use of bridges to external datasets.

6 Conclusions

This paper presented a pragmatic semantic-based approach to the traceability problem in supply-chains. The first prototype is finished and has been successfully tested in a Swiss and Indian supply-chain in the textile industry. However, Fairtrace is still an ongoing work and the roadmap contains many improvements. SWT will continue playing a central role in the future infrastructure. We are currently using the next-generation OWLIM semantic repository to take advantage on the new constructs offered by OWL2 and SPARQL 1.1 UPDATE. We are also implementing important enhancement on the creation of formulars, on the customization of the system and on the primitives for modelling supply-chains. Finally, we are also considering intelligent agent techniques for automatically querying the semantic repositories to bring the benefits of decision support to our customers.

Acknowledgements. We especially thank the Swiss Commission for Technology and Innovation (http://www.kti-cti.ch) who financed a big part of this project under contract number PFES-ES No. 11141.1, and the company Ontotext who supported us with a research license for OWLim SE.

References

1. Alves, B., Schumacher, M.I., Cretton, F., Le Calv'e, A., Cherix, G., Werlen, D., Gapany, C., Baeryswil, B., Gerber, D., Cloux, P.: Fairtrace - a semantic-web oriented traceability solution applied to the textile traceability. In: 15th International Conference on Enterprise Information Systems 1, pp. 101–106 (2013)
2. Werlen, D., Alves, B., Cherix, G., Gapany, C., Schumacher, M.: Procédé d'édition de formulaires pour la saisie de données en différents points de collecte. Swiss patent application CH00104/12 filed on 25 Jan 2012 (2012)
3. Mentzer, J., DeWitt, W., Keebler, J., Min, S., Nix, N., Smith, C., Zacharia, Z.: Defining supply chain management. J. Bus. logistics **22**, 1–25 (2001)
4. Chandra, C., Kumar, S.: Enterprise architectural framework for supply-chain integration. Ind. Manage. Data Syst. **101**, 290–304 (2001)
5. Lambert, D., Cooper, M., Pagh, J.: Supply chain management: implementation issues and research opportunities. Int. J. Logistics Manage. **9**, 1–20 (1998)
6. Lambert, D., Cooper, M.: Issues in supply chain management. Ind. Mark. Manage. **29**, 65–83 (2000)
7. Grubic, T., Fan, I.S.: Supply chain ontology: review, analysis and synthesis. Comput. Ind. **61**, 776–786 (2010)

---

[9] http://www.geonames.org
[10] http://dbpedia.org

8. Fox, M., Barbuceanu, M., Teigen, R.: Agent-oriented supply-chain management. Int. J. Flex. Manuf. Syst. **12**, 165–188 (2000)
9. Christopher, M.: Logistics and Supply Chain Management: Creating Value-Added Networks. Pearson Education, Harlow (2005)
10. Ye, Y., Yang, D., Jiang, Z., Tong, L.: Ontology-based semantic models for supply chain management. Int. J. Adv. Manuf. Technol. **37**, 1250–1260 (2008)
11. Bowersox, D., Closs, D., Cooper, M.: Supply Chain Logistics Management, vol. 2. McGraw-Hill, New York (2002)
12. Kärkkäinen, M.: Increasing efficiency in the supply chain for short shelf life goods using rfid tagging. Int. J. Retail Distrib. Manage. **31**, 529–536 (2003)
13. Kelepouris, T., Pramatari, K., Doukidis, G.: Rfid-enabled traceability in the food supply chain. Ind. Manage. Data Syst. **107**, 183–200 (2007)
14. Kwok, S.K., Wu, K.K.W.: Rfid-based intra-supply chain in textile industry. Ind. Manage. Data Syst. **109**, 1166–1178 (2009)
15. Opara, L.: Traceability in agriculture and food supply chain: a review of basic concepts, technological implications, and future prospects. J. Food Agric. Environ. **1**, 101–106 (2003)
16. Kim, J.W., Jain, R.: Web services composition with traceability centered on dependency. In: Proceedings of the 38th Annual Hawaii International Conference on System Sciences (HICSS'05) - Track 3, HICSS '05, vol. 03, p. 89. IEEE Computer Society, Washington, DC (2005)
17. Mocan, A., Moran, M., Cimpian, E., Zaremba, M.: Filling the gap - extending service oriented architectures with semantics. In: Proceedings of the IEEE International Conference on e-Business Engineering, ICEBE '06, pp. 594–601. IEEE Computer Society, Washington, DC (2006)
18. Paolucci, M., Kawamura, T., Payne, T.R., Sycara, K.: Semantic matching of web services capabilities. In: Horrocks, I., Hendler, J. (eds.) ISWC 2002. LNCS, vol. 2342, pp. 333–347. Springer, Heidelberg (2002)
19. Schumacher, M., Helin, H., Schuldt, H.: CASCOM: intelligent service coordination in the semantic web, 1st edn., Birkhäuser Basel (2008)
20. Ye, Y., Yang, D., Jiang, Z., Tong, L.: An ontology-based architecture for implementing semantic integration of supply chain management. Int. J. Comput. Integr. Manuf. **21**, 1–18 (2008)
21. Virgilio, R., Sciascio, E., Ruta, M., Scioscia, F., Torlone, R.: Semantic-based rfid data management. In: Ranasinghe, D.C.C., Sheng, Q.Z.Z., Zeadally, S. (eds.) Unique Radio Innovation for the 21st Century, pp. 111–141. Springer, Heidelberg (2010), doi:10.1007/978-3-642-03462-6_6
22. Bechini, A., Cimino, M.G.C.A., Marcelloni, F., Tomasi, A.: Patterns and technologies for enabling supply chain traceability through collaborative e-business. Inf. Softw. Technol. **50**, 342–359 (2008)
23. Datta, S., Lyu, J., Ping-Shun, C.: Decision support and systems interoperability in global business management. Int. J. Electron. Bus. Manage. **5**(4), 255–265 (2007)
24. Haller, A., Oren, E., Kotinurmi, P.: m3po: an ontology to relate choreographies to workflow models. In: IEEE International Conference on Services Computing, SCC'06, pp. 19–27. IEEE (2006)

Estimating Sufficient Sample Sizes
for Approximate Decision Support Queries

Amit Rudra[1], Raj P. Gopalan[2(✉)], and N.R. Achuthan[3]

[1] School of Information Systems, Curtin University, Perth, Australia
A.Rudra@curtin.edu.au
[2] Department of Computing, Curtin University, Perth, Australia
R.Gopalan@curtin.edu.au
[3] Independent Consultant, Perth, Australia
achu_tha@yahoo.com.au

Abstract. Sampling schemes for approximate processing of highly selective decision support queries need to retrieve sufficient number of records that can provide reliable results within acceptable error limits. The k-MDI tree is an innovative index structure that supports drawing rich samples of relevant records for a given set of dimensional attribute ranges. This paper describes a method for estimating sufficient sample sizes for decision support queries based on inverse simple random sampling without replacement (SRSWOR). Combined with a k-MDI tree index, this method is shown to offer a reliable approach to approximate query processing for decision support.

Keywords: Decision support queries · Approximate query processing · Sampling · Data warehousing · Inverse simple random sample without replacement (SRSWOR)

1 Introduction

Last two decades have seen significant advances in research to facilitate decision support queries on data warehouses storing huge amounts of data. Such queries often require large processing time to derive information suitable for the present day analysts and decision makers. As time is at a premium for taking effective decisions within enterprises, estimates of query results that are reliable approximations within acceptable error limits and delivered in a timely manner may be more crucial than ensuring absolute accuracy of those results. Relatively small random samples can be used effectively for certain data warehouse queries. But these samples may not adequately represent data sought by highly selective queries. A sufficient sample for such a query should be ideally drawn from a subset of the data warehouse records that satisfy the query's selection conditions. Given a sufficient sample, the query result estimated from it will have accuracy within the specified confidence interval. This paper is focused on estimating the sizes of sufficient samples for data warehouse queries.

Picking records at random from a database without prior organization to facilitate the process is very inefficient [16], as the records to be included in a sample may be scattered across the disk storage resulting in a large number of disk accesses. Several

© Springer International Publishing Switzerland 2014
S. Hammoudi et al. (Eds.): ICEIS 2013, LNBIP 190, pp. 85–99, 2014.
DOI: 10.1007/978-3-319-09492-2_6

researchers have proposed schemes to ameliorate the cost of data access for approximate query processing [1, 8, 10–15, 19]. Joshi and Jermaine [14] proposed a binary tree index structure called the ACE tree for efficiently drawing samples for processing database queries. They demonstrated the effectiveness of this structure for single and two attribute database queries, though they did not deal with multi-attribute aggregate queries. For databases with k key attributes, they [14] proposed to extend the binary ACE tree by splitting the ranges of one attribute after another at consecutive levels starting from the root to level $k + 1$; the splitting process is to be then repeated with each attribute in the same sequence as before until the required number of leaf nodes are reached. The resulting binary tree index will have a very large number of levels for a data warehouse with even a relatively small number of attributes. Rudra et al. [17] proposed the k-MDI Tree, which extends the ACE Tree structure to deal with multi-dimensional data warehouses using k-ary splits of data ranges. It was shown that random samples of rows that satisfy the conditions of a given query could be drawn more efficiently using the k-MDI tree.

The k-MDI tree index [17] allows storing of records for quick retrieval of random samples in given attribute ranges. It thus supports picking of rich samples for queries with highly specific selection conditions. The result of a decision support query to get the average of an attribute can be estimated from a sample containing a sufficient number of records that satisfy the query conditions. But to estimate the sum of an attribute, both the average and the count of the records that satisfy the query in the whole database need to be estimated. Chaudhuri and Mukerjee [4] had proposed an unbiased estimator based on inverse simple random sampling without replacement (SRSWOR) by random sampling of a finite population until a predefined number of domain members are observed. In this paper, the inverse SRSWOR method is adapted to estimate sufficient sample sizes for decision support queries using the k-MDI tree index. The method is empirically evaluated on a large real world data warehouse.

The rest of the paper is organized as follows: In Sect. 2, we define some basic terms, and briefly describe the k-way multi-dimensional (k-MDI) indexing structure and how it is used for estimating query results. Section 3 discusses how to select sufficient samples using inverse SRSWOR. In Sect. 4, the results of our experiments are described. Finally, Sect. 5 concludes the paper and provides some pointers for further research.

2   Dimensions, Measures and the k-MDI Tree Index

In this section, we define some terms pertaining to data warehousing and then review the k-MDI tree index and the process for retrieving relevant samples from a data warehouse.

2.1   Dimensions and Measures

The data for decision support queries is normally structured in large databases called data warehouses. A typical data warehouse based on a star schema consists of a large table in the middle called the fact table connected to other tables called dimension tables. For example, consider the fact table Sales shown as Table 1. A *dimension* table Store linked to StoreNo in this fact table will contain more information on each of the stores such as store name, location, state, and country [9]. Other dimension tables could exist for item and date. The remaining attributes like quantity and amount are typically, but not necessarily, numerical and are termed *measures*. A typical decision support query aggregates a measure using functions such as Sum(), Avg() or Count(). The fact table Sales along with all its dimension tables forms a *star schema*.

Table 1. Fact table SALES.

SALES				
StoreNo	Date	Item	Quantity	Amount
21	12-Jan-11	iPad	223	123,455
21	12-Jan-11	PC	20	24,800
24	11-Jan-11	iMac	11	9,990
77	25-Jan-11	PC	10	12,600

In decision support queries a measure is of interest for calculation of averages, totals and counts. For example, a sales manager may like to know the total sales quantity and amount for certain item(s) in a certain period of time for a particular store or even all (or some) stores in a region. This may then allow her to make decisions to order more or less stocks as appropriate at a point in time.

2.2 k-MDI Tree Index

The k-ary multi-dimensional index tree (k-MDI tree) proposed in [17] extends the ACE tree index [14] for multiple dimensions. As shown in Fig. 1, the ACE tree is a binary tree of potentially unlimited height. In the example shown (Fig. 1), the root node $I_{1,1}$ with its range $I_{1,1}.R$ labeled as [0–64] signifies the key value range of the whole data set. The key of the root node partitions the range $I_{1,1}.R$ into $I_{2,1}.R = [0–32]$ and $I_{2,2}.R = [33–64]$. This partitioning of ranges is propagated down the tree among the descendants of respective nodes. The ranges associated with a section of a leaf node are determined by the ranges associated with each internal node on the path from the root node to the leaf. If we look at the path from $I_{1,1}$ i.e. the root node down to the leaf node L_4, we come across the following ranges 0–64, 0–32 and 17–24. A leaf node is partitioned into sections (S_1, S_2, ...), their number depending on the number of dimensions indexed. Thus, the first section $L_4.S_1$ has a random sample of records in the range 0–64; $L_4.S_2$ has them in the range 0–32; $L_4.S_3$ in the range 17–32 and $L_4.S_4$ in the range 25–32. The size of each leaf is chosen as the number of records that can be stored in a disk block and so the number of leaf nodes depends on the size of the database, which also determines the height of the index tree itself.

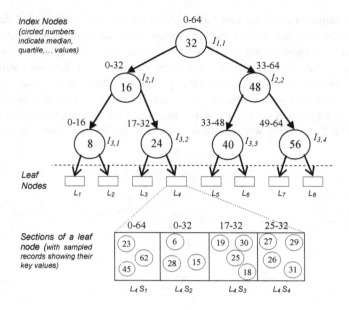

Fig. 1. Structure of the ACE tree.

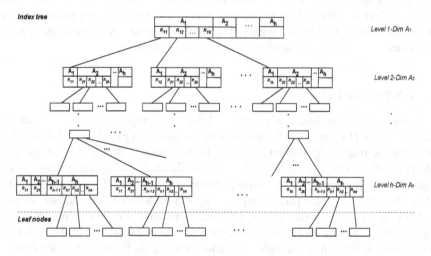

Fig. 2. General structure of the *k*-MDI tree.

As opposed to the unlimited height of the ACE tree, the height of the *k*-MDI tree (Fig. 2) is limited to the number of key attributes. As a multi-way tree index, it is relatively shallow even for a large number of key value ranges and thus, requires only a small number of disk accesses to traverse from the root to the leaf nodes.

The *k*-MDI tree is a *k*-ary balanced tree [2] as described below:

1. The root node of a k-MDI tree corresponds to the first attribute (dimension) in the index.
2. The root points to k_1 ($k_1 \leq k$) index nodes at level 2, with each node corresponding to one of the k_1 splits of the ranges for attribute a_1.
3. Each of the nodes at level 2, in turn, points to up to k_2 ($k_2 \leq k$) index nodes at level 3 corresponding to k_2 splits of the ranges of values of attribute a_2; similarly for nodes at levels 3 to h, corresponding to attributes $a_3, \ldots, a_h$.
4. At level h, each of up to k^{h-1} nodes points to up to k_h ($k_h \leq k$) leaf nodes that store data records.
5. Each leaf node has $h + 1$ sections; for Sects. 1 to h, each section i contains random subset of records in the key range of the node i in the path from the root to the level h above the leaf; section $h + 1$ contains a random subset of records with keys in the specific range for the given leaf.

Thus, the dataset is divided into a maximum of k^h leaf nodes with each leaf node, in turn, consisting of $h + 1$ sections and each section containing a random subset of records. The total number of leaf nodes depends on the total number of records in the dataset and the size of a leaf node (which may be chosen as equal to the disk block size or another suitable size). More details on leaf nodes and sections are given in Subsect. 2.3. In real data sets, the number of range splits at different nodes of a given level i need not be the same. For convenience, the number of splits at all levels are kept as k in Fig. 1 that shows the structure of the general scheme for k-MDI multilevel index tree of attributes $A_1, A_2, \ldots, A_h$ with k ranges ($R_{11}, R_{12}, \ldots, R_{1k}$), ($R_{21}, R_{22}, \ldots, R_{2k}$), $\ldots$ ($R_{h1}, R_{h2}, \ldots, R_{hk}$) respectively at levels ($1, \ldots, h$). In other words, R_{ij} is the i-th attribute's j-th range high water mark (HWM).

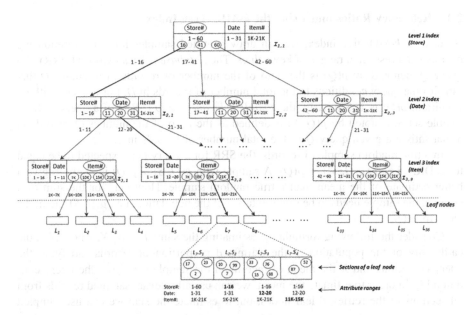

Fig. 3. A leaf node (changes in range values for attributes are indicated in bold).

An example of the k-MDI tree for a store chain dataset with three dimensions – store, date sold and item number is shown in Fig. 3. The number of range splits and hence branches from non-leaf nodes vary between 3 and 4 in this example.

2.3   Leaf Nodes

The lowest level nodes of a k-MDI tree point to leaf nodes containing data records. The data records are stored in $h + 1$ sections, where h is the height of the tree. Section S_1 of every leaf node is drawn from the entire database with no range restriction on the attribute values. Each section S_i ($2 \le i \le h + 1$) in a leaf node L is restricted on the range of key values by the same restrictions that apply to the corresponding sub-path along the path from the root to L. Thus for section S_2, the restrictions are the same as on the branch to the node at level 2 along the path from the root to L and so on.

Figure 3 shows an example leaf node projected from the sample k-MDI tree. The sections are indicated above the node with attribute ranges for each section below the node. The circled numbers in each section indicate record numbers that are randomly placed in the section. The range restrictions on the records are indicated below each section, where the first section S_1 has records drawn from the entire range of the database. Thus, it can contain records uniformly sampled from the whole dataset. The next section S_2 has restriction on the first dimension viz. store (for leaf node L_7 this range is store numbers 1–16). The third section S_3 has restrictions on both first and second dimensions viz. store and date. While the last section S_4 has restrictions on all the three dimensions – store, date and item. The scheme for selection of records into various leaf nodes and sections is explained in detail in the following section.

2.4   Relevancy Ratios and Using the k-MDI Tree Index

By using a k-MDI tree index, we can draw stratified samples for data warehousing queries from restricted ranges of key values. The *database relevancy ratio* (DRR) of a query Q, denoted by $\rho(Q)$ is the ratio of the number of records in a dataset D that satisfies the query conditions to the total number of records in D. For a query with no condition, $\rho(Q)$ is 1. Similarly, the *sample relevancy ratio* (SRR) of a query Q for a sample set S, denoted by $\rho(Q, S)$ is defined as the ratio of the number of records in S that satisfy a given query Q to the total number of records in S.

In a true random sample of records, the SRR for a query Q is expected to be equal to its DRR, i.e., $E(\rho(Q, S)) = \rho(Q)$. A sample with $\rho(Q, S) > \rho(Q)$ is likely to give a better estimate of the mean than a true random sample. However, for the sum of a column, the sample needs to be representative of the population, i.e., $\rho(Q, S)$ should be close to $\rho(Q)$.

Consider the following formula for estimating the sum: $\hat{T} = N\hat{p}\bar{X}$, where N is the cardinality of the population, $\hat{p}$ the estimated proportion of records satisfying the query conditions and $\bar{X}$ the mean of records in the sample satisfying the query condition [3]. In order to estimate the mean, we can use all relevant sampled records from all sections of the retrieved leaf nodes, but to estimate the sum we can use sampled records only from section S_1, which is the only section with records drawn randomly from the entire dataset. For estimating the sum for a query with conditions on some of the indexed dimensions we use appropriate sections of the retrieved leaf nodes to get a better estimate of the mean; the records from section S_1 are used to get a fair estimation of the proportion of records that satisfy the query conditions.

2.5   Effect of Sectioning on Relevancy Ratio

As discussed earlier, sections S_1 to S_{h+1} of each leaf node contain random collections of records with the difference that S_1 contains records from the entire dataset while other sections contain random records from restricted ranges of the key attributes. Consider a query with the same range restrictions on all three dimensions (store, date and item) as section $L_7.S_4$ in Fig. 2. We are then likely to get more relevant records in the sample from the second section $L_7.S_2$ than from S_1 since records of S_2 have restrictions on the first dimension of store that matches the query condition. Records in S_3 will have restrictions on both store and date dimensions that match that of the query and so likely to contain more relevant records than in S_2. All records in section $L_7.S_4$ will satisfy the query since the range restrictions on S_4 exactly match the query. Mathematically, for a query Q having restrictions as mentioned above:

$$\rho(Q) = E(\rho(Q, L_7.S_1)) \leq E(\rho(Q, L_7.S_2))$$
$$\leq E(\rho(Q, L_7.S_3)) \leq E(\rho(Q, L_7.S_4))$$

Using this property of the k-MDI tree, it is possible to quickly increase the size of a sample that is too small, by including more records from other sections of the retrieved leaf nodes.

2.6   Record Retrieval to Process a Query

The objective of using the k-MDI tree is to retrieve a significant number of relevant records (i.e. records that satisfy the query conditions) in the sample drawn for processing a given query. The query conditions may span sections of one or more leaf nodes, which can be reached from index nodes that straddle more than one range of attribute values. Traversing the tree from the root using the attribute value ranges in the query conditions can access these leaf nodes. Sections from multiple leaf nodes are then combined to form the sample.

We describe the retrieval process using an example query on the sample database of Fig. 3. Consider a query Q_0 about sales in store 12 for date range 1–13 and item range 12K–20K. The retrieval algorithm finds the sections of leaf nodes for this query as follows:

1. Search index level 1 to locate the relevant store range. Store 12 is in the left most range of 1–16.
2. Traverse down to index level 2 (date), indicated by a dashed arrow in Fig. 4, along the first store range. Since there is a condition on date (1–13), compare the

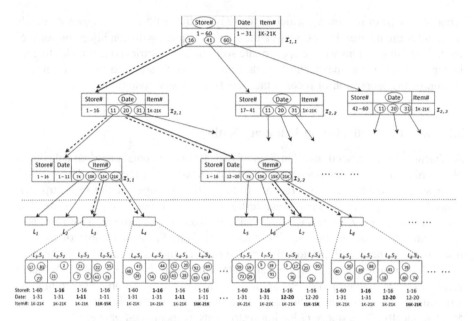

Fig. 4. Navigation down index tree nodes for conditions on three dimensions.

HWMs (high water marks) of the three ranges and find that it fits into two date ranges viz. the first and the second. Make a note of these date ranges.

3. Traverse down using the first date range to the next index level, which has item ranges. Since there is a condition on item numbers (12K–20K), compare this range with HWMs and find that it fits into two ranges viz. the third and the fourth. Make a note of these item ranges.

4. Traverse down using the third item range to relevant leaf pages and make a note of them.

5. Iterate step 4, except this time using the fourth item range.

6. Next, repeat the above three steps i.e. steps 3 through 5; but this time using the second date range instead.

7. Now retrieve records from the relevant sections in the four leaf nodes (viz. L_3, L_4, L_7 and L_8) to form a sample for the given query.

3   Sampling to Sufficient Levels Using Inverse SRSWOR

An important question to be answered is how much sampling is sufficient to estimate some property of a population. For business analytics on very large data [5], it is valuable to provide the analytic query user with incremental feedback of the ongoing progress of an approximate query [6, 7]. The method described below for determining if a sufficient sample size has been retrieved is based on the works of Chaudhuri and Mukerjee [4] and Sangngam and Suwatee [18]. Their research established that inverse simple random sampling without replacement (or inverse SRSWOR) method provides an unbiased estimate of the number of data points (M) satisfying property P, if sampling is continued until a pre-assigned number, say m, of data points satisfying property P are present in the sample. For a commonly raised query Q we need to establish an acceptable pre-assigned number m. Such an m is established only once (the first time the query Q is raised). If the underlying market situation changes significantly then one might have to revise the value of m. We first discuss some of the necessary concepts. In the present case, property P would be the conditions imposed on a query viz. the dimension ranges. For a given query Q, assume that we have determined the estimate of $\rho(Q)$. Recall that

$$\rho(Q)=\frac{\text{Number of cases satisying conditions of query Q}}{\text{Sample size n}}.$$

We could also choose the above sample size n as follows: Fix the proportion of error we are ready to tolerate, say e. Then choose $n = \frac{z_{\alpha/2}^2 \rho(Q)(1-\rho(Q))}{e^2}$, where e is a number such as 0.01, 0.02, or 0.05 etc. and $Z_{\alpha/2}$ is the normal ordinate such that $\text{Prob}\left\{ P(Q) - \rho(Q) > z_{\alpha/2}\sqrt{\frac{\rho(Q)(1-\rho(Q))}{n}} \right\} = \frac{\alpha}{2}$ where P(Q) is the random variable representing $\rho(Q)$. Usually, we take for 95 % confidence interval.

Now estimate $\rho(Q)$ again using this new sample size. Henceforth, assume that we have this new estimate with error bounded by e. In fact, when the true value of $\rho(Q)$ is not too close to zero (0) or one (1), and sample size n is large enough we know that the random variable P(Q) representing $\rho(Q)$, follows approximately the Normal distribution with mean $\rho(Q)$ and standard deviation $\sqrt{\frac{\rho(Q)(1-\rho(Q))}{n}}$. Now assume that the true value of is not too close to zero (0) or one (1), then we can get 95 % confidence interval for true value of $\rho(Q)$ as

$$\left(\rho(Q) - 1.96\sqrt{\frac{\rho(Q)(1-\rho(Q))}{n}}, \rho(Q) + 1.96\sqrt{\frac{\rho(Q)(1-\rho(Q))}{n}} \right) \qquad (1)$$

Using the confidence interval (1) we can choose about 5 to 10 possible values for P(Q). These values may correspond to 10, 25, 50, 75, 90 percentile points of the random variable P(Q). Let us denote these values by $\rho_1(Q)$, $\rho_2(Q)$, $\rho_3(Q)$, $\rho_4(Q)$, and $\rho_5(Q)$.

Using these 5 percentiles, choose 10 % or 20 % of the corresponding M values as possible choice of values for m. More specifically,

$$m_{1,1} = 0.10\rho_1(Q)N, m_{2,1} = 0.20\rho_1(Q)N;$$
$$m_{1,2} = 0.10\rho_2(Q)N, m_{2,2} = 0.20\rho_2(Q)N;$$
$$m_{1,3} = 0.10\rho_3(Q)N, m_{2,3} = 0.20\rho_3(Q)N;$$
$$m_{1,4} = 0.10\rho_4(Q)N, m_{2,4} = 0.20\rho_4(Q)N; \text{ and}$$
$$m_{1,5} = 0.10\rho_5(Q)N, m_{2,5} = 0.20\rho_5(Q)N.$$

We now describe the *Basic Find_M* or *BF_M* algorithm. There are five steps in the *BF_M* algorithm, which are as follows:

1. *Initialization:* In this step, various variables, like counts and cumulative totals, are initialized.
2. *Sampling:* Records are sampled iteratively and those meeting the given condition i.e. satisfying the given property, say *P*, are used for calculating the sum and the count of the value(s) in the query.
3. *Check & iterate:* This step checks if sufficient number of samples have been retrieved. In case, it has not reached the targeted number of samples, it iterates the sampling step, else it terminates further sampling.
4. *Estimation:* In this step, unbiased estimators of M, average and sum, and their variances are computed.
5. *Best estimate:* Choose the best estimate as the one that minimizes the desired variance.

In the step 4 the unbiased estimators of M, average and sum, and their variances are computed using the following formulae from Chaudhuri and Mukerjee [4]:

Let the current sample size be *n* and the number of transactions satisfying the property *P* be *m*. Define set $\text{sum}' = \text{sum}(X_i)$ and $Z = (\text{Sum}(X_i^2))/m$,

$$\hat{M} = N\frac{m-1}{n-1}, \ v(\hat{M}) = N^2\left(\frac{m-1}{n-1}\right)\left[\left(\frac{m-1}{n-1}\right) - \frac{N-1}{N}\left(\frac{m-2}{n-2}\right) - \frac{1}{N}\right], \ \bar{x} = \frac{\text{sum}'}{m}, \ \hat{T} = \hat{M}\bar{x},$$

$$s^2 = \frac{m}{m-1}\left(Z - (\bar{x})^2\right), \ v(\bar{x}) = \frac{\hat{M} - m}{\hat{M}(m-1)}\left(Z - (\bar{x})^2\right), \ R = N^2\left(\frac{m-1}{n-1}\right)\left[\frac{N-1}{N}\left(\frac{m-2}{n-2}\right) + \frac{1}{N}\right], \text{ and}$$

$$v(\hat{T}) = \hat{T}^2 - \left[R(Z - s^2) + \hat{M}s^2\right].$$

Note that unbiased estimators of M, average and sum are given by $\hat{M}, \bar{x}, \text{and } \hat{T}$ respectively. Furthermore, unbiased estimators of $\hat{M}, \bar{x}, \text{and } \hat{T}$ are given by $v(\hat{M}), v(\bar{x}) \text{ and } v(\hat{T})$ respectively.

Now, for a given query *Q*, we can use the above method to recommend the appropriate value of *m* that yields the smallest variance for the estimate of M. To determine the number of sections to retrieve, frequency tables for all dimensions are used. In case the query involves more than one dimension, information in frequency tables for all dimensions involved in the query condition is utilized.

4 Experimental Results

To evaluate the effectiveness of the proposed sampling technique based on the *k*-MDI tree, experiments were performed on real life supermarket retail sales data [20] for a month from 150 outlets. The data warehouse is structured as a star schema shown in Fig. 5, with the fact table (Itemscan) consisting of over 21 million rows and three dimension tables viz. StoreInfo, ItemDesc and StoreMemberVisits.

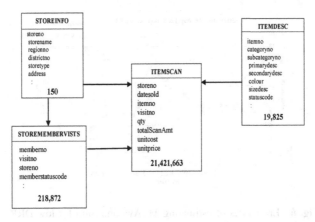

Fig. 5. The schema for experimental retail sales data warehouse.

In Sect. 3, the concept of inverse random sampling without replacement [4, 18] along with unbiased estimation techniques was introduced for estimating the mean, Sum and M, the count of records satisfying a property P in the database. Next, the results of the experiments are shown using the k-MDI tree to facilitate random retrieval of records to estimate M.

We considered a set of three queries (modified version of TPC-H Query 1 [21]) containing the SQL functions – avg(), sum(), count() with varying database relevancy ratios (or DRR, as defined in Sect. 2.4), viz. low (<0.01), medium (0.01–0.1) and high (>0.1) DRRs. The queries were of the form:

```
Select Avg(totscanAmt),Sum(totscanAmt),Count(*)
From  itemscan, storeinfo, itemdesc
Where  storeno between s1 and s2
And itemscan.storeno=storeinfo.storeno
And itemscan.itemno=itemdesc.itemno
And datesold between d1 and d2
And itemno between i1 and i2;
```

Table 2. Error rates of M, Avg and Sum for low DRR queries.

Sampling rate	Est. value of M	Error in estimating M	Error Avg	Error Sum
m1,1	3231	6.61	4.1	14.68
m1,2	2758	9.01	2.21	12.02
m1,3	2757	9.05	3.12	19.08
m1,4	3286	8.42	2.59	15.46
m1,5	3353	10.61	2.19	15.4
m2,1	2670	11.9	1.78	12.87
m2,2	3340	10.18	1.36	14.65
m2,3	3262	7.62	1.27	9.86
m2,4	2782	8.21	1.69	9.28
m2,5	3241	6.92	1.59	8.94

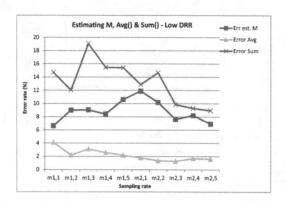

Fig. 6. Error rates of estimating M, Avg and Sum for low DRR.

Table 3. Error rates of M, Avg and Sum for medium DRR queries.

Sampling rate	Est. of M	Err est. M	Error Avg	Error Sum
m1,1	11683	3.12	2.06	4.02
m1,2	11582	2.22	2.63	3.88
m1,3	11600	2.38	2.66	3.86
m1,4	11621	2.57	2.11	3.42
m1,5	11575	2.16	2.13	3.24
m2,1	11602	2.4	2.31	2.64
m2,2	11500	1.5	2.22	2.22
m2,3	11391	0.54	2.03	2.86
m2,4	11558	2.01	2.01	2.1
m2,5	11526	1.73	1.64	2.08

Table 2 and the corresponding graph in Fig. 6 show the accuracy levels achieved by the sampling scheme using inverse SRSWOR for low DRR queries, using the 10 different sampling rates pertaining to 5 percentile values of $\rho(Q)$ at the 0.10 rate and 5 for 0.20 rate as per the sampling and estimation schemes discussed in Sect. 3. Here, $m_{1,1}$ refers to 0.10 rate for the 10th percentile value of $\rho(Q)$; $m_{1,2}$ for the 25th percentile value; $m_{1,3}$ for the 50th; $m_{1,4}$ for 75th; and $m_{1,5}$ for 90th; while $m_{2,1} - m_{2,5}$ for the same percentile values respectively but at 0.20 rate. It is observed that the error rates for calculation of Avg are below 5 %, but estimates of both the M and the Sum are not within the acceptable error limits of 5 %.

Table 3 and the corresponding graph in Fig. 7 shows the accuracy levels achieved by the sampling scheme as described for inverse SRSWOR on medium DRR queries. It can be observed that for medium DRR queries, the count M, the Avg and the Sum are within the acceptable error rate limits of 0–5 %.

Table 4 and the corresponding graph in Fig. 8 shows the accuracy levels achieved by the sampling scheme for inverse SRSWOR on high DRR queries. It can be

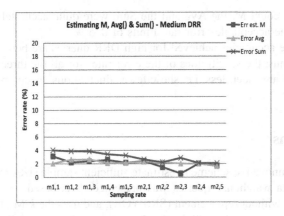

Fig. 7. Error rates of estimating M, Avg and Sum for medium DRR.

Table 4. Error rates of M, Avg and Sum for high DRR queries.

Sampling rate	Est. of M	Error M	Error Avg	Error Sum
m1,1	329333	1.97	2.45	3.06
m1,2	331819	1.23	2.01	2.87
m1,3	342099	1.83	2.44	2.05
m1,4	339680	1.11	1.98	2.56
m1,5	328997	2.07	1.82	2.32
m2,1	329803	1.83	1.1	2.18
m2,2	329299	1.98	1.44	2.28
m2,3	331449	1.34	1.29	1.05
m2,4	339949	1.19	0.52	0.76
m2,5	339546	1.07	0.63	1.11

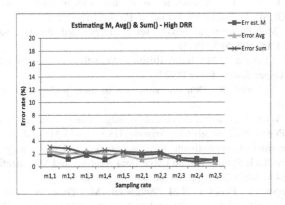

Fig. 8. Error rates of estimating M, Avg and Sum for high DRR.

observed that the count M, the Avg and the Sum were quite accurately estimated as they are within the acceptable error rate limits of 0–5 %.

In general, the accuracies achieved for high DRR queries are better than those of medium DRR. Thus, the sensitivities of the error rates for all the three statistics viz., Avg, Sum and M are much less, i.e. show fewer fluctuations, as compared to that of the medium DRR.

5   Conclusions

In this paper, an innovative scheme to estimate sufficient sample sizes for approximate processing of data warehouse queries was presented. It is based on inverse simple random sampling without replacement (SRSWOR), and uses the k-MDI tree index for drawing the relevant samples efficiently. In order to experimentally evaluate this technique, typical queries on a relatively large data warehouse were used. For each query, the total number M of records in the whole database satisfying the query conditions was estimated along with the mean and sum of relevant quantitative attributes. It was found that for queries of low database relevancy ratio (DRR) of less than 0.01, the estimated values of average were within the acceptable error limit of 5 %, but not the estimates of sum and the total number of relevant records M. However, for queries of both medium DRR (0.01–0.1) and high DRR (greater than 0.1), all the three statistics viz. the value of M, the average and the sum were estimated with error rates below 5 % as shown in Sect. 4. These results indicate that the approach proposed in this paper can be highly effective for estimating sufficient sample sizes of specific decision support queries on large data warehouses. In future research, it is proposed to incorporate in our algorithm the probabilistic approaches similar to those in [1, 7].

References

1. Aouiche, K., Lemire, D.: A comparison of five probabilistic view-size estimation techniques in OLAP. In: DOLAP'07, Lisboa, Portugal (2007)
2. Bentley, J.L.: Multidimensional binary search trees used for associative searching. Commun. ACM **18**, 509–517 (1975)
3. Berenson, M.L., Levine, D.M.: Basic Business Statistics - Concepts and Applications. Prentice Hall, Upper Saddle River (1992)
4. Chaudhuri, A., Mukerjee, R.: Domain estimation in finite populations. Aust. J. Stat. **27**, 135–137 (1985)
5. Chaudhuri, S.: What next? a half-dozen data management research goals for big data and the cloud. In: PODS 2012, Scottsdale, Arizona, USA, 21–23 May 2012
6. Fisher, D.: Incremental, approximate database queries and uncertainty for exploratory visualization. In: IEEE Symposium on Large Data Analysis and Visualization, Providence, RI, USA, 23–24 October 2011, pp. 73–80 (2011)
7. Fisher, D., Popov, I., Drucker, S.M., Schraefel, M.: Trust me, i'm partially right: incremental visualization lets analysts explore large datasets faster. In: CHI 2012, Austin, Texas, USA, 5–10 May 2012, pp. 1673–1682 (2012)

8. Heule, S., Numkesser, M., Hall, A.: HyperLogLog in practice: algorithmic engineering of a state of the art cardinality estimation algorithm. In: EDBT/ICDT'13 2013, Genoa, Italy, 18–22 March 2013

9. Hobbs, L., Hillson, S., Lawande, S.: Oracle9iR2 Data Warehousing. Elsevier Science, Boston (2003)

10. Jermaine, C.: Random shuffling of large database tables. IEEE Trans. Knowl. Data Eng. **18**(1), 73–84 (2007)

11. Jermaine, C.: Robust estimation with sampling and approximate pre-aggregation. In: VLDB Conference Proceedings 2003, pp. 886–897 (2003)

12. Jermaine, C., Pol, A., Arumugam, S.: Online maintenance of very large random samples. In: SIGMOD Conference Proceedings 2004 (2004)

13. Jin, R., Glimcher, L., Jermaine, C., Agrawal, G.: New sampling-based estimators for OLAP queries. In: Proceedings of the 22nd International Conference on Data Engineering (ICDE'06), Atlanta, GA, USA (2006)

14. Joshi, S., Jermaine, C.: Materialized sample views for database approximation. IEEE Trans. Knowl. Data Eng. **20**(3), 337–351 (2008)

15. Li, X., Han, J., Yin, Z., Lee, J.-G., Sun, Y.: Sampling cube: a framework for statistical OLAP over sampling data. In: Proceedings of ACM SIGMOD International Conference on Management of Data (SIGMOD'08), Vancouver, BC, Canada, June (2008)

16. Olken, F., Rotem, D.: Random sampling from database file: a survey. In: Michalewicz, Z. (ed.) SSDBM 1990. LNCS, vol. 420, pp. 92–111. Springer, Heidelberg (1990)

17. Rudra, A., Gopalan, R.P., Achuthan, N.R.: Efficient sampling techniques in approximate decision support query processing. In: Proceedings of the International Conference on Enterprise Information Systems - ICEIS 2012, Wroclaw, Poland, June 28–July 2 2012

18. Sangngam, P., Suwatee, P.: Modified sampling scheme in inverse sampling without replacement. In: 2010 International Conference on Networking and Information Technology, pp. 580–584 . IEEE Press, New York (2010)

19. Spiegel, J., Polyzotis, N.: TuG synopses for approximate query answering. ACM Trans. Database Syst. (TODS) **34**(1), 1–56 (2009)

20. TUN: Teradata University Network. http://www.teradata.com/TUN_databases (2007). Accessed 12 Jun 2007)

21. TPC-H: Transaction Processing Council. Decision Support Queries. http://www.teradata.com/TUN_databases (2007). Accessed 23 Apr 2007

A Data-Driven Prediction Framework for Analyzing and Monitoring Business Process Performances

Antonio Bevacqua[1], Marco Carnuccio[1], Francesco Folino[2],
Massimo Guarascio[2], and Luigi Pontieri[2(✉)]

[1] DIMES Department, University of Calabria,
via P. Bucci 41C, 87036 Rende, CS, Italy
{abevacqua,mcarnuccio}@deis.unical.it
[2] ICAR-CNR, National Research Council of Italy,
via P. Bucci 41C, 87036 Rende, CS, Italy
{ffolino,guarascio,pontieri}@icar.cnr.it

Abstract. This paper presents a framework for analyzing and predicting the performances of a business process, based on historical data gathered during its past enactments. The framework hinges on an inductive-learning technique for discovering a special kind of predictive process models, which can support the run-time prediction of a given performance measure (e.g., the remaining processing time/steps) for an ongoing process instance, based on a modular representation of the process, where major performance-relevant variants of it are modeled with different regression models, and discriminated on the basis of context variables. The technique is an original combination of different data mining methods (ranging from pattern mining, to non-parametric regression and predictive clustering) and ad-hoc data transformation mechanisms, allowing for looking at the log traces at a proper level of abstraction, in a pretty automatic and transparent way. The technique has been integrated in a performance monitoring architecture, meant to provide managers and analysts (and possibly the process enactment environment) with continuously updated performance statistics, as well as with the anticipated notification of likely SLA violations. The approach has been validated on a real-life case study, with satisfactory results, in terms of both prediction accuracy and robustness.

Keywords: Data mining · Prediction · Business process management

1 Introduction

In most real application contexts, business processes are bound to the achievement of business goals expressed in terms of performance measures (or Key Performance Indicators), which are monitored continuously at run-time. In principle, historical log data, gathered during past enactments of a process, are a valuable source of hidden information on its behavior, which can be extracted

© Springer International Publishing Switzerland 2014
S. Hammoudi et al. (Eds.): ICEIS 2013, LNBIP 190, pp. 100–117, 2014.
DOI: 10.1007/978-3-319-09492-2_7

with the help of process mining techniques [1], and eventually exploited to improve the process, and meet performance-oriented goals. In particular, it appears really relevant, to this regard, the recent research stream on the automated discovery of predictive process models (see, e.g., [3,7,9]) for estimating some given performance measure over new instances of a process. The interest towards such novel mining tools stems from the observation that performance forecasts can highly improve process enactments, through, e.g., task/resource recommendations [14] or risk notification [5]. In general, these approaches try to induce some kind of prediction model for the given performance measure, based on a suitable trace abstraction function (mapping, e.g., the trace onto the set/multiset of process tasks appearing in it). For example, a non-parametric regression model is used in [7] to build the prediction for a new (possibly partial) trace, based on its similarity towards a set of historical ones – where the similarity between two traces is evaluated by comparing their respective abstract views. However, such instance-based schemes are likely to be unpractical in real environments, due to their long prediction times. A model-based prediction scheme is conversely followed in [3], where an annotated finite-state machine (AFSM) model is induced from the input log, with the states corresponding to abstract representation of log traces. The discovery of such AFSM models was combined in [9] with a context-driven (predictive) clustering approach, so that different execution scenarios can be discovered for the process, and equipped with distinct local predictors.

A key point in the induction of such models, especially in the case of complex business processes, is the definition of a suitable trace abstraction function, allowing to focus on the properties of log events that impact the more on its performance outcomes. In fact, as discussed in [3], choosing the right abstraction level is a delicate task, requiring to reach an optimal balance between the risks of overfitting (i.e., having an overly detailed model, nearly replicating the training set, which will hardy provide accurate forecasts over unseen cases) and of underfitting (i.e., the model is too abstract and imprecise, both on the training cases and on new ones). In current approaches, the responsibility to tune the abstraction level is left to the analyst, who can select the general form of trace abstractions (e.g., set/lists of tasks), while possibly fixing a maximal horizon threshold h — i.e., only the properties of the h more recent events in a trace may appear in its abstract view. Further, FSM-like models cannot effectively exploit non-structural (context) properties of the process instances — in fact, including such data in trace abstractions would lead to a combinatorial explosion of model states.

Contribution. First of all, we try to overcome the above limitations, by devising a novel approach which can fully exploit "non structural" context data, and find a good level of abstraction over the history of process instances, in a pretty automated and transparent fashion. Our core idea is that handy (and yet accurate enough) prediction models can be learnt through various model-based regression methods (either parametric, such as, e.g., [11,13], or non-parametric, such as, e.g., [12,15]), rather than resorting to an explicit representation of process states (like in [3,9]) or to an instance-based approach (like in [7]). This clearly requires that an adequate propositional representation of the given traces be preliminary build, capturing both structural (i.e., task-related) and ("non-structural") aspects. To this end, we convert each process trace into a set or a multi-set of process tasks, and let the regression method decide automatically how the basic structural elements of such an abstracted trace view are to be used to make a forecast.

Leveraging the idea of [9], of combining performance prediction with a *predictive clustering* technique, we also try to equip different context-dependent execution scenarios ("variants") of the analyzed process with separate regression models. In fact, such an approach brings, in general, substantial gain in terms of readability and accuracy, besides explicitly showing the dependence of discovered clusters on context features, and speeding up (and possibly parallelize) the computation of regression models. In fact, as confirmed by the empirical results in Sect. 6, even very simple regression methods could furnish robust and accurate predictions, when combined with an effective clustering procedure. Notably, the target features used in the clustering (where context variables conversely act as descriptive attributes) are derived from frequent structural patterns (still defined as sets or bags of tasks), rather than directly using the abstract representations extracted by the log, as done in [9]. Notably, such an approach frees the analyst from the burden of explicitly setting the abstraction level (i.e., the size of patterns, in our case), which is determined instead in a data-driven way.

Finally, we devise a novel Business Process Analysis architecture, where the predictive performance models obtained with the proposed learning approach are used as a basis for the provision of advanced monitoring and analysis functionalities. In particular, in this architecture, the high-level information captured in the different kinds of process models discovered (i.e., frequent execution patterns, predictive clustering models, and cluster-wise regressors), can be exploited to better comprehend how the real behavior of the process depends on processing steps and on context factors. Moreover, such models can be reused to deploy advanced forecast services, capable to estimate, at run-time, the performance outcomes of new process instances, as well as to notify likely violations of Service Level Agreements, in advance.

Organization. The remainder of the paper is structured as follows. We first introduce some preliminaries (Sect. 2), and formally define a series of key concepts (Sect. 3). The proposed learning algorithm is then illustrated in details in Sect. 4, while Sect. 5 describes the implemented system prototype. After discussing an empirical analysis conducted on a real-life case study in Sect. 6, we finally draw a few concluding remarks and future work directions in Sect. 7.

2   Preliminaries

Log data. As usually done in the literature, we assume that for each process instance (a.k.a "case") a *trace* is recorded, storing the sequence of *events* happened during its unfolding. Let $\mathcal{T}$ be the universe of all (possibly partial) traces that may appear in any log of the process under analysis. For any trace $\tau \in \mathcal{T}$, $len(\tau)$ is the number of events in τ, while $\tau[i]$ is the i-th event of τ, for $i = 1 .. len(\tau)$, with $task(\tau[i])$ and $time(\tau[i])$ denoting the task and timestamp of $\tau[i]$, respectively. We also assume that the first event of each trace is always associated with task A_1, acting as unique entry point for enacting the process. This comes with no loss of generality, seeing as, should the process not have such a such a unique initial task, it could be added artificially at the beginning of each trace, and associated with the starting time of the corresponding process instance.

Let us also assume that, like in [9], for any trace τ, a tuple $context(\tau)$ of data is stored in the log to keep information about the execution context of τ, ranging from internal properties of the process instance to environmental factors pertaining the state of the process enactment system. For ease of notation, let $\mathcal{A}^{\mathcal{T}}$ denote the set of all the tasks (a.k.a., activities) that may occur in some trace of $\mathcal{T}$, and $context(\mathcal{T})$ be the space of context vectors — i.e., $\mathcal{A}^{\mathcal{T}} = \cup_{\tau \in \mathcal{T}} tasks(\tau)$, and $context(\mathcal{T}) = \{context(\tau) \mid \tau \in \mathcal{T}\}$.

Further, $\tau(i)$ is the *prefix* (sub-)trace containing the first i events of a trace τ and the same context data (i.e., $context(\tau(i) = context(\tau))$, for $i = 0 .. len(\tau)$.

A *log* L is a finite subset of $\mathcal{T}$, while the *prefix set* of L, denoted by $\mathcal{P}(L)$, is the set of all the prefixes of L's traces, i.e., $\mathcal{P}(L) = \{\tau(i) \mid \tau \in L$ and $1 \leq i \leq len(\tau)\}$.

Let $\hat{\mu} : \mathcal{T} \to \mathbb{R}$ be an (unknown) function assigning a performance value to any (possibly unfinished) process trace. For the sake of concreteness, we will focus hereinafter on two particular instances of such a function, where the performance measure corresponds to the *remaining time* (denoted by μ_{RT}) or the *remaining steps* (denoted by μ_{RS}), i.e., the time (resp., steps) needed to finish the corresponding process enactment. In general, we assume that performance values are known for all prefix traces in $\mathcal{P}(L)$, for any given log L. This is clearly true for the two measures mentioned above. Indeed, for each trace τ, the (actual) remaining-time of $\tau(i)$ is $\hat{\mu}_{RT}(\tau(i)) = time(\tau[len(\tau)]) - time(\tau[i])$, while the number of remaining steps is $\hat{\mu}_{RS}(\tau(i)) = len(\tau) - i$.

A (predictive) *Process Performance Model (PPM)* is a model that can predict the unknown performance value (i.e., the remaining time/steps in our setting) of a process enactment, based on the contents of the corresponding trace. Such a model can be viewed as a function $\mu : \mathcal{T} \to \mathbb{R}$ estimating $\hat{\mu}$ all over the trace universe — including the prefix traces of all possible process instances. Learning a PPM hence amounts to solving a particular induction problem, where the training set takes the form of a log L, and the value $\hat{\mu}(\tau)$ of the target measure is known for each (sub-)trace $\tau \in \mathcal{P}(L)$. Current approaches to this problem [3,7,9] relies on applying some abstraction functions to process traces, capturing only those facets of the registered events that influence the most process performances, while disregarding minor details.

Trace Abstraction. An abstracted (structural) view of a trace summarizes the tasks executed during the corresponding process enactment. Two simple ways to build such a view consist in regarding the trace as a tasks' set or multiset (a.k.a. bag), as follows.

Definition 1 (Structural Trace Abstraction). Let $\mathcal{T}$ be a trace universe and $A_1, \ldots, A_n$ be the tasks in $\mathcal{A}^{\mathcal{T}}$. A *structural (trace-) abstraction function* $struct^{mode} : \mathcal{T} \to \mathcal{R}_{\mathcal{T}}^{mode}$ is a function mapping each trace $\tau \in \mathcal{T}$ to an *abstract representation* $struct^{mode}(\tau)$, taken from an *abstractions' space* $\mathcal{R}_{\mathcal{T}}^{mode}$. Two concrete instantiations of the above function, denoted by $struct^{bag} : \mathcal{T} \to \mathbb{N}^n$ (resp., $struct^{set} : \mathcal{T} \to \{0,1\}^n$), are defined next, which map each trace $\tau \in \mathcal{T}$ to a bag-based (resp., set-based) representation of its structure: *(i)* $struct^{bag}(\tau) = \langle count(A_1, \tau), \ldots, count(A_n, \tau) \rangle$, where $count(A_i, \tau)$ is the number of times that task A_i occurs in τ; and *(ii)* $struct^{set}(\tau) = \langle occ(A_1, \tau), \ldots, occ(A_n, \tau) \rangle$, where $occ(A_i, \tau) = 1$ iff $count(A_i, \tau) > 0$, for $i = 1, \ldots, n$. $\qquad\square$

The two concrete abstraction "modes" (namely, *bag* and *set*) defined above summarize any trace τ into a vector, where each component corresponds to a single process task A_i, and stores either the number of times that A_i appears in the trace τ, or (respectively) a boolean value indicating whether A_i occur in τ or not. Notice that, in principle, we could define abstract trace representations as sets/bags over another property of the events (e.g., the executor, instead of the task executed), or even over a combination of event properties (e.g., the task plus who performed it).

Example 1. Let us consider a real-life case study pertaining a transshipment process, also used for experiments of Sect. 6. Basically, for each container c passing through the harbor, a distinct log trace τ_c is stored, registering all the tasks applied to c, such as: moving c by means of either a straddle-carrier (MOV), swapping c with another container (SHF), and loading c onto a ship by a shore crane (OUT). Let τ be a log trace encoding a sequence $\langle e_1, e_2, e_3 \rangle$ of three events such that $task(e_1) = task(e_2) = MOV$ and $task(e_3) = OUT$. With regard to the abstract trace representations of Def. 1, it is easy to see that $struct^{bag}(\tau) = [2, 0, 1]$, and $struct^{set}(\tau) = [1, 0, 1]$ — where the traces are mapped into a vector space with dimensions $A_1 \equiv MOV$, $A_2 \equiv SHF$, $A_3 \equiv OUT$. $\qquad\triangleleft$

The structural abstraction functions in Definition 1 are a subset of those used in previous approaches to the discovery of predictive process models [3,7,9]. To be more precise, [7] also considers the possibility to map a trace into a vector of task durations, as well as to combine multiple structural abstractions with data attributes of the traces, while the other two approaches also allow for abstracting a trace into the list of tasks appearing in it (as an alternative to bag/set -oriented abstractions).

3   Formal Framework

Clustering-Based PPMs. The core idea of predictive clustering approaches [4] is that, based on a suitable clustering model, predictions for new instances can be based on the cluster where they are estimated to belong. Two kinds of features are considered for any element z in a given instance space $Z = X \times Y$: *descriptive* features and *target* features (to be predicted), denoted by $descr(z) \in X$ and $targ(z) \in Y$, respectively. Then, a *predictive clustering model* (PCM), for a given training set $L \subseteq Z$, is a function $q : X \to Y$ of the form $q(x) = p(c(x), x)$, where $c : X \to \mathbb{N}$ is a partitioning function and $p : \mathbb{N} \times X \to Y$ is a (possibly multi-target) prediction function. Clearly, whenever there are more than one target features, q encodes a multi-regression model.

Similarly to [9], we here consider a special kind of PPM model, based on a clustering of process traces. The model, described below, is in fact a predictive clustering one, where context data play the role of descriptive attributes, while the target variables are derived by certain performance values of the traces.

Definition 2 (Clustering-Based Performance Prediction Model (CB-PPM)). Let L be a log (over $\mathcal{T}$), with context features $context(\mathcal{T})$, and $\hat{\mu} : \mathcal{T} \to \mathbb{R}$ be a performance measure, known for all $\tau \in \mathcal{P}(L)$. Then a *clustering-based performance prediction model* (CB-PPM) for L is a pair $M = \langle c, \langle \mu_1, \ldots, \mu_k \rangle \rangle$, encoding the unknown performance function $\hat{\mu}$ through a predictive clustering model (where k is the number of clusters found for L). Specifically, c is a partitioning function, which assigns any (possibly novel) trace to one of the clusters (based on context data), while each μ_i is the *PPM* of the i-th cluster — i.e., $c : context(\mathcal{T}) \to \{1, \ldots, k\}$, and $\mu_i : \mathcal{T} \to \mathbb{R}$, for $i \in \{1, \ldots, k\}$. The performance $\hat{\mu}(\tau)$ of any (partial) trace τ is eventually estimated as $\mu_j(\tau)$, where $j = c(context(\tau))$. $\qquad\square$

Notice that each cluster has its own PPM model, encoding how $\hat{\mu}$ depends on the structure (and, possibly, on the context) of a trace, within that cluster. The prediction for each trace is then made with the predictor of the cluster it is assigned to (by function c).

In general, such an articulated kind of PPM can be built by inducing a predictive clustering model and multiple PPMs (as the building blocks implementing c and all μ_i, respectively). In particular, in [9], the latter task is accomplished by using the method in [3], so that each cluster is eventually provided with an AFSM model. As mentioned in Sect. 1, in order to develop an easier-to-use and data-adaptive approach, we will not use AFSM models (which typically require a careful explicit setting of the abstraction level), and will rather employ one of the various regression methods available for propositional data. To this purpose, an ad-hoc view of the log needs to be produced, where both the context-oriented and structure-oriented (cf. Definition 1) features of a trace are used as descriptive attributes, whereas the target attributes are derived by projecting the trace onto a space of structural patterns. These patterns, eventually computed with an ad-hoc data mining method, are described in detail in the following.

Structural Patterns. In our setting, structural patterns are meant to capture regularities in the structure of log traces, and they correspond to (constrained) sub-sets or sub-bag of tasks appearing frequently in the log traces (viewed as well as tasks' sets/bags). More precisely, let $mode \in \{bag, set\}$ be a given abstraction criterion, $\mathcal{T}$ be the reference trace universe, and $\mathcal{A}^{\mathcal{T}} = \{A_1, \ldots, A_n\}$ be its associated process tasks. Then, a *(structural) pattern* w.r.t. $\mathcal{T}$ and *mode* simply is an element p of the *abstractions' space* $\mathcal{R}_{\mathcal{T}}^{mode}$ – over which function $struct^{mode}$ ranges indeed. The size of p, denoted by $size(p)$, is the number of distinct tasks in p, i.e., the number of p's components with a positive value.

Having a structural pattern the same form as a (structural) trace abstraction, we can apply usual set/bag containment operators to them all. Specifically, given two elements p and p' of $\mathcal{R}_{\mathcal{T}}^{mode}$ (be them patterns or representations of entire traces), we say that p_2 *contains* p_1 (and that p_1 is contained in p_2), denoted by $p_1 \preceq p_2$, if $p_1[j] \leq p_2[j]$, for $j = 1, \leq, n$, and for $i = 1, 2$ — where $p_i[j]$ is the j-th component of vector p_i, which ranges over $\{0, 1\}^n$ or $\mathbb{N}^n$ depending on the chosen abstraction mode (cf. Definition 1).

Since such patterns are to be eventually used for clustering purposes, we are interested in those capturing significant behavioral schemes. In particular, an important requirement is that they occur frequently in the given log (otherwise, little, low significant clusters will be found), as specified in the following notion of support.

Definition 3 (Pattern Support and Footprint). Let $\tau \in \mathcal{T}$ be a trace, *mode* be a given abstraction mode, and p be pattern (w.r.t. $\mathcal{T}$ and *mode*). Then, τ *supports* p, denoted by $\tau \vdash p$ if its corresponding structural abstraction contains p (i.e., $p \preceq struct^{mode}(\tau)$). In this case, a *footprint* of p on τ is subset $F = \{f_1, \ldots, f_k\} \subseteq \{1, \ldots, len(\tau)\}$ of positions in τ, such that $struct^{mode}(\langle \tau[f_1], \ldots, \tau[f_k] \rangle) = p$. Moreover, $gap(F)$ denotes the number of events in τ which correspond to none of the positions in F but appear in between a pair of matching events, i.e., $gap(F) = \max_{f_i \in F}\{f_i\} - \min_{f_i \in F}\{f_i\} - |F| + 1$. We finally denote $gap(p, \tau) = \min \{\{\infty\} \cup \{ gap(F) \mid F \text{ is a footprint of } p \text{ on } \tau \} \}$.   □

A footprint F of a pattern p, on a trace τ supporting it, identifies a subsequence of τ which contains all the elements of τ marked by F (i.e., appearing in one of the positions of F). Clearly, the structural representation of such a subsequence coincides with p. As a special case, if τ does not support p, then $gap(p, \tau)$ is infinite.

In order to focus on significant patterns, w.r.t. a given log L, one could simply set a minimal support threshold, say $minSupp \in [0, 1)$, and discard all patterns getting a support lower than $minSupp \times |L|$ by the given log traces (viewed as tasks' bags or sets). In addition, an upper threshold $maxGap \in \mathbb{N} \cup \{\infty\}$ can be specified for the maximal gap admitted between patterns and traces, in order to focus on patterns that fit well enough the actual sequencing of tasks in the latters. Both constraints can be specified through a variant of the classical support function (actually coinciding with the latter when $maxGap = \infty$), defined as follows:

$$supp^{maxGap}(p, L) = \frac{|\{\tau \in L \mid \tau \vdash p \text{ and } gap(p, \tau) < maxGap + 1\}|}{|L|} \quad (1)$$

Let L be a log, p be a structural pattern for a given abstraction mode *mode* (BAG or SET), $minSupp$ be a minimum support threshold, and $maxGap$ be a maximum gap threshold. Then, p is a *(minSupp, maxGap)-frequent* pattern w.r.t. L

Input: A log L over a trace universe $\mathcal{T}$, with associated tasks $AS = A_1, \ldots, A_n$ and target
performance measure $\hat{\mu}$ (known over $\mathcal{P}(L)$), an abstraction mode $m \in \{set, bag\}$
(cf. Def. 1), three thresholds, $minSupp \in [0, 1)$, $maxGap \in \mathbb{N} \cup \{\infty\}$, and $K_{top} \in$
$\mathbb{N}^+ \cup \{\infty\}$, and a base regression method $REGR$.

Output: A CB-PPM model for L (fully encoding $\hat{\mu}$ all over $\mathcal{T}$).

Method: Perform the following steps:

1   Let $context(\tau)$ be the vector of context data associated with each $\tau \in L$;
2   Build a *structural view* S_L of $\mathcal{P}(L)$, by replacing each $\tau \in \mathcal{P}(L)$ with a transaction-like
representation of $struct^m(\tau)$;
3   $RSP := \mathtt{minePatterns}(S_L, m, minSupp, maxGap)$;
4   $RSP := \mathtt{filterPatterns}(RSP, kTop)$;
6   Let $RSP = \{p_1, \ldots, p_s\}$;
7   Build a *log sketch* P_L for L, by using both context data and RSP-projected performances;
8   Learn a PCT T, using $context(\tau)$ (resp., $val(\tau, p_i)$, $i=1..s$) as descriptive (resp., target)
features for each $\tau \in L$;
9   Let $L[1], \ldots, L[k]$ denote the discovered clusters;
10 **for each** $L[i]$ **do**
11   Induce a regression model ppm_i out of $\mathcal{P}(L[i])$, using method $REGR$ — regarding,
for each $\tau \in \mathcal{P}(L[i])$, $context(\tau)$ and $struct^m(\tau)$ as the input values, and the performance
measurement $\hat{\mu}(\tau)$ as the target value;
10   Store ppm_i as the implementation of the prediction function $\mu_i : \mathcal{T} \to M$ (for cluster i);
11 **end**
12 **return** $\langle c, \{ \mu_1, \ldots, \mu_k \} \rangle$.

Fig. 1. Algorithm AA-PPM Discovery.

if $supp^{maxGap}(p, L) \geq minSupp$. In our approach, such patterns are considered as
interesting behavioral features, useful for finding a performance-relevant partitioning of the log traces.

4   Learning Algorithm

Figure 1 illustrates the main steps of our approach to the discovery of a CB-PPM
model, in the form of an algorithm, named AA-PPM Discovery. Essentially, the
problem is approached in three main phases.

In the first phase (Steps 1–5), a set of (frequent) structural patterns are
extracted from the log, which are deemed to capture the main behavioral schemes
of the process, as concerns the dependence of performance on the execution of
tasks. To this end, after converting the structure of each (possibly partial) trace
τ into an itemset (Step 2), we compute all the structural patterns (i.e., subsets, of various sizes) that occur frequently in the log and effectively summarize
the behaviors in the log — in particular, in the case of bag abstractions, notice
that any $s = struct^{bag}(\tau) \in \mathbb{N}^n$ can be represented as $\{(A_i, k_j) \mid 0 \leq i \leq n,$
$s[i] > 0$ and $1 \leq j \leq s[i] \}$.

More precisely, we first compute the set $\{p \in \mathcal{R}_{\mathcal{T}}^m \mid supp^{maxGap}(p, S_L) \geq$
$minSupp\}$ (cf. Definition 3), by using function $\mathtt{minePatterns}$, which is stored
in RSP — note that this set will never be empty, since (as an extreme case)
at least a singleton pattern with A_1 is frequent (no matter of $minSupp$, m and

maxGap). These patterns are then filtered by function `filterPatterns`, which selects the *kTop* most relevant patterns among them. Notably, we can still use all the discovered patterns, by fixing $maxGap = \infty$ (no real filter is applied in this case). Both these functions are explained in details later on.

In the second phase, the selected patterns are used to associate a series of numerical variables with all traces (Step 7), and to carry out a predictive clustering of them (Step 8). To this end, a propositional view of the log, here named *log sketch*, is produced by transforming each trace into a tuple, where context properties play as are descriptive attributes and the projection onto the space of selected patterns are the target numerical features. Specifically, any selected pattern p gives rise to a target (performance) feature, such that the value $val(\tau, p)$ taken by it on any trace τ is be computed as follows: **(i)** $val(\tau, p) =$ NULL, if $\tau \nvdash p$, or **(ii)** $val(\tau, p) = \hat{\mu}(\tau(j^*))$, where j^* is the biggest index $j \in \{1, \ldots, len(\tau)\}$ such that $\tau(j) \vdash p$. Like in [9], the clustering is computed by inducing a Predictive Clustering Tree (PCT) [4] from the log sketch (Step 8).

Finally, each cluster is equipped with a basic (not clustering-based) PPM model, by using some suitable regression method (chosen through parameter *REGR*), provided with a dataset encoding all the prefixes that can be derived from the traces assigned to the cluster. Specifically, each such prefix τ is encoded as a tuple where $context(\tau)$ and $struct^m(\tau)$ are regarded as input values, while the associated performance measurement $\hat{\mu}(\tau)$ represents the value of the numerical target variable that is to be estimated.

Function `minePatterns`. This function is devoted to compute a set of ($minSupp$, $maxGap$)-frequent patterns of any size — i.e., patterns getting a support score (according to Eq. 1) equal to or higher than $minSupp$, over a transaction-oriented view of the log. Notably, the function does not require the analyst to specify the size of each pattern (differently from the horizon threshold h of previous methods), which is actually chosen automatically, in a data-driven way. However, it allows for possibly fixing a finite $maxGap$ threshold for the gaps admitted between patterns and traces, in case she/he wants to keep more details on the actual tasks' sequencing. All the specified constraints are enforced along the computation, in order to shrink the amount of patterns generated, as well as the computation time. Further details are omitted for lack of space.

Function `filterPatterns`. This function is meant to select a subset of significant and useful patterns, as to make the computation of clusters more effective and more scalable, by preventing the PCT learning algorithm to work with a sparse and high-dimensional target space. Hence, we allow the analyst to ask for only keeping the *kTop* patterns that seems to discriminate the main performance profiles at best. To this end, we employ a variant of the scoring function ϕ proposed in [9] (giving score 0 to every feature not positively correlated with context data), which gives preference to patterns ensuring higher values of the following measures: (i) support, (ii) correlation with the context attributes and (iii) and variability of the associated performance values (i.e., $val(p, \tau)$, with τ ranging over L). Further details can be found in [9].

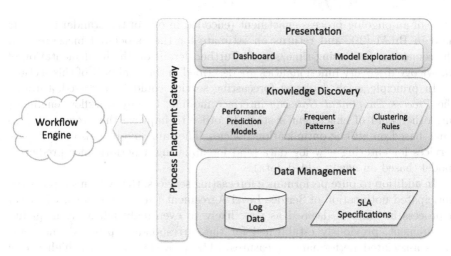

Fig. 2. Conceptual architecture of the *AA-TP* system prototype.

5 System AA-TP (Adaptive-Abstraction Time Prediction)

The learning approach described so far has been integrated into a prototype system, aimed at providing advanced services for the analysis and "anticipated" (i.e., predictive) monitoring of process performances. The current implementation of the system focuses on the two time-oriented process performance measures considered in this paper: the remaining processing time (μ_{RT}), and the number of remaining processing steps (μ_{RS}).

Looking at the right part of Fig. 2, it can be seen that the system features a three-layer conceptual architecture. The lowest level implements basic *Data Management* modules, which are responsible for storing both historical process logs and different kinds of data (e.g., structural log views and log sketches), derived from them prior to the application of the inductive learning mechanisms described in the previous section. In fact, such data, originated by past enactments of a business process, provide a basis for the automated discovery of three different kinds of knowledge about the process: (i) frequent (structural) execution patterns, (ii) predictive clustering models (capturing the existence of diverse execution scenarios for the process, as well as their correlation with major context factors), and (iii) a series of *PPM* models (one for each discovered scenario). All these pieces of knowledge, built and handled in the *Knowledge Discovery* layer, can help better comprehend and analyze the real behavior of the process, and the dependence of its performances on both processing steps and facets of the execution context. On the other hand, thanks to their predictive nature, each clustering model and its associated local *PPMs* can be reused to configure a forecasting service for the process they were discovered from, in order to estimate (at run time and step-by-step) the performance outcome of any new instance of that process. Essentially, based on a given performance prediction model, the service implements a core method, which takes as input the partial trace of an ongoing process enactment (encoded in one of the standard formats used in ProM [2]), and returns an estimate for the associated measure (i.e., the remaining processing time/steps). Further details on the implementation of knowledge discovery functionalities are described in the final part of this section.

In principle, each deployed forecasting service could be accessed, through the *Process Enactment Gateway* interface module, by any workflow engine or any other kind of enactment system, in order to improve the process at runtime, based on ad-hoc optimization policies. The same module also offers basic services for entering new log data, and for updating a performance prediction model (based on newly added data).

In addition to pure performance forecasting services, the system supports the anticipated notification of Service Level Agreement (SLA) violations, whenever a process instance is deemed as very likely to eventually fail a given quality requirement, previously established for the corresponding process (and some of its associated performance measures). The provision of such a higher-level prediction service requires that an SLA model can be defined for any process P and performance measure μ, and be kept in a suitable repository of the Data Management layer. Basically, such a model is meant to encode information about: (i) the procedure for computing the value of μ for any historical (completely executed) instance of P; (ii) a violation criterion, stating which are values that μ is not admitted to take on P's instances; (iii) the degree of sensitiveness in the notification of possible violations. A simple approach to the specification of SLA models and associated triggering mechanisms is explained later on.

Finally, the *Presentation Layer* (still at an incomplete stage of development) is in charge of providing the user (analyst or manager) with summarized information on the past and current behavior of the analyzed business processes. In particular, it allows the user to inspect and navigate all kinds of process models and patterns extracted out of log data, as well as to create and access SLA specifications. Moreover, a customizable dashboard can be build to provide the user with aggregated statistics computed over the instances of a given process or on predefined groups of them (e.g., cases enacted for the same customer), possibly mixing predicted performance outcomes with historical ones.

SLA Models. Currently the system allows for specifying a simple kind of SLA model over two types of performance measures: the total processing time and the total number of processing steps. In particular, for each chosen process and performance measure, it is possible to set a maximum threshold M (identifying the legal range of values for the measure), and a risk tolerance threshold γ — the greater the threshold, the lower the sensitivity in detecting SLA violations (w.r.t. to the performances of the process).

Let $\tau(i]$ denote a trace, encoding the history of an ongoing process instance up to the (current) execution step i. Then, an SLA violation for $\tau(i]$ can be predicted on the basis of the likelihood $\ell_M(\tau(i])$ that the total time (or number of steps) needed to fully handle the case corresponding to τ will not exceed M (like in [5]). In more details, letting $elapsed(\tau(i])$ denote the time already spent (resp. steps already performed), this likelihood is computed as follows:

$$\ell_M(\tau) = \begin{cases} 1 - \frac{M}{elapsed(\tau(i)) + \mu(\tau(i))} & \text{if } elapsed(\tau(i)) + \mu(\tau(i)) > M \\ 0 & \text{otherwise} \end{cases}$$

where $\mu(\tau(i))$ is the remaining processing time (resp., nr. of steps) estimated for $\tau(i)$.

Then, an alert can be eventually triggered for the process instance associated with $\tau(i)$, if $\ell_M(\tau(i)) > \gamma$. In such a case, the user (or even the enactment system) will get aware of the fact that an SLA is likely to be infringed, so that some suitable optimization policy could be proactively put in place, in order to possibly prevent the occurrence of such a requirement violation.

Details on the Knowledge Discovery Layer. The core learning mechanism in this layer have been implemented as a plugin of the framework ProM [2]. As mentioned above, the plugin specializes algorithm AA-PPM Discovery to the case where the target performance measure coincides with the remaining processing time/steps. The plugin features the following major modules: (a) *Scenario Discovery* module, which is in charge of identifying behaviorally homogeneous groups of traces, in terms of both context data and remaining times; and (b) *Time Predictors Learning* module, which implements a range of classical regression algorithms (including, in particular, IB-k, Linear Regression, and RepTree), eventually used to induce the local predictor (i.e., PPM) of each discovered cluster — all of these predictors will compose (along with the logical rules discriminating among the clusters) the overall CB-PPM model, returned as main result.

More specifically, the former module consists of the following submodules: (i) the *Predictive Clustering* submodule, which groups traces sharing similar descriptive and target values, leveraging system CLUS [6] (a framework for inducing PCT models from propositional data); (ii) the *Log-View Generator* submodule, which right converts all log traces into propositional tuples, according to the ARFF format used in CLUS, relying on the explicit representation of both context data and target attributes (derived from the original log); and (iii) the *Pattern Mining* module, which exploits a transactional representation of these context-enriched traces in order to extract a set of relevant patterns out of them. In fact, these patterns are the target features used by the *Log-View Generator* in order to build a training set for the induction of a clustering model.

6   Case Study

This section illustrates a series of experimental activities that we conducted, with the prototype system AA-TP, on some logs of a real transshipment system (already mentioned in Example 1), keeping trace of major logistic activities applied a sample of 5336 containers, which passed through the system in the first third of year 2006. Essentially, each container is unloaded from a ship and temporarily placed near to the dock, until it is carried to some suitable yard slot for being stocked. Symmetrically, at boarding time, the container is first placed in a yard area close to the dock, and then loaded on a cargo. Different kinds of vehicles can be used for moving a container, including, e.g., cranes, "straddle-carriers", and "multi-trailers". This basic life cycle may be extended with additional transfers, devoted to make the container approach its final embark point or to leave room for other ones. Several data attributes are available for each container as context data (of the corresponding process instance), including: the origin and final ports, its previous and next calls, various properties of the ship unloading it, physical features (such as, e.g., size, weight), and some information about its contents. Like in [9], we also considered a few more (environment-oriented) context features for each container: the hour (resp., day of the week, month) when it arrived, and the total number of containers that were in the port at that moment.

Considering the remaining processing time/steps as the target performance measure, we evaluated the effectiveness of predictions via three classic error metrics (computed via 10-fold cross validation): *root mean squared error (rmse)*, *mean absolute error (mae)*, and *mean absolute percentage error (mape)*. For ease of interpretation, the results reported next for the former two metrics have been normalized w.r.t. the average processing time/steps (computed over all the containers passed through the terminal).

Tuning of Parameters. First of all, we tried our approach with different settings of its parameters, including the base regression method (*REGR*) for inducing the PPM of each discovered cluster. For the sake of simplicity, we here only focus on the usage of two basic regression methods: classic *Linear* regression [8], and the tree-based regression algorithm *RepTree* [15]. In addition, we consider the case where each PPM model simply encodes a k-NN regression procedure (denoted by *IB-k* hereinafter), as a rough term of comparison with the family of instance-based regression methods (including, in particular, the approach in [7]). For all of the above regression methods, we reused the implementations available in the popular data-mining library Weka [10].

Figure 3 allows for analyzing how the *rmse* scores[1] vary when using different regression methods (distinct curves are depicted for them), and different values of the parameters (namely, $maxGap \in \{0, 4, 8, \infty\}$, $kTop \in \{4, \infty\}$, and $minSupp \in \{0.1, \ldots, 0.4\}$).

Clearly, the underlying regression method is the factor exhibiting a stronger impact on precision results. In particular, the disadvantage of using linear regression is neat (no matter of the error metrics), whereas both *IB-k* and *RepTree* methods performs quite well, and very similarly. This is good news, especially for the *RepTree* method, which is to be preferred to *IB-k* for scalability reasons. Indeed, this latter may end up being too time-consuming at run-time, when a large set of example traces must be kept – even though, differently from pure instance-based methods (like [7]), we do not need to search across the whole log, but only within a single cluster (selected via context data).

As to the remaining parameters, we notice that poorer results are obtained when $minSupp = 0.1$ and $kTop = 4$, as well as when $minSupp = 0.4$. As a matter of fact, the former case epitomizes the cases where we cut little (according to frequency) during the generation of patterns, while trying to reduce their

---

[1] Notice that similar trends of behavior were discovered for the *mae* and *mape* metrics.

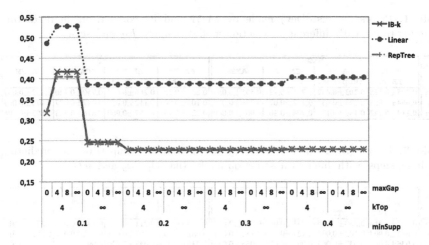

Fig. 3. The effect of parameters on `rmse` results.

number in the filtering phase; the latter, instead, is an opposite situation where a rather high threshold support threshold is employed, at a higher risk of loosing important pieces of information on process behaviour. Remarkably, when *minSupp* gets a value from [0.2, 0.3], the remaining two parameters (namely *kTop* and *maxGap*) do not seem to affect the quality of predictions at all. In practice, it suffices to choose carefully the regression method (and a middling value of *minSupp*) to ensure good and stable prediction outcomes, no matter of the other parameters – which would be, indeed, quite harder to tune in general.

Comparison with Competitors. In order to assess the effectiveness of our approach, we compared it with two other ones, defined in the literature for the discovery of a PPM: CA-TP [9] and AFSM [3]. Tables 1 and 2 report the average errors and standard deviations made by system AA-TP, while varying the base regression method (namely, and *IB-k* and *RepTree*), when predicting both remaining times and remaining steps, respectively. In particular, the first half of tables regards the case when *bag* representations are used for abstracting traces, while the second to the usage of *set* abstractions. These values were computed by averaging the ones obtained with different settings of the parameters *minSupp*, *kTop*, and *maxGap*. Similarly, for both of the approaches CA-TP and AFSM, we computed the average of the results obtained using different values of the history horizon parameter *h* (precisely, $h = 1, 2, 4, 8, 16$), and the best-performing setting for all the remaining parameters.

Interestingly, the figures in Tables 1 and 2 indicate that our approach is more accurate than both competitors, no matter which abstraction strategy is adopted. It is worth noticing that the best results (shown in bold in the tables), for all the error metrics, are obtained when AA-TP is used with the *bag* abstraction mode. In particular, by looking at values in Table 1 it is easy to notice that, if we combine this abstraction mode with the *IB-k* regressor, AA-TP manages to lower the prediction error by about 65.88 % on average w.r.t. CA-TP, and

Table 1. Errors (avg±stdDev) made by AA-TP and its competitors in predicting remaining times, with different abstraction modes (namely, *bag* and *set*).

Metric	BAG				SET			
	AA-TP (IB-k)	AA-TP (RepTree)	CA-TP	AFSM	AA-TP (IB-k)	AA-TP (RepTree)	CA-TP	AFSM
rmse	**0.205±0.125**	**0.203±0.082**	0.291±0.121	0.505±0.059	0.287±0.123	0.286±0.084	0.750±0.120	0.752±0.037
mae	**0.064±0.058**	0.073±0.033	0.142±0.071	0.259±0.008	0.105±0.061	0.112±0.035	0.447±0.077	0.475±0.009
mape	**0.119±0.142**	0.189±0.136	0.704±0.302	0.961±0.040	0.227±0.131	0.267±0.060	2.816±0.303	2.892±0.206

Table 2. Errors (avg±stdDev) made by AA-TP and its competitors in predicting remaining steps, with different abstraction modes (namely, *bag* and *set*).

Metric	BAG				SET			
	AA-TP (IB-k)	AA-TP (RepTree)	CA-TP	AFSM	AA-TP (IB-k)	AA-TP (RepTree)	CA-TP	AFSM
rmse	**0.192±0.014**	0.209±0.010	0.241±0.042	0.278±0.022	**0.193±0.013**	0.211±0.018	0.286±0.056	0.322±0.016
mae	**0.082±0.004**	0.102±0.007	0.127±0.039	0.151±0.021	**0.082±0.008**	0.103±0.028	0.172±0.051	0.201±0.013
mape	**0.035±0.003**	0.042±0.003	0.060±0.025	0.056±0.016	**0.035±0.003**	0.043±0.030	0.094±0.036	0.110±0.008

by an astonishing 77.51 % w.r.t. AFSM, on average (w.r.t. all the error metrics). Again, good results are obtained when using *RepTree* (still with bag abstractions), where a reduction of 59.10 % (resp., 73.04 %) is achieved w.r.t. to CA-TP (resp., AFSM). An even higher degree of improvement is achieved when using set-oriented abstractions. Indeed, in this case, the reduction in the average of prediction errors is of 84.58 % w.r.t. CA-TP and of 84.97 % w.r.t. AFSM, when using our approach with the *IB-k* regressor; moreover, when using it with *RepTree*, these reductions become 83.43 % and 83.86 %, respectively.

As to the prediction of remaining steps, the best outcomes are obtained when using AA-TP with the *IB-k* regressor (see Table 2). Improvements are, in general, less noticeable than those observed for the prediction of remaining times, but still substantial. Indeed, AA-TP manages to shrink the prediction error of 26.89 % (resp. 16.49 %) w.r.t. CA-TP and of 36.70 % (resp. 27.68 %) w.r.t. AFSM, when using the *IB-k* (resp. *RepTree*) regressor and bag abstractions. Finally, in the case of set abstractions, an error reduction of 43.77 % (resp. 35.39 %) w.r.t. CA-TP, and of 51.04 % (resp. 43.74 %) w.r.t. AFSM is observed when AA-TP is used in combination with *IB-k* (resp., *RepTree*) regressors.

SLA Violation Results. We next focus on a specific kind of SLA violations, corresponding to the overcoming of maximal threshold M on the total processing time. In the context of container management systems, such a maximum processing ("dwell") time is typically set within predefined agreements, on service quality, between the shipping lines and the terminal handler. In our tests we considered a parametric specification of this threshold: $M = \alpha \times ADT$, where ADT is the average dwell time computed over all containers, and α is an integer ranging over $\{1, 2, 3\}$ (allowing us to simulate three different settings of the agreement level). It is important to notice that cases requiring an excessively long processing time imply high monetary costs, and detecting them in advance

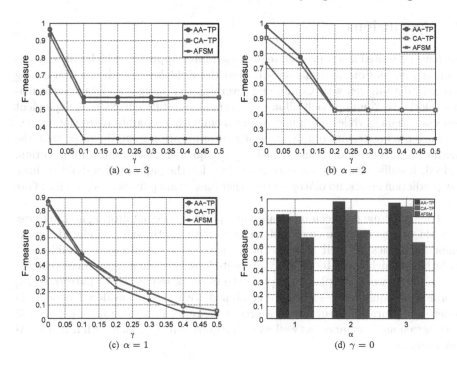

Fig. 4. F-measure scores for the prediction of overtime faults by `AA-TP` and by baseline methods, when varying γ and the factor α.

can allow for undertaking suitable counter-measures, possibly exploiting additional (storage/processing) resources, which are not used in normal conditions. Since, however, such a remedial policy as well come with a cost, even though it is typically lower than SLA-violation penalties, such an overtime prediction mechanism must exhibit a good trade-off between precision and recall, in order to ensure the whole approach to be really convenient economically.

Figure 4 sheds light on the ability our approach to discriminate "overtime" from "in-time" containers. To this purpose, we report the F-measure scores for different values of the risk threshold γ, when a fixed, good-working, configuration is used for both our approach and the baseline ones, respectively `CA-TP` [9] and `AFSM` [3]. As expected, F-measure tends to worsen when increasing γ, whatever the factor α is. Interestingly, when using lower values of γ (i.e., a more aggressive warning policy) the capability of our approach to recognize real overtime cases is ever better than the baseline predictors – in particular, a more evident improvement is obtained for $\alpha = 2$ when an astonishing F-measure of 0.98 is reached w.r.t. 0.90 and 0.74 reached by `CA-TP` and `AFSM`, respectively.

7   Conclusions

We have presented a new predictive process-mining approach, which fully exploits context information, and manages to find the right level of abstraction on log traces in data-driven way. Combining several data mining and data transformation methods, the approach allows for recognizing different context-dependent process variants, while equipping each of them with a separate regression model.

Encouraging results obtained on a real application scenario show that the method is precise and robust enough, yet requiring little human intervention. Indeed, it suffices not to use extreme values for the support threshold to have low prediction errors, no matter of the other finer-grain parameters (i.e., $maxGap$ and $kTop$).

The technique has been integrated in a performance monitoring architecture, capable to provide managers and analysts with continuously updated performance statistics, as well as with the anticipated notification of possible SLA violations, which could be possibly prevented via suitable improvement policies.

As future work, we plan to explore the usage of sequence-like patterns (e.g., k-order subsequences) — possibly combined with those considered here — in order to capture the structure of a process instance in a more precise (but still abstract enough) manner, as well as to integrate our approach with a real BPM environment.

References

1. van der Aalst, W.M.P., van Dongen, B.F., Herbst, J., Maruster, L., Schimm, G., Weijters, A.J.M.M.: Workflow mining: a survey of issues and approaches. Data Knowl. Eng. **47**(2), 237–267 (2003)
2. van der Aalst, W.M.P., et al.: ProM 4.0: comprehensive support for *Real* process analysis. In: Kleijn, J., Yakovlev, A. (eds.) ICATPN 2007. LNCS, vol. 4546, pp. 484–494. Springer, Heidelberg (2007)
3. van der Aalst, W.M.P., Schonenberg, M.H., Song, M.: Time prediction based on process mining. Inf. Syst. **36**(2), 450–475 (2011)
4. Blockeel, H., Raedt, L.D.: Top-down induction of first-order logical decision trees. Artif. Intell. **101**(1–2), 285–297 (1998)
5. Conforti, R., Fortino, G., La Rosa, M., ter Hofstede, A.H.M.: History-aware, real-time risk detection in business processes. In: Meersman, R., et al. (eds.) OTM 2011, Part I. LNCS, vol. 7044, pp. 100–118. Springer, Heidelberg (2011)
6. DLAI Group: CLUS: a predictive clustering system (1998). http://dtai.cs.kuleuven.be/clus/
7. van Dongen, B.F., Crooy, R.A., van der Aalst, W.M.P.: Cycle time prediction: when will this case finally be finished? In: Meersman, R., Tari, Z. (eds.) OTM 2008, Part I. LNCS, vol. 5331, pp. 319–336. Springer, Heidelberg (2008)
8. Draper, N.R., Smith, H.: Applied Regression Analysis. Wiley Series in Probability and Statistics. Wiley, New York (1998)
9. Folino, F., Guarascio, M., Pontieri, L.: Discovering context-aware models for predicting business process performances. In: Meersman, R., et al. (eds.) OTM 2012, Part I. LNCS, vol. 7565, pp. 287–304. Springer, Heidelberg (2012)

10. Frank, E., Hall, M.A., Holmes, G., Kirkby, R., Pfahringer, B.: Weka - a machine learning workbench for data mining. In: Maimon, O., Rokach, L. (eds.) The Data Mining and Knowledge Discovery Handbook, pp. 1305–1314. Springer, New York (2005)
11. Hardle, W., Mammen, E.: Comparing nonparametric versus parametric regression fits. Ann. Stat. **21**(4), 1926–1947 (1993)
12. Harlde, W.: Applied NonParametric Regression. Cambridge University Press, Boston (1990)
13. Quinlan, R.J.: Learning with continuous classes. In: Proceedings of 5th Australian Joint Conference on Artificial Intelligence (AI'92), pp. 343–348 (1992)
14. Schonenberg, H., Weber, B., van Dongen, B.F., van der Aalst, W.M.P.: Supporting flexible processes through recommendations based on history. In: Dumas, M., Reichert, M., Shan, M.-C. (eds.) BPM 2008. LNCS, vol. 5240, pp. 51–66. Springer, Heidelberg (2008)
15. Witten, I.H., Frank, E.: Data Mining: Practical Machine Learning Tools and Techniques, 2nd edn. Morgan Kaufmann Publishers Inc., San Francisco (2005)

An Overview of Experimental Studies on Software Inspection Process

Elis Montoro Hernandes[1(✉)], Anderson Belgamo[1,2],
and Sandra Fabbri[1]

[1] LaPES - Software Engineering Research Lab, UFSCar, São Carlos, SP, Brazil
{elis_hernandes,sfabbri}@dc.ufscar.br
[2] Science and Technology, IFSP - Federal Institute of Education,
Piracicaba, SP, Brazil
anderson@ifsp.edu.br

Abstract. Software inspection process is an effective activity to find defects on software artifacts as soon as they are introduced. The development of experimental knowledge on this area is useful to everyone who needs to make decisions about inspection activity. This paper aims to map the empirical studies conducted in the software inspection process area. The steps of the Systematic Mapping (SM) process was performed with the support of the StArt tool. Seventy nine papers were accepted in this SM and attributes related to inspection process, techniques, tools, inspected artifacts, research groups and universities were extracted. The results show different inspection processes, which have been experimentally investigated. Fagan's process is the most investigated of them. In relation to inspected artifacts, requirements document and source code were the most used. Moreover, different tools and techniques have been used to support these processes.

Keywords: Systematic mapping · Software inspection process · Experiments · Empirical software engineering · Experimental software engineering

1 Introduction

The inspection activity is a systematic approach that aims to detect defects in software artifacts as soon as they are committed. Since it was introduced in IBM around 70's, by Michael Fagan, the inspection activity is considered one of the best software engineering practices to identify defects [1].

One of the inspection activity advantages is that it can be applied on many kinds of software artifacts, as soon as these are constructed, decreasing defects transfer to other artifacts, besides the possibility of being applied them before the testing activities [2].

The software inspection process proposed by Fagan [3] has been modified and adapted, generating other versions such as [4–11].

Although each different version of the software inspection process has proposed new and different roles and activities, all of them share the same goal: allow inspectors identifying defects, analyzing them and establishing the real defects for correction.

© Springer International Publishing Switzerland 2014
S. Hammoudi et al. (Eds.): ICEIS 2013, LNBIP 190, pp. 118–134, 2014.
DOI: 10.1007/978-3-319-09492-2_8

When an enterprise decides to adopt an inspection process, it is necessary to identify which process and which techniques fit better for its development process and team.

A way to search for evidence about what process or technique to use, is to look for experimental studies related to them. According to [12], software engineering experimental studies aim to characterize, evaluate, foresee, control and improve products, process, resources, models and theories. In addition, Basili et al. [13] argue that "the only way to discover how applicable a new method, technique, or tool is in a given environment is to experiment with its use in that environment".

Thus, the importance of experimental studies is clear for software engineering researchers and enterprises that want to adopt or adapt processes and techniques in their business environment. Well-known techniques to find this kind of knowledge are Systematic Review (SR) (a.k.a. Systematic Literature Review (SLR)) and Systematic Mapping (SM).

Although the research process is benefited by these techniques, the SR process is considered laborious to be planned and conducted [14]. It demands a high maturity level from the researcher to define the right research question to be answered, leading novice researchers to opt for an ad hoc literature review.

According to Bailey et al. [15], Systematic Mappings (SM), also known as Scoping Review [16], should be conducted before a SR, since its goal is to identify the features and the kind of publications to be investigated on a particular theme.

The main goal of Systematic Mapping studies is to provide an overview of a research area, and identify the quantity and type of research and results available within it as well as mapping the frequencies of publication over time to see trends. [17]. These authors also mentioned that a secondary goal is to identify the forums where the research topic has been published. Furthermore, Systematic Mapping studies can help in refining the question for the full review and estimating the resources that will be needed [16].

The goal of this paper is to describe a Systematic Mapping of experimental studies related to software inspection process. The objective was to identify techniques, tools, artifacts and the inspection process usually employed in the published experimental studies. Moreover, the intention was to identify the process and techniques more explored in the experimental studies, their respective authors and the places where the studies are usually published.

The remaining of this paper is organized as follows: Sect. 2 presents the methodology; Sect. 3 presents the systematic mapping conducted; Sect. 4 presents some of the software inspection processes experimentally investigated and finally, Sect. 5 presents the discussions regarding the study.

2 Methodology

Briefly, SM allows creating an overview of an interest area based on the definition of research questions and the identification and quantification of the collected data.

Petersen et al. [17] present the following steps as the essential process steps for a Systematic Mapping study (Fig. 1):

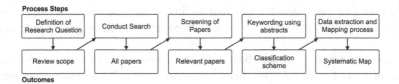

Fig. 1. The Systematic mapping process [17].

(1) *Definition of research question:* In this step, one or more research questions should be defined, reflecting the expected answer at the end of the mapping. The outcome of this step is the review scope.

(2) *Conduct Search:* In this step, search strings are defined based on the research questions established in the previous step. The search strings are then applied to different online scientific databases to identify relevant papers for the mapping. The outcome of this step is a list of papers.

(3) *Screening of Papers*: In this step, inclusion and exclusion criteria should be applied based on the research questions. These criteria are intended to identify those primary studies that provide direct evidence about the research question. In order to reduce the likelihood of bias, selection criteria should be established during the protocol definition, although they may be refined during the search process [18]. The outcome of this step is a list of relevant papers to the research theme.

(4) *Keywording using Abstracts:* In this step, the researcher must read the abstract of accepted papers and identify keywords that characterize various aspects of the studies, like the research method, type of conducted study, research area, research group, method and/or tool used, etc. After the reading, a set of keywords is created and used to classify all papers in different features. The outcome of this step is a Classification Scheme.

(5) *Data Extraction and Mapping Process:* the accepted papers in step 3 are classified according to the categories previously identified in step 4. The classification scheme may evolve during the data extraction, either by adding new categories or merging or splitting existing categories. After that, the categories are grouped into facets, which in turn are related between each other to generate a map (as a bubble plot, for example) so to allow the researcher to visualize various aspects of the studied research topic. The outcome of this step is the generated map.

3   Systematic Mapping

Following the process previous presented, next sections present the details of the conducted systematic mapping.

3.1   Definition of Research Questions

According to the intention of this SM, presented in Sect. 1, the research questions were:

- RQ.1) *Which software inspection processes were investigated through experimental studies?*
- RQ.2) *Which techniques and tools have been used in experimental studies that investigated software inspection processes?*

Petersen et al. [17] suggest that a protocol is filled as it is in Systematic Reviews to enable the registration of the study decisions, as well as the auditing and replication.

Aiming to use a computational support for conducting this SM, the StArt tool [19–21] was used. Hence, the protocol was based on Kitchenham's proposal [18], since this is the model provided by the tool. Although the protocol data can be adjusted during the process execution, in this step the research questions, the inclusion and exclusion studies criteria and the information extraction form fields were defined.

3.2   Search Conduction

The definition of the search string is relevant to ensure that the studies to be analyzed support the answer to the research question. The online scientific database SCOPUS was selected to perform essays till an effective search string was reached.

SCOPUS was chosen because it offers facilities that allow operations with a set of strings besides analyzing relevant data as: list of research area, authors, conferences/journals and keywords most frequent in the papers retrieved. Furthermore, Dieste et al. [22] argue that it has fewer weaknesses than the other online scientific databases. After some essays, the search string defined was:

TITLE-ABS-KEY("software inspection process" OR (("inspection process" OR "inspection technique") AND "software engineering")) AND TITLE-ABS-KEY("-primary stud" OR "experiment*" OR "empirical stud*" OR "controlled stud*")*

After performing the query in SCOPUS and exporting the results (papers) to a .bib file, the same search string was adapted to be applied to the other online scientific database defined in the protocol: IEEExplore, ACM Digital Library and Web of Science.

These four online scientific databases were inserted into the StArt tool protocol such that a respective search session was created for each one. Aiming to enable replications of this study, for each search session the respective search string was registered in the tool, as well as the BibTex file was imported.

Dieste et al. [22] exposed that the results of an ACM DL search cannot be exported either to text or Reference Manager formats which represents a significant impediment for a SR. To workaround this problem we used the Zotero Firefox plug-in (www.zotero.org) to import the ACM DL results and generate the BibTex file.

When the user imports a .bib file to a search session of StArt, duplicated papers (with the same title and authors) are automatically identified. In addition, the tool sets a score for each papers, which is based on the frequency that each keyword (defined in the protocol) appears in the title, abstract and keywords of the paper.

After all .bib files were imported, 249 papers were inserted under this SM, having 116 as duplicated papers (indexed by more than one online scientific database).

3.3 Screening of Papers

The computational support of the StArt tool makes the screening of papers easier. The tool offers an interface that allows the reading of the abstracts (retrieved by .bib reference file); shows the inclusion and exclusion criteria (defined on the protocol); enables the attribution of these criteria to the papers; and allows setting the papers as accepted or rejected. The StArt also allows the user setting a reading priority (very high, high, low and very low), deduced from the reading of the abstract, which will be useful when the full paper should be read, for example, in a Systematic Review.

In order to revise the inclusion and exclusion criteria and the data extraction form (both defined in the protocol - Step 1), first of all the five high scored and five low scored papers were analyzed.

The criteria were satisfactory and no change was made. By the other hand, a new field was added to the data extraction form: "Which process phase (or activity) is supported by the technique?" (more details in Sect. 3.5).

Although Petersen et al. [17] suggest that this SM step is conducted based on the paper abstract (or some paper sections), there are cases where the abstract is not enough for applying the inclusion and exclusion criteria. In these cases, reading the full text can be a good option, like in the Systematic Review process [14, 18].

At the end of this step, 54 papers were rejected and 79 were accepted. Table 1 shows the inclusion and exclusion criteria applied and the number of papers related to each one. There are some papers that were related to more than one criterion.

Table 1. Inclusion and exclusion criteria applied in the SM.

Type	Criterion	# of papers
Inclusion	Presents or uses some tool/technique to support the experimental studies	31
	Presents a experimental study related to software inspection process	56
Exclusion	Proceedings introduction	1
	Not written in English or Portuguese	1
	Full paper not available on web neither in the university commutation service	4
	Not presents an inspection process related to software	14
	Not related to software	16
	Not presents an experimental study related to software inspection process	18

It is important to mention that this systematic mapping has focused just in papers about software inspection process and its variants – papers about peer review, as example, were not considered.

3.4   Keywording of Abstracts

Although Petersen et al. [17] suggest that the classification schema should emerge while the step *Keywording of Abstracts* is being conducted, in this SM it was defined when the protocol was filled. In this way, we tried to ensure that the required data to answer the research question would be extracted.

In this SM the *Keywording of Abstract* was conducted in parallel to the Screening of Papers. Hence, if a paper was accepted, as the abstract was read, the *Classification Scheme* (data extraction form) defined in the protocol was revised aiming to: (i) identify if the paper would fill all items of the schema; (ii) identify values to compose a list of possible categories for each classification schema item.

Again, the StArt tool makes this task easier, once it gives two possibilities to define the classification schema items in the data extraction form (resource available in the tool): textual classification or itemized classification.

If the user set a classification item as textual, this field will be a text and probably, different for each papers. If the user set a classification item as itemized, a list of categories must be created and only one category can be chosen when the item is filled. Of course, the list of categories can be updated if necessary.

The itemized item is a good option to ensure standardization of answers. For instance, in this SM the classification item "study type" was an itemized item and its categories were updated as the *Keywording of abstracts* was conducting.

3.5   Data Extraction and Mapping of the Studies

In this step the 79 accepted papers were categorized in 8 classification items: (i) study classification, according to [23]; (ii) inspection process used, (iii) artifact inspected; (iv) tool used in the study; (v) step (s) of the process supported by the tool; (vi) techniques used in the study; (vii) step (s) of the process supported by the technique; and (viii) research group or university.

In addition to the map based on data collected through the classification schema, using the StArt tool it is possible to map the research area taking into account other data, for example: publication year, conferences or journals, and authors. These fields are available when the .bib file is imported to the tool.

Considering the research question, the bubble chart that maps the research allows identifying the techniques used in experimental studies related to software inspection process and which activities are supported by these techniques.

Charts and tables show the publications evolution, processes and tools more used, artifacts commonly inspected, and so on.

When the StArt tool is used, besides the characterization of the papers by means of the Classification Schema, the papers can be characterize by additional and relevant information. This is possible since relevant information can also be registered in a memo field provided by the tool, for each paper. We emphasize that any scientific methods to Thematic Synthesis as mentioned by Cruzes and Dyba [24] were considered.

As secondary studies should be accessible to the community [18, 25] the package of this study is available at: www.dc.ufscar.br/~lapes/packs/inspecao5.1.rar.

3.6   Results

The results will be commented according to the research questions. The first question is related to the software inspection process that have been used in experimental studies: RQ.1) "Which software inspection processes were investigated through experimental studies?".

According to Fig. 2, that shows the identified processes and how many papers cited them, we observe that few authors mentioned the process used in the experimental study (23 occurrences).

The Fagan process [3, 4] was the most mentioned (22 occurrences), mainly if some adaptations of this process are also considered (7 occurrences) [26–31].

The process presented by Sauer et.al [9] was also highlighted among the accepted papers (7 occurrences). Some adaptations of this process [32–34] were also mentioned (3 occurrences).

The inspection process presented by Gilb and Graham [7] (3 occurrences), hyperCode [35, 36] (2 occurrences) and N-fold (2 occurrences) [37, 38] were the other processes also explicitly cited among the accepted papers.

As mentioned before, although the secondary study that was carried out was a SM, which does not require the full reading of papers, some of them were completely read aiming to extract more detailed information.

As mentioned before, there were cases where a brief reading of the full text was needed. Although different processes were identified among the experimental studies, all of them propose activities to plan the inspection, find defects, analyze the defects and select the ones for rework. The main differences between the processes stayed on the roles, intermediate activities, strategies to collect and analyze defects and tools to support them.

It is important to notice that some papers used more than one inspection process. In addition, a process was considered "adapted" when some of its steps were not performed.

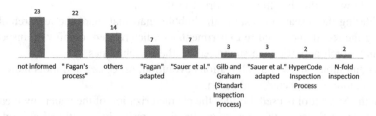

Fig. 2. Software inspection process used in the experimental studies.

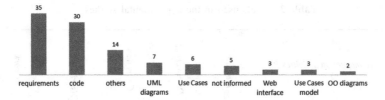

Fig. 3. Artifacts inspected in the experimental studies.

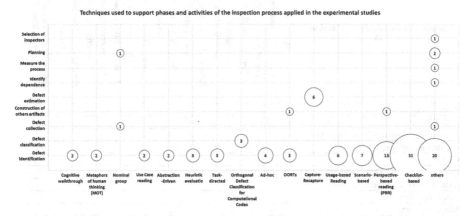

Fig. 4. Techniques x Inspection Process phase/activity map.

As software inspection can be applied to all kind of software artifact, the artifacts referred in the experimental studies were of different types. Figure 3 shows this information and highlights that the most investigated artifacts are requirement documents and code. The reviewers have decided maintain the name of the artifacts mentioned by each author, which led to present UML diagrams, Use Cases, Use Cases model and OO diagrams as different items.

The secondary question is related to techniques and tools that have been used in experimental studies: RQ.2) "Which techniques and tools have been used in experimental studies that investigated software inspection processes?"

Figure 4 shows a bubble chart that shows the most mentioned techniques and the respective activities supported by them. Table 2 shows the tools and what features each one provides. Only 25 papers mentioned some tool and which one was used.

Related to the techniques, as expected, most of them are reading techniques or techniques defined for other purpose but used to find defects [39].

The outstanding reading techniques of this SM were Checklist and Perspective-Based Reading (PBR). PBR is a systematic technique for defect detection in requirement documents and Checklist is a reading technique that can be applied for reading different types of artifacts. Notice that this result is aligned with the one showed in Fig. 3, since the requirements document was mentioned as the most inspected artifact in the experimental studies.

Table 2. Tools used in the experimental studies.

Software inspection activities [9] → / Activities mentioned by the authors →	Planning			Discovering			Collection		Discrimination						Rework	Follow-up
	Planning	Artifacts / documents sharing	Individual preparing	Defect identification	Automatic defect identification	Defect identification form	Defects collection	Analysis and defect priorization	Defects discrimination	Data analysis	Meeting (asynchronous)	Meeting (synchronous)	Inspection review	Simulations of the process	Rework	Capture-recapture techniques application
Adobe Acrobat 5.0		✓								✓						
ASSIST	✓		✓				✓									
Assistent to Usability Inspection Process	✓			✓			✓	✓	✓							
Capture-Recapture; CARE																✓
CRISTA				✓		✓			✓	✓						
Document Quality Defect Detection tool				✓		✓										
Extend Software Modeling tool														✓		
FindBugs; Jlint				✓												
Electronic form							✓									
Gerdame / NosePrints					✓				✓							
GRIP	✓						✓	✓								
GroupSystems	✓						✓	✓								
hyperCode																
InspectA							✓	✓	✓				✓			
Internet-Based Inspection System (IBIS)	✓			✓			✓	✓	✓							
ISPIS	✓			✓			✓	✓	✓						✓	
Spreadsheet							✓									
SUIT	✓			✓			✓					✓				
Ventana Corp.'s Group Outliner tool				✓								✓				
VisionQuest; GSS anonymous software							✓	✓				✓				
WAIT	✓			✓			✓	✓	✓							
WIPS							✓	✓								

Other technique commonly used in the experimental studies was Capture-Recapture [34, 40–44]. This technique is related to statistic methods used to quantify remaining defects in the artifact after the inspection. The use of Capture-Recapture in software inspection was proposed by Eick et al. [45] and some studies and improvements were presented thereafter.

Related to the tools mentioned in the papers, they usually provide support to the software inspection process in different ways.

Regarding inspection meeting or defects discrimination activity, in general, the tools adopt asynchronous communication. The roles involved in these activities communicate and share opinions by means of forums created to enable discussions about the defects identified during the inspection, for example. A score previously assigned to each defect by inspectors assists the discussion and also helps the moderator in defining if a defect is a false-positive or a real-defect [46–48].

Two studies applied synchronous communication to support these activities. Tyran and George [49] have used a GSS tool (Group Support System) to allow that a group of inspectors discuss the process outcomes in a synchronous way. A similar study was presented by Vitharana and Ramamurthy [29], who used a GSS tool to enable the roles involved in the inspection joining in the discussion activity anonymously.

Although both studies presented appropriate results using this kind of tool, these tools do not assist other inspection activities such as defects identification.

Porto et al. [31] presented CRISTA (Code Reading with Stepwise Abstraction) that supports the inspection meeting and defect discrimination activity. Despite the discussions can be performed by groups, they must be coordinated by the moderator who inserts the decision into the tool.

As mentioned before, for SM it is also important to identify the sources where the papers were published and outstanding authors. Table 3 shows the conferences and journals that published the accepted papers - those which published only one paper were grouped in the row "Other conferences and journals". The outstanding in this classification was the Empirical Software Engineering Journal.

Table 3. List of journals/conferences which published experimental studies on software inspection.

Journals	Number of papers
Empirical Software Engineering	7
IEEE Transactions on Software Engineering	5
ACM Transactions on Software Engineering and Methodology (TOSEM)	2
Information and Software Technology	2
Lecture Notes in Computer Science	2
SIGSOFT Software Engineering Notes	2
Software Testing Verification and Reliability	2
Conferences	
International Conference on Software Engineering (ICSE)	5
International Software Metrics Symposium	4
ACM/IEEE International Symposium on Empirical Software Engineering	3
Conference of the Centre for Advanced Studies on Collaborative research	3
International Symposium on Empirical Software Engineering (ISESE)	3
Asia-Pacific Software Engineering Conference	2
Euromicro Conference	2
EUROMICRO Conference on Software Engineering and Advanced Applications	2
International Conference on Automated Software Engineering (ASE)	2
International Conference on Quality Software (QSIC)	2
International Conference on Software Engineering and Knowledge Engineering	2
Nordic Conference on Human-computer Interaction	2
Brazilian Symposium on Software Engineering	2
Other conference and journals	23

Table 4 shows the universities and research groups that have conducted experimental studies related to software inspection. The outstanding in this classification were the Vienna University of Technology and the University of Maryland.

Table 4. Universities and research groups highlighted on the SM.

University/research group	# Papers	University/research group	# papers
Vienna University of Technology	13	Mississippi State University	3
University of Maryland	8	University of Bari	3
Fraunhofer Kaiserslautern	6	Federal University of São Carlos	2
University of Strathclyde	7	Fraunhofer Maryland	2
Federal University of Rio de Janeiro	4	Technical University Vienna	2
Johannes Kepler University Linz	4	University of Copenhagen	2
Lund University	4	University of Oulu	2
Royal Military College of Canada	4	University of Sannio	2
Università di Bari	4	Other universities /research groups	40
AT&T Bell Labs	4		

According to the categories presented by Wieringa [23], the studies fitted to three categories: proposal (5 studies), validation (25 studies) and evaluation (49 studies). Considering that this SM is about experimental studies that investigated software inspection processes, as expected, most of the papers corresponded to a validation or evaluation of some process. The *"proposal"* category represents the studies that presented a new proposal and also an empirical study to evidence the proposal advantages.

3.7   Threats to Validity

Although a research protocol have been filled and evaluated by other members of the research group, some threats to validity can be identified.

Basically, the main threats are of internal validity as: (i) researcher's bias when analyzing the primary studies; (ii) the possibilities provided by the online scientific databases of constructing the search string, which may not catch all representative papers from the database; and (iii) the researcher's university permission related to the online scientific databases access, which may cause non access to full papers and, consequently, their rejection.

Some actions were taken for minimizing these threats, for example, assessing the protocol during the screening of papers to certificate that it portrayed the correct selection criteria; and the conduction of pilot study for reaching an acceptable search string.

Regarding the details present in this paper and the study package available, we believe that a replication of this study is feasible. Even the replication date can affect the outcome and threats to validity, we believe the underlying trends should remain unchanged.

4 Main Differences Among Software Inspection Processes Experimentally Investigated

The software inspection process proposed by Fagan in the 70s [3] and revisited by the same author in the 80s [4] is composed by six activities:

- *Planning*: the inspection team is defined and the roles are assigned to the members;
- *Overview*: the inspection team is informed about the product and artifact. This activity is optional;
- *Preparation*: individually, the inspectors review the artifact aiming to learn about it and be prepared to the inspection meeting;
- *Inspection Meeting*: guided by the moderator, the inspectors about defects on the artifact aiming to find the high number them, but not aiming to find solutions. After the meeting, the moderator prepares a list of all identified defects aiming to ensure that all them will be addressed to the author;
- *Rework*: all the real defects are resolved by the author;
- *Follow-up*: The moderator checks and verifies each defect correction.

The Fagan's process is the basis of a lot of other software inspection process and until now, it is frequently investigated in experimental studies, as mentioned in the previous section.

Figure 5 shows the activities of other four highlighted inspection processes indentified in this systematic mapping

Based on experimental studies, Sauer and others [9] have proposed a new version of the Fagan's inspection process, aiming to reduce the cost and time of the inspection activity. These authors replaced the preparation and inspection meeting of Fagan's process with three inline activities: detection, collection and discrimination. During

Processes	Activities					
Fagan	Presentation	Preparation	Inspection meeting		Rework	Follow Up
Sauer et al.	Presentation	Detection	Collection	Discrimination	Rework	Follow Up

Fagan	Presentation	Preparation	Inspection meeting		Rework	Follow Up
Gilb & Graham	Presentation	Preparation	Inspection meeting	Development process brainstorming meeting	Rework	Follow Up

Fagan	Presentation	Preparation		Inspection meeting	Rework	Follow Up
N-Fold	Presentation	Preparation (performed by n teams)		Inspection meeting	Rework	Follow Up

Fagan	Presentation	Preparation	Inspection meeting	Rework	Follow Up
hyperCode	Initial preparation	Preparation & Collection	Resolution & Repair		

Fig. 5. Activities of some inspection process in relation to Fagan's process.

the detection activity inspectors should individually find defects, which are grouped in the collection activity. During the discrimination activity, the moderator, authors and inspectors discuss the defects list generated in the collection activity and define which are real defects or false positives.

Gilb and Graham's software inspection process [41] is similar to Fagan's process, except for the introduction of a new activity after the inspection meeting: the process brainstorming meeting. During this activity the participants should discuss about the causes of the detected defects, aiming to improve the software development process.

The N-Fold inspection process [37] is based on formal inspection, as Fagan's inspection process. The difference on it process is on inspection activity – in other process this activity is performed by one team of inspectors, but the N-Fold process replicates the inspection activity using N independent teams, which uses the same artifact. According to Martin and Tsai [37], this process is suggested for the initial phase of critical software development, since its cost is higher than other process.

The hyperCode inspection process is based on a web system to support the software inspection: the hyperCode system. According to [35] the differences of hyper-Code are the inspection preparation, collection and repair phases. The preparation and collection are done at the same time by means of hyperCode system, which provides the automatic collection of defects. The decision about the real defects and false positives is done by the moderator and author as part of the repair phase.

5 Discussions, Lessons Learned and Future Works

This paper presented a systematic mapping of experimental studies on software inspection process.

The search string was applied in four online scientific databases and 249 papers were retrieved. Taking title and authors into account, the StArt tool, used as computational support to conduct this study, identified 116 duplicated papers. After analyzing the 133 remaining papers and applying the inclusion and exclusion criteria, 79 papers were accepted.

The data extracted from these papers showed that the inspection process presented by Fagan [3, 4] was the most experimentally investigated. The other processes identified in the studies are based on the Fagan's process, as it was mentioned in the previous section.

Although software inspection can be applied to all kind of software artifact, requirement documents and code were highlighted as the most investigated artifacts.

In relation to the techniques, the most mentioned were the reading techniques. Checklist and Perspective-Based Reading (PBR) were highlighted.

Concerning the tools, a wide list of tools with different purposes was identified. Some tools were specific to the software inspection process, such as CRISTA [31], ISPIS [47], hyperCode [36], InspectA [8] and IBIS [46]. Other tools were used in the experimental studies but were not for supporting the software inspection process properly, such as Capture-Recapture [40] and FindBugs [50].

Some lessons learned deserve attention: the importance of good abstracts and the registration of some details about any object under evaluation through experimental studies. This is very important for reaching the objective of a SM.

Although the SM process suggests that the Classification Schema is created on the basis of papers abstract, few of them provide basic information about the conducted study. Hence, the only way to get the necessary information is to read the full paper or some section of it.

Even so, there were papers that did not exhibit relevant details about the conducted study, such as: the process used (or the way that the process was performed), artifacts inspected, how the data was analyzed and the threats to validity. Thus, the lack of information for filling the classification schema established by the investigators can jeopardize the research area characterization.

These hardships faced by the authors (lack of information both in the abstracts and the full paper) emphasize the importance of topics already explained by other authors: structured abstracts [51] and guidelines to report empirical studies [52].

Considering that this SM was conducted in the context of a PhD research that aims to give better support to the inspection meeting and defect discrimination activities, as future work the most used inspection processes will be investigated more deeply. Hence, systematic reviews are being planned and will be conducted as future work.

Acknowledgements. Our thanks to the Brazilian funding agencies CAPES and CNPq and INEP (*Observatório da Educação*, project 3280). E.M.H thanks CAPES foundation (BEX 11833/12-2).

References

1. Anderson, P., Reps, T., Teitelbaum, T.: Design and implementation of a fine-grained software inspection tool. IEEE Trans. Softw. Eng. **29**(8), 721–733 (2003)
2. BooSerd, C., Moonen, L.: Prioritizing software inspection results using static profiling. In: 6th IEEE International Workshop on Source Code Analysis and Manipulation. IEEE Computer Society, Los Alamitos (2006)
3. Fagan, M.E.: Design and code inspections to reduce errors in program development. IBM Syst. J. **15**(7), 182–211 (1976)
4. Fagan, M.E.: Advances in software inspections. IEEE Trans. Softw. Eng. **12**(7), 744–751 (1986)
5. Humphrey, W.S.: Managing the Software Process. Addison-Wesley Longman Publishing Company, Boston (1989)
6. NASA. http://www.cs.nott.ac.uk/~cah/G53QAT/fi.pdf
7. Gilb, T., Graham, D.: Software Inspection. Addison-Wesley, England (1993)
8. Murphy, P., Miller, J.: A process for asynchronous software inspection. In: 8th IEEE International Workshop on Software Technology and Engineering Practice. IEEE Press, Los Alamitos (1997)
9. Sauer, C., Jeffery, D., Land, L., Yetton, P.: The effectiveness of software development technical review: a behaviorally motivated program of research. IEEE Trans. Softw. Eng. **1**(26), 1–14 (2000)

10. Halling, M., Biffl, S., Grunbacher, P.: A groupware-supported inspection process for active inspection management. In: Euromicro Conference. IEEE Press, Los Alamitos (2002)
11. Denger, C., Elberzhager, F.: Unifying inspection processes to create a framework to support static quality assurance planning. In: 33rd Euromicro Conference on Software Engineering and Advanced Applications. IEEE Press, Los Alamitos (2007)
12. Travassos, G.H., Gurov, D., Amaral, E.: Introdução à Engenharia de software experimental. Technical report, UFRJ (2002)
13. Basili, V.R., Green, S., Laitenberger, O., Shull, F., Sørumgård, S., Zelkowitz, M.: The empirical investigation of perspective-based reading. Empir. Softw. Eng. 1(2), 133–164 (1996)
14. Kitchenham, B.A.: Procedures for performing systematic reviews. Technical report, Keele University (2004)
15. Bailey, J., Budgen, D., Turner, M., Kitchenham, B., Brereton, P., Linkman, S.: Evidence relating to object-oriented software design: a survey. In: International Symposium on Empirical Software Engineering and Measurement. IEEE Press, Los Alamitos (2007)
16. Petticrew, M., Roberts, H.: Systematic Reviews in the Social Sciences - a practical guide. Blackwell Publishing, Malden (2006)
17. Petersen, K., Feldt, R., Mujtaba, S., Mattson, M.: Systematic mapping studies in software engineering. In: International Conference on Evaluation and Assessment in Software Engineering (2008)
18. Kitchenham, B.A.: Guidelines for performing systematic literature reviews in software. Technical report, Keele University (2007)
19. Hernandes, E.C.M., Zamboni, A.B., Thommazo, A.D., Fabbri, S.C.P.F.: Avaliação da ferramenta StArt utilizando o modelo TAM e o paradigma GQM. In: 7th Experimental Software Engineering Latin American Workshop (2010)
20. Zamboni, A.B., Thommazo, A.D., Hernandes, E.C.M., Fabbri, S.C.P.F.: StArt Uma Ferramenta Computacional de Apoio à Revisão Sistemática. In: Brazilian Conference on Software: Theory and Practice - Tools session (2010)
21. Fabbri, S., Hernandes, E., Di Thommazo, A., Belgamo, A., Zamboni, A., Silva, C.: Managing literature reviews information through visualization. In: 14th International Conference on Enterprise Information Systems. SciTePress, New York (2012)
22. Dieste, O., Grimán, A., Juristo, N.: Developing search strategies for detecting relevant experiments. Empir. Softw. Eng. 14(5), 513–539 (2009)
23. Wieringa, R., Maiden, N., Mead, N., Rolland, C.: Requirements engineering paper classification and evaluation criteria: a proposal and a discussion. Requir. Eng. 11(1), 102–107 (2005)
24. Cruzes, D., Dyba, T.: Recommended steps for thematic synthesis in software engineering. In: International Symposium on Empirical Software Engineering and Measurement. IEEE Computer Society, Los Alamitos (2011)
25. Pai, M., McCulloch, M., Gorman, J.D., Pai, N., Enanoria, W., Kennedy, G., Tharyan, P., Colford Jr, J.M.: Clinical research methods - systematic reviews and meta-analyses: an illustrated, step-by-step guide. Natl. Med. J. India 17(2), 86–95 (2004)
26. Porter, A., Siy, H., Mockus, A., Votta, L.: Understanding the sources of variation in software inspections. ACM Trans. Softw. Eng. Methodol. 7(1), 41–79 (1998)
27. Kelly, D., Shepard, T.: Task-directed software inspection technique: an experiment and case study. In: Conference of the Centre for Advanced Studies on Collaborative Research. IBM Press, Palo Alto (2000)
28. Harjumaa, L.: Distributed software inspections - an experiment with Adobe Acrobat. In: 26th International Conference on Computer Science and Technology. IASTED, New York (2003)

29. Vitharana, P., Ramamurthy, K.: Computer-mediated group support, anonymity, and the software inspection process: an empirical investigation. IEEE Trans. Softw. Eng. **29**(2), 167–180 (2003)

30. Torner, T., Ivarsson, M., Pettersson, F., Öhman, P.: Defects in automotive use cases. In: ACM/IEEE International Symposium on Empirical Software Engineering. ACM Press, New York (2006)

31. Porto, D., Mendonca, M., Fabbri, S.: The use of reading technique and visualization for program understanding. In: 21st International Conference on Software Engineering and Knowledge Engineering. ACM Press, New York (2009)

32. Bernardez, B., Genero, M., Duran, A., Toro, M.: A controlled experiment for evaluating a metric-based reading technique for requirements inspection. In: 10th International Symposium on Software Metrics. IEEE Press, Los Alamitos (2004)

33. Winkler, D., Biffl, S., Thurnher, B.: Investigating the impact of active guidance on design inspection. In: Bomarius, F., Komi-Sirviö, S. (eds.) PROFES 2005. LNCS, vol. 3547, pp. 458–473. Springer, Heidelberg (2005)

34. Walia, G., Carver, J.: Evaluation of capture-recapture models for estimating the abundance of naturally-occurring defects. In: 2nd ACM-IEEE International Symposium on Empirical software Engineering and Measurement. ACM Press, New York (2008)

35. Perpich, J., Perry, D., Porter, A., Votta, L., Wade, M.: Anywhere, anytime code inspections: using the web to remove inspection bottlenecks in large-scale software development. In: International Conference on Software Engineering. IEEE Computer Society, Los Alamitos (1997)

36. Perry, D., Porter, A., Wade, M., Votta, L., Perpich, J.: Reducing inspection interval in large-scale software development. IEEE Trans. Softw. Eng. **28**(7), 695–705 (2002)

37. Schneider, M., Martin, J., Tsai, W.T.: An experimental study of fault detection in user requirements documents. ACM Trans. Softw. Eng. Methodol. **1**(2), 188–204 (1992)

38. He, L., Carver, J.: PBR vs. checklist: a replication in the n-fold inspection context. In: ACM/IEEE International Symposium on Empirical Software Engineering. ACM Press, New York (2006)

39. Frøkjær, E., Hornbæk, K.: Metaphors of human thinking for usability inspection and design. ACM Trans. Comput.-Hum. Interact. **14**(4), 1–33 (2008)

40. Runeson, P., Wohlin, C.: An experimental evaluation of an experience-based capture-recapture method in software code inspections. Empir. Softw. Eng. **3**(4), 381–406 (1998)

41. Miller, J.: Estimating the number of remaining defects after inspection. Softw. Test. Verif. Reliab. **9**(3), 167–189 (1999)

42. Freimut, B., Laitenberger, O., Biffl, S.: Investigating the impact of reading techniques on the accuracy of different defect content estimation techniques. In: 17th Software Metrics Symposium. IEEE Press, Los Alamitos (2001)

43. Thelin, T.: Empirical evaluations of usage-based reading and fault content estimation for software inspections. Empir. Softw. Eng. **8**(3), 309–313 (2003)

44. Thelin, T.: Team-based fault content estimation in the software inspection process. In: 26th International Conference on Software Engineering. IEEE Computer, Washington (2004)

45. Eick, S., Loader, C., Long, D., Votta, L., Vander Wiel, S.: Estimating software fault content before coding. In: 14th International Conference on Software Engineering. IEEE Computer Society, Los Alamitos (1992)

46. Lanubile, F., Mallardo, T., Calefato, F.: Tool support for geographically dispersed inspection teams. Softw. Process: Improv. Pract. **8**(4), 217–231 (2004)

47. Kalinowski, M., Travassos, G.H.: A computational framework for supporting software inspections. In: 19th Conference on Automated Software Engineering. IEEE Press, Los Alamitos (2004)

48. Ardito, C., Lanzilotti, R., Buono, P., Piccinno, A.: A tool to support usability inspection. In: 11th Working Conference on Advanced Visual Interfaces. ACM Press, New York (2006)
49. Tyran, C.K., George, J.F.: Improving software inspections with group process support. Commun. ACM **45**(9), 87–92 (2002)
50. Wojcicki, M., Strooper, P.: Maximising the information gained from an experimental analysis of code inspection and static analysis for concurrent java components. In: ACM/ IEEE International Symposium on Empirical Software Engineering. ACM Press, New York (2006)
51. Budgen, D., Kitchenham, B., Charters, S., Turner, M., Brereton, P., Linkman, S.: Presenting software engineering results using structured abstracts: a randomised experiment. Empir. Softw. Eng. **13**(4), 435–468 (2008)
52. Jedlitschka, A., Pfahl, D.: Reporting guidelines for controlled experiments in software engineering. In: International Symposium on Empirical Software Engineering. IEEE Press, Los Alamitos (2005)

Artificial Intelligence and Decision Support Systems

Coordinating Agents in Dynamic Environment

Richardson Ribeiro[1]([⊠]), Adriano F. Ronszcka[2],
Marco A.C. Barbosa[1], and Fabrício Enembreck[3]

[1] Department of Informatic, Federal University of Technology,
Pato Branco, Parana, Brazil
{richardsonr,marcocb}@utfpr.edu.br
[2] Graduate School in Electrical Engineering & Industrial Computer Science
(CPGEI), Federal University of Technology, Curitiba, Parana, Brazil
ronszcka@gmail.com
[3] Post-Graduate Program in Computer Science,
Pontificial Catholical University, Curitiba, Parana, Brazil
fabricio@ppgia.pucpr.br

Abstract. This paper presents strategies for speeding up the convergence of agents on swarm. Speeding up the learning of an agent is a complex task since the choice of inadequate updating techniques may cause delays in the learning process or even induce an unexpected acceleration that causes the agent to converge to a non-satisfactory policy. We have developed strategies for updating policies which combines local and global search using past policies. Experimental results in dynamic environments of different dimensions have shown that the proposed strategies are able to speed up the convergence of the agents while achieving optimal action policies, improving the coordination of agents in the swarm while deliberating.

Keywords: Coordination · Ant-colony algorithms · Dynamic environments

1 Introduction

Learning and coordination of agents have been receiving attention of the artificial intelligence community. Even in seemingly simple applications becomes often difficult or even impossible to predict behavior to ensure acceptable performance to an agent throughout its life cycle. Because of this difficulty, it is usually necessary to adapt some agents with learning abilities for changing their behavior in the light of experience and of the possible coordination model available. The coordination in this case, is necessary to ensure broadly consistent behavior for systems formed by individuals who share goals, resources and skills.

In multiagent systems, one important ability of an agent is to be able to coordinate effectively with other agents towards desirable outcomes, since the outcome not only depends on the action it takes but also the actions taken by other agents that it interacts with. When properly applied, coordination between agents can help to make the execution of complex tasks more efficient. Proper coordination can help to avoid such complications as finding redundant solutions to a sub-problem, inconsistencies of

© Springer International Publishing Switzerland 2014
S. Hammoudi et al. (Eds.): ICEIS 2013, LNBIP 190, pp. 137–153, 2014.
DOI: 10.1007/978-3-319-09492-2_9

execution (such as up-dating obsolete sub-problems), loss of resources, and deadlocks (waiting for events which will probably not occur) [1, 24].

Real-world activities which require coordinated action include traffic environments [2], sensor networks [3], supply chain management [4], environmental management, structural modeling, and dealing with the consequences of natural disasters. In such applications agents act in uncertain environments which change dynamically. Thus, autonomous decisions must be taken by agents themselves in the light of what they perceive locally.

In such applications, agents must decide upon courses of action that take into account the activities of other agents, based on knowledge of the environment, limitations of resources and restrictions on communication. Methods of coordination must be used to manage consequences that result when agents have inter-related objectives: in other words, when agents share the same environment or share common resources.

The paradigm for coordination based on swarm intelligence has been extensively studied by a number of researchers [5–7, 25, 26]. It is inspired by the behavior of colonies of social insects, with computational systems reproducing their behavior exhibited when solving collective problems: typically the colonies are those of ants, bees, woodlice or wasps. Such colonies have desirable characteristics (adaptation and coordination) which find solutions to computational problems needing concerted activity. Earlier research on the organization of social insect colonies and its applications for the organization of multi-agent systems has shown good results for complex problems, such as combinatorial optimization [8].

However, one of the main difficulties with such algorithms is the time required to achieve convergence, which can be quite expensive for many real-world applications. In such applications, there is no guarantee that reward-based algorithms will converge, since it is well known that they were initially developed and used to cope with static problems where the objective function is invariant over time. However, few real-world problems are static in which changes of priorities for resources do not occur, goals do not change, or where there are tasks that are no longer needed. Where changes are needed through time, the environment in which agents operate is dynamic.

The use of methods based on insect behavior, of ant colonies in particular, has drawn the attention of researchers who reproduce sophisticated exploration strategies which are both general and robust [8]; but in most cases such approaches are not able to improve coordination between agents in dynamic conditions due to the need to provide adequate knowledge of changes in environment.

The work reported here re-examines and extends principles presented in [2, 9], which discussed approaches for updating policies in dynamic environments and analysed the effects of strengthening learning-algorithm parameters in dynamic optimization problems. To integrate such approaches into updating strategies, as proposed in this paper, a test framework was developed to iteratively demonstrate the influence of parameters in the *Ant-Q* algorithm [10], whilst agents respond to the system using updating strategies, further discussed in Sect. 3.

One important aspect is to investigate whether policies learned can be used to find a solution rapidly after the environment has been modified. The strategies proposed in this paper respond to changes in the environment. We cite as one example of dynamic alteration the physical movement of the vertex in a graph (the environment): i.e., the change in vertex coordinates, in a solution generated with a Hamiltonian cycle. Such strategies are based on rewards (pheromones) from past policies that are used to steer agents towards new solutions. Experiments were used to compare the utilities of policies generated by agents using strategies proposed. The experiments were run using benchmark.

2 Ant-Colony Algorithms

The inspiring source of Ant Colony Optimization (ACO) is the foraging behavior of real ants colonies [5]. When searching for food, ants initially explore the area surrounding their nest in a random manner. One of the main ideas underlying this approach is the indirect communication among the individuals of a colony of agent, called (*artificial*) ants, based on an analogy with pheromone trails that real ants use for communication (pheromones are an odorous, chemical substance). The (artificial) pheromone trails are a kind of distributed numeric information that is modified by the ants to reflect their accumulated experience while solving a particular problem.

Ant-colony algorithms such as *Ant System* [5], *Ant Colony System* [8] and *Ant-Q* [10] have been applied with some success to combinatorial optimization problems, including the traveling salesman problem, graph coloring and vehicle routing. Such algorithms are based on the foraging behavior of ants (*"agents"*) which follow a decision pattern based on probability distribution [12].

Gambardella and Dorigo [10] developed the algorithm *Ant-Q*, inspired by the earlier algorithm *Q-learning* of Watkin and Dayan [13]. In *Ant-Q*, the pheromone is denoted by *AQ-value* ($AQ(i,j)$). The aim of *Ant-Q* is to estimate $AQ(i,j)$ as a way to find solutions favoring collectivity. Agents select their actions based on transition rules, as given in Eqs. 1 and 2:

$$
s = \begin{cases} \arg \max_{j \in N_k(t)} \left\{ [AQ(i,j)]^\delta \times [HE(i,j)]^\beta \right\} & if\ q \le q_0 \\ S & otherwise \end{cases} \tag{1}
$$

where the parameters δ and β represent the weight (influence) of the pheromone $AQ(i,j)$ and of the heuristic $HE(i,j)$ respectively; q is a value selected at random with probability distribution $[0,..,1]$: the larger the value of q_0, the smaller is the probability of the random selection; S is a random variable drawn from the probability function $AQ(i,j)$; and the $HE(i,j)$ are heuristic values associated with the link (i,j) (edge) which helps in the selection of adjacent states (vertices). In the case of the traveling salesman problem, it is taken as the reciprocal of the Euclidean distance.

Three different rules were used to choose the random variable S: (i) *pseudo-random*, where S is a state selected at random from the set $N_k(t)$, following a uniform distribution; (ii) *pseudo-random-proportional*, in which S is selected from the distribution given by Eq. 2 and; (iii) *random-proportional*, such that, if q had the value 0 in Eq. 1, then the next state is drawn at random from the distribution given by Eq. 2.

$$S = \begin{cases} \dfrac{[AQ(i,j)]^{\delta} \times [HE(i,j)]^{\beta}}{\sum\limits_{a \in N_k(t)} [AQ(i,a)]^{\delta} \times [HE(i,a)]^{\beta}} \end{cases} \tag{2}$$

Gambardella and Dorigo [10] showed that a good rule for choosing actions with the *Ant-Q* algorithm is based on *pseudo-random-proportional*. The $AQ(i,j)$ is then estimated by using the updating rule in Eq. 3, similar to the *Q-learning* algorithm:

$$AQ(i,j) = (1 - \alpha) \times AQ(i,j) + \alpha \left(\Delta AQ(i,j) + \gamma \times \max_{a \in S(j)} AQ(j,a) \right) \tag{3}$$

where the parameters γ and α are the discount factor and learning rate respectively.

When the updating rule is local, the updated $AQ(i,j)$ is applied after the state s has been selected, setting $\Delta AQ(i,j)$ to zero. The effect is that $AQ(i,j)$ associated with the link (i,j) is reduced by a factor γ each time that this link appears in the candidate solution. As in the *Q-learning* algorithm, therefore, this approach tends to avoid exploration of states with lower probability (pheromone concentration), making the algorithm unsuitable for situations where the present solution must be altered significantly as a consequence of unexpected environmental change.

Other methods based on ant-colony behavior have been proposed for improving the efficiency of exploration algorithms in dynamic environments. Guntsch and Middendorf [14] propounded a method for improving the solution when there are changes in environment, using local search procedures to find new solutions. Alternatively, altered states are eliminated from the solution, connecting the previous state and the successor to the excluded state. Thus, new states are brought into the solution. The new state is inserted at the position where the cost is least or where the highest cost in the environment is reduced, depending on the objective. Sim and Sun [15] used multiple ant-colonies, such that one colony is repelled by the pheromone of the others, favoring exploration when the environment is altered. Other methods for dealing with a dynamic environment change the updating rule of the pheromone to enhance exploration. Li and Gong [16], for example, modified local and global updating rules in the *Ant Colony System* algorithm. Their updating rule was altered as shown in Eq. 4:

$$\tau_{ij}(t+1) = (1 - p(\tau_{ij}(t)))\tau_{ij}(t) + \Delta\tau_{ij}(t) \tag{4}$$

where $p_l(\tau_{ij})$ is a function of τ_{ij} at time t, with $\theta > 0$; for example:

$$p_1(\tau_{ij}) = \frac{1}{1 + e^{-(\tau_{ij} + \theta)}} \tag{5}$$

Such methods can be used as alternatives for finding solutions where the environment is changing. By using probabilistic transition rules, the ant-colony algorithm widens the exploration of the state-space. In this way a random transition decision is used and some parameters are modified, with new heuristic information influencing the selection of the more desirable links.

High pheromone values are reduced by introducing a dynamic evaporation process. Thus when the environment is altered and the solution is not optimal, pheromone concentration in the corresponding links is diminished over time. Global updating proceeds in the same way, except that only the best and worst global solutions are considered; i.e.:

$$\tau_{ij}(t+1) = (1 - \rho_2(\tau_{ij}(t)))\tau_{ij}(t) + \gamma_{ij}\Delta\tau_{ij}(t) \tag{6}$$

where:

$$\gamma_{i,j} = \begin{cases} +1 & \text{if } (i,j) \text{ is the best global solution} \\ -1 & \text{if } (i,j) \text{ is the worst global solution} \\ 0 & \text{otherwise} \end{cases} \tag{7}$$

A similar global updating rule was used by Lee et al., [17]. Other strategies for changing the pheromone value have been proposed to compensate the occurrence of stagnation in ant-colony algorithms. Gambardella et al., [18] proposed a method for re-adjusting pheromone values with the values initially distributed. In another strategy, Stutzle and Hoos [19] suggested proportionally increasing the pheromone value according to the difference between it and its maximum value.

Thus, a number of methods based on ant-colony algorithms have been developed for improving efficiency of algorithm exploration in dynamic environments. They can be used as alternatives for improving the solution when the environment is changed. The proposed approaches are based on procedures that use strategies to improve exploration using the probabilistic transition of the *Ant Colony System* algorithm to widen exploration of the state space. Thus, the most random transition decision is used, varying some parameters where the new heuristic information influences the selection of the more desirable links.

Some papers apply updating rules to links of a solution, including an evaporation component similar to the updating rule of *Ant Colony System*. Thus the pheromone concentration diminishes through time, with the result that less favorable states are less likely to be explored in future episodes. For this purpose, one alternative would be to re-initialize the pheromone value after observing the changes to the environment, maintaining a reference to the best solutions found. If the altered region of the environment is identified, the pheromone of adjacent states is re-initialized, making them more attractive. If a state is unsatisfactory, rewards can be made smaller (generally proportional to the quality of the solution), thus becoming less attractive over time because of loss of pheromone by evaporation.

It can be seen that most of the works mentioned concentrate their efforts on improving transition rules using sophisticated strategies to obtain convergence. However, experimental results shown that such methods do not yield satisfactory results in environments that are highly dynamic and where the magnitude of the space to be searched is not known. In Sect. 3 we present strategies developed for updating policies generated by rewards (pheromones) in dynamic environments.

In these problems, it is only possible to find the optimum solution if the state space is explored completely, so that the computational cost increases exponentially as the state-space increases.

3 Strategies for Updating Policies Generated by Algorithms which Simulate Ant-Colonies

In Ribeiro and Enembreck [6] it was found that algorithms based on rewards are efficient when the learning parameters are satisfactorily estimated and when modifications to the environment do not occur which might change the optimal policy. An action policy is a function mapping states to actions by estimating a probability that a state e' can be reached after taking action a in state e. In dynamic environments, however, there is no guarantee that the Ant-Q algorithm will converge to an acceptable policy. Before setting out the strategies for updating policies, we give a summary of the field of application, using a combinatorial optimization problem frequently used in computation to demonstrate problems that are difficult to solve: namely the Traveling Salesman Problem (TSP). In general terms, the TSP is defined as a closed graph $A = (E,L)$ (representing the agent's environment) with n states (vertices) $E = \{e_1,...,e_n\}$, in which L is the set of all linkages (edges) between pairs of states i and j, where $l_{ij} = l_{ji}$ under symmetry. The goal is to find the shortest Hamiltonian cycle which visits every state, returning to the point of origin [20]. It is typically assumed that the distance function is a metric (e.g., Euclidean distance).

One approach to solving the TSP is to test all possible permutations, using exhaustive search to find the shortest Hamiltonian cycle. However given that the number of permutations is $(n-1)!$, this approach becomes impracticable in the majority of cases. Unlike such exhaustive methods, heuristic algorithms such as Ant-Q therefore seek feasible solutions in less computing time. Even without guaranteeing the best solution (the optimal policy), the computational gain is favorable to finding an acceptable solution.

The convergence of ant-colony algorithms would occur if there were exhaustive exploration of the state space, but this would require a very lengthy learning process before convergence was achieved. In addition, agents in dynamic environments can adopt policies which delay the learning process or which generate sub-optimal policies. Even so, the acceleration to convergence of swarm-based algorithms can be accelerated by using adaptive policies which avoid unsatisfactory updating. The following paragraphs therefore set out strategies for estimating current policy which improve convergence of agents under conditions of environmental change.

These strategies change pheromone values so as to improve coordination between agents and to allow convergence even when there changes in the cartesian position of environmental states. The objective of the strategies is to find the optimum equilibrium of policy reformulation which allows new solutions to be explored using the information from past policies. Giving a new equilibrium to the pheromone value is equivalent to adjusting information in the linkages, giving flexibility to the search procedure which enables it to find a new solution when the environment changes, thereby modifying the influence of past policies to construct new solutions.

One updating strategy that has been developed is inspired by the approaches set out in [17, 20], in which pheromone values are reset locally when environmental changes have been identified. This is termed the *global mean* strategy. It allocates the mean of all pheromone values of the best policy to all adjacent linkages in the altered states. The *global mean* strategy is limited because it fails to take in account the intensity of environmental change. For example, good solutions when states are altered can often make the solution less acceptable since it is only necessary to update part of action policy. The *global distance* strategy updates the pheromone concentrations of states by comparing the Euclidean distances between all states, before and after the environmental change. If the cost of the policy increases with increasing rate of environmental change, the pheromone value is decreased proportionately; otherwise it is increased. The *local distance* strategy is similar to the *global distance* strategy, but updating the pheromone is proportional to the difference in Euclidean distance of states that were altered.

Before discussing how strategies allocate values to the current policy in greater detail, we discuss how environmental changes are occurring. Environmental states can be altered by factors such as scarcity of resources, change in objectives or in the nature of tasks, such that states can be inserted, excluded, or simply moved within the environment. Such characteristics are found in many different applications such as traffic management, sensor networks, management of supply chains, and mobile communication networks.

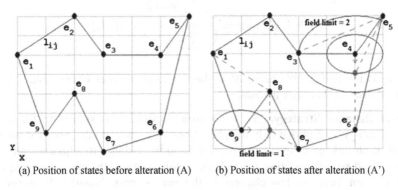

(a) Position of states before alteration (A)   (b) Position of states after alteration (A')

Fig. 1. Changing environmental states.

Figure 1 gives a simplified representation of a scenario with 9 states in a cartesian plane. Figure 1(a) shows the scenario before alteration; Fig. 1(b) shows the scenario after altering positions of states. It can be seen that altering the positions of states e_4 and e_9 will add six new linkages to the current policy. The changes to the environment were made arbitrarily by altering the cartesian positions of states whilst restricting them to lie within the field limit: i.e., adjacent to a cartesian position. Field limit is used to restrict changes in addition to adjacent states.

Thus, introducing environmental change can modify the position of a state, which can introduce differences between the current and the optimal policies giving rise, temporarily, to undesirable policies and errors. The strategies must update the pheromone values of linkages between the altered states, according to the characteristics of each.

A. Mean Global Strategy. The mean global strategy takes no account of the intensity of environmental change, whilst detecting that states have been altered. The mean pheromone value of all linkages to the current best policy Q is attributed to linkages to the modified states. In contrast to other reports where the pheromone was re-initiated without taking account of the value learned, the mean global strategy re-uses values from past policies to estimate updated values. Equation 8 shows how the values are computed for this strategy:

$$mean\_global = \frac{\sum\limits_{l \in Q} AQ(l)}{n_l} \qquad (8)$$

where n_l is the number of linkages and $AQ(l)$ is the pheromone value of the l linkages.

B. Global Distance Strategy. The global distance strategy calculates the distance between all states and the result is compared with the distance between states in the modified environment. This strategy therefore takes into account the total intensity of environmental change. If the distance between states increases, the updated pheromone value is inversely proportional to this distance. If the cost of the distance between states is reduced, the pheromone value is increased by the same proportion. Equation 9 is used to estimate the updated values for linkages between states in the modified environment A′.

$$global\_distance = \frac{\sum\limits_{i=1}^{n_e} \sum\limits_{j=i+1}^{n_e} d_A(l_{ij})}{\sum\limits_{i=1}^{n_e} \sum\limits_{j=i+1}^{n_e} d_{A'}(l_{ij})} \times AQ(l_{ij}) \qquad (9)$$

where n_e is the number of states, A′ is the environment after change and d is the Euclidean distance between the states.

C. Local Distance Strategy. The local distance strategy is similar to the global distance strategy, except that only the pheromone of linkages to the modified states is updated. Each linkage is updated in proportion to the distance to adjacent states that were modified so that updating is localized in this strategy, thereby improving convergence when there are few changes to the environment. Equation 10 is used to compute updated values for the linkages:

$$local\_distance = \frac{d_A(l_{ij})}{d_{A'}(l_{ij})} \times AQ(l_{ij}) \qquad (10)$$

The Pseudocode 1 gives the algorithm for the strategies mentioned above. An important aspect of the algorithm in Pseudocode 1 is the method for updating the learning table, which can occur either globally or locally. Global updating occurs at the end of each episode, when the least-cost policy is identified and the state values are updated using the reward parameter.

Equation 11 is used to calculate the value of $\Delta AQ(i,j)$, the reward for global updating.

$$\Delta AQ(i,j) = \begin{cases} \dfrac{W}{L_{best}} \end{cases} \qquad (11)$$

where W is a parameterized variable with value 10 and L_{best} is the total cost of the shortest Hamiltonian cycle in the current episode. Local updating occurs at agent action, the value of $\Delta AQ(i,j)$ being zero in this case.

4 Experimental Results

Experiments are reported here which evaluate the strategies discussed in Sect. 3 and the effects of the learning parameters on *Ant-Q* performance. These experiments evaluate algorithm efficiency in terms of: (i) variations in learning rate; (ii) discount factor; (iii) exploration rate; (iv) transition rules; (v) number of agents in the system; and (vi) the proposed updating strategies. Results and discussions are given in subSects. 4.1 and 4.2.

Algorithm. *Ant-Q with strategies* ().

Require:
Learning table $AQ(i,j)$; Environment E; #Changes, $t_w := 100$; Number of agents m_k; Number of states S; Number of episodes t_n; Learning parameters:$\{\alpha, \beta, \gamma, q_0, \delta, W\}$;   Updating   strategies: {*mean_global*,   *global_distance*, *local_distance*}

Ensure:
Randomize the states in E;
Use $\dfrac{1}{avg \times n}$ to compute the initial value of the pheromone and
assign it to $AQ(i,j)$;
// avg is the average of the Euclidean distances between state
pairs (i,j).
For all episode **Do:**
  Set the initial position of the agents in the states;
  While there are states to be visited **Do:**
   For all agent **Do:**
   If (q(**rand**(0..1) <= q_0) **Then**
    Choose an action according to Eq. 1;
    Else
     Choose an action according to Eq. 2;
    end If
   Update $AQ(i,j)$ using the rule in place upgrade (Eq.3);
   end For
  end While
 Compute the cost of the best policy of the episode t_x;
 Compute the global update, using equations 3 and 11;
 If #changes are supposed to occur **Then**
  For all linkage (i,j) of altered states **Do:**
   Switch (strategy):
   Case *mean_global* strategy:
    Value := strategyA(); //Eq. 8
   Case *global_distance* strategy:
    Value := strategyB(); // Eq. 9
   Case *local_distance* strategy:
    Value := strategyC(); // Eq. 10
  end For
 end If
 For all linkage (i,j) incident to the altered state **Do:**
  AQ(i,j) := Value;
 end For
 Otherwise continue()
end For
Return(.,.)

The experiments were run on benchmark: eil51 and eil76, found in the online library TSPLIB[1] [11]. The datasets eil51 and eil76 have 51 and 76 states respectively and were constructed by [21]. Such datasets have important characteristics for simulating problems of combinatorial optimization, such as, for example, the number of states and the presence of neighboring states separated by similar distances. They were also used by [5, 6, 10]. We also analyse the efficiency of the algorithm in three different scenarios, using 35, 45 and 55 states, in which the states were randomly positioned (Fig. 2).

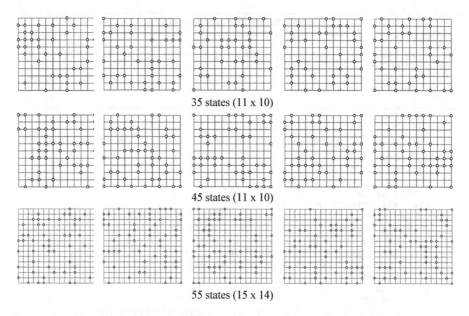

35 states (11 x 10)

45 states (11 x 10)

55 states (15 x 14)

Fig. 2. Scenarios used in the simulations, with states given as points in a 2D Euclidean coordinate system.

Learning by the algorithm in each set of instances was repeated 15 times, since it was found that doing experiments in one environment alone, using the same inputs, could result in variation between results computed by the algorithm. This occurs because agent actions are probabilistic and values generated during learning are stochastic variables. The action policy determined by an agent can therefore vary from one experiment to another. The efficiency presented in this section is therefore the mean of all experiments generated in each set of instances. This number of replications was enough to evaluate the algorithm's efficiency, since the quality of policies did not change significantly ($\pm$ 2.4 %).

The learning parameters were initially given the following values: $\delta = 1$; $\beta = 2$; $\gamma = 0.3$; $\alpha = 0.1$; $q_0 = 0.9$ and $W = 10$. The number of agents in the environment is equal to the number of states. Stopping criteria were taken as 400 episodes ($t = 400$).

---

[1] www.iwr.uni-heidelberg.de/groups/comopt/software/TSPLIB95/

It should be noted that because of the number of states and the complexity of the problems, the number of episodes are not enough for the best policy to be determined. However the purpose of the experiments was to evaluate the effects of parameters on the algorithm *Ant-Q* and on the utility of the final solution from the strategies given in Sect. 3.

To evaluate the performance of a technique, a number of different measures could be used, such as time of execution, the number of episodes giving the best policy, or a consideration only of the best policies identified. To limit the number of experiments, the utility of policies found after a given number of episodes was used, taking the minimum-cost policy at the end of the learning phase.

Before discussing the results obtained when learning factors are varied, recall that the best policies are identified after only a small number of episodes. This is because of the heuristic influence which was set at double the value of the pheromone influence. The plots in Fig. 3 show how policy evolved after each 50 episodes, in the 55-state environment.

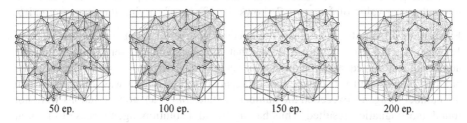

| 50 ep. | 100 ep. | 150 ep. | 200 ep. |

Fig. 3. Policy evolution after each 50 episodes.

Preliminary results discussed in Subsect. 4.1 are for the original version of the *Ant-Q* algorithm, whilst experiments with dynamic environments and updating strategies are given in Subsect. 4.2.

4.1 Preliminary Discussion of the Learning Parameters

Initial experiments were generated to evaluate the impact of the learning parameters and consequently were adjusted to the proposed strategies. Preliminary discussions are related in sub subsections A to E.

A. Learning Rate. The learning rate α shows the importance of the pheromone value when a state has been selected. To find the best values for α, experiments were conducted in the set of instances for values of α between 0 and 1. Best results were found for α between 0.2 and 0.3. For larger values, agents tend to no longer make other searches to find lower-cost trajectories once they have established a good course of action in a given environmental state. For lower values, learning is not given the importance that it requires, so that agents tend to not select different paths from those in the current policy. The best α-value for policy was 0.2, and this was used in the other experiments. It was also seen that the lower the rate of learning, the lower is the variation in policy. Figure 4 shows the efficiency of learning rates over the interval [0,.,1].

B. Discount Factor. The discount factor determines the time weight relative to the rewards received. The best values for the discount factor were between 0.2 and 0.3 as shown in Fig. 5. Smaller values led to inefficient convergence, having little relevance to agent learning. Values greater than 0.3 the discount factor receives too much weight, leading agents to local optima.

C. Exploration Rate. The exploration rate, denoted by the parameter q_0, gives the probability that an agent selects a given state. Experiments showed that the best values lay between 0.8 and 1. As the parameter value approaches zero, agent actions become increasingly random, leading to unsatisfactory solutions. The best value found for q_0 was 0.9. Agents then selected leading to lower-cost trajectories and higher pheromone concentrations. With $q_0 = 0.9$ the probability of choosing linkages with lower pheromone values was 10 %. Figure 6 shows results for q_0 in the interval $[0,..,1]$.

D. Transition Rule. The factors δ and β measure the importance of the pheromone and of the heuristic (distance) when choosing a state. The influence of the heuristic parameter β is evident. To achieve best results, the value of β must be at least 60 % lower than the value of δ. Figure 7 shows the effects of varying the factors δ and β.

E. Number of Agents. To evaluate the effect of number of agents in the system, 26 to 101 agents were used. Figure 8 shows that the best policies were found when the number of states is equal to the number of agents in the system ($m_k = x$), where x is the number of states and x_i is the number of agents in the system. It was found that when the number of agents exceeded the number of states ($m_k > x$), good solutions were not found and stagnation resulted. Thus having found a solution, agents cease to look at other states, having found a local maximum. When the number of agents is lower than the number of states ($m_k < x$), the number of episodes must increase exponentially if the best solutions are to be found.

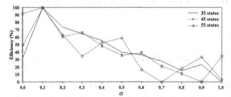

Fig. 4. Efficiency of learning rate (α).

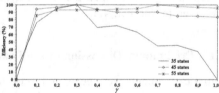

Fig. 5. Efficiency of the discount factor (γ).

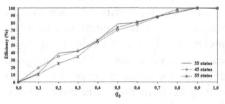

Fig. 6. Results for the parameter q_0.

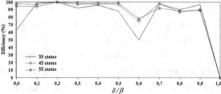

Fig. 7. Results for the transition rule δ and β.

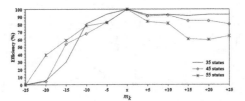

Fig. 8. Number of agents (mk).

4.2 Performance of Agents with Updating Strategies

To evaluate the strategies set out in Sect. 3, dynamic environments were generated in the set of instances eil51. Agent performance was evaluated in terms of the percentage change (percent of changes (10–20 %) in environment for a window $t_w = 100$) generated in the environment after each 100 episodes. This time window $t_w = 100$) was used because past studies have shown that the algorithm converged well in environments in around 60 states [6].

Change was introduced as follows: at each 100 episodes, the environment produces a set of alterations. The changes were made arbitrarily in a way that simulated alterations in regions that were partially-known or subject to noise. Thus, environments with 51 states had 10 states altered when 20 % change occurred. Moreover, alterations were then simulated for the space with limiting field of depth 1 and 2, so that change in state positions was restricted, thus simulating the gradual dynamically changing problems of the real world. Equation 12 is used to calculate the number of altered states in $t_w = 100$.

$$\text{changes}_{t_w=100} = \frac{\#\text{states}}{100} \times \#\text{percent} \tag{12}$$

The results of the experiments compare the three strategies with the policy found using the original *Ant-Q* algorithm. The learning parameters used in simulation were the best of those reported in Subsect. 4.1. In most cases, each strategy required a smaller number of episodes, since the combination of rewards led to better values by which agents reached convergence when policies were updated. Figures 9, 10, 11 and 12 show how the algorithm converged in the set of instances eil51. The X-axis in these figures shows the t_i episodes; the Y-axis shows policy costs (Hamiltonian cycle as a percentage) obtained in each episode, which 100 % refers to the best policy compute (optimal policy).

Figures 9, 10, 11 and 12 show that the global policy obtained when the strategies are used is better than that of the original *Ant-Q*. The *mean global* strategy is seen to be most adequate for environments where changes are greater (Figs. 10 and 12). This is because this strategy uses all the reward values within the environment. However, agents reach convergence only slowly when the environment is little changed, since altered states will have lower rewards in their linkages than the linkages that define the current best solution. Nevertheless the *global distance* strategy was also more robust in environments with few changes (Figs. 9 and 11). When the environment is altered, the strategy seeks to modify rewards in proportion to the amount of environmental

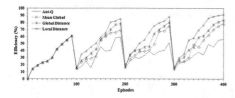

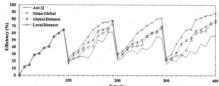

Fig. 9. Limiting field = 1; Change = 10 %.   **Fig. 10.** Limiting field = 1; Change = 20 %.

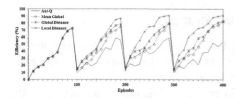

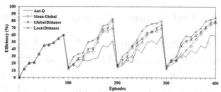

Fig. 11. Limiting field = 2; Change = 10 %.   **Fig. 12.** Limiting field = 2; Change = 20 %.

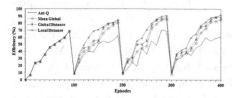

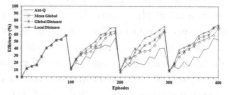

Fig. 13. Limiting field = **5**; Change = 10 %.   **Fig. 14.** Limiting field = **5**; Change = 20 %.

change. Thus, the effect of updating reduces the impact resulting from change, causing agents to converge uniformly. The *local distance* strategy only takes account of local changes, so that updating of policies by means of this strategy works best when the reward values are larger, as in later episodes.

In general, the strategies succeed in improving policy using fewer episodes. They update global policy, and accumulate good reward values, when the number of episodes is sufficiently large. When learning begins, policy is less sensitive to the strategies, so that policy performance is improved after updating. Some strategies can estimate values that are inappropriate for current policy, mainly after many episodes and environmental changes result in local maxima.

One point concerns the effect of the limiting field (adjacent to the cartesian position) on strategies. Even with the limiting field restricted, the strategies improve the algorithm's convergence. In other experiments where the limiting field was set to 5, the efficiency of the *Ant-Q* algorithm is lower (19 %) when compared with the best strategy (Figs. 13 and 14).

The *mean global* strategy is better when the limiting field is less than 5 (as in Figs. 9, 10, 11 and 12). Since updating uses the mean of all pheromone values, the value for linkages between altered states is the same. The *global distance* and *local distance* strategies converge rapidly when the limiting field is 5 (Figs. 13 and 14).

This is because updating is proportional to the length of each linkage connected to an altered state. Thus linkages which are not part of the best policy have their pheromone values reduced.

We also generate experiments in others environments of different dimensions, 35, 45 and 55 states. Note that a number of states S can generate a long solution space, in which the number of possible policy is $|A||^S|$. The quality of policies in such environments did not change significantly ($\pm$ 1.9 %) and the efficiency of best strategy compared with the results of the set of instances eil76 is lower (14 %).

5   Conclusions and Discussions

Collective behavior when coordinated assign individual a system skills (rewards) and patterns of behavior that enhance the interaction. In a system with social features coordination among individuals is necessary because the exchange of information should benefit both the individual and collective behavior. The social behavior is when two or more individuals are mutually dependent on each other for the execution of tasks in a social environment.

Methods for coordination based on learning by rewards have been the subject of recent research by a number of researchers, who have reported various applications using intelligent agents [9, 13, 22]. In this scheme, learning occurs by trial and error when an agent interacts with the surrounding environment, or with its neighbors. The source of learning is the agent's own experience, which contributes to defining a policy of action which maximizes overall performance.

Adequate coordination between agents that use learning algorithms depends on the values of fitted parameters if best solutions are to be found. Swarm-based optimization techniques therefore use rewards (pheromone) that influence how agents behave, generating policies that improve coordination and the system's global behavior.

Applying learning agents to the problem of coordinating multi-agent systems is being used more and more frequently. This is because it is generally necessary for models of coordination to adapt in complex problems, eliminating and/or reducing deficiencies in traditional coordinating mechanisms [23].

Results obtained when the updating strategies for policies in dynamic environments are used show that performance of the *Ant-Q* algorithm is superior to its performance at discovering best global policy in the absence of such strategies. Although individual characteristics vary from one strategy to another, the agents succeed in improving policy through global and local updating, confirming that the strategies can be used where environments are changing over time.

Experiments using the proposed strategies show that, although their computational cost is greater, their results are satisfactory because better solutions are found in a smaller number of episodes. However further experiments are needed to answer questions that remain open. For example, coordination could be achieved using only the more significant parameters. A heuristic function could be used to accelerate *Ant-Q*, to indicate the choice of action taken and to limit the space searched within the system. Updating the policy could be achieved by using other coordination procedures, avoiding stagnation and local maxima. Some of these strategies are found in

[2, 9]. A further question is concerned with evaluating the algorithm under scenarios with more states and other characteristics. These hypotheses and issues will be explored in future research.

Acknowledgements. This research is supported by the Program for Research Support of UTFPR - campus Pato Branco, DIRPPG (Directorate of Research and Post-Graduation) and *Fundação Araucária* (Araucaria Foundation of Parana State).

References

1. Wooldridge, M.J.: An Introduction to MultiAgent Systems. Wiley, Chichester (2002)
2. Ribeiro, R., Favarim F., Barbosa, M.A.C., Borges, A.P., Dordal, B.O., Koerich, A.L., Enembreck, F.: Unified algorithm to improve reinforcement learning in dynamic environments: an instance-based approach. In: 14th International Conference on Enterprise Information Systems (ICEIS'12), Wroclaw, Poland, pp. 229–238 (2012)
3. Mihaylov, M., Tuyls, K., Nowé, A.: Decentralized learning in wireless sensor networks. In: Taylor, M.E., Tuyls, K. (eds.) ALA 2009. LNCS, vol. 5924, pp. 60–73. Springer, Heidelberg (2010)
4. Chaharsooghi, S.K., Heydari, J., Zegordi, S.H.: A reinforcement learning model for supply chain ordering management: an application to the beer game. J. Decision Support Syst. **45**(4), 949–959 (2008)
5. Dorigo, M.: Optimization, Learning and Natural Algorithms. Ph.D. thesis, Politecnico di Milano, Itália (1992)
6. Ribeiro, R., Enembreck, F.: A sociologically inspired heuristic for optimization algorithms: a case study on ant systems. expert systems with applications. Expert Syst. Appl. **40**(5), 1814–1826 (2012)
7. Sudholt, D.: Theory of swarm intelligence. In: Proceedings of the 13th Annual Conference Companion on Genetic and Evolutionary Computation (GECCO '11), pp. 1381–1410. ACM, New York (2011)
8. Dorigo, M., Gambardella, L.M.: A study of some properties of Ant-Q. In: Proceedings of PPSN Fourth International Conference on Parallel Problem Solving From Nature, pp. 656–665 (1996)
9. Ribeiro, R., Borges, A.P., Enembreck, F.: Interaction models for multiagent reinforcement learning. In: International Conference on Computational Intelligence for Modelling Control and Automation - CIMCA08, Vienna, Austria, pp. 1–6 (2008)
10. Gambardella, L.M., Dorigo, M.: Ant-Q: a reinforcement learning approach to the TSP. In: Proceedings of ML-95, Twelfth International Conference on Machine Learning, pp. 252–260 (1995)
11. Reinelt, G.: TSPLIB - a traveling salesman problem library. ORSA J. Comput. **3**, 376–384 (1991)
12. Dorigo, M., Maniezzo, V., Colorni, A.: Ant system: optimization by a colony of cooperting agents. IEEE Trans. Syst., Man, Cybern.-Part B **26**(1), 29–41 (1996)
13. Watkins, C.J.C.H., Dayan, P.: Q-Learning. Mach. Learn. **8**(3), 279–292 (1992)
14. Guntsch, M., Middendorf, M.: Applying population based ACO to dynamic optimization problems. In: Proceedings of Third International Workshop ANTS, pp. 111–122 (2003)
15. Sim, K.M., Sun, W.H.: Multiple ant-colony optimization for network routing. In: Proceedings of the First International Symposium on Cyber Worlds, pp. 277–281 (2002)

16. Li, Y., Gong, S.: Dynamic ant colony optimization for TSP. Int. J. Adv. Manuf. Technol. **22**(7–8), 528–533 (2003)
17. Lee, S.G., Jung, T.U., Chung, T.C.: Improved ant agents system by the dynamic parameter decision. In Proceedings of the IEEE International Conference on Fuzzy Systems, pp. 666–669 (2001)
18. Gambardella, L.M., Taillard, E.D., Dorigo, M.: Ant colonies for the QAP. Technical report, IDSIA, Lugano, Switzerland (1997)
19. Stutzle, T., Hoos, H.: MAX-MIN Ant system and local search for the traveling salesman problem. In: Proceedings of the IEEE International Conference on Evolutionary Computation, pp. 309–314 (1997)
20. Guntsch, M., Middendorf, M.: Pheromone modification strategies for ant algorithms applied to dynamic TSP. In: Proceedings of the Workshop on Applications of Evolutionary Computing, pp. 213–222 (2001)
21. Christofides, N., Eilon, S.: Expected distances in distribution problems. Oper. Res. Q. **20**, 437–443 (1969)
22. Tesauro, G.: Temporal difference learning and TD-Gammon. Commun. ACM **38**(3), 58–68 (1995)
23. Enembreck, F., Ávila, B.C., Scalabrin, E.E., Barthes, J.P.: Distributed constraint optimization for scheduling in CSCWD. In: International Conference on Computer Supported Cooperative Work in Design, Santiago, vol. 1, pp. 252–257 (2009)
24. Hao, J., Leung, H.-F.: The dynamics of reinforcement social learning in cooperative multiagent systems. In: Proceedings of the 23rd. International Joint Conference on Artificial Intelligence (IJCAI'13), Beijing, China, pp. 184–190 (2013)
25. Kötzing, T., Frank, N., Röglin, H., Witt, C.: Theoretical analysis of two ACO approaches for the traveling salesman problem. Swarm Intell. **6**(1), 1–21 (2012)
26. Brambilla, M., Ferrante, E., Birattari, M., Dorigo, M.: Swarm robotics: a review from the swarm engineering perspective. Swarm Intell. **7**(1), 1–41 (2013)

Optimizing Power, Heating, and Cooling Capacity on a Decision-Guided Energy Investment Framework

Chun-Kit Ngan[1]([X]), Alexander Brodsky[1], Nathan Egge[1], and Erik Backus[2]

[1] Department of Computer Science, George Mason University, 4400 University Drive, Fairfax, VA 22030, USA
{cngan, brodsky, negge}@gmu.edu
[2] Facilities Management Department, George Mason University, 4400 University Drive, Fairfax, VA 22030, USA
ebackus@gmu.edu

Abstract. We propose a Decision-Guided Energy Investment (DGEI) Framework to optimize power, heating, and cooling capacity. The DGEI framework is designed to support energy managers to (1) use the analytical and graphical methodology to determine the best investment option that satisfies the designed evaluation parameters, such as return on investment (ROI) and greenhouse gas (GHG) emissions; (2) develop a DGEI optimization model to solve energy investment problems that the operating expenses are minimal in each considered investment option; (3) implement the DGEI optimization model using the IBM Optimization Programming Language (OPL) with historical and projected energy demand data, i.e., electricity, heating, and cooling, to solve energy investment optimization problems; and (4) conduct an experimental case study for a university campus microgrid and utilize the DGEI optimization model and its OPL implementations, as well as the analytical and graphical methodology to make an investment decision and to measure trade-offs among cost savings, investment costs, maintenance expenditures, replacement charges, operating expenses, GHG emissions, and ROI for all the considered options.

Keywords: Decision guidance · Energy investment · Optimization model

1 Introduction

Sustainable enterprise development has been considered a significant and competitive strategy of corporate growth in manufacturing and service organizations. A significant part of sustainable development involves new technologies for local electricity, heating, and cooling generation. Making optimal decisions on planning and invest-ment of these technologies to support commercial and industrial facilities is an involved problem because of complex operational dependencies of these technologies. This is exactly the focus of this paper.

Currently, the existing approaches to support the optimization of energy plants can be divided into two categories: (1) optimal operation of an energy system and (2)

© Springer International Publishing Switzerland 2014
S. Hammoudi et al. (Eds.): ICEIS 2013, LNBIP 190, pp. 154–173, 2014.
DOI: 10.1007/978-3-319-09492-2_10

a better plant-process design [1]. The former category is related to the optimized scheduling of an electric power plant. Some researchers, such as Bojic and Stojanovic [2], proposed an optimization procedure based on a MILP solver [3] to provide an operation diagram which allows users to find an optimum composition of energy consumption that minimizes the operating expenses of an energy system [4–9]. The latter approach includes the analysis of simulations carried out to determine the most suitable matching between a plant and its loads that could increase the plant power output. Some researchers, e.g., Savola et al. [10], did extensive research to propose an off-design simulation and mathematical modelling of the operation at part loads and a Mixed-Integer Non-Linear Programming (MINLP) optimization model for increasing power production [11, 12]. However, neither of the above approaches considers optimizing the complex interactions between the existing components and the newly added energy equipment that would result in a higher operating cost, such as the charges on electricity and gas consumptions, as well as significant environmental impacts, i.e., greenhouse gas (GHG) emissions, e.g., carbon dioxide (CO_2) and mono-nitrogen oxide (NO_x). Without considering such interactions for every time interval over an investment time horizon, it would be impossible to make optimal recommendations on energy planning and investment.

Thus this paper focuses on addressing the above shortcomings. More specifically, the contributions of this paper are as follows. First, we propose a Decision-Guided Energy Investment (DGEI) Framework. Given electricity, heating, and cooling generation processes, utility contracts, historical and projected demand, facility expansions, and Quality of Service (QoS) requirements, the DGEI framework is designed to recommend optimal settings of decision control variables. These decision control variables include the amount of electricity, heating, and cooling that is generated by the supply of water and gas, which is inputted to each deployed component in every time interval. The goal of the DGEI framework is to learn optimal values of those decision control variables in order to minimize the total operating cost within the required quality of service and within the bound for GHG emissions, as well as to take into account all components' interactions. Second, to support the DGEI framework, we develop a DGEI optimization model, i.e., a MILP formulation construct, to solve the adjusted cost minimization problem. Furthermore, we implement the DGEI optimization model by using the IBM Optimization Programming Language (OPL) [13, 14]. Third, we propose an analytical and graphical methodology to determine the best available investment option based upon the evaluation parameters. The parameters include investment costs, maintenance expenditures, replacement charges, operating expenses, cost savings, return on investment (ROI), and GHG emissions. Finally, we use the methodology and the DGEI framework to conduct an experimental case study on the microgrid at the Fairfax campus of George Mason University (GMU). This study has been conducted and used by the GMU Facilities Management Department (FMD) to make actual investment decisions.

The rest of the paper is organized as follows. Using the GMU Fairfax campus microgrid as an example, we describe its energy investment problem in Sect. 2. We explain our DGEI framework and optimization model in Sect. 3 and demonstrate the OPL implementation in Sect. 4. In Sect. 5, we present the analytical and graphical methodology to determine an optimal investment option. In Sect. 6, we conduct the experimental analysis on the GMU energy investment case and illustrate the relationships among the investment costs, ROI, and GHG emissions of the various options in tabular and graphical formats. We also explain and draw the conclusion for the investment options from the graphs and tables in detail on the GMU energy investment problem. In Sect. 7, we conclude and briefly outline the future work.

2   Problem Description of Real Case Study

Consider the real case study at GMU, in which the GMU Facilities Management Department (FMD) is planning to extend and or expand the existing energy equipment in order to meet the current and future demand of electricity, heating, and cooling across the expanding Fairfax campus in Virginia. Presently, the GMU existing energy facilities at the Fairfax campus operate a centralized heating and cooling plant (CHCP) system and utilize the electricity purchased from the Dominion Virginia Power Company (DVPC) to satisfy all the energy demand. Over the past 10 years, the campus has experienced a significant growth on a square-foot basis in terms of land use. Since the campus continues its expansion at a rapid rate, the existing CHCP system and the electricity consumption have reached a saturated point where the current capacity and facilities will not be able to satisfy the future energy demand, i.e., electricity, heating, and cooling. For these reasons, a study has been conducted to determine the best available investment option, e.g., a new cogeneration (CoGen) plant, with regards to a possible methodology to meet the current and future electricity, heating, and cooling demand, while also addressing the optimal operations of the newly added facility with the existing energy equipment.

The diagram in Fig. 1 depicts the GMU energy generation process which supplies heating, cooling, and electricity to the entire Fairfax campus. The GMU energy facilities have a CHCP system to supply the hot and cold water (see the red and blue resources) which are distributed across the facilities to the campus buildings to meet the heating and cooling demand (see the upper two sub-processes on the right), i.e., heating and air-conditioning to the buildings. To supply the heating and cooling to the campus buildings, the CHCP system needs the inputs, i.e., natural gas (see the yellow resource on the left), water (see the light blue resource on the left), and electric power (see the green resource on the left). These resources come from the gas supply, i.e., Washington Gas Light Company (WGLC), the water supply, i.e., Fairfax County Water Authority (FCWA), and the electricity supply, i.e., Dominion Virginia Power Company (DVPC), correspondingly. In addition, the facilities also need to satisfy the electricity demand across the entire campus, where the electricity demand is beyond the demand from the CHCP consumption. Any excessive electric power supply can also be resold to the DVPC (see the electricity resell on the right). Furthermore, the facilities also commit a curtailment demand (see the curtailment demand on the right) to the energy curtailment program through EnergyConnect (EC), Inc. Both the electricity resell and the curtailment commitment can bring certain revenues and savings to offset the overall operational costs on a monthly basis and the capital expenditures in the long run. The facilities also generate greenhouse gas (GHG) emissions, such as carbon dioxide (CO_2) (see the black resource at the bottom right).

Given the expansion of the GMU Fairfax campus, in addition to the increasing electricity demand, the heating and cooling demand is also expected to increase. The CHCP system will not have enough capacity to meet the future need. The GMU plan is to employ a procurement strategy, i.e., the deployment of the best available investment option, which will satisfy projected demand and minimize investment costs, maintenance expenditures, replacement charges, operating expenses, and GHG emissions, as well as maximize cost savings and return on investment (ROI) at the same time. The FMD managers are now considering some viable options. One of the considerable options is to integrate a new cogeneration (CoGen) plant (see the lower sub-process in the middle), i.e., the Combined Heating and Power (CHP) Plant [1, 15], into the existing facilities shown in Fig. 1. The new CoGen plant has turbines to generate electricity to complement the electricity demand, uses the generated heat as a by-product to complement the heating demand, and collaborates with the ammonia process technology [16] to supply the cooling demand. Now, the challenging question is how to analytically determine the best investment option that satisfies all the energy demand, i.e., electricity, heating, and cooling, at the lowest operating costs.

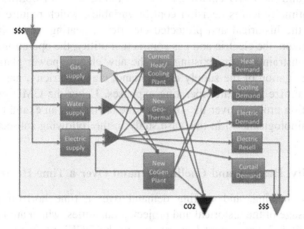

Fig. 1. Prospective heating, cooling, and electric power facilities at the GMU Fairfax campus.

3 Decision-Guided Energy Investment (DGEI) Framework and Optimization Model

To answer the above question, we propose the DGEI framework. This framework is composed of six energy-investment libraries, i.e., Energy Generation Process (EGP), Energy Contractual Utility (ECU), Energy Historical Demand (EHD), Energy Future Demand (EFD), Energy Facility Expansion (EFE), Quality of Service (QoS) requirements, and a DGEI optimizer. The EGP is an extensible library that enables domain experts to construct an energy generation process to supply electricity, heating, and cooling. The ECU is a library that contains energy contractual terms for calculating bill utilities, e.g., an electricity bill, a water bill, and a gas bill. The EHD and EFD are the libraries that store historical and projected energy demand respectively. The EFE library archives the facility expansion of an organization in terms of square-footage increase. The QoS library stores the QoS requirements that the energy facilities of an organization need to meet, e.g., the maximal power interruptions allowed per monthly pay period in an organization. The DGEI optimizer supports energy managers to utilize all the libraries, i.e., EGP, ECU, EHD, EFD, EFE, and QoS, as inputs to the decision optimization process, which minimizes operating expenses and maximize cost savings. This decision optimization process not only optimizes the interactions between the existing and the considerable energy facility options but also minimizes the environmental impacts on the surroundings, i.e., minimizing the GHG emissions. In addition to the GHG emissions, energy managers also utilize (1) return on investment (ROI), i.e., the gain return efficiency among different investments, (2) the investment costs, i.e., an amount spent to acquire a long-term asset, and (3) equipment expenses, i.e., maintenance expenditures plus replacement charges, to evaluate all the available investments and then to determine the best option.

To solve an energy investment optimization problem in terms of minimizing the operating cost and the GHG emissions is to formulate a DGEI optimization model. This model optimally learns decision control variables, which require several input data sets, i.e., the historical and projected electricity, heating, and cooling demand over a time horizon, the electric and gas contractual utility, the operational parameters and capacity constraints of the existing and the new electric power plants, as well as the energy aggregation of the supply and demand, e.g., electricity, gas, heating, and cooling, to minimize the entire operating expenses. Using the GMU energy investment optimization problem over the 10-year time horizon as an example, we explain the above terminologies used in this case study in the following subsections.

3.1   Electricity, Heating, and Cooling Demand Over a Time Horizon

The electricity, heating, and cooling demand over a time horizon is the input, including the usage of the historical and projected quantities, which are provided from the GMU Facilities Management Department, to the DGEI optimization model that requires the domain users to define all (i.e., past plus future), past, and future power intervals over the 10-year time horizon respectively.

- AllPowerIntervals is a set of all powerIntervals, where each powerInterval is a tuple which includes several attributes, i.e., pInterval, payPeriod, year, month, day, hour, and weekDay. We use negative and zero integers to represent the past time horizon and positive integers to denote the future time horizon. For example, pInterval is an hourly time interval of the energy demand, where $-8759 \leq$ pInterval ≤ 78840. payPeriod is a monthly pay period of the energy demand, where $-11 \leq$ payPeriod ≤ 108. Other attributes' intervals include $2011 \leq$ year ≤ 2020, $1 \leq$ month ≤ 12, $1 \leq$ day ≤ 31, $0 \leq$ hour ≤ 23, and $0 \leq$ weekDay ≤ 6.
- PastPowerIntervals is a set of past powerIntervals of tuples, where $-8759 \leq$ pInterval ≤ 0, $-11 \leq$ payPeriod ≤ 0, year $= 2011$, $1 \leq$ month ≤ 12, $1 \leq$ day ≤ 31, $0 \leq$ hour ≤ 23, and $0 \leq$ weekDay ≤ 6.

- FuturePowerIntervals is a set of future powerIntervals of tuples, where $1 \leq$ pInterval ≤ 78840, $1 \leq$ payPeriod ≤ 108, $2012 \leq$ year ≤ 2020, $1 \leq$ month ≤ 12, $1 \leq$ day ≤ 31, $0 \leq$ hour ≤ 23, and $0 \leq$ weekDay ≤ 6.

After declaring the power intervals, the quantities of electricity, heating, and cooling demand can be stored in their arrays over their power intervals. These three quantities of demand are provided by the GMU Facilities Management Department.

- demandKw[AllPowerIntervals] ≥ 0 is an array of electricity demand over the AllPowerIntervals. This array stores both the historical and the projected demand over the PastPowerIntervals and the FuturePowerIntervals respectively.
- demandHeat[FuturePowerIntervals] ≥ 0 is an array of projected heating demand over the FuturePowerIntervals.
- demandCool[FuturePowerIntervals] ≥ 0 is an array of projected cooling demand over the FuturePowerIntervals.

3.2   Electric and Gas Contractual Utility

To determine the total operating cost, we need to compute the consumption expenses of electricity and gas supply according to their utility contracts. The consumption expenses of electricity include both the peak demand charge and the total power consumption charge that are explained in detail as follows.

3.2.1   Peak Demand Charge

For the electricity supply, utilityKw[AllPowerIntervals] ≥ 0 is an array of electricity supplied from the DVPC over the AllPowerIntervals.

historicUtilityKw[i] is an array of past electricity demand from the GMU, i.e., `historicUtilityKw[i] = demandKw[i]`, which satisfies the constraint, i.e., `utilityKw[i] == historicUtilityKw[i]`, where i $\in$ PastPowerIntervals. This constraint is to assure that the electricity consumed by the GMU in the past year, i.e., 2011, is equivalent to the supply from the DVPC.

payPeriodSupplyDemand[p] is the peak demand usage per future pay period (p). This peak demand usage meets the below contractual constraints (C1 and C2) and is determined based upon the highest of either (C1) or (C2):

C1: The highest average kilowatt measured in any hourly time interval of the current billing month during the on-peak hours of either between 10 a.m. and 10 p.m. from Monday to Friday for the billing months of June through September or between 7 a.m. and 10 p.m. from Monday to Friday for all other billing months.

C2: 90 % of the highest kilowatt of demand at the same location as determined under (C1) above during the billing months of June through September of the preceding eleven billing months.

The logic constraints of both *C1* and *C2* can be expressed as follows:

```
if (i.payPeriod == p ∧ i.weekDay ≥ 1 ∧ i.weekDay ≤ 5 ∧ ((i.month ≥ 6
∧ i.month ≤ 9 ∧ i.hour ≥ 10 ∧ i.hour ≤ 22) ∨ (i.month ≤ 5 ∧ i.month ≥
10 ∧ i.hour ≥ 7 ∧ i.hour ≤ 22)))
    payPeriodSupplyDemand[p] ≥ utilitykW[i]
else if (i.month ≥ 6 ∧ i.month ≤ 9 ∧ i.payPeriod ≥ p - 11 ∧
i.payPeriod ≤ p ∧ i.weekPay ≥ 1∧ i.weekDay ≤ 5 ∧ i.hour ≥ 10 ∧ i.hour
≤ 22)
    payPeriodSupplyDemand[p] ≥ 0.9 * utilitykW[i];, where i ∈
```

AllPowerIntervals, p ∈ FuturePayPeriods, and $1 \leq$ FuturePayPeriods ≤ 108. Using these logic constraints, we can determine the optimal peak demand usage per future pay period, which consumes more than the expected electricity supply per powerInterval from the DVPC.

generationDemandCharge[p], i.e., `generationDemandCharge[p]` $= 8.124 *$ `payPeriodSupplyDemand[p];`, is the Electricity Supply (ES) service charge, i.e., the peak demand charge, where p ∈ FuturePayPeriods, and 8.124 is the dollar charge per kW.

3.2.2   Total Power Consumption Charge

payPeriodKwh[p] is the total power consumption per future pay period, i.e., `pay-PeriodKwh[p]` $= \sum$`utilitykW[i];`, where i ∈ AllPowerIntervals, p ∈ FuturePayPeriods, and i.payPeriod = p.

payPeriodKwhCharge[p] is the total kWh charge per future pay period, i.e., payPeriodKwhCharge[p] ≥ 0, which satisfies the below contractual constraints:

```
if (payPeriodKwh[p] ≤ 24000)
    payPeriodKwhCharge[p] = 0.01174 * payPeriodKwh[p]
else if (payPeriodKwh[p] ≤ 210000)
    payPeriodKwhCharge[p]   =   0.01174   *   24000   +   0.00606   *
    (payPeriodKwh[p] - 24000)
else
    payPeriodKwhCharge[p]  =  0.01174  *  24000  +  0.00606  *  186000  +
    0.00244 * (payPeriodKwh[p] - 210000);,
```

where p ∈ FuturePayPeriods, 0.01174 is the dollar charge of the first 24000 kWh consumed, 0.00606 is the dollar charge of the next 186000 kWh consumed, and 0.00244 is the dollar charge of the additional kWh consumed. Note that if payPeriodSupplyDemand[p] is 1000 kW or more, 210 kWh for each peak demand usage over 1000 kW is added to the total power consumption to calculate payPeriodKwhCharge[p].

3.2.3   Total Electricity Cost

The total electricity cost per future pay period is the sum of payPeriodKwhCharge[p] and generationDemandCharge[p], i.e., `electricCostPerFuturePayPeriod` $= ($`payPeriodKwhCharge[p]` $+$ `generationDemandCharge[p]`$);$, where p ∈ FuturePayPeriods.

The total electricity cost of all the FuturePayPeriods is the aggregations of all the total electricity costs per future pay period, i.e., `electricCost =` $\sum$ `(payPeriodKwhCharge[p] + generationDemandCharge[p]);`, where p $\in$ FuturePayPeriods.

Table 1. Descriptions for the constant values in the DGEI optimization model of the GMU energy investment problem.

Constant	Description
0.9	Percentage of the highest kW of demand during the billing months of June through September of the preceding 11 billing months
8.124	Amount ($) of Electricity Supply (ES) demand charged per kW
24000	First ES kWh
0.01174	Amount ($) of the first 24000 ES kWh charged per kWh
186000	Next ES kWh
0.00606	Amount ($) of the next 186000 ES kWh charged per kWh
210000	Sum of the first ES kWh and the next ES kWh
0.00244	Amount ($) of the additional ES kWh charged per kWh
210	kWh for each ES kW of demand over 1000 kW

Table 1 summarizes the descriptions of all the constant values from the electric utility contract used in the DGEI optimization model for the GMU energy investment problem.

3.2.4   Total Gas Consumption Charge

Regarding the gas supply, utilityGas[FuturePowerIntervals] ≥ 0 is an array of gas supplied from the WGLC over the FuturePowerIntervals. The total gas cost of all the FuturePowerIntervals is the aggregations of all the total gas utility per future power interval, i.e., `gasCost = (`$\sum$`(utilityGas[i]/btuPerDth)) *` `gasPricePerDth;`, where i $\in$ FuturePowerIntervals, btuPerDth = 1000000 BTU, which is the amount of energy per decatherm, and gasPricePerDth = $6.5, which is the gas charge per decatherm.

3.2.5   Total Operating Cost

The total operating cost is the sum of the total electricity cost of all the future pay periods and the total gas cost of all the future power intervals, i.e., `totalCost = electricCost + gasCost;`.

3.3   Operational Parameters and Capacity Constraints of the CHCP and the Cogen Plant

In addition to the supply and demand of gas and electricity, the operational parameters and the capacity constraints of the CHCP and the CoGen plant are also considered.

3.3.1 The CHCP Plant

For the CHCP plant, gasIntoCHCP[FuturePowerIntervals] ≥ 0 is an array of natural gas input to the CHCP over the FuturePowerIntervals to generate the heat supply. kwIntoCHCP[FuturePowerIntervals] ≥ 0 is an array of power input to the CHCP over the FuturePowerIntervals to generate the cool supply. heatOutCHCP[FuturePower-Intervals] ≥ 0 is an array of heat output from the CHCP over the FuturePowerIn-tervals to satisfy the partial heating demand. coolOutCHCP[FuturePowerIntervals] ≥ 0 is an array of cool output from the CHCP over the FuturePowerIntervals to satisfy the partial cooling demand. The CHCP constraints include:

- `heatOutCHCP[i] * gasPerHeatUnit` $\leq$ `gasIntoCHCP[i]` ;, i.e., the amount of gas consumed to generate the heat cannot be more than that of the gas input;
- `coolOutCHCP[i] * kwhPerCoolUnit` $\leq$ `kwIntoCHCP[i]` ;, i.e., the amount of electric power consumed to generate the cool cannot be more than that of the power input;
- `heatOutCHCP[i]` $\leq$ `chcpMaxHeatPerHr` ;, i.e., the amount of heat generated cannot be more than the maximal heat output of the CHCP; and
- `coolOutCHCP[i]` $\leq$ `chcpMaxCoolPerHr` ;, i.e., the amount of cool generated cannot be more than the maximal cool output of the CHCP, where i $\in$ Future-PowerIntervals, gasPerHeatUnit = (1 /0.78), and kwhPerCoolUnit = (1 /0.94).

3.3.2 The CoGen Plant

For the CoGen plant, gasIntoCogen[FuturePowerIntervals] ≥ 0 is an array of gas input to the CoGen plant over the FuturePowerIntervals to generate the power supply. kwOutCogen[FuturePowerIntervals] ≥ 0 is an array of power output from the CoGen plant over the FuturePowerIntervals to satisfy the partial electricity demand. hea-tOutCogen[FuturePowerIntervals] ≥ 0 is an array of heat output from the CoGen plant over the FuturePowerIntervals to satisfy the partial heating demand. coolOut-Cogen[FuturePowerIntervals] ≥ 0 is an array of cool output from the CoGen plant over the FuturePowerIntervals to satisfy the partial cooling demand. The constraints of the CoGen plant include:

- `kwOutCogen[i] * cogenGasPerKwh` $\leq$ `gasIntoCogen[i]` ;, i.e., the amount of gas consumed to generate the power cannot be more than that of the gas input;
- `kwOutCogen[i]` $\leq$ `cogenMaxKw`;, i.e., the amount of power generated cannot be more than the maximal electricity output of the CoGen plant;
- `heatOutCogen[i]` $\leq$ `cogenHeatPerKwh * kwOutCogen[i]`;, i.e., the amount of heat generated cannot be more than the maximal heat supply that is restricted by the power output of the CoGen plant;
- `heatOutCogen[i]` $\leq$ `cogenMaxHeatPerHr * (kwOutCogen[i]/co-genMaxKw)` ;, i.e., the amount of heat generated cannot be more than the maximal heat output of the CoGen plant;
- `coolOutCogen[i]` $\leq$ `(cogenMaxHeatPerHr * (kwOutCogen[i]/co-genMaxKw) - heatOutCogen[i]) * cogenHeatToCoolRatio`;, i.e., the amount of cool generated cannot be more than the maximal cool supply that is restricted by the power and heat output of the CoGen plant; and

- coolOutCogen[i] ≤ cogenMaxCoolPerHr;, i.e., the amount of cool generated cannot be more than the maximal cool output of the CoGen plant,

where i ∈ FuturePowerIntervals, cogenMaxKw = 7200 kW is the maximal power output, cogenHeatPerKwh = 10300 kWh is the amount of heat generated per kWh, cogenHeatToCoolRatio = cogenMaxCoolPerHr/cogenMaxHeatPerHr is the ratio of converting heat to cool supply, cogenMaxHeatPerHr = 40000000 BTU is the maximal heat supply of the CoGen plant per hour, cogenMaxCoolPerHr = 2400 Tons is the maximal cool supply of the CoGen plant per hour, cogenGasPerKwh = gasB-TUPerGallon/kWhPerGallon/cogenGasToKwhEfficiency is the amount of natural gas consumed per kWh, for gasBTUPerGallon = 114000 BTU is the amount of energy generated per gallon of gas, kwhPerGallon = 33.41 is the amount of kWh generated per gallon of gas, and cogenGasToKwhEfficiency = 0.33 is the efficiency of the CoGen plant to generate power from natural gas.

3.4 Energy Aggregations of Supply and Demand

The aggregations of energy supply and demand within the entire energy system include:

- kwIntoCHCP[i] + demandKw[i] ≤ utilityKw[i] + kwOutCogen[i];, i.e., the amount of power input to the CHCP and the power demand from the GMU cannot exceed the amount of power supply provided from the DVPC and the power output generated from the CoGen plant, where i ∈ FuturePowerIntervals.
- demandReduction[i] ≤ (utilityKw[i] + kwOutCogen[i]) - (kwInto CHCP[i] + demandKw[i]);, i.e., the power supply reduction cannot exceed the difference between the total power supply (utilityKw[i] + kwOutCogen[i]) and the total power demand (kwIntoCHCP[i] + demandKw[i]), where demand Reduction[FuturePowerIntervals] ≥ 0 is an array of extra power supply that can be cut from the power inputs over the FuturePowerIntervals, and i ∈ Future PowerIntervals.
- ∑demandReduction[i] ≤ maxKwReductionPerPayPeriod;, i.e., the total power reductions over the future power intervals cannot exceed the allowable maximal power interruptions per future pay period, where i ∈ FuturePowerInter-vals, p ∈ FuturePayPeriods, and i.payPeriod = p.
- utilityGas[i] ≥ gasIntoCogen[i] + gasIntoCHCP[i];, i.e., the gas input to the CoGen plant and to the CHCP cannot exceed the gas supply provided from the WGLC, where i ∈ FuturePowerIntervals.
- heatOutCogen[i] + heatOutCHCP[i] ≥ demandHeat[i];, i.e., the heat demand from GMU cannot exceed the heat supply generated from the CoGen plant and the CHCP, where i ∈ FuturePowerIntervals.
- coolOutCogen[i] + coolOutCHCP[i] ≥ demandCool[i];, i.e., the cool demand from GMU cannot exceed the cool supply generated from the CoGen plant and the CHCP, where i ∈ FuturePowerIntervals.

3.5 DGEI Optimization Model

After declaring all the input data sets and the above constraints, which the input data sets need to satisfy, the DGEI optimization model for the GMU energy investment problem can be formulated as follows in Fig. 2.

Fig. 2. The DGEI optimization model for the GMU energy investment problem.

4 OPL Implementation for DGEI Optimization Model

The DGEI optimization model has been implemented by using the OPL language. Using the GMU historical data of power usage in the past year, i.e., 2011, and its projected electricity, cooling, and heating demand over a future time horizon from 2012 to 2020, we use the OPL language to implement and demonstrate the DGEI optimization model to solve the GMU energy investment problem and minimize the operating cost.

The intuition of using the OPL language is that its optimization formulation looks like the DGEI optimization model. When comparing the DGEI optimization model in Fig. 2 with the OPL formulation from Figs. 3.1, 3.2, 3.3, 3.4, 3.5, 3.6, 3.7, 3.8, 3.9, we realize that both models are very similar to each other. Only some notations and syntaxes are different that is shown in Table 2. For example, instead of using the summation sign ($\sum$) in the DGEI optimization model, the OPL language uses the keyword, "sum", to perform the aggregation. Rather than using the if-then statement in the mathematics, the OPL uses the specific construct with the implication operatior (=>).

More specifically, the OPL implementation construct is described as follows. In Fig. 3.1, from the line number 9 to 12, the value 12, i.e., the total 12 months of 2011, is assigned to the variable nbPastPayPeriods, the value 108, i.e., the total 108 months from 2012 to 2020, is assigned to the variable nbPayPeriods, and the value 0 is assigned to the maximal power interruptions, i.e., maxKwReductionPerPeriod.

Table 2. Differences between DGEI Optimization model and OPL formulation model.

DGEI optimization model	OPL formulation model
Notation: Summation Sign $\sum$ Example: $\sum(\text{demandKw}[i] - \text{kW}[i]) \leq$ $2 * \text{annualBound}$	Syntax: sum Example: sum(i in PowerIntervals : i.pInterval >= 1) (demandKw[i] − kW[i]) <= annualBound * 2
Notation: If-then Statement Example: if (payPeriodKwh[p] $\leq$ 24000) payPeriodKwhCharge[p] = 0.01174 * payPeriodKwh[p]	Syntax: => Example: (payPeriodKwh[p] <= 24000) = > (payPeriodKwhCharge[p] == 0.01174 * payPeriodKwh[p])
Notation: Where clause Example: peakDemandBound[p] $\leq$ payPeriodSupplyDemand[p], where p $\in$ PayPeriods	Syntax: forall Example: forall (p in PayPeriods) peakDemandBound[p] <= payPeriodSupplyDemand[p]

The FuturePayPeriods is ranged from 1 to 108. From the line number 15 to 23, we declare a tuple of a power interval that has the attributes, including pInterval, pay-Period, year, month, day, hour, and weekDay. The line number 25 to 27 declares and initializes AllPowerIntervals that include both PastPowerIntervals and FuturePower-Intervals. The line number 30 to 32 declares and initializes the demandKw[AllPow-erIntervals], the demandHeat[FuturePowerIntervals], and the demandCool[Future PowerIntervals] arrays.

```
 1 /***********************************************
 2  * OPL 12.4 Cogeneration Plant Analysis     *
 3  * Author: Alex Brodsky and Chun-Kit Ngan   *
 4  * Creation Date: July 24, 2012 at 8:28PM   *
 5  * Updated Date: August 12, 2012 at 03:15PM *
 6  ***********************************************/
 7
 8  //General Input Data
 9  int nbPayPeriods = ...;
10  int nbPastPayPeriods = ...;
11  float maxKwReductionPerPayPeriod = ...;
12  range FuturePayPeriods = 1 .. nbPayPeriods ;
13  float intervalSize = 1.0;
14
15  tuple powerInterval{
16      int pInterval;
17      int payPeriod;
18      int year;
19      int month;
20      int day;
21      int hour;
22      int weekDay;
23  }
24
25  {powerInterval} AllPowerIntervals = ...;
26  {powerInterval} PastPowerIntervals = {i | i in AllPowerIntervals : i.pInterval <= 0};
27  {powerInterval} FuturePowerIntervals = {i | i in AllPowerIntervals : i.pInterval >= 1};
28
29  //Demand Input Data
30  float demandKw[AllPowerIntervals] = ...;
31  float demandHeat[FuturePowerIntervals] = ...;
32  float demandCool[FuturePowerIntervals] = ...;
33
```

Fig. 3.1. General and demand input data.

Figure 3.2 declares the decision control variables, i.e., utilityKw[AllPowerInter-vals], payPeriodSupplyDemand[FuturePayPeriods], and payPeriodKwh[Futur-ePayPeriods], to compute payPeriodKwhCharge[FuturePayPeriods] and generation

DemandCharge[FuturePayPeriods] that are summed together to determine the total electricity cost over all the future pay periods while satisfying the electric contractual constraints.

```
34  //Electric Cost
35  dvar float+ utilityKw[AllPowerIntervals];
36  dvar float+ payPeriodSupplyDemand[FuturePayPeriods];
37  float historicUtilityKw[i in PastPowerIntervals] = demandKw[i];
38  dvar float+ demandReduction[FuturePowerIntervals];
39
40  dexpr float payPeriodKwh[p in FuturePayPeriods] =
41        sum(i in AllPowerIntervals : i.payPeriod == p) utilityKw[i];
42  pwlFunction kwhCost = piecewise {0.01174-> 24000; 0.00606 -> 210000; 0.00244};
43  dexpr float payPeriodKwhCharge[p in FuturePayPeriods] = kwhCost(payPeriodKwh[p]);
44  dexpr float generationDemandCharge[p in FuturePayPeriods] = 8.124 * payPeriodSupplyDemand[p];
45  dexpr float electricCost = sum(p in FuturePayPeriods)
46              (payPeriodKwhCharge[p] + generationDemandCharge[p]);
47
```

Fig. 3.2. Total electricity cost.

Figure 3.3 declares the constants, i.e., gasPricePerDth and btuPerDth, and utilityGas[FuturePowerIntervals] to calculate the total gas cost over all the future power intervals.

```
48  //Gas Cost
49  float gasPricePerDth = 6.5;
50  float btuPerDth = 1000000.0;
51  dvar float+ utilityGas[FuturePowerIntervals];
52  dexpr float gasCost = (sum(i in FuturePowerIntervals)
53              (utilityGas[i]/ btuPerDth)) * gasPricePerDth;
54
```

Fig. 3.3. Total gas cost.

Figure 3.4 declares the objective function to minimize the total operating cost, i.e., the total electricity cost plus the total gas cost.

```
55  //Objective Function
56  dexpr float totalCost = electricCost + gasCost;
57  minimize totalCost;
58
```

Fig. 3.4. Total operating cost.

Figure 3.5 declares the constants, i.e., gasPerHeatUnit, kwhPerCoolUnit, chcpMaxHeatPerHr, and chcpMaxCoolPerHr, and the arrays, i.e., gasIntoCHCP[FuturePowerIntervals], kwIntoCHCP[FuturePowerIntervals], heatOutCHCP[FuturePowerIntervals], and coolOutCHCP[FuturePowerIntervals], used in the CHCP capacity constraints.

```
59  //Central Heating and Cooling Plant
60  float gasPerHeatUnit = (1 / 0.78); //GasBTU / heatBTU
61  float kwhPerCoolUnit = (1 / 0.94); //ton / kWH
62  float chcpMaxHeatPerHr = 108000000.0;   //Total Existing Capacity Btu/hr
63  float chcpMaxCoolPerHr = 11880;      //Total Existing Capacity Ton/hr
64
65  dvar float+ gasIntoCHCP[FuturePowerIntervals];
66  dvar float+ kwIntoCHCP[FuturePowerIntervals];
67  dvar float+ heatOutCHCP[FuturePowerIntervals];
68  dvar float+ coolOutCHCP[FuturePowerIntervals];
69
```

Fig. 3.5. Operational parameters and data structures of the CHCP plant.

Figure 3.6 declares the constants from the line number 71 to 79, and the arrays, i.e., gasIntoCogen[FuturePowerIntervals], heatOutCogen[FuturePowerIntervals], coolOutCHCP[FuturePowerIntervals], and kwOutCHCP[FuturePowerIntervals], which are used in the capacity constraints of the CoGen plant.

```
70  //New Cogeneration Plant
71  float cogenMaxHeatPerHr = 40000000.0;    //Btu/hr
72  float cogenMaxCoolPerHr = 2400.0;        //ton/hr
73  float cogenMaxKw = 7200.0;               //kW
74  float cogenGasToKwhEfficiency = 0.33;
75  float gasBTUPerGallon = 114000.0;
76  float kWhPerGallon = 33.41;
77  float cogenGasPerKwh = gasBTUPerGallon/kWhPerGallon/cogenGasToKwhEfficiency; //BTU/kWh
78  float cogenHeatPerKwh = 10300.0;         //Btu/kWh - Net Heat Rate
79  float cogenHeatToCoolRatio = cogenMaxCoolPerHr / cogenMaxHeatPerHr;
80
81  dvar float+ gasIntoCogen[FuturePowerIntervals];
82  dvar float+ heatOutCogen[FuturePowerIntervals];
83  dvar float+ coolOutCogen[FuturePowerIntervals];
84  dvar float+ kwOutCogen[FuturePowerIntervals];
85
```

Fig. 3.6. Operational parameters and data structures of the CoGen plant.

Figure 3.7 defines all the capacity constraints for the CHCP and the CoGen plant.

```
86  subject to{
87  //Central Heating and Cooling Plant Constraints
88      forall (i in FuturePowerIntervals){
89          heatOutCHCP[i] * gasPerHeatUnit <= gasIntoCHCP[i];
90          coolOutCHCP[i] * kwhPerCoolUnit <= kwIntoCHCP[i] * intervalSize;
91          heatOutCHCP[i] <= chcpMaxHeatPerHr * intervalSize;
92          coolOutCHCP[i] <= chcpMaxCoolPerHr * intervalSize;
93      }
94
95  //New Cogeneration Plant Constraints
96      forall (i in FuturePowerIntervals){
97          kwOutCogen[i] * intervalSize * cogenGasPerKwh <= gasIntoCogen[i];
98          kwOutCogen[i] * intervalSize <= cogenMaxKw;
99          heatOutCogen[i] <= cogenHeatPerKwh * kwOutCogen[i] * intervalSize;
100         heatOutCogen[i] <= cogenMaxHeatPerHr * intervalSize * (kwOutCogen[i]/cogenMaxKw);
101         coolOutCogen[i] <= (cogenMaxHeatPerHr * intervalSize * (kwOutCogen[i]/cogenMaxKw)
102                            - heatOutCogen[i]) * cogenHeatToCoolRatio;
103         coolOutCogen[i] <= cogenMaxCoolPerHr * intervalSize;
104     }
105
```

Fig. 3.7. Capacity constraints of the CHCP and the CoGen plant.

Figure 3.8 defines the contractual constraints for the electricity bill.

```
106  //Electric Contractual Utility Constraints
107      forall(i in PastPowerIntervals) utilityKw[i] == historicUtilityKw[i];
108
109      forall(p in FuturePayPeriods)
110          forall(i in AllPowerIntervals : i.payPeriod == p && i.weekDay >= 1 && i.weekDay <= 5
111          && ((i.month >= 6 && i.month <= 9 && i.hour >= 10 && i.hour <= 22) ||
112              (i.month <= 5 && i.month >= 10 && i.hour >= 7 && i.hour <= 22)))
113                  payPeriodSupplyDemand[p] >= utilityKw[i];
114
115      forall(p in FuturePayPeriods)
116          forall(i in AllPowerIntervals : i.month >= 6 && i.month <= 9 &&
117          i.payPeriod >= p - 11 && i.payPeriod <= p &&
118          i.weekDay >= 1 && i.weekDay <= 5 && i.hour >= 10 && i.hour <= 22)
119                  payPeriodSupplyDemand[p] >= 0.9 * utilityKw[i];
120
121
```

Fig. 3.8. Contractual electricity utility constraints.

Figure 3.9 defines the constraints for the energy aggregations of electric power, gas, heat, and cool.

```
122  //Electric Power Aggregation
123      forall (i in FuturePowerIntervals){
124          (kwIntoCHCP[i] + demandKw[i]) <= (utilityKw[i] + kwOutCogen[i]);
125          demandReduction[i] <= (utilityKw[i] + kwOutCogen[i]) - (kwIntoCHCP[i] + demandKw[i]);
126      }
127
128      forall (p in FuturePayPeriods) {
129          (sum(i in FuturePowerIntervals: i.payPeriod == p)
130              demandReduction[i]) <= maxKwReductionPerPayPeriod;
131      }
132
133  //Gas Aggregation
134      forall (i in FuturePowerIntervals)
135          utilityGas[i] >= gasIntoCogen[i] + gasIntoCHCP[i];
136
137  //Heat Aggregation
138      forall (i in FuturePowerIntervals)
139          heatOutCogen[i] + heatOutCHCP[i] >= demandHeat[i];
140
141  //Cool Aggregation
142      forall (i in FuturePowerIntervals)
143          coolOutCogen[i] + coolOutCHCP[i] >= demandCool[i];
144  }
```

Fig. 3.9. Energy aggregations of supply and demand.

5   Analytical Methodology on Evaluation among Energy Investment Options

For domain experts being able to formulate and implement the above DGEI optimization model to determine the best investment option, we propose an analytical methodology that guides the domain experts to achieve this goal. The methodology includes six steps.

STEP 1: Collect historical energy demand, such as electricity, heating, and cooling, from each building unit, and forecast those demands in terms of growth on a square-foot basis over the future time horizon.

STEP 2: Identify all the possible energy investment options, such as the expansion of current facilities and the procurement of cogeneration plants.

STEP 3: Formulate, implement, and execute the DGEI optimization model that integrates historical and projected energy demand, electric and gas contractual utility, operational parameters and capacity constraints of energy equipment, as well as energy aggregations of supply and demand in each considered option under the assumption of optimal interactions among available resources.

STEP 4: Compute the annualized evaluation parameters for each option based upon the results from the optimization process in STEP 3.

The parameters include the investment cost (I_i), equipment cost (E_i), i.e., maintenance expenditure (M_i) plus replacement charge (R_i), operating expense (C_i), i.e., the charges on electricity and gas consumptions, cost saving (S_i), i.e., $C_0 - C_i$, where $i \geq 0$ denotes an investment option and C_0 is the operating cost of a base investment option that the other available options compare with, and return on investment (ROI_i), i.e., $S_i /(I_i - I_0)$, as well as the GHG emissions ($MTCDE_i$), i.e., $G_i * 0.053$ MTCDE/ Million-Btu $+ P_i * 0.513$ MTCDE/Million-Wh, shown in Table 3, against the various investment options, where 0.053 and 0.513 are the factors, which are calculated from the historical data.

Note that the base investment option is the option that the current capacity of the existing facilities is expanded without procuring any new energy equipment.

Using the ROI and GHG emissions, domain users and experts can plot the analytical graphs to illustrate the relationships among the ROI, GHG emissions, and investment expenses, which enable the domain experts to determine the best investment option among all of the options being considered.

STEP 5: Remove any option that is dominated by the other options in terms of the evaluation parameters.

STEP 6: Construct a trade-off graph to evaluate the options that are not dominated among others and then make a final decision.

Note that although STEP 1, 2, 4, 5, and 6 are typical processes of evaluations, STEP 3 is not typical at all as the problem that we solve is a non-trivial optimization problem.

Table 3. Evaluation parameters of ROI and GHG emissions for determining the best investment option.

Parameter	Symbol	Parameter	Symbol
Investment Cost	I_i	Cost Saving	S_i
Maintenance Expenditure	M_i	Return on Investment	ROI_i
Replacement Charge	R_i	Average Annual Gas Consumption MBTU	G_i
Equipment Cost	E_i	Average Annual Electric Power Consumption MWh	P_i
Operating Expense	C_i	GHG Emission	$MTCDE_i$

6 Analytical Methodology on Experimental Case Study

After the process from STEP 1 to STEP 3 in the experimental case study at GMU, the four investment options, including ① the expansion of the existing CHCP only, ② the addition of a CoGen plant to the existing CHCP, ③ the half capacity of the Option with the half planned capacity of the CoGen plant, and ④ the full capacity of the

Table 4. Evaluation parameters of ROI and GHG emissions for determining the GMU energy Investment options.

Investment Option	Investment Cost ($M)	Annual Maintenance Cost ($)	Annualized Replacement Cost ($M)	Annualized Equipment Cost ($M)	Annualized Average Operational Cost ($M)	Annualized Saving over the Expanded CHCP ($M)	ROI (%)
1 Expanded CHCP	$34.293	$343,200	$3.429	$3.772	$6.244	$0.000	0.000%
1 CoGen Plant + 1 Current CHCP	$65.328	$655,600	$3.850	$4.506	$5.494	$0.016	0.052%
½ CoGen Plant + ½ Expanded CHCP	$46.995	$499,400	$4.699	$5.199	$5.557	-$0.740	-5.827%
1 CoGen Plant + 1 Expanded CHCP	$99.621	$998,800	$7.279	$8.278	$5.492	-$3.754	-5.747%

Investment Option	Investment Cost ($M)	Average Annual Gas Consumption (MBTU)	Average Annual Electric Power Consumption (MWh)	GHG Emission (MTCDE)
1 Expanded CHCP	$34.293	510,500.00	141,433.33	99611.799
1 CoGen Plant + 1 Current CHCP	$65.328	523,622.22	141,333.33	100255.977
½ CoGen Plant + ½ Expanded CHCP	$46.995	520,888.89	141,344.44	100116.811
1 CoGen Plant + 1 Expanded CHCP	$99.621	523,600.00	141,333.33	100254.799

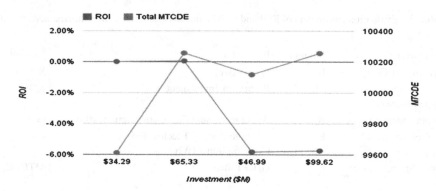

Fig. 4. ROI (%) and GHG emissions (MTCDE) vs. investment cost ($M) across the four investment options.

Option with the full planned capacity of the CoGen plant, have been chosen to be evaluated to meet the electricity, heating, and cooling demand of the Fairfax campus over the next 9 years from 2012 to 2020.

In STEP 4, using the evaluation parameters, i.e., ROI and GHG emissions, discussed in Sect. 5 and the OPL to solve the GMU energy investment problem in Sect. 4, we obtained Table 4 and Fig. 4 that can be used to determine the best investment option.

In STEP 5, the Option ③ and ④ are the dominated cases that can be removed from our consideration list because of the negative ROI.

In STEP 6, according to the Table 4 and Fig. 4, we can conclude that the Option ① should be chosen because of the three observations. First, the GHG emissions and the equipment cost of the Option ① are the lowest. Second, even though the ROI of the Option ②, i.e., 0.052 %, is marginally better than that of the Option ②, the GHG emissions of the Option ② is the highest among all the options being considered. Third, it is not economical at all for GMU to invest $31 million dollars, i.e., the Option ② investment cost minus the Option ① investment cost, more to earn only 0.052 % ROI in the next 9-year timeframe. Thus, the Option 1 is the best long-term option for GMU.

7   Conclusions and Future Work

In this paper, we propose a Decision-Guided Energy Investment (DGEI) Framework to optimize power, heating, and cooling capacity. The DGEI framework is designed to support energy managers to (1) use the analytical and graphical methodology to determine the best investment option that satisfies the designed evaluation parameters, such as ROI and GHG emissions; (2) develop a DGEI optimization model to solve energy investment problems that the operating expenses are minimal in each considered investment option; (3) implement the DGEI optimization model using the IBM OPL language with historical and projected energy demand data, i.e., electricity, heating, and cooling, to solve energy investment optimization problems; and

(4) conduct an experimental case study on the Fairfax campus microgrid at George Mason University (GMU) and utilize the DGEI optimization model and its OPL implementations, as well as the graphical and analytical methodology to make the investment decision and trade-offs among the cost savings, investment costs, maintenance expenditures, replacement charges, operating expenses, GHG emissions, and return on investment (ROI) for all the considered options.

Technically, the core challenge is the development of the DGEI optimization model that is very accurate in terms of the contractual terms and engineering constraints, and yet efficient and scalable, which is done by the careful modelling of mainly continuous decision variables and using constructs that avoid introduction of combinatorics, e.g., explicit or implicit binary variables, into the model. However, the DGEI optimization problem that we formulate is implemented by using the OPL language. This OPL construct is then sent to the IBM CPLEX solver which is the branch-and-bound-based algorithm with the exponential time complexity, i.e., $O(k2^N)$, where k is the number of decision control variables, and N is the size of the learning data set. Thus the future research focus will develop a new algorithm that will be able to solve the energy investment problems at a lower time complexity.

Concerning the real case study at George Mason University and its CHCP system, it is clear that GMU must develop and research other available options beyond those discussed in the analysis of this paper in order to meet the future needs of the Fairfax campus demand. Thus, the DGEI framework further developed will aid the GMU energy decision makers to determine the optimal solutions that will satisfy the GMU short- and long-term power, heating, and cooling demand. Note that our framework is applicable to solve any energy investment problem in different domains of industry. Therefore, the future work includes the advanced development of the DGEI libraries and optimization models that enable domain users and experts to integrate more clean and efficient energy equipment, such as geothermal electric power facilities, into the existing plants optimally in order to support the continuous development of enterprises and organizations.

Appendix: Abbreviation

Abbreviation	Full Name	Abbreviation	Full Name
CHCP	Centralized Heating and Cooling Plant	ES	Electricity Supply
CO_2	Carbon Dioxide	FCWA	Fairfax County Water Authority
CoGen	Cogeneration	FMD	Facilities Management Department
DGEI	Decision-Guided Energy Investment	GHG	Greenhouse Gas
DVPC	Dominion Virginia Power Company	MILP	Mixed Integer Linear Programming

(continued)

(Continued)

EC	EnergyConnect	MINLP	Mixed Integer Non-Linear Programming
ECU	Energy Contractual Utility	NO_x	Mono-Nitrogen Oxide
EFD	Energy Future Demand	OPL	Optimization Programming Language
EFE	Energy Facility Expansion	QoS	Quality of Service
EGP	Energy Generation Process	ROI	Return On Investment
EHD	Energy Historical Demand	WGLC	Washington Gas Light Company

References

1. Broccard, M., Girdinio, P., Moccia, P., Molfino, P., Nervi, M., Pini Prato, A.: Quasi static optimized management of a multinode CHP plant. J. Energy Convers. Manag. **51**(11), 2367–2373 (2010)
2. Bojić, M., Stojanović, B.: MILP optimization of a CHP energy system. J. Energy Convers. Manag. **39**(7), 637–642 (1998)
3. SAS Institute Inc.: SAS/OR(R) 9.22 User's Guide: Mathematical Programming (2012) http://support.sas.com/documentation/cdl/en/ormpug/63352/HTML/default/viewer. htm#ormpug_milpsolver_sect001.htm. Accessed 29 April 2012
4. Brodsky, A., Wang. X.S.: Decision-guidance management systems (DGMS): seamless integration of data acquisition, learning, prediction, and optimization. In: Proceedings of the 41st Hawaii International Conference on System Sciences, Waikoloa, Big Island, Hawaii, USA (2008)
5. Brodsky, A., Bhot, M.M., Chandrashekar, M., Egge, N.E., Wang, X.S.: A decisions query language: high-level abstraction for mathematical programming over databases. In: Proceedings of the 35th SIGMOD International Conference on Management of Data, RI, USA (2009)
6. Brodsky, A., Cherukullapurath, M., Awad, M., Egge, N.: A decision-guided advisor to maximize ROI in local generation and utility contracts. In: Proceedings of the 2nd European Conference and Exhibition on Innovative Smart Grid Technologies, Manchester, UK (2011)
7. Brodsky, A., Egge, N., Wang, X.S.: Reusing relational queries for intuitive decision optimization. In: Proceedings of the 44th Hawaii International Conference on System Sciences, Koloa, Kauai, Hawaii, USA (2011)
8. Brodsky, A., Henshaw, S.M., Whittle, J.: CARD: a decision-guidance framework and application for recommending composite alternatives. In: Proceedings of the 2nd ACM International Conference on Recommender Systems, Lausanne, Switzerland (2008)
9. Brodsky, A., Alrazgan, A., Nagarajan, A., Egge, N.: Learning occupancy prediction models with decision-guidance query language. In: Proceedings of the 44th Hawaii International Conference on System Sciences, Koloa, Kauai, Hawaii, USA (2011)
10. Savola, T., Keppo, I.: Off-design simulation and mathematical modeling of small-scale CHP plants at part loads. J. Appl. Therm. Eng. **25**(8–9), 1219–1232 (1997)
11. Tuula Savola, T., Fogelholm, C.: MINLP optimization model for increased power production in small-scale CHP plants. J. Appl. Therm. Eng. **27**(1), 89–99 (2007)
12. Tuula Savola, T., Tveit, T., Fogelholm, C.: A MINLP model including the pressure levels and multiperiods for CHP process optimization. J. Appl. Therm. Eng. **27**(11–12), 1857–1867 (2007)

13. Hentenryck, P.V.: The OPL Optimization Programming Language. MIT Press, Cambridge (1999)
14. The IBM Corporation: Optimization Programming Language (OPL) (2012). http://pic.dhe. ibm.com/infocenter/cosinfoc/v12r4/index.jsp?topic=%2Filog.odms.ide.help%2FOPL_ Studio%2Fmaps%2Fgroupings_Eclipse_and_Xplatform%2Fps_opl_Language_1.html
15. Biezma, M., San Cristobal, J.: Investment criteria for the selection of cogeneration plants – a state of the art review. J. Appl. Therm. Eng. **26**(5–6), 583–588 (2006)
16. American Electric Power Inc.: CCS front end engineering & design report American electric power mountaineer CCS II Project Phase 1, Columbus, Ohio, USA (2012). http:// cdn.globalccsinstitute.com/sites/default/files/publications/32481/ccs-feed-report-gccsi-final. pdf

Combining Fuzzy Ontology Reasoning and Mamdani Fuzzy Inference System with HyFOM Reasoner

Cristiane A. Yaguinuma[1]([✉]), Walter C.P. Magalhães Jr.[2],
Marilde T.P. Santos[1], Heloisa A. Camargo[1], and Marek Reformat[3]

[1] Department of Computer Science, Federal University of São Carlos,
São Carlos, SP, Brazil
[2] Embrapa Dairy Cattle, Juiz de Fora, MG, Brazil
[3] Department of Electrical and Computer Engineering, University of Alberta,
Edmonton, AB, Canada
{cristiane_yaguinuma,marilde,heloisa}@dc.ufscar.br,
walter@cnpgl.embrapa.br, reformat@ualberta.ca

Abstract. Representing and processing imprecise knowledge has been a requirement for a number of applications. Some real-world domains as well as human subjective perceptions are intrinsically fuzzy, therefore conventional formalisms may not be sufficient to capture the intended semantics. In this sense, fuzzy ontologies and Mamdani fuzzy inference systems have been successfully applied for knowledge representation and reasoning. Combining their reasoning approaches can lead to inferences involving fuzzy rules and numerical properties from ontologies, which can be required to perform other fuzzy ontology reasoning tasks such as the fuzzy instance check. To address this issue, this paper describes the HyFOM reasoner, which follows a hybrid architecture to combine fuzzy ontology reasoning with Mamdani fuzzy inference system. A real-world case study involving the domain of food safety is presented, including comparative results with a state-of-the-art fuzzy description logic reasoner.

Keywords: Knowledge representation and reasoning · Fuzzy ontology · Mamdani fuzzy inference system · Hybrid reasoner

1 Introduction

A number of applications have been using ontologies for knowledge representation, aiming to deal with semantic information that can be shared among people, software agents and systems. In special, ontologies support not only representational primitives but also reasoning tasks that reveal implicit knowledge from assertions, axioms and defined concepts and relationships.

Some real-world applications as well as human subjective perceptions require representation and reasoning involving concepts whose meaning cannot be fully

© Springer International Publishing Switzerland 2014
S. Hammoudi et al. (Eds.): ICEIS 2013, LNBIP 190, pp. 174–189, 2014.
DOI: 10.1007/978-3-319-09492-2_11

captured by conventional ontologies. For instance, it is difficult to model concepts like *creamy, dark, hot, large* and *thick*, for which a clear and precise definition is not possible, as they involve so-called fuzzy or vague concepts [1]. Therefore, concepts from the fuzzy set theory [2] should be incorporated to ontologies in order to represent and reason over imprecise or vague information.

According to Lukasiewicz and Straccia [3], there is a number of fuzzy extensions of ontologies that have been developed recently. Some proposals have considered ontologies extended with fuzzy variables and linguistic terms, as they capture the vagueness inherent in some real-world situations and in human language. In computational intelligence research, these concepts have been largely exploited by Mamdani Fuzzy Inference Systems (Mamdani FIS) [4] to infer numerical outputs based on fuzzy variables and fuzzy rules. As stated by Loia [5], the design of advanced decision making systems requires that fuzzy knowledge be embeded in a high-level inference engine able to infer novel information by exploring fuzzy relationships through well-defined computational intelligence methods. In this sense, the Mamdani FIS reasoning approach could be employed in combination with fuzzy ontologies, providing numerical property values inferred by fuzzy rule reasoning. In addition, the inferred values can collaborate with other fuzzy ontology reasoning tasks, such as the fuzzy instance check depending on specific property values.

Even though the combination of fuzzy ontology and fuzzy rule reasoning has been researched in the literature [6–13], there are still some important issues to be addressed. Fuzzy rule semantics and defuzzification methods should meet application requirements in order to obtain meaningful inferences. The set of fuzzy inferences should not be restricted to fuzzy rule reasoning, since fuzzy ontology reasoners also provide relevant inferences regarding fuzzy concept knowledge. It is important to incorporate fuzzy rule inferences to the fuzzy ontology, as they may collaborate with other fuzzy ontology reasoning tasks.

Focusing on these issues, this paper describes the HyFOM reasoner (*Hybrid Integration of Fuzzy Ontology and Mamdani reasoner*), extending the research initiated by Yaguinuma *et al.* [14]. The HyFOM reasoner is based on a hybrid architecture to combine fuzzy ontologies and Mamdani rules, providing meaningful inferences involving numerical property values to fuzzy ontology-based applications. The developed approach is explained in the following sections. Section 2 discusses some related work on the combination of fuzzy ontologies and fuzzy inference systems. Section 3 describes the integration approach and components of the HyFOM reasoner. A case study about the domain of food safety is presented in Sect. 4, including comparative results with a state-of-the-art fuzzy description logic reasoner. Finally, Sect. 5 concludes this paper and points out ongoing research.

2   Related Work

In relation to the current approaches aiming to combine fuzzy ontologies and fuzzy inference systems, there are some issues that should be considered:

1. Does the semantics provided to represent and reason over fuzzy rules meet the application needs?
2. Are fuzzy rule inferences integrated to the fuzzy ontology so that they can contribute to other ontology reasoning tasks?
3. Does the set of possible fuzzy inferences comprise both fuzzy ontology and fuzzy rule reasoning?

Some fuzzy ontology languages based on expressive fuzzy description logics, e.g. [8,10], provide implication operators that can be used to represent fuzzy rules. As described by Guillaume and Charnomordic [15], these rules are called implicative rules, which are combined conjunctively. Nevertheless, such semantics can be too restrictive depending on the application, possibly resulting in knowledge base inconsistency even for allowed property values (question 1). Another approach provided by the fuzzyDL reasoner [8] is representing fuzzy rules using fuzzy concept definitions along with a query interface to call defuzzi-fication methods. However, the defuzzification methods available are not based on the shape of the fuzzy sets, thus the results may not correspond to the appli-cation requirements.

There are proposals, such as [9,11], that consider a *crisp* ontology integrated with Mamdani rules. In this context, an ontology reasoner is used for consistency checking regarding crisp definitions but the set of fuzzy inferences is limited to fuzzy rule reasoning (question 3).

Some studies [6,7] have adopted the *Fuzzy Markup Language* (FML) [16] to express FIS-related information such as fuzzy rules, linguistic variables and fuzzy rule reasoning methods. OWL-FC [13] also represents these elements with a high-level specification for fuzzy control systems that enables links to domain ontology concepts. In general, these proposals focus on fuzzy rule reasoning, mainly using the fuzzy ontology to represent a FIS knowledge base. Thus, their set of fuzzy inferences does not include fuzzy concept reasoning provided by fuzzy ontology reasoners, a limitation related to questions 2 and 3.

Bragaglia *et al.* [12] propose a hybrid architecture combining forward rules and fuzzy ontology reasoning. Although the set of fuzzy inferences covers both fuzzy ontological and fuzzy rule reasoning, their proposal does not exploit Mam-dani reasoning neither defuzzification methods. As mentioned earlier, Mamdani FIS provides useful inferences that can complement the set of fuzzy inferences demanded by some applications and not provided directly by ontology reasoning mechanisms - an issue related to question 1.

Aiming to deal with the discussed limitations, the HyFOM reasoner is described in Sect. 3, combining fuzzy ontology and Mamdani reasoning based on a hybrid architecture.

3 The HyFOM Reasoner

The HyFOM reasoner aims at combining fuzzy ontology and fuzzy rule reason-ing to provide expressive inferences that are not obtained through typical fuzzy ontology reasoning. Specifically, a Mamdani FIS can be used to infer numerical

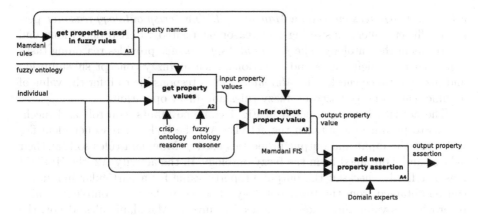

Fig. 1. Main steps for combining fuzzy ontology and Mamdani FIS reasoning with HyFOM reasoner.

property values based on fuzzy rules combining different properties and their respective linguistic terms. In this sense, when applications require knowledge associated with a numerical property value, it can be inferred based on a Mamdani FIS by getting inputs from the fuzzy ontology. The inferred output is then returned to the ontology, possibly contributing to other fuzzy ontology reasoning tasks. Figure 1 presents a SADT diagram [17] describing the HyFOM reasoner approach to integrate fuzzy ontology and Mamdani FIS reasoning

According to Fig. 1, the main inputs and controls of the HyFOM reasoner are *Mamdani rules* representing a Mamdani rule base; a *fuzzy ontology*; and an *individual* of the fuzzy ontology. The Mamdani rule base contains a set of rules combining numerical properties and linguistic terms in the antecedent (input properties) to infer the value of a property in the consequent (output property). An example of a Mamdani rule is: If `property1` is *high* and `property2` is *medium* then `property3` is *low*, where *property1* and *property2* are input properties and *property3* is an output property, all of them described by linguistic terms (*high, medium* and *low*, respectively).

The fuzzy ontology models a specific domain in terms of concepts, properties, relationships, instances and linguistic terms associated with numerical properties. The properties and linguistic terms used in Mamdani rules should be defined in the fuzzy ontology with equal names, for mapping purposes. Applications pass an individual of the fuzzy ontology to check if it has any property value that can be inferred based on Mamdani reasoning. If a class is passed as input, the integration approach is done for all its individuals.

The mechanisms (arrows at the bottom of activity boxes) are the resources required to complete a process, which may include people with particular skills and computational tools, according to the SADT specification. In the proposed approach, the mechanisms are inference engines and domain experts who supervise the outputs of the integration process. Following a hybrid architecture, inference engine implementations are reused, including a *crisp ontology reasoner*, a *fuzzy ontology reasoner* and a *Mamdani FIS*. The *crisp ontology reasoner* performs efficient query answering and reasoning related to crisp definitions and assertions in the ontology. The *fuzzy ontology reasoner* provides reasoning tasks regarding fuzzy definitions and assertions, such as fuzzy concept subsumption and fuzzy instance check. The *Mamdani FIS* is responsible to infer the value of a numerical property based on fuzzy rules and fuzzy operations.

The activity boxes presented in Fig. 1 combine inputs, controls and mechanisms to produce outputs. In the activity A1, the HyFOM reasoner identifies which are the input and output properties used in Mamdani rules so that their values can be obtained from the fuzzy ontology. In the activity A2, the HyFOM reasoner firstly checks if the output property value for a particular individual can be obtained from the fuzzy ontology. If so, then the fuzzy ontology is able to provide its value thus there is no need to involve Mamdani rules. If not, the appropriate input property values should be obtained from the fuzzy ontology so that the Mamdani FIS can be invoked to infer the output property value.

Still in the activity A2, property values (either output or input) are obtained from the fuzzy ontology based on the function `getPropValue` presented in Algorithm 1. The crisp ontology reasoner is invoked to check if the property value is either asserted or inferred based on crisp definitions. The main reason for using a crisp ontology reasoner is due to its optimized access to assertions and conventional ontology reasoning tasks. Still, if property values cannot be obtained, the fuzzy ontology reasoner is invoked because fuzzy concept definitions and implications can support reasoning associated with property values. For example, a fuzzy concept definition such as `C1` ≡ ∃ `property1.high` along with an assertion `C1(ind1)` indicates that individual `ind1` has value `high` for `property1`. Thus, even if property values are not explicit, they may be inferred based on fuzzy ontology axioms and definitions. The function `getPropValue` is invoked in two situations:

1. to check if the fuzzy ontology already provides the output property value;
2. to obtain input property values to be sent to FIS. In such situation, the hybrid reasoner can be configured to handle either crisp or fuzzy inputs to FIS.

Algorithm 1: `getPropValue`.

---

    input   : Fuzzy ontology individual ind, Property prop;
    output : prop value for ind
    initialize:
        fuzOnt ← Fuzzy ontology;
        crispOntR ← Crisp Ontology Reasoner;
        fuzOntR ← Fuzzy Ontology Reasoner;

1 propValue ← crispOntR.`getPropValue`(fuzOnt,ind,prop);
2 **if** propValue = ∅ **then**
3 | propValue ← fuzOntR.`getPropValue`(fuzOnt,ind,prop);
4 **end**
5 **if** propValue ≠ ∅ **then return** propValue **else return** ∅

After the input values are obtained, the activity A3 invokes the Mamdani FIS to infer the corresponding output based on Mamdani rules. In the Mamdani FIS, the fuzzy operations considered are min-max composition, minimum for rule semantics and maximum for aggregation of outputs [4]. Several defuzzification methods are provided to obtain a numerical value from the aggregated fuzzy output, such as Center of Area (COA), Moment defuzzification and Mean of Maxima (MOM). Finally, a new property assertion involving the output property, the individual and the defuzzified value is added to the fuzzy ontology under domain expert supervision (activity A4). As a result, the output generated by Mamdani FIS will be available for other fuzzy ontology reasoning tasks that may depend on it.

The HyFOM reasoner was implemented using reasoners and frameworks available for fuzzy ontology-based applications and FIS. The crisp ontology reasoner is based on the OWL API [18] and Hermit [19], an optimized reasoner providing efficient access to crisp ontology assertions and inferences. The fuzzy ontology reasoner used is the fuzzyDL reasoner [8], which supports fuzzy concepts, linguistic terms and fuzzy axioms, with a Java API to access reasoning tasks. The Mamdani FIS is provided by FuzzyJ Toolkit and Fuzzy Jess [20], including a Java API for handling fuzzy sets, fuzzy rules, Mamdani inference and defuzzification methods.

Based on this platform, domain experts can model the fuzzy ontology using the Protégé ontology editor with the FuzzyOWL2 plugin [21]. The resulted ontology can be processed by OWL API, Hermit and fuzzyDL, provided that it is parsed to the fuzzyDL syntax to allow fuzzy ontology reasoning. The results inferred by the Mamdani FIS are integrated to the fuzzy ontology using the OWL API support for including new assertions.

In order to demonstrate some contributions of the HyFOM reasoner, Sect. 4 describes a real-world case study concerning fuzzy rule reasoning semantics and integration issues.

4   Case Study on Food Safety

The HyFOM reasoner was applied in a case study to support domain experts in evaluating the chemical risk of analytes (residues and contaminants) detected in food samples. The experiments were sponsored by the Brazilian Ministry of Agriculture, Livestock and Supply (MAPA), focusing on the National Plan for Control of Residues and Contaminants (PNCRC). PNCRC is responsible for monitoring the presence of residues of pesticides and veterinary drugs as well as environmental contaminants in food products. More details on MAPA and PNCRC are available in [22].

According to the methodology explained by Magalhães Junior *et al.* [22], laboratory analyses obtain the concentration of different analytes in food samples. For each analyte, there is a *maximum level* established by the Codex Alimentarius Commission, which is the maximum concentration of that substance officially permitted in a specific food. Each analyte concentration is confronted with its respective maximum level (in percentage) to obtain the *Concentration Risk* (CR) of the analyte detected in a food sample. In this sense, if an analyte concentration is lower than or equal to its maximum level it is called a *compliant* analyte in the sample; otherwise it is called *non-compliant*. In addition to CR, there are other risk factors determined by PNCRC experts:

- Trends associated with analyte concentration: indicate whether the analyte concentration has a tendency of decreasing, stabilizing or increasing in a short, medium or long period of time, according to its toxicological profile;
- Adjustment period: estimated time for the provider of the food sample to be brought into compliance with MAPA's requirements concerning a specific analyte;
- Adjustment cost: estimated costs for the provider of the food sample to be brought into compliance with MAPA's requirements concerning a specific analyte.

The Chem-risk approach [23] combines the risk factors to obtain the Aggregate Risk (AR) associated with an analyte detected in a food sample. Although Chem-risk provides appropriate results, it is based on a mathematical model which is not easily interpretable for domain experts, who need to understand the context and the causes associated with AR values. In this sense, fuzzy ontology and fuzzy rules can contribute to make the whole process more transparent and interpretable, as they consider semantic structures and linguistic terms that are closer to the human language. Thus, the HyFOM reasoner was instantiated in such context and its results were compared with Chem-risk, which is the reference in relation to the data available.

With supervision of PNCRC experts, the main concepts related to the chemical risk of analytes were modeled in a fuzzy ontology. The relation among risk factors to derive aggregate risk was modeled using Mamdani rules. Both the fuzzy ontology and fuzzy rules are described in the next subsection.

4.1   Modeling Fuzzy Ontology and Fuzzy Rules

Initially, Protégé and FuzzyOWL2 plugin were used to model the main concepts and properties of the domain (Fig. 2). In the left part of Fig. 2, the main concepts of the domain are listed, such as *FoodCommodity*, *Analyte*, *Sample*, *SampleLot* and *AnalyteSampleAnalysis*. The key concept *AnalyteSampleAnalysis* is the main unit of information representing an analyte detected in a sample and contains the respective values of risk factors. There are different types of analytes, represented as subclasses of *Analyte* (*Contaminant* and *Residue*). A specific type of *Residue*, named *Mycotoxin*, is associated with a rule saying that analyses about a *Mycotoxin* have a concentration trend risk of value 0, which represents the tendency to decrease or stabilize the detected concentration. In addition, there are some concepts to represent compliant and non-compliant analysis and possible interventions that should be applied to the providers of food samples depending on the calculated AR value. Some types of intervention are:

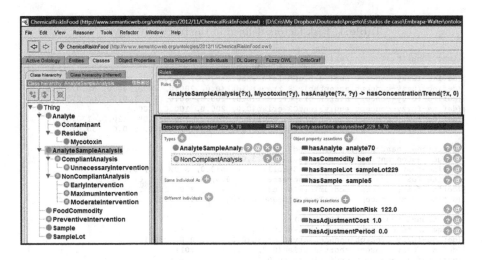

Fig. 2. Main concepts related to the chemical risk of analytes modeled with Protégé.

- *UnnecessaryIntervention* for compliant analytes with negligible AR;
- *EarlyIntervention* for non-compliant analytes with low AR;
- *PreventiveIntervention* for analytes with a short-term increasing trend and medium AR;
- *ModerateIntervention* for non-compliant analytes that have high AR and
- *MaximumIntervention* for non-compliant analytes that have intolerable AR.

An instance of *AnalyteSampleAnalysis* (*analysisBeef_229_5_70*) is illustrated in Fig. 2, relative to the *analyte70* detected in the beef *sample5* of lot *sampleLot229* along with its respective risk factor values. Note that, for confidential purposes with regard to MAPA's data, analyte names are masked with identifiers.

After modeling the main concepts with Protégé, the ontology is parsed to the fuzzyDL syntax to enable fuzzy ontology reasoning. Table 1 shows how the risk factors were modeled in the fuzzy ontology, all of them associated with linguistic terms defined with support of experts. At the moment, the linguistic terms related to the properties *hasConcentrationTrend*, *hasAdjustmentPeriod* and *hasAdjustmentCost* are nominal (crisp) values due to the data available, but there is an ongoing work with PNCRC experts to fuzzify such definitions. Table 2 describes concept definitions representing the types of intervention, which are based on the risk factors and their linguistic terms.

Instead of using the Chem-risk approach [23] to compute AR, domain experts were requested to express their knowledge using Mamdani rules combining the risk factors to infer AR. In this case study, fuzzy rules contribute to make the process more transparent and interpretable for PNCRC and MAPA decision makers, due to the linguistic terms that are closer to human language. A total of 17 Mamdani rules were modeled, some of them illustrated in Table 3 using Fuzzy Jess.

Table 1. Risk factors defined in the fuzzy ontology.

```
(functional hasConcentrationRisk )
(range hasConcentrationRisk *real* 0.0 200.0 )
(define-fuzzy-concept negligibleCR left-shoulder(0.0, 200.0, 20.0, 40.0) )
(define-fuzzy-concept acceptableCR trapezoidal(0.0, 200.0, 20.0, 40.0, 80.0, 90.0) )
(define-fuzzy-concept nearCR trapezoidal(0.0, 200.0, 80.0, 90, 100.0, 100.0) )
(define-fuzzy-concept equivalentCR crisp(0.0, 200.0, 100.0, 100.0) )
(define-fuzzy-concept highCR trapezoidal(0.0, 200.0, 100.0, 100, 120.0, 130.0) )
(define-fuzzy-concept intolerableCR right-shoulder(0.0, 200.0, 120.0, 130.0) )

(functional hasConcentrationTrend )
(range hasConcentrationTrend *real* 0.0 3.0 )
(define-fuzzy-concept decreaseOrStabilize crisp(0.0, 3.0, 0.0, 0.0) )
(define-fuzzy-concept longTermIncrease crisp(0.0, 3.0, 1.0, 1.0) )
(define-fuzzy-concept mediumTermIncrease crisp(0.0, 3.0, 2.0, 2.0) )
(define-fuzzy-concept shortTermIncrease crisp(0.0, 3.0, 3.0, 3.0) )

(functional hasAdjustmentPeriod )
(range hasAdjustmentPeriod *real* 0.0 3.0)
(define-fuzzy-concept unnecessaryAP crisp(0.0, 3.0, 0.0, 0.0))
(define-fuzzy-concept shortAP crisp(0.0, 3.0, 1.0, 1.0))
(define-fuzzy-concept mediumAP crisp(0.0, 3.0, 2.0, 2.0))
(define-fuzzy-concept longAP crisp(0.0, 3.0, 3.0, 3.0))

(functional hasAdjustmentCost )
(range hasAdjustmentCost *real* 0.0 3.0 )
(define-fuzzy-concept unnecessaryAC crisp(0.0, 3.0, 0.0, 0.0))
(define-fuzzy-concept lowAC crisp(0.0, 3.0, 1.0, 1.0))
(define-fuzzy-concept mediumAC crisp(0.0, 3.0, 2.0, 2.0))
(define-fuzzy-concept highAC crisp(0.0, 3.0, 3.0, 3.0))

(functional hasAggregateRisk )
(range hasAggregateRisk *real* 1.0 15.0 )
(define-fuzzy-concept negligibleAR crisp(1.0, 15.0, 1.0, 1.5) )
(define-fuzzy-concept veryLowAR triangular(1.0, 15.0, 1.5, 1.5, 4.75) )
(define-fuzzy-concept lowAR triangular(1.0, 15.0, 1.5, 4.75, 8.0) )
(define-fuzzy-concept mediumAR triangular(1.0, 15.0, 4.75, 8.0, 11.25) )
(define-fuzzy-concept highAR triangular(1.0, 15.0, 8.0, 11.25, 14.5) )
(define-fuzzy-concept veryHighAR triangular(1.0, 15.0, 11.25, 14.5, 14.5) )
(define-fuzzy-concept intolerableAR crisp(1.0, 15.0, 14.5, 15.0) )
```

Table 2. Concept definitions in the fuzzy ontology.

```
(define-concept CompliantAnalysis
(and AnalyteSampleAnalysis (<= hasConcentrationRisk 100.0 )))

(define-concept NonCompliantAnalysis
(and AnalyteSampleAnalysis (> hasConcentrationRisk 100.0 )))

(define-concept UnnecessaryIntervention
(and CompliantAnalysis (some hasAggregateRisk negligibleAR)))

(define-concept EarlyIntervention
(and NonCompliantAnalysis (some hasAggregateRisk lowAR)))

(define-concept PreventiveIntervention
(and (some hasConcentrationTrend shortTermIncrease) (some hasAggregateRisk mediumAR)))

(define-concept ModerateIntervention
(and NonCompliantAnalysis (some hasAggregateRisk highAR)))

(define-concept MaximumIntervention
(and NonCompliantAnalysis (some hasAggregateRisk intolerableAR)))
```

Table 3. Mamdani rules to infer aggregate risk.

```
(defrule rule1
(hasAdjustmentCost ?c&:(fuzzy-match ?c "unnecessaryAC"))
(hasConcentrationRisk ?v&:(fuzzy-match ?v "negligibleCR")) =>
(assert (hasAggregateRisk (new FuzzyValue ?*hasAggregateRiskFvar* "negligibleAR"))))

(defrule rule2
(hasAdjustmentCost ?c&:(fuzzy-match ?c "unnecessaryAC"))
(hasConcentrationRisk ?v&:(fuzzy-match ?v "acceptableCR")) =>
(assert (hasAggregateRisk (new FuzzyValue ?*hasAggregateRiskFvar* "veryLowAR"))))

(defrule rule3
(hasAdjustmentCost ?c&:(fuzzy-match ?c "unnecessaryAC"))
(hasConcentrationRisk ?v&:(fuzzy-match ?v "nearCR")) =>
(assert (hasAggregateRisk (new FuzzyValue ?*hasAggregateRiskFvar* "veryLowAR"))))

(defrule rule4
(hasAdjustmentCost ?c&:(fuzzy-match ?c "unnecessaryAC"))
(hasConcentrationRisk ?v&:(fuzzy-match ?v "equivalentCR")) =>
(assert (hasAggregateRisk (new FuzzyValue ?*hasAggregateRiskFvar* "lowAR"))))

(defrule rule5
(hasAdjustmentCost ?c&:(fuzzy-match ?c "lowAC"))
(hasAdjustmentPeriod ?p&:(fuzzy-match ?p "unnecessaryAP"))
(hasConcentrationRisk ?v&:(fuzzy-match ?v "negligibleCR")) =>
(assert (hasAggregateRisk (new FuzzyValue ?*hasAggregateRiskFvar* "veryLowAR"))))

(defrule rule6
(hasAdjustmentCost ?c&:(fuzzy-match ?c "lowAC"))
(hasAdjustmentPeriod ?p&:(fuzzy-match ?p "unnecessaryAP"))
(hasConcentrationRisk ?v&:(fuzzy-match ?v "acceptableCR")) =>
(assert (hasAggregateRisk (new FuzzyValue ?*hasAggregateRiskFvar* "veryLowAR"))))
```

Using the fuzzy ontology and Mamdani rules, the HyFOM reasoner was applied to provide recommendations on aggregate risk and intervention actions related to food samples. Following the approach described in Sect. 3, individuals of the concept *AnalyteSampleAnalysis* (see an example in Fig. 2) are passed to the HyFOM reasoner to obtain AR values based on Mamdani rules. The fuzzy ontology is firstly checked for AR values; if they can not be obtained this way, the Mamdani FIS is invoked to compute AR based on inputs provided by the fuzzy ontology. Under expert supervision, the output values are returned to the fuzzy ontology so that they can be used in the fuzzy instance check to recommend the appropriate type of intervention.

Based on this case study, some experiments were conducted using data provided by PNCRC. A total of 114 beef sample analyses were available, involving 19 different analytes. The HyFOM reasoner was executed with the 114 individuals of *AnalyteSampleAnalysis* defined in the fuzzy ontology, using the Moment and COA defuzzification methods for generating the AR values. The results obtained with the HyFOM reasoner were compared with the results provided by Chem-risk approach, which represents the control data in this context.

Among the related work, the fuzzyDL reasoner was chosen for comparison since it is one of the state-of-the-art fuzzy description logic reasoners that also supports FIS semantics with 3 defuzzification methods - Smallest of Maxima (SOM), Largest of Maxima (LOM) and MOM (Middle of Maxima). Note that the HyFOM reasoner already uses fuzzyDL as a fuzzy ontology reasoner, but only for inferences related to fuzzy concept knowledge. Therefore, a "stand-alone" fuzzyDL reasoner is compared with the hybrid reasoner. Two fuzzyDL approaches for modeling fuzzy rules were considered: (1) fuzzy implications and (2) fuzzy concept constructors with MOM defuzzification. In these two situations, the fuzzy ontology (Tables 1 and 2) is reused but the fuzzy rule set is replaced by the corresponding fuzzy rule syntax according to the two fuzzyDL approaches.

In the following subsections, the main contributions of the HyFOM reasoner are discussed using the case study on food safety, focusing on the integration approach, numerical output generation and overall AR results.

4.2   Combining Fuzzy Ontology and Mamdani FIS Reasoning

The integration approach provided by the HyFOM reasoner considers two situations in which fuzzy ontology reasoning and Mamdani FIS collaborate with each other: ontology reasoning providing appropriate inputs for FIS and FIS providing outputs that are required by some fuzzy ontology reasoning tasks. These two situations are illustrated within the domain of chemical risk of analytes, considering the individual shown in Fig. 2 that describes the *analyte70* detected in the beef *sample5* of *sampleLot229*. In this context, suppose that an expert would like to know the appropriate intervention action for such analysis.

According to the integration approach described in Sect. 3, the HyFOM reasoner firstly attempts to obtain the AR value for the individual *analysis-Beef_229_5_70* from the fuzzy ontology. If it does not have enough information to provide such value, the HyFOM reasoner should call the Mamdani FIS to infer the aggregate risk based on fuzzy rules. In order to do that, the appropriate inputs regarding the individual *analysisBeef_229_5_70* should be obtained from the fuzzy ontology. As illustrated in Fig. 2, all risk factor values are explicitly asserted in the ontology, except for the *concentrationTrend* risk factor. Since the HyFOM reasoner also relies on the crisp ontology reasoner to infer the input values, the *concentrationTrend* value can be obtained through the domain rule that assigns the *decreaseOrStabilize* (trend risk of value 0) for analyses about analytes of the *Mycotoxin* class, such as *analyte70*. Specifically, this inference was performed by the crisp ontology reasoner HermiT, as it involves crisp definitions and rules. Therefore, this situation illustrates that ontology reasoning contributes to infer inputs to be sent to Mamdani FIS. In this context, other approaches that do not consider ontology reasoning to obtain the inputs would not be able to provide complete data to FIS. Consequently, they would not infer the appropriate AR value and the corresponding intervention action. FuzzyDL reasoner standalone would not be able to perform this inference because it does not support crisp rules like the one shown in Fig. 2.

After fuzzy rule reasoning was performed by Mamdani FIS, the generated outputs should be integrated with the fuzzy ontology, possibly contributing to other fuzzy ontology reasoning tasks. For example, consider that a domain expert would like to know if the analysis *analysisBeef_229_5_70* should have an early intervention action. This query corresponds to a fuzzy instance check task involving the individual *analysisBeef_229_5_70* and the concept *EarlyInterven-tion* defined in the fuzzy ontology. In order to infer the appropriate membership degree, the fuzzy ontology reasoner should consider the AR inferred by fuzzy rule reasoning. According to the integration approach provided by the HyFOM reasoner, the AR value inferred by Mamdani FIS is returned to the fuzzy ontol-ogy as a new property assertion. As a consequence, the fuzzy ontology reasoner is able to perform the fuzzy instance check with the AR value inferred by fuzzy rule reasoning.

Hence, as illustrated by the example in the case study, the HyFOM reasoner is able to deal with the two situations in which the fuzzy ontology reasoning and Mamdani FIS collaborate with each other.

4.3   Numerical Output Generation

Another relevant issue related to the semantics of fuzzy rule reasoning is how a numerical output is generated from the fuzzy set resulting from rule aggregation. The HyFOM reasoner used in the case study supports Center of Area (COA), Moment defuzzification and Middle of Maxima (MOM), which are the methods available in the underlying FIS implementation based on FuzzyJ Toolkit and Fuzzy Jess. COA and Moment defuzzification generate an output that reflects the shape of the fuzzy set which resulted from different rules contributing to a joined solution that balances outputs from individual rules.

When using fuzzyDL with concept definitions, the defuzzification queries available are SOM, MOM and LOM, which consider the extremes of maximum degree. Depending on the situation, they may lose information compared with other defuzzification methods that are based on the shape of the fuzzy set. Figure 3 illustrates two analyses in which the fuzzy set obtained by Mamdani reasoning is better defuzzified with COA and moment defuzzification than with the methods based on the interval of maximum degree.

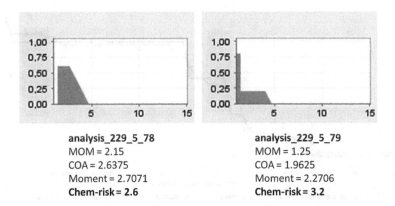

analysis_229_5_78
MOM = 2.15
COA = 2.6375
Moment = 2.7071
Chem-risk = 2.6

analysis_229_5_79
MOM = 1.25
COA = 1.9625
Moment = 2.2706
Chem-risk = 3.2

Fig. 3. Information loss with defuzzification methods based on maximum degree.

In both cases, there is a greater information loss when MOM is considered to generate the numerical output. Specially in *analysis_229_5_79*, it is possible to notice that more than one fuzzy rule was fired, the small interval of maximum degree causes a greater error for MOM compared with the other methods.

Implicative rules in fuzzyDL generate a numerical output corresponding to the minimum value in the domain of discourse which belongs to the conjunction of rule consequents. Thus, the numerical output is not based on the shape of the fuzzy set, unlike COA and Moment defuzzification.

Therefore, for the context regarding the chemical risk of analytes, the HyFOM reasoner can be considered more appropriate as it provides defuzzification methods that deal with the shape of fuzzy sets, corresponding to the application semantics.

4.4   Comparative Evaluation

Some tests were performed to evaluate AR values inferred by the HyFOM reasoner and fuzzyDL, compared with the results provided by Chem-risk approach. The experiments were restricted to analyses relative to beef samples from lots 226 and 229, which cover a comprehensive range of risk values. To ensure that all approaches work with the same set of fuzzy rule inputs, risk factor values were explicitly asserted in the fuzzy ontology, since fuzzyDL does not support rules like the one shown in Fig. 2.

Figure 4 presents the results obtained with HyFOM reasoner, fuzzyDL and Chem-risk, which is the reference for comparison. Some individuals of *Analyte-SampleAnalysis* are omitted because the AR values remain unchanged for individuals with $id \leq 66$. In terms of mean squared error (*mse*), the HyFOM reasoner achieved a better overall performance with moment defuzzification (*mse* = 0.195) and COA (*mse* = 0.199) against fuzzyDL implications (*mse* = 0.295)

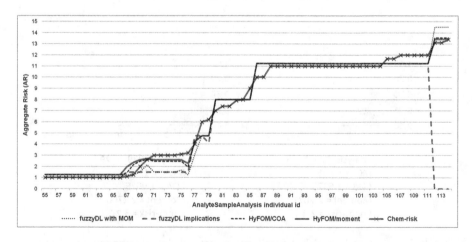

Fig. 4. Aggregate risk obtained with fuzzyDL, HyFOM reasoner and Chem-risk.

and fuzzyDL with MOM ($mse = 0.342$). The Friedman test was applied over
the squared error values, concluding that at least one of the means differs from
the rest. Dunn's post test revealed that the fuzzyDL implications results are
significantly different from the rest, reflecting the distinct reasoning semantics
involved (Mamdani rules with defuzzification versus implication rules). However,
it is important to analyze the specific situations in which one approach performs
better than the others, to have a comprehensive understanding of the results.

For analyses with $AR = 1$ according to Chem-risk, the results from fuzzyDL
implications are more precise than results provided by Mamdani rules with
defuzzification. Implicative rules in fuzzyDL generate a numerical output corresponding to the minimum value in the domain of discourse which belongs to the
conjunction of rule consequents. Thus, the numerical output is not influenced by
the shape of the fuzzy set, as it happens with COA, Moment and MOM defuzzification methods, which generate a $mse = 0.0625$ in this specific situation. On
the other hand, such characteristic favored the HyFOM reasoner results when
$1 < AR \leq 5$ according to Chem-risk. In this case, the defuzzification methods based on shape of the fuzzy sets provided more precise results, differently
from the fuzzyDL implications and MOM that are influenced by the extremes
of maximum degree.

For analyses with $5 < AR \leq 12$, there is no difference in the results provided by both HyFOM reasoner and fuzzyDL. In such situation, the fired rules
involve input properties with nominal values (*hasConcentrationTrend*, *hasAdjustmentPeriod* and *hasAdjustmentCost*), thus fuzziness is not considered in the
results. As it was mentioned previously, there is an ongoing work to fuzzify these
properties with support of PNCRC experts, so that more precise results can be
obtained in comparison with Chem-risk approach.

Finally, the HyFOM reasoner presents better results for analyses with $AR >
12$. In this situation, fuzzyDL implications do not infer AR values due to knowl-
edge base inconsistency, since different rule consequents not having an intersection are combined *conjunctively*. This problem does not happen with Mamdani
rules, which are able to infer pertinent outputs. In addition, the defuzzification
methods provided by the HyFOM reasoner generate a better approximation than
MOM, one of the methods available in fuzzyDL. Therefore, in relation to question 1 (Sect. 2), the HyFOM reasoner can be considered more appropriate for
this case study as it provides rule semantics and defuzzification methods that
better meet the application needs.

5   Conclusions and Future Work

The proposed hybrid reasoning system was designed to address issues discussed
in Sect. 2, which are not fully accomplished by related work. Regarding rule
semantics, the HyFOM reasoner is based on Mamdani rules while some fuzzy
description logic reasoners support implicative rules that can be too restrictive
for some applications. Moreover, the defuzzification methods provided are based
on the shape of the fuzzy set, generating outputs that represent a suitable balance
among multiple fired rules.

The case study involving the domain of food safety demonstrated that the HyFOM reasoner produces appropriate results comparable with the Chem-risk approach already used in this domain. Fuzzy ontologies and Mamdani rules are interesting for this context as they provide advantages regarding interpretability and treatment of imprecision, inherent in expert knowledge.

In terms of integration approach, the HyFOM reasoner automatically provides Mamdani FIS outputs to other fuzzy ontology reasoning tasks. Since the HyFOM reasoner includes a fuzzy ontology reasoner (fuzzyDL), the set of possible fuzzy inferences comprises both fuzzy ontology and fuzzy rule reasoning. As illustrated by the case study, the integration of the outputs from Mamdani FIS is important for the fuzzy instance check task involving intervention actions that depend on aggregate risk values.

As for future work, more real-world applications of the HyFOM reasoner are being developed. In addition, there is an ongoing research about an integration architecture involving a fuzzy tableau-based reasoner and a fuzzy inference system. Other types of fuzzy inference systems can be considered as well, such as the non-parametric fuzzy system model proposed by [24], which is a new type of simplified fuzzy rule-based system as an alternative to the Mamdani and Takagi-Sugeno models.

Acknowledgements. The authors would like to thank the Brazilian research agency CAPES for supporting this research. Special thanks to the Embrapa Dairy Cattle and the Brazilian Ministry of Agriculture, Livestock and Supply for providing real-world data and domain expert support for the case study.

References

1. Straccia, U.: A fuzzy description logic for the semantic web. In: Sanchez, E. (ed.) Fuzzy Logic and the Semantic Web. Capturing Intelligence, pp. 73–90. Elsevier, Amsterdam (2006)
2. Zadeh, L.A.: Fuzzy sets. Inf. Control **3**, 338–353 (1965)
3. Lukasiewicz, T., Straccia, U.: Managing uncertainty and vagueness in description logics for the semantic web. J. Web Semant. **6**(4), 291–308 (2008)
4. Mamdani, E.H., Assilian, S.: An experiment in linguistic synthesis with a fuzzy logic controller. Int. J. Man-Mach. Stud. **7**(1), 1–13 (1975)
5. Loia, V.: Fuzzy ontologies and fuzzy markup language: a novel vision in web intelligence. In: Mugellini, E., Szczepaniak, P.S., Pettenati, ChM, Sokhn, M. (eds.) AWIC 2011. AISC, vol. 86, pp. 3–10. Springer, Heidelberg (2011)
6. Lee, C.S., Wang, M.H., Acampora, G., Hsu, C.Y., Hagras, H.: Diet assessment based on type-2 fuzzy ontology and fuzzy markup language. Int. J. Intel. Syst. **25**(12), 1187–1216 (2010)
7. Huang, H.D., Acampora, G., Loia, V., Lee, C.S., Kao, H.Y.: Applying FML and fuzzy ontologies to malware behavioural analysis. In: IEEE International Conference on Fuzzy Systems, pp. 2018–2025 (2011)
8. Bobillo, F., Straccia, U.: fuzzyDL: An expressive fuzzy description logic reasoner. In: International Conference on Fuzzy Systems, Hong Kong, China, pp. 923–930. IEEE Computer Society (2008)

9. Bobillo, F., Delgado, M., Gómez-Romero, J., López, E.: A semantic fuzzy expert system for a fuzzy balanced scorecard. Expert Syst. Appl. **36**(1), 423–433 (2009)
10. Bobillo, F., Straccia, U.: Fuzzy description logics with general t-norms and datatypes. Fuzzy Sets Syst. **160**(23), 3382–3402 (2009)
11. Wlodarczyk, T.W., O'Connor, M., Rong, C., Musen, M.: SWRL-F: a fuzzy logic extension of the Semantic Web Rule Language. In: International Workshop on Uncertainty Reasoning for the Semantic Web (URSW), Shanghai, China. Springer (2010)
12. Bragaglia, S., Chesani, F., Ciampolini, A., Mello, P., Montali, M., Sottara, D.: An hybrid architecture integrating forward rules with fuzzy ontological reasoning. In: Graña Romay, M., Corchado, E., Garcia Sebastian, M.T. (eds.) HAIS 2010, Part I. LNCS, vol. 6076, pp. 438–445. Springer, Heidelberg (2010)
13. de Maio, C., Fenza, G., Furno, D., Loia, V., Senatore, S.: OWL-FC: an upper ontology for semantic modeling of fuzzy control. Soft. Comput. **16**(7), 1153–1164 (2012)
14. Yaguinuma, C.A., de Magalhães Jr., W.C.P., Santos, M.T.P., Camargo, H.A., Reformat, M.: HyFOM reasoner: Hybrid integration of fuzzy ontology and Mamdani reasoning. In: International Conference on Enterprise Information Systems, Angers, France, vol. 1, pp. 372–380. SciTePress (2013)
15. Guillaume, S., Charnomordic, B.: Fuzzy inference systems: an integrated modeling environment for collaboration between expert knowledge and data using FisPro. Expert Syst. Appl. **39**(10), 8744–8755 (2012)
16. Acampora, G., Loia, V.: Fuzzy control interoperability and scalability for adaptive domotic framework. IEEE Trans. Ind. Inform. **1**(2), 97–111 (2005)
17. Marca, D.A., McGowan, C.L.: SADT: Structured Analysis and Design Technique. McGraw-Hill Inc., New York (1987)
18. Horridge, M., Bechhofer, S.: The OWL API: a Java API for OWL ontologies. Seman. Web **2**(1), 11–21 (2011)
19. Motik, B., Shearer, R., Horrocks, I.: Hypertableau reasoning for description logics. J. Artif. Intell. Res. **36**, 165–228 (2009)
20. Orchard, R.: Fuzzy reasoning in Jess: the FuzzyJ Toolkit and Fuzzy Jess. In: International Conference on Enterprise Information Systems, Setubal, Portugal, pp. 533–542 (2001)
21. Bobillo, F., Straccia, U.: Fuzzy ontology representation using OWL 2. Int. J. Approximate Reasoning **52**(7), 1073–1094 (2011)
22. de Magalhães Jr., W.C.P., Bonnet, M., Feijó, L.D., Santos, M.T.P.: Risk-off method: improving data quality generated by chemical risk analysis of milk. In: Cases on SMEs and Open Innovation: Applications and Investigations, pp. 40–64. IGI Global (2012)
23. de Magalhães Jr., W.C.P.: Chem-risk approach: assessment, management and communication of chemical risks in food by employing knowledge discovery in databases, fuzzy logics and ontologies. Master's thesis, Federal University of São Carlos (2011) (in portuguese)
24. Angelov, P., Yager, R.: A new type of simplified fuzzy rule-based system. Int. J. Gen. Syst. **41**(2), 163–185 (2012)

Business Intelligence for Improving Supply Chain Risk Management

Lingzhe Liu[1]([⊠]), Hennie Daniels[2], and Wout Hofman[3]

[1] Rotterdam School of Management, Erasmus University,
Burg. Oudlaan 50, 3062 PA Rotterdam, The Netherlands
lliu@rsm.nl
[2] CenTER, Tilburg University, Warandelaan 2, 5037 AB Tilburg,
The Netherlands
daniels@uvt.nl
[3] Technical Sciences, TNO, Brasserplein 2, 2612 CT Delft,
The Netherlands
wout.hofman@tno.nl

Abstract. The risk management over a supply chain has to be founded on the management controls in each of the partner companies in the chain. Inevitably, the business relationship and operations dependence bind the control efforts of partner companies together. This proposes challenges for supply chain risk management and at the same time for the BI application. In this paper we analyse the management control situations where business intelligence technology can be applied and describe the concepts of systematic risk analysis to improve the management controls, based on causal analysis of business exceptions. The analysis process is driven by diagnostic drill-down operations following the equations of the information structure in which the data are organised. Using business intelligence, the analysis method can generate explanations supported by the data. A "risk template" is provided to assist analysts to fully comprehend the risk scenario in the practical business setting, so as to evaluate and re-design the existing controls, and to apply BI for management improvement.

Keywords: Risk management · Supply chain exceptions · Business intelligence · Collaboration

1 Introduction

In many supply chains world-wide, the parties are becoming aware that their complex supply chains also become vulnerable for various type of risk. Companies are striving for secure, robust, and less vulnerable supply chains, and their SCM strategies more and more "risk-oriented". Risk management is closely related to the management of business exceptions. The exceptional incidents, themselves albeit not necessarily risky, are early risk indicators and will possibly escalade to severe accident if they are not properly detected and corrected in time.

Risk management addresses the vulnerability of the business system (a company, or a supply chain), which is the condition in which an exception will turn into a risk.

© Springer International Publishing Switzerland 2014
S. Hammoudi et al. (Eds.): ICEIS 2013, LNBIP 190, pp. 190–205, 2014.
DOI: 10.1007/978-3-319-09492-2_12

Since a system is only "as strong as its weakest link", the risk management over a supply chain has to be founded on the risk management in each of partner companies in the chain. Decision made in a partner company influences, and can be influenced by those in other organizations. This is common in today's supply chains: business activities are highly specialized because of the complexity of the international trade, logistics and transport. Lots of operations involve outsourcing and service-providing, in the form of delegating responsibilities and handling process on trade partner's behalf [1], which creates problems like low visibility in supply chain management, loss of confidence [2], sub-optimal supply chain management [3] and supply chain vulnerabilities [4]. With low visibility, business exceptions and disruption may occur without being noticed by the management [5].

Business intelligence (BI) is playing a fundamental role in supporting decision-making and risk management in business organizations [6]. It enhances managers' visibility on the status and performance of the organization, enabling proper management control. A well-known philosophy of control is so-called "Management by exceptions", in which management can be described as a reflex arc of monitor-control loop: the manager perceives the environment of a company, forms an expectation, and decides on the operations planning; additional decisions will be made when deviations occur. Once an exception is detected, the manager needs an explanation "why the exception occurred", so that he or she can make informed decisions on subsequent (re-) actions – whether and how to treat the exception.

BI provides good facility supporting and automating the exception analysis. In recent years, with the prevalence of Enterprise Resource Planning (ERP) systems and the rising awareness of the strategic value of business data, companies continuously collect data about its internal operations and external environment. BI and analytics has been vigorously applied in industry, translating data into a competitive edge [7]. "Management by exceptions" is then endowed with new implication of "detecting and managing risks proactively", rather than the old ways of "reactive fire-fighting" [8], with the new terms of Risk Management or Risk Based Decision Making.

The analysis of exceptions is an important exercise to understand the risk propagation, especially in the supply chain context: how a seemingly small exception causes a catastrophic system-wide failure (see e.g. [9], Chap. 13). If such weak signal of risk can be detected early in time, it leaves more space for reaction and mitigation [8]. Presumably, the pattern of risk propagation must be implied in the historical events records of business exception. Yet, to our best knowledge, currently there is hardly any research on the general methodology for systematically analysing business exceptions in supply chains.

In this paper we focus on the role of BI in risk management and work towards a general methodology to improve the management of exceptions taking place in and across companies. The paper is organized as follows. The next section reviews the requirements of risk management. Section 3 discusses how BI can be applied in the analysis of risk. A case study is shown in Sect. 4 to investigate the real world application and implementation, with discussion and conclusion in Sect. 5.

2 Requirements for Business Intelligence in Risk Management

In modern supply chains, risk assessment is a collaborative effort, as the operations dependency inevitably binds the management control efforts of partner companies together. This proposes new challenges for risk management and at the same time for the BI application. Here lists two of these challenges. First, the collaborative management needs "distributed intelligence" from both internal and external sources (distributed BI), that is, sharing intelligence across organization borders [10]. Second, management on the quality of shared information also becomes more challenging [11], because the quality of BI analysis result is bounded by the quality of input data, and because external control power is weaker in general to ensure data quality.

2.1 Data Analysis in Supply Chains

In the supply chain context, the analysis of exceptions involves heterogeneous data shared by multiple companies, i.e. the event logs which are shared during business transactions between trading partners (see the data pipeline in Fig. 1). Integrating these data to form a data view gives rise to the challenges of interoperability [12]. Here we limit the discussion to logistic services. Interoperability comprises three aspects that are closely interrelated, namely (1) the logistic services resulting in business transactions, (2) the semantics of shared data, and (3) the choreography of business. The semantics of data is a precondition for processing data automatically. The choreography needs to be known to derive the status of physical processes and the

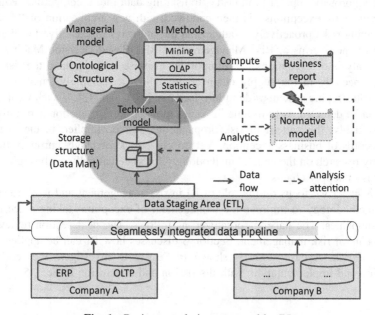

Fig. 1. Business analytics supported by BI.

business transactions which refer to logistic activities that are performed, e.g. transport of cargo containers. As such, these three aspects are part of the managerial model relevant for monitoring supply chain networks.

Under the assumption that companies share data electronically, a data capture algorithm can crawl these event logs regularly. And the data can be fused to compose a supply chain view, organized in a "business event store". A condition is that all the involved companies adhere to the same semantic model. Transformations can be implemented in case a company adheres to another semantic model than agreed.

The business event store may contain duplicated data for different business events, i.e. (almost) identical data can be stored for two or more business events that are related to different companies. For instance, two reports for a container may be stored, referring to the delivery and the acceptance events of the container. The data fusion component needs to identify that these two reports are related, referring to the same business transaction involving the logistics service provider and the cargo receiver.

The data fusion functionality has to mine the association amongst the event logs by matching the following properties of logistic service:

- Business transaction identifier: e.g. a Unique Consignment Number assigned to each complete chain of transportation
- Sender/recipient: which construct the customer/service provider relation for each transaction
- Place and time: each business event associates to a place and time, e.g. place and time of acceptance and of delivery
- Transaction hierarchy: this allows for decomposition of logistic activities, e.g. a journey of container transport may consist of several stretches of transportation

2.2 Risk Assessment in Supply Chains

We focus on the operational aspect of risk, i.e. the event or organizational behaviour that disrupts normal business operations. A risk-based management control for a networked organization, such as companies in a supply chain, requires the integrated "Governance, Risk and Compliance" approach (GRC). Control is to align the behaviours of a company's internal departments' as well as its partners'. Meanwhile, as a member of the supply chain, it must also make sure its own behaviour complies with external norms and regulations.

Inter-organizational cooperation and control is based on trust [13, 14]. In lights of accounting theory, the risk assessment in a networked organization is in fact the assessment on the "trustworthiness" of an organization, i.e. whether the organization under question has enough capability in controlling its operations so that the uncertainty of deviation is contained within certain level. Thus, risk assessment is the auditing analysis on the focal organization itself and on its partners, and the assessment has to be done on three tiers:

1. Operations tier: assessing the risk level of the business operation (in the *controlled system*), according to operations standards.

2. Compliance tier: assessing the risk level of the management system (or, the *controlling system*), i.e. its capability to align the operations with regulations.
3. Governance tier: assessing the risk level of the configuration of the business network (the *design of controlling system*), with criteria of how the management system adapt itself and maintain its control capability for new risks.

Risky events and impacts on the first tier can be directly measured and assessed by analysing the shared data. The second tier assessment may be done by internal or external auditors; sometimes external audit is required by law. BI could lend support to these two assessments with its analytical power. The third tier assessment can be simulated [15], but it remains an open question how it can be done analytically with BI.

Information quality can be a risk source itself that subjects to assessment. The quantitative assessment can be done on the first and second tier, on the capability of the data provider for the quality assurance. Alternatively, the qualitative assessment may find some indicator from third party reference: if a trusted partner uses the same shared information for managing its own risk, this information should be reliable [5]. Later in Sect. 3, we will discuss how the quantitative assessment can be supported by BI.

2.3   Risk Assessment for Compliance Management

Compliance has been identified as a requirement for risk management [6]. For a networked organization, the compliance requirement may originate either externally from regulations like Sarbanes-Oxley Act, or from self-imposed imperatives for implementing its business model. For the latter, the focal organization would like to control its business process according to its customer's compliance requirement, so as to offer value-adding service beyond the value of a business service output. For example, a freight forwarder can provide extra value to its importer client if it properly makes use of its knowledge of preferential trade agreement to reduce import tariffs.

Information technology can automate the verification of operational compliance against the requirements. Turetken, Elgammal, Van den Heuvel and Papazoglou [16] introduced a conceptual model to facilitate the adaptable compliance management. The model allows specifying compliance rules formally, which can be used for checking on operations data. The model explicitly decouples compliance management from business process management (BPM), which suits the second tier of risk management and introduces an opportunity for distributed BI application. Meta control, i.e. controlling BPM system's capability for compliance, can be supported by BI, for instance, in discovering of exceptional operations that are not yet restricted by current compliance specification and leading to the derivation of (new) risk rules.

3   Business Intelligence Supported Risk Analytics

Modern management system, such as ERP, records business data in large volume, but overloaded information is a problem for human decision maker, as it confounds him/her from realizing the true status of the system, causal relationship between exceptions, and the effect of treatment measures [17]. To avoid this, reports are generated by aggregating the data before presented to the manager. When the manager is examining the report, he/she is looking for extreme or unexpected items and tries to find explanations using analytics, i.e. reversing the process of report generation, drilling down in a managerial model, or using additional knowledge possibly from external sources.

The use of analytics in business can be roughly grouped into two parts. First, *descriptive* analytics captures the pattern of systematic emergence in the company or the environment. The description usually supports prediction. Examples are the data mining algorithms like clustering, classification and association, applied to identify the events which can possibly lead to disasters. Although descriptive analytics does not presume any expectations, the analyst usually looks for "interesting" patterns when interpreting the results. In this process, implicit background knowledge is applied in searching for (mental) exceptions [18].

Secondly, *diagnostic* analytics reason about the causal relations of those patterns. The goal for this type of the analysis is to restore or verify the mechanism of a sequence of events [18], e.g. the operations in the company. The conclusion usually leads to decisions for adjustment and improvement of the system. Exemplary analysis questions are "why the company performance is not as expected" – for improving performance of the managed system, and "why certain exceptions have not been detected by current monitors" – for adjusting the management system. Audit analytics also falls in this category, analysing the risk of fraud and/or unintentional errors in accounting systems [19, 20].

3.1 Business Intelligence and the Organization of Information

Business Intelligence is the collection of procedures to reduce the volume of information that the manager need to take into account when making decision. The information-reduction is done by organizing (extract-transform-load, ETL) transactional data into a multi-dimensional database (data warehouse or OLAP), in which large volume of operational details can be abstracted, aggregated or computed into business reports, using BI techniques (see Fig. 1).

This process involves both the *managerial model* and the *technical model of information organization*. On one hand, the organizing of information is in essence driven by managerial purpose, i.e. the managerial model. For example, the accounting process, which in general is a BI process, aggregates transaction records in various documents such as journals, general ledgers and financial statements for operating, financing and investing purposes respectively [20]. The organization of these documents codifies the managerial model. For instance, the general ledger, recorded using double-entry book-keeping, is a codified management system which internally controls balance between two accounts involved in each transaction [20]. On the other hand, the technical model organizes information for an analytical purpose. Organizing business data in the form of tables helps to highlight contextual similarities among the data, providing important support for the business analyst. For instance, aligning records chronically, e.g. transport volume in multiple periods, can show the temporal changes and trends in the record set. As a special case, OLAP is a useful tool to analyse multi-dimensional, hierarchical data interactively, with the standard drill-down, roll-up and slice operations [21]. From an analytics viewpoint, the managerial model provides an *ontological structure* of the information [12], while the technical model gives a *storage structure*, also known as data structure in computer science. Combining these two models gives a data view of the business activities taking place in the managed and the management systems.

3.2   The Learning Cycles

We argue that risk analytics is an important component of the control mechanism for risk management, as a strategic process of organizational learning that extends the philosophy of "management by exception". The importance of analytics lies in the necessity of "meta-control", that is, adapting the existing management control system to cope with the internal and external changes and risks.

The management system (e.g. the ERP in a company) monitors and controls the business processes, which deliver value to customers and form competitive competence. It automates the routine tasks of detecting and treating operational exceptions, because the business knowledge are codified into the build-in controls of the system (in form of business rules or constraints) in a "plan-do-check-adjust" cycle. With automation, management systems can help with handling these routine tasks in large volume, e.g. managing thousands of transactions. However, their monitor-control capability is limited to the codified business rules and constraints, so they cannot deal with the "new" changes or the exceptions out-of-scope of the rules. These exceptions are left to the responsibility of human managers.

The "new" exceptions are on a higher system level than the management system ergo not directly visible, but they affect the output of the managed system (e.g. the performance of the company): therefore, they must be detectable by analysing the data collected or generated by current management system. The analysis results in new business knowledge that equips the management system for controlling similar exceptions in the future. Ideally, the managers hope to continuously meta-control the management system, automating the process using BI [19].

Figure 2 reflects the logic of the control and meta-control mechanisms. It depicts the monitor and control activities as the centre of supply chain risk management. Here, we interpret monitoring as all activity, instruments, models and procedures dedicated to the task of observing, inspecting or supervising supply chain processes. Monitoring takes actual data about stakeholders, transactions, logistical operations and security status as inputs together with norm data (the business knowledge of what is normal). Subsequently, it interprets any discrepancies between actual and norm data, and infers about the likelihood that risk events occur. Control takes the resulting assessments and uses risk rules to determine if and which risk mitigation measures are needed. The mentioned risk rules are primarily imperative rules that define preconditions or control triggers and a mitigation action. The mitigation action could be a local corrective measure, to be taken by the actor according to predefined norms, or it could be a signalling action to communicate with stakeholders.

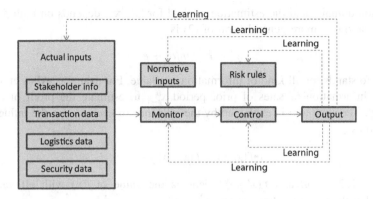

Fig. 2. Integrated monitor and control in supply chain risk management.

3.3 A General Model for Business Analytics

Before the analytic process can be automated, its procedure should first be formalized. The lexical definition of exception is *"an instance that does not conform to a rule or generalization"* (thefreedictionary.com), which implies the comparison of the *actual* instance to a *norm*. Our discussion on business analytics is largely based on previous works of causal analysis and explanations, based on the assumption that the data are organized in an OLAP structure [21–24]. In general, one can always organize the information of the analysis context into an OLAP-like structure, and then start to analyse.

The analysis of exceptions takes the canonical format of [24]:

$$\langle a, F, r \rangle \text{ because } C^+, \text{ despite } C^- \tag{1}$$

where $\langle a, F, r \rangle$ is the triple for exception detection, and the exception is to be explained by the non-empty set of contributing causes C^+ and the (possibly empty) set of counteracting causes C^-. The diagnosis analysis is to explain why the instance a (e.g. the ABC-company) has property F (e.g. having a low profit) when the other members of reference class r (e.g. other companies in the same branch or industry) do not.

The information structure of r has the general form of $y = f(\mathbf{x})$, where $\mathbf{x} = (x_1, x_2, \cdots, x_n)$ is an n-component vector. In words, certain property value of a which is important for decision making, denoted by y, is dependent on other property values $\mathbf{x}$ in the information structure of r.

We can use the information structure to estimate the norm value of y, given the actual values of $\mathbf{x}$. Exception-detection is done by studying the difference between the actual and the norm value of y.

$$y^a = \mathbb{E}(y|x^a) + e, \tag{2}$$

where $e \sim N(0, \sigma)$. If the difference e is significant, i.e. $|e| > \delta\sigma$, y^a is viewed as a *symptom* to be explained. The user defined threshold parameter δ depends on the application domain, and the estimation method for $\mathbb{E}(y|\mathbf{x}^a)$ depends on both $f(\mathbf{x})$ and the application. A more general form of (2) is

$$y^a = \mathbb{E}(y|info) + e \tag{3}$$

where info stands for all kind of information available. For example, Alles et al. [25] uses the information of sales of prior period $\mathbf{x}_{t-1}^a$ to estimate the profit of current period y_t^a. The symptom is explained by the influence of each x_i, and the influence is measured as

$$inf(x_i, y) = f\left(x_{-i}^r, x_i^a\right) - y^r, \tag{4}$$

where $i = 1, 2, \cdots, n$, and $f\left(\mathbf{x}_{-i}^r, x_i^q\right)$ denotes the value of $f(\mathbf{x})$ with all variables evaluated at their norm values, except x_i.

For clarity, we distinguish the technical model from the managerial model in the information structure. For example in OLAP (see equation system (5)), the variables in a managerial model (shown as the functional relation g) can be organised into a hierarchy by aggregation, such as summation or average (shown as the functional relation h). Vertically, all variables in the managerial model are organised based on the same aggregation relation h. Given that, the variables on a specific level of aggregation follow the same business relation g, just as those variables on other aggregation levels horizontally do.

In (5), the variables y and $\mathbf{x}$ are organized in an OLAP cube with l dimensions. Each dimension has a hierarchy of q_k levels, where $k = 1, 2, \cdots, l$. In a specific dimension k, variables on the hierarchy level q_k are aggregated from the m elements in the lower hierarchy level $(q_k - 1)$, and these elements are denoted respectively as y_j and $\mathbf{x}_j$, where $j = 1, 2, \cdots, m$. Here, $\mathbf{x}_j$ is an n-component vector, whose components are denoted as $x_{i,j}$.

$$
\begin{aligned}
y &= g(x) = g(x_1, x_2, \cdots, x_n) \\
y_j^{q_1 \cdots (q_k-1) \cdots q_l} &= g\left(x_j^{q_1 \cdots (q_k-1) \cdots q_l}\right) \\
&= g\left(x_{1,j}^{q_1 \cdots (q_k-1) \cdots q_l}, \cdots, x_{n,j}^{q_1 \cdots (q_k-1) \cdots q_l}\right) \\
y^{q_1 \cdots q_k \cdots q_l} &= h\left(y_j^{q_1 \cdots (q_k-1) \cdots q_l}\right) = \sum_j y_j^{q_1 \cdots (q_k-1) \cdots q_l} \\
x^{q_1 \cdots q_k \cdots q_l} &= h\left(x_j^{q_1 \cdots (q_k-1) \cdots q_l}\right) = \sum_j x_j^{q_1 \cdots (q_k-1) \cdots q_l}
\end{aligned}
\tag{5}
$$

With the information structure available, we can look at lower level of detail for explanation by drilling down. For example, if there is a significant symptom e_j^y in the OLAP model h, detected by $y^a = \mathbb{E}_h\left(y|y_j^a\right) + e_j^y$, we can drill down the managerial model g for explanations, using $y_j^a = \mathbb{E}_g\left(y_j|\mathbf{x}_j^a\right) + e_j^x$. A necessary condition to obtain sensible explanations by drilling down is consistency of the normative estimation, i.e.

$$\mathbb{E}_g(y|x^a) = \mathbb{E}_g\left(h(y_j)|h\left(x_j^a\right)\right) = h\left(\mathbb{E}_g\left(y_j|x_j^a\right)\right) \tag{6}$$

This condition in relation with g usually holds for the OLAP model, but should be checked for (statistical) managerial models in general. This issue is studied in depth for ANOVA models in OLAP databases [21].

3.4   Analytic Procedure

For the analysis of risks, the following two key tasks are the most intricate in the analysis process: (a) How to find an appropriate normative model to detect exceptions, and (b) How to find the real causes to explain the relationship between the exceptions.

The normative model plays a central role in qualifying a feature as normal or exceptional. The firstly used normative models to detect symptoms are usually the codified business constraints in the management system, such as plans or budgets. Peculiarly, in the subsequent diagnostic analysis to explore a sensible explanation, the choice of the normative model for the operational level of analysis relies to a large extent on the choice of the analysis context (i.e. the *reference class*: a class of business object whose common features bares the information of "what is normal"), because the analysis goal is usually an open question. For instance, in analysing "why the monthly transport volumes of this year are low", the decrease in transport volume may due to either the drop in internal efficiency or the deteriorated global economy. In the former case, the figures of the company's monthly volumes in last year are used as reference, while for the latter the reference would be other companies' transport volume figures.

In the exploration for the subsequent normative models, statistics are usually applied to the analysis context. With a data driven (bottom-up) approach, the method for choosing a proper reference class can be "softening" the set of business constraints used in the management system for a particular monitor, using an un-slice operation in OLAP. Softening business constraint is a useful technique for analysis. The un-slice operation takes the union of the data sets which correspond to different parts of the system. It thus expands the analysis scope, so that the patterns on a larger system scale can be revealed. For example, in the time dimension, the trend or fluctuation of a variable over time can only be seen on a time period, but not at a time point. Besides, expanding the scope by un-slicing is in itself an attempt of exploration, for instance in searching for those exceptions whose impact only takes effect after a time lag [19]. This in general helps the analyst to involve extra data by extending the current information structure: in any case, one can always organize the information of the analysis context into an OLAP-like structure, and then start to expand.

The reference class is always defined by a set of constraints. Reminding of the codified business constraints in the first place, the exploration for an appropriate reference class can be regards as a "meta-control" process that diagnoses and reflects upon the detective power of the current set of constraints, performed by the analyst. The exploration thus iteratively applies the detective and diagnostic processes on the design of the analysis method.

To find the causes, correctness and relevance are two important criteria for evaluating the causal explanation. The correctness of the models in the information structure is a premise for finding the real cause. If the model doesn't capture the business correctly, the reference model would be based on a false assumption, and it would then be incapable even in explaining a normal effect. As a result, the model will possibly raise many false alarms. The relevance concerns the usefulness of the explanation for decision support. A counter-example is the explanation presented at the wrong level of detail (also pointed out in [18]). The method for the evaluation of the correctness and relevance generally rely on the background knowledge of the application domain.

Here we propose a general procedure for the analytics, with considering the practical methodology of data analysis [26]:

1. Define problem: define analysis goal and choose the variable which is important for decision.
2. Establish context: abstract and explicitly specify the information structure (or load from a knowledge base, if available). The context is usually connoted by the source of information from which the business report was generated. Sometimes external sources need to be included to enlarge the context, depending on the analysis goal.
3. Identify exceptions: choose appropriate reference class, estimate the norm, and apply it to actual data. Despite the wishes for fully automated analysis, the derivation of the norm remains an interactive process in which several practical aspects demand lots of background knowledge from the analyst (see Sect. 4).
4. Generate explanations: relate the exceptions in different parts of the business system and reason about the causal relations.
5. Interpret results: review the explanations. In case the results does not sufficiently supports decision, repeat step 2 to 5.

4 Illustrative Case

The case study shown here is an on-going research a freight forwarding company (referred as FFco herein after). In this case study, we would like to investigate the way in which the conceptualization of risk management improve the (re-)design of FFco's risk management and progressively improve their operations excellence. The research has two objectives. On the management perspective, we want to research the systematic method for translating the risk-oriented SCM strategy into operable and preferably automatic control mechanisms. On the technical perspective, we are developing a prototypical BI solution to support the collaboration of risk management in supply chains (see Fig. 1).

4.1 Background

Freight forwarding companies resume the orchestrator role in organizing the border-crossing transport of a container [27]. In this case, we focus on FFco's customs brokerage business, as it involves a lot of information processing. As a customs broker, FFco prepares and submits declarations of the containerized cargo on its clients' behalf (c.q. importers or exporters) to obtain clearance through customs frontier. The declarations have to provide evidence that the cargos are in compliance with international trade regulations, such as safety and security, tax and tariff, veterinary, phytosanitary and/or food inspections.

The correctness of the information stated on the declaration is a major concern. Although an incorrect declaration may be merely a result of human error, it could be regarded as an intentional fraud, resulting in penalties or other legal charges to either FFco or its client. This will bring damage to its reputation and customer relations besides the financial losses. What makes the situation more intricate is that FFco as a broker is dependent on the client to provide the correct information while it as a declarer is responsible for the correctness. For mitigating this risk, FFco endeavour to streamline its information systems to assure the data integrity during internal exchange. However, lots of domain knowledge is required to verify the correctness of declarations, therefore a specialist is appointed to do this task manually.

4.2 Approach

We apply a so-called "risk template" to fully comprehend the risk scenario in the supply chain setting (see Table 1). The template is also a risk registration that documents and reflects the way risk management solutions have been developed and

Table 1. Risk template for FFco's customs declaration procedure.

Risk or exceptions:	*Non-compliance of customs declaration*			**Risk owner:**	*FFco, its client*
Business activity:	*Customs declaration*	Impact	High/Medium/Low	Probability	High/Medium/Low
Risk Indicator(s):	*Incorrect information provided by the client and used for the customs declaration*	Party(-ies) involved in the transaction:	*FFco, its client, government agencies*	Party(-ies) to be notified (in case of exception)	*1. ex-ante: consult with the client to verify the info 2. ex-post: notify government agencies of errors, and re-submit a corrected declaration*
Required normative doc / info	*brokerage knowledge: 1. regulations 2. knowledge on the client's (historical) business*	Current practice of check / control (using what info/doc as norm?)	*Manual check: 1. ex-ante verification (using brokerage knowledge) 2. ex-post audit (feedback from gov.)*	Suggested practice of check / control (using what info/doc as norm?)	*Manual checks supported by data analysis tools: Suggestions on possible errors using the normal patterns of the client's business (Inferred from historical transactions using data mining)*
Required monitor measure(s), or check / control	*Check correctness of information on each declaration*				

implemented, serving as a record trail for meta-controlling the capability of risk management solutions. As the risk and its indicators have been identified in the research background, we first analyse the business relations, by identifying the parties whose interest may be harmed by the risky incidence and thus will be benefited from improved risk management. In this case, the improvement will not only contribute to FFco's operations excellence, but also strengthen its cooperative relationship with the client [13, 14], because the incorrectness in declaration information could be an indicator of SCM problems in the client's operations. Secondly, we map the processes to understand in which step /business activity the risk could occur (see Fig. 3), and further analyse and evaluate the current monitor-control mechanism at that step, including the information (exchange) requirement for detecting and correcting the risk. From these analyses we can lastly conclude whether current mechanism is sufficient or not and derive the desired monitor-controls.

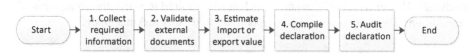

Fig. 3. Internal processes for the customs declaration.

4.3   Business Intelligence (Re-)Design

The analyses in the risk template suggest that the best mitigation would be to control the information quality at the source, that is, at the client's SCM processes. However, this is out of reach of FFco's operations management. FFco decided to improve the analytical capability of its information systems, as part of its risk-oriented continuous management improvement.

The BI's role in decision support in FFco is twofold. It is first of all a detection measure. Data mining techniques such as exploratory data analysis (EDA) [28] and Apriori algorithm can be applied to extract the normal patterns in historical declarations and help detecting possible errors in a (new) declaration. Exemplary exceptions could be a numerical value which deviates significantly from its historical average e.g. a container carrying shoes being impossibly over-weighted, or a rare combination of categorical values e.g. the combination of an exporter and a type of product it never sells indicating a possible error. In the analysis on the correctness of customs value, an OLAP-like structure can be used, in combination with the EDA method, to investigate the calculation procedure of customs value. This can further trace the error to the information sources with which the custom value is determined (e.g. the accounting system which documents the transactions of international trades).

The second role of BI is a "knowledge distiller". The normal patterns extracted by BI can be codified and stored in a knowledge base. Although the capability of the knowledge base is still too limited to replace human decision making, it could anyhow grow asymptotically and complement the work of human specialists by making suggestions. Such knowledge management, as a preventive measure, can add to FFco's learning cycle for operations excellence.

5   Discussion and Conclusions

When applied to support collaborative decision-making in supply chains, business intelligence technology enhances the reflex-arc of management control on operations level with its analytical power. It can also be used in a learning cycle to improve the management control system on the governance and compliance level. Current business databases contain massive amounts of data that carry important explicit and implicit information about the underlying business process. In this paper we analysed the management control situations where business intelligence technology can be applied, and we have shown how general statistical methods can be applied to automatically detect implicit patterns that are interesting to be investigated further for risk assessment. In many cases the data itself include enough information to discover unusual patterns or trends to be explored further, like in an OLAP database. The process of examination is driven by accounting equations or drill-down equations and can generate explanations supported by the data.

As part of the learning cycle for management improvement, the design and implementation of BI in risk management have to base on a thorough understanding of the supply chain operations, management control and the sources of risks in the company. In the on-going case research, we want to evaluate the pragmatic usefulness of the proposed methodology. The evaluation will contribute to the change management for adapting the existing management control, which ensures a successful deployment of the BI solution. There are three domains of evaluation: procedural evaluation, behavioural evaluation, and analytical evaluation of risk effects.

The *procedural* evaluation deals with procedures and design choices of the risk-based monitor control. It systematically records the way risk management solutions have been developed and implemented, i.e. the actual and desired monitoring and control process, using the risk template. *Behavioural* evaluation considers the adoption of the monitor-control implementations in daily operations. This part of the evaluation looks into how people work with the implementations, how their decisions are affected by these implementations, and how they perceive the increased visibility of the supply chain could be utilized for the benefit of operations enhancement. This is important because, in the end, even technically advanced systems may not be used to their full extent, if people are unwilling or unable to adopt the technology offered to them. The *analytical* evaluation bears upon the measurement of risk effects following the implementation of developed monitor-control instruments. The emphasis is on the effects *on* risk, i.e. how the monitor-controls reduce the risk occurrence or its impact. In addition to empirical data, simulation studies can be employed to obtain a generic view of the consequences of the developed instruments.

Acknowledgements. This work was supported by the EC FP7 project CASSANDRA (Grant agreement no: 261795). We are thankful to Dr. Jan van Dalen and Dr. Marcel van Oosterhout for their constructive advice, and to Ron Triepels for his help in developing the case study.

References

1. Rushton, A.: International Logistics and Supply Chain Outsourcing: From Local to Global. Kogan Page Publishers, London (2007)
2. Christopher, M., Lee, H.L.: Mitigating supply chain risk through improved confidence. Int. J. Phys. Distrib. Logist. Manag. **34**, 388–396 (2004). doi:10.1108/09600030410545436
3. Bartlett, P.A., Julien, D.M., Baines, T.S.: Improving supply chain performance through improved visibility. Int. J. Logist. Manag. **18**, 294–313 (2007). doi:10.1108/09574090710816986
4. Peck, H.: Drivers of supply chain vulnerability: an integrated framework. Int. J. Phys. Distrib. Logist. Manag. **35**, 210–232 (2005). doi:10.1108/09600030510599904
5. Hulstijn, J., Overbeek, S.: International Logistics and Supply Chain Outsourcing: From Local to Global. Advanced Information Systems Engineering Workshops, pp. 351–365. Springer, Berlin (2012)
6. Lee, G., Kulkarni, U.: Business intelligence in corporate risk management. AMCIS (2011)
7. Davenport, T.: Competing on analytics. Harv. Bus. Rev. **84**, 98–107 (2006)
8. Sodhi, M.S., Tang, C.S.: Managing supply chain disruptions via time-based risk management. In: Wu, T., Blackhurst, J. (eds.) Managing Supply Chain Risk and Vulnerability, pp. 29–40. Springer, London (2009)
9. Lund, M.S., Solhaug, B., Stølen, K.: Model-Driven Risk Analysis: The CORAS Approach, 460 pp. Springer, Berlin (2011). doi:10.1007/978-3-642-12323-8
10. Rizzi, S.: Collaborative business intelligence. In: Aufaure, M.-A., Zimányi, E. (eds.) eBISS 2011. LNBIP, vol. 96, pp. 186–205. Springer, Heidelberg (2012)
11. Van Baalen, P., Zuidwijk, R., van Nunen, J.: Port inter-organizational information systems: capabilities to service global supply chains. Foundations and Trends® in Technology. Inf. Oper. Manag. **2**, 81–241 (2009). doi:10.1561/0200000008
12. Hofman, W.: Compliance management by business event mining in supply chain networks. VMBO (2013)
13. Das, T.K., Teng, B.-S.: Between trust and control: developing confidence in partner cooperation in alliances. Acad. Manag. Rev. **23**, 491–512 (1998)
14. Tomkins, C.: Interdependencies, trust and information in relationships, alliances and networks. Acc. Organ. Soc. **26**, 161–191 (2001). doi:10.1016/S0361-3682(00)00018-0
15. Laurier, W., Poels, G.: Invariant conditions in value system simulation models. Decis. Support Syst. (2013). doi:10.1016/j.dss.2013.06.009
16. Turetken, O., Elgammal, A., van den Heuvel, W.J., Papazoglou, M.: Enforcing compliance on business processes through the use of patterns. ECIS 2011 Proceedings, Paper 5 (2011)
17. Milliken, F.J.: Three types of perceived uncertainty about the environment: state, effect, and response uncertainty. Acad. Manag. Rev. **12**, 133 (1987). doi:10.2307/257999
18. Von Wright, G.: Explanation and understanding. Annu. Rev. Psychol. **57**, 227–254 (1971). doi:10.1146/annurev.psych.57.102904.190100
19. Vasarhelyi, M.A., Alles, M.G., Kogan, A.: Principles of analytic monitoring for continuous assurance. J. Emerg. Technol. Acc. **1**, 1–21 (2004). doi:10.2308/jeta.2004.1.1.1
20. Bay, S., Kumaraswamy, K., Anderle, M.G., Kumar, R., Steier, D.M.: Large scale detection of irregularities in accounting data. In: Sixth IEEE International Conference on Data Mining, 2006. ICDM'06, pp 75–86. IEEE (2006)
21. Caron, E.A.M.: Explanation of Exceptional Values in Multi-dimensional Business Databases. Erasmus University Rotterdam (2012)
22. Caron, E.A.M., Daniels, H.A.M.: Business analysis in the OLAP context. In: Cordeiro, J., Filipe, J. (eds) ICEIS 2009, Milan, Italy, pp. 325–330 (2009)

23. Caron, E.A.M., Daniels, H.A.M.: Explanation of exceptional values in multi-dimensional business databases. Eur. J. Oper. Res. **188**, 884–897 (2008). doi:10.1016/j.ejor.2007.04.039
24. Feelders, A., Daniels, H.A.M.: A general model for automated business diagnosis. Eur. J. Oper. Res. **130**, 623–637 (2001). doi:10.1016/S0377-2217(99)00428-2
25. Alles, M.G., Kogan, A., Vasarhelyi, M.A., Wu, J.: Analytical Procedures for Continuous Data Level Auditing: Continuity Equations (2010)
26. Feelders, A., Daniels, H.A.M.: Methodological and practical aspects of data mining. Inf. Manag. **37**, 271–281 (2000). doi:10.1016/S0378-7206(99)00051-8
27. Van Oosterhout, M.P.A.: Organizations and flows in the network. In: van Baalen, P., Zuidwijk, R., van Nunen, J. (eds.) Port Inter-Organizational Information Systems: Capabilities to Service Global Supply Chains, pp. 176–185. Now Publishers, Hanover (2009)
28. Pham, D.A.: EDA & Data Mining for Supply Chain Security: Risk Analysis at the Dutch Customs. Erasmus University Rotterdam (2008)

Information Systems Analysis
and Specification

Bayesian Prediction of Fault-Proneness of Agile-Developed Object-Oriented System

Lianfa Li[1,2] and Hareton Leung[2(✉)]

[1] LREIS, Institute of Geographical Sciences and Resources Research,
CAS, Beijing, China
lspatial@gmail.com
[2] Department of Computing, The Hong Kong Polytechnic University,
Hong Kong, China
hareton.leung@polyu.edu.hk

Abstract. Logistic regression (LR) and naïve Bayes (NB) extensively used for prediction of fault-proneness assume linear addition and independence that often cannot hold in practice. Hence, we propose a Bayesian network (BN) model with incorporation of data mining techniques as an integrative approach. Compared with LR and NB, BN provides a flexible modeling framework, thus avoiding the corresponding assumptions. Using the static metrics such as Chidamber and Kemerer's (C-K) suite and complexity as predictors, the differences in performance between LR, NB and BN models were examined for fault-proneness prediction at the class level in continual releases (five versions) of Rhino, an open-source implementation of JavaScript, developed using the agile process. By cross validation and independent test of continual versions, we conclude that the proposed BN can achieve a better prediction than LR and NB for the agile software due to its flexible modeling framework and incorporation of multiple sophisticated learning algorithms.

Keywords: Fault-proneness · Agile process · Object-oriented systems · Software quality · Data mining

1 Introduction

As an important measure of software quality, fault-proneness refers to the probability a software component contains at least one fault. For its prediction in object-oriented systems, it is essential to have informative predictive factors [1] and a good prediction model. There are many choices for predictive factors, including product metrics, processing and external metrics, and other combinations of factors [2]. There are also many choices for the prediction model which is as important as the predictive factors in determining the accuracy of the fault-proneness prediction [3].

Logistic regression has been extensively used for fault-proneness prediction as a benchmark method [4]. Recently, other learners such as decision tree [5], random forest [6], naive Bayes (NB) [3], neural network [7] and support vector machine [8] have been successfully used to predict fault-proneness.

These prediction methods have some shortcomings. For example, logistic regression [9] assumes a linear and addictive relationship between predictors and the

© Springer International Publishing Switzerland 2014
S. Hammoudi et al. (Eds.): ICEIS 2013, LNBIP 190, pp. 209–225, 2014.
DOI: 10.1007/978-3-319-09492-2_13

dependent variable (fault-proneness) on a logistic scale. This assumption is simplistic and presents a critical constraint on the model [10]. Further, the form of logistic regression also makes it difficult to combine qualitative predictors such as processing or external factors with numeric product metrics. NB has the constraints of assuming the conditional independence of predictors and the normal distribution of continuous product metrics as predictors [11]. Recently, Pai and Dugan [2] used LR to construct and parameterize their BN model which didn't avoid the typical constraints associated with LR. Other approaches such as random forest and neural network were black-box models and less interpretable although having a good prediction performance.

In this paper, we present a Bayesian network as a flexible modelling approach. We examine the performance of BN with its optimal learning algorithm (genetic algorithm) in comparison with the LR and NB using the continual versions of the open-source JavaScript tool, Rhino which has been developed using the agile software development process. Our study shows that the learned BN was mostly better than the LR and NB from the cross-validation test and from the independent test of the continual Rhino versions. The results suggest that our proposed BN modelling approach is valuable as a prediction model of fault-proneness.

The agile software development strategy is an iterative and incremental approach to software development which is performed in a highly collaborative manner that is cost effective and meets the changing needs of its stakeholders [12–14]. Agile Alliance defined 12 principles for the agile development process [14]. Olague *et al.* argued that Rhino was a typical software product using the agile development strategy [15]. Their study showed that product metrics (e.g. C-K metrics) at the class level were useful for the fault-proneness prediction of the agile OO systems. Therefore, our case study uses the C-K metrics and the cyclomatic complexity metrics to examine the difference in performance of the predictions (LR, NB and our proposed BN).

This paper makes the following contributions. First, we present the BN modelling framework with data mining techniques for learning and optimization and demonstrate its distinguishing features and advantages (more flexible network topology for including quantitative and qualitative predictors, and wide choices and incorporation of optimal learning algorithms) in comparison to the LR and NB models. Second, based on the cross-validation with sensitivity analysis and the independent test of the continual versions of Rhino, we show the superior performance of the learned BN. Third, with detailed analysis of implication of the BN modelling approach in combination with our series of studies, this study adds to the body of empirical knowledge about the prediction models of fault-proneness.

2 Background

This section briefly introduces the metrics used, the agile-developed Rhino system used for our study and the collection of metrics.

2.1 Metrics Used

We use the Chidamber and Kemerer's (C-K) metric suite and the cyclomatic complexity metrics at the class level as predictors. The C-K metric suite has been empirically validated to be useful for the fault-proneness prediction in many studies [4, 15, 16] and so are the cyclomatic complexity metrics [17]. It is assumed that the higher the metric value, the more fault-prone is the class.

In the C-K metrics implemented for this study, LCOM represents a later variation of the original LCOM that has been shown to have a better predictability [18]. The C-K metrics are listed below:

- WMC (Weighted Methods per Class): The number of methods implemented in a class.
- DIT (Depth of Inheritance Tree): Maximum number of edges between a given class and a root class in an inheritance graph (0 for a class which has no base class).
- NOC (Num. Children): A count of the number of direct children of a given class.
- CBO (Coupling Between Objects): Counts other classes whose attributes or methods are used by the given class plus those that use the attributes or methods of the given class.
- RFC (Response For a Class): A count of all local methods of a class plus all methods of other classes directly called by any of the methods of the class.
- LCOM (Lack of Cohesion of Methods): Number of disjoint sets of local methods, no two sets intersect, and any two methods on the same set share at least one local variable (1998 definition).

The cyclomatic complexity can be computed for each of the methods [19].

- CCMIN: Minimum of all cyclomatic complexity of the methods for a class.
- CCMAX: Maximum of all cyclomatic complexity of the methods for a class.
- CCMEAN: Arithmetic average of all cyclomatic complexity of the methods for a class.
- CCSUM: Sum of all cyclomatic complexity of the methods for a class.

2.2 System Under Study

Rhino [20], tested in this study, is an open-source implementation of JavaScript completely written in Java. This system has been developed following an iterative cycle from 2 to 16 months. The core components and their bug data of versions 1.5R3, 1.5R4, 1.5R5, 1.6R1, and 1.6R2 of Rhino were analyzed in our study. Fault reports of Rhino were extracted from the online Bugzilla repository [21]. The change logs of each version of Rhino listed the post-release bugs that were resolved for the next version. Bug fixes were cross-referenced with classes affected by each bug/fix.

2.3 Collection of Metrics

We used the open-source Java metric toolkits for extracting the product metrics from Rhino. Spinellis's CKJM [22] has been integrated in our program to collect the C-K metrics, and CYVIS, a software complexity visualiser [23] has been adapted to extract the cyclomatic complexity metrics at the class level from the Java class files.

Our initial analysis shows that, among the complexity metrics, CCMIN has little contribution to the prediction and hence it is removed from the set of predictors. Also, there is a large correlation between CCMAX, CCMEAN and CCSUM. This leads to the problem of multicollinearity [15]. After comparing their correlation with the C-K metrics, we select the complexity metric with a good predictability and less redundancy of information. Consequently, CCMAX is chosen for our case study.

The metric data were generated from the core components used for our study. Table 1 presents the descriptive statistics of predictive factors.

Table 1. Descriptive statistics of predictive factors used.

Version	Items	WMC	DIT	NOC	CBO	RFC	LCOM	CCMAX
1.5R3	Mean	14.79	0.81	0.35	6.04	37.29	228.27	20.75
	STDEV	19.55	0.84	1.29	7.24	47.13	811.4	43.88
1.5R4	Mean	14.76	0.85	0.32	6.08	26.91	236.45	21.58
	STDEV	20.06	0.81	1.28	7.61	48.13	851.95	47.72
1.5R5	Mean	14.85	0.86	0.34	5.96	36.86	234.21	19.24
	STDEV	19.93	0.85	1.34	6.84	47.68	914.97	42.29
1.6R1	Mean	15.53	0.82	0.33	6.12	38.87	300.16	20.5
	STDEV	22.84	0.82	1.56	7.54	53.7	1475.65	44.82

3   Modeling Techniques

This section describes the Bayesian modeling approach proposed in this study and briefly introduces other methods used for comparison.

3.1   Learned Bayesian Network

Bayesian network (BN) has a flexible network topology. We can use techniques of data mining and optimization to search for an optimal network and parameters to generate a better model. Further, we can use optimal discretization techniques to convert continuous metrics into discrete inputs for the BN.

3.1.1   Basic Model

Definition 1. A Bayesian Network B over the set of variables, V, is an ordered pair (B_S, B_P) such that

(1). $B_S = G(V, E)$ is a directed acyclic graph, called *the network structure* of B ($E \in V \times V$ is the set of directed edges, representing the probabilistically conditional dependence relationship between random variable (rv) nodes that satisfies the *Markov property*, i.e. there are no direct dependency in B_S which are not already explicitly shown via edges, E) and

(2). $B_P = \{\gamma_u : \Omega_u \times \Omega_{\pi_u} \to [0...1]u \in V\}$ is a set of *assessment functions*, where the
state space Ω_u is the finite set of values for the variable u; π_u is the set of parent
nodes of variables for u, indicated by B_S; if X is a set of variable, Ω_X is the
Cartesian product of all state spaces of the variables in X; γ_u uniquely defines the
joint probability distribution $P(u|\pi_u)$ of u conditional on its parent set, π_u.

Let c be the "faulty" rv of a class and its state space Ω_c be binary, then
$\Omega_c = \{$"faulty", "faultless"$\}$. In a specified BN, if some evidences are given, we can
get the posterior probability or belief of $c =$ "faulty" as the fault-proneness by calculating the marginal probability:

$$Bel(c = \text{``faulty''}) \sum_{u_i \in V, u_i \neq c} p(u_1, u_2, \ldots, c, \ldots, u_n) \tag{1}$$

where $p(u_1, \ldots, u_n) = \prod_{u_i \in V} p(u_i|\pi_{u_i})$ is the joint probability over V.

In practice, we often use the efficient algorithm of exact inference or approximate
inference rather than the marginalization of the joint probability to compute *Bel*.

3.1.2   Optimal Discretization by Learning
According to Definition 1, we need to generate the discrete state space Ω_u of u as
inputs to the BN when the predictor u is continuous. As the predictive factors used in
our study are quantitative metrics, discretization is necessary. There are two classes of
discretization methods: supervised and unsupervised. We used a supervised method,
the optimal multi-splits algorithm proposed by Elomaa and Rousu [24], which is based
on the information theory. This algorithm finds the optimal cut-points of a continuous
predictor based on the discretization's contribution to the classification prediction. The
algorithm is recursively run to identify the optimal splits [25].

3.1.3   GA for the Network Structure
There are two kinds of learning methods for a BN structure: the conditional independence test and the search of the scoring space. Since our goal is to obtain a BN
with the best performance, we prefer the latter because it can generate a BN satisfying
the Markov property and achieve an optimal prediction. In learning of an optimal BN,
a quality score is required to measure the network's quality. There are three kinds of
score measures that bear a close resemblance [26]: Bayesian approach, information
criterion approach, and minimum description length approach. We used the Bayesian
approach that uses the posterior probability of the learned network structure given the
training instances as a measure of the structure's quality.

There are different algorithms for searching the optimal Bayesian network. In our
study, we used the genetic algorithm (GA) because it can better explore the search
space and therefore has a lower chance of getting stuck in local optima [27]. It is more
likely to find the globally optimal solution.

GA is based on the mechanics of natural selection and genetics ("survival of the
fittest") and it aims to find the optimum with structured yet randomized information
exchange among encoded string structures. It evolves by repeating the following
steps: initialization or re-formation of the population, evaluation and selection of

individuals, crossover and mutation for generation of offspring until the maximum quality score is obtained or the maximum evolution time is used up. To learn an optimal BN, a connectivity matrix $C = (c_{ij})_{i,j\,=\,1,...,n}$ is used to encode the BN: if j is a parent node of i and $i > j$, $c_{ij} = 1$; otherwise, $c_{ij} = 0$. Then the BN can be represented by the string that consists of the elements of C [28]. The inequality $i > j$ ensures the assumed ancestral order between the variables. Using the general GA for the strings that encode the network structures, we can find the optimal BN. For details, see [27, 28].

In our study, the GA parameters were set as follows: descendant population size $= 100$, population size $= 20$, crossover probability $= 1$, mutation probability $= 0.1$, random seed $= 1$, and run time $= 50$.

3.1.4 Learning of the Network Parameters
After the network structure is found, the conditional probability table (CPT), i.e. implementation of assessment functions in B_P of the BN (Definition 1) needs to be estimated from the database of instances. We used the Bayesian estimator which assumes that the conditional probability of each rv node corresponding to its parent instantiation conforms to the Dirichlet distribution [29] with local parameter independence: $D(\alpha_1, \cdots, \alpha_i, \cdots, \alpha_\tau)$ with α_i being the hyperparameter for state i.

The Dirichlet-based parameter estimator assumes independence of local parameters which may not be true in practice. This can result in biased parameters. We can use classification tree to improve learning while avoiding the assumption [29].

3.1.5 Probabilistic Inference
The constructed BN model can be used to make an inference of the probability prediction of the query (target) variable ("faulty" or "fault-free"), given the nodes of predictors. There are two kinds of inference: exact inference and approximate inference. Exact inference uses all the information of nodes in the BN to make the probability inference. It has a higher prediction accuracy than the approximate inference, which makes the inference through sampling [29]. For a large-scale connected BN, the exact inference is a NP problem and the approximate inference is preferred. But, in our study, as the learned network is relatively simple (with less than 8 nodes), the exact inference of the BN's polytree [29] is used, partly because it is more efficient than the marginalization of the joint probability.

3.2 Other Methods for Fault-Proneness Prediction

We also used logistical regression and naïve Bayes for comparison with the Bayesian approach described in Sect. 3.1.

Logistic regression (LR) is a technique of probability estimation based on maximum likelihood estimation. In this model, let Y be the fault-proneness of a class as the dependent variable ($Y = 1$ indicating "faulty" and $Y = 0$ "fault-free") and X_i ($i = 1, 2, ..., n$) be the predictive factors. LR assumes that Y follows a Bernnouli distribution and the link function relating X_i and Y is the *logit* or log-odds. Also, the predictive factors, X, are linearly and addictively related to Y on a logistic scale. This may be too simplistic and can introduce bias [10]. Further, LR uses only quantitative factors for the prediction and constrains the inclusion of other factors such as processing or external factors.

Naïve bayes is a simplified Bayesian approach with a single structure of a target node and multiple evidence nodes with the assumption that the predictive factors are conditionally independent given the class attribute ($C =$ "fault-free" or "faulty"). The two assumptions of naïve Bayes, namely, the conditional independence and the normal distribution of continuous predictors, may not hold for some domains (predictive metrics) [11], thus affecting its prediction performance.

4 Data Analysis

The data analysis involves four steps: feature selection, multicollinearity analysis, modeling and prediction, and evaluation.

4.1 Feature Selection

Feature selection selects the correlative and informative features (factors) for learning and prediction. As Pearson's correlation only measures the linear correlation and may omit nonlinear information, we use the information-based feature selector, Information Gain Ratio (GR) [30]. GR takes into account the information that each feature contains and measures the gain ratio given the feature to be assessed.

If a predictor is continuous, it is discretized before computing its GR. Table 2 shows the GR of the metrics used for each of the chosen Rhino versions. CCMIN with GR of 0 will be removed from the set of predictors.

4.2 Multicollinearity Analysis

For multicollinearity analysis, we can use the combination of predictive factors with less redundancy information for a better learning and prediction for LR and NB.

Table 2. GR of C-K and cyclomatic complexity.

Metrics	1.5R3	1.5R4	1.5R5	1.6R1	1.6R2
WMC	0.23	0.21	0.14	0.23	0.26
DIT	0	0.09	0	0.18	0.12
CBO	0.36	0.24	0.13	0.22	0.2
RFC	0.49	0.24	0.22	0.3	0.26
LCOM	0.28	0.29	0.26	0.2	0.13
NOC	0	0.18	0	0	0
CCMIN	0	0	0	0	0
CCMAX	0.51	0.21	0.12	0.18	0.16
CCMEAN	0.29	0.18	0.12	0.17	0.12
CCSUM	0.11	0.22	0	0.16	0.13

The variance inflation factor (VIF) is often used to diagnose the multicollinearity and weaken it [31]. If multicollinearity exists, by comparing the Pearson's correlation and removing one of the strongly correlative independent variables, or removing the predictor with the maximum VIF value, the multicollinearity can be gradually weakened until VIFs of all the predictors are equal to or smaller than 3. We directly used the result of multicollinearity analysis in [15] since it analyzed the same system (Rhino) and similar versions (1.5R3, 1.5R4 and 1.5R5) as ours. Thus, two combinations of C-K metrics were chosen as sets of predictive factors (with VIF < 3):

- C-K model 1: CBO, DIT, LCOM, NOC, and WMC;
- C-K model 2: CBO, DIT, LCOM, NOC, and RFC.

For the cyclomatic complexity metrics, Table 2 shows that CCMAX has a larger GR for almost all the Rhino versions, which indicates its higher contribution to the prediction. Further, there are large correlations between CCMAX, CCSUM and CCMEAN (CCMIN is removed as its GR is 0). We select CCMAX as the predictor of complexity because it has a better GR value and a weak correlation with the C-K metrics (as shown in Table 3). Thus, CCMAX will be combined with those metrics in C-K model 1 and model 2 to generate new sets of predictors.

Table 3. CCMAX's correlation with CK-metrics.

Version	WMC	DIT	CBO	RFC	LCOM	NOC
1.5R3	0.45*	−0.21*	0.47*	0.56*	0.25*	0.22*
1.5R4	0.46*	−0.09*	0.44*	0.57*	0.25*	0.04*
1.5R5	0.50*	−0.07*	0.36*	0.55*	0.29*	0.023
1.6R1	0.46*	−0.05	0.37*	0.53*	0.21*	0.072
1.6R2	0.47*	0	0.38*	0.54*	0.22*	0.074

*: Correlation is significant at the 0.01 level (2-tailed).

4.3 Modeling and Prediction

For LR and NB, we choose informative combinations of predictive factors with less redundancy information according to Table 2 and the above multicollinearity analysis. As BN can model the complex probabilistic dependent (conditional) relationships between predictors with its flexible network topology, we do not consider the multicollinearity issue and choose all the predictors with nonzero GR values.

The procedure of modeling and prediction follows the techniques described earlier in Sect. 3. For the LR, the continuous product metrics are directly used as inputs since its model is based on continuous attributes; for the NB, we use the pdf of a normal (Gaussian) distribution for estimation. But for the BN, the continuous predictors are discretized first, and then used in the modeling with fault data.

We evaluate the performance of these prediction methods in two ways. The first method applied the usual 10×10 cross-folder validation. In this validation, the dataset was randomly divided into 10 buckets of equal size. Nine buckets were used for training and the last bucket was used for the test. The procedure was iterated 10 times and the final result was averaged. For the construction of model, we used all the instances for learning. The second method used the prediction model of one version to predict the fault-proneness of the relevant classes of the next version (i.e. 1.5R3 for 1.5R4, 1.5R4 for 1.5R5, 1.5R5 for 1.6R1, and 1.6R1 for 1.6R2).

Besides, for the 10 × 10 cross validation, we also conducted sensitivity analysis to test variation of the prediction using different sampling schemes to get the folds of different training samples. Then, the statistics (mean, variance and confidence intervals) of performance measures for the learning models were used to examine the modeling uncertainty.

4.4   Evaluation Methods

We use the receiver operative characteristic (ROC) as the evaluation method. ROC was originated from the signal detection theory and statistical decision theory. It assumes that the binary signal is corrupted by Gaussian noise and the recognition accuracy depends on the strength of signal, noise variance, and desired hit rate or false alarm rate.

In a ROC graph, the horizontal axis represents 1-specificity and the vertical axis the sensitivity. If we register whether an artifact is fault-prone as the signal (0 regarded as "fault-free" and 1 as "faulty"), the 1-specificity refers to the ratio of the instances detected as "faulty" among all the fault-free instances (a.k.a. probability of false alarms, pf) and the sensitivity refers to the ratio of the instances also detected as "faulty" among all the faulty instances (a.k.a. probability of fault detection, pd). *Precision* (p) is the proportion of the correctly predicted cases.

According to the definition of pd and pf, their range must be within the interval [0, 1]. A larger pd with a lower pf indicates a good prediction performance. When the ROC point (pf, pd) is closer to the upper-left corner (0, 1), called "sweet spot" where $pf = 0$ and $pd = 1$, the prediction model has a better performance. Often we cannot simultaneously achieve a high pd and low pf. The balance is based on the Euclidean distance from the sweet spot (0,1) to a pair of (pf, pd):

$$balance = 1 - \sqrt{((pf - 0)^2 + (pd - 1)^2)/2} \tag{2}$$

A higher balance indicates being closer to the sweet spot and a better prediction performance.

ROC curve corresponds to a sensitivity analysis. We can set different values of the threshold of the fault-proneness, p_0, from 0 to 1, to calculate the value pairs (pf, pd) for each threshold. Then we use these pairs to construct a curve with pf varying from 0 to 1. If the curve is closer to the sweet spot and more convex than another curve, then its performance is better; if the curve is close to the diagonal line from (0, 0) to (1, 1), its prediction performance is no better than a random guess [32].

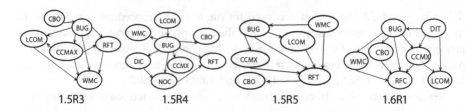

Fig. 1. Network topologies of the learned BN for the chosen Rhino versions.

5   Results and Discussion

5.1   Learned Models

Our result shows that model 2 of NB had a better performance than model 1. Thus, it is used for comparison against the LR and BN models.

Figure 1 shows the network topology of the learned BN for each of the four test versions (1.5R3, 1.5R4, 1.5R5, 1.6R1).

5.2   Comparison by Cross Validation

Table 4 gives the comparison of the prediction models (LR, NB and BN) from the 10×10 cross-folder validation. The BN achieves a better *pd* (0.55–0.792) than the NB, LR-model 1 and LR-model 2 for the chosen Rhino versions (1.5R3, 1.5R4, 1.5R5, 1.6R1 and 1.6R2). Further, for each version, the proposed BN keeps its *pd* above 0.5 which demonstrates a high stability of prediction performance.

Relatively, for the test versions, both LR and NB have a lower and unstable *pd* value (the LR's *pd* ranges from 0.31 to 0.648 and the NB's *pd* ranges from 0.345 to 0.519). Also, the BN's *balance* is better and more stable than that of both LR and NB although its precision is slightly lower than theirs.

ROC curves of the prediction models indicates that the ROC of the BN is mostly closer to the sweet spot and more convex (also bigger ROC values) than those of the LR or NB, which further indicates its better performance.

Our sensitivity analysis in 10×10 cross validation showed that different sampling schemes resulted in the bias that could in turn affect the effectiveness of the prediction. Further, even with small variation, BN still remained a better prediction performance for fault-proneness, with an improvement in ROC of 10–14 % for LR and 10–11 % for NB (1.5R3), 6–7 % for LR and 9–10 % for NB (1.5R4), 5–7 % for LR and 10–15 % for NB (1.5R5), 6–7 % for LR and 5–8 % for NB (1.6R1), and 2–4 % for LR and 6–7 % for NB (1.6R2).

5.3   Validation by Continual Versions

For the fault-proneness prediction, a better validation is to use the prediction model learned from one version to test the next version. This validation by continual versions

Table 4. Comparison of the models by cross validation.

Version	Model	pd	pf	Precision	ROC Area	balance
1.5R3	LR-model1	0.4	0.031	0.727	0.784	0.399
	LR-model2	0.4	0.031	0.727	0.755	0.399
	NB-model2	0.55	0.061	0.647	0.778	0.546
	BN	0.55	0.061	0.647	0.867	0.546
1.5R4	LR-model1	0.63	0.157	0.756	0.834	0.598
	LR-model2	0.648	0.143	0.778	0.832	0.62
	NB-model2	0.519	0.071	0.848	0.803	0.514
	BN	0.722	0.129	0.813	0.89	0.694
1.5R5	LR-model1	0.276	0.052	0.615	0.756	0.274
	LR-model2	0.31	0.052	0.643	0.767	0.308
	NB-model2	0.345	0.063	0.625	0.697	0.342
	BN	0.552	0.042	0.8	0.806	0.55
1.6R1	LR-model1	0.623	0.152	0.767	0.785	0.594
	LR-model2	0.642	0.182	0.739	0.79	0.598
	NB-model2	0.377	0.061	0.833	0.785	0.374
	BN	0.792	0.242	0.724	0.84	0.681
1.6R2	LR-model1	0.627	0.231	0.681	0.796	0.561
	LR-model2	0.609	0.185	0.721	0.804	0.567
	NB-model2	0.392	0.046	0.87	0.77	0.39
	BN	0.784	0.323	0.656	0.824	0.611

is more useful for testing software developed with a highly-iterative or agile evolutional strategy [15]. We used the models of LR-model 1, LR-model 2, NB-model 2 and BN learned with the class instances of the core components of one version to test those of the next version with the same predictors (1.5R3 for 1.5R4, 1.5R4 for 1.5R5, 1.5R5 for 1.6R1 and 1.6R1 for 1.6R2). Table 5 shows the results.

For Rhino versions 1.5R3 and 1.5R5, all LR, NB and BN models present a low *pd* and *balance*. However, for these two versions, the BN has a higher *pd* and *balance* than those of LR and NB. For the other versions (1.5R4 and 1.6R1), the BN achieves a much better *pd* and *balance*. The ROC areas of all the models are above 0.7, indicating moderate to high precision.

Figure 2 shows changes of *pd*, *balance* and *precision* of the prediction models in the cross-folder validation (a, b and c) and the validation of continual versions (d, e and f). As seen in Fig. 2(a vs. d, and b vs. e), the *pd* and *balance* curves of the models keep the same shape (two linked "V") and trend. The difference in shape between the *pd* and *balance* curves is not large. Further, the core components of Rhino version 1.5R5 have the worst prediction performance either by the cross-folder validation or by the validation of continual versions. According to the change log of Rhino [21], since version 1.6R1, there was a major revision (to support ECMAScript for XML (E4X) as specified by ECMA 357 standard) which represented a large change from the

Table 5. Comparison of the models by validation by continual versions.

Version	Model	pd	pf	Precision	ROC Area	balance
1.5R3	LR-model1	0.204	0.014	0.917	0.779	0.204
	LR-model2	0.185	0.014	0.909	0.79	0.185
	NB-model2	0.333	0.029	0.9	0.842	0.332
	BN	0.407	0.014	0.957	0.847	0.407
1.5R4	LR-model1	0.724	0.281	0.438	0.795	0.606
	LR-model2	0.724	0.292	0.429	0.795	0.598
	NB-model2	0.552	0.156	0.516	0.745	0.526
	BN	0.862	0.365	0.417	0.806	0.61
1.5R5	LR-model1	0.1892	0.015	0.909	0.78	0.189
	LR-model2	0.208	0.015	0.917	0.758	0.208
	NB-model2	0.245	0.03	0.867	0.822	0.244
	BN	0.283	0.03	0.882	0.825	0.282
1.6R1	LR-model1	0.647	0.215	0.702	0.816	0.587
	LR-model2	0.647	0.215	0.702	0.827	0.587
	NB-model2	0.392	0.031	0.909	0.818	0.391
	BN	0.843	0.338	0.662	0.832	0.627

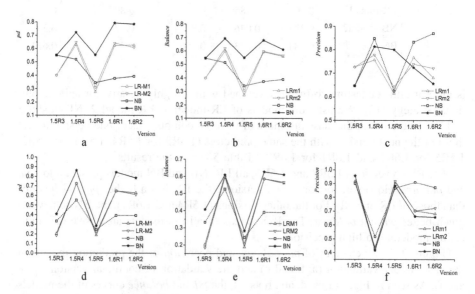

Fig. 2. Changes of *pd*, *balance* and *precision* by the cross-validation (a, b, c) and the validations of continual versions (d, e, f).

earlier versions. This additional functionality (non-fault cause) may result in the low *pd* and *balance* of the models for this version 1.5R5 when making prediction for the next version, 1.6R1 (Fig. 2d and e).

As can be seen in Fig. 2(a vs. d, b vs. e), the performance of the prediction models (LR-model 1, LR-model 2, NB-model 2 and BN) by the cross-folder validation is similar to that by the validation of continual versions. Overall, the performance by the cross-folder validation is slightly better than that by the continual validation but for the BN model, this is not the case for version 1.5R4 and 1.6R1. Further, the difference in performance of the prediction models between the cross-folder validation and the validation of continual versions is similar. The BN has achieved a better prediction performance (a larger *pd* and *balance*) for each of the chosen Rhino versions either by the cross-folder validation or by the validation of continual versions. The performance of the NB and LR models is inconsistent (for version 1.5R3 and 1.5R5, NB is better than LR; but for version 1.5R4 and 1.6R1, LR is better than NB).

On the other hand, the *precision* curves of the prediction models present an unstable trend either by the cross-folder validation (Fig. 2c) or by the validation of continual versions (Fig. 2f). There is no one model whose precision always keeps a better value across the releases of the continual versions. Our analysis suggests that precision is not a good measure for evaluation of the prediction models due to its large standard deviations (instability) [33]. Although the BN's precision is sometimes not as good as the LR or NB, it's larger and more stable *pd* and *balance* show that it is valuable for fault-proneness prediction.

5.4 Implications

The BN has the advantages of a flexible network structure and wide choices of the learning and optimization algorithms. It also avoids the constraints of LR (logistical-scale linear and addictive relationships between predictors and the fault-proneness), and the assumptions of NB (the conditional independence and the normal distributions of predictors). Our 10×10 cross-validation and the independent test of continual versions of the test system showed that the prediction results of the BN learned by the GA are *positively encouraging*: compared with the NB and LR, the BN has a better and stable *pd* and *balance*. The comparison between the ROC values of the prediction models also strengthened this conclusion.

In the previous studies on using BN for fault-proneness, Liu et al. [34] used spanning tree to construct their BN, Fenton et al. [35] constructed the network based on the domain knowledge, and Pai and Dugan [2] used LR to construct and parameterize their BN model. Compared with the previous studies, we adopted optimal discretization and genetic algorithm (GA) to improve the network (avoiding missing of domain knowledge for construction of network and local optimization since GA is a globally optimal solution).

Further, BN, as an integrative method, is capable of capturing critical domain knowledge and using multiple learners to strengthen the ability of processing uncertainty in modelling that mainly originated from missing or incomplete training samples. However, the uncertainty deriving from learning and modelling was seldom considered in previous studies [2, 3, 6, 8, 15]. In this study, we conducted sensitivity analysis to test the uncertainty in 10×10 cross validation that showed an improvement of BN by 2–14 % over LR and by 6–11 % over NB. This provided additional support for superiority of BN. In our earlier study [36], we employed Occam's window to select highly-qualified models [37] and Bayesian model averaging (BMA) [38] to get an integrative and robust prediction of fault-proneness. In the test of NASA's MDP dataset (http://mdp.ivv.nasa.gov/), the BN models were selected based on the heuristic learning algorithms (K2, Hill-climbing, Tan and Tabu) [29] and the BN integrative prediction was statistically significantly comparable to or better than many other learning algorithms including LR, NB, J48, sequential minimal optimization, normalized Gaussian radial basis function network, multilayer perceptron and random forest. Our studies demonstrated the advantages and superiority of BN over other single learning algorithms due to its flexible modelling framework and capability of processing uncertainty.

Our study also used continual versions of Rhino to extensively validate the learning models as independent tests. In many previous studies, the same model had varying performances across different contexts and software products [3] that presented the issue of validating usefulness of the learning algorithms for fault-proneness prediction. By independent tests of continual versions, the learned BN method is particularly valuable for the quality evaluation of the mainstream OO systems developed with the highly-iterative or agile strategy. By cross validation and independent test, our study demonstrated applicability and advantages of employing the BN modelling approach to evaluate fault-proneness, a critical measure for software quality for OO systems.

5.5 Threats to Validity

There are several threats to validity. The first threat is that only version series of one software product (Rhino) were used to train and test the model. But the paper's focus is on examination of the learners in agile process software (not generalization of the method to general software modules). We have examined our models across other different software products and statistically demonstrated our approach's advantages in previous studies [36, 39]. The second threat is that selection of different predictive factors for different models may damage the validity of the models. But learning was conducted to achieve the optimal prediction performance. Using the same methods of feature selection and optimal learning algorithms for different models, the prediction performance of the models could be comparable no matter what different predictors were used. The third threat is use of cross validation that may result in over-optimism due to sampling bias. We performed sensitivity analysis and independent test of continual versions of the test product (Rhino) as extensive validity that could diminish or remove bias by cross validation.

6 Conclusions

This paper presents an integrative learned BN that is based on the data mining techniques of optimal discretization and genetic algorithm for prediction of fault-proneness of the agile OO systems. D'Ambros et al. [1] illustrated the importance of predictors and Menzies et al. [3] showed the importance of learners such as naïve Bayes. We extended the previous work by illustrating the improvement of fault-proneness prediction by learning algorithms for feature selection and flexible network structure. Using five continual versions of the open-source Rhino system, we empirically validated the proposed prediction model and compare its performance with LR and NB.

Using additional benchmark datasets (e.g. NASA's MDP) from public domain, we also conducted more empirical validation of the BN in comparison with other models for the fault-proneness prediction. With this study, the previous test [36] illustrated the superiority and stability of BN for quality assessment of software products including agile software.

Further, we have been investigating the contribution of more sophisticated learning algorithms such as GA used in this study and simulation annealing as parts of the integrative learners as well as more effective predictors, qualitative or quantitative in BN to improve fault-proneness prediction. We will also explore predictability and effectiveness of BN with the learning algorithms (discretization, adjustment of network structure and parameters by multiple learning algorithms in combination with domain knowledge) for other aspects (e.g. reliability) of software quality.

Acknowledgements. This research is partly supported by the Hong Kong CERG grant PolyU5225/08E, NSFC grant 1171344/D010703, MOST grants (2012CB955503 and 2011AA120305-1).

References

1. D'Ambros, M., Lanza, M., Robbes, R.: Evaluating defect prediction approaches: a benchmark and an extensive comparison. Empir. Softw. Eng. **17**, 531–577 (2012)
2. Pai, G.J., Dugan, J.B.: Empirical analysis of software fault content and fault proneness using Bayesian methods. IEEE Trans. Software Eng. **33**, 675–686 (2007)
3. Menzies, T., Greenwald, J., Frank, A.: Data mining static code attributes to learn defect predictors. IEEE Trans. Software Eng. **33**, 2–13 (2007)
4. Briand, L.C., Wust, J., Daly, J.W., Porter, D.V.: Exploring the relationships between design measures and software quality in object-oriented systems. J. Syst. Softw. **51**, 245–273 (2000)
5. Singh Y., Kaur, A., Malhotra, R.: Application of decision trees for predicting fault proneness. In: International Conference on Information Systems, Technology and Management-Information Technology, Ghaziabad, India (2009)
6. Guo, L., Ma, Y., Cukic, B., Singh, H.: Robust prediction of fault proneness by random forests. In: 15th International Symposium on Software Reliability Engineering, pp. 417–428. IEEE Computer Society, Washington, DC (2004)

7. Singh, Y., Kaur, A., Malhotra, R.: Predicting software fault proneness model using neural network. In: Jedlitschka, A., Salo, O. (eds.) PROFES 2008. LNCS, vol. 5089, pp. 204–214. Springer, Heidelberg (2008)

8. Singh, Y., Kaur, A., Malhotra, R.: Software fault proneness prediction using support vector machines. In: Proceedings of the World Congress on Engineering (2009)

9. Hosmer, D., Lemeshow, S.: Applied Logistic Regression. Wiley, New York (2000)

10. Gokhale, S.S., Lyn, M.R.: Regression tree modeling for the prediction of software quality. In: Proceedings Of Third ISSAT Intl. Conference on Reliability, pp. 31–36 (1997)

11. John, G.H., Langley, P.: Estimating continuous distributions in Bayesian classifiers. In: the Eleventh Conference on Uncertainty in Artificial Intelligence, pp. 338–346 (1995)

12. Ambler, S.W.: Agile Modeling: Effective Practices for Extreme Programming and the Unified Process. Wiley, New York (2002)

13. Herbsleb, J.D.: Global software development. IEEE Softw. 18, 16–20 (2001)

14. http://www.agilealliance.org

15. Olague, H.M., Etzkorn, L.H., Gholston, S., Quattlebaum, S.: Empirical validation of three software metrics suites to predict fault-proneness of object-oriented classes developed using highly iterative or agile software development processes. IEEE Trans. Softw. Eng. 33, 402–419 (2007)

16. Basili, V.R., Briand, L.C., Melo, W.L.: A validation of object-oriented design metrics as quality indicators. IEEE Trans. Softw. Eng. 22, 751–761 (1996)

17. Cardoso, J.: Process control-flow complexity metric: an empirical validation. In: IEEE International Conference on Services Computing (IEEE SCC 06), pp. 167–173. IEEE Computer Society (2006)

18. Harrison, R., Counsell, S., Nithi, R.: An evaluation of the MOOD set of object oriented software metrics. IEEE Trans. Softw. Eng. 24, 150–157 (1998)

19. McCabe, T.J.: A complexity measure. IEEE Trans. Softw. Eng. 2, 308–320 (1976)

20. http://www.mozilla.org/rhino

21. https://bugzilla.mozilla.org/

22. Spinellis, D.: Code Quality: The Open Source Perspective. Addison Wesley, Boston (2006)

23. http://cyvis.sourceforge.net/index.html

24. Elomaa, T., Rousu, J.: Finding optimal multi-splits for numerical attributes in decision tree learning (1996)

25. Li, L., Wang, J., Leung, H., Jiang, C.: Assessment of catastrophic risk using bayesian network constructed from domain knowledge and spatial data. Risk Anal. 30, 1157–1175 (2010)

26. Bouckaert, R.R.: Bayesian Belief Network: from Construction to Inference (1995)

27. Kabli, R., Herrmann, F., McCall, J.: A Chain-Model Genetic Algorithm for Bayesian Network Structure Learning. GECCO, London (2007)

28. Larranaga, P., Murga, R., Poza, M., Kuijpers, C.: Structure learning of Bayesian network by hybrid genetic algorithms. In: Fisher, D., Lenz, H.J. (eds.) Learning from Data: AI and Statistics. Springer, New York (1996)

29. Korb, K.B., Nicholson, A.E.: Bayesian Artificial Intelligence. Chapman & Hall/CRC, Boca Raton (2004)

30. Quinlan, J.R.: C4.5: Programs for Machine Learning. Morgan Kauffman, San Francisco (1993)

31. Dirk, V.P., Bart, L.: Customer attrition analysis for financial services using proportional hazard models. Eur. J. Oper. Res. 157, 196–217 (2004)

32. http://white.stanford.edu/ ~ heeger/sdt/sdt.html

33. Menzies, T., Dekhtyar, A., Distefano, J., Greenwald, J.: Problems with precision: a response to "comments on 'data mining static code attributes to learn defect predictors'". IEEE Trans. Softw. Eng. **33**, 637–640 (2007)
34. Liu, Y., Cheah, W., Kim, B., Park, H.: Predict software failure-prone by learning Bayesian network. Int. J. Adv. Sci. Technol. **1**, 33–42 (2008)
35. Fenton, N., Neil, M., Marsh, W., Hearty, P., Radlinski, L., Krause, P.: On the effectiveness of early life cycle defect prediction with Bayesian nets. Empir. Softw. Eng. **13**, 499–537 (2008)
36. Li, L., Leung, H.: Mining static code metrics for a robust prediction of software defect-proneness. In: ACM /IEEE International Symposium on Empirical Software Engineering and Measurement Anaheim, CA (2011)
37. Cox, A.L.: Risk Analysis: Foundations, Models and Methods. Springer, Heidelberg (2001)
38. Hoeting, A.J., Madigan, D., Raftery, E.A., Volinsky, T.C.: Bayesian model averaging: a tutorial. Stat. Sci. **14**, 382–417 (1999)
39. Li, L., Leung, H.: Using the number of faults to improve fault-proneness prediction of the probability models. In: 2009 World Congress on Computer Science and Information Engineering, Los Angeles/Anaheim (2009)

Foundation for Fine-Grained Security and DRM Control Based on a Service Call Graph Context Identification

Ziyi Su[1](✉) and Frédérique Biennier[2]

[1] Department of Computer Science and Information Technology,
Northeast Normal University, Changchun, China
[2] Lab. LIRIS CNRS, INSA-lyon, Avenue Albert Einstein, Villeurbanne, France
suziyi@nenu.edu.cn, frederique.biennier@insa-lyon.fr

Abstract. Maintaining service/data providers' protection requirements in a dynamic service composition context requires a collaborative business process slicing method to capture the assets derivation pattern. Based on a brief discussion of sub-context modes in collaborative enterprise scenarios, we propose a service composition context identification method with Service Call Graph (SCG) model, extending the System Dependency Graph, to describe dependencies among partners in a business process. This graph is then analyzed to group partners into sub-context thanks to asset-based and request-based slicing strategies. By this way, downstream consumers' security profile can be compared with upstream asset providers' policies so that security requirements can be fulfilled.

Keywords: Web Service composition · Workflow · Service Call Graph · Context slicing · Dependency

1 Context

Service-Oriented Architecture provides an environment for partners to share digital assets, including computing capability (e.g. Web Service) and information (e.g. data), in order to produce final artifacts (e.g. composed service or new information generated from data aggregation). As assets are shared beyond ownership boundary, the risk of intellectual property infringement (e.g. circumventing of trade secret, or even leakage to a competitor) associated to 'loss of governance' is a major barrier for moving toward collaborative business model [2,5,6]. Therefore security requirement is brought to an end-to-end scale, to ensure the protection of corporate patrimony value during its full lifecycle (covering the creation, dissemination, aggregation and destruction stages), paying attention to the way assets are used and protected.

In a web-based business collaborative context, such requirements involve first to control the way partners are selected to define the way downstream recipients

© Springer International Publishing Switzerland 2014
S. Hammoudi et al. (Eds.): ICEIS 2013, LNBIP 190, pp. 226–241, 2014.
DOI: 10.1007/978-3-319-09492-2_14

must gain assets provider's approval for re-disseminating such assets (or a new digital asset including it) [1,9], ensuring that all the providers' security criteria are maintained during the full lifecycle of their assets.

To this end we propose a method for analyzing complex collaborative context and applying fine-grained security policy to manage assets sharing activities. The basic thoughts involve that security foundation for a successful collaborative process is built when each provider's policy upon its asset is fulfilled during the whole business process.

After presenting the extended security policy management challenges in Sect. 2, we present our solution based on a Service Call Graph (SCG) [12] extending the System Dependency Graph (SDG), for mining partners asset sharing relations in collaborative business processes, thanks to a 'service call tuple' data structure used to capture dependencies among partners in Sect. 3. Then the asset-based and request-based context slicing methods are used to mine the 'assets aggregation' and 'requests aggregation' from the service call tuple list that represents a business process (Sect. 4). We analyze the sub-context developments, using 'pre-processing' and 'on-the-fly processing' strategies, and describe how down-stream provider assets security is achieved by managing sub-context developments.

2   Extended Security Policy Management

Web Services enable the openness of corporate Information System, the interoperable interaction, agile work-flow and efficient values exchange. Such federated business paradigm brings new concerns about how to configure security among decentralized partners and how to protect resources in a life-long vision. Fitting the open and collaborative Internet-based system paradigm, more adaptive attribute-based security policies [7,10] have been brought forward to express enriched security factors as well as consumption 'actions' upon resources. To ensure the required protection even after dynamic service composition includes business process analysis challenges.

2.1   Attribute-Based Security Policy Model

An attribute-based security policy has the ability to express fine-grained security factors related to system entities, through elements as Rights, Conditions and Obligations (see formula 1).

$$Assertion = (O, S, R, C, Rn, Ob, L) \tag{1}$$

The semantics of the factors are as follows: 'O' (Object) is the resource bearing corporate asset value (service or information). 'S' (Subject) is the party that requests accessing the Right to the resource. 'R' (Right) is the Operation upon the resource that the Subject can be allowed to exercise. 'Rn' (Restriction) is the constraints upon the Right. For example a restriction 'three times' may be used to refine the right 'rendering a piece of multi-media file'. 'C' (Condition) is the requirements that must be satisfied for the Subject to access Rights upon the Object, including subject attributes (SAT), object attributes (OAT) or context related attributes ($CNAT$) – attributes of transaction context, environment, infrastructure, etc. 'Ob' (Obligations) is the action that 'must' be exercised. For example the obligation 'to delete acquired data in 10 days' can be associated to rights like 'read stock amount' and 'read client data'. 'L' (Logic Operator) represents the logic operators as 'imply' ($\leftarrow$), 'and' ($\wedge$) and 'or' ($\vee$).

Such a policy model, usually called Attribute-Based Access Control policy (ABAC) [13], has the ability to accommodate 'point-to-point' security factors such as the subjects and environment attributes. The 'due use' factors can also be expressed to regulate consumption actions. In deployment stage, an assets owner uses such policy models to declare its "Requirement of Protection (RoP)", namely the requirements about the security attributes of the asset-requester and the consumption actions that are allowed on the asset. And an assets consumer uses such policy models to declare its "Quality of Protection (QoP)", that is, its security attributes and the consumption actions it requests to exert on the asset.

Nonetheless, such a security model is oriented to the one-to-one cooperation scenario. In a Web Service composition scenario, security requires that an upstream provider's policy should be met by downstream consumers that directly or indirectly receive information assets from the provider, in order to guarantee end-to-end security to assets. In such contexts the asset sharing pattern in the service composition should be analyzed.

2.2 Sub-Context Modes

In a service composition scenario, only partners correlated by (both direct or indirect) exchanged assets are deemed as in one sub-context [11]. Therefore, a diagrammatical analysis can differentiate a service composition scenario into 4 type of sub-context modes, as discussed in the following. For convenience of discussion, we denote the assets provided by partners as 'Original Assets' ('O-Assets' for short) and the artifacts of collaborative work (aggregating several O-Assets) as 'Collaboration Assets' ('C-Assets' for short). Security management with the asset aggregation viewpoint follows such principles:

1. Providers for the same C-Asset are deemed as the same sub-context.
2. A participant can belong to more than one sub-context at the same time. It must follow the RoP (resulting from the aggregation of providers' RoPs) of that sub-context.
3. All consumers having the same rights upon the C-Asset(s) are deemed as in one group.

With above principles, the provider-consumer relations among partners can be specified. Analyzing a collaborative context in this way, one can encounter several situations (denoted as 'sub-context modes' [11]) (Fig. 1):

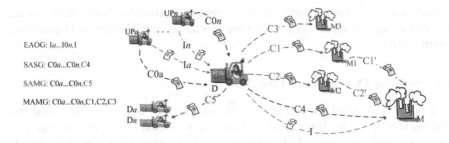

Fig. 1. Sub-context modes in service composition scenario.

- 'Each Asset One Group (EAOG)' mode:
  When all providers **can distinguish** their own asset (O-Assets) in the artifact of business collaboration (C-Asset), there is no asset aggregation. Each
  partner works in a separate sub-context. An example is when the inventory
  information from upstream providers are concatenated into one XML file, each
  of them as a separate node. Then each provider's policy is attached to the
  node containing its inventory information. Downstream partner reading one
  node must follow the due policy of that node.
- 'Single-Asset Single-Group (SASG)' mode:
  If the O-Assets in C-Asset are **not identifiable**, their providers are deemed
  as in one sub-context. Besides, all the consumers will be given the same rights,
  that is, the most privileged rights required among the consumers. An example
  is when production information from different providers is merged to a global
  scheduling information. A downstream consumer must fulfill the policies of all
  the providers in order to read the global scheduling information.
- 'Single-Asset Multi-Group (SAMG)' mode:
  If the O-Assets in C-Asset are not identifiable and their providers have defined
  multiple rights. Different consumers are given different rights (nevertheless,
  they should fulfill the condition corresponding to that right). Then each right
  manages a group of consumers.
- 'Multi-Asset Multi-Group (MAMG)' mode:
  If there are multiple C-Assets in the context, we should track the O-Assets
  dissemination and see which C-Assets include which O-Assets. The providers'
  policies must be maintained on the C-Assets.

These 4 patterns generally exist in many collaborative contexts, as long as
the issue of information asset protection and consumption exists. Imagining
to change above supply chain scenario to others, e.g. switching the materials
providers as Cloud providers or Service providers, the asset exchange pattern
still falls in the 4 modes. Security governance is achieved in each sub-contexts,
by examining if the QoPs of the consumers for the C-Asset fulfill the RoPs of
the providers, based on a policy aggregation and negotiation strategy [10].

The central issue in this paper is to develop a method that analyzes the
collaborative business process to partition sub-contexts and allocates partners

according to asset sharing patterns. We develop a method for this task, borrowing and modifying the method used for programm slicing with System Dependency Graph (SDG).

2.3   System Dependency Graph

In a business federation context, service composition is used to set collaborative business process, leading to exchange information assets across organization boundaries and possibly to merge them with other assets. In order to give a full lifecycle protection to an asset, the asset derivations must be captured. Asset derivation is analogous to program slicing [3,14] based on System Dependency Graph (SDG) [3,4]. Program slicing asks about which statements influence (backward slicing), or are influenced by (forward slicing), the current statement under exam, whereas collaborative process analysis asks about which processes (functionalities provided by a partner can be seen as a process, e.g. implemented with a Web Service) influence which processes, therefore tracing asset exchanges and derivations.

We use a similar approach to 'slice' a collaborative context into sub-contexts, confining a scope of partners interrelated by assets exchanges (in other words, partners in different sub-contexts don't exchange asset, although they are in the same collaborative process). We firstly give an overview of the sub-context modes we may encounter when analyzing a collaborative context, before introducing the analysis method.

3   Service Call Graph-Based Service Composition Representation

We use a simple use case (see Fig. 2) of Web Service composition to support our discussions.

Use Case 1. A manufacturing enterprise 'Direct Device' (D) consults 'logistic schedule' (h) and 'Price' (p) from 'Bonétat Transport' (B). Part of the price information 'p_2' and the 'due transportation' (s) are taken from 'Clear railway transport' (C). The business process includes the following steps:

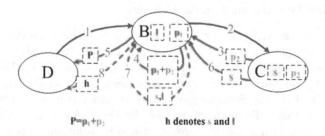

Fig. 2. Service composition represented with SCG (Color figure online).

(1) D contacts B, requiring h and p;
(2) B contacts C, requiring s and p_2, in order to reply D;
(3) C sends p_2 to B;
(4) B provides p_1 and merges (sum up) it with p_2 to produce p;
(5) B sends p to D;
(6) C sends s to B;
(7) B provides l and combines it with s;
(8) B sends the combined logistic schedule information (denoted as h) to D.

As B and C are asset (information) providers in this use case, a full lifecycle security management means that their policies should be respected during the whole lifecycle of their assets. This involves answering two questions:

(1) By which partners will an asset be accessed? Such as "The 'railway scheduling info' provided by C will be accessed by B or D, or both of them?"
(2) Which assets will a party be given access to? Such as "Will D access the assets provided by B and C, either directly or indirectly?".

While both of these questions can be answered intuitively for our use case, the pondering procedure reflects the goal and method of context slicing. Question (1) is related to Quality of Protection (QoP) aggregation among partners. Question (2) is linked to Requirement of Protection (RoP) aggregation. The goal is to enable down-stream asset security [1], so that consumers should comply with the policies of the O-Assets (original assets provided by partners) involved in the C-Asset (namely, the collaborative-context's asset, which aggregates several O-Assets) they want to access. Our method is based on a Service Call Graph resulting from the modification and extension of System Dependency Graph (SDG) [3,4].

3.1 Service Call Graph

A participant in a collaborative context is analogous to a procedure in SDG: it receives calling information and yields results. We use $P_i \xleftarrow{c} P_j$ to denote that a party P_i depends on another party P_j with 'control dependency': whether P_i will be activated or not depends on P_j. We use $P_i \xleftarrow{d} P_j$ to denote that a party P_i depends on another party P_j with 'data dependency': data provided by P_j are involved in data produced by P_i. We propose a data structure 'Service Call Graph' (SCG) based on extensions of SDG to represent partners interactions in the collaboration context. These extensions can be illustrated with use case 1 (Fig. 2 is a SCG of use case 1):

- The first extension in our SCG model is that data dependency can belong to two types:
  - an **aggregation dependency** means that P_i involves data of P_j (the same as SDG);
  - a **non-aggregation dependency** denotes that data produced by P_i do not involve data from P_j (an extension of SDG).

For example, in the SCG presented in Fig. 2, the blue edges (step 1 and 2) represent control dependency. The green edges (steps 3, 4, 5, 6, 7 and 8) represent data dependency. Besides, the solid green lines (edge 4 and 5) mean that the output data (responses) **include** information from the input data (aggregation dependency). The dashed green line (edge 7, 8) means that the output data **does not** include information from the input data (non-aggregation dependency).

- The second extension is that the **assets** carried by the message exchanges are attached directly to the edges in SCG (see edges 3, 4, 5, 6, 7 and 8 in Fig. 2).

Furthermore, to capture assets derivation pattern, the **indirect dependency** relation should be retrieved, based on partner service calls in a business collaboration: $\forall P_i, P_j, P_k, \forall \alpha \in \{c, d\}$ where P_i, P_j and P_k are partners in a collaboration, c and d are *control dependency* and *data dependency* relations respectively, then P_i is **indirectly dependent** on P_k if $P_i \xleftarrow{\alpha} P_j \wedge P_j \xleftarrow{\alpha} P_k$.

There are two types of indirect dependency.

- *Indirect **data** dependency* is the situation where each relation in a dependency chain is *data dependency*. We sum it up as an axiom:

Axiom 1 (Indirect Data Dependency).

$$\forall P_i, P_j, P_k: P_i \xleftarrow{d} P_j \wedge P_j \xleftarrow{d} P_k \Rightarrow P_i \xleftarrow{d} P_k$$

For example, in use case 1, whether D gets the results or not depends on the response of B. B's response in turn depends on response from C.

- *Indirect **control** dependency* is the situation where (one or more) *control dependency* relations exist in the dependency chain:

Axiom 2 (Indirect Control Dependency).

$$\forall P_i, P_j, P_k, \forall \alpha \in \{c, d\}: (P_i \xleftarrow{c} P_j \wedge P_j \xleftarrow{\alpha} P_k) \vee (P_i \xleftarrow{\alpha} P_j \wedge P_j \xleftarrow{c} P_k) \Rightarrow P_i \xleftarrow{c} P_k$$

As an example for indirect control dependency, in use case 1, whether C will be called or not depends on B. In turn, whether B will be called or not depends on D. So C is indirectly 'control dependent' on D.

We can see the slight difference between Axiom 1 and Axiom 2: Data dependency is transitive only when the edges in the dependency chain are all associated to 'data dependency', whereas when control dependency exists in a dependency chain, it propagates 'control dependency' to the chain.

When analyzing complex business process, e.g. those defined using WS-BPEL, one must consider the impact of 'variables', which are used to carry information inside the process. As information carried by variables are eventually exchanged between partners, the information exchanges between variables (e.g. through 'value assignment') also lead to assets derivation.

These variables can be complex data type (e.g. defined by XML schema). In this case, if a part of one variable is valued-assigned to a part of another variable (see the 'sample process' in WS-BPEL specification [8]), the later variable is 'data dependent' on the former one. Thus we have the following axiom:

Axiom 3 (Direct Data Dependency Between Variables).
$$\forall V_i.c_m, V_j.c_n, c_m \xleftarrow{d} c_n \Rightarrow V_i \xleftarrow{d} V_j$$

where P_i and P_j stand for variables. c_m is a component of (a part of) P_i. c_n is a component of P_j.

This axiom describes the situation that, as in WS-BPEL a "variable" can have plural components, each of them a container that can be assigned value, the value exchange between components of two "variables" incurs data dependency between the two "variables". There are only data dependency relations between variables, as the only form of interactions between variable is data exchange. Therefore the conditions leading to indirect data dependency between variables can be described by Axiom 1. In the following discussion about dependency relation, we don't need to differentiate variables from partners (i.e. 'partnerLink' in WS-BPEL), as we can see that dependency relations for partners and for variables can be described by the same set of axioms.

3.2   Service Call Tuple

We use a tuple $< P_i \xleftrightarrow{t} P_j, \Delta >$ to denote the service call from P_i to P_j, Δ being the exchanged asset. We can have the following basic types of service call tuple:

- $< P_i \xrightarrow{c} P_j >$ denotes that P_i calls P_j with a message carrying no asset.
- $< P_i \xleftarrow{c} P_j >$ denotes that P_i receives a message from P_j that carries no asset.

  An example scenario including these two types of service call is when a mail agent queries a mail service for whether a mail is sent or not, and receives confirmation from the server. In such case the calling message and the response message are deemed as not carrying any asset (i.e. information needing protection). We can see that whether a message carries asset or not depends on the straining criteria of security in a specific application context.

- $< P_i \xrightarrow{d} P_j, \Delta_i >$ denotes that P_i calls P_j, by sending asset Δ_i.
- $< P_i \xleftarrow{d} P_j, \Delta_o >$ denotes that P_i receives a response from P_j that carries asset Δ_o.
- $< P_i \xleftrightarrow{\alpha} P_j, \Delta_i, \Delta_o >$ denotes that P_i calls P_j, sending asset Δ_i, receiving response carrying asset Δ_o, where Δ_o includes information from Δ_i.
- $< P_i \xleftrightarrow{\alpha} P_j, \Delta_i, \Delta_o, \not\subset >$ denotes that P_i calls P_j, sending asset Δ_i and receives a response carrying asset Δ_o, where Δ_o does not include information from Δ_i.

- $< P_i \xleftrightarrow{f} P_j, \not\subset >$ denotes that the interaction between P_i and P_j is failed, due to negative result of policy negotiation.

These tuples represent the edges of SCG. We can see that asset exchanges (and aggregations) occur with service calls.

3.3   Assets Aggregation

Usually, assets derivations (basically, either 'merging' or 'splitting') occur with partners' interactions. Therefore, recognizing assets derivation relations involves firstly formalizing partner interactions with service call tuples. Then the service call tuples list can be analyzed to track the asset merging or splitting activities. There are three situations that may incur such activities:

– If X sends information containing asset value to Y, who aggregates it with its own information (expressed as Y calling itself) and further sends it to Z. In this situation, we can identify the following service call tuple sequence:

$$< X \xrightarrow{d} Y, \Delta_X >$$
$$< Y \xleftarrow{d} Y, \Delta_X, \Delta_Y > \qquad (2)$$
$$< Y \xrightarrow{d} Z, \Delta_Y >$$

– If X sends information within its request to Y and gets response(s) from Y that includes X's information. This situation is represented by the following service call tuple:

$$< X \xleftarrow{d} Y, \Delta_X, \Delta_Y > \qquad (3)$$

Extra attentions should be paid in this case, as we can not be sure that the response message includes information from the request message. Whether the output (responses) from a partner integrates the input (request) or not depends on the business logic of this partner's system. An example of such a case is when X sends some personal information to Y to calculate the insurance premium. If the response from Y consists in the insurance premium and the person's information, there is an assets derivation, otherwise if Y answers with only the insurance premium, there is no assets derivation. The decision of which information includes 'asset value' and should be protected is closely related to the application domains. In any case, we need to know relations between inputs and outputs to conclude whether assets derivation exists during a direct interaction or not. This can be done by analyzing partner's service functional description, e.g. WSDL in a Web Service context. It can also be done at the business process level, by adding extra indicators to a WS-BPEL script. In the modeling level, we use the following notations to define whether the partner's response includes information from a request or not:

• Most of the time, request information (or part of it) is included in the response, therefore we use the default tuple to represent it:

$$< Y \xleftarrow{d} Y, \Delta_i, \Delta_o > \qquad (4)$$

• whereas $\not\subset$ is used to indicate that no information of the request is included in the response:

$$< Y \xleftarrow{d} Y, \Delta_i, \Delta_o, \not\subset > \qquad (5)$$

- If X fetches (expressed by '$\xrightarrow{c}$', as there is no asset value in the request) information from Y and aggregates its own information with it. We get the following tuples:

$$< X \xrightarrow{c} Y >$$
$$< X \xleftarrow{d} Y, \Delta_Y >$$
$$< X \xleftrightarrow{d} X, \Delta_Y, \Delta_X >$$

(6)

As an example, we build the list of service call tuples for our use case (the tuples are indexed by the steps of business process):

$$< \tau 1, D \xrightarrow{c} B >$$
$$< \tau 2, B \xrightarrow{c} C >$$
$$< \tau 3, B \xleftarrow{d} C, (p_2) >$$
$$< \tau 4, B \xleftrightarrow{d} B, (p_2), (p = p_1 + p_2) >$$
$$< \tau 5, D \xleftarrow{d} B, (p) >$$
$$< \tau 6, B \xleftarrow{d} C, (s) >$$
$$< \tau 7, B \xleftrightarrow{d} B, (s), (s, l) >$$
$$< \tau 8, D \xleftarrow{d} B, (h) >$$

(7)

The assets derivation relations between partners are equivalent to data dependency relations between them. Therefore assets derivation trail, which decides the sub-context pattern, can be mined from the list of service call tuples.

4   Sub-context Slicing

Like the information *reachability* questions in SDG, the assets derivation trail can be tracked by scanning the service call tuples list, paying particular attention to asset aggregation. Based on this, providers' policies upon assets can be maintained during assets derivations. This involves firstly allocating correlated assets in the same sub-contexts.

We use a data structure 'context development tuple' $< N_C, V_C, P_C, L_A, L_P, \tau >$ to record the information of sub-context development, where:

- N_C is the name of the sub-context,
- V_C its version,
- P_C its parent sub-context,
- L_A a list of all the asset involved in the sub-context,
- L_P the collection of policies in the sub-context,
- τ the step of business process.

This tuple is built by the sub-context slicing process which scans the SCG (e.g. service call tuple list) according to two strategies: asset-based slicing and request-based slicing.

4.1   Asset-Based Slicing

The asset-based slicing method focuses on capturing the aggregation relation among assets. Using this method, a sub-context is created when the first O-Asset is launched into the collaborative context by the owner. When a new partner joins the context with a new O-Asset, the sub-context consisting of the existing asset is updated, if the new partner's O-Asset is merged with the existing C-Asset. Otherwise (i.e. the new partner's O-Asset is not merged with existing C-Asset), a new sub-context is created. In use case 1, the list of sub-context tuples is as following:

$$
\begin{aligned}
&< p_{CB}, 1, (\phi), (p_2), (RoP_C), \tau 3 > \\
&< p_{CB}, 2, (p_{CB}.1), (p_1 + p_2), (RoP_C, RoP_B), \tau 4 > \\
&< p_{CB}, 3, (p_{CB}.2), (p), (RoP_C, RoP_B), \tau 5 > \\
&< s_{CB}, 1, (\phi), (s), (RoP_C), \tau 6 > \\
&< s_{CB}, 2, (s_{CB}.1), (s, l), (RoP_C, RoP_B), \tau 7 > \\
&< s_{CB}, 3, (s_{CB}.2), (h), (RoP_C, RoP_B), \tau 8 >
\end{aligned}
\tag{8}
$$

We can see that in step 3 (represented by $\tau 3$), the first sub-context is created, including the asset p_2 and its related RoP_C. We name the context after the interaction leading to the creation of it, i.e. p_{CB} ('price' sent from C to B). Its version is '1'. It has no parent context (ϕ). Then in step 4, as a new asset p_1 merges with P_2, the sub-context $p_{CB}.1$ is updated to $p_{CB}.2$. In step 5, it remains unchanged.

This list describes the evolution of the sub-contexts. The first cub-context can be represented with an assets derivation diagram (see Fig. 3).

In step 6 (represented by $\tau 6$), the second sub-context is created, when partner C sends another asset s to B. We name the context with s_{CB} ('s' sent from C to B). Its version is '1'. Being a created sub-context, It has no parent context (ϕ). Then in step 7, B receives s and provides asset l, the sub-context $p_{CB}.1$ is updated to $p_{CB}.2$. In step 8, B sends the combined s and l (denoted as h) to D.

Using the asset-based slicing method, policy negotiation and aggregation (including conflicts detection) can not be done until the first asset is launched into the context (step 4 of use case 1). If there is a conflict, steps $\tau 2$ and $\tau 3$ are actually wastes of partners' resources and don't need to be proceeded. Therefore the asset-based slicing method should be used for pre-processing a business process script (e.g. WS-BPEL documents) before it is executed. To analyze a collaborative context on-the-fly, we need a request-based slicing method.

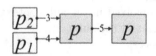

Fig. 3. Assets derivation in the sample use case.

4.2   Request-Based Slicing

The request-based slicing method creates a sub-context when the first request is made. Then, when a new partner joins the business process, either its QoP can be aggregated into an existing sub-context, or it will lead to the creation of a new sub-context. The decision is also straight forward: the QoPs of two partners should be aggregated, if they will access the same asset in future steps of the collaboration context. By this method, we get the following list of sub-context tuples for use case 1:

$$< Q_{DB}, 1, (\phi), (QoP_D), \tau 1 >$$
$$< Q_{DB}, 2, (Q_{DB}.1), (QoP_D, QoP_B), \tau 2 > \tag{9}$$

This tuple list captures QoP aggregations. When the first request is made by D in step 1, a sub-context is created, including the QoP of D. We name the context after the interaction leading to the creation of it, e.g. Q_{DB} ('query' sent from D to B). In step 2, as B is requesting assets from C 'on behalf of' D, QoP_B and QoP_C are aggregated. Therefore sub-context $Q_{DB}.1$ is updated to $Q_{DB}.2$.

However, deciding who will access the same asset is more tricky than it may firstly look like, especially when partners work asynchronously, (e.g. if after a partner X receiving a request from partner Y, another partner Z also sends request to X, before X responding to Y). We provide basic protocols for dealing with such cases:

– **Protocol 1.** *After X receiving a request from Y, all the requests X sends to other partners are deemed as being **on behalf of** Y, until X responds to Y, or X receives a request from another partner Z.* This involves that a request from Y to X establishes an 'on behalf of' relation. Consequently, the QoP_Y should be aggregated into QoP_X for all the requests X sends after receiving the request from Y, until that X gets the result and responds to Y. The 'on behalf of' relation between X and Y ends when X responds to Y. It also can, however, be interrupted before that X responds to Y. The following two protocols regulate such cases.
– **Protocol 2.** *An 'X on behalf of Y' relation is interrupted by another 'X on behalf of Z' relation if Z makes a request after that X receives a request from Y and before that X responds to Y.*
– **Protocol 3.** *An 'X on behalf of Y' relation interrupted by another request from Z can be resumed after X responding to Z, if X receives a response from a partner P, who was called by X 'on behalf of Y'.* This means that the 'on behalf of' relation can be **nested**. For example, with the following request-response sequence (i.e. service call tuple list in formula 10), we can say that the 'on behalf of' relation between X and Y is restored after X responding to Z (step 5), by the interaction where 'P responds to X', as P is a partner that X has requested on behalf of Y.

$$< \tau1, Y \xrightarrow{c} X, \Delta_{i1} >$$
$$< \tau2, X \xrightarrow{c} P, \Delta_{i2} >$$
$$< \tau3, Z \xrightarrow{c} X, \Delta_{i3} >$$
$$< \tau4, X \xleftarrow{d} Q, \Delta_{i4}, \Delta_{o4} > \qquad (10)$$
$$< \tau5, Z \xleftarrow{d} X, \Delta_{o3} >$$
$$< \tau6, X \xleftarrow{d} P, \Delta_{o2} >$$
$$< \tau7, Y \xleftarrow{d} X, \Delta_{o1} >$$

These are basic protocols because they handle the primary cases in service composition. When dealing with real-world complex business federations, more information concerning the business process and partner's functionalities should be taken into consideration. Nevertheless this basic reasoning process remains in accordance with those described in these protocols.

In the following we discuss the employment of asset-based and request-based methods for context slicing. For this, we firstly give an overview of sub-context developments that can occur in a collaborative business process.

4.3   Context Development

During each step (partner interaction) of the business process, different types of sub-context development are caused by the partners' service calls:

- **Create.** The creation of a new sub-context is always based on an independent QoP or RoP from a partner. In other words, if the partner provides an asset which is not aggregated with other assets in the *current step*, a new sub-context consisting of this asset and the corresponding RoP is created. Analogously, if the partner is calling others **on its own behalf** (i.e. not because it is doing so for responding to another partner) a new sub-context consisting of its QoP should be created.
- **Update.** On the contrary, updating an existing sub-context happens if the partner's asset has data dependency (according to discussions in Sect. 3.3) with the assets belonging to an existing sub-context, or if this partners' assets are merged with existing assets. It also happens when the partner is requesting assets on behalf of another 'former' requestor, that is, it's QoP and the QoP of the former requestor should be 'transmitted' to the requested party. Therefore the QoPs are in the same sub-context.
- **Merge.** Merging sub-contexts is a special kind of update operation. It happens when two existing assets in two sub-contexts merge, or when the request sent by a partner is on behalf of several former requestors from different sub-contexts. In the later case, the different sub-contexts are correlated by the asset value in the responding message.
- **Split.** While 'splitting' a sub-context, several new sub-contexts are created. They all 'inherit' the assets and policies of the previous context. Context splitting can be caused by three types of interactions:
  - a party sends copies of the same asset to several partners and the copies are developed differently;

- a party sends copies of the same request to several partners at the same time;
- the business process has a control structure defining parallel activities.
- **End.** Ending a sub-context occurs when it is *merged, split* or when the whole *business process ends.*

These sub-context developments occur as asset sharing relations change, hence the context analysis is proceeded according to business process logic. In the Web Service contexts, one need to consider both scenarios of service orchestration guided by WS-BPEL and on-the-fly service compositions. We propose both a pre-processing method and an on-the-fly processing method for these scenarios.

4.4   Pre-processing and On-the-Fly Processing

In context slicing, *pre-processing* refers to the circumstances where a pre-defined business process (e.g. WS-BPEL script) is analyzed before the execution, to see whether it can be carried out or not, w.r.t. partners' security profile-request satisfiability. This can be done with the asset-based slicing method, using the policies and attributes of partners.

On the contrary, for *on-the-fly* processing, partners' RoPs and QoPs must be aggregated as soon as they join the collaboration context, in order to find out security policy conflicts more timingly. This requires using both asset-based and request-based slicing methods.

In our use case 1, on-the-fly slicing strategy first builds the QoP tuples (see formula 9) from the beginning of the business process, using request-based slicing. Then from step '$\tau 3$', RoP tuples are built (see formula 8), using asset-based slicing.

The RoP aggregation relations and QoP aggregation relations are used to generate the security polices and profiles of each sub-context. When a new partner joins the collaboration context, it is allocated to a sub-context according to whether it's an asset provider or consumer (or both). Its policy and profile are aggregated to the security policy and profile of that sub-context.

5   Conclusions and Future Work

This paper develops a method for analyzing information assets sharing patterns in Web Service composition scenarios, therefore security configuration can be done in a fine-grained manner and ensure the overall security level in inter-enterprise level business federation. We introduce a 'Service Call Graph (SCG)' and a corresponding data structure 'service call tuple' extending the System Dependency Graph (SDG), to capture asset aggregation (and derivation) in a collaborative business process. A 'context slicing' operation can be made based on the SCG, to categorize partners that have direct and indirect assets exchange relations to the same 'sub-contexts'. Security policy negotiation and aggregation in the scope of each sub-context can ensure the full lifecycle security for assets. A detailed discussion has been given on the rational of our method, facilitated by a sample use case. Basically, 'data dependency' between partners incurs assets (and RoP policies) aggregation, whereas 'control dependency' between partners leads to the 'on behalf of' relation and QoP aggregation. According to data dependency, 'asset-based' slicing is sufficient for pre-processing a business process script (e.g. WS-BPEL script). Nevertheless our on-the-fly processing strategy applied to a business federation (e.g. dynamic service composition) requires both 'request-based' (due to control dependency) and 'asset-based' slicing. Future work involves the construction of security management paradigm with assets tagging systems and the context slicing engine for both asset-based and request-based analysis.

Acknowledgements. This work is supported by "the Fundamental Research Funds for the Central Universities" under grant Number 12QNJJ025.

References

1. Bussard, L., Neven, G., Preiss, F.-S.: Downstream usage control. In: 11th IEEE International Symposium on Policies for Distributed Systems and Networks, pp. 22–29. IEEE Computer Society, Washington, DC (2010)
2. Daniele, C., Giles, H.: Cloud computing: benefits, risks and recommendations for information security. Technical report, European Network and Information Security Agency (2009)
3. GrammaTech.: Dependence graphs and program slicing-codesurfer technology overview. Technical report, GrammaTech Inc.
4. Gu, L., Ding, X., Deng, R.H., Xie, B., Mei, H.: Remote attestation on program execution. In: 3rd ACM Workshop on Scalable Trusted Computing, pp. 11–20. ACM, New York (2008)
5. Kagal, L., Abelson, H.: Access control is an inadequate framework for privacy protection. In: W3C Privacy Workshop. W3C (2010)
6. Linda, B.B., Richard, C., Kristin, L., Ric, T., Mark, E.: The evolving role of IT managers and CIOs–findings from the 2010 IBM global IT risk study. Technical report, IBM (2010)
7. OASIS: eXtensible Access Control Markup Language (XACML) version 2.0 (2005). http://docs.oasis-open.org/xacml/2.0/
8. OASIS: Web Services Business Process Execution Language (WS-BPEL) (2007). http://docs.oasis-open.org/wsbpel/2.0/wsbpel-v2.0.html
9. Park, J., Sandhu, R.: Originator control in usage control. In: 3rd International Workshop on Policies for Distributed Systems and Networks, pp. 60–66. IEEE Computer Society, Washington, DC (2002)
10. Su, Z., Biennier, F.: End-to-end security policy description and management for collaborative system. In: 6th International Conference on Information Assurance and Security, pp. 137–142 (2010)
11. Su, Z., Biennier, F.: Toward comprehensive security policy governance in collaborative enterprise. In: Frick, J., Laugen, B.T. (eds.) APMS 2011. IFIP AICT, vol. 384, pp. 350–358. Springer, Heidelberg (2012)

12. Su, Z., Biennier, F.: Service Call Graph (SCG)-information flow analysis in Web service composition. In: 15th International Conference on Enterprise Information Systems, pp. 17–24. SciTePress (2013)
13. Zhang, X., Li, Y., Nalla, D.: An attribute-based access matrix model. In: 20th ACM Symposium on Applied Computing, pp. 359–363. ACM, Santa Fe, NM (2005)
14. Zhao, J., Rinard, M.: System dependence graph construction for aspect-oriented programs. Technical report MIT-LCS-TR-891, Laboratory for Computer Science. MIT (2003)

SourceMiner: Towards an Extensible Multi-perspective Software Visualization Environment

Glauco de Figueiredo Carneiro[1](✉)
and Manoel Gomes de Mendonça Neto[2]

[1] Computer Science Department, Salvador University (UNIFACS),
Salvador, BA, Brazil
glauco.carneiro@unifacs.br
[2] Computer Science Department, Federal University of Bahia (UFBA),
Salvador, BA, Brazil
mgmendonca@dcc.ufba.br

Abstract. In spite of the available resources provided by modern IDEs, program understanding remains as a difficult task in software engineering. This paper presents a software visualization environment named SourceMiner. Implemented as an Eclipse plug-in to enhance software comprehension activities, SourceMiner is an extensible, interactive and coordinated multi-perspective environment. This paper describes the principles behind the design of SourceMiner, and discusses how it has been used to support software comprehension activities such as the identification of code smells and the characterization of object-oriented software systems.

Keywords: Software visualization · Software comprehension · Multiple view environments

1 Introduction

Many researchers have pointed out the important role that visualization plays in interactive data analysis and information exploration [2, 4]. Humans have the natural ability to track and detect visual patterns and this ability can be exploited to improve software comprehension. Software visualization (also known as SoftVis) is a means to provide perceivable cues to several aspects of software systems in order to reveal patterns and behaviors that would otherwise remain hidden to the programmer [33].

The design and use of software visualization environments should take into account three important issues. The first is that software is eminently complex, hindering many of the software comprehension activities. The second, described by Lehman's second law [19], is that software evolves as it is subject to modifications over time. It is difficult to follow those changes and more resources are needed to understand them. The third is that software is intangible, having no physical shape [3]. Considering that humans acquire more information through vision than through all the other senses combined [35], the comprehension is affected by the lack of visual

© Springer International Publishing Switzerland 2014
S. Hammoudi et al. (Eds.): ICEIS 2013, LNBIP 190, pp. 242–263, 2014.
DOI: 10.1007/978-3-319-09492-2_15

presence that characterizes software as an entity. This difficulty is increased by the complexity and constant evolution of software systems.

Common software engineering tasks, such as the identification of code smells, usually require analyzing the software from multiple perspectives [7]. Moreover, to be effective, software visualization environments must provide complementary perspectives which together can support diverse software engineering tasks. Each perspective should present the software from a certain point of view that focuses on the comprehension of specific software properties. If these properties are complex, the perspective itself may require multiple views. A single visual metaphor may not be sufficient to portray the relevant peculiarities of such properties.

Multiple coordinated views can facilitate comparison [15]. The usage of multiple views is very difficult if the views are not coordinated among themselves and with the environment in which they operate. It is confusing, for example, if two views have different meanings for the same visual attribute (e.g., node color). Also, visual elements from different views should be linked to each other when they represent the same software entity. The selection or change in one such element of a view must be reflected in the others. One should also be able to easily navigate between visual elements from different views. And actions in these visual elements should have consistent response over all the views. Although, view coordination is a requirement for the use of multiple views in information visualization [2, 15], and well used in modern IDEs, it is still a concept that needs to be better explored in software visualization environments [33].

Views are based on visual metaphors that must match the data and task at hand. Graphs, for example, are very useful to visualize relational data, but do not scale well if the number of entities and relations grows. Information visualization and software visualization researchers have proposed many metaphors to visually present data. Unfortunately, it is not yet clear what sets of visual metaphors are best suited for most software engineering tasks. For this reason, a software visualization environment should facilitate the inclusion of new visual metaphors to its workbench. The purpose of this extensibility should be more than simply facilitating the growth of the number of views in an environment. It should aid experimentation and support the identification of which sets of views can be effectively combined for common software engineering tasks.

Software visualization environments must also be highly interactive. Good visualization needs to exploit the visual and cognitive systems of human beings. Programmers need to interact with the environment in order to configure the visual scenario to best fit their needs. They need widgets to filter, zoom, navigate and browse through visual metaphors. These mechanisms should support users in adjusting visual scenarios in aspects such as information content, visual mapping, and view configuration [6, 10, 15, 30].

The use of multiple views in SourceMiner better handles the diversity of attributes, user profiles, and levels of abstraction needed in software visualization. It enables users to configure and effectively combine views to bring out correlations and or disparities that might otherwise remain hidden in the code. The use of multiple views splits complex data into more manageable chunks of information, and this information can be further filtered and explored through interaction with the different visual scenarios.

This paper presents SourceMiner, a software visualization environment that provides a set of easy to comprehend, complementary, coordinated and highly interactive views. It uses code as its main data source and was implemented as an Eclipse plug-in to interactively visualize Java projects, complementing the native views and resources provided by the Eclipse IDE. It provides programmers with several ways to interact with the views: filters to visually present information that match filtering criteria, semantic and geometric zooming to better adjust the views to the canvas, arranging them in accordance with the preference of the programmer, and transparent navigation from the visual representation to the source code.

The rest of this paper is organized as follows. Section 2 motivates the work with a scenario of use of an IDE with and without SourceMiner. Section 3 introduces information visualization concepts that are relevant to the design of multiple view environments. Section 4 presents a conceptual model for multiple view environments. Section 5 presents SourceMiner architecture and design. Section 6 describes SourceMiner perspectives and their respective views. Section 7 presents examples of use of SourceMiner. And, Sect. 8 has the final remarks of the paper.

2 Current versus Proposed Scenario

This section motivates the integration of extensible software visualization environments into modern IDEs. It first describes an example of the use of the Eclipse IDE. In the sequence, it illustrates how a software visualization environment can improve this use.

Modern IDEs are very sophisticated, but in spite of the resources they provide, program understanding remains a very difficult task, especially on large and complex software systems. Typically, different types of information are required for executing software engineering tasks, such as fixing errors, changing or adding new features, or improving the code and design.

Consider the information about the code structure presented by the Eclipsés package explorer (package-file-class-methods and attributes hierarchy) as an example. This information is useful but limited. The package explorer alone is insufficient to support most development or maintenance tasks. One has to combine it with other views. Moreover, the package explorer itself could be augmented with more information. It does not present data related to software metrics, such as code size or complexity for example. In fact, most of the modern IDEs do not yet have specific views to show this type of property. This is very useful information and it is desirable to expand the IDEs with them. The question is how to do that. There are many forms in which an IDE can be visually enriched. Eclipse itself provides a comprehensive infrastructure to develop such features. A possible approach is to extend this infrastructure further to support common information visualization functionalities [2, 6], on top of that enrich the IDE with diverse but integrated software visualization resources, and finally evaluate them in different software engineering tasks.

In order to discuss some of the limitation of modern IDEs, Fig. 1 shows a snapshot example of the Eclipse IDE on a typical software engineering task. This snapshot was taken from a real world case study on the detection of bad smells. During the

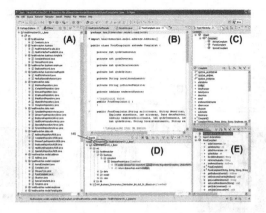

Fig. 1. Eclipse IDE on a typical task.

execution of this task, the Package Explorer view (Part A) may include hundreds of nodes just after a few navigational clicks through project files and classes. Hierarchical relationships, in this case, are no longer visible without manually scrolling through the tree. In part thanks to how easy Eclipse makes navigating over structural relations, the number of open files in the editor (Part B) can also increase quickly, making the instances of the editor a poor representation of the files currently relevant to the task. The search in Eclipse for references to a class within the project (Part D) can return hundreds of items and there is no convenient way to search only for those elements related to the task at hand. Instead, the search results (145 in our example) require manual inspection, if someone wants to find the elements of interest. Even the Outline view (Part E), that shows only the structure of the current file, can be overloaded with dozens of elements that might not be relevant to the task.

Modern IDEs also need to better explore interaction resources as mentioned earlier in this paper. The work presented here addresses these issues from a software visualization perspective. It enhances the IDE with an extensible software visualization environment. Its views are integrated among themselves and with the IDE.

In order to illustrate the solution, Fig. 2 shows a screenshot of SourceMiner. The arrows indicate how a specific class of a Java software system called HealthWatcher [14] is portrayed in multiple views. The editor (in Part B) shows part of the source code of the class and the Package Explorer (Part A) shows the structure comprised of packages, classes, methods and attributes using a traditional structural view. These are native views of the Eclipse IDE. The Parts D, E and F show three different views of SourceMiner. Like the Package Explorer, the view in Part D represents the package-class-method perspective of the system. However, it does so using treemaps [28], a hierarchical visualization metaphor that represents all packages, classes and methods of a project as nested rectangles. Programmers do not need to scroll to see any element of the structure because they are all there. The view in Part E represents an inheritance hierarchy perspective of the project using a polymetric view [18]. Eclipse does not have a native view to portray the inheritance hierarchy of the software system. The view in Part F represents a coupling perspective of the system using a grid (chessboard like) view to indicate the most coupled modules of the software project.

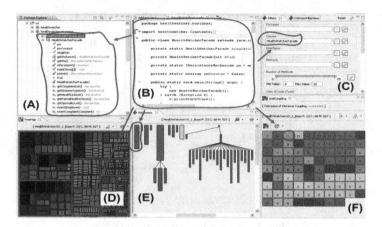

Fig. 2. An example of use of SourceMiner.

Views D, E and F are directly affected by the view in Part C. This filtering view enables users to apply filtering criteria to views D-F simultaneously. In the example, a user typed the string HealthWatcherFacade as a class name filtering option to highlight occurrences that match the typed string in all views. This is an example of the data transformation interaction level discussed earlier, a filtering resource that is not natively available in modern IDEs.

The goal here was to highlight that the proposed approach portrays the software from several perspectives, enhancing IDE native views and resources. And, that it does so with a fully integrated set of views that support several levels of interactions, as it will be discussed next.

3   Information Visualization Concepts

Software visualization is a specialization of information visualization. For this reason, a reference model for a Multi-Perspective Environment (MVE) must use concepts drawn from the InfoVis field. Information visualization researchers identified three main levels of interactions in multi-perspective environments [6]. The first, and most common, is interface interaction for view configuration. It is related to how the visual elements are configured and arranged in the visual scenario.

The second level of interaction deals with the dynamic mapping between the real attributes (of the software, in our case) and the visual attributes that are used to represent them on the canvas. Users should be able to configure the way software properties such as size or complexity will be represented on the views. The third level consists in dynamically filtering and selecting the data to be represented on the canvas. Selective data visualization is very useful to locate relevant information, to restrict visualization to interesting portions of the data and to control the level of detail at which the information is presented. Too much data may hinder visual scene interpretation, and too little neglects potentially important information.

As mentioned before, information visualization systems usually require this process to be highly interactive. In it, the user should be able to change the selected data to be presented on the canvas, modify the mapping between real and visual attributes, and alter the way views are rendered on the canvas (zooming or panning over it). To be effective, the response time between these interactions and reassembling the views should be as short as possible.

3.1 Multiple Perspectives and Multiple Views

A view is a particular visual representation of a data set. Complex data sets typically require multiple views, each revealing a different aspect of the data. Multiple view systems have been proposed to support the investigation of a wide range of information visualization topics. The reference model proposed by Card and colleagues is adapted in this paper to explicitly emphasize the use of multiple views on software visualization.

Distinct views should be used if they reveal dissimilar aspects of the conceptual entity presented. In complex domains, such as software engineering, no single all-inclusive view is likely to lead to insight. In this context, multiple view systems portray complementary information that supports complementary cognitive processes. One view can be used to constrain possible (mis)interpretations in the use of another. In fact, multiple views encourage users to construct a deeper understanding of the analyzed data.

Multiple views must be consistently designed to provide integration and coordination among themselves. Users should be able to select a subset of views in a coordinated fashion to perform a task [2]. The visualization environment should support the interactive exploration of views to uncover facts or relationships that otherwise would remain hidden [2]. Each single view should have affordances (e.g. selection capabilities or navigation functionalities such as panning and zooming). These affordances should be tied together so that actions in one view have an effect in another view [2]. These observations are expressed as three important concepts proposed by information visualization researchers and adopted in our work: (a) navigational slaving – multiple views systems should enable that actions in one view are automatically propagated to the others [29]; (b) linking – multiple views systems should connect data in one view with data in the other views [29]; (c) brushing – multiple views systems should enable that corresponding data items in different views are highlighted simultaneously [29].

4 A Conceptual Model for Multiple View Software Visualization

Many software visualization projects have been conceived as standalone systems, but we consider IDEs as the ideal substrata on which a Multiple View Environment (MVE) should reside. Integrating software visualization environments into IDEs is a natural way to support software comprehension activities. In fact, current IDEs already offer several resources to support software comprehension. Most of them offer at least a syntax directed editor that uses pretty printing and colour textual representation of the code, as well as some sort of hierarchical representation of the project structure. Usually, several other views present valuable information to programmers, representing the software from many different perspectives (e.g., the package explorer of Eclipse and outliner). They also provide different ways of searching, navigating and browsing software entities. A natural consequence of using an IDE as an MVE substratum is that programmers will be able to interchangeably and concurrently access source code, the views originally provided by the IDE and the views from the MVE [20].

Figure 3 illustrates how we adapted the Card et al. reference model to the software engineering domain. The goal here is to provide a set of coordinated and cross-referenced views integrated to a modern IDE. Similarly to the original, the adapted model also has three main interaction levels: data transformations, visual mapping and view transformation interactions.

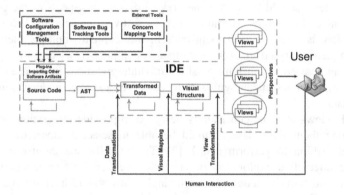

Fig. 3. A reference model for software visualization.

The multiple views are used to represent different properties of the software. For example, one can build a visualization of module inheritance and another of module coupling. Different representations can also be employed to portray the same property in various ways. For example, module coupling can be represented by interactive graphs or relationship matrices. In this case, each representation should emphasize a different aspect of the property under analysis or should have complementary affordances to facilitate the visual interpretation of the portrayed information. In order to be precise, we use the expression multiform visualization when referring to different views (forms) being used to describe the same software property. Also, as discussed previously in this paper, multiple views should be coordinated so an action taken in one view should be reflected on all the other views of the environment. In this scenario, we use the expression multiple coordinated views as opposed to simply multiple views.

Figure 3 also emphasizes view coordination in the model. The feedback arrows around the views indicate this fact. The use of multiple coordinated views and multiform representations are suitable to support programmers in exploring over complex information spaces [13, 36]. The idea of having multiple coordinated views strives for visually combining different aspects of data in different displays [4]. In software engineering, multiple views are intended to help raising the level of abstraction and reduce the amount of information required to perform recurrent software engineering tasks, especially when they are coordinated and cross referenced [33].

The model also emphasizes that the IDE is the main data source of a software system. The data available at the IDE is accessed, transformed, mapped to visual structures and rendered as views. Current IDEs allow for easy extraction of source code information from native resources such as the software system Abstract Syntax Tree (AST). Additional information – such as concern maps, churning information and defect data – can be captured from external data sources and used to enrich the views, as shown on the top-left box of Fig. 3.

5 A Multiple Visualization Environment for the Eclipse IDE

The challenge of building and coordinating multiple views and multiform systems far exceeds the challenge of building a single view system. Figure 4 presents the layers and the modules of SourceMiner. This high level architecture is divided into a two layers. The Rendering and Visualization (RV) Layer is responsible for rendering the views provided by SourceMiner. The Core Visualization Environment (CVE) is responsible to capturing information from the IDE and structuring it for the RV Layer. It also coordinates all views among themselves and the IDE. The following subsections describe the functionalities provided by each of these layers.

The **Core Visualization Environment (CVE)** is the kernel of SourceMiner. It is responsible for extracting data from a project source code using the resources provided by the Eclipse Java Development Tool (JDT) to this end. JDT provides

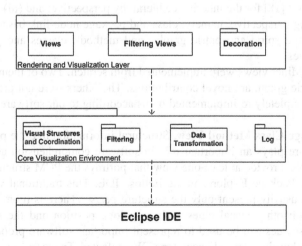

Fig. 4. SourceMiner layers.

fundamental information on software entities avoiding the creation of such functionality from scratch. This made it possible to focus most of our efforts on how to extend the environment with views, coordination and interaction resources, and it is a clear advantage of using an open IDE as a substratum for a MVE. Besides extracting and structuring data about the software system under analysis, the CVE provides services of coordination among views, filters the data to be presented in the views and logs the primitive operations performed by the users while they use the environment. The CVE uses IDE resources to coordinate the environment with the IDE itself. The next subsections present the modules that comprise the CVE layer.

The **Rendering and Visualization (RV)** layer is responsible for rendering the views in SourceMiner. To accomplish this task, this layer relies on the services provided by the Core Visualization Environment (CVE). The modules that comprise the RV layer are the Views, the Filtering Views and the Decorator modules. The following subsections describe these modules.

6   Perspectives and Views in SourceMiner

Views are key resources in SourceMiner. Views are the result of using some visualization metaphor to present the data stored in the visual structures. Views implement a certain visualization model and affordances to present software related data on the canvas. View instantiates visual scenarios. A visual scenario is instantiated based on data, a decoration and a graphical setup selected by the user to a certain view.

Currently SourceMiner has three classes of views or perspectives: the **package class method, inheritance hierarchy** and **coupling views.** As described earlier, a perspective is a set of views that represent the same type of software properties. The combined use of these perspectives provides a broad range of information to programmers when executing software engineering tasks.

We considered several metaphors from the InfoVis and we ended-up adopting the following ones: (i) treemaps [28] for the package-class-method perspective; (ii) polymetric views [18] for the inheritance hierarchy perspective; and (iii) several views for the coupling perspective, namely, class and package node-link-based dependency graphs, grids and spiral egocentric graphs, and methods, classes and package relationship matrices.

All SourceMiner views were implemented from scratch. Two of them, the grid and spiral egocentric graph, are novel contributions. The others were not proposed by the authors, but completely re-implemented by us according to our software visualization needs.

The **Package Class Method View.** Structural information like the package-class-method structure plays an important role in software comprehension activities [33]. Most of the IDEs provide at least one view that portrays the PCM structure. One such example is the Package Explorer in the Eclipse IDE. This traditional view does not scale well and usually present only the structure per se. There is room for enriching such views with other visual clues such as colors, position and the size of figure elements. These cues can be used to represent important software properties such as size, version, churning, and element type. We selected Treemaps as an alternative visual metaphor to create a PCM view in SourceMiner. Treemaps are 2D visualizations that map a tree structure using recursively nested rectangles [28].

They are a very effective way of representing large hierarchies. And, besides the hierarchy itself, they can show other data attributes using the rectangle size (area) and color. Each rectangle of the treemap portrays a node of the represented the PCM hierarchy. The structure is scalable and facilitates the discovery of patterns and outliers. It makes it easy to spot outliers in terms of module size and number of sub modules, for example. An example of treemap in SourceMiner is portrayed in Fig. 5.

As with any SourceMiner view, users can apply filtering criteria to eliminate elements from the treemap PCM view. The views provide direct access to their corresponding source code. For that, the user has just to control-click on a graphical element. The RV layer will then request that the Integration and Coordination Module on the CVE Layer activates the Eclipse Editor for the corresponding source code element (method, class or interface).

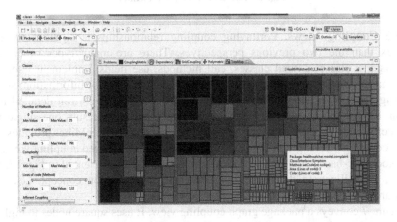

Fig. 5. Treemaps in SourceMiner.

The **Inheritance Hierarchy View.** The polymetric view [17] was selected to portray the inheritance hierarchy of a software system. It portrays inheritance relationships between the software entities (class/interface) as a forest of round rectangles. Originally proposed for this very purpose, polymetric views help to understand the structure and detect problems of a software system in the initial phases of a reverse engineering process [17]. As can be seen in Fig. 6, the view is a two-dimensional display that uses rectangles to represent software entities, such as classes and interfaces, and edges to represent inheritance relationships between them. The dimensions of the rectangles are used to represent properties of the entities. In SourceMiner, the width corresponds to the number of methods while the height to the number of lines of code of a class or interface. The color is used for decoration just like discussed before. A geometric zoom is available to better display the polymetric view in accordance with the number of elements on the canvas. A semantic zoom can also be used to navigate over specific sub-trees of a portrayed hierarchy.

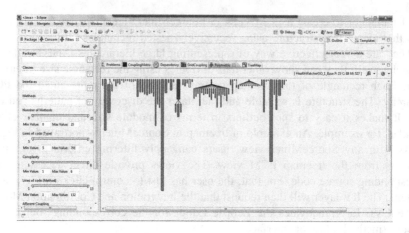

Fig. 6. Polymetric in SourceMiner.

The **Coupling Views.** Portraying coupling relationships is significantly more complex than the two previous perspectives. There are many types of coupling relationships: classes extend classes, call methods, use fields, implement interfaces, just to name a few. One may also be interested in other types of information, such as coupling direction or strength. Also, some views are good to portrait detailed information, but for this very reason they do not scale well. As a result, one single view cannot efficiently support all coupling visualization goals. SourceMiner provides three sets of coupling views: graph-based coupling views, matrix-based coupling views and grid/egocentric-based coupling views. All these views are represented in Figs. 7, 8, 9, and 10. They illustrate the use of the multiform visualization concept, i.e., many views are used to represent the same type of property.

Figure 7 conveys a package graph coupling view. It uses square nodes to highlight this fact. As seen in the figure, any of the peripheral package nodes can be selected to

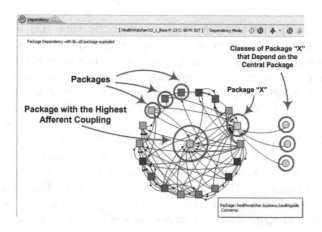

Fig. 7. Package dependency in SourceMiner.

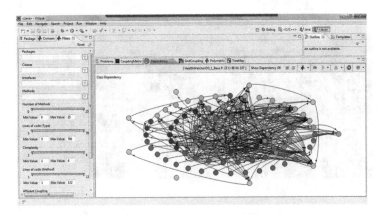

Fig. 8. Class dependency in SourceMiner.

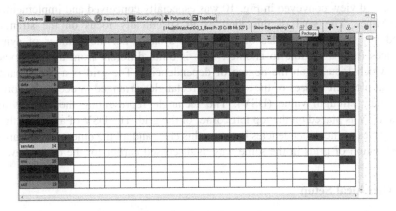

Fig. 9. Package dependency matrix in SourceMiner.

have its composing classes revealed as round nodes. In this case, SourceMiner only shows the classes that justify the coupling relations with the central node. The node-link-based graph in Fig. 8 clearly exhibits a high amount of visual clutter as a result of edge congestion. We decided to implement matrix views as an option to the graph views. They have a cleaner and more uncluttered layout. In SourceMiner, a matrix of rows and columns are configured to show different levels of coupling relationships between software elements (package, classes and methods). Figure 9 portrays an example of a package dependency matrix.

SourceMiner also allows for semantic zooming over the matrices. This is achieved by double clicking on a gray cell. This action brings out a new coupling matrix that semantically details the selected dependency. For example, by clicking on a package dependency cell of Fig. 9, the user will obtain a class dependency matrix involving all classes. This type of action also works from class to method dependency matrices. The transition is bidirectional, meaning that the user can backtrack to the original matrix by simply right clicking on the view canvas.

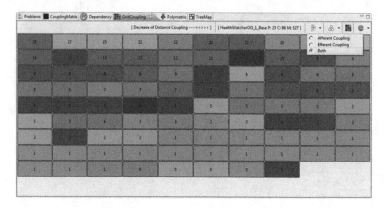

Fig. 10. Grid view in SourceMiner.

The grid view conveyed in Fig. 10 was especially conceived and implemented for SourceMiner. The goal of this view is to specifically focus on the strength of dependency between modules of a software system, i.e. the number of syntactic references from a module to another. This is quite different from the previous two views which focused on the degree of dependencies. The grid is a chessboard-like view that plots all classes of the system as rectangles arranged in decreasing order of dependency strength value (DSV). The rectangle representing the class with the highest DSV is placed on the top left corner of the grid. The DSV of a class is the sum of the values of the dependencies between this class and all the others. Colors are used for decoration of grids in the same way as discussed earlier for the other views.

6.1 Graphical Setup

All views have a set of controls to adjust their rendering parameters. Most of those controls, such as the use of sliders for view panning, are familiar to general audiences and need no further explanations. However, there is a concept that deserves some explanation. SourceMiner's views use both geometric and semantic zooms. As expected, geometric zoom is used to scale up and down the visual elements of a view. Zooming in will increase the number of pixels per visual element. Zooming out will do the opposite. Semantic zoom, on the other hand, refers to changing the level of detail in which a set of elements is presented. Zooming in and out will navigate on the inheritance and structural trees, or expand and collapse the amount of dependency information shown in graphs and matrices.

The meaning conveyed by the new view as a result of a semantic zoom differs from that conveyed by the previous one [30]. Section 6 will show examples of these operations when it discusses the views of SourceMiner.

6.2 The Filtering Views

Filtering views allow programmers to filter software elements out of the canvas according to specific criteria. Filtering operations are based on numerical and

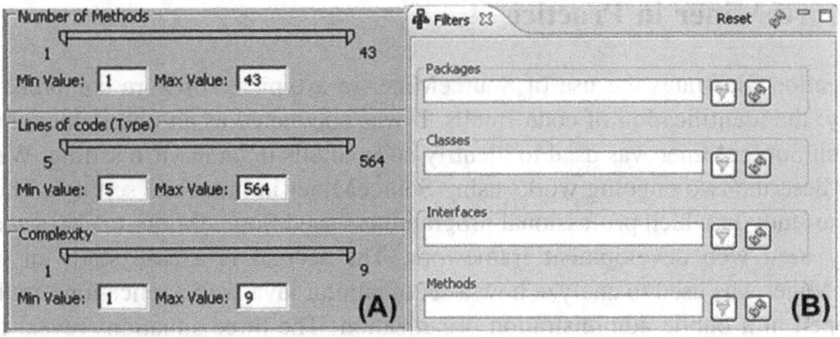

Fig. 11. Filtering using range sliders (Part A) and text boxes (Part B).

categorical values as shown in Parts A and B of Fig. 11, respectively. The global filtering criterion is the conjunction of all the partial filtering criteria. Filter controls have a reset button to set filter options to their default, full selection, values.

6.3   The Decoration

Visual elements can be decorated with visual attributes such as size and color. SourceMiner uses colors as its main means of decoration. Color is an important visual attribute in multiple view environments, because it is transversal to all views. Most if not all visual metaphors can use colors to efficiently differentiate among its visual elements.

SourceMiner uses a common module to consistently color the elements represented in the views. This decoration module can currently use colors to represent software properties such as being affected by a concern, element size, cyclomatic complexity, and element type (e.g., concrete, abstract, inner or external classes). Figure 12 presents the same view decorated by element type (Part A) and concerns (Part B). In part B, the number in each rectangle indicates the number of concerns that affects a given class.

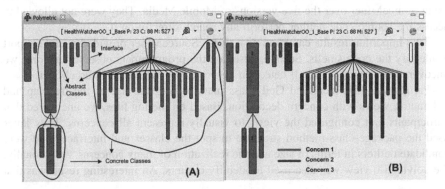

Fig. 12. Decoration using Colors in SourceMiner.

7 SourceMiner in Practice

This section illustrates the use of SourceMiner in a typical software comprehension activity: the identification of code smells. It was conducted as an observational study in which SourceMiner was used to identify code smells in an in vitro setting. We also briefly describe two ongoing works using SourceMiner in industrial settings. The first is a case study in which professional programmers used SourceMiner to characterize a heavily used web development framework. The second is a case study in which SourceMiner was used to analyze how a set of similar java-web applications are being developed in a public administration organization. The three situations reveal initial evidences that the execution of the described activities would be harder or even impossible to do through the use of a single view.

The first study illustrates how SourceMiner aids the identification of code smells. It consisted of an observational study [7], where developers identified a set of well-known code smells on an open source system called Mobile Media. Participants were asked to identify the following code smells using SourceMiner: God Class (GC) [18], Divergent Change (DC) [12] and Feature Envy (FE) [18].

The following descriptions of the code smells summarize the ones presented to the study participants. Feature Envy (FE) occurs when a piece of code seems more interested in a class other than the one it actually is in [12]. This code smell can be seen as a misplaced piece of concern code, i.e., code which does not implement the main concern of its class. Hence, the concern realized by this misplaced code is probably located mainly in a different class. God Class (GC) is characterized by non-cohesiveness of behavior and the tendency of a class to attract more and more features [24]. In a different perspective, we can look at GC as classes that implement too many concerns and, so, have too many responsibilities. It violates the idea that a class should capture only one key abstraction, and breaks the principle of separation of concerns. Divergent Change (DC) occurs when one class commonly changes in different ways for different reasons [12]. Depending on the number of responsibilities of a given class, it can suffer unrelated changes. The fact that a class suffers many kinds of changes can be associated with a symptom of concern tangling. In other words, a class that presents mixed concerns is likely to be changed for different reasons.

In the context of the study, programmers were asked to detect these code smells using SourceMiner over the five versions of Mobile Media. They were not allowed to access the source code neither perform any search directly on it.

Two important results came out of it. First, SourceMiner provided useful support to identify the code smells. Second, based on the programmers observed actions, we uncovered strategies for smell detection supported by the use of SourceMiner.

Participants that identified God Class made synergistic use of the treemap and polymetric views with concern decoration. Based on the log files, we uncovered that participants first configured the views to visually represent all concerns. They latter used the package-class-method structure to spot the classes and interfaces that were candidate outliers in terms of size and the realization of many concerns. Additionally, the polymetric view was also used to identify outliers. An interesting result was that

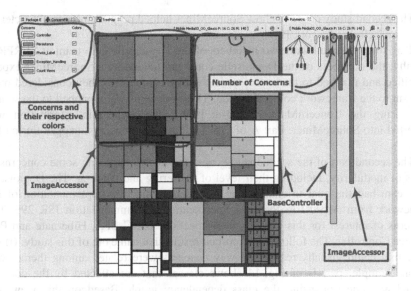

Fig. 13. Identifying outlier classes with SourceMiner.

all participants successfully identified BaseController as a God Class of Mobile Media (MM) using this strategy.

Figure 13 portrays a scenario of MM version 3 where BaseController and ImageAccessor clearly stand out as God Class candidates. In Fig. 13, BaseController is the largest rectangle as indicated by the arrows in Treemap and Polymetric View. Moreover, it contains methods with different concerns (colors). The same is true for the class ImageAccessor, also indicated by arrows in the figure.

In the case of the Feature Envy, the grid and the spiral views were used to spot the code smell. Considering that these views present classes and interfaces in decreasing dependency order, the grid view was used to first present classes with higher dependency weight. In this view, the user selected the BaseController class (Fig. 13) and then double clicked on it so that the spiral view could display its dependency relationships. Using these two sets of views, it is possible to easily spot BaseController as Feature Envy candidate as presented in Fig. 13. This class stands out due to its interest in other classes.

An uncovered strategy to identify Divergent Change candidates was the combined use of the Treemap and Polymetric views to spot classes that may have been frequently changed for different reasons.

A concern is tangled when it is mixed with other concerns within a module which can easily be observed in the treemaps. Moreover, if the ascendants of a given class realize different concerns, this class is change prone, a characteristic that can be observed in the polymetric view. This is again the case of the BaseController class in MM version 3 as illustrated in Fig. 13.

The results that came out from this study present initial evidences that SourceMiner can play an important role in software characterization and, in this particular case, helped to detect God Class, Divergent Class and Feature Envy code smells.

The second study describes how SourceMiner helped programmers to characterize the Demoiselle framework [9].

This study was run with two members of the Demoiselle core team at SERPRO. Initially, the members of the Demoiselle core team, aided by a SourceMiner expert, identified and mapped to the source code a set of 13 concerns they considered most relevant to the framework comprehension. These concerns were mapped to the source code using the ConcernMapper plug-in [27]. Afterwards, this information was imported into SourceMiner. Part A of Fig. 14 shows the concerns mapped during the study.

The second part of the second study consisted in characterizing some concerns in terms of modularity, including their level of scattering and tangling. The Demoiselle core team had the goal to change the dependency injection implementation of the framework from AspectJ to the Java Specification Recommendation JSR 299. The concerns of interest for this activity were injection, JDBC, JPA, Hibernate and Persistence Controller. The following important results that came out of this study: (i) the specialists could visually realize the way concerns were related among themselves. As an example, part B of Fig. 14 shows classes that are affected by the concern dependency injection using the class dependency graph. Based on this view, the specialists were able to identify classes that have any relationship with the dependency injection concern and which other concerns affected these same classes; (ii) considering the results presented before, the specialists were then able to plan and execute the change of the dependency injection technology without any major incident.

The third study describes the use of SourceMiner to support the characterization of Java web-based systems developed in an organization. The organization where the case study took place is a Brazilian public company which has its own development sites settled in different cities. The sites develop software systems to their internal clients. The central office provides a core Java web-based system upon which all sites develops web applications. SourceMiner was used to analyze to which extent the applications followed the original structure of the core java web-based system and in which cases it did modify or did not follow it. The idea was to use SourceMiner to detect such occurrences and to support the decision to develop applications in the

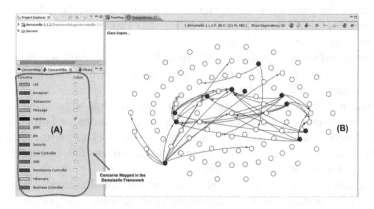

Fig. 14. Characterizing concerns in SourceMiner.

company using a framework such as the one mentioned before. Two versions of the core Java web-based system and three applications developed using them were analyzed. The applications 1 and 2 were developed using the first version of the core java web-based system, while application 3 used the second version. We compared the applications using the three perspectives from SourceMiner: package class method, inheritance and coupling.

The analysis indicated that the approach adopted in the organization is not suitable for code reuse and contributes to degenerate the original architecture of the core Java basic project. Figures 17 and 18 in [8] show an example of a utility class that increased from 701 lines of code and 47 methods in the first version core system to 2089 lines of code and 160 methods in the derived application. This increase is due to new utility functionalities that were added by the application development team. These utility functionalities should have been requested from the core system development team, or at the very least fed back to them, by the application development team, in order to make them available to other applications. In interviews, we found that as the software systems developed in different sites evolve, they tend to include functionalities that originally were to be provided by the basic project. That revealed a clear flaw of this approach of application derivation.

8 Related Works

Software visualization has been extensively studied as a means to support software engineers to build mental models of software systems [10, 16, 31]. Software has been visualized at various levels of detail, from the module granularity seen in Rigi [22] to the individual lines of code depicted in SeeSoft [11]. Many interesting and novel metaphors have been proposed, but much debate and study are still needed to validate them. Consider software visualization techniques that use 3D representations as an example. These techniques attempt to make more efficient use of the available screen space and apply intuitive metaphors to represent data [34]. In spite of their positive points, they also have negative points such as user adaptation and cognition overload. The interaction with 3D presentations and possibly the use of special devices demand considerable adaptation efforts to these technologies [34]. These trade-off scenarios are common for any family of visualization metaphors. For this reason, it is useful that software visualization infrastructures provide means of extensibility and resources to empirically evaluate its use and effectiveness in software engineering tasks, as we have implemented in SourceMiner.

While there are many works on the use of novel metaphors, there is not that many on the combination of metaphors in multiple views environments. Rigi was one of the pioneers in this aspect [22]. It uses multiple views in a reverse engineering environment. It is extensible in the sense that new visualization techniques can be included in the environment through the use of Rigi Command Language (RCL), which is based on the Tcl/Tk scripting language. Several tools were implemented on top of it, where SHriMP is probably the most known [32]. They all employ multiform visualization using module relationships as their main software analysis perspective.

Mature open standard IDEs, such as Eclipse, are nowadays the substratum of many software engineering tool implementations. However, the number of software visualization tools that explore it is still relatively small [5, 21]. Among the main initiatives to move software visualization closer to practitioners, by integrating them in popular IDEs, one can mention Creole [5], an Eclipse plugin by Lintern et al. and X-Ray [21]. Most of those were developed as Eclipse's plug-ins. Unfortunately they cannot be classified as interactive and coordinated multiple view environments, as they do not completely explore environment integration, having limited roundtrip, multiple view coordination and interactive dynamic filtering resources.

As a concluding remark, it is important to observe that the use of multiple, interactive, and coordinated visualization resources are by no means a novel idea in the information visualization field [1, 2, 4, 23, 25, 26]. They just have not fully reached the software visualization field yet.

9 Conclusions

Most software visualization published work focuses on introducing new metaphors to represent software data, behavior and evolution. This work highlights that the study and implementation of extensible, interactive, and coordinated multi-perspective software visualization environments is an important part of the software visualization research. Software is very complex and multi-faceted. The literature has already shown that no single view is able to depict all software properties of a software system [33]. One needs several views. Moreover, it is not clear what the best metaphors are for presenting many of these properties. One needs to test many view combinations and those views need integration and coordination.

We believe that only part of software visualization promising benefits are being observed in practice by the software development industry, because we have not yet seen a tight integration of software visualization tools with current popular software development environments. This paper described SourceMiner as an extensible multiple view environment to enhance software comprehension activities. In its development, we considered guidelines proposed and already used in the information visualization domain to bring forth relevant information from the software source code and associated information.

The model envisioned for SourceMiner is based on the reference model by [6] and allows for consistent coordination among the views. SourceMiner and the model upon which it was built have the following characteristics: (i) views that represent a specific software property are grouped in perspectives to portray information of relevant software properties such as coupling, inheritance and the package-class-method structure; (ii) through the use of multiple view and interaction mechanisms, users to configure visual scenarios suitable to the task at hand; (iii) the model was conceived considering the IDE as its substratum; (iv) the source code is the main data source for the visualization environment; (v) other data sources are used to enrich the views with information such as concerns, and bug track information. We foresee the use of several other types of data in SourceMiner as way to broaden the range of software comprehension activities supported by the multiple view interactive environment;

(vi) the environment is extensible, in the sense that it is designed to support the inclusion of new views. During its development, new views were included following this principle.

The use of multiple views in SourceMiner better handles the diversity of attributes, user profiles, and levels of abstraction needed in software visualization. It enables users to configure and effectively combine views to bring out correlations and or disparities that might otherwise remain hidden in the code. The use of multiple views splits complex data into more manageable chunks of information, and this information can be further filtered and explored through interaction with the different visual scenarios. Despite its focus on static software visualization, we believe that the lessons learned in the design of SourceMiner can be applied to other types of software visualization, such as those that represent dynamic software behavior or evolution [10].

The environment was built for experimentation and we plan to continue to empirically studying it to determine whether or not it actually decreases cognitive load and increases performance on specified software engineering tasks. SourceMiner is being expanded to convey software evolution attributes, churning and bug analysis information. In addition, we are adapting it to support collaborative software comprehension activities in a distributed environment. This paper described SourceMiner that is available at www.sourceminer.org.

References

1. Ainsworth, S.: The functions of multiple representations. Comput. Educ. **33**(2–3), 131–152 (1999)
2. Baldonado, M., Woodruff, A., Kuchinsky, A.: Guidelines for using multiple views in information visualization. In: ACM AVI 2000, Italy, pp. 110–119 (2000)
3. Ball, T., Eick, S.: Software visualization in the large. Computer **29**(4), 33–43 (1996)
4. Becks, A., Seeling, C.: SWAPit: a multiple views paradigm for exploring associations of texts and structured data. In: AVI'2004, Italy (2004)
5. Callendar, C.: Creole: integrating shrimp to the eclipse IDE. http://www.thechiselgroup.org/creole (2012). Accessed May
6. Card, S.K., Mackinlay, J., Shneiderman, B.: Readings in Information Visualization Using Vision to Think. Morgan Kaufmann, San Francisco (1999)
7. Carneiro, G., Silva, M., Mara, L., Figueiredo, E., Sant'Anna, C., Garcia, A., Mendonca, M.: Identifying code smells with multiple concern views. In: Proceedings of the 24th Brazilian Symposium on Software Engineering (SBES) (2010)
8. Carneiro, G., Mendonça, M.: SourceMiner. Technical report (2013). http://www.sourceminer.org/screenshots.html
9. Demoiselle, F.: Demoiselle framework (2013). http://demoiselle.sourceforge.net/
10. Diehl, S.: Software Visualization Visualizing the Structure, Behaviour, and Evolution of Software, 1st edn. Springer, Heidelberg (2007)
11. Eick, S., Steffen, J., Eric, S.: SeeSoft—a tool for visualizing line oriented software statistics. IEEE Trans. Softw. Eng. **18**(11), 957–968 (1992)
12. Fowler, M.: Refactoring: Improving the Design of Existing Code. Addison Wesley, Menlo Park (1999)
13. Graham, M., Kennedy, J.: Multiform views of multiple trees. In: CMV2008, London (2008)

14. Greenwood, P., Bartolomei, T., Figueiredo, E., Dosea, M., Garcia, A., Cacho, N., Sant'Anna, C., Soares, S., Borba, P., Kulesza, U., Rashid, A.: On the impact of aspectual decompositions on design stability: an empirical study. In: Ernst, E. (ed.) ECOOP 2007. LNCS, vol. 4609, pp. 176–200. Springer, Heidelberg (2007)

15. Heer, J., Shneiderman, B.: Interactive dynamics for visual analysis. Commun. ACM **55**(4), 45–54 (2012)

16. Koschke, R.: Software visualization in software maintenance, reverse engineering, and re-engineering: a research survey. J. Softw. Maint. Evol. Res. Pract. **15**, 87–109 (2003)

17. Lanza, M., Ducasse, S.: Polymetric views - a lightweight visual approach to reverse engineering. IEEE Trans. Softw. Eng. **29**(9), 782–795 (2003)

18. Lanza, M., Marinescu, R.: Object-Oriented Metrics in Practice - Using Software Metrics to Characterize, Evaluate, and Improve the Design of Object-Oriented Systems. Springer, Heidelberg (2006)

19. Lehman, M., Belady, L.: Program Evolution: Processes of Software Change. Academic Press, London (1985)

20. Lintern, R., Michaud, J., Storey, M.-A., Wu, X.: Plugging-in visualization: experiences integrating a visualization tool with eclipse. In: Proceedings of SoftVis'03, pp. 47–56. ACM Press (2003)

21. Malnati, J.: X-ray open source software visualization. http://xray.inf.usi.ch/xray.php (2012). Accessed May

22. Müller, H.A., Klashinsky, K.: Rigi: a system for programming-in-the-large. In: Proceedings of the 10th International Conference on Software Engineering, Singapore, pp. 80–86 (2008)

23. Pattison, T., Phillips, M.: View coordination architecture for information visualization. In: Proceedings of the Australian Symposium on Information Visualization, Sydney, Australia, pp. 165–171 (2001)

24. Riel, A.: Object-Oriented Design Heuristics. Addison-Wesley Professional, Reading (1996)

25. Roberts, J.C.: Multiple-view and multiform visualization. In: Erbacher, R., Pang, A., Wittenbrink, C., Roberts, J. (eds.) Visual Data Exploration and Analysis VII, Proceedings of SPIE, vol. 3960, pp. 176–185. SPIE Press, Bellingham (2000)

26. Roberts, J.C.: State of the art: coordinated & multiple views in exploratory visualization. In: CMV'07: Proceedings of the Fifth International Conference on Coordinated and Multiple Views in Exploratory Visualization, Washington, DC, USA, pp. 61–71. IEEE Computer Society (2007)

27. Robillard, M., Murphy, G.: Representing concerns in source code. ACM Trans. Softw. Eng. Methodol. **16**(1), 1–38 (2007)

28. Shneirderman, B.: Tree visualization with tree-maps: A 2-D space-filling approach. ACM Trans. Graph. (ToG) **11**(1), 92–99 (1992)

29. Shneiderman, B., Plaisant, C.: Designing the User Interface: Strategies for Effective Human-Computer Interaction, 5th edn. Addison-Wesley Professional, Reading (2009)

30. Spence, R.: Information Visualization: Design for Interaction, 2nd edn. Person Education, Essex (2007)

31. Storey, M., Fracchia, F., Muller, H.: Cognitive design elements to support the construction of a mental model during software exploration. J. Syst. Softw. **44**(3), 171–185 (1999)

32. Storey, M.D., Müller, H.A.: Manipulating and documenting software structures using SHriMP views. In: 11th IEEE International Conference on Software Maintenance, ICSM'95, pp. 275–284 (1995)

33. Storey, M.: Theories, tools and research methods in program comprehension: past, present and future. Softw. Q. J. **14**(3), 187–208 (2006)

34. Teyseyre, A.R., Campo, M.R.: An overview of 3D software visualization. IEEE Trans. Vis. Comput. Graph. (TVCG) **15**(1), 87–105 (2009)
35. Ware, C.: Information Visualization: Perception for Design. Morgan Kaufmann Publishers Inc., San Francisco (2004)
36. Wu, J., Storey, M.-A.: A Multi-perspective software visualization environment. In: Proceedings of CASCON'2000, November 2000, pp. 41–50 (2000)

Capturing Semiotic and Social Factors
of Organizational Evolution

Alysson Bolognesi Prado[(⊠)] and Maria Cecilia Calani Baranauskas

Institute of Computing, State University of Campinas,
Campinas, São Paulo, Brazil
{aprado,cecilia}@ic.unicamp.br

Abstract. Enterprises are always subject to internal and external pressures for change. Organizational Semiotics explains the structure of social norms, which allows a group of people to act together in a coordinated way for certain purposes. When a novelty requires reshaping this structure, Actor-Network Theory provides sociological insights to understand the involved factors. This paper delineates a method combining these theoretical sources for clarifying and representing the social forces involved in organizational changes. All actors – people, technical devices and other objects – are modeled in the same social level, tracing the flow of interests back to their sources, enabling to negotiate changes with the appropriate stakeholders.

Keywords: Actor-Network Theory · Organizational semiotics · Organizational evolution · Social factors

1 Introduction

Enterprises and organizations are always subject to internal and external pressures for change. Market and politics from one side, and managerial decisions and personal preferences from the other make the propagation of novelties and collective evolution a non-linear process, with forces acting in several directions [18]. The pervasive adoption of an always evolving Information Technology brings more complexity to the scenario [25].

Organizational Semiotics – OS for short – describes an organization as a "structure of social norms, which allows a group of people to act together in a coordinated way for certain purposes" [15, p. 109]. The OS seeks for the cognitive and behavioral universals of the participants of the organization to a better understanding of the environment in which an information system will be deployed and run. However, when studying the readiness of an enterprise for the adoption of new technology, this theory may not reach factors such as support to managers and business process [10].

Some organizational researchers [8, 9] argue that collective phenomena are not defined by previous structure but instead are the result of reciprocal actuation between individuals. The recently proposed branch of Sociology called Actor-Network Theory – or ANT – claims that *social* is not a specific domain of reality or some particular attribute of people, but rather is the name of "a movement, a displacement,

© Springer International Publishing Switzerland 2014
S. Hammoudi et al. (Eds.): ICEIS 2013, LNBIP 190, pp. 264–279, 2014.
DOI: 10.1007/978-3-319-09492-2_16

a transformation, a translation, an enrollment" [13, p. 64] that occurs involving the stakeholders, their interests and the means used to achieve them. This dynamic point of view contributes to understand situations in which the state of affairs is not well stabilized and the social structure is being reconfigured.

The potential of using ANT and OS together have been already pointed out by Soares and Sousa [22] aiming at balancing social and engineering approaches to introduce technology in organizations, and explored by Underwood [27] to understand the diffusion of shared meanings, a prerequisite to the success of Information Systems. These trials provide good examples of positive aspects of merging both theories and encourage the expansion to address social, pragmatic and normative issues.

This paper details and extends a previously published proposal of a method to trace the social forces involved in organizational changes [20]. By unveiling the network of interferences and mediations present in a social scenario and locating the sources of conflicting interests, it is possible to drive the actions needed to improve the organizational structure by redesigning existing software or building new one.

In the following sections we present Organizational Semiotics and Actor-Network Theory and discuss how they can complete each other to be used as support for understanding changes in organizations. Case studies are presented for illustrative purpose, followed by discussion and conclusion.

2   Theoretical Background

Changes in organizations can be seen as social activities, since they require discussion and negotiation among the involved people. To understand social phenomena in general, the Sociology traditionally takes one of two opposite approaches: structuralism or agency. The first defends the primacy of a social "field of forces" that shapes human behavior, while the latter sees the individual actions and choices as the sources of the perceived social reality [7].

The structuralist approach begins with the definition of *social fact*, recognized by the "power of external coercion which it exercises or is able to exercise over individuals" [6, p. 10] giving rise to a *structure* that is beyond people but directs their behavior.

The agency-based approach sees the capacity of individuals to act independently and to make their own free choices as the source of social phenomena [28]. The social structure is just a consequence of the use of physical and cognitive abilities of individuals according to their interests and intentions.

In the following sections we present the two theoretical sources that support this work: Organizational Semiotics and Actor-Network Theory that, when properly combined, have the potential to address the structural and dynamic aspects of organizational evolution.

2.1   Organizational Semiotics

Organizational Semiotics is widely used to provide conditions to develop and deploy software into enterprises and for social groups [16]. It proposes to see an organization as an information system that uses signs and norms to coordinate people working together. Norms capture patterns of behavior and signs carry meaning and promote communication.

At first, organized groups of people can be seen as driven by informal norms, whose performance relies on oral culture, constant negotiation of meaning, and individual abilities, beliefs and patterns of action. Some situations ruled by literate culture, bureaucratic procedures, and normalized behavior constitute an inner structure, that is captured in formal norms. Within this structure, some tasks can be automated and humans replaced by computers or other technical information systems. These three layers are nicknamed "organizational onion" (Fig. 1a). Each layer emerges, relies and depends on the outer ones.

Wright [29] identified and conceptualized six distinct types of norms: rules, prescriptions, directions, customs, moral principles and ideals. Prescriptions and customs define the conducts of people; while the former are characterized by having an explicit issuer or authority and attached sanctions in case of disrespect, the later have no such features, being acquired and forwarded by members of a community by means of imitation and social pressure and becoming regularities in individuals' behavior.

Norms can also be classified as perceptual, evaluative, cognitive or behavioral, according to the nature of the phenomenon they govern: to identify things, to attach a value to things, to grasp causality in flows of events, and to coordinate activities, respectively [24]. Liu [15] shows a general syntax to represent behavioral norms in organizations:

```
whenever <condition>
if <state>
then <agent>
is <obliged | permitted | prohibited>
to do <action>.
```

Semiotic is the science that studies signs as units of signification and communication. According to Morris [17], Semiotics is organized in three levels: syntactic, semantic and pragmatic. The first deals with the structures and relations between signs, the second with their meanings and the third with the intentions and contexts of use. Stamper [23] added a physical and an empirical level on the lower end and a social level to the upper level. This is called the semiotic framework or "ladder" (Fig. 1b).

The three lower levels (shaded) of the semiotic framework are often related to the computational structure of organizations, encompassing hardware, networks, protocols, data encoding, logic and software. The three upper levels correspond to human

Fig. 1. (a) Organizational layers of social norms; (b) semiotic framework, depicting levels in which signs' presence and activity can be studied (adapted from Liu [15]).

attributions: in the semantic layer data is comprehended and meaning is assigned; in the pragmatic layer the system is used with a certain purpose; and if this purpose presupposes or implies other people participating on the system, it reaches the social level. This last level is responsible for negotiation of the meanings of signs and the definition of norms of behavior.

2.2   Actor-Network Theory

The Actor-Network Theory is rooted in the principle that the basic human social skills are able to generate only weak, near reaching, and fast decaying ties [13, p. 65]. It is also asserted that all the forces responsible for sustaining the social aggregations come from the participants of the phenomenon. Therefore, to explain social structures such as organizations, that are expected to last longer and mobilize many different people to work together, it claims that *non-human* elements must be equally addressed.

The participants of the social realm create *associations* among each other, intending to obtain support to propagate forces, share intentions, and mobilize other allies. These aggregates must be between humans, between non-humans, frequently are heterogeneous, but these distinctions are not considered relevant. Instead, it is fundamental to identify the role they fulfill in the associations, when transporting meaning or intentions: as intermediaries or as mediators.

An actor is an *intermediary* in a chain of associations when he or she or it forwards the actions received without transformation. The behavior of an intermediary is predictable and the outputs are determined by the inputs. On the other hand, a *mediator* inserts some new behavior to the system. Mediators modify, distort, enhance or translate the inputs received. They are creative and show some variability and unpredictability when acting upon the others. While faithful intermediaries often fade out in the studied scenarios, mediators appear resolving asymmetries and conflicts between the other actors.

According to ANT, social groups are performative, their existence relies on the constant action of the participants upon each other. Therefore, all the elements involved in a social phenomenon are *actors*, in a broader sense that encompass both human and non-human. The process of building the associations among actors is named *translation* and depends on the success of steps in which an actor, in the desire to change a certain state of affairs, looks for other actors whose acting skills are beneficial, stimulate their interests to join, defines roles and ensures compliance with the responsibilities assumed. A successful translation must follow four well-defined steps of problematisation, interessment, enrollment and mobilization of allies [4] that culminate with the establishment and maintenance of associations.

The strength with which these movements unfold and mechanisms to ensure its stability and preservation define the success of the formed *network* as a whole. When actors become connected, the consequences of success or failure spread through, creating a mutual interest that the group succeeds. When the translation is effective and the various actors are driven to act as one through the mechanisms of mutual control, their complexity is abstracted in a black box. So the network becomes itself an actor.

From the methodological viewpoint, ANT proposes to "follow the actors in their weaving through things they have added to social skills so as to render more durable the constantly shifting interactions" [13, p. 68]. The observer is always accounted as part of the representation and explanation of the studied phenomena. Each actor studied has his own frame of reference and shifting from one frame to another always adds some uncertainty. ANT recommends that we follow the actors closely, investigating the circulating entities that make people act, understanding how each actor is recruiting the others, looking myopically to the phenomena in order to grasp details and covering the whole scenario.

3 Identifying and Representing Social Forces Involved in Organizational Evolution

For an organization to work properly, it is necessary to share meanings, concepts, interests and goals among its members. Precision in semantics [27] allows efficient communication between the participants, while social norms afford them to know what actions, attitudes and behaviors are expected from them and what they can expect from the others [3]. This universality and predictability lead to give up individual meanings and intentions, and rendering impersonal fields of forces that allow people to work together towards some goal.

However, this is a provisional equilibrium between several forces and interests. There are moments when such balance is disturbed: when new players or new interests come to participate, changing the dynamics of the organization. Interests can be understood as expectations on the behavior of the others, as an actor expects that someone else does something useful for him or her, and for the group.

This paper agrees with the scenario described by Sani et al. [21] in which innovation and changes come from the informal layer of the semiotic onion, as the place for discussion, negotiation and uncertainties. Since at this point norms may be conflicting and provisional, there are behaviors and concepts that are not universal, but localized in individuals or subgroups with shared opinions. The source of these forces must be retrieved and understood when it is necessary to change the way they work or to promote consensus. Only when a state of affairs is stable, norms can be formalized and shifted successively to the formal and technical layers. In this section we propose a mechanism to capture and represent such scenario, drawing on tools from Organizational Semiotic and Actor-Network Theory.

3.1 Rationale for Combining ANT and OS

ANT comes as a conciliatory proposal between agency and structure, in a position that can be named *structurationist* [28]. For being focused on actors and the means by which they can interfere in the course of actions, ANT proposes that one of the goals of actors' movements is to build a stable structure that, once established, governs future actions in a certain degree.

Patterns strengthened by the passage of time and the creativity required by uncertainties in the future are the essentials for society. Latour [12] metaphorically represented this by the figure of Janus, a two-faced roman deity who simultaneously looks to the past and to the future, a metaphor for the ambivalent character of the social aggregates: existing structures mold behavior, represented by ancient face looking to the past, and new behavior redefines structures, represented by younger face looking to the future (Fig. 2). Knowing the sources of these patterns is funda-mental when someone is interested in changing them. Besides, knowing the nature of these reservoirs of rules, examples, laws and models – as human or non-human – allows us to choose an approach to tackle the change.

Fig. 2. Two-faced Janus, from roman mythology Extracted from Yonge [30].

ANT argues that norms are not impersonally produced by the fields of forces [2], but are instead the sum of social forces generated, stored and replied by actors and conducted through the associations between them, regardless of being human or not. Customs are not seen as anonymous anymore: they reach people through the asso-ciations each actor has. Although they do not have an authoritative issuer and neither an explicit penalty for being broken, ANT affirms that there is a process of translation that make people behave accordingly and that can be observed and studied. This process is better perceived in moments of group creation or of instability.

Norms and interests can be embodied in documents and devices. Although it is not controversial to say that technology is a kind of consequence of human action, and it is capable of carrying human intentions, it can be controversial to assume that these artifacts may contribute to a state of things for themselves. Kroes [11] defends the agency of objects, in particular, technological devices, arguing that they can change the way people think and act, sometimes in different ways than they were designed for, sometimes unexpectedly. Sharing patterns of behavior is not always a face-to-face phenomenon; in this sense, both OS and ANT share a semiotic-materialistic viewpoint [14], in which non-human can act upon other actors by physical or cognitive means.

3.2 A Representational Mechanism

The momentary structure of the involved actors and their associations compounding a network can be represented as a graph [19]. Each actor is represented by a vertex that, in a visual presentation, can have its nature encoded by its shape: human actors are represented as circles, non-human as squares and entities with undefined nature are depicted as triangles. This notation is shown in Fig. 3.

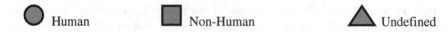

● Human   ■ Non-Human   ▲ Undefined

Fig. 3. Graphical notation for vertices according to the nature of the actors they represent.

This distinction of actors according to their nature does not intend to impose different treatment or positioning. It only records possibilities to information extraction and future actuation. For instance, human actors can be subject to interviews or answer to forms, as well as direct observation. Non-human can be inspected and observed, but can also be copied, read or disassembled. Actors with undefined nature, in this proposal, can be used to represent composite entities that it is not necessary or is not possible to be decomposed. For instance, companies and departments whose internal structure is not relevant or known, although composed by people, machines and documents, are examples of an actor that receive such representation.

When two actors interact in such way that an association is established between them, this is represented by an edge in the graph. From the ANT viewpoint, this means that the behavior of one of the actors is benefic to the other, or potentially configures mutual benefit. In our proposal, it can be seen that over this edge one or more norms are being promoted or intended to be enforced. This can be seen in Fig. 4, in which we represented the flow of interests as arrows and provide an identifier for each norm [26] for the sake of faster referencing. Solid arrows (Fig. 4a) represents successful translations with verified patterns of behavior, while dashed arrows (Fig. 4b) represents unsuccessful or planed translations.

Fig. 4. Proposed representation for the norms of behavior that actors exhibit and enforce. The edge linking the nodes represents an existing association between them, while the arrow represents successful (a) or unsuccessful (b) translations. In this example we used non-human actors, but any type of actor can be used as well.

The roles of the actors, therefore, need to be distinguished: the one that is effectively fulfilling the actions predicted by the norm is called *focal actor* [5], while the ones that are surrounding, expecting such behavior, are named *associates*. The interests on establishing some pattern of behavior on the focal actor can depart from one or more associates. This influence can occur directly through the association between the two actors, as shown in Fig. 4, but can also follow a chain of heterogeneous actors, as studied by Akrich and Latour [1].

In addition to the graphical representation, we propose to extend the syntax of textual representation of norms to encompass the now necessary elements – an identifier for the norm and the list of associated actors:

```
Norm <norm-id>:
whenever <condition>
if <state>
then <focal-actor>
is <obliged | permitted | prohibited>
by <associates>
to do <action>.
```

As an example of the combined use of these representations, consider the scenario of a developer building commercial software that requires the user to fill a form in which the date fields must be in the format "dd/mm/yyyy". This behavior can be oriented by applying masks on the fields before and while the user is typing or by means of a visual calendar; also, the format can be enforced by validation messages and the denial of submission of the form as long as the date format is incorrect. Once the behavior of the user fulfills the expectation of the developer, this must be considered a successful translation. This example is represented in Fig. 5 along with the textual norm representation. A chain of associations can be observed, with the software S acting as an intermediary for norm N1.

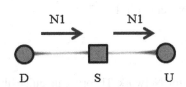

```
Norm N1:
whenever filling the form
if in a date field
then user
is obliged
by developer, software
to use format dd/mm/yyyy.
```

Fig. 5. Example of a chain of associations and a related norm. A developer (D) relies on a software (S) to mold the actions of a user (U) according to norm N1.

Now suppose a researcher wants to use the data already gathered by the above mentioned form to build some monthly statistics using the date field. As the software works properly and grants that the month is informed in the expected positions, the researcher can rely on the data and is allowed to use the data without any previous processing or cleanup. This is represented in Fig. 6. As the software S participates in the possibilities of action for R, the norm N1 is converted into N2 and addressed to R. This characterizes S as a mediator between R and U. Notice that being an intermediary or a mediator is not an internal attribute of the actor, but a consequence of the applied norms, relative to the flows of interests.

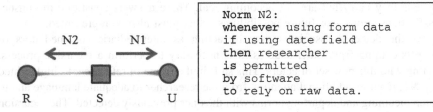

Fig. 6. Example of a mediation in a chain of associations. A researcher (R) relies on raw data input by a user (U), since the software (S) is already guiding the actions of the user according to N1. This enables R to behave according to N2.

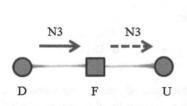

```
Norm N3:
whenever using the forum
if writing text
then user
is prohibited
by developer, forum software
to use bad language.
```

Fig. 7. Example of another chain of associations and a related norm. A developer (D) relies on an Internet Forum (F) to mold the actions of a user (U) according to norm N3. However, users find ways to work around such constraint and behave disregarding the developer intentions.

Finally, consider the example of an Internet Forum software package in which the developer trusts the available automatic filters to deny the users from cursing, using bad language or a list of forbidden words. As soon as the users perceive that the filters can be cheated by replacing some letters with numbers or special characters while keeping the readability – as for instance change "E" for "3" or "S" for "$" – the pattern of behavior desired by the developer cannot be obtained and therefore the translation was unsuccessful. This scenario is represented in Fig. 7.

3.3 Gathering Data for the Analysis

The methodological framework provided by Actor-Network Theory can guide the observations necessary for the understanding of the social phenomenon corresponding to organizational evolution. ANT adopts an ethnographic stance, proposing a detailed scrutiny of every particular participant, prior to any generalization.

Beginning within the business processes to be understood, changed or improved, we must follow each actor through the daily activities, identifying patterns of behavior and representing them as the existing norms. Ask the actors to explain what motivates or constraints such behavior, in order to elicit the presence of the associated actors. These justifications may include desires, favors, orders or imitations, as originating from a human actor, or laws, handbooks and signs as non-humans acting semiotically, or even the physical layout of workplace and machines, as a non-human acting physically.

The results of this step are a set of focal actors, a set of norms of behavior related to them, and a set of newly identified associates that participate in the promotion of such norms. For each of the actors, ask about unfulfilled intentions, or seek the interests they carry but are not becoming real. These answers constitute the unsuccessful translations – or future possibilities – that must also be represented.

As the detected associates may be acting as intermediaries or mediators of interests coming from other sources, it is necessary to perform a recursive process, starting with this new set of actors. This shift in the frame of reference, as highlighted by ANT, requires additional attention from the researcher to adequate language and to match incoming and departing norms with the ones previously detected. The recursion goes until the behavior of the original focal actors can be explained. The presence of the researcher must be also made clear, adding her as an actor, and representing direct contact with other actors as associations.

4   Case Studies

Two case studies were conducted, following the IT team of a public University during their activities of building or improving software. The focus of the participants was in producing changes in a real-world situation and improving the practices of an organization. ANT and OS were used as tools when applicable, and the successive trials and cases of success informed the method described in this paper.

4.1   Understanding the Role of a Legacy System

The IT team was requested by the Human Resources Department (HR) of the same institution to build a web version of a legacy system, already used in client-server mode, which was custom built by a third-part software factory fifteen years ago. This moment was seen by the managers as an opportunity to document, review and improve business processes.

The dialogues below were simplified and translated from a series of conversations with the involved actors, following their own daily activities. We started from the main user of the system, member of the Human Resources Department staff, who we will refer to as *HR-STAFF-1:*

> *HR-STAFF-1: When I use this screen, I must first type the teacher's name and ID, set the status to '1' and click 'save'. Then change the status to '2' and click 'save'. Again, change the status to '3' and 'save', and only now I can input the other data: workplace, date of admittance and so on. Then click 'save' again and it's done.*

When asked about the reason for that behavior, she just replied:

> *HR-STAFF-1: When I started to work here, my colleagues told me to do so. And also, see: when I insert a new teacher, the only value the system left for me to choose for 'status' is '1'. And only when 'status' reaches '3', the system enables the other fields for me.*

In fact, analyzing the available source code, the IT team confirmed that such behavior was deliberated, but produced no intermediary effect or outcome other than enabling and disabling fields on the form. This brings us to the first recorded norm:

```
Norm N1:
whenever teacher data is inserted into HR database
if it is a new teacher
then HR-STAFF
is obliged
by SYSTEM, HR-STAFF (coworkers)
to set the status to 1, 2 and 3 in sequence.
```

The HR staff member was sometimes advised by a senior consultant, who worked there since the time the legacy system was being developed. Although she does not use the system anymore, she provided some additional information about the motivations for the development of that software:

> *HR-SENIOR-CONSULTANT: there is a Deliberative Act that says the hiring process of a new teacher must begin at a Faculty, and then wait for approval by the Legal Department. Only if approved, HR proceeds with registration. The former HR Director believed that the system must reflect such rule, and all the involved workers must use the system.*

The Deliberative Act is an official document, available at the local intranet for the researcher's inspection. Analyzing the text and the senior consultant's story, new norms were detected:

Norm N2:
whenever hiring a new teacher
if the process is beginning
then FACULTY
is obliged
by DELIBERATIVE-ACT
to send the filled forms to
Legal Department.

Norm N3:
whenever hiring a new teacher
if the forms are filled by
Faculties
then LEGAL-DEPARTMENT
is obliged
by DELIBERATIVE-ACT
to verify their content. If
approved, send them to Human
Resources; if rejected, send
them back to Faculty.

Norm N4:
whenever hiring a new teacher
if the forms are approved by
Legal Department
then Human Resources
Department
is obliged
by DELIBERATIVE-ACT
to insert teacher's data on
the database.

Norm N5:
whenever hiring a new teacher
if the forms moved in workflow
then FACULTY, LEGAL-
DEPARTMENT, Human Resources
Department
are obliged
by FORMER-HR-DIRECTOR
to inform process status,
meaning:
1-Forms filled by Faculty;
2-Legal Dept. approval;
3-Registering in the HR
database.

The senior consultant also informed that norm N5 was not accepted by Faculties and Legal Department, since they were not interested in using the Human Resources software only to inform the hiring process' situation. Therefore the FACULTY and LEGAL-DEPARTMENT actors chose not to follow N5, being subject only to N2 and N3. Figure 8 represents all actors studied and the scenario of norms they are enforcing and to which they are subject.

The detection of these points of conflict in the norms and in the flow of interests lead to the situation where an organizational structured can be improved: either N5 is discarded, by negotiation with the current Human Resources Director, or its translation is completed by convincing Faculties and Legal Department to use the system. This decision is to be taken by the current Human Resources Director, in negotiation with Legal Department and Faculties.

4.2   Clarifying the Interests on a New Software

Every year, the University publishes its Statistical Yearbook summarizing the achievements of the previous year, as a physical paper book and also as a PDF file available at its website. Data from several sources as Human Resources, Finances and Academic Board are received by the yearbook Editor and arranged in a single document layout. The tables and charts available in the book are used by University

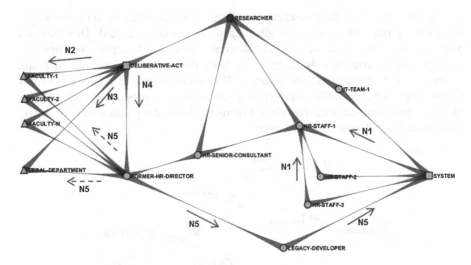

Fig. 8. Actor-Network and the norms gathered during case study. Some arrows, although existing in the real data, were omitted for the sake of readability.

managers to support decisions, and for social scientists to study academic activities. Due to the static nature of this type of publication, the users of the data often ask the sources of information to send updated versions of those data; users also request for the same data in electronic spreadsheets that allow custom sorting and filtering.

In 2011, the Brazilian federal government issued the Law on Access to Information[1], which required all public agencies to provide broad access to data related to public affairs, using websites among other media. Briefly, this current state of affairs can be represented in Fig. 9, along with the following norms:

Norm N1:
whenever a new year has begun
if asked by EDITOR
then DATA-SOURCE
is obliged
by EDITOR
to provide data for the yearbook, relative to the previous year.

Norm N2:
whenever during the current year
if analyzing academic activities
then USER
is permitted
by YEARBOOK
to know details about the academic activities of the previous year.

Norm N3:
whenever in need for up to date data
if not available in YEARBOOK
then DATA-SOURCE
is obliged
by USER
to provide updated data.

Norm N4:
whenever performing bureaucratic activities
if data is generated
then UNIVERSITY
is obliged
by LAW
to made this data publically available on the web.

---

[1] In portuguese: http://www.planalto.gov.br/ccivil_03/_ato2011-2014/2011/lei/l12527.htm

The Vice-President for University Development realized this as an opportunity to make managerial data publically available and continuously updated. Therefore, she proposed to build a new web portal, under the premise of meeting the new law requirements, to continuously receive data from the sources and publish in proper formats, including electronic spreadsheets. This intended state of affairs can be represented by adding the WEB-PORTAL as a new actor in the network and relaying to it the expectations of the Vice-President. Figure 10 shows the planned state of affairs, along with the following intended norms:

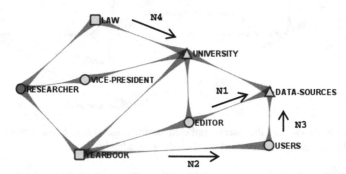

Fig. 9. Actor-Network and the norms representing the current state of affairs of the case study.

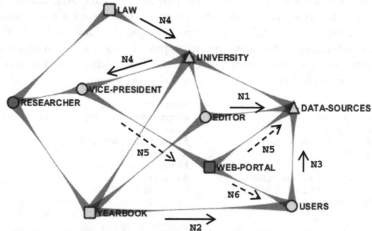

Fig. 10. Planned Actor-Network and the norms representing the desired behavior.

Norm N5:
whenever new data is available
if is data of public interest
then DATA-SOURCE
is obliged
by VICE-PRESIDENT
to send data to the WEB-PORTAL.

Norm N6:
whenever necessary
if analyzing academic activities
then USER
is permitted
by WEB-PORTAL
to know up to date details about the academic activities.

5 Discussion

By knowing the role of the actors as intermediaries or mediators, and being aware of the process of translation, we are able to find the trials of introducing innovations. For instance, in the first Case Study, the former HR Director translated norms N4 to N5 according to his own interests, being a mediator. The legacy software developer, on the other hand, acted as a faithful intermediary, implementing such behavior on the system (see Fig. 8). Non-human actors share the responsibility of keeping the others acting as expected by their designers. The SYSTEM kept HR-STAFF performing according to the FORMER-HR-DIRECTOR's intentions, although the other stake-holders, who were not connected to the system, ignored the norm N5.

During the representation of the actor-network, associations between actors do not always carry norms. They represent the flows of information and interests among all the involved entities. For instance in the case study, HR-SENIOR-CONSULTANT does not enforce or is subject to any norm. She provided de path through which the norms N2 to N5 became known. The ANT representation makes explicit the presence of this informant as a source of uncertainty. The role of the researcher is also high-lighted as an active actor.

Although incomplete translations do not exist as a global shared behavior, they play an important role in the dynamics of organizations, because from the ANT point of view, they are precursor of norms or, as seen in the case study, generate local patterns of action that may be obsolete and subject to improvement. Using ANT, local sub-cultures can be disassembled, analyzed and explained; for example, the existence of norm N1 was maintained by the SYSTEM and the HR-STAFF by means of a custom, although the justification for such behavior, FORMER-HR-DIRECTOR, was not directly acting anymore.

It is also noteworthy that the passage of norms from the formal to the technical layer is not a passive process of diffusion, but instead subject to the active interference of actors' interests, capabilities and comprehension, for instance, the sequence of translations N4 → N5 → N1. Norms always reach people through a network of associations that may be heterogeneous in actors' nature and intentions.

Since the insertion of a computer system as a new actor implies in a reshaping of the surrounding network, to understand the requirements for system development, from the ANT point of view, goes beyond eliciting what the system is supposed to do; instead, it is necessary to inquiry what it is expected to change in the behavior of the other actors.

For instance, in the second case study, the goal of the VICE-PRESIDENT is not merely building a new WEB-PORTAL, but benefit from an external need generated by LAW to promote a more dynamic flow of information from DATA-SOURCES to the USERS, mediated by the WEB-PORTAL. Plans and intentions were modeled as intended norms (dashed arrows in Fig. 10). The VICE-PRESIDENT translated norm N4 into N5, planning a new behavior for the DATA-SOURCES. It is also desired that the existence of the system allows a distinct behavior of the USERS, represented as N6. The analysis also shows that as long as the new web portal works, the association between users and data sources may become unnecessary, and so does norm N3. And as N6 replaces N2, the function of the YEARBOOK may be reconsidered.

6 Conclusions

System design for an evolving organization is far from being a solved problem. The Actor-Network Theory argues that individuals' intentions are the source of social structure and provides a good methodological and theoretical support to find those interactions and understand how such structure emerges and is maintained. Organizational Semiotics, on the other hand, has a long tradition in providing a deep understanding of the enterprises and, once behavioral patterns are established, guiding the software development.

By seeing the whole organization as a single information system and considering that all involved actors – people, technical devices and other objects – may have the same importance in the social level, through the proposed method and representation, we were able to trace the flow of interests through the network of actors and reach their sources, enabling to negotiate the change with the appropriate stakeholders. The proposed method also allows following intended norms forward through new planned actors, eliciting the interests they are supposed to mediate.

References

1. Akrich, M., Latour, B.: A summary of a convenient vocabulary for the semiotics of human and nonhuman assemblies. In: Bijker, W.E., Law, J. (eds.) Shaping Technology/Building Society: Studies in Sociotechnical Change. MIT Press, Cambridge (1992)
2. Al-Rajhi, M., Liu, K., Nakata, K.: A conceptual model for acceptance of information systems: an organizational semiotic perspective. In: Proceedings of the Sixteenth Americas Conference on Information Systems (2010)
3. Bicchieri, C.: The Grammar of Society – The Nature and Dynamics of Social Norms. Cambridge University Press, New York (2006)
4. Callon, M.: Some elements of a sociology of translation: domestication of the scallops and the fishermen of St. Brieuc Bay. In: Law, J. (ed.) Power, Action and Belief: A New Sociology of Knowledge. Routledge, London (1986)
5. Carroll, N., Richardson, I., Whelan, E.: Service science: an Actor-Network Theory approach. Int. J. Actor-Netw. Theor. Technol. Innov. **4**(3), 51–69 (2012)
6. Durkheim, E.: The Rules of Sociological Method. Ed. Martins Fontes, Brazilian Portuguese edition (2007)
7. Hewege, C.R.: Resolving structure-agency dichotomy in management research: case for adaptive theory research methodology. In: Proceedings of the 24th Annual Australian and New Zealand Academy of Management Conference (2010)
8. Holt, D.T., Armenakis, A.A., Field, H.S., Harris, S.G.: Readiness for organizational change: the systematic development of a scale. J. Appl. Behav. Sci. **43**(2), 232–255 (2007)
9. Jacobides, M.G., Winter, S.G.: Capabilities: structure, agency, and evolution. Organ. Sci. **23**(5), 1365–1381 (2012)
10. Jacobs, A., Nakata, K.: Organisational semiotics methods to assess organisational readiness for internal use of social media. In: Proceedings of the 18th Americas Conference on Information Systems (2012)

11. Kroes, P.: The moral significance of technical artefacts. In: Technical Artefacts: Creations of Mind and Matter. A Philosophy 163 of Engineering Design, Philosophy of Engineering and Technology. Springer, Netherlands (2012). Chapter 6, Springer Science+Business Media B.V

12. Latour, B.: Science in action: how to follow scientists and engineers through society. Ed. UNESP (2000)

13. Latour, B.: Reassembling the Social: an Introduction to Actor-Network-Theory. Oxford University Press, Oxford (2005)

14. Law, J.: Actor-Network Theory and Material Semiotics. The New Blackwell Companion to Social Theory. Blackwell Publishing Ltd, Rowley (2009)

15. Liu, K.: Semiotics in Information Systems Engineering. Cambridge University Press, Cambridge (2000)

16. Liu, K., Benfell, A.: Pragmatic web services: a semiotic viewpoint. In: Cordeiro, J., Ranchordas, A., Shishkov, B. (eds.) ICSOFT 2009. CCIS, vol. 50, pp. 18–32. Springer, Heidelberg (2011)

17. Morris, C.W.: Foundations of the Theory of Signs. Chicago University Press, Chicago (1938)

18. Pastuszak, J., Orłowski, C.: Model of rules for IT organization evolution. In: Nguyen, N.T. (ed.) Transactions on Computational Collective Intelligence IX. LNCS, vol. 7770, pp. 55–78. Springer, Heidelberg (2013)

19. Prado, A.B., Baranauskas, M.C.C.: Representing scientific associations through the lens of Actor-Network Theory. In: Proceedings of IEEE CASoN (2012)

20. Prado, A.B., Baranauskas, M.C.C.: Perspectives on using Actor-Network Theory and organizational semiotics to address organizational evolution. In: Proceedings of ICEIS (2013)

21. Sani, N.K., Ketabchi, S., Liu, K.: The co-design of business and IT systems: a case in supply chain management. In: Dua, S., Gangopadhyay, A., Thulasiraman, P., Straccia, U., Shepherd, M., Stein, B. (eds.) ICISTM 2012. CCIS, vol. 285, pp. 13–27. Springer, Heidelberg (2012)

22. Soares, A.L., Sousa, J.P.: Modeling social aspects of collaborative networks. In: Camarinha-Matos, L.M., Afsarmanesh, H. (eds.) Collaborative Networked Organizations: a Research Agenda for Emerging Business Models. Springer, New York (2004)

23. Stamper, R.K.: Signs, information, norms and systems. In: Holmqvist, P., Andersen, P.B., Klein, H., Posner, R. (eds.) Signs of Work: Semiotics and Information Processing in Organisations. Walter de Gruyter, New York (1996)

24. Stamper, R., Liu, K., Hafkamp, M., Ades, Y.: Understanding the roles of signs and norms in organisations. J. Behav. Inf. Technol. 19, 15–27 (2000)

25. Stirna, J., Grabis, J., Henkel, M., Zdravkovic, J.: Capability driven development – an approach to support evolving organizations. In: Sandkuhl, K., Seigerroth, U., Stirna, J. (eds.) PoEM 2012. LNBIP, vol. 134, pp. 117–131. Springer, Heidelberg (2012)

26. Sun, L., Chong, S. Liu, K.: Articulation of information requirements in e-business systems. In: Proceedings of AMCIS (2001)

27. Underwood, J.: Translation, betrayal and ambiguity in IS development. In: Liu, K., Clarke, R.J., Andersen, P.B., Stamper, R.K., Abou-Zeid, E.-S. (eds.) Organizational Semiotics. IFIP, vol. 94, pp. 91–108. Springer, Boston (2002)

28. Vandenberghe, F.: Review of the book Structure, Agency and the Internal Conversation by Margaret S. Archer. Revue du Mauss (2008). www.journaldumauss.net

29. Wright, G.H.: Norm and Action (1958). www.giffordlectures.org/Browse.asp?PubID=TPNORM

30. Yonge, C. M.: Young Folks' History of Rome. Project Gutenberg (1880)

The Change Impact Analysis in BPM Based Software Applications: A Graph Rewriting and Ontology Based Approach

Mourad Bouneffa and Adeel Ahmad[✉]

Université Lille Nord de France, Laboratoire d'Informatique Signal et Image de la Côte d'Opale, 50, rue Ferdinand Buisson, BP 719, 62228 Calais Cedex, France
{bouneffa,ahmad}@lisic.univ-littoral.fr
http://www-lisic.univ-littoral.fr

Abstract. The Business Process Models describe and formalize the operations, constraints and policies of an organization. These models have firstly been used as abstract views of all the processes implied in an organisation. These served as inputs and outputs of the business analysis and re-engineering activities with no explicit relationship with the IT infrastructures which have been implementing business processes. In this paper, we deal with the BPM as higher abstraction level artefacts of software applications implementing the organisation processes. It presents our approach dealing with the change management of such applications. The approach is based on the graph based formalisation of all the software artefacts including the BPM ones. It provides an explicit management of various relationships conducting the change impact. The change operations are then formalized by graph rewriting (or transformation) rules. These rules implement both the change and the change impact propagation. The semantic knowledge concerning the various artefacts and the change operations is represented by an ontology. This ontology is intended to be able to automatically generate some change management rules. We use graph rewriting system (AGG) as a mean to formally specify and validate the result of our approach. The resulting specifications are then implemented using an integrated software change management platform appearing as a set of the Eclipse Workbench plug-ins.

Keywords: BPM · Change impact propagation · Graph Rewriting Rules · Ontology · Process Change Management

1 Introduction

The Business Process Models (BPMs) and their components have first been used as first class entities of the Business Process Management activities. The BPM generally encapsulate semi-formal specifications describing the activities of an organisation. Which may lead to build an artefact repository serving as a knowledge base used by the various activities of the Business Management, also

© Springer International Publishing Switzerland 2014
S. Hammoudi et al. (Eds.): ICEIS 2013, LNBIP 190, pp. 280–295, 2014.
DOI: 10.1007/978-3-319-09492-2_17

including the Business Process Re-engineering. Such activities may be viewed as a part of the job of a business analyst with no explicit relationship to the Information Technology Infrastructures supporting the organisation's information system. During the last decade, BPMs have also been used as the first class entities of a new software development methodology based on the transformation of the BPMs into executable programs. It led to the semergence of new software development tools and approaches based on the BPM [1,2] concept. In these approaches the BPMs are specified by means of some standard notations like BPMN [3,4] and XPDL [5,6]. The BPMs are then transformed into executable programs that are generally deployed as multi-tiered distributed applications using platforms like J2EE, .NET, etc. The executable programs are often built as macro programs implementing the well known concept of *programming in the large* [7]. These programs contain invocations of web services [8] provided by the various software applications which have been deployed inside or sometimes outside the information system boundaries. The Business Process Execution Language (BPEL) [9] is one of the most known *programming in the large* language. The main motivation of such an approach is to eliminate the gap between the activities involved in Business Analysis and Information Technology making it more easy and rapid to implement business change requirements.

In a recent paper [10], we considered the study of this new generation of applications and we demonstrate the feasibility of the implementation of a process to control the change impact which may affect these applications. Our approach is mainly based on the use of attributed typed graphs to represent the business process model and software artefacts and the use of graph rewriting system for a formal specification of the BPM changes.

In this paper we enrich our approach by the use of ontologies to explicitly represent more knowledge concerning the BPM, the software artefacts, and the changes affecting them. We consider the fact that a specific relationship between a BPM artefact and a software one conducts the change impact in certain direction. We represent the knowledge concerning the structure of an enterprise and associate BPM artefacts to its one or more structural units. It may respond to queries like which BPM artefacts are affected by a change concerning the particular structural unit? And which software artefact are affected by this change? We can also specify queries like what are the change operations concerning a specific artefact type? etc. In this work, we focus on the change impact propagation aspect which can be achieved by associating more semantic information to the relationship types.

Our approach is mainly based on an ontology, which is built in an interactive and incremental manner. This ontology concerns both the business analysts and software engineers. For this purpose we have been using a simple tool to build such an ontology. For instance, we used the Protégé tool[1] as an assistance to build OWL[2] ontologies using graphical and interactive user interface. We also developed a semantic annotation tool to assist the business analysts and

---

[1] Protégé: http://protege.stanford.edu/.
[2] OWL Web Ontology Language: http://www.w3.org/TR/owl2-profiles/.

software engineer to annotate the business models and software artefacts with those belonging to ontologies. In fact, all the artefacts are yet stored as graph elements of attributed and typed graphs [10]. The annotation mechanism provide help to add more semantical information to these elements.

In Sect. 2 we present, the meta-model for the BPM formalization and the notions relevant to BPM and BPM-based software applications. The Sect. 3 specifies a taxonomy of BPM change operations and we formalize these operations with the help of graph rewriting rules. The Sect. 4 presents the change impact analysis and propagation process along with its formalization by the graph rewriting rules. The Sect. 5 explains the use of ontology to associate more semantic information to BPM and software artefact. It also presents a generic algorithm we used to automatically generate graph rewriting rules in order to manage the change impact propagation. The Sect. 6 shows the prototype implementation of our specifications regarding the integrated platform to control the software changes [11]. The Sect. 7 summarizes the contribution with the conclusion and the perspectives of this work.

2   BPM Formalization and Meta-Modeling

Before explaining the formalization and meta-modeling of BPM, we first explain the concept of BPM and especially the life cycle of BPM based software applications. As shown in Fig. 1 the development, deployment, and evolution of BPM based software applications obey a life cycle. The different phases of BPM life cycle are described in the following sections:

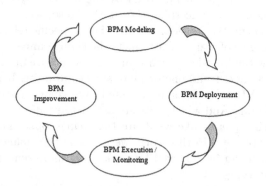

Fig. 1. The life cycle of BPM based applications.

2.1   The BPM Modeling

This phase involves BPM Modeling in terms of tasks or activities which are necessary to implement the process, the order of tasks accomplishment, the human actors involved in the performance of these tasks, etc. In recent years, several models or notations have been defined to model the BPM. At first, designing a BPM is an activity within the scope of the information system cartography. It was most often performed as a part of BPR (Business Process Re-engineering) projects [12]. Thus, many models and methods have been used such as the OSSAD method [13], etc. Our present work is particularly related to the BPM as a means of specification, development, and deployment of automated processes. We selected the widely considered and used notations in this area, in particular the BPMN [14]. Figure 2 shows an example of such a process. In this figure, the process is a partial description of the *Sales Chain Management*. We first distinguish two important actors: the *Client* and the *Process Order*. At the beginning, a start event represent the fact that *Place Order* is the first task. This first task performed by the *Client* consists of the generation of an order that is sent as a *message* to the *Check Availability* task, which is linked to a gateway involving the *Check Payment* task. If the products are available or the *Cancel Order*, otherwise. The process ends by end events linked with *Confirm Order* and *Cancel Order* tasks.

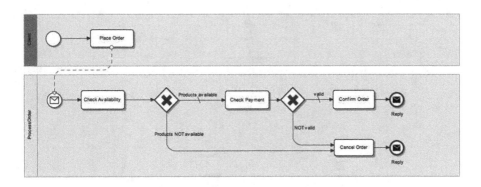

Fig. 2. An example of Business Process Model Notation.

2.2   The Development and the Deployment of the BPM

The development and the deployment of a BPM are two separate activities that can be performed manually, automatically, or usually semi-automatically. In principle, these activities can be considered as classical operations for code generation, where the BPM plays the role of a detailed design and the code is represented by an application, deployed most often on a web platform. There exists also software tools to automate the deployment of such applications almost transparently. Some of these tools are Bonita[3], Intalio[4], BizAgi[5] and Barium Live![6], etc. In these tools a web application is generated and is hosted in form

---

[3] Bonita Open Solution url: http://www.bonitasoft.com/.
[4] Intalio—BPMS: http://www.intalio.com/.
[5] Bizagi BPM Suite: http://www.bizagi.com/.
[6] Barium Live!: http://www.bariumlive.com/.

of dynamic web pages, a Java servlet engine, or ASP.NET pages, etc. Without going to the full automation and complete transparent development and deployment of BPM based applications, there are intermediate languages playing the role of orchestrators or macro programs involving software components already encapsulated by web services. BPEL is one of the main languages of this type and appears like a sort of standard in the matter. In one perspective of Model Driven Engineering (MDE) [15], BPMN can be considered as a Platform Independent Model (PIM) and BPEL as a Platform Specific Model (PSM) consisting of implementing BPMN in an environment using web services as a means of communication and interoperability.

Figure 3 shows an example of BPEL implementing the BPM shown in Fig. 2. In this figure the BPEL is a kind of web services orchestration. To do this, the BPEL contains calls or invocations to web services like *Check Availability*, *Check Payment* and *Cancel Order* and flow management nodes like *sequence* for a sequential execution of web services invocations or *If* for conditional branches. It is useful to remark that the *programming in the large* concepts are quite

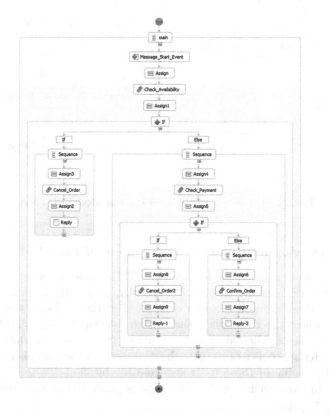

Fig. 3. An example of Business Process Execution Language.

similar to the *programming in the small* [16] ones. For our example, the tasks or activities of the BPMs are implemented by web service calls while *gateways* are implemented by *If* nodes.

2.3   The Execution and Monitoring of the BPM

The execution of the application is generally assured by a web platform which is usually on multi-tiered architecture etc. The BPM execution provides generally some interesting data such as response time, resource consumption, etc. These data are necessary for the purpose of analyzing the process quality. Indeed, business managers define performance indicators (Key Performance Indicator [17]) for each process, to measure the performance of activities implemented by processes. Some of these informations can be obtained by dynamic analysis by means of program profiling techniques [18–20]. Other information are exclusively provided by human experts and will be explicitly taken into account by some organizational process. They are generally the derived data from activities within the framework of customer satisfaction, etc.

2.4   The BPM Improvement

The process improvement is a generic term that refers primarily to the evolution of BPM processes. In reality, the improvement is expected but what is actually done, is an evolution of a process embodied by the change affecting the BPM processes. The goal is to fix certain performance anomalies or simply to complete the automation of processes, a part of which is manual, etc. In the literature, the improvement is seen only on the process side and it ignores the software implementation problems. In our case, we consider both aspects, analyzing in particular the BPM change impacts on the software and *vice versa.*

2.5   A Meta-Model of Graph-Based BPM

We propose a meta-model to represent the concepts involved in the definition of BPMs. This meta-model has been formalized by a typed graph that we implement particularly in the context of the AGG[7]. The result of this modeling is shown schematically in the Fig. 4. This figure represents the main concepts emerging from the BPMN. The process concept represents the processes that contain what is called *flow objects*. These objects can be *tasks* or *activities, subprocesses* or *macro-tasks*, refined by the *processes, events* or *gateways*. A process has an actor which is called the *owner* which can be one user, or more, who has defined the process and is authorized to change this process. The process is implemented by an application which is deployed and which can host the execution of multiple instances or cases of this process. Every instance involves actors that are the users interacting with the various tasks performed during the instance life cycle. The typed attributed graph formalism may be viewed as

---

[7] http://user.cs.tu-berlin.de/~gragra/agg/

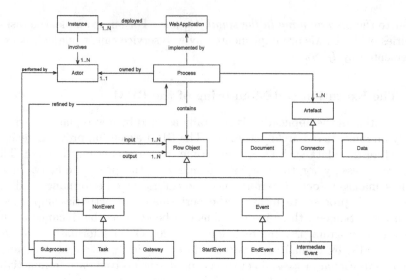

Fig. 4. A UML based representation of BPM meta-model.

a mean to check the BPM artefacts consistency. In fact these artefacts are also formalized by graphs.

3   The Taxonomy of Change Operations

In the development and the deployment of BPM-oriented applications, the change seems inevitable. It enrolls in fact, in the usual life cycle of this kind of applications. We define it as a taxonomy of change operations that may affect one of the important components of these applications to know the BPM. We consider two kind of changes: the atomic change operations and the composite (or complex) change operations.

3.1   The Atomic Change Operations

The formalization of a BPM as a typed attributed graph allows us to compile a list of atomic change operations. It is important to notify that, "each change operation corresponds to an insertion, deletion or modification of a node or an edge of this graph". We thus obtain the following change operations:

- Insert or Delete or Modify a process.
- Insert or Delete or Modify a task.
- Insert or Delete or Modify an Event.
- Insert or Delete or Modify a Gateway
- Insert or Delete an edge or link (between two flow objects)
- *Et cetera.*

Each defined atomic change operation is then formalized by graph rewriting rules. A graph rewriting rule is in fact a production rule where the left and right sides of the rule are graphs. In other words, a production rule that transform a part of the graph which match or corresponds to the Left Hand Side (LHS) of the production by another subgraph represented by the Right Hand Side (RHS) of the production. There are also preconditions called negative or NAC, which specify the need for non existence of certain sub-graph for the rule to run.

Visually such a rule can be outlined as in the Fig. 5. This figure depicts the partial creation or insertion of a new task. It shows the three components of a rule called *InsertTask* which represents the insertion of a task in a process. The LHS of the rule states that there must be a node in the graph of process type. It would then match a process node of the graph with that of the rule. This matching can be done manually by the user or automatically by the graph rewriting system following many methods that are out of the scope of this paper. The RHS of the rule shows the creation of a task called x connected to the process by the relationship *"contains"*. The NAC of the rule prohibits the creation of a task named x if there is already a task in the process with the same name.

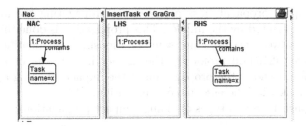

Fig. 5. A rule to insert a task.

3.2   The Composite Change Operations

The composite change operations can be expressed in the form of compositions of atomic operations. We did not set a precise or exhaustive taxonomy of these operations but we consider the most significant and frequent ones. It is also possible to define new composite change operations. A comosite operation may be the merger of two tasks, the decomposition of a task into two tasks, the merger of two processes or the breaking down of a task into a subprocess.

4   The Change Impact Analysis

This section deals with the BPM change impact management. A simulation of the change impact generation is presented formerly, using graph rewriting rules and then in later part impact propagation is elaborated to the various artifacts through the different type of relationships.

4.1 The Change Impact Generation

All change operations are defined by the preconditions, which in the case of a graph rewriting rules consist of the LHS (positive preconditions) and the NAC (negative preconditions) and the post-conditions symbolized by the RHS. We therefore consider the impact of a change M given the result of its execution (symbolized as the RHS), in the case of a violation of the precondition. In the case of graph rewriting rules, this is translated into the creation of a node of *Impact* type, connected to the nodes affected by the impact and containing an attribute called *explanation* which contains a narrative of the impact (see Fig. 6). We simulate the creation of the impact by setting rules without NAC and therefore tolerate the enforcement of the rule with the result, in addition to that provided by the original rule, appending a node of impact type linked to the nodes it affects. In Fig. 6, we define a rule to delete a task that provokes the creation of an *Impact* node affecting the tasks related to the task that has been deleted.

4.2 The Change Impact Propagation

The change impact propagation is a process of propagating the impact to all nodes indirectly affected by the impact. This propagation is done through a link or relationship between nodes. Thus, some relationships are identified as *change impact conductor* [21] and propagate the impact in one way or another. For example, the Fig. 7 shows the propagation of the impact affecting a task to the author of this task with the associated explanation.

We distinguish here two types of change impact propagations:

- The horizontal change impact propagation is to propagate the change impact between artifacts belonging to the same phase of the development life cycle of an application. This is the case of the rule as shown in Fig. 7. It shows the impact propagation between tasks and actors.
- The vertical change impact propagation corresponds to the change impact flow between artifacts belonging to different phases of the development life cycle of an application. This is the case of the change impact propagation between a task and a web service that implements a part of this task and *vice versa*.

To show how we deal the vertical change impact propagation, we first define a kind of mapping relationships that are useful for the traceability purpose. These relationships are:

- The *mapedTo* relationship between a BPMN process and a BPEL process. In fact, we defined a meta-model of BPEL processes like we have done with the BPMN but the BPEL process contains objects like web services, etc.
- The *ImplementedBy* relationship between a task of the BPM and a web service of the BPEL.

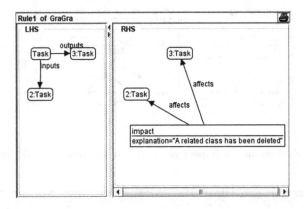

Fig. 6. A rule for change impact analysis of a task deletion.

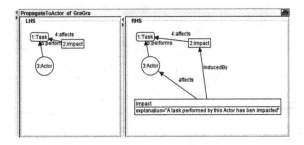

Fig. 7. A rule for change impact propagation.

We know that this set of mapping relationships is a restrictive one since it is generally possible that a task may be implemented by more than one web service, it may also be implemented by a process. In another hand a BPMN process may be implemented by a set of BPEL, ones.

The mapping relationships are then used by the graph rewriting rules generating or propagating the impact. So, the Fig. 8 shows the impact generated by the composite change consisting of the merging of two tasks. The question here is what to do with web services implementing these tasks?

On the other hand, we consider three kinds of change impact propagation processes.

- The total change impact propagation simulates the change operation and then execute all possible rules of its impact propagation.
- The selective change impact propagation only propagates the change impacts induced by a subset of nodes relationships.
- The Propagation of type *changes-and-fix* [22,23] which is to simulate a change, directly addresses the impact of this operation (in terms of direct neighbours).

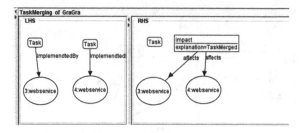

Fig. 8. Rule for the impact generated by the composite change.

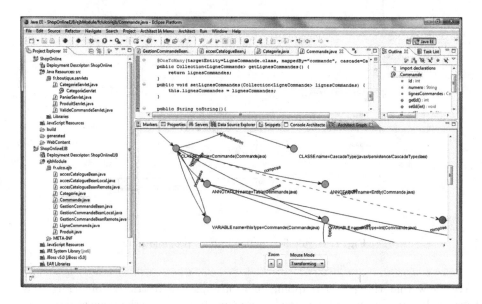

Fig. 9. Screen shot of a change impact propagation scenario in *Architect*.

This treatment or correction of the change impact will be a transaction which itself will directly impact the address, and so on.

5 The BPM and Software Artefacts Change Ontology

The use of graph rewriting rules may help to specify a formal and flexible implementation of the BPM change propagation analysis. Such rules serve as a validation tool and are mainly syntactical since they are only based on the application of syntactical morphisms between artefacts represented by graph elements and the left and right hand sides of the rules. We also want to find a mean to automatically or semi-automatically generate such syntactical rules. The generation of such rules need a more semantic data concerning both the artefacts affected by the change or the change itself. It is therefore we decided to use ontologies allowing the representation and the manipulation of semantic knowledge associated to BPM and software artefacts. This ontology has been used to semantically annotate the artefacts that are represented by graph elements (Fig. 9) and to generate the graph rewriting rules managing the change impact propagation.

The ontology we defined may be viewed as a transcription of the BPM meta-model (Fig. 4) using the OWL. The significant difference consists of the fact that relationships between artefacts are also described by an *ISA* hierarchy. The relationships are also described by some semantic attributes like "is the relationship symmetric, antisymmetric, reflexive, transitive, etc.". Such attributes can be very useful for the change propagation process. We defined two hierarchies; one hierarchy concerns the artefacts and the second concerns the relationships. The current work is focused on the relationship hierarchy based on aspects relevant to the change impact analysis and propagation (Fig. 10). Considering the change impact propagation we define five relationship types:

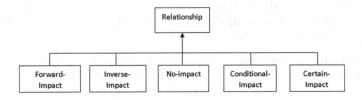

Fig. 10. Relationship hierarchy.

- *ForwardImpact* relationships are those conducting the impact from their source or themselves to their destination. That means if a change affect the source of the relationship or affect the relationship itself, the impact may generate and it may also impact the destination of the relationship.
- *InverseImpact* relationships are the relationship conducting the impact from the destination to the source. That means if the destination of the relationship is affected by a change then an impact of this change may generate and this impact may affect the source of the relationship.
- *NoImpact* relationships do not conduct the impact of a change. That means if a change affects the source or destination of the relationship no impact my generate through this relationship.
- *CertainImpact* relationships are those conducting certainly the impact.
- *ConditionalImpact* relationships are those conducting the impact in some cases only.

These relationship types are not disjunctives. That means a relationship may be at the same time *ForwardImpact* and CertainImpact or *InverseImpact* and *ConditionalImpact* or *ForwardImpact* and *InverseImpact*, etc. For instance the *MappedTo* relationship is a *ForwradImpact*. A change affecting a BPM can affect the BPEL implementing it. This relationship is also *InverseImpact* since a change affecting a BPEL may have an impact affecting the corresponding BPM. This relationship is also a *ConditionalImpact* since it is not sure that a change affecting a BPM will really cause a change affecting the corresponding BPEL. With the help of an ontology language it is then possible to define the new relationship types by combining these.

In our ontology we also represent some descriptions concerning the different kind of changes (as described in the Sect. 3. We add complementary information regarding the artefacts affected by a change, the author of the change, etc. We then define and implement a generic algorithm that generates automatically graph rewriting rules implementing the change impact propagation (Listing 1.1). In this algorithm we assume the existence a function called *generateImpact(ImpactType:String, AffectedNode: Node)* associated to a relationship Ri. This function generates a rule in which:

- the *LHS* of the rule is a subgraph containing the source and destination of the relationship Ri as linked by the relationship Ri.
- The *RHS* of the rule contains the source and destination of Ri that are not linked (directly related) by Ri and a node of type *ImpactType* is then created and linked (indirectly related) to the affected node that may be the source or the destination of the relationship Ri.

This algorithm has also been designed to assess the change impact propagation without the use of the graph rewriting rules. In this case the function *generateImpact* does not generate a rule but manipulates directly the artefacts stored in the XML repository as graph nodes and edges using the GXL data model.

Listing 1.1. Algorithm impactGeneration(artefact:a change:c).

```
1   R=relationships where a is source or destination artefact
2   forAll Ri in R {
3       if Ri.forward then
4           if Ri.impact then
5               forAll d in  Ri.destination {
6                   Ri.generateImpact('certainImpact', d)
7                   }
8           else
9               forAll d in Ri.destination {
10                  Ri.generateImpact('conditionalImpact', d)
11                  }
12          endif
13      endif
14
15      if Ri.inverse then
16          if Ri.impact then
17              forAll s in Ri.source {
18                  Ri.generateImpact('certainImpact', s)
19                  }
20          else
21              forAll s in  Ri.source {
22                  Ri.generateImpact('conditional ',  s)
23                  }
24          endif
25      endif
26  }
```

6   The Prototype of Validation

The prototype we developed can be divided on two main parts:

- the first part concerns the graph rewriting implementation and the ontology construction. For this part we mainly used tools such as AGG and Protégé, which allow the graph rewriting specification (and execution) and the ontology construction, respectively. These two tools concerns the specification and formalization of the concepts used by our approach. These tools are not supposed to be actually used in a real project but these help in developing the second part.
- the second part of our validation concern the integration of the results of our approach on a platform we developed to deal with the change management of large distributed software applications. This platform called *Architect* is built as a set of *Eclipse*[8] IDE plug-ins. An Eclipse project manages a set of resources that can be source code files, libraries, BPEL, and BPMN files etc. *Architect* analyzes these heterogeneous sources and parses their elements to represent them as a homogenous interactive graph. The *Architect Graph* extension of eclipse visualizes the elements of the corresponding editor view. This prototype contains a graph editor which provides in a very simple way the nodes and arcs of the structural graph.

We have used the *Java Universal Network/Graph (JUNG)*[9] Framework. It is a software library that can be re-used for the modeling, analysis, and the visualization of data as a graph or network. This library allows to define the structure of data *Graph* and also to use certain graph primitives for the construction of user interfaces associated with the graph manipulation tools. We used it in interaction with the built-in capabilities of Java API, as well as those of other existing third party Java libraries i.e. *Drools*[10]. We have specialized the class *Graph* available in the *JUNG* library in a class that we called *ArchitectGraph*. By using our platform, one can friendly specify a change affecting a node. Which may be a BPM task, a web service specification, or a Java class, etc. The various rules implementing the change impact propagation may then be fired. As a result the new graph is displayed containing nodes of type "impacted" related to the different impacted artifacts along with the explanation of the propagated impact.

7   Concluding Remarks and Future Work

In this paper, we present an approach based on a BPM meta-model intended to serve as a BPM artifacts repository data schema. We also defined the initial BPM change operations taxonomy. It involves the formalization of the change and the analysis of its impact propagation by graph rewriting rules. The graph rewriting

---

[8] http://www.eclipse.org/
[9] http://jung.sourceforge.net/
[10] http://www.jboss.org/drools/

rules have been implemented with AGG that is a graph rewriting system. This implementation can be considered as an operational or constructive specification. The use of the an ontology language (OWL) provides more semantic information about the various artefacts. The significant semantic information concerns the role of the various relationship types in the impact propagation. We especially define a relationship class hierarchy considering several relationship types from the perspective of the change impact propagation. This allows us to define a generic algorithm that has been used to both generate graph rewriting rules managing the change impact propagation or to directly implement the change impact propagation. The main concept of our approach is validated using a set of tools integrated as ECLIPSE plug-ins. These plugins are parts of a more general integrated framework which is built to deal with the software artifacts change impact propagations.

We are continuing the work by enriching the approach, in a more detailed way, with the different kind of mapping relationships related to the BPM artifacts and their implementation. The main goal is to be able to automatically track the change impact propagation. To achieve this, we must explicitly enrich the knowledge concerning the semantic of BPM elements and their relationships. We are then using the BPMN ontology [24] that is expressed using the OWL [25]. We plan to enrich this ontology by concepts representing the various aspects of change impact and the relationships propagating such impacts. Another goal is to provide some forward and reverse engineering tools in order to implement some important tasks like defining flexible and adaptable tools for the generation of BPM implementations and some others for the generation of BPMs from the process implementations.

References

1. Weske, M.: Business Process Management Concepts, Languages, Architectures, 1st edn. Springer, Heidelberg (2007)
2. Weske, M.: Business process management architectures. In: Business Process Management, pp. 333–371. Springer, Heidelberg (2007)
3. Silver, B.: BPMN Method and Style: A Levels-Based Methodology for BPM Process Modeling and Improvement using BPMN 2.0. Cody-Cassidy Press, CA (2009)
4. Allweyer, T.: BPMN 2.0: Introduction to the Standard for Business Process Modeling. Books on Demand, Norderstedt (2010)
5. Van der Aalst, W.M.P.: Patterns and XPDL: a critical evaluation of the XML process definition language. Technical report BPM-03-09, BPMcenter.org (2003)
6. Haller, A., Gaaloul, W., Marmolowski, M.: Towards an xpdl compliant process ontology. In: Services I, pp. 83–86 (2008)
7. Emig, C., Momm, C., Weisser, J., Abeck, S.: Programming in the large based on the business process modeling notation. In: Jahrestagung der Gesellschaft für Informatik (GI), Bonn (2005)
8. Gottschalk, K., Graham, S., Kreger, H., Snell, J.: Introduction to web services architecture. IBM Syst. J. 41, 170–177 (2002)

9. Juric, M.B.: Business Process Execution Language for Web Services BPEL and BPEL4WS, 2nd edn. Packt Publishing, Birmingham (2006)
10. Bouneffa, M., Ahmad, A.: Change management of bpm-based software applications. In: 15th International Conference on Enterprise Information Systems (ICEIS 2013), pp. 37–45 (2013)
11. Hassan, M.O., Deruelle, L., Basson, H., Ahmad, A.: A change propagation process for distributed software architecture. In: ENASE 2010: Proceedings of the 5th International Conference on Evaluation of Novel Approaches to Software Engineering (2010)
12. Lee, Y.C., Chu, P.Y., Tseng, H.L.: Corporate performance of ict-enabled business process re-engineering. Ind. Manage. Data Syst. **111**, 735–754 (2011)
13. Dumas, P., Charbonnel, G., Calmes, F.: La méthode OSSAD - Pour maîtriser les technologies de l'information - Tome 2: Guide pratique. Les Editions d'Organisation, Paris (1990)
14. OMG: Business process model and notation (bpmn) version 2.0 (2011) OMG Document Number: formal/2011-01-03, Standard document URL: http://www.omg.org/spec/BPMN/2.0 Accessed 18 March 2011
15. Schmidt, D.: Guest editor's introduction: model-driven engineering. Computer **39**, 25–31 (2006)
16. DeRemer, F., Kron, H.: Programming-in-the large versus programming-in-the-small. SIGPLAN Not. **10**, 114–121 (1975)
17. Parmenter, D.: Key Performance Indicators (KPI): Developing, Implementing, and Using Winning KPIs. John Wiley & Sons Inc., New York (2007)
18. Ahmad, A., Basson, H., Deruelle, L., Bouneffa, M.: Towards a better control of change impact propagation. In: INMIC'08: 12th IEEE International Multitopic Conference, pp. 398–404. IEEE Computer Society (2008)
19. Ahmad, A., Basson, H.: Software evolution modelling: an approach for change impact analysis. In: Proceedings of the 7th International Conference on Frontiers of Information Technology, FIT '09, pp. 56:1–56:4. ACM, New York (2009)
20. Ahmad, A., Basson, H., Bouneffa, M.: Rule-based approach for software evolution management. In: IEEE APSSC 2009: IEEE Asia-Pacific Services Computing Conference (2009)
21. Ahmad, A., Basson, H., Bouneffa, M.: Software evolution control: towards a better identification of change impact propagation. In: ICET'08: Proceedings of the 4th IEEE International Conference on Emerging Technologies, pp. 286–291. IEEE Computer Society (2008)
22. Rajlich, V., Gosavi, P.: Incremental change in object-oriented programming. IEEE Softw. **21**, 62–69 (2004)
23. Rajlich, V.: A model for change propagation based on graph rewriting. In: Proceedings of the International Conference on Software Maintenance, pp. 84–91. IEEE Computer Society, Washington, DC (1997)
24. Penicina, L.: Choosing a bpmn 2.0 compatible upper ontology. In: The 5th International Conference on Information, Process, and Knowledge Management, Nice, France, IARIA, pp. 89–96 (2013)
25. Motik, B., Grau, B.C., Horrocks, I., Wu, Z., Fokoue, A., Lutz, C.: Owl 2 web ontology language: Profiles. w3c recommendation, 27 Oct 2009 (2012)

Reengineering of Object-Oriented Software into Aspect-Oriented Ones Supported by Class Models

Paulo Afonso Parreira Júnior[1]($\boxtimes$), Rosângela Dellosso Penteado[1]($\boxtimes$),
Matheus Carvalho Viana[1]($\boxtimes$), Rafael Serapilha Durelli[2]($\boxtimes$),
Valter Vieira de Camargo[1]($\boxtimes$),
and Heitor Augustus Xavier Costa[3]($\boxtimes$)

[1] Departament of Computer Science, Federal University of São Carlos,
São Carlos, Brazil
{paulo_junior,rosangela,matheus_viana,
valter}@dc.ufscar.br
[2] Computer Systems Department, University of São Paulo, São Carlos, Brazil
rdurelli@icmc.usp.br
[3] Departament of Computer Science, Federal University of Lavras,
Lavras, Brazil
heitor@dcc.ufla.br

Abstract. Object-Oriented Software Reengineering (OO) into Aspect-Oriented Software (AO) is a challenging task, mainly when it is done by means of refactorings in the code-level. The reason is that direct transformation from OO code to AO one needs of several design decisions due to differences of both paradigms. To make this transformation more controlled and systematic, we propose the use of concern-based refactorings, supported by class models. It allows design decisions to be made during the reengineering process, improving the quality of the final models. An example is presented to assess the applicability of the proposed refactorings. Moreover, we also present a case study, in which AO class models created based on the refactorings are compared with another obtained without the aid of them. The data obtained indicated that the use of the proposed refactorings improved the efficacy and productivity of maintenance groups during the process of software reengineering.

Keywords: Concern-based refactorings · Class models · Aspect-Orientation · Reengineering

1 Introduction

Aspect-Orientation (AO) can be used in the revitalization of Object-Oriented (OO) legacy software. AO allows encapsulating the so-called "crosscutting concerns" (CCC) - software requirements whose implementation is tangled and scattered by functional modules - in new abstractions such as pointcuts, aspects, advices and inter-type declarations [12].

© Springer International Publishing Switzerland 2014
S. Hammoudi et al. (Eds.): ICEIS 2013, LNBIP 190, pp. 296–313, 2014.
DOI: 10.1007/978-3-319-09492-2_18

Reengineering from OO to AO in code-level is not an easy task due to existing differences between concepts related to both approaches. However, if the reengineering process was supported by models, it could facilitate future maintenance. In this paper we propose the use of concern-based refactorings on OO class models annotated with information of CCC to obtain AO models. In the context of this paper, annotated OO class models are UML OO class models whose elements (classes, interfaces, attributes and methods) are annotated with stereotypes corresponding to the CCC that exist in the software. The main idea is that concern-based refactorings can be applied to transform these models into AO models.

There are many studies in the literature that present code-based refactorings [8, 10, 13, 14, 19]. Our main reasons to create and apply **concern-based refactorings supported by models** ("model-based refactorings" in the rest of this paper) are:

(i) code-level refactorings can be applied to transform OO software in AO ones. However, this transformation is usually done in one step, which has as input an OO code and as output an AO one. It makes the reengineering process less flexible, because the responsibility to generate a code that follows good design practices of AO is on the refactorings. The transformation supported by model-based refactorings introduces at least one more step in the process before generating the final code. Thus, to ease the inflexibility of the process, in this step the outcome AO model can be modified by the software engineer according to the environment and stakeholder requirements;

(ii) generally, the source code is the only available artifact of the legacy software. Applying model-based refactorings, both the legacy software and the generated software will have a new type of artifact (i.e., UML class models), improving their documentation; and

(iii) unlike the code-based refactorings, model-based ones are platform independent. Thus, models can be transformed and good designs can be produced regardless of programming language.

A set of nine model-based refactorings was developed [1]. It is subdivided into: (i) three generic refactorings, which are concern-independent refactorings; and (ii) six specific refactorings to the following concerns: persistence (subdivided into connection, transaction and synchronization management), logging and Singleton and Observer design patterns [6]. Due to the limitation of space, only five of them are presented in more details in this paper. The AO class models presented in this paper are based on AOM (Aspect-Oriented Modeling) approach proposed by Evermann [4].

The remainder of this paper is structured as follows. Some concepts related to the AOM approach proposed by Evermann, the annotated OO class models and the computational support DMAsp [3], used to generate automatically annotated OO class models, are discussed in Sect. 2. The generic and specific refactorings are presented in Sect. 3. An example that illustrates the use of one generic refactoring is shown in Sect. 4 and an evaluation of whole set of refactorings is presented in Sect. 5. Some related works are summarized in Sect. 6. Finally, conclusions and suggestions for future work are presented in Sect. 7.

2   Background

ProAJ/UML (UML Profile for AspectJ) is one of the most used approaches to model AO software [4]. This approach consists of a set of stereotypes that can be applied on UML class models, such as:

- <<CrossCuttingConcern>>: it is an extension of the *Package* meta-class, in the UML meta-model. Its aim is to encapsulate aspects related to the same cross-cutting concern;
- <<Aspect>>: it extends the UML *Class* meta-class. Its goal is to cluster *pointcuts* and *advices* in an aspect and to allow aspects to extend classes or aspects and implement interfaces;
- <<Advice>>: it is a *BehavioralFeature* meta-class extension. Its aim is to associate advices with aspects; and
- <<PointCut>>: it is a *StructuralFeature* meta-class extension, whose goal is to specify a static behavior. Its modelling is performed by concrete subclasses of *PointCut*, such as *CallPointCut* and *ExecutionPointCut*.

These stereotypes are used in the AO class models generated with the application of the refactorings proposed in this work. Furthermore, OO class models annotated with information of CCC are used in the proposed refactorings. These annotations are represented using stereotypes on the left side of the classes, interfaces, attributes and methods identifiers. Figure 1 illustrates a class annotated with indications of persistence CCC. The DMAsp (Design Model to Aspect) tool [3], developed in a previous work, is used to generate automatically the annotated OO class models.

Based on the concept of annotated OO class models, the following concepts, proposed by Figueiredo [5], were adapted to the context of this work and are commented in the refactoring descriptions.

- **Components Affected by a Concern** are software elements such as classes, interfaces, attributes and methods which have indications of this concern. These elements are annotated with stereotypes of the concern that affect them;
- **Primary Concern** is the main concern of a component and it is related to the reason by which it was created. For example, the openConnection method (Fig. 1) was created to open database connections. Then "Persistence" is the primary concern of this method. The primary concerns are identified by the prefix "Pri_" in the stereotypes;
- **Secondary Concern** of a component corresponds to functions that this component plays. However, these functions are not directly related to the reason for which it was created. The Account class and its method withdraw, Fig. 1, were created to perform the business rules of a hypothetical banking system. Thus "Persistence"

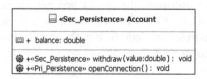

Fig. 1. An UML class annotated with information about persistence CCC.

is a secondary concern in these components. The secondary concerns are identified by the prefix "Sec_" in the stereotypes; and

- **Well-modularized Components** are software elements composed only by the primary concern for which they were created. For example, the `openConnection` method (Fig. 1) is considered well-modularized, because the only type of stereotype of this method is a primary concern related to "Persistence" concern.

3 Model-Based Refactorings

Hannemann [9] proposed the following classification of AO software refactorings:

(i) **conventional OO refactorings adapted for AO software**. These refactorings only involve OO elements. The difference between these refactorings and the well-known OO refactorings is they are aware of the existence of AO elements;

(ii) **specific refactorings for AO software**. These refactorings involve OO and AO elements and they are specific to lead to the AO abstractions, such as aspects, pointcuts, etc.; and

(iii) **crosscutting concerns refactorings**. Also called concern-based refactorings, they should take all the elements (classes, aspects, interfaces, etc.) that participate in a crosscutting concern and their relationships into consideration. This happens, because concerns usually are manifested in several components.

A set of nine concern-based refactorings is shown in Table 1. Only five of them are described in this paper with more details. The remaining refactorings were omitted for reasons of limitation of space and can be found in [16].

The refactorings are presented with: (i) Acronym and Name of the Refactoring; (ii) Application Scenario, which defines the situations the refactoring can be applied; (iii) Motivation, which presents some problems caused by tangling and scattering of CCC; and (iv) ProAJ/UML Mechanism, which is a set of steps to obtain an AO class model from an OO one, according to the ProAJ/UML profile.

3.1 Generic Refactorings

The generic refactorings are responsible for transforming an annotated OO class model to a partial AO class model. The generated model is named "partial", because

Table 1. Model-based refactorings.

Name	Description
Generic Refactorings	
R-1	Encapsulating a Secondary Concern with Association Relationships.
R-2	Encapsulating a Secondary Concern with Generalization/Specialization Relationships.
R-3	Extracting a Primary Concern.
Specific Refactorings	
R-Connection	Encapsulating the CCC responsible for managing database connections.
R-Transaction	Encapsulating the CCC responsible for managing database transactions.
R-Sync	Encapsulating the CCC responsible for managing database synchronization.
R-Logging	Encapsulating the CCC responsible for controlling the application of logging record.
R-Singleton	Encapsulating the CCC corresponding to the Singleton design pattern.
R-Observer	Encapsulating the CCC corresponding to the Observer design pattern.

the existing CCC may not be well-modularized yet. In this case, there still can exist classes/interfaces, methods and/or attributes affected by crosscutting concerns. All three generic refactorings are presented as follows.

R-1. Encapsulating a Secondary Concern with Association Relationships.

Application Scenario: when there are classes with Primary Concerns (Crosscutting Concerns) which are Secondary Concerns in other classes and these classes are related through association/aggregation relationships.

Motivation: the invocation of methods of classes which Primary Concern is a Crosscutting Concern can improve the tangling/scattering of this concern, hurting the software maintenance.

ProAJ/UML Mechanism: 1) Create a *CrossCuttingConcern* element called "CCC", in which "CCC" represents the concern name that is being modularized; **2)** Inside the element created previously, add an *Aspect* element called "CCCAspect"; **3)** Move each well-modularized attribute and method from the classes affected by the concern to the "CCCAspect" element; and **4)** Move all classes that have the concern in analysis as a Primary Concern to the "CCC" element.

R-2. Encapsulating a Secondary Concern with Generalization/Specialization Relationships.

Application Scenario: when there are classes with Primary Concerns (Crosscutting Concerns) which are Secondary Concerns in other classes and these classes are related through generalization/specialization relationships.

Motivation: the override of methods of classes which Primary Concern is a Crosscutting Concern can improve the tangling/scattering of this concern, hurting the software maintenance.

ProAJ/UML Mechanism: 1) Create a *CrossCuttingConcern* element called "CCC", in which "CCC" represents the concern name that is being modularized; **2)** Inside the element created previously, add an *Aspect* element called "CCCAspect"; **3)** Move each well-modularized attribute from the classes affected by the concern to the "CCCAspect" element; **4)** For each well-modularized method from the classes affected by the concern, create a "IntroductionMethod" element to add this method to the aspect "CCCAspect"; and **5)** Move the inherence and interface realization to the aspect "CCCAspect", using "DeclareParents" elements.

R-3. Extracting a Primary Concern.

Application Scenario: when there are classes with Secondary Concerns, which are Crosscutting Concerns and these ones are not Primary Concerns in any classes.

Motivation: some crosscutting concerns can be scattered in several classes and there are not specific classes that implement them. One concern of this type is not a Primary Concern in any class of the application. This scenario represents a high level of concern tangling and a low level of software modularization.

ProAJ/UML Mechanism: 1) Create a *CrossCuttingConcern* element called "CCC", in which "CCC" represents the concern name that is being modularized; **2)** Inside the element created previously, add an *Aspect* element called "CCCAspect"; and **3)** Move each well-modularized attribute and method from the classes affected by the concern to the "CCCAspect" element.

Looking at the application scenarios of these refactoring we understand that: "no matter what concern we are dealing, the scenario described above represent a low level of modularization".

R-Singleton. **Encapsulating the CCC corresponding to the Singleton Design Pattern.**

Application Scenario: when there are classes dedicated to implementation of Singleton pattern.

Motivation: the Singleton pattern can cause problems of tangling and scattering of concerns in OO application. The modularization using AO is one alternative to solve these problems [7].

ProAJ/UML Mechanism: 1) Identify the "CCCAspect" aspect related to implementation of the singleton concern and verify if this aspect is abstract. If not, transform it into abstract one; **3)** Create, inside the element "CCC" related to the singleton concern, an empty interface called `Singleton`; **4)** Define an execution pointcut called `instance` that intercepts the calls to constructor of the classes that realize the `Singleton` interface and add it to the "CCCAspect"; **5)** Identify the set of classes, "S", that implement the Singleton pattern, *i. e.*, the classes whose instance must be unique in the application. If the constructor of these classes be *private*, transform it into *public*; **6)** For each class "N" ∈ "S", create an aspect "CCCAspectN", where "N" corresponds to the class name and create inheritance relationships from the aspects "CCCAspectN" to the aspect "CCCAspect"; **7)** Each aspect "CCCAspectN" created previously must declare an interface realization relationship between the class "N", represented by this aspect, and the interface `Singleton`; and **8)** Create an around advice that returns a `Singleton` object and associate it to the `instance` pointcut. This advice implements the logic of the Singleton pattern: if there exists an instance, return it; otherwise, create one instance and return it.

R-Transaction: **Encapsulating the CCC corresponding to the Database Transaction Management.**

Application Scenario: when there are classes dedicated to implementation of Transaction CCC as a Secondary concern.

Motivation: applications generally have transactional methods that cause a high rate of concern tangling/scattering in the software. The modularization of these concerns can facilitate the software understanding, maintenance and reusability.

ProAJ/UML Mechanism: 1) Identify the "CCCAspect" aspect that corresponds to concern of transaction control and verify if this aspect is abstract. If not, transform it into abstract one; **2)** Define an abstract pointcut, called `transactionalMethods()`, and one around advice related to this pointcut; **3)** For each class "N" affected by this concern, create an aspect "CCCAspectN", where "N" corresponds to the class name and create inheritance relationships from the aspects "CCCAspectN" to the aspect "CCCAspect"; **4)** Identify the transactional methods of these classes and create one concrete appropriate pointcut for each aspect, called `transactionalMethods()`.

For example, based on the *R-3* refactoring, we already can apply a modularization strategy to this concern, whatever it is, putting all the well-modularized elements (attributes and methods) related to this concern in a specific module, in this case, an aspect. In all refactorings presented above, only well-modularized elements are moved to the aspect, avoiding problems related to the dependence of other concerns.

3.2   Specific Refactorings

The specific refactorings are responsible for transforming partial AO class models in final ones. These refactorings are named "specific", because they only can be applied to a specific type of concern. For example, there is a specific refactoring to the transaction management concern that generates an AO class model with the modularization of this concern using aspects. Six specific refactorings were developed, as presented in Table 1.

These refactorings were created based on the most common strategies for implementing these types of crosscutting concerns. For example, the database connection concern is usually implemented with a class responsible for creating connections and each persistent method must open the connection at the beginning of its execution and close it at the end. In another example, the singleton pattern is generally implemented as follows [6]: (i) create an attribute of the same type of the Singleton class; (ii) become private the constructor of the Singleton class; and (iii) create a method responsible for keeping only one instance of the Singleton class. Therefore, it is possible to define some steps for modularization of this type of concern, based on the most common strategies for implementing them.

The specific refactorings are applied on the models generated by the generic refactorings. Thus, in ProAJ/UML Mechanism description, aspects created previously are mentioned. To illustrate this case the refactorings *R-Singleton* and *R-Transaction* are presented.

Unlike the generic refactorings, in this case, we can use some more specific steps to modularize the CCC, because they are well-known concerns. Thus, for example, in the case of the Singleton concern, the aspect created by a generic refactoring has been transformed into an abstract one and for each class affected by this concern one aspect has been created. This strategy follows a good practice for AO design suggested by Piveta [18]. Furthermore, it is similar to Hannemann and Kiczales' solution [7] and was adapted to the context of annotated OO class models.

3.3   Considerations About the Refactorings

Some of the main reasons to apply generic refactorings are: **(i) the application of generic refactorings can facilitate the achievement of a better AO model**: wrong decisions made by software engineers, due to their inexperience, can prejudice the AO model quality. Thus, an initial modularization strategy offered by these refactorings can minimize this problem; and **(ii) generic refactorings can be applied to any type of concern, even to those concerns that are not widely known as crosscutting**

concerns: it is not easy to identify whether a particular concern is or not a crosscutting concern. Thus, with the help of generic refactorings, we can identify scenarios that demonstrate or provide evidence of the existence of crosscutting concerns in software. For example, the application scenario for the refactoring *R-3* states a configuration that can evidence the existence of a crosscutting concern (many classes of software related to a secondary concern in these classes).

There is not a specific sequence to apply generic refactorings proposed in this work. The steps created for refactoring are applied when a specific element is well-modularized, *i.e.*, when there is no interference of other concerns in this element. Moreover, some modularization strategies described in the steps of the refactoring were considered to avoid interference in the order of execution of the refactoring. Similarly to what happens with the generic refactorings, the order in which the specific refactorings are applied does not interfere in the final AO class model. It happens because each refactoring acts only on a particular concern at a time, not compromising elements related to other concerns.

The manual execution of the steps described in the refactoring presented on class models of software for medium and large scale can be hard and error-prone. Thus, an Eclipse plug-in called MoBRe (Model-Based Refactorings) was developed to perform tasks related to refactoring of crosscutting concerns in a semi-automatic way. MoBRe [17] allows transforming an annotated class model into a partial AO class model, when the generic and specific refactorings are applied. The AO class models generated can be visualized within the Eclipse.

4 Example of Use

To present the applicability of the proposed refactorings, an example, using the Health Watcher software [20], is presented. This software registers complaints in the health area and it was chosen because it: (i) has an OO and an AO version; and (ii) was modularized by expert software engineers by using best practices of AO design.

The crosscutting concern partially modularized in this example is the Singleton pattern, represented by the "Singleton" stereotype. Other crosscutting concerns affect this application, such as connection and transaction management, represented by the "Conn" and "Trans" stereotypes, but the modularization of them is not performed in this paper because of limitations of space.

One part of Health Watcher OO class model, responsible for the maintenance of the patient complaints, is presented in Fig. 2. This model is annotated by using stereotypes of the concerns that affect the software classes, according to the information provided by Soares et al., [20].

The `HealthWatcherFacade` class provides methods necessary for execution of the business logic of the application, as complaints registration, diseases, and symptoms. The `singletonHW` and `singletonPS` attributes and the `getInstanceHW` and `getInstancePS` methods have "Singleton" as Primary Concern, because they were created specifically for implementing the Singleton pattern. The same way, "Conn" and "Trans" are Primary Concerns of the `IPersistenceMechanism` interface and the `PersistenceMechanism` class, because they were

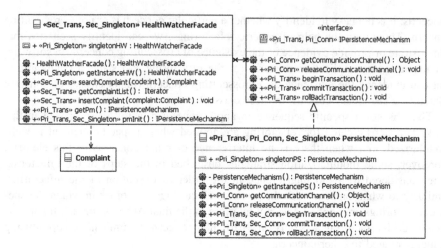

Fig. 2. A UML class stereotyped with CCC indications.

created for implementing these concerns. The `HealthWatcherFacade` class has "Trans" and "Singleton" as Secondary Concerns, because this class was not created for implementing these concerns, but it is affected by them. This information about what concerns are primary or secondary one was provided by the Health Watcher developers.

According to the scenario of tangling/scattering of the model presented in Fig. 2, the singleton concern can be initially refactored by the *R-3* refactoring. This happens because "Singleton" is a Secondary Concern in some classes of this model and it is not a Primary Concern in none other classes. After applying the *R-3* refactoring to the "Singleton" concern, the partial AO class model presented in Fig. 3 was obtained.

The changes made were: (i) the `SingletonAspect` aspect was created; and (ii) the `singletonHW` and `singletonPS` attributes and the `getInstanceHW` and

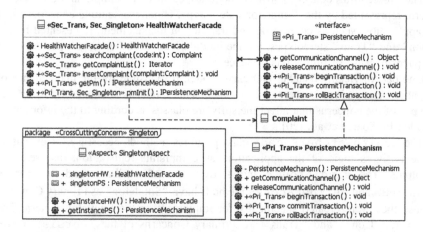

Fig. 3. Health watcher AO class model obtained through R-3 refactoring.

`getInstancePS` methods were moved to the `SingletonAspect` aspect. It is because these elements are well-modularized in the `HealthWatcherFacade` and `PersistentMechanism` classes.

The application of the *R-Singleton* refactoring was omitted for reasons of limitation of space and can be found in [1].

5   Evaluation

The crosscutting concern modularization may be performed with or without the assistance of refactorings. In the second case, the process of modularization is extremely dependent on the expertise of the software engineer. He/She must have knowledge about the crosscutting concerns to be modularized and best practices and strategies for the modularization of these concerns. Refactorings minimize this dependence, making the final product (modularized software) more standardized and improving its quality.

The question we want to answer with this case study is: *how much can the refactorings affect the efficacy of the modularization process and the productivity of the maintenance group?* In this context, productivity is defined as the time that a group takes to modularize the crosscutting concerns of a software product. Besides, efficacy consists in verifying whether all crosscutting concerns were suitably modularized or not. Thus, the case study was carried out and it is shown in the next subsections.

5.1   Case Study Definition

The efficacy and productivity evaluation of the refactorings was performed in two ways:

(i)   comparing the generated AO class models with another version of them, obtained from a reverse engineering using the AO code found in the literature (in this study, we use the JSpider AO code available in [11]). To do this, a set of seven **Metrics for Modularization** were used to compare both versions of the application AO class model (Table 2). All of them, except *MQ* and *AVG(MQ)*, accept the following values: 1.0 – Completely Compliant; 0.5 - Partially Compliant; and

Table 2. Metrics for modularization.

Metric	Metric Description
CC_As	Correctly Created Aspects: specifies if all needed aspects were correctly created.
CM_AM	Correctly Modularized Attributes and Methods: specifies if all attributes and methods affected by a concern were correctly modularized.
CC_PA	Correctly Created Pointcut and Advices specifies if all needed pointcuts and advices were correctly created.
CC_GSR	Correctly Created Generalization and Specialization Relationships: specifies if all needed relationships were correctly created.
CS_PC	Correctly Specified Profile Concepts: specifies if all ProAJ/UML concepts were correctly used.
MQ	Modularization Quality: CC_As + CM_AM + CC_PA + CC_GSR + CS_PC.
AVG(MQ)	Average of the Metric *MQ*.

0.0 – Not Compliant. These values are assigned to the metrics for modularization by specialists after comparing the models created by the participants of this experiment to the models obtained from the literature. The metrics *MQ* and *AVG(MQ)* accepts values between [0.0; 5.0] and the higher the value of them, the better is the modularization of a concern; and

(ii) comparing the time spent by each participant to complete the modularization of a given OO class model. For this, we used the metric *Productivity* (*Pr*), given to the Formula (1). The higher the value of *Pr*, the better is the productivity of a participant.

$$Pr = AVG(MQ) / T, \tag{1}$$

where *AVG(MQ)* is the average of the metric *Modularization Quality* and *T* is the time (in hours) spent by a participant to modularize the crosscutting concerns.

5.2   Case Study Planning

(a) Selection of Context and Formulation of Hypothesis. The study was carried out with graduate students at the Federal University of São Carlos. The system used as object of study was JSpider [11], a highly configurable and customizable Web Spider engine. The participants had to modularize the Logging and Singleton crosscutting concerns and generate an AO class model from the OO model classes of the JSpider application.

Four hypotheses were elaborated (Table 3), two of which refer to the efficacy and two ones refer to the productivity. Besides, the metrics *MQ* and *Pr* were used for formulating the hypotheses.

(b) Selection of Variables and Participants. Independent variables are those manipulated and controlled during the experiment. In this context, they are the way how the participants performed the modularization: with or without the use of the refactorings. Dependent variables are those under analysis, whose variations must be

Table 3. Hypotheses of the case study.

Hypotheses for Efficacy	
H_{0Ef}	There is no difference of using refactorings or not using them, regarding the efficacy. H_{0Ef}: $MQ_{WR} = MQ_{WOR}$
H_{1Ef}	There is difference of using refactorings or not using them, regarding the efficacy. H_{1Ef}: $MQ_{WR} \neq MQ_{WOR}$
Hypotheses for Productivity	
H_{0Pr}	There is no difference of using refactorings or not using them, regarding the productivity. H_0: $Pr_{WR} = Pr_{WOR}$
H_{1Pr}	There is no difference of using refactorings or not using them, regarding the productivity. H_0: $Pr_{WR} \neq Pr_{WOR}$
Legends:	
• X_{WR}, where X is a metric, means: the value of X obtained by a specific participant using the refactorings proposed in this paper (WR = With Refactorings). • X_{WOR}, where X is a metric, means: the value of X obtained by a specific participant that did not use the refactorings proposed in this paper (WOR = Without Refactorings).	

observed. In this experiment, they are the efficacy and productivity. The participants were selected through a convenient non-probabilistic sampling.

(c) Design of the Experiment. The distribution of the participants in groups was done by using a profile characterization questionnaire.

The questions were about their level of experience in OO and AO, modularization and UML profile to modelling AO software. All questions had the possible answers: 1 - None; 2 - Basic; 3 - Medium; 4 - Advanced; 5 - Expert. The obtained values are plotted in the graph shown in Fig. 4.

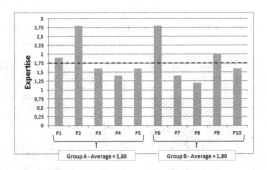

Fig. 4. Expertise of the participants.

The groups were created as follows: Group A - participants P1 to P5; Group B - participants P6 to P10. The average of expertise of Group A is approximately 1.86 and Group B, 1.80, representing that the groups were balanced. To separate the experts and novices we have defined the value 1.75 (horizontal line in Fig. 4). This value was defined according to our experience with the required knowledge to perform the modularization of CCCs. Above this value the participants were considered experts (P1, P2, P6 and P9) and below novices (P3, P4, P5, P7, P8 and P10). It is important to notice that both groups have the same number of expert and novice participants.

The documents used in this experiment were: (i) a registry form to be filled out with information related to the execution of the study; (ii) a script of execution with the steps to be followed to perform the experiment; and (iii) the description of the proposed refactorings. The registry form contained the participant name, the application to be modularized, the starting time and the observations and/or problems noticed by the participant. The script of execution contained a list of tasks that the participants should carry out and had the goal of assisting them and minimizing the possibility of failures during the execution. The description of the proposed refactorings presents the refactoring according the template used in Sect. 3.

The experiment was divided in three phases. In the first phase (*Training*), we conducted a training aimed at homogenizing the knowledge of the participants on the modularization of crosscutting concerns using hypothetical applications. In the second phase (*Pilot*) all participants had to discover how to modularize the persistence concern that crosscuts pieces of the HealthWatcher application manually and using the proposed refactorings. The goal of the pilot was to minimize the difficulties of following the steps described in the refactorings. Besides, the pilot also was intended to avoid that problems related to the filling out of the forms could interfere in the results of the experiment. In the third phase (*Execution*) the goal was to modularize the Logging and Singleton concerns in the JSpider application. Different types of concern between *Execution* and *Pilot* phases were used to avoid that the knowledge on the persistence concern obtained in the previous phase (*pilot*) to influence the results.

(d) Collected Data. Tables 4 and 5 show the data obtained in third phase of the experiment (*Execution*) by the Groups A and B, respectively (AoE means *Average of the Experts* and AoN means *Average of the Novices*).

Table 4. Execution of the case study – Group A (with refactorings

Data	P1	P2	P3	P4	P5	AVG	AoE	AoN
Time (m)	35	47	60	60	60	52	41	60
Time (h)	0,58	0,78	1,0	1,0	1,0	0,87	0,68	1,0
Singleton Pattern								
CC_As	1,0	1,0	1,0	1,0	1,0			
CM_AM	1,0	1,0	1,0	1,0	1,0			
CC_PA	1,0	1,0	0,5	1,0	0,5			
CC_GSR	1,0	1,0	1,0	1,0	1,0			
CS_PC	1,0	1,0	1,0	1,0	1,0			
MQ	5,0	5,0	4,5	5,0	4,5	4,8	5,0	4,7
Logging								
CC_As	1,0	1,0	1,0	1,0	1,0			
CM_AM	1,0	1,0	1,0	1,0	1,0			
CC_PA	1,0	1,0	0,5	0,5	0,5			
CC_GSR	1,0	1,0	1,0	1,0	1,0			
CS_PC	1,0	1,0	1,0	1,0	1,0			
MQ	5,0	5,0	4,5	4,5	4,5	4,7	5,0	4,5
Results								
AVG(MQ)	5,0	5,0	4,5	4,8	4,5	4,8	5,0	4,6
Pr	8,57	6,38	4,5	4,8	4,5	5,75	7,48	4,6

Table 5. Execution of the case study - Group B (without refactorings).

Data	P6	P7	P8	P9	P10	AVG	AoE	AoN
Time (m)	38	45	60	60	30	46	49	45
Time (h)	0,63	0,75	1,0	1,0	0,5	0,78	0,69	0,83
Singleton Pattern								
CC_As	1,0	1,0	0,0	0,0	1,0			
CM_AM	1,0	1,0	0,0	0,0	1,0			
CC_PA	0,0	0,0	0,0	0,0	0,0			
CC_GSR	0,0	0,0	0,0	0,0	0,0			
CS_PC	0,0	0,0	0,0	0,0	1,0			
MQ	2,0	2,0	0,0	0,0	3,0	1,4	1,0	1,7
Logging								
CC_As	1,0	1,0	0,5	0,0	1,0			
CM_AM	1,0	1,0	0,0	0,0	0,5			
CC_PA	0,5	1,0	0,0	0,0	0,0			
CC_GSR	0,0	0,0	0,0	0,0	0,0			
CS_PC	0,0	0,0	0,0	0,0	1,0			
MQ	2,5	3,0	0,5	0,0	2,5	1,7	1,3	2,0
Results								
AVG(MQ)	2,3	2,5	0,3	0,0	2,8	1,6	1,1	1,8
Pr	3,63	3,33	0,3	0,0	5,6	2,57	3,48	1,97

The participants, assigned by "P#", and the titles of the table columns are presented in first line. The time used by the participants for performing the modularization is presented in lines from 2 to 3. The concern names are presented in lines 3 and 10 and the values of the metrics described in Table 2 are presented in lines from 5 to 10 (for the Singleton concern) and from 12 to 17 (for the Logging concern). The average of the metric *MQ* and the value of the metric *Pr* are presented in lines 19 and 20. The columns that contain the data of participants classified as experts were highlighted in gray color.

(e) Data Analysis. Regarding the *Efficacy* and *Productivity*, Tables 4 and 5 show that most of participants that used the proposed refactorings got better results than those ones that do not used them.

Regarding the *Productivity*, just one of the participants that used the proposed refactorings was less productive. Although there was an extra task to be carried out (to follow the steps described in the refactorings), the developer will need to modify the models during the process of refactoring less times, thus minimizing the final time to perform the activity.

As it can be observed in Fig. 5, the average of metric *MQ*, when the participants had the aid of the refactorings was higher than the one when they did not have this aid. According to this chart, the value of the metric *MQ* was 206 % higher, in average, for all participants, and 344 % higher, in average, for participants classified as experts and 150 % higher, in average, for participants classified as novices).

Analogously, in Fig. 6, the average of metric *Pr* also was better when the participants used the refactorings. This chart presents productivity 124 % higher, in average, for all participants, and 115 % higher, in average, for participants classified as experts and 134 % higher, in average, for participants classified as novices).

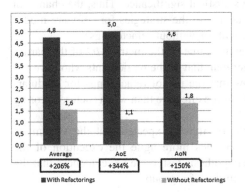 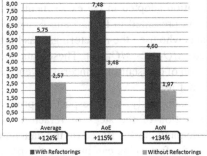

Fig. 5. Average of the metric MQ.   **Fig. 6.** Average of the metric Pr.

It is also possible to notice in Figs. 5 and 6 that the refactorings helped more expert participants than non-expert ones. It happened maybe because the description of the proposed refactorings was not well detailed enough to guide non-expert participants to modularize the concerns correctly.

(f) Hypothesis Testing. After outlier analysis, it was noticed that none outlier was identified and the hypotheses tests were performed. The verification of the normality of the distribution sample data was made using the non-parametric test called Shapiro-Wilk [15].

The aim of the hypothesis test is to verify if the null hypothesis (H_{0Ef} and H_{0EPr}) can be rejected, with some significance degree, in favor of an alternative hypotheses (H_{1Ef} or H_{1Pr}) based in the set of data obtained.

The *t-test* test was applied to the set of sample data in two stages, because of the existence of two dependent variables, *Efficacy* and *Productivity* were observed. In first stage, the sample relative to the values of the metric *Pr* was compared. In second one, the comparison was made using samples referring to the values of *MQ* metric. For the purpose of this study, the minor degree of significance α was used in both stages to reject the null hypothesis and the maximum degree of significance equal to 5 % was considered.

First Stage. Based in two independent samples (Pr_{WR} and Pr_{WOR}) with averages equals to 5.75 and 2.57, respectively in Tables 4 and 5, the null hypothesis (H_{0Pr}) could be rejected with 0.0151 % of significance. In others words, it is possible to assure with 99.9 % of accuracy that the average of the values of the productivity obtained by the participants that used the refactorings is different.

Second Stage. Based in two independent samples (MQ_{WR} and MQ_{WOR}) with averages equals to 4.8 and 1.6, respectively, the null hypothesis (H_{0Ef}) could be rejected with 0.0007 % of significance. In others words, it is possible to assurance with 99.9 % of accuracy that the average of the values of the efficacy obtained using the refactorings is different as compared to not using the refactorings.

With the rejection of H_0, it can be stated that the observed differences in the average of *efficacy* and *productivity* of the participants who used the refactorings and participants who have not use them, have statistical significance. Thus, the change in efficacy and productivity of the groups was due to the strategies for software modularization adopted in the experiment, *i.e.*, with or without refactorings.

As presented in Figs. 5 and 6, the average value of the metric *MQ* of the participants who used the refactorings was higher than that of the participants who have not used ($MQ_{WR} > MQ_{WOR}$). These data show that the use of refactorings for modularization of crosscutting concerns is generally more effective than when such refactoring are not used.

Analogously, with respect to productivity, it was expected that the systematic description of the steps of refactorings becomes more agile the execution of the participants' tasks. Based on the data and hypothesis test, there are evidences that the use of refactorings can increase the productivity of a group.

(g) Threats to the Validity of the Study. *Concluding Validity*: the *t-test* was adopted because our study was a project with one factor with two treatments. This is the most suitable test for projects with this configuration, which the aim is to compare the obtained averages from two distinct treatments. The *t-test* usually requires normally distributed data. So, the Shapiro-Wilk test was applied and the result was positive for our study.

Internal Validity: a point that may have influenced the results of the experiment is the use of graduate students as participants. However, they were not influenced by the conductors of this study and we did not show any expectation in favor or against the refactorings proposed in this paper. Besides, the students were properly grouped according to their experience levels in order to have homogeneous groups. This was done to avoid that a group could finish the tasks much earlier than other group. The participants did not receive any grade for the participation.

External Validity: an important bias is the choice of the concerns to be modularized in the experiment. Different types of concern were used to avoid that the knowledge on a specific concern obtained in the training phase to influence the results in other phases of the experiment. Another bias in this case study is that the proposed refactorings have been applied in software of fairly small size that cannot reflect the real scenario of a company that develops/maintains software. It is intended to replicate such experiment with different participants, concerns and applications, in order to isolate the obtained results from these possible influences.

6 Related Works

Many works have been proposed for refactoring of OO software to AO ones and the refactorings are only applied at source-code level, from OO to AO [8, 10, 13, 14, 19]. Moreover, it was noted a lack of related works related to model-based refactorings.

Boger [2] developed a plug-in for the CASE tool ArgoUML that support UML model-based refactorings. The refactoring of class, states and activities is possible, allowing the user to apply refactorings that are not simple to apply at source-code level. Van Gorp [21] proposed a UML profile to express pre and post-conditions of source-code refactorings using Object Constraint Language (OCL) constraints. The proposed profile allows that a CASE tool: (i) verify pre and post-conditions for the composition of sequences of refactorings; and (ii) use the OCL consulting mechanism to detect bad smells.

The differential of this work in relation to others is the proposal to construct an AO model considering OO class models annotated with stereotypes representing cross-cutting concerns.

From the conducted case study was performed an evaluation of the obtained results with the support of AO metrics. It was realized that the use of proposed refactorings allows to obtain high quality AO models because: (i) it provided a step by step guide to modularization of certain CCC; and (ii) the proposed refactorings were elaborated considering good design AO practices. Therefore, the use of these refactorings can lead to build high quality AO models, because it prevents software engineers to choose inappropriate strategies for modularization of crosscutting concerns. The limitations of this study is considered: (i) lack of a more quantitative evaluation of the computational support and the proposed refactorings; (ii) the need for new metrics to improve the evaluation process of the refactorings; (iii) lack of studies about the security semantics of legacy software after the application of refactorings; and (iv) a little amount of refactorings for CCC.

7 Final Considerations and Future Works

The idea of using annotated OO class models to build AO models was adopted because they can bring the following benefits: (i) it helps to visualizing possibilities for modularization without using AO; (ii) provides higher level of abstraction by helping the software understanding; (iii) the generated models serves as documentation for the AO software and legacy ones and are independent of programming language.

As future works we intend: (i) to determine if, by means of a controlled experiment, the AO project model generated with the use of refactorings has better benefits than an AO project only obtained with code refactorings; (ii) to develop new specific refactorings for other types of concerns such as security, exception handling, among others; (iii) to create a module for detecting the impacts that can cause a refactoring on a particular software before being applied; and (iv) to proposed strategies for guarantee the behaviour-preservation of OO and AO models after using the refactorings.

Acknowledgements. The authors would like to thank CNPq for the financial support (Proc. No. 133140/2009-1 and 560241/2010-0).

References

1. Parreira Júnior, P.A., et al.: Concern-based refactorings supported by class models to reengineer object-oriented software into aspect-oriented ones. In: International Conference on Enterprise Information Systems (ICEIS), 2013, Angers/FR (2013)
2. Boger, M., Sturm, T.: Tools-support for model-driven software engineering. In: Proceedings of Practical UML-Based Rigorous Development Methods (2001)
3. Costa, H.A.X., Parreira Júnior, P.A., Camargo, V.V., Penteado, R.A.D.: Recovering class models stereotyped with crosscutting concerns. In: Session Tool of XVI Working Conference on Reverse Engineering, Lille, France (2009)
4. Evermann, J.: A metalevel specification and profile for aspectj in UML. In: AOSD. Victoria University Wellington, Wellington (2007)
5. Figueiredo, E., Sant'Anna, C., Garcia, A., Lucena, C.: Applying and evaluating concern-sensitive design heuristics. In: Brazilian Symposium on Software Engineering, Fortaleza (2009)
6. Gamma, E., Helm, R., Johnsn, R., Vlisside, J.: Design Patterns: Elements of Reusable Object-Oriented Software. Addison-Wesley, Reading (1995)
7. Hannemann, J., Kiczales, G.: Design pattern implementation in java and aspectj. In: Conference on Object-Oriented Programming Systems, Languages and Applications. SIGPLAN Notices, Vol. 37(11), pp. 161–173. ACM (2002)
8. Hannemann, J., Murphy, G.C., Kiczales, G.: Role-based refactoring of crosscutting concerns. In: AOSD, New York, pp. 135–146, (2005)
9. Hannemann, J.: Aspect-oriented refactoring: classification and challenges. In: International Workshop On Linking Aspect Technology and Evolution, Bonn (2006)
10. Iwamoto, M., Zhao, J.: Refactoring aspect-oriented programs. In: International Workshop On Aspect-Oriented Modeling With UML, Boston, pp. 1–7 (2003)
11. JSpider. j-spider.sourceforge.net/. Accessed January 2013
12. Kiczales, G., Lamping, J., Mendhekar, A., Maeda, C., Lopes, C., Loingtier, J.-C., Irwin, J.: Aspect-oriented programming. In: Akşit, Mehmet, Matsuoka, Satoshi (eds.) ECOOP 1997. LNCS, vol. 1241, pp. 220–242. Springer, Heidelberg (1997)
13. Marin, M., Moonen, L., Van Deursen, A.: An approach to aspect refactoring based on crosscutting concern types. Sigsoft Softw. Eng. Notes **30**(4), 1–5 (2005)
14. Monteiro, M.P., Fernandes, J.M.: Towards a catalogue of refactorings and code smells for aspectj. In: Rashid, A., Akşit, M. (eds.) Transactions on Aspect-Oriented Software Development I. LNCS, vol. 3880, pp. 214–258. Springer, Heidelberg (2006)
15. Montgomery, D.C.: Design and Analysis of Experiments, 5th edn. Wiley, New York (2000)
16. Parreira Júnior, P.A.: Recovering aspect-oriented class models from object-oriented systems by model-based refactorings. Master Dissertation. UFSCar, São Carlos. Brazil (2011) (in Portuguese)
17. Parreira Júnior, P.A., Penteado, R.A.D., Camargo, V.V., Costa, H.A.X.: Mobre: refactoring from annotated OO class models to AO class models. In: CBSoft Tools Session, São Paulo/ SP (2011) (in Portuguese)
18. Piveta, E., Moreira, A., Pimenta, M., Araújo, J., Guerreiro, P., Price, T.: Avoiding bad smells in aspect-oriented software. In: International Conference on Software Engineering and Knowledge Engineering, Boston, pp. 81–87 (2007)

19. Da Silva, B.C., Figueiredo, E., Garcia, A., Nunes, D.: Refactoring of crosscutting concerns with metaphor-based heuristics. Electron. Notes Theor. Comput. Sci. (Entcs) **233**, 105–125 (2009)
20. Soares, S., Laureano, E., Borba, P.: Implementing distribution and persistence aspects with AspectJ. In: ACM Conference OOPSLA'02, pp. 174–190 (2002)
21. Van Gorp, P., Stenten, H., Mens, T., Demeyer, S.: Towards Automating Source-Consistent UML Refactorings. In: Stevens, P., Whittle, J., Booch, G. (eds.) UML 2003. LNCS, vol. 2863, pp. 144–158. Springer, Heidelberg (2003)

Re-learning of Business Process Models from Legacy System Using Incremental Process Mining

André Cristiano Kalsing$^{(\boxtimes)}$, Cirano Iochpe, Lucinéia Heloisa Thom, and Gleison Samuel do Nascimento

Department of Informatics,
Federal University of Rio Grande do Sul, UFRGS, Porto Alegre, Brazil
{ackalsing, ciochpe, lucineia,
gsnascimento}@inf.ufrgs.br

Abstract. Several approaches have already been proposed to extract both business processes and business rules from a legacy source code. These approaches usually consider static and dynamic source code analysis for re-learning of these models. However, business processes have components that cannot be directly extracted by static analysis (i.e., process participants and concurrent tasks). Moreover, most of well-known process mining algorithms used in dynamic analysis do not support all required operations of incremental extraction. Re-learning of large legacy systems can benefit from an incremental analysis strategy in order to provide iterative extraction of process models. This paper discusses an approach for business knowledge extraction from legacy systems through incremental process mining. Discovery results can be used in various ways by business analysts and software architects, e.g. documentation of legacy systems or for re-engineering purposes.

Keywords: Process mining · Incremental process mining · Legacy systems

1 Introduction

Extraction of business processes from legacy systems can become a very complex task when the continuous evolution of business processes is required. Business processes usually translate the current business needs of a company and they are made up of business rules, tasks (i.e. a concrete activity), control flows, roles and systems. When these business needs change, it is likely that the structure of the process will also change. Consequently, the process models discovered during the mining task, either partial or complete, should also reflect these changes. So, in this case the extraction of business processes cannot be done in one step, but several incremental ones. Moreover, this scenario could be even more complex when the re-engineering process must handle large legacy system with constant maintenance. In this case incremental discovery helps to keep the system maintenance lives while it is modernized.

To overcome these limitations, incremental process mining techniques [1, 2, 5, 6] are designed to allow continuous evolution of the discovered process models.

© Springer International Publishing Switzerland 2014
S. Hammoudi et al. (Eds.): ICEIS 2013, LNBIP 190, pp. 314–330, 2014.
DOI: 10.1007/978-3-319-09492-2_19

Evolution means that new events executed and recorded in the log can generate new dependencies among activities or remove old ones. Thus, using these techniques we can significantly improve the discovery process from legacy allowing an iterative approach and also more accurate results.

1.1 Problem Statement

Although some techniques for incremental process mining have already been proposed, there are still aspects to be improved. The main aspect is the better support for update operations during incremental mining of logs, such as removing elements from previously discovered process model when they are considered obsolete elements (e.g. tasks and transitions removed from process definition).

After the discovery of a partial or complete process model from legacy system, any changes contained in modified process instances (e.g. modified business rules in source code) must be merged in those models. Those kinds of changes can be seen in the example of the execution logs shown in Fig. 1 and described next. The logs were generated by the execution of a legacy information system. These logs are divided into three logical parts: *Initial Traces*, *New Traces* and *Updated Traces* (*see* Fig. 1). We can check that the generation of the *Initial Traces* and the *New Traces* log occur when users (i.e. Mary, Paul and Mark) execute specific use cases scenarios within an information system (e.g. cases A, B and C) presented in Fig. 1. The logs are composed by business rules instances executed and recorded from the system.

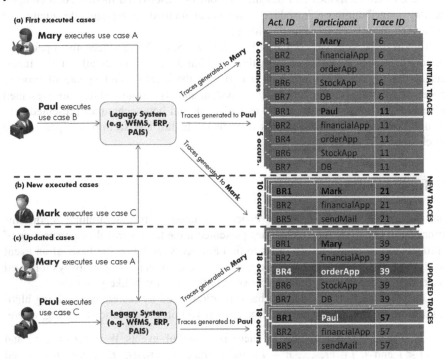

Fig. 1. Information system logs generation.

The final log (i.e. *Updated Traces*) represents new executions of previously scenarios, but this time generating modified process instances (i.e. see changes highlighted in Fig. 1c). We can see modified traces in this log, where task BR3 was replaced by task BR4. These changes were generated by the legacy system and are related to changes in the business rules. In this case, the BR3 was removed from the system source code. In addition, case C, which was originally executed by user Mark, is now performed by Paul. This specific kind of change is usually not present in source code and can be represented by an organizational change.

1.2   Contribution

In our previous work [1, 2] we propose an incremental algorithm which is able to perform the incremental mining of process logs (i.e. only the discovery of new process elements) generated from legacy systems or any other kind of system. In this paper, we are revising these mining algorithms and improving the original ones to detect new and also obsolete elements on discovered process models. We use different heuristics to analyze new and modified process instances recorded in the log in order to incrementally discover process models and mainly update previous discovered process models. This distinguishes our approach from all previous works. Thus, the main contribution of this work is the creation of algorithms that introduce new mining techniques, capable to (i) add new discovered activities to an existing model and (ii) remove obsolete activities and transitions from the discovered model. As a complementary contribution we introduce a statistical method to measure the quality of discovered models on incremental mining.

The next sections are organized as follow: Sect. 2 introduces the operations supported by the incremental algorithm. Section 3 introduces details of the incremental mining algorithm and how it performs the creation and update of process models. Experiments using a real legacy system and also simulated logs are presented in Sect. 4. Section 5 introduces the related work and how techniques presented here include considerable improvements over them. In the last section, we present the conclusions and future work.

2   Basic Concepts

This section introduces the basic concepts related to process mining algorithms described in our work. The techniques presented mine the control-flow perspective of a process model from logs. In order to find a process model on the basis of an event log, it must be analyzed for causal dependencies, e.g., if an activity is always followed by another, a dependency relation between both activities is likely to exist.

Our previous work [2] defined basic relations used by incremental mining algorithm. Here we introduce a new relation to represent obsolete relations in a log, where:

(1) $[a > wc]_{a \mapsto wb}$ if and only if there is a log of events $W = \sigma_1\sigma_2\sigma_3...\sigma_n$ and $i < j$ and $i, j \in \{1, ..., n - 1\}$ and a trace $\sigma = t_1t_2t_3...t_n$, where $t_i = a$ and $t_{i + 1} = (b$ or $c)$ and $\sigma_i \subset a > wc$ and $\sigma_j \subset a \mapsto wb$. The relation $\mapsto w$ represents

the sibling relation of $> w$ derived from log of events W, where the relation $> w$ represents a relation older than (i.e. that occurs chronologically before in the log) the sibling relation $\mapsto w$.

We also introduce here the update operations that may occur during incremental mining. The first operations (i.e. rows $a–d$ of Table 1) represent the insertion of structures in a process model, such as the inclusion of tasks, gateways and participants. These operations were already supported by our previous algorithm and will be complemented here with new removal operations (i.e. rows $e–h$ of Table 1).

Table 1. Update operations of incremental mining.

Operation	When it occurs
(a) Add a new task to the model {john} {finApp} {db} **{Mary}**	It occurs when $a \rightarrow wb$ introduces a new transition into the graph, where b (task D) is a new task.
(b) Add a new participant to the model {john} {finApp} {db} {Mary, **Paul}**	It occurs when a participant (human or system) starts executing a new task.
(c) Add a new gateway (control flow) to the model {john} {finApp} {db} {Mary, Paul}	It occurs when $a \rightarrow wb$ introduces a new transition into the graph, where a (task B) has two causal relations (e.g. B $\rightarrow$ C and B $\rightarrow$ D).
(d) Add a new transition to the model {John} {finApp} {db} {Mary, Paul}	It occurs when $a \rightarrow wb$ introduces a new transition into the graph, where a and b were already in the graph.
(e) Remove transition from the model {John} {finApp} {db} {Mary, Paul}	It occurs when $a \rightarrow wb$ represents a transition that does not belong more to the graph anymore, but a (C) e b (C) must be kept in the graph;
(f) Remove a participant from the model {John} {finApp} {db} {Mary, P̶a̶u̶l̶}	It occurs when a participant (human or system) does not execute some task anymore.
(g) Remove a gateway from the model {John} {finApp} {db} {Mary, Paul}	It occurs when $a \rightarrow wb$ represents a transition that does not belong to the graph anymore, where a (B) has now just *one* causal relation (task C).
(h) Remove a task from the model {John} {finApp} {db} {Mary}	It occurs when $a \rightarrow wb$ represents a transition that does not belong more to the graph anymore, where b (D) must be removed from the graph.

3 Incremental Mining

We consider two main phases to extract business process models from legacy: (i) identification and annotation of business rules in the source code and (ii) incremental mining process. The steps are shown in Fig. 5. First, the source code of the system is analyzed by static methods [13, 14] in order to identify business rules in the source. After identified, the business rule is annotated to enable the output of its behavior to log (i.e. as show in Figs. 2 and 3). So, the main objective of the identification of business rules is to generate log information about its behavior as input for the next step. Thus, all business process models extracted from legacy systems will be composed by business rules (i.e. tasks) extracted from the source code. The last main step in the process is the incremental process mining approach. It is used to extract dynamic behavior of process from the legacy system. This phase output is a set of business process structures and task participants, similar to the structures in Fig. 6.

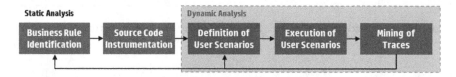

Fig. 2. Knowledge extraction process.

3.1 Mining of Execution Traces

Our mining algorithm uses a heuristic approach to extract the dependency relations from logs. These heuristics use a frequency based metric to indicate how certain we are that there is a truly dependency relation between two events. The main algorithm is presented in Algorithm 1 (i.e. see Fig. 8) and can be divided in three main steps: (1) mining of dependency graph (i.e. mining of relations $> w\|,w$ and $>> w$) and control-flow semantics; (2) discovery of obsolete relations and 3) mining of participants. The first step discovers all dependency relations from events log, such as sequences,

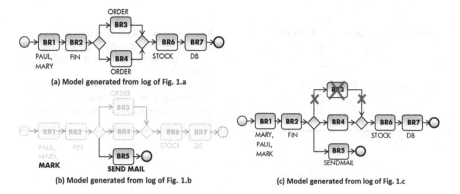

Fig. 3. Process model generated from the log in Fig. 1.

parallelism and control-flows (i.e. see item *2.a.iv* of algorithm 1). Then, in the next step, the algorithm discovers obsolete dependency relations from log. These relations represent elements removed from process definition and must be excluded from previous discovered model. In the last main step, we mine the task participants. It is a simple step to discovery and to manage the set of all participants that perform one task. This behavior is covered by algorithm 7 (i.e. ProcessParticipant).

3.2 Starting the Mining of Logs

The *IncrementalMiner* algorithm uses three basics information from logs to perform the mining: Task Id, Participant and Trace Id (i.e. log in Fig. 1). To exemplify how the mining of logs is performed, consider the partial log $W = \{BR1BR2BR3BR6BR7^6, BR1BR2BR4BR6BR7^5\}$ (i.e. column Act. ID values of the log shown in Fig. 1a). IncrementalMiner starts iterating on each process instance in the log. Each instance is composed by a set of events (i.e. an execution trace). For each pair of events (i.e. e_1 and e_2) in this trace, we apply a set of heuristics to discover likely relations (i.e. ProcessRelation algorithm). Considering the pair of two first events (e.g. BR1 and BR2) in the log, the first heuristic to be applied is heuristic (1) named Dependency Relation heuristic. It verifies if a dependency between the two elements in the trace exists. Let W be an event log on T, and $a, b \in T$. Then $|a > wb|$ is the partial number of times $a > wb$ occurs in W, and:

$$a \Rightarrow wb = \left(\frac{|a > wb| - |b > wa|}{|a > wb| + |b > wa| + 1} \right) \tag{1}$$

The Dependency Relation heuristic calculates the Partial Confidence (i.e. the Confidence value at some point of the algorithm) of this relation, using the support of $a > wb$ (e.g. partial number of times that *BR1* comes before *BR2*) and the support of $b > wa$ (e.g. partial number of times that *BR2* comes before *BR1*). In this example, $a \Rightarrow wb = (11 - 0) / (11 + 0 + 1) = 0.916$ is the partial confidence for the relation BR1 → BR2. After calculated, this value and all the associated data of dependency relation are inserted in the Dependency Tree. Dependency tree is an AVL tree (Adelson-Velskii and Landis' tree) that keeps the candidate relations (i.e. relations that could be considered in the final process graph) together with their confidence and support values, respectively. Figure 6 shows the Dependency Tree for the heuristic $a \Rightarrow wb$ calculated above (i.e. see node *BR2*, in the dependency tree *BR1*) and all further dependency relations. IncrementalMiner uses AVL trees because of satisfactory time for searching, insertion and removal operations, which is required by the incremental approach.

The result of this and all other heuristics of IncrementalMiner has values between -1 and 1, where values near to 1 are considered good confidences. The next two heuristics below (i.e. heuristics 2 and 3) verify the occurrence of short loops in the trace. That is, it checks the existence of iterations in the trace. Heuristic (2) calculates the confidence of short loops relations with size one (i.e. only one task, e.g. BR1BR1) and heuristic (3) considers loops of size two (i.e. two tasks, e.g. BR1BR2BR1).

Let W be an event log over T, and $a, b \in T$. Then $|a >_{W}a|$ is the number of times $a > wa$ occurs in W, and $|a \gg_{W}b|$ is the number of times $a \gg_{W}b$ occurs in W:

$$a \Rightarrow wa = \left(\frac{|a > wa|}{|a > wa| + 1} \right) \quad (2)$$

$$a \Rightarrow 2wb = \left(\frac{|a \gg wb| - |b \gg wa|}{|a \gg wb| + |b \gg wa| + 1} \right) \quad (3)$$

The heuristic (4) is used to verify the occurrence of non-observable activities in the log (i.e. AND/XOR-split/join semantic elements). Let W be an event log over T, and $a, b, c \in T$, and b and c are in dependency relation with a. Then:

$$a \Rightarrow wb^{\wedge}c = \left(\frac{|b > wc| + |c > wb|}{|a > wb| + |a > wc| + 1} \right) \quad (4)$$

$|a > wb| + |a > wc|$ represents the partial number of positive observations and $|b > wc| + |c > wb|$ represents the partial number of times that b and c appear directly after each other. Considering the partial event log $W = \{..., BR1BR2BR3..., BR1BR2BR4...\}$ extracted from Fig. 1a, the value of $a \Rightarrow wb^{\wedge}c = (0 + 0) / (6 + 5 + 1) = 0.0$ indicates that BR3 and BR4 are in a XOR-relation after BR2. Low values from $a \Rightarrow wb^{\wedge}c$ indicate a possible XOR-relation and high ones an AND-relation.

The above defined heuristics are used to calculate the candidate relations that can be added to the final dependency graph. In order to select the best relations, we used the best relations trees (see Fig. 7). These trees keep the best dependency and the best causal relations (i.e. relations with the highest confidence value, as presented in Fig. 6) of each dependency tree. Like the dependency tree, the best relations trees are updated after the evaluation of each dependency relation, calculated by (1), (2) and (3).

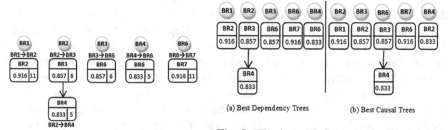

Fig. 4. Dependency trees.

(a) Best Dependency Trees   (b) Best Causal Trees

Fig. 5. The best relations trees extracted from dependency tree of Fig. 6.

The first step to update the best relation tree is to update the best dependency tree for the current relation. Considering the current relation of the example (i.e. BR1 → BR2), we first check if the confidence value of this relation (i.e. 0.916) is lower than the confidence value of the relations in the best dependency tree of BR1 (i.e. see tree BR1 in Fig. 7a). If it is the case, we remove it from the final dependency graph (i.e. see algorithm UpdateBestRelation). Besides, we check if its confidence value is greater than the one of the current best relations in the dependency tree of *BR1* and remove all the older relations from it (i.e. the older relations have confidence values smaller than the one of the current relation). Finally, we add the current relation to the end of the best dependency tree of *BR1*. The same process is carried out for the second element (i.e. BR2). Instead we use the best causal tree of BR2 (see Fig. 7b). All the elements of the dependency tree are considered best dependencies in this simple example. So, both trees (Fig. 7a and Fig. 6) are very similar. At the end, we discovered the partial process model (i.e. dependency graph), as shown in Fig. 5a.

3.3 Adding New Elements to the Model

In an incremental discovery of process models, adding new entries to the log (e.g., new process instances) may reveal additional behavior that should be incorporated into the process model already discovered. Thus, after process the log of initial traces as described in the previous section (i.e. log of Fig. 1a), we still need to process the complementary log traces of Fig. 1b, represented by the log set $W = \{BR1BR 2BR5^{10}\}$. After running IncrementalMiner over this log, we will obtain the final dependency graph of Fig. 5b. The dependency graph shows additional structures extracted from the new traces (i.e. BR5 activity and participants Mark and sendMail).

3.4 Removing Elements from Model

A process model is considered complete when it replays all events recorded in a complete log [7]. In this case, new traces added to the log will not change and neither will add new behavior to the model. However, this definition could not be true when changes occur in the process structure, recording possibly modified instances.

The problem in identifying modified process instances is that this information is often not recorded in the log. What happens in this case is the empirical analysis to check the likelihood of obsolete events (events related to elements that are no longer in the process definition, and consequently they also no longer occur). Thus, the main goal of the algorithms presented in this section and also one of the main contributions of this work is the ability to identify and remove obsolete dependency relations from discovered process models during the incremental mining.

To demonstrate how these algorithms work, we shall return to the log of Fig. 1c. This log contains modified versions of initial process instances and it was recorded by the execution of modified source code presented in Fig. 3. The first change can be observed in the log generated by case A (i.e. executed by the user Mary). This case generates 18 occurrences of trace BR1BR2BR4BR6BR7. However, we can see in Fig. 1a that this case originally used to record the trace BR1BR2BR3BR6BR7. The change in this case is the replacement of task BR3 by task BR4.

Process instances changes as described above can be often imperceptible during the mining task, because they depend on several factors such as frequency of related events (i.e. events related to task BR4), incidence of noise, etc. Thus, *ComputeOld*

Fig. 6. Pseudocode of incremental mining algorithms.

SiblingRelation and *CheckOldSiblingRelation* enable the identification of obsolete relations based on previous discovered model, modified process instances and its frequency. An obsolete relation is basically a dependency relation $> w$ presented in the dependency graph which is not executed anymore. The algorithm *Compute-OldSiblingRelation* is responsible for calculating the confidence of the candidate obsolete relations and it is used by the algorithm *ProcessRelation* (i.e. see item 15 of algorithm 2). To perform this, it uses the heuristic (5) defined bellow. The heuristic calculates the confidence of relation $> w$ to be an obsolete relation against its sibling relations $\mapsto w$.

To demonstrate this, we can see the relation BR2 $\rightarrow$ BR3 in Fig. 9a. The sibling relations of BR2 $\rightarrow$ BR3 are BR2 $\mapsto$ BR4 and BR2 $\mapsto$ BR5 (i.e. dashed transitions). Thus, we need to apply the heuristic for each sibling relation of BR2 $\rightarrow$ BR3. So, let W be a log of events T, and $a, b, c \in T$. So $|a > wb|$ is the partial number of times that $a > wb$ occurs in W, $|a > wc|$ is the partial number of times that $a > wc$ occurs in W, $|[a > wc]_{a \mapsto wb}|$ is the partial number of times that $[a > wc]_{a \mapsto wb}$ occurs in W and:

$$a \Rightarrow wb \mapsto c = \left(\frac{\left(1 + \frac{|a > wb|}{|a > wc|}\right) \times \left(|a > wb| - |[a > wc]_{a \mapsto wb}|\right)}{\left(1 + \frac{|a > wb|}{|a > wc|}\right) \times \left(|a > wb| - |[a > wc]_{a \mapsto wb}|\right) + 1} \right) \quad (5)$$

Another important point of heuristic (5) presented above is that as more events are available in the log greater is the confidence of obsolete relations. This behavior is introduced by the partial expression $1 + (\langle a > wb \rangle / \langle a > wc \rangle)$ presented in (5). It is used as a factor to maximize the value calculated by $a \Rightarrow wb \mapsto c$.

Considering the log with modified instances $W = \{..., \text{BR1BR2BR4BR6BR7}^{18}, \text{BR1BR2BR5}^{18}\}$, presented in Fig. 1c, we can check that the task BR3 was replaced by BR4. All dependency relations in the dependency graph which have task BR3 as a causal relation is likely to be an obsolete relation. In the example, the relation BR2 $\rightarrow$ BR3 is the only relation having task BR3 in the causal relation. To confirm if it is an obsolete relation, we need to analyze it from the sibling relations perspective (i.e. BR2 $\mapsto$ BR4 e BR2 $\mapsto$ BR5). Thus, we apply the heuristic (5) for each of them. The first sibling relation BR2 $\rightarrow$ BR4 has the support of $a > wb$ as the partial number of times that BR2 $\rightarrow$ BR4 occurs in the log (i.e. 23 times), the support of $a > wc$ as the partial number of times that BR2 $\rightarrow$ BR3 occurs in the log (i.e. 6 times), and $[a > wc]_{a \mapsto wb}$ as the support of sibling relation BR2 $\mapsto$ BR4 before the last occurrence of BR2 $\rightarrow$ BR3. Figure 9a shows that the support of sibling relation BR2 $\mapsto$ BR4 was zero (i.e. no occurrences) in the last time that BR2 $\rightarrow$ BR3 occurs. After that, we can calculate the confidence of BR2 $\rightarrow$ BR3 to be an obsolete relation against BR2 $\mapsto$ BR4 as $a \Rightarrow wb \mapsto c = ((1 + 23/6) \times (23 - 0)) / (((1 + 23/6) \times (23 - 0)) + 1) = 0.991$. We repeated the same process to the next sibling relation BR2 $\mapsto$ BR5, where $a \Rightarrow wb \mapsto c = ((1 + 28/6) \times (28 - 0)) / (((1 + 28/6) \times (28 - 0)) + 1) = 0.993$. As result of the execution of *ComputeOldSibling Relation* for both sibling relations BR2 $\mapsto$ BR4 and BR2 $\mapsto$ BR5 we have obtained values 0.991 and 0.993, respectively.

To check if the relation above (i.e. BR2 → BR3) can really be defined as an obsolete dependency relation, we execute the algorithm 4 (i.e. see *CheckOldSiblingRelation* at item *2.a.v*). The algorithm checks the confidence of each sibling relation ↦ *w* of dependency relation > *w* calculated by *ComputeOldSiblingRelation*. To set the minimum acceptable value calculated by the heuristic (5), the threshold *Obsolete Relation* uses the following definition:

Definition 1 (Obsolete Relation). Let > *w* be a relation with two or more sibling relations ↦ *w*, a dependency relation is considered obsolete if and only if all sibling relations have $a \Rightarrow wb \mapsto c$ result above threshold *Obsolete Relation*.

The definition above is followed by algorithm 4, as presented at item *5.c* and *5.d*. Moreover, we set the threshold *Obsolete Relation* value to 0.990 to get only obsolete relation candidates with high confidence. So, if all sibling relations ↦ *w* of > *w* reach heuristic results above threshold, then we need to remove > *w* from dependency process graph, as presented in items *5.d* and *5.e.ii* of algorithm 6. Back to the example, we can see that relation BR2 → BR3 presented in Fig. 9a has both of sibling relations with heuristic result above 0.990 (i.e. 0.991 for BR2 ↦ BR4 and 0.993 for BR2 ↦ BR5). Thus, it means that we need to remove the relation from dependency graph, such as presented in the final discovered model in Fig. 5c.

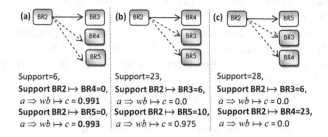

Fig. 7. Calculating the candidate obsolete relations.

4 Experiments

The experiments in this section were implemented in Java language and divided into two groups. The first group shows the quality of models mined from logs generated by a process execution simulator (i.e. see Sect. 4.1). The second group demonstrates the quality of models mined from logs of a real legacy system.

4.1 Experiments on Simulated Data

Obtaining practical data for incremental mining is not a trivial task. Therefore, we have used a simulation tool [11] to generate data about process models definitions and their execution logs. The models are generated in a recursive way. First *n* parts are generated. Each part is a task (with probability 50 %), a parallel structure (20 %), an alternative structure (20 %) or a loop (10 %). We also included noise in 5 % of all traces in the log. Additionally, each task has a performer that represents a process participant. For a parallel or an alternative structure the simulation randomly generates b branches. Usually there are no more than 100 tasks in a workflow model [9], so we set $n = 4$ and $2 \leq b \leq 4$ to limit the scale. Each model has at least one loop and at most three alternative structures and at most three parallel structures. The simulation randomly generates each task's waiting time and execution time. At the choice point it enters each branch with the same probability. Each generated model has also a modified version. It was used to simulate the evolution of the process model and to perform the incremental mining with modified process instances. At the end, we generated 400 models (i.e. 200 original process models and 200 modified versions of them) and 200 log files, with an average of 47.6 tasks. In each log dataset there are 500 simulated instances made up by 300 new process instances (i.e. from original process model) and 200 modified process instances, generated from the modified version of these processes.

4.2 Quality of Non Incremental Mining

For measuring the correctness of our method in a non-incremental scenario, we have used the conformance checking metrics for models and logs [10]. The result is evaluated from aspects of *Token Fitness* (i.e. which evaluates the extent to which the workflow traces can be associated with valid execution paths specified in the model), *Behavioral Appropriateness* (i.e. which evaluates how much behavior is allowed by the model but is never observed in the log) and *Structural Appropriateness* (i.e. which evaluates the degree of clarity of the model). We use the conformance checker plug-in of ProM 5.2 [4]. The average results from the mining of 200 datasets (i.e. considering just original process instances without changes from the logs) are shown in Table 2.

The Token Fitness and the Structural Fitness metric values suggest that our method has nearly the same precision as α-algorithm [7] and Behavioral Appropriateness slightly lower than α-algorithm and the method proposed by [5].

Table 2. Quality metrics values.

Metric	Our method	α-algorithm	Ma et al. [5]
Token Fitness	0.998	0.882	0.953
B. Appropriateness	0.851	0.865	0.854
Structural Fitness	1.000	1.000	0.901

4.3 Quality of Incremental Mining

Because of a lack of techniques to measure the models conformance during the incremental mining with modified process instances, it was necessary to use an alternative technique. Kappa [3] was used to give a quantitative measure of agreement between the input process models which generate the log records (i.e. observer 1) and the process model mined by the *IncrementalMiner* (i.e. observer 2). Here, this measure of agreement defines the level of similarity between the process structures of both models. The reason to use Kappa to check process graph similarity instead other methods like [12] is that we must also consider the organizational aspects of process such as participants of process, which is not part of the graph structure.

The values obtained from Kappa range from -1 (i.e. complete disagreement or low similarity) to $+1$ (i.e. perfect agreement or full similarity). The statistic formula is presented by Eq. (6), where P(A) is the empirical probability of agreement between two observers for one aspect of the process, and P(E) is the probability of agreement between two observers who performed the classification of that aspect randomly (i.e. with the observed empirical frequency of each mapping aspect). Thus, high Kappa values suggest high similarity between the input and output models. In this work, we applied the agreement over six different aspects, as shown in Table 3.

$$K = \frac{P(A) - P(E)}{1 - P(E)} \tag{6}$$

The first aspect checks the mapping of activities in the model. It identifies whether all activities presented in the mined models belongs to the process definition. The second aspect refers to the mapping of participants to the tasks of the process. It defines whether the participant associated with a task actually performs the activity in the process. The next two aspects define the mapping of incoming and outgoing transitions of an activity. These aspects define if all input and output transitions associated with an activity are correct. The last two aspects evaluate whether the semantics of input and output activities (e.g. AND/XOR-split/join) are correct. So, we can check whether control flows associated to the process are correct.

Table 3. Kappa results for real and simulated data.

Aspect	Simulated logs	Real legacy system logs
Activity mapping	1.000	0.920
Participants mapping	**0.710**	1.000
Input transitions	0.950	0.930
Output transitions	0.910	0.900
Output semantics	1.000	1.000
Input semantics	1.000	1.000

The Kappa verification of models is divided into three main steps which are represented in Fig. 10. First, we perform the mining of initial log (i.e. new traces without changes, generated by simulator, as described in Sect. 4.1) through IncrementalMiner to generate the intermediate models. After that, we submit to IncrementalMiner both intermediate model (i.e. generated in first step) and the log with modified instances of processes, also generated by simulator. The result is a set of updated process models containing all new dependencies and the updated ones. As the last step, we submit both modified process definition and updated discovered process model to Kappa for similarity verification. In column *Precision with Simulated Logs*

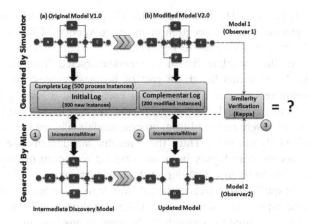

Fig. 8. Incremental mining verification process.

of Table 3, we can check the results. We have obtained high values for Kappa in the majority of aspects (i.e. values above 0.8 are considered good agreement [16]), what suggests that the discovered models and the designed models that generate the logs are similar. This means that the incremental mining of logs was conducted efficiently for the main aspects.

4.4   Experiments on Real Legacy System

To demonstrate how effective this approach on a real scenario is, we use a real legacy system. So, the process logs were generated from successive executions of an ERP legacy system written in COBOL language. It has more than 2,000,000 lines of source code and several modules (i.e. Financial Management, Sales Management, etc.). Moreover, each module implements several implicit (i.e. no formal process models defined) and interrelated business processes.

In order to start the discovery of business processes from legacy system, we followed the process defined in Fig. 4. On this experiment each module of legacy system was annotated and recompiled to generate trace events to the log. They were instrumented in such a way that each executed business rule (i.e. task) records an event into the log. Moreover, use case scenarios were defined to coordinate both the system execution and the log generation.

We have split and executed the user scenarios in seven groups. Each group represented all the scenarios related to one specific user of legacy system. Following the successive execution of these system scenarios, seven incremental dataset (i.e. one per user) with approximately 30,000 trace instances were generated. The datasets were named respectively as A, B, C, D, E, F and G. The datasets A, B recorded incremental logs related to execution of Financial Management module. Therefore, dataset C recorded process instances from execution of Sales Management. Dataset D recorded process instances of Service Management module. The next two datasets E and F recorded process instances of modules Production Management and Warehouse

Management, respectively. The last dataset (i.e. G) perhaps introduce modified process instances, generated from execution of modified version of Sales Management module (i.e. version 2 as illustrated in Fig. 11).

Table 4 shows the complete list of elements extracted from the incremental mining of logs. All elements listed are part of business process model structure. Incremental mining reveals new elements after each mined dataset, gradually generating a more complete model. On the other hand, the last dataset log (i.e. G) revel obsolete elements that were removed from process models (i.e. see negative values on rows Tasks and XOR-split/join). Thus, these results can demonstrate that we can extract process models from legacy in an incremental way even on those situations where the system has to be modified during the mining process.

To measure the quality of models extracted from legacy, we have also used Kappa statistic. The same aspects considered on Sect. 4.3 and shown on Table 3 were used. Here, these aspects were used to demonstrate the level of business analysts agreement on the business process structures obtained from legacy. So, in experiments using two different business analysts, Kappa values between 0.90 and 1.00 were obtained, as shown in column *Precision with Real Legacy System Logs* of Table 3. That means the business analysts agree with most of process models structures mined from legacy, during the incremental discovery.

Table 4. Elements extracted from legacy.

| | Log file | | | | | | | |
Element	A	B	C	D	E	F	G	Total
Biz processes structures	+2	+1	+2	+1	+4	+3	–	13
System participants	+3	+1	+1	+1	+1	+1	–	8
Human participants	+1	+1	+1	+1	+1	+1	+1	7
Tasks (Business Rules)	+20	+8	+15	+11	+24	+1	+2 (−4)	77
XOR-split/join	+10	+5	+5	+1	+3	+3	+3 (−2)	28
AND-split/join	+1							1

5   Related Work

Gunter [8] introduced the mining of ad hoc process changes in adaptive Process Management Systems (PMS). This technique introduces extension events in the log (e.g. insert task event, remove task event, etc.) that record all changes in a process instance. So change logs must be interpreted as emerging sequences of activities which are taken from a set of change operations. It is different from conventional execution logs where the log content describes the execution of a defined process. The problem here is that sometimes legacy information systems and WfMS do not generate process change information into the log. Thus, it is very hard to discovery process changes from these systems. Although, Bose [15] introduced concept drift applied to mining processes. He applied techniques for detection, location and classification of process modifications directly in the log without the need for specialized log containing such modifications as proposed by Gunter. After that, Luengo [17] proposed a new approach using clustering techniques. He uses the starting time of each process instance as an additional feature to those considered in traditional clustering approaches.

The work presented here supports the main operations of evolutionary learning (e.g. insert and exclusion operations) using an incremental mining approach. Moreover, our technique does not require extra information in the log to detect process changes. Thus, it makes possible to avoid the reprocessing of the complete set of logs, reducing its total processing time.

6 Summary and Outlook

This paper proposed an incremental process mining algorithm for mining of process structures in an evolutionary way from legacy systems. This is an important step for the incremental legacy modernization because it keeps the system maintenance live while the system is modernized. The algorithm enables the discovery of new and obsolete relations from log as new or modified traces are executed and recorded in the log. Thus, we can keep all process models discovered updated with the process definition when it changes.

In quality experiments using non-incremental simulated data and conformance metrics, the models discovered by IncrementalMiner present good accuracy. Regarding the incremental approach, IncrementalMiner also shows good precision for the models discovered from logs with modified process instances. During the discovery of process models from real legacy system and also simulated logs, the algorithm shows good results on the extracted models (i.e. Kappa values above 0.900). Thus, our approach could be an effective alternative for incremental mining of process models during the re-engineering of legacy systems.

Altogether, the main contribution of this work was the creation of a mechanism that introduces the incremental mining of logs with support to (i) the discovery of new dependency relations (i.e. new tasks) and participants in order to complement a partial or complete process model, and (ii) the identification and removal of obsolete dependency relations in order to update an existent process model. We also introduced an alternative way to measure the quality of models generated during the incremental process mining.

As future work we include the improvement of the identification of obsolete participants in the model (i.e. see low kappa value in simulate data of Table 3) and the integration of algorithm and the incremental approach in ProM tool.

References

1. Kalsing, A.C., Iochpe, C., Nascimento, G.S., Thom, L.H.: Evolutionary learning of business process models from legacy systems using incremental process mining. In: 15th International Conference on Enterprise Information Systems, pp. 58–69 (2013)

2. Kalsing, A.C., Nascimento, G.S., Iochpe, C., Thom, L.H.: An incremental process mining approach to extract knowledge from legacy systems. In: 14th IEEE EDOC 2010, pp. 79–88 (2010)
3. Cohen, J.: A coefficient of agreement for nominal scales. Educ. Psychol. Measur. **20**(1), 37–46 (1960)
4. van Dongen, B.F., de Medeiros, A.K.A., Verbeek, H., Weijters, A., van der Aalst, W.M.: The ProM framework: a new era in process mining tool support. In: Ciardo, G., Darondeau, P. (eds.) ICATPN 2005. LNCS, vol. 3536, pp. 444–454. Springer, Heidelberg (2005)
5. Ma, H., Tang, Y., Wu, L.: Incremental mining of processes with loops. Int. J. Artif. Intell. Tools **20**(1), 221–235 (2011)
6. Sun, W., Li, T., Peng, W., Sun, T.: Incremental workflow mining with optional patterns and its application to production printing process. Int. J. Intell. Control Syst. **12**(1), 45–55 (2007)
7. van der Aalst, W.M.P., Weijters, A.J.M.M., Maruster, L.: Workflow mining: discovering process models from event logs. IEEE Trans. Knowl. Data Eng. **16**(9), 1128–1142 (2004)
8. Gunther, C.W., Rinderle-Ma, S., Reichert, M., van der Aalst, W.M.P.: Using process mining to learn from process changes in evolutionary systems. Int. Bus. Process Integr. Manag. **3**(1), 61–78 (2008). (Inderscience)
9. Weijters, A.J.M.M., van der Aalst, W.M.P., Medeiros, A.K.: Process mining with the heuristics miner algorithm. Technical Report WP, Eindhoven, vol. 166 (2006)
10. Rozinat, A., Medeiros, A.K., Gunther, C.W., Weijters, A.J.M.M., van der Aalst, W.M.P.: Towards an evaluation framework for process mining algorithms. BPM Center Report BPM-07-06, BPMcenter. Org (2007)
11. Burattin, A., Sperduti, A.: PLG: a framework for the generation of business process models and their execution logs. In: Muehlen, M., Su, J. (eds.) BPM 2010 Workshops. LNBIP, vol. 66, pp. 214–219. Springer, Heidelberg (2011)
12. Dijkman, R., Dumas, M., García-Bañuelos, L.: Graph matching algorithms for business process model similarity search. In: Dayal, U., Eder, J., Koehler, J., Reijers, H.A. (eds.) BPM 2009. LNCS, vol. 5701, pp. 48–63. Springer, Heidelberg (2009)
13. Sneed, H.M., Erdos K.: Extracting business rules from source code. In: Proceeding of the Fourth IEEE Workshop on Program Comprehension, pp. 240–247 (1996)
14. Wang, C., Zhou, Y., Chen, J.: Extracting prime business rules from large legacy system. In: International Conference on Computer Science and Software Engineering, vol. 2, pp. 19–23 (2008)
15. Bose, R.C., van der Aalst, W.M., Žliobaitė, I., Pechenizkiy, M.: Handling Concept Drift in Process Mining. In: Mouratidis, H., Rolland, C. (eds.) CAiSE 2011. LNCS, vol. 6741, pp. 391–405. Springer, Heidelberg (2011)
16. Landis, J.R., Koch, G.G.: The measurement of observer agreement for categorical data. Int. Biom. Soc. **33**, 159–174 (1977)
17. Luengo, D., Sepúlveda, M.: Applying Clustering in Process Mining to Find Different Versions of a Business Process That Changes over Time. In: Daniel, F., Barkaoui, K., Dustdar, S. (eds.) BPM Workshops 2011, Part I. LNBIP, vol. 99, pp. 153–158. Springer, Heidelberg (2012)

On the 'Impossibility' of Critical and Emancipatory Design Science Research

J. Marcel Heusinger[✉]

Institute for Computer Science and Business Information Systems,
University of Duisburg-Essen, Universitaetsstr. 9, 45141 Essen, Germany
marcel.heusinger@icb.uni-due.de

Abstract. Popper's [1] 'piecemeal social change' is an approach manifesting itself in science as critical and emancipatory (C&E) research. It is concerned with incrementally removing manifested inequalities to achieve a 'better' world. Although design science research in information systems seems to be a prime candidate for such endeavors, respective projects are clearly underrepresented. This can be attributed to the demand of justifying research ex post by an evaluation in practical settings. From the perspective of C&E research it is questionable if powerful actors grant access to their organization and support projects which ultimately challenge their position. Within the present inquiry it is argued that the idea of Lewis's [2] 'possible worlds' can be leveraged as basis for C&E design science research. It is suggested that a theoretical approach, based on a synthesis of justificatory knowledge and 'organizational options', can complement the practical oriented design science research focus by allowing to design technical systems not only for factually existing contexts, but also for theoretically grounded, more desirable structures.

Keywords: Critical and emancipatory research · Possible world · Design science · Socio-technical system design · Reference architecture

1 Introduction

Critical and emancipatory (C&E) research projects, i.e., projects concerned with the identification and removal of manifested injustices [3], are recognized as an important application area of information systems research (ISR) [4]. However, within ISR in general and design science research in information systems (hereinafter: design science research (DSR)) in particular, there is a clear lack of such projects [5, 6]. Furthermore, most often C&E lack a constructive or transformative component, that is, they result in a form of 'destructive negativism' by solely focusing on criticism [6]. DSR, aiming to change existing structures and processes [4, 7–9], seems to be a prime candidate for a more satisfying endeavor, if combined with the research stream that conceptualizes information systems (IS) as socio-technical systems [e.g., 10–15]. This stream recognizes that information and communication technology (ICT) applications are embedded in an action system, comprising human beings and processes, and does not, as the much narrower view, exclude almost anything but ICT applications [e.g., 16–20]. Although both streams are concerned with transforming action systems to IS

© Springer International Publishing Switzerland 2014
S. Hammoudi et al. (Eds.): ICEIS 2013, LNBIP 190, pp. 331–348, 2014.
DOI: 10.1007/978-3-319-09492-2_20

or change existing IS, the broader perspective can account for the dialectic relationship between technical and social systems. This clearly locates DSR in the overarching endeavor of socio-technical system design or engineering [cf. 21–24]: DSR is the methodological[1] foundation for approaches developing technical systems, supporting or enabling the emerging social system. Despite the widespread belief that methodical suggestions such as 'participatory research' in DSR and socio-technical system design [cf. 14, 19, 28–32] are compatible with C&E goals, they can address them only superficially. On the one side, participatory approaches neglect what in reference to Sen [33] can be called the downward adaptation of employees' expectations in respect to what is possible because of continual exploitation. On the other side, it is unreasonable to assume that powerful actors grant access to their organization and devote resources to a research project, which ultimately challenges their position [34, 35], something DSR and, by implication, derived methodical support presuppose by demanding an ex post justification in a practical setting. This internal tension inhibits DSR to unfold its full potential and explains the lack of C&E DSR.

To overcome this limitation and to counterbalance the abuse of participatory approaches, the present paper, based on a critical reflection of the conventional notion of DSR, sketches a complementary approach which, in reference to Lewis [2], is called the design of 'possible worlds', a concept introduced to ISR by Frank [36]. The paper suggests that the idea of a theoretically 'possible world' provides an adequate basis for more progressive C&E DSR by indicating possible alternatives to factually existing circumstances, an essential prerequisite for questioning existing structures and processes [cf. 36–38], and by allowing to design technical systems, supporting and enabling these more desirable structures, based on these 'possible worlds'. More precisely, a designed 'possible world' can function as a domain or 'reference model' [39] from which the requirements for the development of 'facilitating reference architectures' [40] can be elicited. In short, the 'possible world' can be considered as a sketch of a desirable, not yet realized structure, used to design technical systems; both together inform the practice of socio-technical system design and practical DSR by providing normatively justified 'patterns' or safeguards.

Such an approach represents a valuable contribution to the disciplinary knowledge base, because it addresses both of the above mentioned issues in the traditional conceptualization and it connects DSR more clearly to the overarching endeavor of socio-technical system design. Furthermore, despite being 'merely' theoretical, the approach helps ISR to 'enlighten society', a duty all scientific disciplines have to fulfill [41]. Therefore, the present inquiry is highly relevant, however, relevance is a characteristic attributed by the target audience [42], who has to pass the final judgment. The audiences most likely to benefit from the following discussion are scientists, especially design science researchers who need an approach to conduct C&E DSR projects and those who are interested in a critical reflection of the methodological self-conception of DSR.

---

[1] The terms 'method' and 'methodical' refer to the general procedure involved in conducting a study, which differs from the concrete 'research strategy' or technique, used to collect and analyze data [cf. 25–27]. In this perspective, the terms 'methodology' and 'methodological' refer to the theoretical underpinning of methods captured in the disciplinary body of knowledge.

The remainder is structured as follows: the next section explicates the limitations of the traditional conceptualization of DSR in general and in respect to C&E. Based on this rationale, the third section puts forward the design of 'possible worlds' as an approach for C&E DSR and relates it to complementary approaches. Before the final section concludes the discussion and outlines further research options, the fourth section provides a brief illustrative application of the method.

2 The 'Impossibility' of C&E DSR

Design science research (DSR) has the aspiration to be a methodology that bridges both, relevance and rigor. It tries to achieve this goal by demanding that DSR deals with problems and opportunities articulated in practice (relevance) and that designed artifacts are evaluated in practical settings (rigor). As indicated before, those demands prevent DSR to fully unfold its potential, especially in respect to C&E research. Elucidating limitations inherent to this narrow definition provides the basis for the suggested complementary approach. Therefore, the following critical reflection questions that (1) a 'rigorously' evaluation of a designed artifact provides a comprehensive justification of the 'effectiveness' or 'validity' of the implied claim and that (2) 'relevance', defined as 'problems and opportunities articulated in practice', is a comprehensive conceptualization.

The first aspect tends to be the most pressuring as almost all DSR approaches demand an evaluation [e.g., 5, 14, 15, 18–20]. The goal of an evaluation is to assess the efficacy or consequences of the artifact's instantiation in use [16] by either employing empirical-quantitative [7] or interpretive [43] methods. Instantiation and evaluation are mandatory activities for a valid research project [44]. This is a common tenor in DSR: from more general instructions such as Hevner et al.'s [14] third guideline (i.e., "[t]he utility, quality, and efficacy of a design artifact must be rigorously demonstrated via well-executed evaluation methods") to the more specific demands in theory development [18] (i.e., the "[v]alidation of the artifact generates information that is used to assess the correctness of the entire reasoning/circumscription chain") [see also 13, 15, 19, 43, 45]. The ultimate concern is the 'effectiveness' or 'validity' of the claim(s) manifested in the artifact, that is, the evaluation is performed to justify all non-evident or unshared assumptions embodied in the artifact [46]. In sum, the answer to how novel research results are justified, the central question of the context of justification [25, 47], in DSR is verificatory, like the answer of the empirical-quantitative tradition [38]. Justification through 'post-construction evaluation' is well-established, but not perfect. There is room for complementary approaches such as 'justification through evidence synthesis'.

An argument for this pluralistic perspective of justification can be derived from difficulties associated with the conventional approach. The central challenge originates from the 'amplified contingency' [42] of DSR's unit of analysis leading to the insight that "the evaluation process in design science is task and situation specific" [45]. In other words, the evaluation of the effectiveness is spatially and temporally bound to a specific context. This corresponds to the second moment of the scientific enterprise, the moment of 'open-systemic application of theory' [48]. In the 'moment of theory', the first moment, knowledge is gained in controlled environments (i.e., closed systems such as laboratories), which is then leveraged to measure or predict events in uncontrollable environments (i.e., open systems such as organizations). As it is impossible to control all influencing variables to isolate the effects of specific causes within open systems, observed events and their magnitude are always the result of multiple amplifying and/or curtailing influences. Because of the context's contingency, the 'practical/technological utility' [49] ascertained in the evaluation in one context, does not guarantee practical utility in another. Furthermore, the suggestion to exclude trail-and-error descriptions from research reports to preserve the reader's motivation [25] makes it impossible to reconstruct and explain processes in open systems—a prerequisite to derive transcontextual knowledge. This in turn has the consequence that neither the possibility of transferring an artifact to another context nor the effectiveness of this transfer can be explained scientifically; they are based on experience or 'assumed rationality' [48]. Finally, focusing on 'practical utility' at the expense of the first moment's 'epistemtic utility' [49] inhibits eliminating hypotheses from the body of knowledge [25, 41, 50], because the practical application of the artifact and its successful evaluation does not give an indication of the truth of the embedded theoretical propositions [50]. For example, it might be possible that only some part of the theoretical knowledge embedded in the artifact holds in practice or the evaluation is successful despite false theoretical statements (i.e., spurious correlation). This in turn maintains the (insufficient) state of the knowledge base which forces DSR to "rely on intuition, experience, and trial-and-error methods" [14] or 'assumed rationality'.

Relevance in DSR, the second aspect mentioned above, is mainly concerned with the grounding of a DSR project's purpose in practical problems and opportunities [e.g., 13, 14]. These practice demands articulated by 'important stakeholders', predominantly managers responsible for deciding if organizational resources are committed to the construction, procurement, and usage of artifacts [11, 43], enter DSR projects in form of goals or context-specific requirements. According to the postulate of the 'absence of value judgments', which should ensure objectivity, justification has to be free from value judgments [25]. A common interpretation of this demand is to be personally detached from values and solely focus on selecting the 'objectively' most effective means to achieve given goals. This move is possible because values have no binding force [49]. In reference to Habermas [51] this perspective can be called 'purposive or means-end rationality'. An extension of this type of rationality—'normative rationality'—would discuss goals and means in reference to commonly shared and acceptable social values.

Such an extended perspective seems reasonable, because science in general and applied sciences in particular have considerable societal consequences and side-effects. Nobel laureate North [52], for example, argues that introducing new technology often leads to the "deliberate deskilling of the labor force", that is, highly skilled employees, with high bargain power, are substituted with less skilled and less powerful employees [see also 28, 32, 53, 54]. In the same vein, Chmielewicz [25] argues that it is hard to accept that researchers, despite these social consequences, work on goals and means without a normative position. He further argues that, because researchers' obligations are different from those of politicians and managers, they should consider the normative implications of their research. Similarly, Niiniluoto [49] notes that a researcher "contributing to applied science is *morally responsible* for" his or her contribution. The exclusion of 'normative rationality', by solely focusing on 'purposive rationality' implies that human beings, an immanent part of IS, are merely treated as objects. To some degree and in special circumstances such a perspective might be acceptable for analytical purposes; however, it is a serious deficit if normative considerations are completely excluded, especially from applied disciplines. It not only makes the discipline morally questionable, it also confines intellectual curiosity—the source of important scientific research [50] —to purposive rationality; it makes demarcation of DSR and consulting/design practice fuzzy; and it neglects the duty of scientists to enlighten society [41].

This is not a call to fundamentally revise the foundations of the discipline and its methodological repertoire, but to recognize the inherent 'imperfect obligation'. To make ISR more accountable to one of its largest stakeholders, viz. society at large, 'relevance' cannot only be defined in relation to the needs of 'important stakeholders' devoting resources to a project. Furthermore, a practical evaluation is not the only way to conduct research rigorously. Within the next section a sketch of the design of 'possible worlds' method [34] is presented, a complementary approach that allows to conduct C&E DSR projects.

3   The Design of 'Possible Worlds' and Related Approaches

The tension between C&E research's aim to challenge entrenched injustices and the demand of DSR to conduct 'relevant' projects 'rigorously' can be resolved by broadening the understanding of 'rigor' and 'relevance'. Such an extension, feasible as explicated above, will admit C&E DSR projects. The present section strives to realize this goal by (i) arguing that 'relevant' research is based on normatively justified criticism of existing circumstances, the principle underpinning the design of 'possible worlds' method, and by (ii) substituting the ex post evaluation through the successfully applied 'realist synthesis' [55] and a simplified version of 'applicability checks' [56], together providing equally appropriate justificatory evidence. Finally, to locate the proposal in the existing body of knowledge, the closing section relates the methodical suggestion to overarching socio-technical design approaches and practical DSR projects, i.e., efforts realizing technical systems in practical settings.

3.1   The Design of 'Possible Worlds'

The design of 'possible worlds' is divided into three steps, similar to the suggestions for interpretative C&E research [see 57, 58]: firstly, the 'factual world', a representative abstraction of the structure of a selected unity of analysis, is 'carved out'; secondly, the idea of a 'possible world' as well as its underpinning value position are sketched and utilized to criticize the 'factual world'; finally, the 'realist synthesis' is employed to gather (i) justificatory evidence for the theoretical possibility of the identified differences (i.e., avoiding the 'utopian counterclaim' [34]) as well as

(ii) knowledge of 'organizational options' [28] from which the requirements for the design of technical systems, supporting the more desirable social system, are elicited. Based on this preparatory work, a technical artifact can be designed and assessed for 'accessibility' and 'applicability' as proposed by Rosemann and Vessey [56]. 'Importance', the third suggested criterion, can be left out, because the identified differences are considered to be intrinsically 'important' or 'relevant'. The rationale, unfolded below, behind this claim is that if, seen from a reasonable value position, particular circumstances are considered to be unjust, there is a strong argument or even an imperfect obligation to deal with these injustices.

As both, employing applicability checks and designing technical systems are well established in ISR [e.g., 8, 12, 19, 20, 39], an elaboration at the expense of less well-established activities tends to be unrewarding. Therefore, the remaining discussion will be confined to the activities required for developing the 'possible world', functioning as a 'domain/reference model' [39] for the design of the technical artifact.

Step 1: Abstraction. The relationship between the envisioned 'possible world' and the existing real world exhibits similarities to incommensurable theories, which are different models of the world and, due to a shift of terminology, use different languages to explicate their conceptualization [59]. Therefore, comprehending the 'possible world' requires a shift of thinking, which according to Sen [60] is a dual task: using a conformist language to communicate clearly, while simultaneously expressing non-conformist ideas. Correspondingly, it seems to be most fruitful to start the design of a 'possible world', the non-conformist idea, by creating a conformist abstraction of the real world segment of concern (hereinafter: 'factual world'). The pre-existing conditions within it not only determine interventions' efficacy [55], they also provide the basis for critical analysis [6]. Abstraction in this context must not be mistaken with unrealistic or far from reality, a common misunderstanding. An abstraction, as understood in the following, is a goal-oriented process that captures the necessarily related elements and processes of a subject of investigation [see 27, 42, 61, 62, for excellent discussions]. It excludes contingently related elements, attributes of elements, and relationships to be applicable in multiple settings (hereinafter: domain). This implies, when applied in a concrete context the abstraction needs to be complemented and refined by information gathered in real world settings.

Correspondingly, the first task in the design of a 'possible world' is to select a differentiable system of the real world as unit of analysis. The selection needs to be congruent with the purpose and goal of the inquiry, i.e., it is implicitly guided by the idea of the 'possible world'. In contrast to the traditional conceptualization of DSR, the researcher is not restricted to a particular organizational setting. However, to avoid unnecessary complexity, the following will be confined to this more familiar case. For the selected unit of analysis the general structure and relevant contextual influences are explicated (schematically depicted in Fig. 1). This entails decomposing structures into relevant elements (i.e., the element on the left side) and identifying relationships between elements [58], together representing the system's structure. For all identified elements relevant powers, i.e., the non-contingent properties [61], or relevant 'organizational options' are be explicated.

Such an abstraction exhibits similarities to conceptual frameworks guiding empirical-quantitative research or the structural context descriptions used in explanatory case study research [see 58]. In other words, the 'factual world' could also be used for examining concrete settings in a domain to identify predominantly occurring tendencies and relate them to ascertained powers, resulting in a "model [...] of a mechanism, which *if* it were to exist and act in the postulated way would account for the phenomena in question [...]" [63, p. 19]. As such it would provide a model for an explanation of "why what happens actually does happen" [61, p. 44]. However, the study's primary interest is not the explanation of a certain event, but the design of a more desirable 'possible world'. Sketching out this alternative, intuitively used to specify the research's purpose and goal as well as to select the unit of analysis, is subject of the second step.

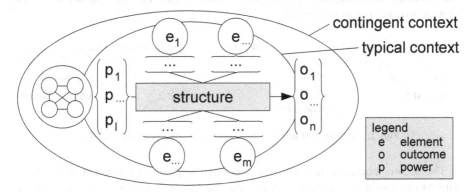

Fig. 1. Abstraction of the unit of analysis, adapted from: [27].

Step 2: Critical Analysis. Artifacts, such as the 'possible world', can be seen as means to achieve given ends [64]. However, there are no means or ends in themselves; they are only meaningful in a certain sphere, which is set through delineating normative value judgments [25]. In C&E research the realm encompasses the removal of manifested injustices [3], which are identified by scrutinizing the believed to be legitimate circumstances for preconceptions and biases [60]; in the current terminology, by criticizing the 'factual world'. In other words, the end of a C&E DSR project is derived from criticizing the current situation, that is, criticism as the reason for change [25, 38, 42, 65]. It could even be argued that this should be the maxim not only of C&E DSR, but of DSR in general, because "if the starting point of all change is perfect and good, then change can only be a movement that leads away from the perfect and good" [1]. However, this line of reasoning is not further pursued here; instead it is taken as given that criticism is a vital prerequisite for C&E DSR. As Habermas [37] points out, the legitimacy of an existing order can be criticized only from the perspective of an, at least hypothetically, existing alternative (i.e., the 'possible world'). This 'possible world' serves as contrasting background or instrument to explicate the shortcomings of the 'factual world'. Correspondingly, the first step of the critical analysis is to make explicit the guiding idea of a 'possible world' by briefly sketching its key points in a form adequate for the critical analysis. This draft will be iteratively revised during the realist synthesis in the subsequent step. Before going into the details of the critical analysis, a briefly discussion of the relationship between the 'factual world', the 'possible world', and concrete contexts is intersected to avoid potential misunderstandings.

As indicated by 'contingent context' and 'typical context' in Fig. 1, there is no 1-to-1 correspondence between the 'factual world' and abstracted factually existing contexts. The 'factual world' is merely a representative cross-section of contexts in a domain, which might differ from context abstractions in two ways (see Fig. 2): (i) the 'factual world' comprises entities not present in the context abstraction or (ii) the context abstraction already exhibits entities of the 'possible world'. This might raise two objections: first, it can be argued that by excluding ramifications the implied understanding of development is teleological, and second, that the 'factual world' is not as representative as suggested.

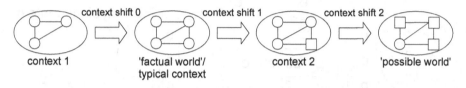

Fig. 2. Sequence of interventions leading to the 'possible world'.

The second objection refers to the shortened sequence of 'context shifts' [34] required to transform a particular setting into the 'possible world'. A 'context shift', more fully elaborated in the succeeding step, can be understood as an intervention changing the structure of a social system in a certain way (e.g., by assigning an additional responsibility to an element or by changing the rules governing interactions within the system), practically resulting in a new context. Therefore, in contrast to the context 2, which is still included in the sequence, context 1 is not covered. Therefore, 'possible worlds' have to be seen as fallible interim results of a 'theorizing' effort [66]: the "emergent products [of theorizing] summarize progress, give direction, and serve as placemarkers". Correspondingly, a single research project is teleological, but succeeding projects can, and probably should, refine the interim result by suggesting different development paths, which can, for example, be utilized for the analysis of trade-offs. Presently the focus is on the methodical support of a single research project. Therefore, the investigation of the prerequisites of an integration of research projects is left for future research and the discussion turns to the actual critical analysis, the second activity in this step.

The aim of this task is to identify entry points for interventions by either criticizing the consequences of inhibited powers and/or the system's structure. The difference between both can be illustrated on the basis of an assumed 'factual world' representing the formal structure of a political system: whereas concentrating on the inhibited powers could, for example, reveal that a group of people is systematically excluded from participating, an intrinsically valuable freedom, in particular decisions, because they are not adequately informed, a structural criticism might explicate that the system's structure grants absolute control to a particular actor, violating the democratic principle of separation of powers. Despite the different direction, both analyses indicate "immanent possibilities for action" [26] (hereinafter: intervention entry points), because the 'possible world', as a hypothetical alternative has a different structure, suggesting at least one possible resolution. As such an analysis goes beyond the 'tendency' or outcome focus, often found in C&E ISR studies [6], it does not run the danger of degenerating into a 'destructive negativisim' [6]. However, what was presupposed in the preceding tasks is that the 'possible world' is indeed more desirable and not a departure from the 'perfect and good'. Such a justification is achieved by explicating the underlying value position [cf. 6, 42], which is ideally supported by arguments, which 'cannot reasonably rejected' [67]. This ensures what Popper [65] calls 'control through critique', a control from which implicit or camouflaged values elude themselves. In the above example a democratically value position was indicated by referring to the intrinsic value of participation and democratic principles respectively.

In sum, the second step involves three tasks: (i) sketch the idea of the 'possible world', (ii) explicate the value position underpinning the 'possible world' to provide a rationale for its desirability, and (iii) criticize the 'factual world' from the perspective of the sketched alternative to identify intervention entry points. The last activity is what makes the research relevant: it is not relevant because it deal with problems articulated by 'important stakeholders', but because there are reasonable normative arguments to characterize the structure as unjust. Having the opportunity to contribute to the removal of this identified injustice entails a certain responsibility or imperfect obligation to do exactly this [34, 60, 68, 69].

Step 3: Possibility Assessment and Synthesizing Design. Up to this point, the idea of the 'possible world' is just a hypothetical alternative to the 'factual world', which might or might not be realizable. The goal of this final step is to indicate which interventions, expressed as technological proposition [cf. 11, 25, 37, 49, 50, 70], are suitable to exploit the identified entry points to create a structure as outlined in the 'possible world'. In other words, if the result of the design of 'possible worlds' is summarized as "If you are in the factual world and want to remove limitation (L) by exploiting entry point (E), intervention (I) might result in structure (S)", then the identification of interventions realizing the context shifts (see Fig. 2) is subject of this step. As Heusinger [34] points out it is important to distinguish 'possible worlds' from 'utopias' by assessing the 'context shifts' in terms of logical, theoretical, technological, economical, and normative possibility. Whereas normative possibility, the guiding principle of the design process, is covered by the preceding step, the remaining four assessments form a hierarchy, because each assessment presupposes an affirmative answer to the respective preceding (e.g., economic possibility presupposes technologies, which determine the involved costs; technologies can be developed only if a change is theoretical possible; theoretical possibility presupposes logical possibility). As the following two lines of reasoning demonstrate, within the design of 'possible worlds' the justification can be confined to the assessment of theoretical possibility.

Firstly, the assessment of logical possibility would essentially require a 'proof' that the formalized versions of the 'possible world' and the 'factual world' do not contradict each other. Such an assessment not only presupposes a mature disciplinary terminology and, assumed such a vocabulary was given, would constitute a self-contained research project, it is also unrewarding: (i) it is non-decisive to realize the aims of C&E, i.e., enlighten actors and inform 'political' action [26] and (ii) not logically possible worlds, the concern of Lewis [2], but those worlds, which are at least theoretically possible, are required to provide a reasonable basis to criticize the 'factual world'.

Secondly, the technological and economic possibility assessment, both addressing the question of "How and at which cost can the 'possible world' be implemented?", are excluded from C&E DSR projects, because subject of socio-technical systems design and practical DSR projects. The main rationale to confine the design of 'possible worlds' to a theoretical endeavor is provided by Habermas [71], who argues that C&E research has to be seen as a 'therapeutical discourse' in which the affected people have the final authority [cf. 37]. In other words, C&E should inform people about possible options, the concrete configuration of change and the initiative for realizing it are the responsibility of affected people themselves. This, in combination with the abstract nature of the 'possible world', restricts the scope of technical arti-facts, which can be developed based on the 'possible world', to 'reference architec-tures' [39, 40], i.e., a form of design patterns, which specify a domain-specific blueprint for context-specific blueprints of concrete ICT applications. In other words, the design of the associated technical systems is, employing the above argument, also confined to the theoretical level, an acceptable DSR output [e.g., 7, 16, 34].

However, the assessment of theoretical possibility is an intricate problem, because the possibility of the intervention sequence leading to the 'possible world' (see Fig. 1) cannot be inferred from those of the comprised interventions as they belong to dif-ferent 'strata' [see 48]. Nevertheless, to justify that the 'possible world' fulfills its role to enlighten society a simplified form of the 'applicability check' [56] is an appro-priate technique. This is compatible with the perspective to see the design of 'possible worlds' as a 'theorizing effort' [66]: 'possible worlds' are fallible interim results, partially grounded through the assessment of the comprised interventions, but they require further development and are subjected to redesign [72]. Such an approach is not scientific because it provides (empirical) evidence for 'truth', impossible in open-systems, but because is conducted with a 'scientific attitude' [3], i.e., systematically, skeptically, and ethically.

This leaves the question of how the theoretical possibility of the 'possible world' can be assessed in a systematic way. Heusinger [34] suggests that the 'realist syn-thesis' [55] provides an adequate technique, also successfully employed in ISR [e.g. 73, 74]. Principally, it is a purposive literature review extracting evidence from the existing body of knowledge to create theories of the working of (policy) interventions; exactly what is required for the assessment. In addition, briefly illustrated in Sect. 4, the 'realist synthesis' also allows to gather knowledge of the 'organizational options' allowing to elicit requirements required for the design of the technical system, completing the IS character of the 'possible world'. In order to illustrate how this proposal contributes to the design of socio-technical systems, the following subsection locates the design of 'possible worlds' in the task structure of such approaches.

3.2 Related Approaches

One well-known and frequently cited method in the socio-technical systems design literature is the 'Effective Technical and Human Implementation of Computer-based Systems (ETHICS)' [28–30, 32], which is used as representative of socio-technical system design approaches. ETHICS is a participatory approach, which conceives technology as a means not an end [28]. It aims at the "successful integration of company objectives with the needs of employees and customers" [28] by designing a completely "new system based on a careful analysis of company, department and individual needs and problems" [28]. In order to achieve this goal, the following steps, partially depicted in Fig. 3, are suggested [28, 29, 32]: (i) analyze business as well as social needs and set efficiency as well as social objectives, (ii) sketch socio-technical solutions achieving these objectives, (iii) select the best fitting alternative, (iv) design the details of this alternative, (v) realize the described system, and (vi) evaluate the implementation [for a more detailed description see 28, 32].

As indicated by the two ellipses in Fig. 3 the 'possible world' (i.e., social system) and the corresponding 'reference architecture' (i.e., technical system) are relevant in the second steps of this socio-technical system design approach. The main tasks involved in this steps are (i) to create 'organizational options' by identifying required work-activities as well as involved skills, governing rules, and distribution of responsibilities [28], (ii) to search for 'technical options' potentially supporting the working environment, and (iii) to evaluate all identified options separately against the goals set in the first step [28]. Next, the shortlisted organizational and technical options are evaluated for their fitting and combined to organizational-technical solutions, which are again evaluated in respect to the set objectives [28]. Finally, the best fitting or 'integrated' solution is selected to be presented to all affected stakeholders and the management level [28], before the details of the new design are worked out in the subsequent steps [28].

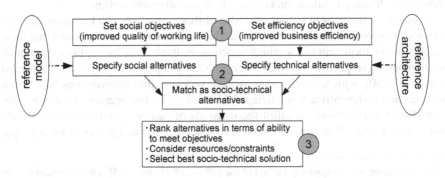

Fig. 3. ETHICS and the design of 'possible worlds', adapted from: [28, 29].

Although only roughly described, ETHICS is prone to, what in reference to Sen [33] can be called, the downward adaption of employees' expectations in respect to what is possible because of continual exploitation. Mumford [28] partially recognizes this by proposing an alternated—in contrast to the design 'expert'—role of the external system designer, an argument equally applying to designers focusing on technical systems: the 'experts' have to be seen as 'facilitators', helping employees to organize the participative design, keeping them interested and motivated, resolving emerging conflicts, and ensuring that nothing important is forgotten and overlooked by informing about organizational as well as technical options [see also 28, 29]. In particular the last mentioned responsibility allows to integrate the design of 'possible worlds' and the implied distinction of 'theoretical and practical ISR' [34] into the design of socio-technical systems: theoretical IS researchers, employing the 'possible world' method in order to design technical options (i.e., reference architectures) for possible organizational options, inform the second step of the socio-technical design process (see Fig. 3). If selected as a suitable solution for certain context, the practical IS researcher (i.e., the 'facilitator' in the socio-technical design process) helps to refine and adapt the technical solution, which functions as a safeguard against the exploitation of downward adapted employees, in cooperation with the employees and other 'facilitators', who are concerned with the realization of the social system.

4 Exemplary Application of the Method

The present section complements the relatively abstract description of the preceding section through an illustrative application[2]. For this purpose the proposal of "community-driven sustainable human development initiatives in 'developed countries'" [76] functions as idea of a 'possible world', guiding the process.

First, as the initiatives are positioned in localities, the 'local development framework' [77] is suitable 'factual world' candidate. The World Bank uses it as a lens to identify development needs of localities in 'less developed' countries. However, if the framework is used as ideal structure against which localities in 'less developed' countries are evaluated it has to capture the minimal structural entities a 'developed' locality exhibits, making it a representative abstraction.

Second, for the present purpose the idea of these initiatives can be summarized as follows: to overcome the limitations of development practice, it is suggested that local people should form initiatives which function as think tank for sustainable human development in respective localities. This proposal is underpinned by Sen's "The Idea of Justice" [60], which, cruelly summarized, proposes that interventions have to be assessed in a comparative, scrutinizing public discourse, considering arguments even from distant perspectives, to fulfill the demands of justice. Contrasting the 'factual world' and the 'possible world' reveals inter alia[3] the inhibited power of local people

---

[2] This application is a summarizing excerpt of the author's Ph.D. thesis [75], which provides a more comprehensive case.

[3] An analysis concerned with structural criticism, e.g., the neglect of environmental resource management [see 75], is not pursued here.

to decide about the development of their locality (i.e., in 'developed' countries development is planned and realized by external organizations, which involve local people, due to resource constraints, only superficially, even in legally mandated projects). What is at stake in this simplified example is (i) that local people can form initiatives at (ii) levels above the community level (i.e., locality), which (iii) are concerned with the development of the respective locality.

Third, in respect to the identified entry point the 'realist synthesis' reveals that the 'development literature' is full of examples of specialized, people-driven initiatives at levels below the locality such as irrigation water user groups, providing evidence that initiatives, concerned with development (ad iii), can be formed by local people (ad i) [e.g., 78]. However, complementary evidence is required to justify that initiatives are possible at higher, less homogenous levels. A review of the 'community cohesion' literature reveals that such initiatives do exist (ad ii), but depend on external actors [e.g., 79]. In sum, it tends to be possible that people have the power to take development into their own hands and that they can form initiatives at the suggested level, if they are adequately supported by external actors. 'Organizational options' in regard to this actor, not part of the initial proposal, are subject of an additional synthesis, indicating the 'possible world's' iterative refinement. However, to keep the example simple, this issue is not further pursued here; instead the focus is put on the relationship between the value position and the 'organizational options' of the, now theoretically justified, initiative extracted during the synthesis. One of the extracted 'organizational options' is the, believed to be comprehensive, description of the initiative's development planning process [80]: name the problem, frame the problem to identify options, make deliberative decisions about which options to turn into action, identify and commit resources, and organize complementary action. Seen from the perspective of the value position, the 'deliberative forums' (i.e., communal meetings) suggested as appropriate platforms for decision making are not sufficient, because they confine arguments taken into account to those made by the local population. However, to meet the demands of justice, the identified options have to be scrutinized from' distant perspectives', that is, by an audience beyond the locality, because, local people might, for example, not be aware that an option destroys the living space of endangered wildlife or that it might cause side-effects such as increased traffic in neighboring localities. This suggests that an additional step, in which potential options are made available for inspection to a larger audience, needs to be added. This ensures scrutiny from 'distant perspectives'., Therefore, the technical system, supporting the desirable structure, should include modules, which (i) publish the results of the framing step on the internet and (ii) collect reviews of options for the decision making step.

Granted, a 'real' research project needs to be underpinned by appropriate techniques and will be much more complex, but even the simplified example illustrates that'possible worlds' can be used for the design of technical systems.

5 Conclusions

The main argument put forward in the present paper is that the conventional conceptualization of DSR systematically disadvantages C&E projects. The principal reason is that powerful actors will not support projects endangering their position. The accustomed response of researchers is to detach themselves from given goals and focus on the practical problems and opportunities articulated by the powerful. This neglects the (imperfect) obligation to consciously consider the social consequences of technological interventions. Although such a move might be acceptable in certain circumstances, a discipline completely excluding C&E endeavors is morally questionable. To overcome this limitation the concepts of 'relevance' and 'rigor' were broadened and it was proposed to add the design of 'possible worlds', as a complementary approach, to the disciplinary knowledge base. The core arguments are that identifying and removing existing and, from the perspective of a reasonable value position, unjust circumstances is intrinsically relevant and that a systematically conducted synthesis of evidence from the existing body of knowledge provides an adequate justification; at least as appropriate as an ex post evaluation in a particular context. Both arguments culminated in a procedure that overcomes the inherent tension between C&E research and DSR through the design of possible alternative structures, which can be used for the design of technical systems (i.e., reference architectures), which support or enable these less unjust social systems. As normative safeguards, these artifacts ensure that the design of socio-technical systems is not abused by powerful actors, who might take advantage of the downward adapted expectations of employees.

However, there are still open questions requiring future research. Particular interesting points are the integration of 'possible worlds' and theory development in DSR [see 34] and the 'mutability' of technical systems [81] in response to different development paths or ramifications in the sequence of interventions transforming the 'factual world' to one of multiple 'possible worlds'. Despite such open questions, the method is still a useful approach for IS researchers, who, driven by their moral obligation, want to contribute to social development, but do not have the resources, in particular time, to conduct practical studies lasting for years. Ph.D. students, such as the author, are a prime example. However, it was not intended to suggest that the problems of the world can be solved theoretically; a practical change is needed. Nevertheless, it is morally questionable to make methodological demands that 'nip C&E ideas in the bud'.

References

1. Popper, K.P.: The Spell of Plato. Open Society and Its Enemies, vol. 1. Routledge, London (1967)
2. Lewis, D.K.: On the Plurality of Worlds. Blackwell, Oxford (1986)
3. Robson, C.: Real World Research: A Resource for Social Scientists and Practitioner-Researchers, 2nd edn. Blackwell, Malden (2002)
4. Iivari, J.: A paradigmatic analysis of information systems as a design science. Scand. J. Inf. Syst. **19**, 39–64 (2007)
5. Carlsson, S.A.: Design science in information systems: a critical realist approach. In: Hevner, A.R., Chatterjee, S. (eds.) Design Research in Information Systems. ISIS, vol. 22, pp. 209–233. Springer, New York (2010)

6. Myers, M.D., Klein, H.K.: A set of principles for conducting critical research in information systems. MIS Q. **35**, 17–36 (2011)
7. Iivari, J.: Twelve theses on design science research in information systems. In: Hevner, A.R., Chatterjee, S. (eds.) Design Research in Information Systems. ISIS, vol. 22, pp. 43–62. Springer, New York (2010)
8. Purao, S., Rossi, M., Sein, M.K.: On integrating action research and design research. In: Hevner, A.R., Chatterjee, S. (eds.) Design Research in Information Systems. ISIS, vol. 22, pp. 179–194. Springer, New York (2010)
9. Sein, M., Rossi, M., Purao, S.: Exploring the limits of the possible: a response to iivari. Scand. J. Inf. Syst. **19**, 105–110 (2007)
10. Bostrom, R.P., Heinen, S.J.: MIS problems and failures: a socio-technical perspective. MIS Q. **1**, 17–32 (1977)
11. Carlsson, S.A.: Through IS design science research: for whom, what type of knowledge, and how. Scand. J. Inf. Syst. **19**, 75–86 (2007)
12. Carlsson, S.A., et al.: Socio-technical IS DSR: developing design theory for IS integration management. IseB **9**, 109–131 (2011)
13. Hevner, A.R.: The three-cycle view of design science research. Scand. J. Inf. Syst. **19**, 87–92 (2007)
14. Hevner, A.R., et al.: Design science in ISR. MIS Q. **28**, 75–105 (2004)
15. Venable, J.R.: A framework for design science research activities. In: Khosrow-Pour, M. (ed.) Emerging Trends and Challenges in Information Technology Management, pp. 184–187. Idea Group, Hershey (2006)
16. Gregor, S.: Building theory in the sciences of the artificial. In: Proceedings of the 4th International Conference on Design Science Research in Information Systems and Technology (DESRIST'09), pp. 1–10. ACM Press, New York (2009)
17. Kuechler, B., Vaishnavi, V.: Characterizing design science theories by level of constraint on design decisions. In: Peffers, K., Rothenberger, M., Kuechler, B. (eds.) DESRIST 2012. LNCS, vol. 7286, pp. 345–353. Springer, Heidelberg (2012)
18. Kuechler, W.L., Vaishnavi, V.: A framework for theory development in design science research: multiple perspectives. J. AIS **13**, 395–423 (2012)
19. Nunamaker, J.F., Chen, M., Purdin, T.D.M.: Systems development in information systems research. J. Manage. Inf. Syst. **7**, 89–106 (1991)
20. Peffers, K., et al.: A design science research methodology for information systems research. J. Manage. Inf. Syst. **24**, 45–77 (2008)
21. Baxter, G., Sommerville, I.: Socio-technical systems: from design methods to systems engineering. Interact. Comput. **23**, 4–17 (2011)
22. Bots, P.W.G.: Design in socio-technical system development: three angles in a common framework. J. Des. Res. **5**, 382–396 (2007)
23. Bots, P.W.G., van Daalen, C.E.: Designing socio-technical systems: structures and processes. In: Proceedings of the 3rd International Engineering Systems Symposium: Design and Governance in Engineering Systems, 18–20 June. Delft University, Delft (2012)
24. Fischer, G., Herrmann, T.: Socio-technical systems: a meta-design perspective. Int. J. Sociotechnology Knowl. Dev. **3**, 1–33 (2011)
25. Chmielewicz, K.: Forschungskonzeption der Wirtschaftswissenschaft. Schäffer-Poeschel, Stuttgart (1994)
26. Comstock, D.E.: A method for critical research. In: Bredo, E., Feinberg, W. (eds.) Knowledge and Values in Social and Educational Research, pp. 370–390. Temple University Press, Philadelphia (1982)
27. Sayer, A.: Method in Social Science. Routledge, New York (1992)

28. Mumford, E.: Designing human systems for new technology: the ETHICS method. Wrigth, Sandbach (1983)
29. Mumford, E.: Effective systems design and requirements analysis: the ETHICS approach. MacMillan, Houndmills (1995)
30. Mumford, E.: A socio-technical approach to systems design. Requirements Eng. 5, 125–133 (2000)
31. Mumford, E.: The story of socio-technical design: reflections on its successes, failures, and potential. Inf. Syst. J. 16, 317–342 (2006)
32. Mumford, E., Weir, M.: Computer systems in work design-the ETHICS method: effective technical and human implementation of computer systems. Associated Business Press, London (1979)
33. Sen, A.K.: The ends and means of sustainability. J. Hum. Dev. Capabilities 14, 6–20 (2013)
34. Heusinger, M.J.: Challenges of critical and emancipatory design science research: the design of 'Possible Worlds' as response. In: Hammoudi, S., et al. (eds.) Proceedings of the 15th International Conference on Enterprise Information Systems, 04–07 July, pp. 233–239. Institute for Systems, Technologies of Information, Control, and Communication (INSTICC), Angers (2013)
35. Stahl, B.C., Brooke, C.: The contribution of critical IS research. Commun. ACM 5, 51–55 (2008)
36. Frank, U.: Die Konstruktion möglicher Welten als Chance und Herausforderung der Wirtschaftsinformatik. In: Becker, J., Krcmar, H., Niehaves, B. (eds.) Wissenschaftstheorie und gestaltungsorientierte Wirtschaftsinformatik, pp. 161–173. Physica, Heidelberg (2009)
37. Habermas, J.: Zur Kritik der funktionalistischen Vernunft, vol. 2. Theorie des kommunikativen Handelns. Suhrkamp, Frankfurt am Main, DE (1987)
38. Zelewski, S.: Kann Wissenschaftstheorie behilflich für die Publikationspraxis sein? Eine kritische Auseinandersetzung mit den "Guidelines" von Hevner et al. In: Lehner, F., Zelewski, S. (eds.) Wissenschaftstheoretische Fundierung und wissenschaftliche Orientierung der Wirtschaftsinformatik, Berlin, DE, Gito, pp. 71–120 (2007)
39. Bass, L., Clements, P., Kazman, R.: Software architecture in practice. Addison-Wesley, Boston (2003)
40. Angelov, S., Grefen, P., Greefhorst, D.: A framework for analysis and design of software reference architectures. Inf. Softw. Technol. 54, 417–431 (2012)
41. Albert, H.: Konstruktion und Kritik: Aufsätze zur Philosophie des kritischen Rationalismus. Hoffmann and Campe, Hamburg (1972)
42. Frank, U.: Towards a pluralistic conception of research methods in information systems research. Technical report 7. Essen, DE (2006)
43. Hevner, A.R., Chatterjee, S.: Design research in information systems: theory and practice. ISIS, vol. 22. Springer, New York (2010)
44. Riege, C., Saat, J., Bucher, T.: Systematisierung von Evaluationsmethoden in der gestaltungsorientierten Wirtschaftsinformatik. In: Becker, J., Krcmar, H., Niehaves, B. (eds.) Wissenschaftstheorie und gestaltungsorientierte Wirtschaftsinformatik, pp. 69–86. Physica, Heidelberg (2009)
45. March, S.T., Vogus, T.J.: Design science in the management discipline. In: Hevner, A.R., Chatterjee, S. (eds.) Design Research in Information Systems. ISIS, vol. 22, pp. 195–208. Springer, New York (2010)
46. Frank, U.: Zur methodischen Fundierung der Forschung in der Wirtschaftsinformatik. In: Österle, H., Winter, R., Brenner, W. (eds.) Gestaltungsorientierte Wirtschaftsinformatik, pp. 35–44. Infowerk, Nuremberg (2010)

47. Ladyman, J.: Ontological, epistemological and methodological positions. In: Kuipers, T. (ed.) Handbook of Philosophy of Science: General Philosophy of Science – Focal Issues, pp. 303–376. North Holland, Oxford (2007)
48. Bhaskar, R.: A Realist Theory of Science, 2nd edn. Routledge, Abingdon (2008)
49. Niiniluoto, I.: The aim and structure of applied research. Erkenntnis 38, 1–21 (1993)
50. Bunge, M.: Technology as applied science. Technol. Cult. 7, 329–347 (1966)
51. Habermas, J.: Handlungsrationalität und gesellschaftliche Rationalisierung, vol. 1. Theorie des kommunikativen Handelns. Suhrkamp, Frankfurt am Main, DE (1987)
52. North, D.C.: Institutions, Institutional Change and Economic Performance. Cambridge University Press, Cambridge (1990)
53. Fountain, J.E.: Building the Virtual State: Information Technology and Institutional Change. Brookings Institution Press, Washington, DC (2001)
54. Stahl, B.C.: The ideology of design: a critical appreciation of the design science discourse in information systems and wirtschaftsinformatik. In: Becker, J., Krcmar, H., Niehaves, B. (eds.) Wissenschaftstheorie und gestaltungsorientierte Wirtschaftsinformatik, pp. 111–132. Physica, Heidelberg (2009)
55. Pawson, P.: Evidence-based policy: a realist perspective. Sage, London (2006)
56. Rosemann, M., Vessey, I.: Toward improving the relevance of information systems research to practice: the role of applicability checks. MIS Q. 32, 1–22 (2008)
57. Alvesson, M., Deetz, S.: Doing critical management research. Sage, London (2000)
58. Wynn Jr., D., Williams, C.K.: Principles for conducting critical realist case study research. MIS Q. 36, 787–810 (2012)
59. Hoyningen-Huene, P.: Paul Feyerabend und Thomas Kuhn. J. Gen. Philos. Sci. 33, 61–83 (2002)
60. Sen, A.K.: The Idea of Justice. Harvard University Press, Cambridge (2009)
61. Danermark, B., et al.: Explaining society: critical realism in the social sciences. Routledge, London (2002)
62. Sayer, A.: Realism and Social Science. Sage, London (2000)
63. Bhaskar, R.: Reclaiming Reality: A Critical Introduction to Contemporary Philosophy. Routledge, Abingdon (2011)
64. Walls, G.J., Widmeyer, G.R., El Sawy, O.A.: Building an information system design theory for vigilant EIS. Inf. Syst. Res. 3, 36–59 (1992)
65. Popper, K.P.: Three Worlds. The Tanner Lecture on Human Values. University of Michigan, Ann Arbor (1978)
66. Weick, K.E.: What theory is not, theorizing is. Admin. Sci. Q. 40, 385–390 (1995)
67. Scanlon, T.M.: What We Owe To Each Other. Harvard University Press, Cambridge (1998)
68. Robeyns, I.: Sen's capability approach and feminist concerns. In: Comim, F., Qizilbash, M., Alkire, S. (eds.) The Capability Approach: Concepts, Measures and Applications, pp. 82–104. Cambridge University Press, Cambridge (2008)
69. Sen, A.K.: The idea of justice. J. Hum. Dev. 9, 331–342 (2008)
70. van Aken, J.E.: Valid knowledge for the professional design of large and complex design processes. Des. Stud. 26, 379–404 (2005)
71. Habermas, J.: Theory and Practice. Beacon Press, Boston (1973). (Trans. J. Viertel)
72. Popper, K.P.: The high tide of prophecy: hegel, marx, and the aftermath. Open Society and Its Enemies, vol. 2. Routledge, London (1967)
73. Carlsson, S.A.: The potential of critical realism in IS research. In: Dwivedi, Y.K., Wade, M.R., Schneberger, S.L. (eds.) Information System Theory. ISIS, vol. 29, pp. 283–304. Springer, New York (2012)

74. Dobson, P., Myles, J., Jackson, P.: Making the case for critical realism: examining the implementation of automated performance management systems. Inf. Res. Manage. J. **20**, 138–152 (2007)
75. Heusinger, M.J.: Design of a reference architecture for decision processes in community-driven sustainable human development initiatives. Ph.D. thesis, University of Duisburg-Essen, Essen, DE (forthcoming)
76. Heusinger, M.J.: practical challenges of sustainable human development: community-driven development as response. In: Human Development and Capability Association (HDCA)'s Annual International Conference: 'Human Development: Vulnerability, Inclusion and Wellbeing', 9–12 September 2013. HDCA, Managua (2013)
77. Helling, L., Serrano, R., Warren, D.: Linking Community Empowerment, Decentralized Governance, and Public Service Provision Through a Local Development Framework. World Bank: Social Protection Paper 535. World Bank, Washington, DC (2005)
78. Huang, Q., et al.: Empirical assessment of water management institutions in Northern China. Agric. Water Manag. **98**, 361–369 (2010)
79. Arandel, C., Wetterberg, A.: Between 'Authoritarian' and 'Empowered' slum relocation: social mediation in the case of Ennakhil. Morocco. Cities **30**, 140–148 (2013)
80. Mathews, D.: What kind of democracy informs community development? In: Brennan, M.A., Bridger, J.C., Alter, T.R. (eds.) Theory, Practice, and Community Development, pp. 138–162. Routledge, New York (2013)
81. Gregor, S., Jones, D.: The anatomy of a design theory. J. Assoc. Inf. Syst. **8**, 312–335 (2007)

Software Agents and Internet Computing

Tweeting Politicians: An Analysis of the Usage of a Micro Blogging System

Matthias Roth[1]([✉]), Georg Peters[1,2], and Jan Seruga[2]

[1] Munich University of Applied Sciences, Munich, Germany
mroth@hm.edu
[2] Australian Catholic University, North Sydney, Australia
georg.peters@cs.hm.edu, jan.seruga@acu.edu.au

Abstract. Political communication via social media is getting more and more important. Besides social websites like Facebook and the video platforms like Youtube, microblogging systems have been increasingly used by politicians as communication tools. Since its introduction in 2007, Twitter has become the leading microblogging system. Today it is used by common people and any kind of celebrity whether they are in the show business, in sports or in any other domain. Twitter is also used by politicians to communicate with their voters. Hence, the objective of our paper is to analyze how elected politicians, i. e. members of parliaments, exploit Twitter in three different countries - namely Australia, Germany and the U.S. For our study, we collected data from more than 1,400 politicians of these countries, in particular their almost one million tweets. Our research gives an insight into the usage of Twitter in politics and discloses areas where the usage of Twitter by parliamentarians, differs between Australia, Germany and the U.S.

Keywords: Social media · Micro blogging · Twitter · Political communication

1 Introduction

In the few years, politicians all over the world have recognized social media as a convenient way to reach and interact with colleagues and supporters. Barack Obama's electoral campaign in 2008 is considered the first campaign where Web 2.0 was intensively used by Smith and Wattal et al. [22,25].

Therefore, the research on social media in politics is emerging and has been focusing on the U.S. primarily. According to Rainie et al. [17] more than 55 % of the adult population in the U.S. get their political news and information through the internet already with a growing interest in micro-blogging systems, which was investigated by Golbeck et al. [11].

In particular, Facebook and Twitter have established themselves as the leading social media platforms in recent years. Their usage covers virtually any purpose of communication and social interaction, e.g. in a private environment

© Springer International Publishing Switzerland 2014
S. Hammoudi et al. (Eds.): ICEIS 2013, LNBIP 190, pp. 351–365, 2014.
DOI: 10.1007/978-3-319-09492-2_21

among friends or as marketing platforms for businesses. In politics, Facebook and Twitter have also gained increasing importance as instruments for political communication and interaction with colleagues and voters.

In our study we concentrate on the usage of Twitter by politicians, in particular elected politicians, i.e. members of parliaments. As already mentioned, most of the research so far has been focused on the U.S. Little research has been directed towards the relevance of social media for politics in countries other than the U.S. and possible comparative analyses of the usage of social media in politics in different countries.

Hence, we examine the relevance of Twitter in political communication in three different countries, i.e. Australia, Germany and the U.S. Furthermore, we compare the country-specific findings to analyze the relative penetration of the usage of Twitter in these countries. Our contribution in this paper especially concentrates on two concepts we recommend for measurement and presentation of trending topics and the impact of politicians: *Mentioned Half-Life (MHL)* and the *Followers & Retweets Matrix (F&RM)*.

The remainder of the paper is structured as follows: In section two we briefly introduce Twitter and survey the related work on political science and social media. We also describe the data we use in our study. In Sect. 3 we give insights into the usage of Twitter in politics. In the final section we discuss key findings and give a brief conclusion.

2   Twitter, Related Work and Data Summary

Twitter is a digital real-time application for the distribution of short messages. It is also described as a communication platform for social networking or as a public online log. Private persons, enterprises, mass media and also politicians use the platform for distribution of short messages. On this basis we will describe in this section the Twitter platform in more detail, we provide a section about related work and also we give a data summary about the data set used in this study.

2.1   Twitter

The mentioned figures about the number of accounts on Twitter show that Twitter is a popular microblogging service. Developed in 2006 by Jack Dorsey, Biz Stone, Evan Williams, and Noah Glass, it rose to prominence in 2007. With respect to the structure of it, the Twitter graph is a directed social network and it is still growing. After registration, each user can submit their own status updates, known as tweets, which are shown in real-time on their own page and also on the pages of their followers. Tweets are messages of up to 140 characters and contain different content like personal information about the user, news or links to content such as images, videos or articles. Also frequently used in tweets are hashtags and mentions. Hashtags are words or phrases prefixed with a "#" sign that are used for simplifying the search for specific topics. Similarly, the "@"

sign followed by a Twitter username is used to mention other users or reply to them. Moreover a retweet is a post originally made by a user that is forwarded by another user. Retweets are useful for propagating interesting posts through the Twitter community. Each user furthermore chooses to follow certain users. Then he is called a follower. The accounts that a user is following are called his "friends" or "followees", as described by Barnett [5].

The usage of a social media platform like Twitter for this study offers the possibility to analyse the direct and unmediated content from politicians or the social media team of a politician. This would not be possible through analysis of traditional media such as newspapers and TV channels.

2.2 Related Work

There has been some prior work on social media sites. Amongst others, Bateman et al. [6] described the public nature of social networking sites and the negative influence for the self-disclosure of social media users.

A deeper insight is provided by Light and McGrath [14] who compiled a study about ethics in social networking sites. Their analysis of Facebook, reveals the complex and diffuse nature of ethical responsibility and the consequent implications for governance of social networking sites. To get an impression of how instant messaging (IM) as social media tool enables employees to be empowered, Ou et al. [15] developed a research model. This model together with a survey about the usage of instant messaging tools by Chinese work professionals shows how instant messaging empowers work teams via shaping the social networks and facilitating the sharing of knowledge in the workplace. Ou et al. come to the conviction, that this leads to a heightened team performance.

Shirazi [21] investigates the role of social media communication in the Islamic Middle East and North African (MENA) countries, by applying the critical discourse analysis (CDA). In the study, Shirazi finds that social media also played an important role in citizens' participation because of the authorities failing against protesters. However, Wiredu [26] evaluates with an empirical study the institutional challenges between the efficiency principle and innovations in information systems (IS) and public bureaucracy.

With regard to blogs, Panteli et al. [16] investigated in a case study the virtual presence in travel blogs. In particular, the study highlights the role played by the audience in shaping the blogging experience and the sense of presence this experience develops. Also regarding blogs, Adar and Adamic [2] focused on the tracking information epidemics in Blogspace whereas Adamic and Glance [1] explored the political Blogosphere during the 2004 U.S. election. As a successor of the original blogging, microblogging has now developed and is the basis of extensive research. As the most famous microblogging service, the research focuses particularly on Twitter. In addition to fundamental questions regarding the construction of Twitter and the communication among the participants, science is also exploring some specific areas such as content of posts and political communication. Finally, Jansen et al. [13] analysed the content in terms of branding and opinions, mentioned by consumers and companies. They found that a large percentage of tweets, 19 %, contain brand information. Of those, a sentiment analysis revealed 50 % contained positive feelings and 33 % were critical. Furthermore, Reyes et al. [19] developed an approach for detecting irony in Twitter. The model is designed along two dimensions: representativeness and relevance. The results of this text analysis provide valuable insight into the figurative issues of tasks such as sentiment analysis, assessment of online reputations, and decision making. Also Bosco et al. [7] have worked in this part of research and developed a corpus of opinion and sentiment analysis, with a special attention to irony. They present a case study of sentiment and irony investigation into politics in social media, too. To learn more about social capital, civic engagement and political participation (see also Zuniga et al. [27]).

Furthermore, there is a lot of research that has been done about trends in social media and influence of social media users. Regarding trends in social media Asur et al. [4] carried out an extensive study of trending topics on Twitter and provide a theoretical basis for the formation, persistence and decay of trends. In addition to the trends the authors try to identify the initiating trend setters by distinguishing the tweet publisher into information sources and information propagators. With respect to the influence of bloggers in a community [3] found that active bloggers are not necessarily influential and therefore tried to create a robust model that qualitatively tells how influential a blogger is. Finally, the authors were able to divide the bloggers into three different groups: active and influential, inactive but influential and active but non-influential. Cha et al. [8] went one step further and measured the user influence on Twitter. Cha et al. also found that the indegree of a Twitter user - the number of people who follow a user - is not a strong indicator of his influence. Furthermore Cha et al. divided their results by three types of influence: indegree, retweet and mention influence.

In addition to the already mentioned work about blogging itself and the trends and influence in social networks, there is also research done about the prediction of elections. For example, Chung and Mustafaraj [10] investigate whether expressed collective sentiment on Twitter can predict political elections. They found that simple methods for predicting election results based on sentiment analysis or tweets text do not allow better predictions than traditional methods. Sang and Bos [20] have tried to predict the results of an election in the special case of the 2011 Dutch election. They also have found no reliable approach that allows good election predictions.

2.3 Data Summary

House Systems. Australia, Germany and the U.S. have two house systems, consisting of upper and lower houses. The upper houses basically represent the federal structure while the lower houses represent the country as a whole. The particular names of the houses and the number of seats are depicted in Table 1.

In the course of this paper we will not distinguish in our analysis, between the upper and lower houses but will speak of parliaments and parliament members, parliamentarians or politicians for simplicity reasons.

Table 1. Houses and seats of the parliaments.

	Australia	Germany	U.S.
Lower House	House of Representatives	Bundestag	House of Representatives
Seats	150	620	435
Upper House	Senate	Bundesrat	Senate
Seats	76	69	100

Table 2. Some indicators of the data set.

	Australia	Germany	U.S.
Members	226	689	535
Accounts	109	283	489
Accounts/Members [%]	48	41	91
Tweets	117,121	291,671	482,945
Followers	2,300,000	500,000	32,700,000
Friends	720,929	105,144	1,369,424
Tweets/Active Accounts	1,583	1,736	1,229
Followers/Active Accounts	31,081	2,976	83,206
Friends/Active Accounts	9,742	626	3,485

Demographic Data. About 60 % of the parliamentarians (881/1,450) had a Twitter account with approximately ten million followers. These accounts are maintained by the politicians and/or by their teams. For each account we obtained the following data via Twitter's Application Programming Interface (API) [23]: forename, surname, Twitter account name, number of tweets, number of followers, number of friends, number of mentions, year of joining, gender, age, political party, house affiliation, content and time stamp of all posts.

This database with 891,737 million records (tweets) is the basis for our analysis. Note, that Twitter limits the number of recordable tweets to a maximum of 3,200 per account. So, for very active users with more tweets (about 6.5 %) we could only access the latest 3,200 tweets. Therefore, our database represents approximately 85 % (= 891,737/1,058,692) of all tweets which can be considered as a representative basis for our analysis.

Data Summary. Some important indicators of the Twitter accounts are summarized in Table 2. The table shows that the U.S. parliament has the highest percentage of Twitter penetration with respect to the *accounts/member*, the *activeaccounts/accounts* and derived from this *activeaccounts/members*. Australia has the second highest penetration followed by Germany.

Surprisingly, German politicians are more active tweeters in comparison to their Australian and U.S. counterparts. The U.S. parliamentarians have the highest number of followers, however taking the number of the population into account Australian parliamentarians have relatively more followers. Australian parliamentarians also lead with respect to their Twitter friends.

3   Insights into the Usage of Twitter in Politics

3.1   Year of Joining

Cheng et al. [9] found that the number of new subscribers to Twitter peaked in 2009. Our study confirms that this also applies for politicians (see Fig. 1). In 2009 the percentage of new members is well above 20 % in Australia and Germany and even at approximately 33 % in the U.S. The 2009 election in Germany seemed to have no significant impact on the number of new tweeting German politicians.

Table 3 shows the cumulated numbers of Twitter joining politicians. The penetration of Twitter accounts in the U.S. is by far the highest in comparison to Australia and Germany in each year. It even outpaces Germany by a factor of around two. The penetration in Australia is higher than in Germany, but it also does not have the distribution observed in the U.S.

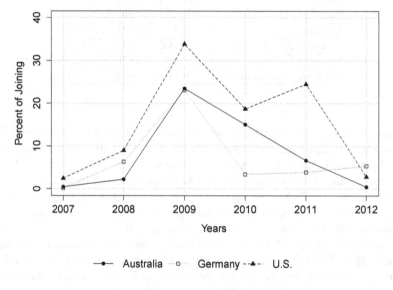

Fig. 1. Year of joining.

Table 3. Number of joining members cumulative per year.

Year	Australia	Germany	U.S.
2007	0.44 %	0.15 %	2,62 %
2008	2.65 %	5.95 %	11.59 %
2009	26.11 %	28.59 %	45.42 %
2010	41.15 %	31.93 %	63.93 %
2011	47.79 %	35.70 %	88.60 %
2012	48.23 %	41.07 %	91.40 %

In the year 2012 91.40 % of the U.S. politicians had Twitter accounts compared to 48.23 % in Australia and 41.07 % in Germany. Such a high percentage of politicians with a Twitter account in the U.S. shows that social media is accepted as a medium for sharing political information in this country. In Australia and Germany, with penetrations of less than 50 %, Twitter plays a rather minor role in comparison to the U.S.

3.2   Trending Topics

Top Three Trending Topics. We define trending topics as words[1] that were most frequently used by the politicians in their tweets. The top three trending topics in 2012 for Australia, Germany and the U.S. are shown in Table 4.

In Australia the most trending topic (see Fig. 2), "Carbon Tax", peaked in July 2012. This is in line with the introduction of the carbon pricing scheme in Australia in the same month. "Health", as trending topic #2, was often used in combination with words like "Denticare", "Medicare" and "Private Health Insurance". The catchphrase "Economy" peaked in May/June, possibly since Moody's reaffirmed Australia's AAA credit rating in May. Its publication as an indicator for a strong domestic economy afterwards was more intensively discussed in Australia.

In the year 2012, in Germany the most trending topic was "Europa" (engl. Europe) followed by "Fiskalpakt" (engl. European Fiscal Compact) and "Griechenland" (engl. Greece) (see Fig. 3). These catchphrases reflect the Euro crisis. The peak of "Europa" in September/October may also have been induced by the award of Nobel Peace Prize to the European Union. The European Fiscal Compact entered into force in June which can explain the peak of this catchphrase in the same month. "Griechenland" peaked in February and in November, the months when the German parliament voted on bail-out packages for Greece.

In the U.S. the most frequently mentioned topic "Jobs" peaked in March 2012, followed by smaller peaks in June and July (see Fig. 4). In these months, the job growth figures were published in the U.S. This explains the increased usage of the catchphrase in these months. The catchphrase "Tax" is frequently used all over the year 2012. However, in September 2012 it peaks as there was an intense discussion on tax plans of the presidential candidates, Barack Obama and Mitt Romney, in the upcoming November election. The topic "Health" (in particular the Patient Protection and Affordable Care Act (PPACA) commonly known as Obamacare) was signed into law already in March 2010. But PPACA contains provisions that became effective after enactment and therefore there was still a regular discussion about this topic in the U.S. parliament in 2012.

Lifetime of Singular Trending Topics. To analyse the lifetime of the trending topics, we introduce the *Mentioned Half-Life (MHL)* metric which is a Thomson Reuters [18] inspired indicator. Thomson Reuters uses the Cited Half-Life indicator to evaluate the impact of journals.

---

[1] Filler words like "is", "the", ... are excluded.

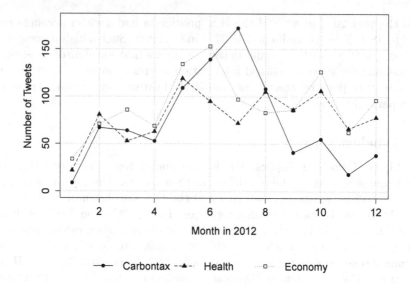

Fig. 2. Australia's trending topics

Table 4. Top trending topics in 2012.

	Top #1	Top #2	Top #3
Australia	Carbon Tax	Health	Economy
Germany	Europa (Europe)	Fiskalpakt (European Fiscal Compact)	Griechenland (Greece)
U.S.	Jobs	Tax	Health

We define the Mentioned Half-Life (MHL) of a topic as the number of days after which 50 % of the lifetime mentions have been posted.

The Mentioned Half-Life implies that we need trending topics that are singular events, at least within a certain time span. Furthermore, they must be globally important events so that we can compare their implications on tweets in Australia, Germany and the U.S. Hence, we identified, for example, Fukushima and the London Olympics as suitable for this MHL analysis.

Fukushima. First, we analyse the earthquake and nuclear disaster in Fukushima, Japan, in 2011 (see Fig. 5). The data reveal that the total number of tweets and the MHL in U.S. is by far bigger than in the other two countries. For Australia and Germany we get similar results but with lower total numbers of tweets about this topic and also lower MHLs.

In particular a comparison of the U.S. and Germany does not support the image of "German Angst" (engl. German fear). Since we would have assumed a higher number of tweets and a longer MHL in Germany in comparison to the U.S. due to "German Angst".

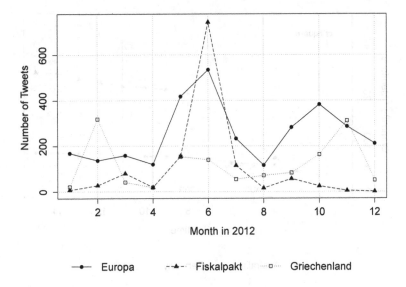

Fig. 3. Germany's trending topics

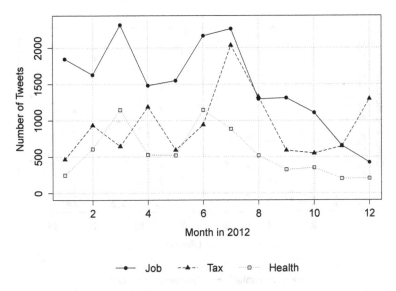

Fig. 4. U.S.' trending topics.

Olympic Games. The London Olympics took place from 27th July to 12th August 2012 with first event on 25th July already. Therefore, we start our observation of the Olympics at the 25th July (see Fig. 6). For the Olympics the MHL in the U.S. is the shortest. Australia comes second with a MHL of eleven days. The topic lasted the longest in Germany. At the first sight this is surprising since Australia is considered to be a "sports nation" par excellence. However, this

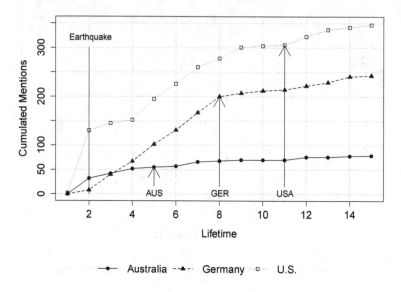

Fig. 5. Daily cumulated mentions of the catchphrase "Fukushima".

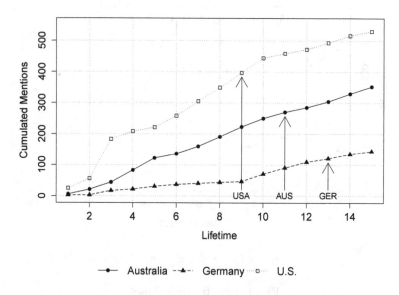

Fig. 6. Daily cumulated mentions of the catchphrase "Olympics".

could be a reason for the low MHL since the Olympics are an important event in these countries but nevertheless not as important as others like American football or even rugby in Australia. Regarding the cumulated numbers of tweets on the Olympics, the U.S. leads followed by Australia and Germany.

Communicative Adaptors	Innovators
post popular content and are therefore frequently retweeted. But on the other hand they are not favoured because they have few followers.	have the highest influence in relation to the number of followers and retweets. They can be regarded as the pioneers of the Twitter trend in politics.
Laggards	**Favored Adaptors**
have a Twitter account, but they cannot take advantage of the trend as yet. They should intensify their activities on Twitter to gain a more influential position in the political network of their parliament.	have already a lot of followers, but their tweets are rarely retweeted. Either they tweet too rare, or their tweets are not interesting.

Retweets (left axis)

Followers

Fig. 7. Followers and retweets matrix.

3.3   Impact of Politicians

Influence. Barack Obama is the most followed politician worldwide on Twitter [24, as of September 2013] and fourth most followed Twitter user overall (Justin Bieber is the leader in this statistic, followed by Katy Perry and Lady Gaga).

In order to show the influence of politicians in their parliaments we adapt the fundamental idea of the quadrants of the Boston Consulting Matrix from Henderson [12] to Twitter's followers and retweets. The *Followers & Retweets Matrix (F&RM)* is depicted in Fig. 7. The results for the five top politicians within the context of the F&RM of each country are shown in Fig. 8. The size of the circles are related to the number of times a politician is mentioned in his parliament.

Note, that due to the dominating position of Barack Obama two Followers & Retweets Matrices are shown for the U.S., one with Obama and one without.

In Australia, Prime Minister Julia Gillard is the most influential politician and the only one whom we consider as an "innovator" in our Followers & Retweets Matrix. Ursula Stephens has a similar number of retweets but not so many followers. So, she is in the top left quadrant and regarded as a "communicative adaptor". In the bottom left quadrant three politicians, Adam Bandt, Joe Hockey and Kate Lundy appear as "laggards".

Like in Australia, in Germany, we only have one "innovator", Sigmar Gabriel, the leader of the opposition party SPD (engl. Social Democratic Party of Germany). Only Peter Altmaier, the Federal Minister for the Environment, Nature Conservation and Nuclear Safety, has more followers among German politicians. Brigitte Zypries and Johannes Vogel are in the top left quadrant and therefore "communicative adaptors". Finally, Uwe Schummer has a similar number of followers but less retweets than the "communicative adaptors". Therefore, he is classified as a "laggard".

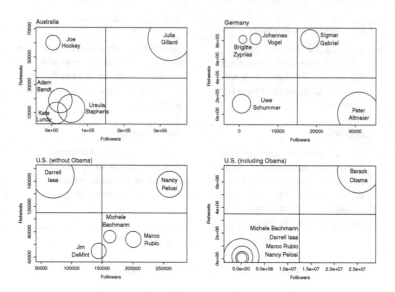

Fig. 8. Influence of politicians.

For the U.S. let us first consider the Followers & Retweets Matrix without Obama (the bottom left sub-figure of Fig. 8). We observe Nancy Pelos as the only "innovator". Darrell Issa has less followers but more retweets and mentions; hence he is a "communicative adaptor". Michele Bachmann and Marco Rubio are "favored adapters", while Jim DeMint is a "laggard" at the borderline to the quadrant of "favored adapters".

The bottom right sub-figure of Fig. 8 shows the top five politicians when Barack Obama is included. This sub-figure confirms Obama's unique position in the American political system. He is an "innovator" with all other politicians of the U.S. parliament becoming (relative) "laggards" in his presence.

4   Discussion and Conclusions

Although we analysed the usage of the microblogging system Twitter in three countries, we discuss four categories: Australia, Germany, the U.S. and Barack Obama.

Barack Obama has such an outstanding position not only in his role as president of the U.S., but also as the leading trendsetter in the use of social media in politics beginning with his, revolutionary 2008 election campaign. Our data shows that he has kept this leading position up to today relatively and absolutely.

– Relative. He is by far the most followed politician in the U.S. with the highest number of retweets world-wide. Of course, this is due to his exposed position as president of the U.S. but also due to his professional and goal-oriented usage of Twitter.

– Absolute. Obama is on the world-ranking of Twitter at position #4. He even improved his rank by one position in the past year. This impressively shows that Twitter is not only a medium for celebrities like Justin Bieber or Lady Gaga but is also deeply integrated into politics.

The year 2009 can be regarded as the year when Twitter had its break-through in politics. However, the penetration of Twitter in Australia and Germany is lagging behind the U.S. Surprisingly, these two countries, show similar characteristics in the usage of Twitter since we would have regarded Australia as culturally closer to the U.S. than to Germany. We would only like to stress two distinct differences in the Twitter usage between Australia and Germany.

– Firstly, in Australia the front benchers seem to use Twitter more actively than in Germany. Even the German chancellor Angela Merkel, is not actively using Twitter.
– Secondly, Australian politicians are far ahead in terms of reaching people by Twitter when compared with German politicians and even U.S. politicians.

However, both, Australia and Germany, have national elections in September 2013. It will be interesting to analyse if the elections will further catalyze the usage of Twitter in these countries.

We also showed that Twitter can be an indicator for hot political topics in a country. While the "carbon tax" has dominated in Australia, the European debt crisis has been the main topic in Germany and classical topics like jobs and tax in the U.S. enriched by an intense discussion on reform of the public health insurance scheme ("Obamacare").

In the long run, it will be interesting to see if and how Twitter and other social media like Facebook establish themselves as platforms for political communication. The past decade has shown that technologies and companies that are considered to be dominant, sometimes decline just after a few years and are replaced by emerging technologies and newly founded companies.

Our study focusses on the impact and usage of Twitter in an international analysis. It excludes any analysis of implications of Twitter on competing and complementary media. Therefore, we believe that the relationship of Twitter and other communication platforms (newspapers, television etc.) in Australia, Germany and the U.S., would be a more insightful field of research which we plan to address in a future project.

References

1. Adamic, L. A., Glance, N.: The political Blogosphere and the 2004 U.S. election: divided they blog. In: Proceedings of the 3rd International Workshop on Link Discovery, LinkKDD '05, pp. 36–43. ACM, New York (2005)
2. Adar, E., Adamic, L.A.: Tracking information epidemics in blogspace. In: Proceedings of the 2005 IEEE/WIC/ACM International Conference on Web Intelligence, WI '05, pp. 207–214. IEEE Computer Society, Washington, DC, (2005)

3. Agarwal, N., Liu, H., Tang, L., Yu, P.S.: Identifying the influential bloggers in a community. In: Proceedings of the 2008 International Conference on Web Search and Data Mining, WSDM '08, pp. 207–218. ACM, New York (2008)

4. Asur, S., Huberman, B.A., Syabo, G., Wang, C.: Trends in social media: persistence and decay. In: 5th International AAAI Conference on Weblogs and Social Media (2011)

5. Barnett, G.A.: Encyclopedia of Social Networks. SAGE Publications Inc., Thousand Oaks (2011)

6. Bateman, P.J., Pike, J.C., Butler, B.S.: To disclose or not: publicness in social networking sites. Inf. Technol. People **24**(1), 78–100 (2011)

7. Bosco, C., Patti, V., Bolioli, A.: Developing corpora for sentiment analysis and opinion mining: the case of irony and senti-tut. IEEE Intelligent Systems 99(PrePrints), 1 (2013).

8. Cha, M., Haddadi, M., Benevenuto, F., Gummadi, K.P.: Measuring user influence in Twitter: The million follower fallacy. In: Proceedings of the Second International Conference on Social informatics, SocInfo'10, pp. 216–231. Springer, Heidelberg (2010)

9. Cheng, A., Evans, M., Singh, H.: Inside Twitter: An in-depth look inside the Twitter world, June 2009. http://www.sysomos.com/insidetwitter/. Accessed 03 Aug 2013

10. Chung, J.E., Mustafaraj, E.: Can collective sentiment expressed on twitter predict political elections? In: Burgard, W., Roth, D. (eds.) AAAI. AAAI Press (2011)

11. Golbeck, J., Grimes, J.M., Rogers, A.: Twitter use by the U.S. congress. J. Am. Soc. Inf. Sci. Technol. **61**(8), 1612–1621 (2010)

12. Henderson, B.: The product portfolio. In: BCG Perspectives, vol. 66. Boston Consulting Group (1970)

13. Jansen, B.J., Zhang, M., Sobel, K., Chowdury, A.: Twitter power: tweets as electronic word of mouth. J. Am. Soc. Inf. Sci. Technol. **60**(11), 2169–2188 (2009)

14. Light, B., McGrath, K.: Ethics and social networking sites: a disclosive analysis of Facebook. Inf. Technol. People **23**(4), 290–311 (2010)

15. Ou, C.X., Davison, R.M., Zhong, X., Liang, Y.: Empowering employees through instant messaging. Inf. Technol. People **23**(2), 193–211 (2010)

16. Panteli, N., Yan, L., Chamakiotis, P.: Writing to the unknown: bloggers and the presence of backpackers. Inf. Technol. People **24**(4), 362–377 (2011)

17. Rainie, L., Smith, A., Lehman-Schlozman, K., Brady, H., Verba, S.: Social media and political engagement, October 2012, http://pewinternet.org/Reports/2012/Political-engagement.aspx. Accessed 22 Aug 2013

18. Reuters, T.: Journal Citation Reports - Quick Reference Card, January 2012. http://ip-science.thomsonreuters.com/m/pdfs/mgr/jcr-qrg.pdf. Accessed 17 Jun 2013

19. Reyes, A., Rosso, P., Veale, T.: A multidimensional approach for detecting irony in twitter. Lang. Resour. Eval. **47**(1), 239–268 (2013)

20. Sang, E.T.K., Bos, J.: Predicting the 2011 dutch senate election results with twitter. In: Proceedings of the Workshop on Semantic Analysis in Social Media, pp. 53–60. Association for Computational Linguistics, Stroudsburg (2012)

21. Shirazi, F.: Social media and the social movements in the Middle East and North Africa: a critical discource analysis. Inf. Technol. People **26**(1), 28–49 (2013)

22. Smith, K. N.: Social Media and Political Campaigns. Honors thesis projects, University of Tennessee (2011). http://trace.tennessee.edu/utk_chanhonoproj/1470. Accessed 15 Aug 2013

23. Twitter: Twitter API Documentation, January 2012. https://dev.twitter.com/. Accessed 10 Sept 2013
24. Twitter: The top 100 most followed on Twitter (2013). http://twittercounter.com/pages/100. Accessed 09 Sept 2013
25. Wattal, S., Schuff, D., Mandviwalla, M., Williams, C.B.: Web 2.0 and politics: the 2008 US presidential election and an e-politics research agenda. MIS Q. **34**(4), 669–688 (2010)
26. Wiredu, G.O.: Information systems innovation in public organisations: an institutional perspective. Inf. Technol. People **25**(2), 188–206 (2012)
27. Gil de Zuniga, H., Jung, N., Valenzuela, S.: Social media use for news and individuals' social capital, civic engagement and political participation. J. Comput.-Mediated Commun. **17**(3), 319–336 (2012)

Cloud-Based Collaborative Business Services Provision

Luis M. Camarinha-Matos[1(✉)], Hamideh Afsarmanesh[2],
Ana Inês Oliveira[1], and Filipa Ferrada[1]

[1] UNINOVA, FCT, Universidade Nova de Lisboa, Campus de Caparica,
2829-516 Monte Caparica, Portugal
cam@uninova.pt
[2] Informatics Institute, University of Amsterdam, Science Park 904,
1098 XH Amsterdam, The Netherlands
h.afsarmanesh@uva.nl

Abstract. The notion of service-enhanced product, representing the association of services to manufactured products, offers an important mechanism for value creation and product differentiation. This is particularly relevant in the case of complex, highly customized and long-life products. Provision of suitable services in this context typically requires collaboration among multiple stakeholders. Furthermore, the involvement of the customer is not limited to service consumption but rather includes contributions to new services design and configuration. In response to these requirements, this paper contributes to the clarification of concepts and definition of a framework for collaborative business services design (co-creation) and delivery. At the base of the framework, a cloud-based collaboration platform supports the establishment and operation of the involved enterprise networks. Application examples are given for the solar energy sector.

Keywords: Collaborative networks · Business services · Service-enhanced products · Service Co-creation

1 Introduction

The principles of collaboration and co-innovation applied to business services open new perspectives of value creation in manufacturing. The notion of service-enhanced product (also known as product-service) and the associated idea of service-enhanced manufacturing represent a growing trend, particularly in the context of complex products. The motivation is that buyers of manufactured products increasingly want more than the physical product itself; they might want finance options to buy it, insurance to protect it, expertise to install it, support to maintain it fully operational during its life cycle, advice on how to maximize returns from it, expertise to manage it, etc. [1]. Thus, a product-service can be thought of as a market proposition that extends the traditional functionality of a product by incorporating additional business services, especially in global markets.

© Springer International Publishing Switzerland 2014
S. Hammoudi et al. (Eds.): ICEIS 2013, LNBIP 190, pp. 366–384, 2014.
DOI: 10.1007/978-3-319-09492-2_22

Service-enhancement of products is closely related to product differentiation. In many industries it is difficult to differentiate manufactured products and thus the profit margins tend to narrow [2]. By associating services that add value to the products, greater forms of differentiation can be achieved and new business opportunities generated. For instance, in the case of the solar energy plants, which have a long life-cycle, typically above 20 years, there are interesting opportunities to introduce new services and particularly new forms of service delivery through collaboration. But similar motivation can be found in many other sectors.

This idea of product "servitization" comes naturally in line with the growing importance of the service sector in our economy. The service sector has been traditionally defined as whatever is not agriculture or manufacturing. During the last century there has been a large shift of jobs, first from agriculture to manufacture, and in the last decades from manufacturing to services. The most advanced economies are dominated by the services sector, which accounts to more than 70 % of the GDP [3]. This is clearly the reality in the case of the USA and most European countries. But this trend can also be observed in countries that have been traditionally more oriented to manufacturing, such as the case of China which is experiencing a rapid growth of the service sector.

Current discussions around the ongoing economic crisis might lead to some level of refocusing on manufacturing and even agriculture, as reflected in some calls for re-industrialization of Europe. Nevertheless, this term is a subject of some controversy, as it might be mistaken by going back to old industrial models, which is not the intended meaning. Certainly one should draw lessons from the economic downturn and appreciate it as an opportunity for the emergence of new business models towards sustainable value creation. Therefore, the discussion should not be manufacturing vs. service provision, but rather taking advantage of both - combining services with manufactured products (including agribusiness products) to enhance and add value to those products.

One of the characteristics of our economy today is that enterprises increasingly need to compete while also collaborate in a global market, using the Internet and other technical means to overcome the traditional barrier of geographical distribution. This perspective also calls for collaboration and **involvement of customers and local suppliers** in target markets. In fact, the notion of *glocal enterprise* represents the idea of thinking and acting globally, while being aware and responding adequately to local specificities. Internet and cloud computing not only facilitate the development of new collaborative processes, but also allow for new ways of (remotely) delivering services associated to products. Another characteristic is the continuous and rapid change and innovation, which may be internal or external to individual enterprises (open innovation and **co-innovation**), but anyway affecting how these enterprises can perform in relation to other enterprises and their market environment [4]. The success of an enterprise, therefore, more and more depends on its ability to seamlessly interoperate with other agile enterprises, and being able to adapt to actual or imminent changes and adjust to local specificities, next to other core competence in making some product or providing a service in the most efficient and sustainable way.

In terms of research on services and service-orientation, earlier periods were characterized by intense but separate activity in different communities, such as the *wave* of works on services marketing in the 1970s and 1980s, promoted by the business schools, or the more recent overwhelming developments in the ICT sector around the web services technologies. Nowadays there is a growing consensus on the need to adopt a multi-disciplinary perspective, as advocated by the efforts to establish *services science* as a new scientific field [5].

In this context, this paper, which is an extended and refined version of a work presented at ICEIS 2013 [6], aims at contributing to the clarification of the main concepts associated to service-enhanced products and their technological support, with particular emphasis on composite services which are collaboratively provided by various stakeholders.

2 Research Context

This work was developed in the context of GloNet, which is a European collaborative project, funded under the ICT-Factories of the Future program. It aims at designing, developing, and deploying an agile virtual enterprise environment for networks of small and medium enterprises (SMEs) involved in highly customized and service-enhanced products through end-to-end collaboration with customers and local suppliers (co-creation) [7]. The notion of *glocal* enterprise is adopted in GloNet for value creation from global networked operations and involving global supply chain management, product-service linkage, and management of distributed production units.

Further to service-based product enhancement, GloNet also considers the growing trend in manufacturing to move towards highly customized products, ultimately one-of-a-kind, which is reflected in the term *mass customization*. In fact, mass customization refers to a customer co-design process of products and services which meet the needs/choices of each individual customer with regard to the variety of different product features. Important challenges in such manufacturing contexts can be elicited from the requirements of complex technical infrastructures, solar energy parks, intelligent buildings, etc.

The main guiding use case in GloNet is the life cycle support of photovoltaic **solar energy parks**. The norm of operation in this industry is that of one-of-a-kind production. The involved systems and services are typically delivered through complementary competences shared between different project participants. A particularly important challenge here is the design and delivery of multi-stakeholder complex services along the product life cycle, which typically spans over 20 years.

Focused issues in this context include: (i) Information/knowledge representation (product catalogue, processes descriptions, best practices, company profiles, brochures, etc.); (ii) User-customized interfaces, dynamically adjusted to assist different stakeholders (smart enterprise approach); (iii) Services provision through cloud; (iv) Broker-customer interaction support: from order to (product/service) design (open innovation approach); (v) Negotiation support; (vi) Workflow for negotiated order solution and its monitoring; and (vii) Risks management support.

In addition to the mentioned use case, and in order to achieve further generalization and thus increase the application potential of the proposed solutions, GloNet requirements are also checked against the needs of other relevant use cases with similar abstract characteristics. As such, and taking into account the competencies and interests of the industrial partners in the consortium, the following additional use cases are analyzed: Intelligent buildings use case; and physical incubator facilities use case.

The project started in Sep 2011 with a planned duration of 3 years, and involves the following partners: CAS (Germany), UNINOVA (Portugal), University of Amsterdam (Netherlands), iPLON (Germany), SKILL (Spain), Steinbeis (Germany), KOMIX (Czech Republic), and PROLON (Denmark).

3   Business Services

Recent efforts, as represented by the Services Science *movement* [2, 5, 8, 9] attempted to formalize the concept of service, but some ambiguity still remains. Two main literature streams - management and computer science - among others, have proposed a number of definitions that often represent a partial perspective of the concept. The ICT developments tend to consider services as some form of "black boxes" that perform some action, being more focused on data, control flow, and interoperability aspects. Other streams look at services from a business perspective, tending to see a service in terms of the added value that is delivered to a customer and the conditions of delivery. Under this perspective, issues such as quality of service (QoS), service level agreement (SLA), terms and conditions, period of availability, interactions with customer, etc., become the focus of attention.

A few recent works have tried to bridge the gap between these two notions of service [10, 11]. Similarly, an ongoing initiative to establish a *Unified Service Description Language* (USDL) [12] makes an attempt to merge various perspectives of service. Although clearly in line with the *"ICT school"*, namely regarding the developments in Service-Oriented Architectures, Web Services and Semantic Web Services, USDL tries to also embed aspects of business services, service networks, and service provision systems.

In our opinion, it makes sense to separate two concepts - *business service* and *software* or *technical service*. Although they can be interrelated, as discussed below, they basically correspond to different views or perspectives that need to be clarified. In GloNet we are particularly interested in business services that add value to the physical product, i.e. that add value to the power plant during its operation (along its 20-year life cycle). Table 1 illustrates typical business services in the operation and maintenance of solar power plants.

Because a business service typically involves some flows of activities and inter-actions with the customer, often the terms 'business service' and 'business process' appear (confusingly) intermixed, although they correspond to different concepts.

What is a **business service**? An earlier definition by Ted Hill [13] states: *"A (business) service is a change in the condition of a person, or a good belonging to some economic entity, brought about as the result of the activity of some other economic entity, with the approval of the first person or economic entity"*. Also according to Hill, (business) services and goods (or physical products) are of different onto-logical categories: while goods are both *transactable* and *transferable*, services are transactable, but not transferable. A number of characteristics can be further identified to distinguish between (business) services and (physical) products [5, 14, 15]:

– Services are intangible;
– Services are interactive, with a high level of customer interaction during the process of service production, delivery and consumption;
– Simultaneity of production (execution) and consumption;

Table 1. Examples of business services in the Photovoltaic Plants Operations and Maintenance.

Service Category	Business Service	Brief description	Typical frequency	Form of provision
Operation monitoring *Collecting and processing real-time data on the plant, combined with control operation*	*Energy monitoring services*	*Allowing to know the energy production in real time, to compare it with expectations, find any issues with equipment, and predict the power generated with increased certainty.*	Continuous	Mostly automated
	Monitoring reports	*Set of relevant reports required for different stakeholders (owner, utility company, insurance company, financial institution, etc.)*	Monthly	Mostly automated
	System performance testing	*To understand plant performance, what drives it, and provide performance testing, benchmarks, power quality analysis, etc.*		Mostly automated
	Site security services	*To detect and to some extent prevent intruders and potential vandalism actions.*	Continuous	Automated and/or manual
	Data analytics services	*To analyse historic data (through data mining) and find methods for enhanced diagnostics, troubleshooting and operation.*	As needed	Mostly automated
Preventive Maintenance *Routine inspection and servicing of equipment and plant site to prevent breakdowns and production losses*	*Panel Cleaning*	*It affects panel's performance. However it highly depends on site conditions – amount of dust, pollen and pollution, frequency of rain and snow, etc.*	1-2 x Times / Year	Mostly manual, with some automatic checks
	Vegetation Management	*Less critical than panel cleaning, it involves cutting grass, bushes, etc., as they might also affect the operation of the equipment, depending on local conditions such as the amount of rain.*	1-3 Times/Year	Mostly manual, with some automatic checks
	Wildlife Prevention	*The development of colonies of wildlife (rats, rabbits, bird nests, etc.) might destroy some equipment.*	Variable	Mostly manual
	Water Drainage	*To ensure proper drainage of water that results from raining or snow melting.*	Variable	Mostly manual
	Retro-Commissioning	*A process for identifying less-than-optimal performance in the facility's equipment, and control systems and making the necessary adjustments (replace outdated equipment, or improve efficiency).*	1 Time / Year	Mostly manual, with some automatic checks
	Upkeep of Data Acquisition and Monitoring Systems	*Maintenance of the sensor network / data collection and communication subsystem.*	Undetermined	Mostly manual, with some automatic checks
	Upkeep of Power Generation System	*Periodic maintenance and provision of proofs of any measures taken, not only to ensure proper operation, but also to comply with regulations and requirements from the utility company. It involves e.g., Inverter Servicing, BOS Inspection, Tracker Maintenance.*	1-2 x Times / Year	Mostly manual, with some automatic checks

(continued)

Table 1. *(Continued)*

Service Category	Business Service	Brief description	Typical frequency	Form of provision
Corrective / Reactive Maintenance *In response to equipment breakdown to mitigate unplanned downtime*	*On-Site Monitoring / Mitigation*	*Implementation of on-site mitigation measures in response to detected weaknesses (e.g. regarding safety and security standards, unforeseen working conditions)*	Variable	Mostly manual, combined with automatic tests
	Critical Reactive Repair	*When a fault / equipment breakdown is detected in a critical component (e.g. inverter, AC subsystems).*	As Needed (High Priority)	Mostly manual, combined with automatic tests
	Non-Critical Reactive Repair	*When a fault / equipment breakdown is detected in a no-critical component (e.g. weather related sensor).*	As Needed	Mostly manual, combined with automatic tests
	Warranty Enforcement	*Since different components have different warranty coverage conditions, with different penalties associated to the levels of criticality, it is important to properly manage them in association to breakdowns.*	As Needed	Mix automatic - manual
Condition-Based Maintenance *Prioritize and optimize maintenance and resources based on real-time data for increased efficiency*	*Active Monitoring - Remote and On-Site*	*Allowing to shift the maintenance process from 'preventive' to 'predictive' model. It involves continuous monitoring and diagnosis of the equipment health / condition, to ensure zero downtime.*	Continuous	Mostly automatic, with option. manual
	Warranty Enforcement	*Management of warranty contracts enforcement based on collected real-time data.*	As Needed	Mostly automatic, with option. manual
	Equipment Replacement	*Different equipment and components have different life-cycles, requiring replacement along the (long) life cycle of the PV plant.*	As Needed	Mostly manual, with some automatic checks
Other Support *Additional services*	*Training services*	*Average industrial technicians are familiar with AC, but often less acquainted with DC power and other specificities of PV plants. Also personnel involved in other services, e.g. panel cleaning, vegetation management, need to be trained on safety protocols.*	As needed	In classroom or remotely via e-learning
	Energy audit services	*Establish pattern of energy use and production; identify losses; and suggest appropriate economically viable engineering solutions to enhance energy efficiency.*	As needed	Mix automatic - manual

Services are bound to a particular time (when they are available and delivered) and place (where they are delivered).

It is important to distinguish between the notions of service providing, service availability and service delivery. Service providing is about the introduction of a service by its provider within the community of its potential customers. This happens for instance through advertising a service in the market, or in the case of the GloNet environment, through the introduction/registration of the service within the collaborative enterprise network. About the difference between service availability and delivery, consider that a customer may keep paying for a corrective maintenance service (thus guaranteeing the availability of the service), while the service might never be delivered if no malfunctioning is ever detected.

Another definition of business service [10] puts the focus on the notions of availability and delivery of the service: "*A (business) service is present at a time T and location L iff, at time T, an agent is explicitly committed to guarantee the execution of some type of action at location L, on the occurrence of a certain triggering event, in the interest of another agent and upon prior agreement, in a certain way*". This definition brings about a number of interesting aspects:

- The notion of *commitment* through which an entity guarantees the execution of some kind of action(s) in the interest of the customer. This notion comes in line with another definition by O'Sullivan [16]: "*A service instance is essentially a promise by one party (the provider) to perform a function on behalf of another party at some time and place and through some channel*".
- *Commitment* and *availability* are different notions. For instance, in the case of malfunctioning periods (of the service provision system) or working pauses, the commitment still holds but the service is not available (temporarily). Specific constraints regarding availability can be defined in the *agreement* (service level agreement) or contract.
- The commitment by an agent to guarantee a service does not necessarily imply that the service is performed by this agent; it can be delegated on other entities, although the responsibility toward the customer remains with the agent that made the "promise".
- Service delivery implies a delivery *location* where the actions take place or the added value is provided. In the case of the solar plants, the effects of several services take place at the actual location of the power plant, although they might be performed remotely (through an ICT channel).
- The actual delivery of the service, i.e. the execution of the associated action(s), is initiated by a *triggering event*. For instance, in the case of a reactive maintenance service, the triggering event can be the detection of a malfunctioning alarm. In the case of a preventive maintenance service, the triggering event can be the scheduled time for the periodic maintenance.

The expression "*execution of some type of action … in a certain way*", which appears in the definition above, implies a *process*. When the service is quite *standardized*, its execution may well be represented by a **business process**. In some cases, the service might be performed through alternative business processes, depending on the triggering event (Fig. 1).

In this sense, we can see the notion of business service as an abstract construct that basically encapsulates the external or customer's view. This "construct" specifies what (value) and under what conditions it would be delivered.

Internal to some "service performance system" we can see the service as materialized by some business sub-processes. In other words, the business (sub)processes (and associated triggering events) represent how the service is performed (its interaction behavioral part).

In the case of less structured services in which the actual set of actions to be performed and their flow strongly depend on the interactions with the customer (during service delivery), it might be difficult to model the interaction behavior of the service through well-defined processes in advance, and thus the processes are

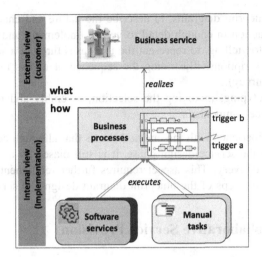

Fig. 1. Views of business service.

dynamically configured "on the fly" during the execution. In this case it is probably more adequate to specify the interaction behavior in terms of a *set of rules*.

The performance of the actions involved in the business service delivery can be done automatically or manually. Automatic solutions can be materialized through the invocation of some *software services*. Manual tasks are human-executed activities ("human tasks").

Service delivery can be subject to a number of *conditions* agreed between the provider and the customer which are typically formalized in a *contract*/agreement and govern the responsibilities of all involved parties.

Since a provider might offer more than one service, it might be convenient to introduce the concept of **service entity** – an *encapsulation* of the various services provided by the same entity; in other words, a representation of a service provider [11, 17].

Service Design. In traditional manufacturing, design has been mainly concerned with the physical product itself, not with services. Given the growing importance of the service sector, a new stream of research emerged mainly in the last decade to provide effective approaches and tools for service design [18]. Given the strong interactions between customer and service providers, service design focuses primarily on: (i) identifying user interactions or "touchpoints"; (ii) designing interfaces and methods to capture the perceived customer experiences; and (iii) service provision management. Typical steps in service design include:

i. Identification of needed business services, through a brainstorming exercise, often based on an analysis of business scenarios.
ii. Design of touchpoints diagram, to identify points of interaction of the customer with the service.

  iii. Design of blueprint diagrams, to describe the nature and characteristics of the service interaction in enough detail to verify, implement, and maintain it.

  iv. Storyboard/storytelling, to represent the use cases through a series of drawings or textual descriptions, illustrating the sequence of events in service delivery (customer journey).

  v. Service prototyping, involving the selection, assembly and integration of the various service components.

Our preliminary experience with this method shows that although coping with multi-stakeholder during the service design phase, it is still biased by a "single provider" model for service delivery. This aspect requires further refinements of the method, namely regarding the steps of the blueprint diagram design and service prototyping.

4 Towards Collaborative Service Provision

Business services can be combined together. A **composite business service** is a collection of related and (to some extent) integrated business services that provide a specific business solution. A lesser definition may consider it as a grouping of related, simpler business services.

Figure 2 illustrates one example of a composite business service. In the case of the solar power plants, a customer might be interested in an integrated *site maintenance service* which is, in fact, a grouping or composition of various simpler services - site security service, wildlife prevention service, vegetation management service, and water drainage service.

The various simpler services that compose an integrated service might be provided by different companies, as also illustrated in Fig. 2. Besides the stakeholders directly involved in the provision of the simpler services, this example also shows the role of a new stakeholder - the *service integrator* - that coordinates the other ones and possibly offers a unique contact point to the customer. The customer would typically establish a single contract with the service integrator and not separate contracts with the other providers.

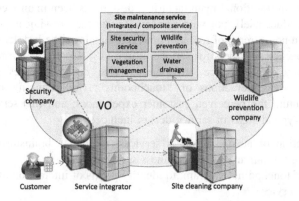

Fig. 2. Example of composite, multi-stakeholder service.

This group of entities together forms a *virtual organization* (VO) [19] for the provision of this composite service, where the service integrator plays the role of virtual organization coordinator. This organizational structure and the role of business service integrator open new business opportunities for SMEs.

In the case of solar energy sector, although a few large companies are able to offer a large number of the services shown in Table 1 [20], most SMEs active in this domain are focused on the provision of just a small subset. This situation limits their capabilities, namely their participation in other geographical markets. Also from the customer perspective, the resulting fragmentation of services is not a desirable situation. A single contract/single interface for a package of services would be preferable.

However, it is important to avoid typical problems with extensive *sub-contracting/ outsourcing* practices. In many contexts, some large corporations have extensively outsourced the provision of their services. However, there is no real collaboration among the involved sub-contracted entities, and whenever there is a need that spans across two or more service areas the lack of seamless integration becomes obvious. The customer then clearly notices the "walls" between providers and a situation where there is no clear responsibility assignment, with each one transferring the responsibilities to the others. Furthermore, the lack of proper support platforms often leads to problems of synchronization among the various providers, which again reflects in a bad quality of the service provided to the customer.

To avoid the risk of such situations, rather than a sub-contracting model, it is necessary to implement a real collaborative network, supported by an environment such as the one envisaged in GloNet. Further to the need of mere workflow coordination, typically performed by the service integrator, it is necessary to have a collaboration space where the various entities can share information and resources, and thus contributing to the building of a sense of co-responsibility. Complementarily, proper involvement of local suppliers, close to the customer location, can increase the sense of proximity.

Often the customer is a *co-creator* of its needed services, closely involved in defining, shaping, and packaging the service. It is important to notice that in the case of products with a long life cycle, these interactions are built around long-term relationships.

Furthermore, although ICT facilitates remote delivery of some services or service components, other parts require local intervention. For instance, in the case of the solar energy plants, a service like "Energy production monitoring" can be delivered remotely. Through a network of sensors and data loggers installed in the plant and some communication channels, it is possible to collect real-time data over Internet (a kind of Internet of Things). However, a service like "Water drainage" will require local (manual) intervention. Other services might combine remote and local operation. For instance, a "Panel cleaning" service might involve some remote actions (e.g. detection of a production performance level lower than expected), a local (manual) activity (the actual cleaning) and possibly another remote action to verify the end result.

In order to give the customer a feeling of *proximity*, and thus a better service *experience*, it is important to involve local suppliers in some components of the service delivery. The services science community uses the term *service experience* "*to encompass all aspects of the production, delivery, and creation of value from the customer's perspective"* [3]. To address the issues above and improve collaboration and proximity, GloNet contributes with a number of elements:

- Mix of collaborative networks. GloNet assumes two base *communities* out of which members will be selected to compose the VO in charge of the service provisioning: The long-term manufacturers' network and the informal community of local stakeholders around the customer (Fig. 3). The service integrator will typically be selected from the manufacturers' network.

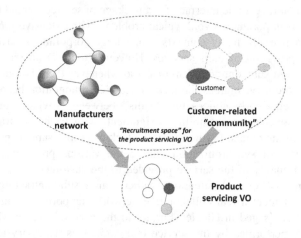

Fig. 3. Recruitment of members for product servicing VO.

- Co-creation business scenario. One of the relevant business scenarios identified in GloNet is aimed at providing an environment that supports and promotes the collaborative design of new business services. It foresees a collaboration environment that helps providing business services based on innovation, knowledge and customer orientation, as well as identifying future needs, through collaboration between manufacturers and the customer and members of the customer's community (open innovation approach).
- Collaboration spaces. The notion of "collaboration space", introduces a sharing space where effective collaboration among the multiple stakeholders involved in the service creation and provision can take place (details bellow).

The approach adopted in GloNet does not follow the traditional company-centric CRM model, but rather a collaborative network/ecosystem model, which is more promising in terms of sustainability and better contributes to the quality of service (in comparison with outsourcing), namely in what concerns the responsibility each entity has within the service that is provided to the customer as a whole.

Naturally technology is not enough to achieve an effective collaborative approach to business services provision; a new culture is needed. This requires other tools such as: Better communication strategy; Team building; Training; etc.; which are not in the core of a technology-oriented project such as GloNet. But technology is an enabler, facilitating sharing, visibility and transparency among the involved stakeholders.

5 Service Packaging

Customers are often interested in a grouping of services, rather than an isolated service. Typically a bundle or package of services is offered for a more competitive price. Two approaches can be considered for this grouping:

- *Free Grouping.* In this case the customer freely selects, from the portfolio of available services, the ones he wants to subscribe. The specific delivery conditions, service level agreement, etc., are negotiated on a case by case basis. Sometimes there are dependencies between services and then the selection of one specific service might mandatorily imply the selection of another one from which this service depends on. For instance, in the solar energy case, the subscription of the service "Monitoring reports" will probably require the service "Energy monitoring" as well, as the latter case provides the base sensorial network that is needed for real-time data acquisition.
- *Pre-packaged Options.* Under this approach, the service provider (service integrator) organizes some pre-configured packages of services, which already take into account all interdependencies and are offered under pre-defined conditions. Often these packages correspond to different levels of coverage, e.g. basic, comfort, and premium. Table 2 shows an example of packages in the solar energy case. The subscription of additional services, not included in a specific package level, would have to be negotiated with the service provider.

6 Implementation Issues

Taking into account the characteristics mentioned above, Fig. 4 introduces the proposed model for business services. The UML diagram also represents the iterative definition of composed business services, through their individual or atomic services.

Table 3 gives a brief description of the elements of the business services that constitute their profiles. Figure 5 shows a simplified diagram of the GloNet system architecture, which follows a SOA approach [21] and is developed using standard blocks of a Java based technology stack, Eclipse, MySQL, Apache Tomcat, etc. The base platform, developed by CAS Software AG, uses an OSGi run-time component based on the Spring framework. The system runs on top of a cloud-based IaaS.

The use of a cloud infrastructure for the target environments, is aimed to facilitate the efficient usage of hardware resources for this purpose while assuring both their fail-safe availability and reliability. Besides the initial lower cost in setting up the cloud's hardware as compared to conventional physical local setups at every organization, ease of servicing, upgrading and maintaining a cloud-based infrastructure fulfill the requirements of this environment in the long term. Nevertheless it is important to notice that cloud computing is not a solution for all consumers of ICT

Table 2. Illustrative example of pre-prepared business service packages in the solar energy case.

Service Category	Business Service	Basic	Comfort	Premium
Operation monitoring	*Energy monitoring services*	X	X	X
	Monitoring reports	X	X	X
	System performance testing		X	X
	Site security services			X
	Data analytics services		X	X
Preventive Maintenance	*Panel Cleaning*		X	X
	Vegetation Management			X
	Wildlife Prevention			
	Water Drainage			
	Retro-Commissioning			
	Upkeep of Data Acquisition and Monitoring Systems	X	X	X
	Upkeep of Power Generation System	X	X	X
Corrective / Reactive Maintenance	*On-Site Monitoring / Mitigation*		X	X
	Critical Reactive Repair		X	X
	Non-Critical Reactive Repair			X
	Warranty Enforcement			X
Condition-Based Maintenance	*Active Monitoring - Remote and On-Site Options*			X
	Warranty Enforcement (Planned and Unplanned)			X
	Equipment Replacement (Planned and Unplanned)			X
Other Support	*Training services*			
	Energy audit services			

services. The result of our analysis of cloud environment and its use for GloNet application domains have left us with some open issues [22]. For example, one relevant fact is that the products in this environment (e.g. the power plants and/or intelligent buildings) have a very long life time and thus the choice of infrastructure for developing their assisting software system should also have the same life expectation or support easy migration. Unfortunately, although some interoperability starts to exist at the Infrastructure as a Service (IaaS) level, the situation at the Platform as a Service (PaaS) level is typically one of vendor lock-in.

7 Collaboration Spaces

In order to facilitate the interaction among stakeholders involved in the achievement of some common goal, GloNet adopts the notion of **collaboration space**. This notion is used in both the physical and virtual worlds. In the physical world, besides the traditional characteristics of a meeting room, it means an environment that supports a

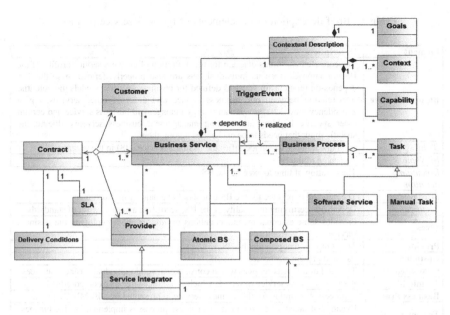

Fig. 4. Simplified business service model in UML.

group of people in working collaboratively, such as doing brainstorming or performing some tasks. It can involve novel design ideas and furniture to inspire creative thinking and provide different sensations according to the objectives of the collaborative activity. In the virtual world we try to mimic some of these aspects allowing a group of geographically disperse participants to work together, mediated by technology. Various other terms are often found in the literature to represent similar notions. Examples include virtual room and virtual co-working space. There are also hybrid versions, which combine physical spaces with advanced technologies to allow both local and remote participation. GloNet is particularly concerned with the virtual world version in order to support the members of a collaborative network, mostly composed of SMEs which are geographically dispersed. As such, two main collaboration spaces were initially identified: Collaborative solution space and Services provision space. In terms of basic characteristics, the two spaces are quite similar, but their purpose and thus the involved support tools are distinct. In summary:

Collaborative Solution Space. This case is envisaged to support a group of stakeholders in the design and development of a new solution, e.g. initial design and development of the product, or co-creation of a new business service. Table 4 shows its main characteristics.

One special instance of this collaboration space corresponds to the business service co-creation scenario. Creation of a new business service can be typically done through a co-creation process carried out by a temporary consortium involving a number of participants selected from the Manufacturers network and Customer "network" or Product Servicing network.

Table 3. Brief description of the elements of business service profiles.

Element	Description
Business Service	The core element in this diagram for the definition of business service profile. If the BS is composed, then its individual BSs are also properly defined. Also the 1..* depends-on relationship which is defined for business services, models the potential inter-relation between one business service and a set of other services, e.g. a dependency may exist between an Energy management business service and certain other specific Lighting and heating management business services, due to the specific input that needs to be exchanged among them.
BS Id	A unique number which identifies the business service (BS) in the registry.
BS Name	The name of the BS.
Execution duration	The duration of time to execute the BS.
Price range	The min and max price for the BS that should be paid by the customer.
Certification	Documents certifying the quality of the BS, according a particular set of standards.
Notes	Provides some essential recommendations or advises about deploying the business service.
Provider	The company that provide the BS.
Customer	Past and present customers of the BS.
Composed BS	The kind of business services which consists of several individual business services.
Atomic BS	A single business service (a service which is not registered as a composed BS).
Business Process	A process description for the business service, represented by a BPMN Diagram.
Trigger Event	Events that launch the execution of business processes implementing the business service.
Service integrator	The entity that offers an integrated or composed business service, coordinates the other involved providers, and possibly offers a unique contact point to the customer.
Contextual Descriptions	Contextual information about the business services.
Goal	Addresses the technical or strategic goals of the business service.
Strategic Goal	Specifies the business targets and benefits of the business service.
Technical Goal	Specifies the operational targets of the business service, which aim at satisfying strategic goals of the business service.
Context	Describes the business or industrial context of the business service.
Capabilities	Addresses the capabilities and capacities of the business service.
Contract	Establishes an agreement between a supplier and a customer, for the provision of one or more business services.
SL Delivery Conditions	Describes the specific conditions during the business service delivery. This element includes facets such pre-conditions, post-conditions, privacy policy, etc.
SLA	Specifies the service level agreement associated to the contracted service(s) provision.

Business Services Provision Space. This class of collaboration spaces is typically aimed at supporting the virtual organizations that will provide services to enhance the product during its life cycle. Table 5 shows its main characteristics.

In terms of the GloNet system, these spaces are accessible through the Stakeholders Space Interface layer (Fig. 5) and are naturally supported by the collaborative networks management functionalities. Other important elements of this environment include common ontologies, an essential element to facilitate collaboration [23, 24], and management of common knowledge and information assets.

To assess the validity of the proposed solution, a demonstrator is built around the use case of solar energy parks. A solar park represents a clear example of a complex and highly customized product, which is expected to have a long life cycle of around $20 \sim 25$ years. During its operation phase, the power plant needs to be supported by a

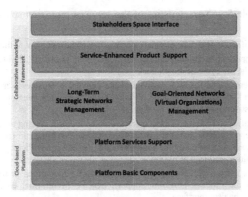

Fig. 5. Main blocks of the GloNet system architecture.

Table 4. Characteristics of the collaborative solution space.

Meeting place	A specific user interface provides a common web access point to the participants.
- Purpose	Joint development of a product or business service.
- Participant group	The members of the VO involved in the development of a specific solution. For instance, it can be the "product development network" (the VO involved in the development of the physical product and design of initial associated business services), or the "service co-creation network" (the dynamic (temporary) VO involved in the design and development of new business services associated to the (physical) product.
Sharing space	A specific information sharing space to allow sharing specific information and knowledge assets that the participants decide to bring in, as well as those assets (e.g. product model, business process models) that they jointly create.
Support tools	Besides generic collaboration tools, the various functionalities provided in the GloNet system for Product Configuration, Service-Enhanced Product Ordering, Service Registering, etc., will be accessible through the user interface.
Privacy and security	The generic protection mechanisms of the platform are used to guarantee protection and access rights to the VO participants. Depending on the access rights of each participant, they might have access to other assets besides the ones included in the shared space.
Occupancy period	The "life" of this space is typically tied to the life cycle of the VO that uses it. Since the aim is to support the creation of a new product or service, the space is created by the starter of the corresponding VO and destroyed when the VO dissolves. Naturally, the objects created by the VO and that need to be kept will be maintained in other information spaces (e.g. product portfolio, or the private spaces of each tenant), depending on the specific asset.

number of business services. In the case of our demonstrator these services are provided by a network of stakeholders located in different continents (Europe and India), which requires both a collaboration platform and proper organizational structures. Figure 6 illustrates the validation approach.

Additional validation, at a smaller scale, is done for the case of intelligent buildings.

Table 5. Characteristics of the services provision space.

Meeting place	A specific user interface provides a common web access point to the participants.
- Purpose	To support collaboration during the delivery of (multi-stakeholder) business services along the life cycle of the product.
- Participant group	The members of the VO involved in the delivery of business services associated to a product. Typically a long-term VO organized to provide integrated (multi-stakeholder) business services along the product life-cycle.
Sharing space	A specific information sharing space is created to allow sharing specific information and knowledge assets that the participants decide to bring in (related to the service provision), and specially the product model, registry of services, and all data related to the business services provision.
Support tools	Besides generic collaboration tools, various functionalities provided in the GloNet system for Product Portfolio Support, Service Monitoring, etc., will be accessible through the user interface.
Privacy and security	The generic protection mechanisms of the platform are used to guarantee protection and access rights to the VO participants. Depending on the access rights, each participant might have access to other assets besides the ones in the shared space.
Occupancy period	This collaboration space is supposed to be available during the operation phase of the life cycle of the product, typically a long duration. It will typically be connected to the duration of the services provision contract. Similar to other collaboration spaces, this one is also created in association to the VO that uses it, i.e. the "product servicing network".

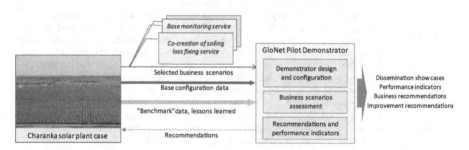

Fig. 6. GloNet validation in the solar plants sector.

8   Conclusions

The development and provision of business services to enhance products offers important business opportunity for SMEs in various economic sectors. These services add value to the product, facilitating a closer fit with customer needs and providing a differentiation factor. Of special relevance is the possibility of developing composite business services that involve the collaboration of a network of stakeholders and provide integrated solutions to the customer.

In this line, the GloNet project addresses the development of a cloud-based environment aimed at supporting collaborative business services design and delivery to enhance complex and highly customized products. The interplay of various strategic and goal-oriented collaborative networks is assumed in these processes. Proposed models and tools are validated in the solar energy plants and intelligent buildings sectors.

Acknowledgements. This work was funded in part by the European Commission through the GloNet project (FP7 programme). The authors also thank the contributions from their partners in these projects.

References

1. Shen, Q.: Research on organization mode selection of service-enhanced manufacturing enterprise. In: Proceedings of 3rd International Conference on Information Management, Innovation Management and Industrial Engineering, 26–28 Nov 2010, Kunming, China, pp. 358–361. IEEE Computer Society (2010)
2. Bitner, M.J., Brown, S.W.: The evolution and discovery of services science in business schools. Commun. ACM **49**(7), 35–40 (2006)
3. Ostrom, A.L., Bitner, M.J., Brown, S.W., Burkhard, K.A., Goul, M., Smith-Daniels, V., Demirkan, H., Rabinovich, E.: Moving forward and making a difference: research priorities for the science of service. J. Serv. Res. **13**(1), 4–36 (2010)
4. Romero, D., Molina, A.: Collaborative networked organisations and customer communities: value co-creation and co-innovation in the networking era. Prod. Plann. Control **22**(5–6), 447–472 (2011)
5. Chesbrough, H., Spohrer, J.: A research manifesto for services science. Commun. ACM **49**(7), 74–78 (2006)
6. Camarinha-Matos, L.M., Afsarmanesh, H., Oliveira, A.I., Ferrada, F.: Collaborative business services provision. In: Proceedings of ICEIS'13 – 15th International Conference on Enterprise Information Systems, Angers, France, 4–7 Jul 2013, vol. 2, pp. 382–392 (2013)
7. Camarinha-Matos, L.M., Afsarmanesh, H., Koelmel, B.: Collaborative Networks in Support of Service-Enhanced Products. In: Camarinha-Matos, L.M., Pereira-Klen, A., Afsarmanesh, H. (eds.) PRO-VE 2011. IFIP AICT, vol. 362, pp. 95–104. Springer, Heidelberg (2011)
8. Spohrer, J., Maglio, P.P.: Service science: towards a smarter planet. In: Karwowski, W., Salvendy, G. (eds.) Service Engineering. Wiley, New York (2009)
9. Wang, S., Li, L., Jones, J.D.: Systemic thinking on services science, management and engineering: applications and challenges in services systems research. IEEE Syst. J. (2012) (in press). doi:10.1109/JSYST.2013.2260622
10. Ferrario, R., Guarino, N.: Towards an ontological foundation for services science. In: Domingue, J., Fensel, D., Traverso, P. (eds.) FIS 2008. LNCS, vol. 5468, pp. 152–169. Springer, Heidelberg (2009)
11. Cardoso, T., Camarinha-Matos, L.M.: Pro-activity in collaborative service ecosystems. In: Camarinha-Matos, L.M., Pereira-Klen, A., Afsarmanesh, H. (eds.) PRO-VE 2011. IFIP AICT, vol. 362, pp. 377–387. Springer, Heidelberg (2011)
12. Oberle, D., Barros, A., Kylau, U., Heinzl, S.: A unified description language for human to automated services. Inf. Syst. **38**, 155–181 (2013)
13. Hill, T.P.: On goods and services. Rev. Income Wealth **23**(4), 315–338 (1977)
14. Engelmann, K.: Services science – where practice meets theory. In: Stauss, B., Engelmann, K., Kremer, A., Luhn, A. (eds.) Services Science - Fundamentals, Challenges and Future Developments, pp. 119–136. Springer, Heidelberg (2008)

15. Sanz, J.L.,Becker, V., Cappi, J., Chandra, A., Kramer, J., Lyman, K., Nayak, N., Pesce, P., Terrizzano, I., Vergo, J.: Business services and business componentization: new gaps between business and IT. In: Proceedings of IEEE International Conference on Service-Oriented Computing and Applications (SOCA'07), pp. 271–278. IEEE Computer Society (2007)
16. O'Sullivan, J.: Towards a precise understanding of service properties. Ph.D. Thesis, Queensland University of Technology (2006). http://eprints.qut.edu.au/16503/1/Justin_O%27Sullivan_Thesis.pdf
17. Franco, R.D., Bas, Á.O., Prats, G., Varela, R.N.: Supporting structural and functional collaborative networked organizations modeling with service entities. In: Camarinha-Matos, L.M., Paraskakis, I., Afsarmanesh, H. (eds.) PRO-VE 2009. IFIP AICT, vol. 307, pp. 547–554. Springer, Heidelberg (2009)
18. Stickdorn, M., Schneider, J.: This is Service Design Thinking: Basics, Tools, Cases. BIS Publishers, Amsterdam (2012)
19. Camarinha-Matos, L.M., Afsarmanesh, H.: Collaborative Networks: Reference Modeling. Springer, Heidelberg (2008)
20. EPRI: Addressing Solar Photovoltaic Operations and Maintenance Challenges - A Survey of Current Knowledge and Practices. Electric Power Research Institute white paper, July 2010, (2010). www.smartgridnews.com/artman/uploads/1/1021496AddressingPVOaM Challenges7-2010_1_.pdf
21. MacKenzie, C.M., Laskey, K., McCabe, F., Brown, P., Metz, R. (eds.) Reference model for service oriented architecture. OASIS Report (2006). www.oasis-open.org/committees/download.php/16587/wd-soa-rm-cd1ED.pdf
22. Camarinha-Matos, L.M., Afsarmanesh, H., Macedo, P., Oliveira, A.I., Ferrada, F.: Collaborative environment for service-enhanced products. In: Proceedings of INDIN 2013–11th International Conference on Industrial Informatics, Bochum, Germany, 29–31 Jul 2013
23. Afsarmanesh, H., Ermilova, E.: The management of ontologies in the VO breeding environments domain. Int. J. Serv. Oper. Manage. 6(3), 257–292 (2010)
24. Unal, O., Afsarmanesh, H.: Schema matching and integration for data sharing among collaborating organizations. J. Softw. 4(3), 248–261 (2009)

An Architecture for Health Information Exchange in Pervasive Healthcare Environment

João Luís Cardoso de Moraes[1(✉)], Wanderley Lopes de Souza[1],
Luís Ferreira Pires[2], and Antonio Francisco do Prado[1]

[1] Department of Computing, Federal University of São Carlos,
São Carlos, SP, Brazil
{joao_moraes, desouza, prado}@dc.ufscar.br
[2] Centre for Telematics and Information Technology,
University of Twente, Enschede, The Netherlands
l.ferreirapires@utwente.nl

Abstract. This paper presents an architecture for health information exchange in pervasive healthcare environments meant to be generally applicable to different applications in the healthcare domain. Our architecture has been designed for message exchange by integrating ubiquitous computing technologies, intelligent agents and healthcare standards, in order to provide interoperability between healthcare systems. We conduct controlled experiments at three cardiology clinics, an analysis laboratory, and the cardiology sector of a hospital located in Marília (São Paulo, Brazil). Three scenarios were developed to evaluate this architecture, and the results showed that the architecture is suitable to facilitate the development of healthcare systems by offering generic and powerful message exchange capabilities. The proposed architecture facilitates health information exchange between various healthcare information systems, contributing in this way to the development of a pervasive healthcare environment that allows healthcare to be available anywhere, anytime and to anyone.

Keywords: Pervasive Healthcare · Intelligent Agents · Ubiquitous Computing · *Open*ehr standard · Interoperability

1 Introduction

In most countries, the conventional healthcare model will soon become inadequate, due to the increasing healthcare costs for the growing population of elderly people, the rapid increase in chronic disease, the growing demand for new treatments and technologies, and the decrease in the number of health professionals relative to the population increase. Recently, the United States Census Bureau estimated that the expected number of inhabitants in the United States older than 65 will be approximately 70 million in 2030, twice than in 2000 [1]. In Ontario, the most populous province of Canada, healthcare is expected to represent 66 % of government expenditure in 2017 and 100 % in 2026 [2].

© Springer International Publishing Switzerland 2014
S. Hammoudi et al. (Eds.): ICEIS 2013, LNBIP 190, pp. 385–401, 2014.
DOI: 10.1007/978-3-319-09492-2_23

The current healthcare model is centred on highly specialized people, located in large hospitals and focusing on acute cases for treatment. It needs to change into a distributed model, in order to produce faster responses and to allow patients to better manage their own health. The centralized healthcare model implies that patients and caregivers have to move to the same place (a hospital or clinic) for the healthcare services to be delivered, and it is often expensive and inefficient. A distributed healthcare model that pervades the daily lives of the citizens is more appropriate to provide less expensive and more effective and timely healthcare, and characterizes Pervasive Healthcare. According to [3], the goal of Pervasive Healthcare is to enable the management of health and wellness by using information and communication technologies to make healthcare available anywhere, at anytime and to anyone.

The exchange of health information among heterogeneous Electronic Healthcare Record (EHR) systems in pervasive healthcare environments requires communication standards that enable interoperability between these systems. Although Health Level Seven (HL7)[1] is a widely used international standard for message exchange between heterogeneous HISs, it has some well-known limitations for representing clinical knowledge, such as its combined use of structured components and coded terms, which can result in inconsistent interpretations of clinical information [4]. *open*EHR[2] is a foundation dedicated to the research of interoperable EHRs that fosters the development of the *open*EHR architecture. This architecture is based on a dual model that separates information from knowledge, thereby addressing some of HL7 known limitations.

Ubiquitous Computing [5] encompasses a group of technologies that explore the advances of wireless connectivity to allow information to move along with the user. In healthcare, these technologies are being mainly employed to build supporting infrastructures for Health Information Systems (HIS), and to develop mobile applications that extend the functionality of healthcare applications formerly limited by traditional computing technologies. Ubiquitous Computing has enabled new healthcare models, such as Distributed and Mobile Healthcare, and is expected to be extremely helpful in the implementation of the Pervasive Healthcare model. However, the Pervasive Healthcare model will only be acceptable for realistic scenarios if it supports efficient and secure information exchange from caregivers to their patients and vice-versa, which requires some more research.

Intelligent agents are software entities that employ techniques from Artificial Intelligence to choose the best set of actions to be performed in order to reach the goals specified by their users. They can communicate with each other, and they have a set of properties, such as sociability and autonomy. In the healthcare domain, intelligent agents can help caregivers exchange and use health information when caring for their patients.

The aim of this paper is to demonstrate the feasibility of designing and implementing an architecture for health information exchange to address realistic pervasive healthcare scenarios. The proposed architecture is based on Intelligent Agents and

---

[1] http://www.hl7.org

[2] http://www.openehr.org

Ubiquitous Computing technologies, and complies with current healthcare standards. This paper particularly addresses the architectural and technical challenges of combining these technologies in order to achieve our goals.

The paper is further structured as follows. Section 2 discusses some related works. Section 3 introduces our proposed architecture. Section 4 describes the scenarios that have been used to evaluate our architecture. Section 5 discusses our evaluation results, in which we assessed the ease of use and perceived usefulness of the applications built using our reusable architecture. Finally, Sect. 6 presents our concluding remarks and gives recommendations for future work.

2 Related Work

Many applications for ubiquitous computing, healthcare standards and intelligent agents in healthcare have been reported in the literature.

A communication system is reported in [6] in which mobile devices recognize the context in which caregivers perform their tasks. The authors propose an extension of the traditional Instant Messaging paradigm by using the Extensible Messaging and Presence Protocol (XMPP) for exchanging XML messages. These messages contain context information that allows the system to deliver messages. Agents are responsible for message exchange. This work has some similarities with ours, since both employ agents and contextual information for message exchange. However, it lacks the definition of a language for the communication amongst agents, and it ignores healthcare standards and the agents' intentionality.

An approach to provide interoperability between self-care systems when exchanging non-clinical information along with clinical data is proposed in [7]. SOAP messages were defined for transporting the Personal Health Record (PHR) contents in so-called Health Diary Entry (HDE) structures. This allowed the use of external vocabularies and ontologies, in order to achieve semantic interoperability. This work has some similarities with ours, since they both deal with the interoperability of heterogeneous systems by means of healthcare standards. However, agent technologies are not used in [7].

A Multi-Agent System (MAS) for controlling the medicine administration to patients as well as the available stock of medicines is proposed in [8]. This work has some similarities with ours, since both use MAS to control clinical tasks. However, in [8] healthcare standards are not employed for message exchange, and contextual information and the agents' intentionality are not considered.

A proposal for the representation and persistence of clinical data of patients as well as context information in ubiquitous applications is described in [9]. The work is based on the *open*EHR dual model, and the persistence solution consists of storing an XML representation of a reference model indexed by data paths defined by archetypes. This work has some similarities with ours, since both use the *open*EHR dual model. However, it does not employ a MAS for message exchange.

3 Architecture Overview

The biggest challenge for our architecture is to support the mobility and collaboration among healthcare professionals when they perform clinical tasks. The main problems to be solved are related to information overload and the heterogeneity of the mobile devices used by such professionals. We use context-awareness, content adaptation, and the technology of intelligent agents to address the challenge and the problems mentioned above.

Figure 1 gives an overview of our architecture, which was developed according to the MVC pattern (*Model-View-Controller*) [10] to separate the business logic from the presentation logic, for the sake of flexibility and reuse. In our architecture, the *view* package contains the *mobileUI* package, which copes with the mobile end-user interactions with other components of the architecture, and the *webUI* package, which displays information to the end-users.

The *controller* package contains the *CAManager* package, which manages the exchange of context-aware messages, the *handler* package, which processes the inputs and outputs and acts as a wrapper to a web service, and the *helper* package, which adapts the data model to the *view*. The *model* package represents the domain models, and contains the *ontology* package, which represents the domain knowledge, the *agent* package, which issues requests and notifications within the architecture, and the *dto* and *dao* packages, which represent the data transfer object and data access object design patterns, respectively. The architecture has also an *external* package with some additional auxiliary packages.

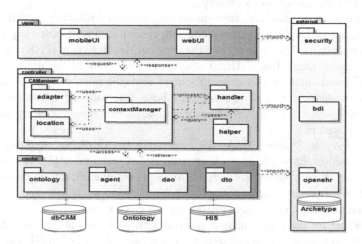

Fig. 1. Architecture overview.

Below we discuss the most distinctive aspects of our architecture, namely the message exchange based on *open*EHR archetypes, the context-awareness support and the use of intelligent agents.

3.1   Message Exchange

In our architecture, the message exchange facilities comply with the *open*EHR standard [11, 12], and have been designed to support message exchange amongst heterogeneous EHR systems in pervasive healthcare environments. *open*EHR has an EHR Extract Information Model (IM)[3] that describes the several ways in which an EHR extract can be built to support interoperability between EHR systems.

The Clinical Knowledge Manager (CKM)[4] is the archetype repository of the *open*EHR Foundation. We have reused some available archetypes provided by CKM, such as *Device* and *Clinical Synopsis*, and we have developed new archetypes to represent clinical concepts from the cardiology domain, such as *Coronary Cardiac Surgery* and *Pacemaker Implantation* [13].

Since the *open*EHR standard [14] consists of a RM part for delivering the container with the needed EHR information, and an AM part for expressing clinical content, the message exchange schema has also a Reference Model Schema (RM-XMLSchema) for representing the constraints in RM, and an Archetype Model Schema (AM-XMLSchema) for representing the clinical archetypes. RM-XMLSchema is the concrete model from which the software can be developed. AM-XMLSchema represents the concrete metamodels of a domain concept, which are expected to be understandable for a domain expert. Figure 2 depicts an overview of the message exchange schema.

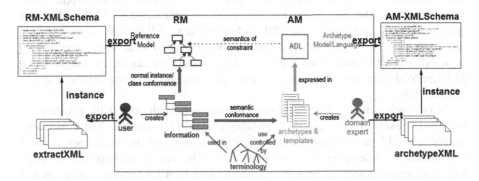

Fig. 2. Message exchange schema based on *open*EHR paradigm.

In our architecture, the *open*EHR Extracts, which contains clinical information related to the patients, are implemented as a type in a Web service environment, to support the semantic interoperability among distributed HIS.

Figure 3 shows the XMLBeans code (*extractXML*) generated according to the '*person_details*' *archetype* instance. In Fig. 3, *birthdate* (1) is an attribute that was generated based on the RM, *xs:date* (2) is the type of this attribute, and the *required* value (3) means that this attribute is mandatory. Further, the generated

---

[3] http://www.openehr.org/programs/specification/releases/1.0.2
[4] http://www.openehr.org/ckm

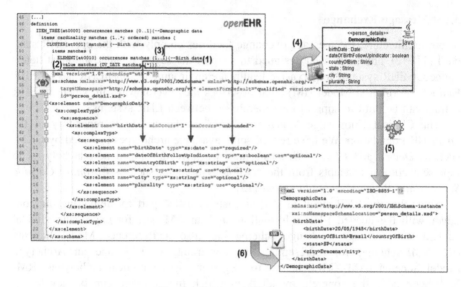

Fig. 3. Generated XML code.

DemographicData (4) is the Java beans class that corresponds to the *person_details* XML Schema is shown and the XML instance (5,6) containing demographic information based on the Java beans instance and in conformance to XML Schema is generated. Due to some available XML technology (e.g., XPath), the output handling and generation have been straightforward. The generated code that represents an *open*EHR extract contains data about a patient. These data can be exchanged using REST*ful* Web services as representational state amongst the components of a distributed HIS.

In our architecture, when the system interoperates with other HIS, *CAManager* and *handler* exchange messages that possibly contain EHR extracts. These messages are represented in accordance with the specification of *open*EHR archetypes, in order to guarantee the interoperability with other HISs. The *handler* package also supports both synchronous and asynchronous communication between architecture agents and HISs. It requests the appropriate content from a legacy HIS, and checks if this content has messages related to the end-user.

3.2   Context-aware

Context-aware systems are highly suitable for delivering healthcare services, especially for Pervasive Healthcare [15]. In some healthcare services, the description of a situation by using 'what' (activity), 'who' (identity), 'where' (location) and 'when' (time) may not be enough, in which case more richness and higher reliability are required. In these cases we may have to include 'how' (process), 'with whom' (source), and 'so what' (needed action). This either increases the complexity of context-aware system or the error probability in the delivery of healthcare services [16]. Increased complexity could also lead to longer response delays, which may not be acceptable for some services, such as e.g., emergency services.

One of the challenges of our architecture has been to cope with the different circumstances in which health professionals have to perform their tasks, including the heterogeneity of their devices. To cope with these different circumstances, we defined a *CAManager* package, which includes the *context-Manager* package to processes the dynamic context information (e.g., end-user's location) and other context information (e.g., identity and user roles) that is obtained from various contextual sources. The *contextManager* package interacts with the *adapter* package to handle content adaptation of the message containing health information, in order to address some of the specific characteristics of the end-user's device. If adaptation is necessary, *contextManager* asks the *view* package to adapt the interface to the particular device.

3.3 Intelligent Agents

An *agent* is a software entity with autonomous behaviour that can achieve its goals through the cooperation and coordination with other agents in a Multi-Agent Systems (MAS) environment [17]. In our architecture, agents interact with each other by using the Agent Communication Language (ACL) [18] to share information and knowledge in the healthcare environment for which our architecture has been designed.

We also applied the BDI model [19] in the development of our architecture. This model is based on *intentionality*, and considers Beliefs, Desires and Intentions as the mental states that generate human action, allowing the agents in this way to operate in an environment according to what they believe, and to perform plans in order to satisfy their desires and intentions. We used JADEX [20] for implementing agents in our architecture, because it supports the formal description of cognitive agents based on the BDI model. The most important agents in the architecture are *Physician-Agent, PatientAgent, LocatorAgent, DeviceAgent, HISAgent,* and *ResourceAgent* components.

The *PhysicianAgent* component is a mobile agent endowed with *intentionality*. This agent is used by the physicians responsible for the patient's healthcare. It helps the medical staff monitor the tasks performed during a workday, and obtain information about patients and the availability of resources, but without requiring the intervention of caregivers. Information about bedridden patients is obtained by agent *ResourceAgent*. Initially, any member of the medical staff can use her mobile device to trigger the *PhysicianAgent*, which is responsible for achieving the goal determined in accordance with the plans, allowing the medical staff to deal with any emergency situation. *PhysicianAgents* are endowed with mobility and can be dispatched by the network in order to achieve their goals. When a *PhysicianAgent* migrates to another container, it keeps its *intentionality* according to its beliefs, so that it can achieve its goals. After achieving its goals, a *PhysicianAgent* returns to its origin (the machine from it was launched) bringing a message consisting of a string value, a serialized Java object containing an extract of an EHR related to an *open*EHR archetype or an *Ontology* object containing the description of the concepts used by the agents (i.e., in FIPA-Semantic Language).

PatientAgent is a component that corresponds to a static agent. This is an intelligent agent, since it has beliefs, desires and intentions and is capable of applying plans to pursue its intentions in the environment where it resides. *PatientAgent* is responsible for the continuous monitoring of the evolution of the patient, and can send and receive messages to and from *PhysicianAgent*.

DeviceAgent and *LocatorAgent* are components responsible for determining the location of patients and caregivers. Bluetooth Access Points (BAPs) has been applied to handle location, namely the capability of discovering devices that are connected. BAPs are co-located with points of interest in the hospitals and clinics, in order to allow both people and devices to be located. Based on the location agents, *PhysicianAgents* can move through the platform in pursuit of their goals.

HISAgent is a component that corresponds to a static agent, since it does not have the ability to migrate between various hosts. This agent analyzes various EHRs and has the ability to retrieve information from the EHR by extracting *open*EHR archetypes that have been requested by a *ResourceAgent*. The main task of *HISAgent* is to ensure interoperability between various HISs through the exchange of messages between agents. The messages exchanged between the agents contain an extract of an EHR, based on constraints imposed by the archetype, and this information is structured according to the *open*EHR reference model.

ResourceAgent is a static agent that runs on a remote server and is responsible for mediating access to resources related to *HISAgent*. This agent is static because it does not have the ability to migrate between various hosts.

Each agent in the architecture is endowed with specialized capabilities and goals in order to perform tasks for the benefit of pervasive healthcare. The architecture allows the caregivers to detect abnormalities in their patients, to check the availability of resources within the healthcare environment, and to obtain information about patients. Caregivers and patients may use any device, anywhere and at anytime.

4   Application Scenarios

We defined a set of application scenarios in order to identify requirements and define experiments to evaluate our architecture. IT professionals described these application scenarios under the guidance and assistance of professional medical experts.

We have conducted a controlled experiment [21] at three cardiology clinics, one analysis laboratory, and the cardiology department of the Santa Casa Hospital of Marília (São Paulo, Brazil), using the three scenarios discussed systematically below. Table 1 gives the number of participants of each scenario. The evaluation period has been from 1 January 2012 to 30 July 2012. These three scenarios have been used to demonstrate the reusability of our architecture.

Table 1. Participants in the different scenarios.

Scenarios / Participants	Caregivers	Patients	Total
Scenario 1: Delivery Laboratory esul	10 cardiology 8 laboratory	235	253
Scenario 2: Pacemaker valuation	7 cardiology	95	102
Scenario 3: Medical Staff eeting	5 cardiology 18 clinical 14 surgical centre	122	179
otal participants	82	452	534

4.1 Delivery of Laboratory Analysis Results

Stakeholders. Dr. Ray (Laboratory worker) and Dr. Call (Cardiac surgeon).

Scenario. Life Institute (LI) is a laboratory that provides chemical analysis to the region of Marília, and has a unit in the Santa Casa Hospital. LI receives and processes daily several requests for clinical analysis. In the case of the Santa Casa Hospital unit, results of the clinical analyses should be directly sent to the medical staff of the hospital.

Solution. In our approach, the daily tasks performed by human agents are delegated to software agents. In this scenario, once Dr. Ray has finished the analysis of specimens requested by Dr. Call, the resulting data are stored in the LI Laboratory Information System (LIS-LI) database. Figure 4 shows the class diagram containing the components of the architecture that have been used to support this scenario.

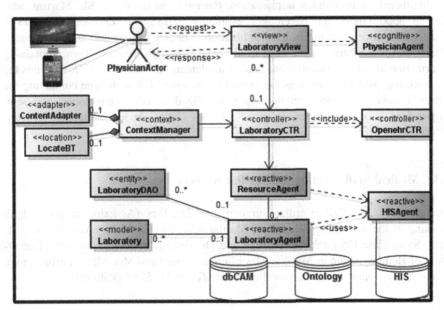

Fig. 4. Laboratory analysis scenario.

PhysicianActor and *PhysicianAgent* represent Dr. Call, who requests the chemical analysis and waits for the results. *HISAgent* represents the LIS-LI and *Laboratory-Agent* represents Dr. Ray, who informs the availability of the analysis results to the *PhysicianAgent* through *ResourceAgent*. *LaboratoryCTR* modifies the message received in accordance with the contextual information, by adapting the content to match the capabilities of the requesting device and by serializing the extract of the EHR related to the *open*EHR archetype that represents analysis results. A message containing a serialized object is enveloped by the agent *ResourceAgent* and represented using the Agent Communication Language (ACL).

4.2   Pacemaker Evaluation

Stakeholders. Dr. Call (Cardiac surgeon) and Mr. Martins (Patient).

Scenario. A pacemaker is a medical device to regulate the beating of the heart. People carrying pacemakers should be checked at regular intervals. The Cardiology Clinic of Marília (CRTB) provides on-going follow-up care for patients with permanent pacemakers, and has a clinical HIS (CRTBSys) to keep track of the care provided to its patients. To schedule of a pacemaker evaluation, a call is made to the patient's phone number. During the pacemaker evaluation, the physician spends a reasonable amount of time consulting the information on the medical history of the patient.

Solution. In this scenario, Dr. Call implanted a pacemaker in Mr. Martins. Figure 5(a) shows the class diagram containing the components of the architecture that have been used to support this scenario. *PhysicianAgent* represents Dr. Call once he has accomplished the pacemaker implantation. *PatientAgent* represents Mr. Martins, who has an appointment for pacemaker evaluation. *HISAgent* represents CRTBSys. *PatientActor* receives a notification in his mobile device to schedule an appointment. *PhysicianAgent* receives a message in his device through *ResourceAgent* containing information about the patients' pacemaker implantation. *PacemakerCTR* modifies the message received and serializes the extract of the *open*EHR archetype containing the patient's data. A message containing a serialized object is enveloped and sent. Figure 5(b) shows the user interface of Dr. Call's device with the received information.

4.3   Medical Staff Meeting for Cardiac Surgery

Stakeholders. Dr. Call (Cardiac surgeon) and Dr. Day (Assisting surgeon), both working at the Cardiology Center of Marília (CCCM); Dr. John (Anesthesiologist) from Santa Casa Hospital; Dr. Marden and Dr. Peter (Physicians) from the Department of Hemodynamic in Marília; Mrs Elienne (Nurse) and Mrs Aline (Perfusionist). These professionals form the so-called *Heart Team*. Mr Silva (Patient).

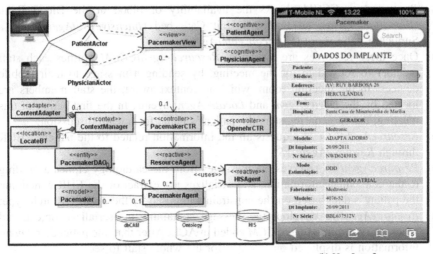

a) Class Diagram   (b) UserInterface

Fig. 5. Pacemaker evaluation scenario.

Scenario. Due to the complexity of the resources involved, cardiac surgery requires the full integration of individual efforts with maximum efficiency to make sure that the surgical action plan is performed successfully.

Solution. The members of the *Heart Team* work together to plan the cardiac surgery of Mr Silva. The notifications necessary to plan this cardiac surgery are exchanged in two phases. Figure 6 shows the interactions between the agents used in this scenario

(1)   *PhysicianAgent* requests the resources required to perform a surgery;
(2)   *ResourceAgent* analyzes the conditions for performing cardiac surgery;

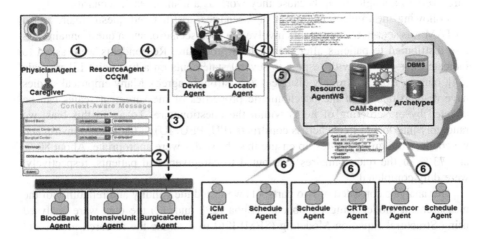

Fig. 6. Medical staff meeting for cardiac surgery scenario.

(3) *ResourceAgentCCCM* checks the availability of blood at the Blood Bank (*BloodBankAgent*), an Intensive Unit Care bed (*IntensiveUnitAgent*) and a Surgical Centre room (*SurgicalCenterAgent*);

(4) Once these resources are available, *Resource-AgentCCCM* notifies each staff member to set a date for the meeting, by sending a message to their mobile devices. In the meeting room, which is context-aware, the staff members are located by the *DeviceAgent* and *LocatorAgent* agents. In the first action of this meeting, the surgeon registers the patient's name for a team discussion;

(5) *ResourceAgentCCCM* requests all the information related to the patient's EHR through *ResourceAgentWS*;

(6) *ResourceAgentWS* receives the messages from the cardiology clinics according to the contextual information, and serializes the extract of the EHR containing the patient's data based on the constraints imposed by the *open*EHR archetype;

(7) *ResourceAgentWS* envelops the message containing the serialized object, and sends it to *ResourceAgentCCCM* coded in ACL. After that, the patient's relevant information is displayed on a screen for the whole staff to see.

The details of the components of the architecture that have been instantiated to support this scenario are discussed in [13].

5 Results and Discussion

In our study we employed the Technology Acceptance Model (TAM) [22], which assumes that *Perceived Usefulness (PU)* and *Perceived Ease of Use (PEU)* can predict the use and *Intentions to Use (IU)* of a particular technology. TAM is known to be a suitable model to explain the technology acceptance process in the healthcare sector [23]. To evaluate the effect on technology acceptance, two groups were selected for analysis, involving a limited but a relevant set of people: caregivers (including physicians, medical students and nurses) and patients. We decided to assign all the caregivers to a single group because they work as a team in each scenario.

Following the implementation of the scenarios, a structured questionnaire based on TAM was sent to the caregivers involved in each scenario, and a questionnaire was also distributed to patients after the medical procedure. Respondents were asked to indicate their opinion with respect to several statements on a five-point Likert scale [24], ranging from 1 (strongly disagree) to 5 (strongly agree). Many empirical studies have demonstrated that the psychometric properties of measurement scales can be affected by the ordering of items within the questionnaire. To avoid this bias, we randomly intermixed items across constructs (PU, PEU, IU) in the questionnaire, and we conducted a group pre-test to ensure that the scales were appropriate. About 80 % and 73 % of the questionnaires distributed to caregivers and patients, respectively, were duly completed.

Our analysis consisted of two parts: (1) we tested the validity and reliability of the measurement model using Cronbach's Alpha [25], and; (2) the data were analysed using Structural Equation Modeling (SEM) [26] to examine the research model and

Table 2. Statistics and reliability of constructs.

Participant	Construct	Items	Mean	Cronbach's Alpha
Caregivers	PEU	4	3.01 to 4.05	0.803 to 0.815
	PU	5	3.12 to 4.70	0.851 to 0.860
	IU	3	3.18 to 4.49	0.799 to 0.854
Patients	PEU	4	3.10 to 4.33	0.850 to 0.895
	PU	5	3.53 to 4.66	0.862 to 0.923
	IU	3	3.04 to 4.16	0.764 to 0.865

the hypotheses. SEM is a statistical method that combines factor analysis and path analysis, enables theory construction and analyses the relationships among variables.

Table 2 shows the results of the validity tests for all scenarios, in which the internal consistency of the constructs were further evaluated for their reliability. The constructs had Cronbach's Alpha values at least close to the limit of 0.700, which is considered very good. Therefore, we concluded that these constructs are reliable to be used in our data analysis. Based on this analysis we concluded that the mean values possessed good validity.

Hereafter, the validated data were analysed using SEM. The users' intentions to use the communication systems in each scenario can be explained or predicted based on their perception of ease of use and usefulness. Figure 7 summarizes the research model of this study. The labels on the arrows show the hypotheses and the path coefficients that measure the relative strength and indicate causal relationships among variables, whereas R^2 gives the percentage of total variance of the independent variables and indicates the predictability of the research model.

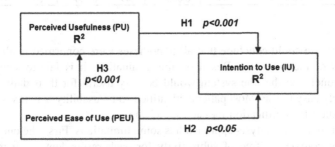

Fig. 7. Research model an hypotheses.

The following three hypotheses have been proposed and tested in each scenario:

H1. Perceived Usefulness positively affects Intention to Use the system.

- *Null hypothesis: H_{1n}: $\mu_{PU} = \mu_{IU}$.*
- *Alternative hypothesis: H_{1a}: $\mu_{PU} \neq \mu_{IU}$.*

H2. Perceived Ease of Use positively affects Intention to Use the system.

- *Null hypothesis: H_{2n}: $\mu_{PEU} = \mu_{IU}$.*
- *Alternative hypothesis: H_{2a}: $\mu_{PEU} \neq \mu_{IU}$.*

H3. Perceived Ease of Use positively affects Perceived Usefulness.

- *Null hypothesis: H_{3n}: $\mu_{PEU} = \mu_{PU}$.*
- *Alternative hypothesis: H_{3a}: $\mu_{PEU} \neq \mu_{PU}$.*

To validate these hypotheses we applied *statistical regression analysis* [27] over the data collected from the users in each scenario. Table 3 summarises our results.

For example, in Scenario 1 (participants = caregivers), we tested H_{3a} to verify if Perceived Usefulness is determined by Perceived Ease of Use. The details of the regression analysis were $R^2 = 0.53$, p = 0.0005, which is highly significant because p < 0.001 and $\alpha = 0.05$. From the result of the regression we could reject the null hypothesis (H_{3n}), meaning that we empirically corroborate that Perceived Usefulness is determinant by Perceived Ease of Use, and that H_{3a} was strongly confirmed. R^2 indicates Perceived Ease of Use explains 53 % ($R^2 = 0.53$) of the variance in Perceived Usefulness. Hypotheses H_{1a} and H_{2a} were accepted, and Perceived Usefulness was a strong determinant of Intention to Use, and Perceived Ease of Use was a significant secondary determinant.

Table 3. Statistic regression analysis.

Scenarios	Hypotheses	H1		H2		H3	
Scenarios	Participants	R^2	p<0.001	R^2	p<0.05	R^2	p<0.001
Scenario 1	Caregivers	0.65	0.0007	0.65	0.010	0.53	0.0005
	Patients	0.23	0.0000	0.23	0.001	0.55	0.0010
Scenario 2	Caregivers	0.72	0.0001	0.72	0.009	0.61	0.0000
	Patients	0.35	0.0000	0.35	0.007	0.55	0.0002
Scenario 3	Caregivers	0.55	0.0002	0.55	0.020	0.54	0.0000
	Patients	0.49	0.0002	0.49	0.019	0.60	0.0005

Therefore, we could conclude that all hypotheses were confirmed in all scenarios at all points of measurement. Based on this evaluation, it is fair to state that the caregivers concluded that the system would be very useful for their daily tasks and was extremely easy to use. Most patients identified some usability benefits, such as the efficient method for notification messages exchange.

However, our data analysis approach has some limitations. First, the questionnaire model is not completely free of subjectivity for each respondent (each respondent reacts in a particular way to a questionnaire). Second, we grouped all caregivers together and generalized the results, while we could have split them in different groups. Third, other factors may affect the decision of people of using a given technology, such as their prior experience and job relevance [28], which we did not take into consideration in our work. However, in this study we considered perceived usefulness and perceived ease of use as the most important factors to explain the intention to use the system in future.

6   Concluding Remarks

Population ageing creates pressure on the healthcare system in various ways. Healthcare environments require efficient and safe information exchange between caregivers and patients. Interoperability can be achieved when there is some level of coordination and communication in the exchange of the healthcare information among different HIS.

This paper has presented a reusable architecture that is based on intelligent agents and uses the *open*EHR standard to exchange messages in order to meet the requirements of interoperability between different HIS. Message exchange between possibly heterogeneous HIS is realized by integrating EHR extracts represented in terms of archetypes into ACL messages, which is a widely used standard for information exchange between agents. Since intelligent agents have cooperation, coordination, and communication capabilities, they were employed for performing tasks on behalf of human agents, and for monitoring the environment in order to ensure the fulfilment of the contextual requirements. They are also capable of taking decisions about the activities to be performed, and when and how to communicate to perform them.

We performed case studies to evaluate the reusability of our architecture, and also the usefulness and ease of use of pervasive healthcare technologies inside healthcare environments. We have presented the scenarios that demonstrated the reusability of the architecture, and showed the potential acceptance of our applications by end-users, which reacted positively in terms of their usefulness.

In further work, we will evaluate the performance of our architecture, especially its scalability, which is a crucial non-functional requirement for realistic applications and for the simultaneous support of multiple scenarios. We will also evaluate whether patient safety is improved during the medical procedure when our architecture is applied. We are planning future experiments to extend the TAM models to investigate the effect of other variables, such as user experience, job relevance and output quality, to moderate the effects of perceived usefulness, perceived ease of use on the intention to use.

Acknowledgements. We thank the National Council of Technological and Scientific Development (CNPq) for sponsoring our research in the context of the National Institute of Science and Technology Medicine Assisted by Scientific Computing (INCT-MACC). We also thank the Coordination of Improvement of Higher Personnel (CAPES) for sponsoring the stay of João Luís Cardoso de Moraes at the University of Twente (Enschede, the Netherlands).

References

1. Jiang, S., Xue, Y., Giani, A., Bajcsy, R.: Robust medical data delivery for wireless pervasive healthcare. In: Eighth IEEE International Conference on Dependable, Autonomic and Secure Computing, Chengdu, China, pp. 802–807 (2009)
2. Skinner, B., Rovere, M.: Paying More, Getting Less: Measuring the Sustainability of Government Health Spending in Canada Fraser Institute (2009)

3. Hansmann, U., Nicklous, M.S., Stober, T.: Pervasive Computing Handbook. Springer-Verlag New York Inc., Secaucus (2001)
4. Browne, E.: openEHR Archetypes for HL7 CDA Documents. Ocean Informatics (2008)
5. Weiser, M.: Some computer science issues in ubiquitous computing. Commun. ACM **36**, 75–84 (1993)
6. Munoz, M.A., Rodriguez, M., Favela, J., Martinez-Garcia, A.I., Gonzalez, V.M.: Context-aware mobile communication in hospitals. Computer **36**, 38–46 (2003)
7. Lahteenmaki, J., Leppanen, J., Kaijanranta, H.: Interoperability of personal health records. In: Annual International Conference of the IEEE Engineering in Medicine and Biology Society, pp. 1726–1729 (2009)
8. Baffo, I., Stecca, G., Kaihara, T.: A multi agent system approach for hospital's drugs management using combinatorial auctions. In: 8th IEEE International Conference on Industrial Informatics (INDIN), pp. 945–949 (2010)
9. Kashfi, H.: An openEHR-based clinical decision support system: a case study. Stud. Health Technol. Inform. **150**, 348–359 (2009)
10. Leff, A., Rayfield, J.T.: Web-application development using the model-view-controller design pattern. In: Fifth IEEE International Enterprise Distributed Object Computing Conference, Proceedings 118–127 (2001)
11. de Moraes, J.L.C., de Souza, W.L., Pires, L.F., do Prado, A.F.: Towards a reusable architecture for message exchange in pervasive healthcare. In: 15th International Conference on Enterprise Information Systems (ICEIS 2013), pp. 393–402. SCITEPRESS - Science and Technology Publications, (2013)
12. de Moraes, J.L.C., de Souza, W.L., Pires, L.F., Cavalini, L.T., do Prado, A.F.: A novel approach to developing applications in the pervasive healthcare environment through the use of archetypes. In: Apduhan, B.O., Carlini, M., Gervasi, O., Misra, S., Murgante, B., Nguyen, H.-Q., Taniar, D., Torre, C.M. (eds.) ICCSA 2013, Part V. LNCS, vol. 7975, pp. 475–490. Springer, Heidelberg (2013)
13. de Moraes, J.L.C., de Souza, W.L., Pires, L.F., Cavalini, L.T., do Prado, A.F.: A novel architecture for message exchange in pervasive healthcare based on the use of intelligent agents. In: 10th IEEE/ACS International Conference on Computer Systems and Applications (AICCSA), p. 8. IEEE, Fez/Ifrane-Marocco (2013)
14. Beale, T., Heard, S.: Archetype Definition Language. openEHR Foundation (2007)
15. Kjeldskov, J., Skov, M.B.: Exploring context-awareness for ubiquitous computing in the healthcare domain. Pers. Ubiquit. Comput. **11**, 549–562 (2007)
16. Varshney, U.: Context-awareness in Healthcare. In: Pervasive Healthcare Computing, pp. 231–257. Springer, NewYork (2009)
17. Jennings, N.R.: Agent-oriented software engineering. In: Imam, I., Kodratoff, Y., El-Dessouki, A., Ali, M. (eds.) IEA/AIE 1999. LNCS (LNAI), vol. 1611, pp. 4–10. Springer, Heidelberg (1999)
18. Labrou, Y., Finin, T., Peng, Y.: Agent communication languages: the current landscape. IEEE Intell. Syst. Appl. **14**, 45–52 (1999)
19. Rao, A.S., Georgeff, M.P.: Modeling rational agents within a BDI architecture. In: Principles of Knowledge Representation and Reasoning: Proceedings of the Second International Conference, pp. 473–484 (1991)
20. Pokahr, Alexander, Braubach, Lars, Lamersdorf, Winfried: A goal deliberation strategy for BDI agent systems. In: Eymann, Torsten, Klügl, Franziska, Lamersdorf, Winfried, Klusch, Matthias, Huhns, Michael N. (eds.) MATES 2005. LNCS (LNAI), vol. 3550, pp. 82–93. Springer, Heidelberg (2005)
21. Hevner, A.R., March, S.T., Park, J., Ram, S.: Design science in information systems research. MIS Q. **28**, 75–105 (2004)

22. Davis, F.D.: Perceived usefulness, perceived ease of use, and user acceptance of information technology. MIS Q. **13**, 319–340 (1989)
23. Chau, P.Y.K., Hu, P.J.H.: Investigating healthcare professionals' decisions to accept telemedicine technology: an empirical test of competing theories. Inf. Manag. **39**, 297–311 (2002)
24. Likert, R.: A Technique for the Measurement of Attitudes. [s.n.], New York (1932)
25. Nunnally, J.C.: Psychometric Theory. Current Contents/Social & Behavioral Sciences (1979)
26. Henseler, J., Chin, W.W.: A comparison of approaches for the analysis of interaction effects between latent variables using partial least squares path modeling. Struct. Equ. Model. Multi. J. **17**, 82–109 (2010)
27. Goldin, R.F.: Review: statistical models-theory and practice. Am. Math. Mon. **117**, 844–847 (2010)
28. Davis, F.D., Venkatesh, V.: Toward preprototype user acceptance testing of new information systems: implications for software project management. IEEE Trans. Eng. Manage. **51**, 31–46 (2004)

Human-Computer Interaction

Dealing with Usability
in Model-Driven Development Method

Lassaad Ben Ammar[✉], Abdelwaheb Trabelsi, and Adel Mahfoudhi

University of Sfax, ENIS, CES Laboratory,
Soukra Road km 3,5, B.P: 1173-3000, Sfax, Tunisia
{lassaad.ben-ammar,adel.mahfoudhi}@ceslab.org,
abdelwaheb@gmail.com

Abstract. Usability is crucial for the acceptance of Interactive Systems (IS) by end users. Unusable User Interfaces (UI) are probably the main reason why IS fail in actual use. This can explains the increasing number of Usability Evaluation Method proposed in the literature. However, most of these methods are focused on the final product which greatly reduced the ability to go back and makes major changes. Recently, and due to the increasing interest in Model Driven Engineering (MDE) paradigm, the conceptual models have become the backbone of the IS development process. Therefore, evaluating the usability from the conceptual models would be a significant advantage with regard to saving time and resources. The present chapter proposes an early usability evaluation method that is based on conceptual models. The usability evaluation can be automated taking as input the conceptual models that represent the system abstractly. As an output it provides a usability report which contains the detected usability problems. The usability report is analyzed in order to identify the source of problems and suggest changes in the development process.

Keywords: Conceptual model · Model Driven Engineering · Early usability evaluation

1 Introduction

Usability is a quality attribute that has been pointed out as being one of the most important factors in the acceptance of Interactive Systems (IS) by end users. It denote the extent to which specific users can use a product to efficiently and effectively achieve specific goals in a specific context of use [1]. For many years, usability has been perceived as related to the User Interface (UI) [2]. Consequently, usability evaluation is considered late at the development process once the UI is implemented. At this stage, the ability to go back and makes major changes in the design is greatly reduced.

Recently, it has been suggested that usability should be performed from the beginning of the development process in order to increase user experience and

© Springer International Publishing Switzerland 2014
S. Hammoudi et al. (Eds.): ICEIS 2013, LNBIP 190, pp. 405–420, 2014.
DOI: 10.1007/978-3-319-09492-2_24

decrease maintenance costs [3–5]. This has motivated the proposition of methods for the *early usability evaluation*. Among these methods, those following the Model-Driven Engineering (MDE) approach seem to be the most appropriate for the early usability evaluation. In a MDE approach, conceptual models are a primary artefact in the development process. The UI code is (semi-) automatically generated by means a model compiler that takes the conceptual model as input. Hence, evaluating the usability from the conceptual models would be a significant advantage with regard to saving time and resources.

The analysis of some research works that deal with usability in an MDE method highlight some gaps. The main limitation is the lack of precise details given (selection of attributes, scores interpretation, etc.) which makes difficult to understand how these approaches could work correctly in practical settings.

This chapter aims to delineate a method for evaluating usability from the early stage of an MDE method by defining metrics for conceptual primitives that constitute conceptual models. The proposed method can be applied automatically taking the conceptual model, that represents a system abstractly, as input. It is based on the usability model presented in [6] which is empirically validated.

The proposed method focuses on the Cameleon reference framework presented in [7] which structure the UI development interface on four level of abstraction, starting from task specification to a running interface: Task and Concepts, Abstract User Interface (AUI) Concrete User Interface (CUI), and Final User Interface (FUI). We have selected the Cameleon framework because it provides a unifying MDE framework for the development of UI that can be able to adapt to the context of use while preserving usability. Such UIs are namely *Plastic*. In this framework, focus is generally placed on data and functional modeling, disregarding usability aspects. Therefore, there is a need to extend the Cameleon framework in order to promotes usability as a first class entity in the development process.

We structure the remainder of this paper as follows. While Sect. 2 presents an outline of the usability evaluation methods quoted in the literature, Sect. 3 provides a description of our proposed method for early usability evaluation. A case study is presented in Sect. 4 in order to show the usefulness of our proposal to the uncovering of potential usability problems. Finally, Sect. 5 presents the conclusion and provides perspectives for future research work.

2 Related Works

Usability evaluation is often defined as methodologies for measuring the usability aspects of a user interface and identifying specific problems [8]. There exist several methods targeting the usability evaluation of user interfaces. In this section, we focus our interest in the analysis of model-based methods since our main motivation is to integrate usability issues into a model driven development approach.

The usability evaluation has attracted the attention of both Human Computer Interaction (HCI) community and Software Engineering (SE) communities.

The SE community proposed a quality model in the ISO/IEC 9126-1 standard [9]. In this model, usability is decomposed into *Learnability*, *Understandability*, *Operability*, *Attractiveness* and *Compliance*. However, the HCI community has shown in the ISO/IEC 9241-11 standard [1] how usability can be measured in term of *Efficiency*, *Effectiveness* and *User Satisfaction*. Although both standards are useful, they are too abstract and need to be extended or adapted in order to be applied in a specific domain.

Some initiatives to extend both standards are proposed over the last few years. Seffah et al. [10] analyzed existing standards and surveys in order to detect their limits and complementarities. Moreover, the authors unify all these standards into a single consolidated model called Quality in Use Integrated Measurement QUIM. The QUIM model includes metrics that are based on the system code as well as on the generated interface. This makes the application of the QUIM to a model driven development process difficult.

Abrahão and Insfrán [3] proposed an extension of the ISO/IEC 9126-1 usability model. The added feature is intended to measure the user interface usability at an early stage of a model driven development process. The model contains subjective measurement which raises the question about its applicability at the intermediate artifacts. Besides, it lacks of any detail about how various attributes are measured and interpreted.

The usability of a multi-platform user interface generated with an MDE approach is evaluated in [11]. The evaluation is conducted in term of effectiveness, efficiency and user satisfaction. The usability evaluation is based on the experiments with end-users. This dependency is incompatible with an early usability evaluation.

Panach et al. [12] proposes an early usability measurement method. The usability evaluation is carried out early in the development process since the conceptual model. The main limitation of this proposal is that metrics are specific to the OO-method [13]. Therefore, they cannot be applied to other method, which is a disadvantage. They need some adaptation in order to be used (adopted) in other similar methods.

The analysis of the related works allows us to underline some limitations. The majority of the existing proposals lack of guidelines about how usability attributes and metrics are measured and how to interpret their scores. Besides, usability has not been defined in a consistent way across the methods just mentioned. The majority of models includes metrics that are based on the system code as well as on the generated interface which makes their application to a model-driven development process difficult.

It becomes clear that usability evaluation in a MDE approach for the development of UI is still an immature area and many more research works are needed. In order to covers this need, we propose to integrate usability issues into the Cameleon framework. The proposed method is intended to evaluate he usability from the conceptual model. For that reason, we opted for the usability model presented in [6] wherein usability metrics are based on the conceptual primitives.

3 Proposed Usability Evaluation Method

3.1 Overview

The Cameleon framework provides a user interface development process which defines four essential levels of abstraction: Task & Domain, Abstract User Interface (AUI), Concrete User Interface (CUI) and Final User Interface (FUI). The development process takes as input the conceptual models in order to generate the final executable user interface. In this framework, the conceptual models covers the AUI and the CUI levels. The CUI model is the most affected by usability. Therefore, we opted to perform the evaluation from this level. To do that, we proposes a set of usability metrics which are based on the conceptual primitives of this model. The usability evaluation is implemented as a model transformation which takes the CUI model as input and the usability model as a parameter. As outcome, it provides a usability report which contains the detected usability problems. Usability problems are analyzed in order to identify their sources and suggest possible changes in order to improve the usability of future UI obtained as part of the transformation process (see Fig. 1).

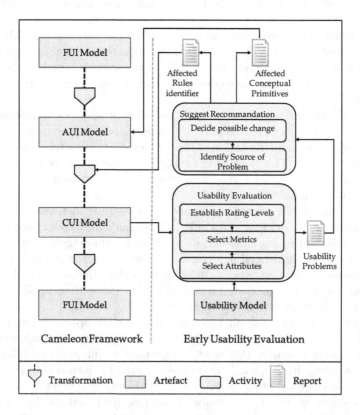

Fig. 1. Incorporating usability into a model-driven development framework.

3.2   Usability Evaluation

Usability evaluation is a process that entails three main steps: (1) Select Attributes, (2) Select Metrics and (3) Establish Rating Levels. In what follows, we briefly describe each step.

Select Attributes. The first step in a usability evaluation method is usually to identify a set of usability attributes. Usability attributes can be either *External* or *Internal*. Attributes which can be measured once the system is implemented are called *External*. Attributes which can be measured before implementing the system are called *Internal*. In this chapter, we focus our interest in the identification of a set of internal attributes. The main objective is to make possible the evaluation without requiring the system implementation. Besides, measuring internal usability can lead to a full automation process.

For the *Learnability* sub-characteristic, which refers to the attributes of a software product that facilitate learning, it can be measured in terms of Prompting, Predictability and Informative Feedback. All these attributes are closely related to the user characteristics. For example, a novice user need to be guided throughout the entire application. Hence, prompting and feedback are essential mechanisms to help user to easily learn the application.

The *Understandability* sub-characteristic refers to the attributes that facilitate understanding. We propose four attributes in order to be able to measure this sub-characteristic. The first attribute is the Information Density which is the degree in which the system will display/demand the information to/from the user in each interface. The Brevity focus on the reduction of the level of cognitive efforts of the user (number of action steps). The short term memory capacity is limited. Consequently, shorter entries reduce considerably the probability of making errors. Besides, the Navigability pertains to the ease with which a user can move around in the application. Finally, Message Concision concerns the use of few words while keeping expressiveness in the error message. Some of these attributes are closely related to the platform features. For example, the screen size has strong influences to the information density and the navigability attributes. Other are related to the users' capacity such as the short term memory.

The *Operability* sub-characteristic includes attributes that facilitate the user's control and operation of the system. Attributes such as Explicit user action, User Operation Cancellability and User Operation Undoability can be used to measure the degree of control that users have over the treatment of their actions. The Error Prevention attribute refers to the means available to detect and prevent data entry errors, command errors, or actions with destructive consequences. The screen size of the platform being used can affect this control when it does not allow displaying button like undo, cancel, validate, etc.

The *Attractiveness* sub-characteristic includes the attributes of software product that are related to the aesthetic design to make it attractive to user. We argue that some aspect of attractiveness can be measured with regard to the Font Style Uniformity and Color Uniformity. The Consistency measure the maintaining of the design choice to similar contexts. The user preferences in term of color or font style are related to the attractiveness attributes. It should be noted that some environment features (e.g. indoor/outdoor, luminosity level) affect the choice of the color in order to obtain a good contrast which give more clear information.

Figure 2 shows an overview of our proposal for attributes specification.

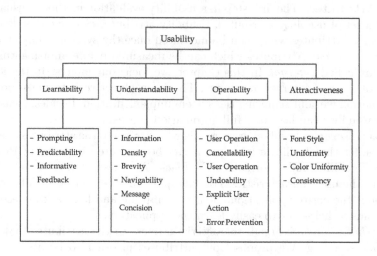

Fig. 2. The proposed usability model.

Select Metrics. All the attributes presented in the previous Section are abstract and can not be measured directly. They need to be more decomposed and detailed in order to be quantified. In order to be able to measure the internal attributes we need to define some *metrics* for each attributes. It should be noted that metrics are intended to measure the internal usability from the conceptual models. Hence, metrics are defined based on the conceptual primitives that constitute the conceptual models of a specific MDE method. The applicability of our method is shown in the present chapter through the MDE method presented in [14]. The main reason of the choice of such method is its compliance to the Cameleon framework and the use of the BPMN notation to describe the user interface models. The BPMN notation is based on the Petri networks which allows the validation of metrics. In what follows, we list the definition of some examples of these metrics. We listed later the indicators defined for each one of the following metric:

– Information Density: The Information Density of a user interface can be measured in terms of the number of the components per user interface. we propose four metric to measure this attribute: average of input element per UI, average of action element per UI, navigation element per UI and total of element per UI.

- Brevity: The human memory capacity is so limited. Hence, each task that require several step will decrease the user satisfaction. The user interface should allow users to accomplish their tasks in a few number of steps. We propose the number of steps (counted in keystrokes) required to accomplish a task as a metric to quantify the brevity.
- Navigability: The navigability measure the level of facilities that the system will provide to navigate throughout several interfaces. We propose the average of navigation elements per UI as an internal metric to measure the navigability attribute.
- Message Concision: Since the quality of the message is a subjective measure, we propose the number of word as an internal metric to measure the quality of the message.
- Error Prevention: To prevent user against error while entering data, we propose to use a drop down list instead of text field when the input element have a set of accepted values.

Establish Rating Levels. The metrics defined previously provides a numerical value that need to have a meaning in order to be interpreted. The mechanism of indicator is restored in order to reach such goal. It consists in the attribution of qualitative values to each numerical one. Such qualitative values can be summarized in: Very Good (VG), Good (G), Medium (M), Bad (B) and Very Bad (VB). For each qualitative value, we assign a numerical range. The ranges are defined build on some usability guidelines and heuristics described in the literature. Next, we detail the numeric ranges associated with some metrics in order to be considered as a Very Good value.

- Information Density: several usability guidelines recommend minimizing the density of a user interface [15]. We define a maximum number of elements per user interface to keep a good equilibrium between information density and white space: 15 input elements (ID1), 10 action elements (ID2), 7 navigation elements (ID3), and 20 elements in total (ID4) [12].
- Brevity: some research studies have demonstrated that the human memory has the capacity to retain a maximum number of 3 scenarios [16]. Each task or goals requiring more than 3 steps (counted in keystrokes) to be reached decreases usability (Minimal Action MA).
- Navigability: some studies have demonstrated that the first level navigational target (Navigation Breadth NB) should not exceed 7 [17].
- Message Concision: since the quality of the message can be evaluated only by the end-user, the number of the word in a message is proposed as an internal metrics to assess message quality (Word Number WN). A maximum of 15 words is recommended in a message [12].
- Error Prevention: The system must provide mechanisms to keep the user from making mistakes [18]. One way to avoid mistakes is the use of ListBoxes for enumerated values. Panach et al. [12] recommend at least 90 % of enumerated values must be shown in a ListBox to improve usability (ERP).

Metrics which are extracted from the proposition of [12] are extracted with their ranges of values. In fact, this ranges are empirically validated. For the others metrics, the ranges of values to consider the numeric value as Very Good are taken into consideration in order to estimate the value to be considered as Very Bad. The Medium, Bad and Good values are equitably distributed once we have the two extremes. The Table 1 shows the list of indicators that we have been defined.

Table 1. Proposed indicators.

Metric	VG	G	M	B	VB
ID1	≺15	$15 \leq ID1 \prec 20$	$20 \leq ID1 \prec 25$	$25 \leq ID1 \prec 30$	$ID1 \geq 30$
ID2	≺10	$10 \leq ID2 \prec 13$	$13 \leq ID2 \prec 16$	$16 \leq ID2 \prec 19$	$ID2 \geq 19$
ID3	≺7	$7 \leq ID3 \prec 10$	$10 \leq ID3 \prec 13$	$13 \leq ID3 \prec 16$	$ID3 \geq 16$
ID4	≺20	$20 \leq ID4 \prec 30$	$30 \leq ID4 \prec 40$	$40 \leq ID4 \prec 50$	$ID4 \geq 50$
MA	≺2	$2 \leq MA \prec 4$	$4 \leq MA \prec 5$	$5 \leq MA \prec 6$	$MA \geq 6$
NB	≺7	$5 \leq NB \prec 10$	$10 \geq NB \prec 13$	$13 \leq NB \prec 16$	$NB \geq 16$
WN	≺15	$15 \leq WN \prec 20$	$20 \leq WN \prec 25$	$25 \leq WN \prec 30$	$WN \geq 30$

3.3 Automatic Usability Evaluation Process

Conducting the usability measurement manually is a tedious task. That is why we propose to automatize this process by implementing it as a model transformation process. The model transformation process requires two model as input (the user interface model and the usability model) and provides as outcome a usability report which contains the detected usability problem. In the model transformation literature, the definition of the meta-model[1] is a prerequisite in order to formalize the approach and use a model in a productive way. With regard to the usability meta-model, Fig. 3 show the proposed meta-model.

With regard to the usability report, we propose a simple meta-model which explain the usability problem using the following scheme: the *description* of the usability problem, the *related attribute* is the sub-characteristic and attribute in the model that are affected by the usability problem, the *level* of the detected problem and the *recommendation* to solve such problem (Fig. 4).

It should be noted that the usability evaluation is implemented as a model transformation that take the usability model as a parameter to the transformation engine. To do this, we reformulate the parameterized transformation principles initiated by [19].

---

[1] A meta-model is a language that can express models. It defines the concepts and relationships between concepts required for the expression of the model.

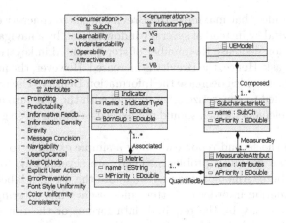

Fig. 3. Usability meta-model.

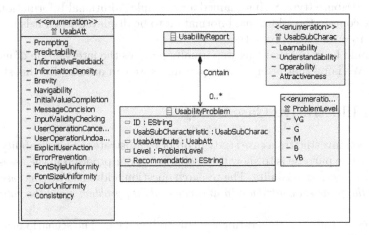

Fig. 4. Usability report meta-model.

3.4   Results Analysis and Suggestion of Recommendations

The main objective of this step is to analysis the *Usability Report* in order to identify the source of the problems and suggest some changes either in the AUI model or in the transformation module. Hence, two reports are produced as an output of this step.

– The first report contains the identifier of the transformation rules that can undergo a slight modification.
– The second report contains the conceptual primitives that have to be modified in order to improve the expressiveness of the AUI model.

As regard to the first report, usability problems that are related to the Brevity and the Information Density attributes usually depend on the transformation rules.

Transformation rules that maximize the Brevity needs to concretize several panels in the some window instead of several window related by a navigation element. Such concretization decrease the number of step (counted in keystroke) required to accomplish a task. Hence, the Brevity is increased. However, the number of widget will be increased which decrease the Information Density. The transformation rule can be modified to concretize several panel with the take into account of the total number of elements which should not exceeds a threshold (e.g., 20 elements per UI).

As regard to the second report, we show a simple example to better explain the impact of the usability problems. There are several way to support the Prompting attribute. Among these way we quote the use of a label that display additional information in order to better guide users while entering data. Additional information may be the required data format or the range of accepted values. The AUI model should provide this information during its transformation. For example, in the underlying method, the UIComponent class should have an attribute (type String) named for example Additional Information. Such attribute contain the additional information to be displayed when it is necessary in order to ensure the prompting.

It should be noted that this step usually requires the intervention of usability experts. We hope that after some experiments we can automatize this step.

4   An Illustrative Case Study

This section investigates a case study in order to illustrate the applicability of our proposal. The purpose is to show the usefulness of our proposal in the assessment of the user interface usability. The research question addressed by this case study is: *Does the proposal contribute to uncover usability problem since the conceptual model?*

The case study is a Requesting a credit to buy a car. The scenario is adapted from [20]. To get information about the credit to buy a car, a bank client does not have to go to the bank branch since the bank portals offer an interactive system which allows resolving such problem. The bank client can perform several tasks using this system: get information about buying tips, simulate a credit to buy a car, request the credit, receive request in line, and communicate with the credit department, etc. For reason of simplicity, we are interested in the <<Request the Credit>> task.

We suppose to have the abstract user interface from Fig. 5 as a result of the transformation of the task model <<Request the Credit>> following the model transformation explained in details in [14]. The result of the transformation is an XML file which is in accordance with the AUI metamodel (left part of Fig. 5). To better clear up the user interface layout, we develop an editor with the Graphical Modeling Framework (GMF) of eclipse. The sketch of the user interface presented by the editor is shown in the right part of Fig. 5.

An ordinary transformation which takes as input the abstract user interface model allows producing the concrete user interface model of Fig. 6. It should

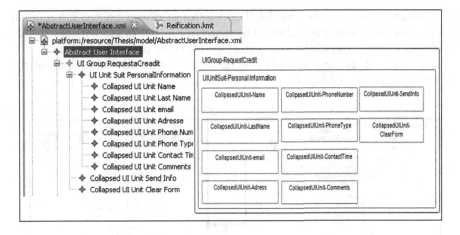

Fig. 5. Abstract user interface.

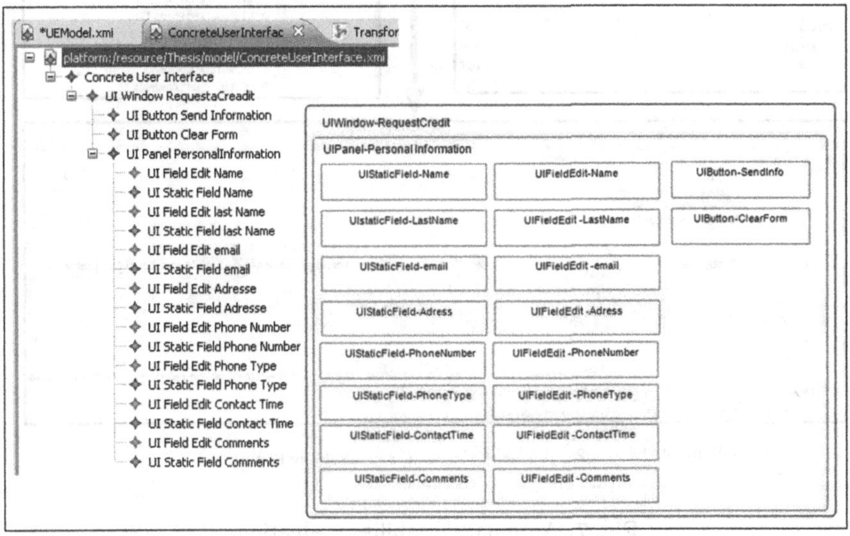

Fig. 6. Concrete user interface.

be noted that this transformation was done taken into account a context of use defined by the analyst. The context is the following: a laptop as an interactive device (normal screen size), an Englishman as a tourist with a low level of experience.

In order to evaluate the concrete user interface, we pursue a reduced version of the usability evaluation process presented in [21]. The *purpose of the evaluation* is to evaluate the usefulness of the proposed model to discover the usability problems presented in the evaluated artifact. The *product part to be evaluated* is the concrete user interface model. The *selected attributes* are the Information Density and the Error Prevention. The *metrics* selected to evaluate the former attributes are ID2 and ERP. The *indicators* are those presented in Table 1.

The result of the evaluation is a usability report model which contains the detected problems (see Fig. 7).

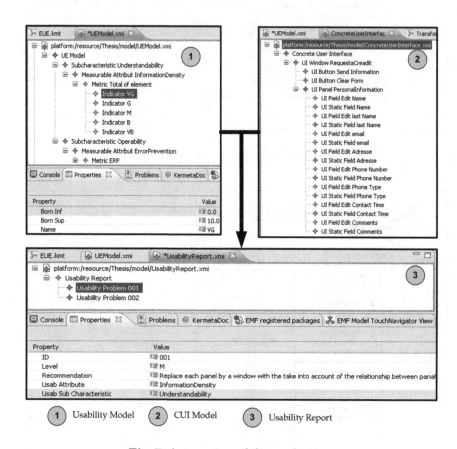

Fig. 7. Automatic usability evaluation.

- Usability problem N1: There are enough elements in the user interface which increase the information density.
  Related attribute: Understandability/Information Density
  Level: M
  Recommendation: Replace each panel by a window with the take into account of the relationship between panel.

- Usability problem N2: There is no means which prevents the user against error while entering data.
  Related attribute: Operability/Error Prevention.

Level:B

Recommendation: Each input element with limited values should be displayed in a dropdown list to protect user against error while entering values (e.g. typos).

The second evaluation to be conducted takes an ≪iPAQ Hx2490 Pocket PC≫ as platform. The migration to such platform raises a new redistribution of the user interface elements. The small screen size (240 × 320) is not sufficient to display all information. The number of the concrete component to be grouped is limited to the maximum number of concepts that can be manipulated (5 in the case of <<iPAQ Hx2490 Pocket PC>>). Therefore, the user interface elements are redistributed on several windows (see Fig. 8).

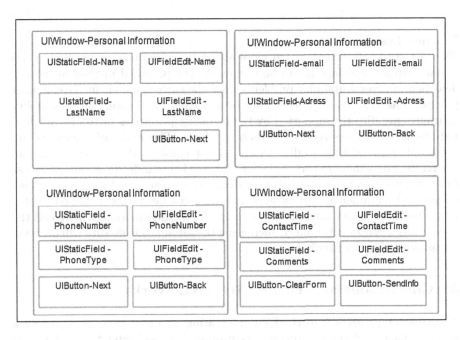

Fig. 8. Concrete user interface for small screen size.

The redistribution of interface elements on several windows will bring more steps to reach the goal. It should be noted that with a small screen size the *Information Density* and the *Brevity* are the most relevant usability attributes to affected. The problem is that these two attributes have a contradictory impact. It is recommended to distribute the concrete components on several screens in order to obtain better *Information Density*. However, redistribute elements from one screen to several will influence negatively the *Brevity* attributes (see Fig. 9).

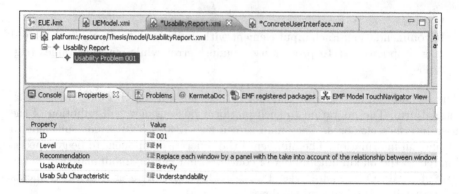

Fig. 9. Usability report.

Learned Lesson

The case study allow us to learn more about the potentialities and limitations of our proposal and how it can be improved. The proposed method allows the detection of several usability problems since the early stage of the development process. The evaluation process may be a means to discover which usability attributes are directly supported by the modeling primitives or to discover limitations in the expressiveness of these artifacts. The ranks of indicators are extracted from existing studies which do not consider the context variation. Therefore, many more experimentations are needed in order to propose a repository of indicators in several cases (medium screen size, small screen size, large screen size). Another important aspect which must be studied is the contradictory affect of usability attributes. For example, the information density and the brevity has a contradictor affect. Increasing the information density will decrease certainly the brevity attribute.

5   Conclusions and Future Research Works

This chapter presents a method for integrating usability issue as a part of a user interface development process. The proposed method extends the Cameleon reference framework. The usability evaluation can be conducted early in the development process (from the conceptual models). The objective is to discover the usability problems presented in the conceptual models. The result of the evaluation is a usability report which contains the usability problems detected during the evaluation step. The analysis of these problems and the identification of their sources allows usability experts to suggest some changes either in the conceptual model or in the model compiler. This can avoid usability problems to occurs in each future UI obtained as part of the development process.

If compared to the existing proposals, our framework presents three main advantages: (1) costs are very low: internal usability evaluation reduce considerably the development costs and maintainability, (2) system does not have to be implemented, (3) it provides a proper details about how to measure attributes and interpret their scores.

The continuity of our research work leads directly to the investigation of the usability-driven model transformation, the relationship between usability attributes and their contradictory influence to the whole usability of the user interface. The automation of the recommendation step is among the perspective that can be investigated in future works.

References

1. ISO/IEC: ISO/IEC 9241. Ergonomic Requirements for Office Work with Visual Display Terminals (VDTs). ISO/IEC (1998)
2. Seffah, A., Metzker, E.: The obstacles and myths of usability and software engineering. Commun. ACM **47**, 71–76 (2004)
3. Abrahão, S.M., Insfrán, E.: Early usability evaluation in model driven architecture environments. In: QSIC, pp. 287–294 (2006)
4. Molina, F., Toval, A.: Integrating usability requirements that can be evaluated in design time into model driven engineering of web information systems. Adv. Eng. Softw. **40**, 1306–1317 (2009)
5. Panach Navarrete, J.I., Juristo Juzgado, N., Pastor, Ó.: Introducing usability in a conceptual modeling-based software development process. In: Atzeni, P., Cheung, D., Ram, S. (eds.) ER 2012 Main Conference 2012. LNCS, vol. 7532, pp. 525–530. Springer, Heidelberg (2012)
6. Ben Ammar, L., Mahfoudhi, A.: An empirical evaluation of a usability measurement method in a model driven framework. In: Holzinger, A., Ziefle, M., Hitz, M., Debevc, M. (eds.) SouthCHI 2013. LNCS, vol. 7946, pp. 157–173. Springer, Heidelberg (2013)
7. Calvary, G., Thevenin, D.: A unifying reference framework for the development of plastic user interfaces. In: Nigay, L., Little, M.R. (eds.) EHCI 2001. LNCS, vol. 2254, pp. 173–192. Springer, Heidelberg (2001)
8. Nielsen, J.: Usability Engineering. Morgan Kaufmann Publishers Inc., San Francisco (1993)
9. ISO/IEC: ISO/IEC 9126. Software engineering - Product quality. ISO/IEC (2001)
10. Seffah, A., Donyaee, M., Kline, R.B., Padda, H.K.: Usability measurement and metrics: a consolidated model. Softw. Qual. Control **14**, 159–178 (2006)
11. Aquino, N., Vanderdonckt, J., Condori-Fernández, N., Dieste, O., Pastor, O.: Usability evaluation of multi-device/platform user interfaces generated by model-driven engineering. In: Proceedings of the 2010 ACM-IEEE International Symposium on Empirical Software Engineering and Measurement, ESEM '10, New York, NY, USA, ACM, pp. 30:1–30:10 (2010)
12. Panach, J.I., Condori-Fernández, N., Vos, T.E.J., Aquino, N., Valverde, F.: Early usability measurement in model-driven development: definition and empirical evaluation. Int. J. Softw. Eng. Knowl. Eng. **21**, 339–365 (2011)
13. Gómez, J., Cachero, C., Pastor, O.: Conceptual modeling of device-independent web applications. IEEE Multimedia **8**, 26–39 (2001)
14. Bouchelligua, W., Mahfoudhi, A., Mezhoudi, N., Daassi, O., Abed, M.: User interfaces modelling of workflow information systems. In: Barjis, J. (ed.) EOMAS 2010. LNBIP, vol. 63, pp. 143–163. Springer, Heidelberg (2010)

15. M. Leavit, Shneiderman, B.: Research Based Web Design & Usability Guidelines (2006)
16. Lacob, M.E.: Readability and Usability Guidelines (2003)
17. Murata, M., Uchimoto, K., Ma, Q., Isahara, H.: Magical number seven plus or minus two: syntactic structure recognition in Japanese and English sentences. In: Gelbukh, A. (ed.) CICLing 2001. LNCS, vol. 2004, pp. 43–52. Springer, Heidelberg (2001)
18. Bastien, J.C., Scapin, D.L.: Ergonomic criteria for the evaluation of human-computer interfaces. Technical report RT-0156, INRIA (1993)
19. Vale, S., Hammoudi, S.: Context-aware model driven development by parameterized transformation. In: Proceedings of the 1st International Workshop on Model Driven Interoperability for Sustainable Information Systems (MDISIS'08) Held in Conjunction with the CAiSE'08 Conference, pp. 121–133. Springer, Heidelberg (2008)
20. Guerrero, J.: A methodology for developing user interfaces to workflow information systems (2010)
21. Ben Ammar, L., Mahfoudhi, A., Abid, M.: A usability evaluation process for plastic user interface generated with an mde approach. Software Engineering Research and Practice, pp. 323–329. CSREA Press, Las Vegas (2012)

Optimizing the User Interface of a First-Aid App: A "Realistic" Usability Study with the Smartphone Application "Defi Now!"

Karin Harbusch[(✉)] and Janine Paschke

Department of Computer Science, University of Koblenz-Landau,
Universitätsstr. 1, 56070 Koblenz, Germany
{harbusch, jpaschke}@uni-koblenz.de

Abstract. Millions of applications (apps) for smartphones exist and are gaining popularity since the introduction of smartphones in 2005. But, merely a small number of these applications were developed in support of *first aid*, in particular the use of a *defibrillation* device. Such apps support passers-by witnessing an emergency situation or allow refreshment of basic first-aid knowledge. Moreover, they inform about publicly available *automatic external defibrillators (AEDs)* and allow charting new devices. After a brief survey of various types of first-aid apps, we consider the question to what extent these apps are really helpful in emergency cases. To begin answering this question, we report the result of a usability study with 74 test subjects who used the "Defi Now!" app. In order to simulate "realistic" conditions where the user is agitated—as is the case when rescuing a person—, we induced fear by a psychologically recommended method. We discuss advantages and disadvantages of the app based on data from our questionnaires and the video material we collected. Basically, the app was judged to be very helpful as a first-aid support tool. Nevertheless, observations during the study suggested several software-ergonomic improvements.

Keywords: First aid · CPR · AED · Bystander effect · Usability study · Induced emotion · Emotion elicitation · Human-computer interaction · Homogeneity · User expectations · Self-descriptiveness · Controllability · Learnability

1 Introduction

According to the Information System of the German Federal Health Monitoring Office [1], sudden cardiac arrest due to ischemic heart disease is the most common cause of death in most Western countries and a major cause of hospital admissions. In the U.S., the number of people dying due to Sudden Cardiac Death even exceeds 250,000 annually—without significant differentiation between the genders.

Cardiac arrest requires immediate help, and defibrillation is mostly inevitable. Nowadays, *automatic external defibrillators (AEDs)* are provided at many public places. Average survival rates of 30 % for defibrillation by first responders within 3 to 5 minutes are reported by the American Heart Association [2]. The probability of

S. Hammoudi et al. (Eds.): ICEIS 2013, LNBIP 190, pp. 421–437, 2014.
DOI: 10.1007/978-3-319-09492-2_25

survival decreases 10 % by the minute when no help is provided (e.g. [3]). Hence, everybody who owns a feature phone or smartphone is obliged to call for help on site. Moreover, passers-by should administer *first aid*, especially *cardiopulmonary resuscitation (CPR)*. This is a procedure serving to restore a person's spontaneous blood circulation and preserve intact brain function in case they are suffering from cardiac arrest or show no vital signs. CPR (either performed as compression-only or with mouth-to-mouth/nose respiration) is a manual treatment, indicated until further treatment, such as defibrillation, is available. High CPR quality (a rhythmic, 5 cm deep compression, with full relaxation after each push) is essential.

In such precarious situations, the *bystander-effect* [4] is more likely to occur than immediate help, i.e. the phenomenon that in emergency cases individuals are the less willing to offer help, the larger the number of bystanders This diffusion of responsibility results in waiting for someone else to take command. Furthermore, bystanders tend to belittle the existing emergency since no one has intervened so far. Thus, in their opinion, no emergency is at hand and no help is necessary. The most common cause for the denial of assistance, however, might be fear of failure or humiliation. This fear discourages many people to help, especially in situations they are unable to judge (e.g., [5]).

A recent survey conducted by Max Planck Institute for Human Development provides results about the recognition of symptoms of heart attack or stroke, and about the behavior induced by the recognition [6]. Merely 33 % of the 10.228 study participants, recruited from nine European countries, would call an ambulance when witnessing a person suffering from heart attack or stroke, as soon as they identify the symptoms. To what extent can a smartphone application (app) help passers-by not to become bystanders but rescuers?

In the following, we collect desirable features of existing *first-aid smartphone app(lication)s* (Sect. 2). In order to answer the question whether or not these apps are really helpful in emergency cases, we conducted a usability study in which 74 participants used the "Defi Now!". We applied *induced agitation* in order to simulate stress, as is the case when being supposed to help a person suffering from cardiac arrest. In Sect. 3, we present the results of our study. Basically, the app was judged to be very helpful. However, observations made during the study suggest important software-ergonomic improvements, described in Sect. 4. In Sect. 5, we draw conclusions and address future work.

2 First-Aid Apps

When searching for "first-aid" applications in the markets *Google play* and *iTunes* of the two main smartphone operating systems, one easily finds more than 1,000 apps. However, this number covers entertainment applications camouflaged with the keywords "first aid", such as a gamers' guide for "World of Warcraft". In the following, we give an overview of desired features exemplified by six systems available in Austria, France, Germany, Switzerland, and the United States:

- *Defi Graz* (Austria [7]; interface only in German);
- *Arrêt Cardiaque 2.0* (France [8]; multi-lingual);

- *AED Locator* (Germany [9]; in German);
- *Defi Now!* (Germany [10]; multi-lingual);
- *Herzsicher* (Switzerland [11]; in German);
- *Pulse Point* (United States [12]; in English).

Here we first outline the features of "Defi Now!" [13–15] in order to familiarize the reader with the system utilized for our study (Sect. 3). Then, we add *best practices* from the other systems in order to propose an optimal interface of a first-aid app (Sect. 4).

The language of "Defi Now!" is automatically adjusted dependent on the user's phone settings. For example, if the user has chosen English as the general language, the app appears in English as well.

The app displays three consecutive steps on the start screen (cf. central panel in Fig. 1 where the three numbers in red attract the users' attention). Pressing the button "(1) Emergency call" automatically activates the national emergency number adapted to the user's whereabouts. However, the button does not immediately dial the emergency number because the rescuer has to affirm first—by pressing "Yes" to the question whether s/he actually want to place the emergency call—in order to avoid hoax calls.

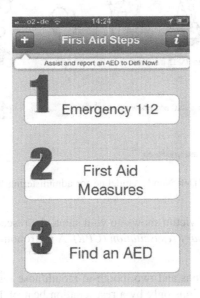

Fig. 1. Start screen of "Defi Now!".

While placing the call, the current address is displayed to the user so that foreigners (and nervous rescuers) can easily provide the location's precise address. (Note that GPS data are not automatically sent in Germany.)

Back in the main menu, after pressing the button "(2) First Aid Measures", the user has to choose between two sequences of first-aid steps, dependent on whether the victim shows vital signs (right branch from topmost node in Fig. 2), or shows no vital

Immediate First-Aid Measures

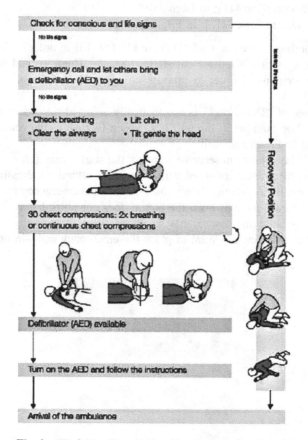

Fig. 2. "Defi Now!" guideline for administering first aid.

signs (left branch). If the victim shows no vital signs, the rescuer receives instructions to perform *cardiopulmonary resuscitation (CPR)*. A metronome for audio support can be set to support either:

1. 30 thorax compressions and two mouth-to-mouth/nose respirations (default), or
2. 100 thorax compressions only by a resuscitation beat of 100 times per minute.

The user has the possibility to switch to the desired rhythm by pushing the wheel button below the diagram (see Fig. 3 outlining the binary pop-up choice along with a canceling option closing it). The other button in the bottom line below the diagram—displaying the currently chosen rhythm—switches a loudspeaker providing this rhythm on or off (cf. button "30:2 Resuscitation Beat (100/min)" in Fig. 3).

Activating step 3 by pressing the button "(3) Find an AED" in the start screen enables the search for AED locations in an interactive map. On the map, the AEDs are

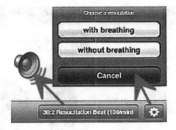

Fig. 3. Buttons displayed below the first-aid guidelines.

depicted by the commonly known pins used in other map applications. The icons are distinguished in four different categories (cf. map in left panel of Fig. 7 below):

1. Green icons 🟢 depict verified AEDs;
2. Grey icons 🔘 signify still unconfirmed AEDs;
3. A red cross on white background 🔺 indicates places where medical staff is available;
4. Blue icons 🔵 denote places retrieved by the database "AED-Kataster".

In order to update this database, the user can add the location of new AEDs. This action can be initiated by pressing the button "+" in the top panel of the start screen (cf. Fig. 1), and does not take place during step 3.

Now, we sum up desirable features that deviate from the ones provided so far in "Defi Now!". Several other systems (e.g. "PulsePoint" and "Herzsicher") provide a *tab(ulator) based interface* (see Fig. 4), i.e. all available functions are permanently visible/selectable. This dialogue strategy renders navigation to the desired choice item superfluous. Such navigation is error prone if the user looses orientation. Therefore, in our study, we evaluate how easily the test subjects navigate in "Defi Now!".

"Defi Graz" and "Arrêt Cardiaque 2.0" support first aid graphically (Fig. 5) rather than textually as in "Defi Now!". "Arrêt Cardiaque 2.0" even provides a video illustrating how to administer heart compression. Therefore, in our study, we asked the test subjects to judge the comprehensibility of the given instructions in emergency situations.

All non-German systems allow for easier emergency call functions due to automatic location of the smartphone.

"Arrêt Cardiaque 2.0" provides social-network integration. The app may be connected with the user's Facebook and/or Twitter account to share the AED they registered with their network. The integration of social media might serve as a fast way of distributing information about AED locations to a large number of users.

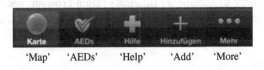

'Map'   'AEDs'   'Help'   'Add'   'More'

Fig. 4. Top-level choice of the "Herzsicher" app, exemplifying a tab-based interface.

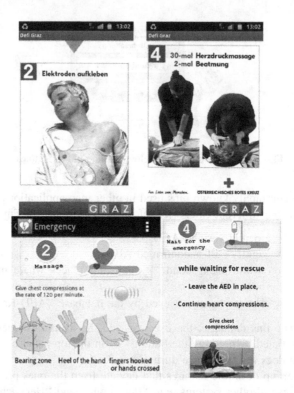

Fig. 5. Upper panel: Graphically supported first-aid instructions in "Defi Graz". Lower panel: CPR details and a CPR instruction video in "Arrêt Cardiaque 2.0".

Hence it might enforce the awareness of social media users for this important information. The more people are aware of such critical issues and involve themselves, the more likely it becomes that they are able to act in an emergency case (cf. conclusions by Mata et al. [6] emphasizing how important appropriate information about first aid is).

In "Arrêt Cardiaque 2.0" and "PulsePoint", the user can register as a first responder (after a special training). This allows the subscriber to be reached in case of a cardiac arrest nearby (radius can be adjusted in an agent-to-agent manner). For example, if a cardiac arrest occurs in a shopping center, a subscriber of such an emergency notification may be present in the same building or in the neighborhood. In "PulsePoint", the alarmed rescuer is shown a route to the emergency case.

In "PulsePoint", by selecting a tab labeled "Incidents", the user receives an overview of all fire department emergencies currently taking place. A "Photos" tab displays a photo gallery of significant incidents (via a browser; see [16]). A "Radio" button enables a streaming radio feed from the dispatch center of the fire department.

3   Realistic Usability Study with "Defi Now!"

Some of the features we outlined above (e.g., graphical support) are obviously very suitable for making a first-aid app supportive for a rescuer. However, more detailed insights in unexpected problems can proceed from a *usability study* (e.g., [17]). This applies, in particular, to first-aid apps because any time delay due to a suboptimal user interface may be fatal. The system has been tested in conditions simulating the stress elicited by real emergencies.

3.1   Test Set-Up

Participants were tested in individual sessions. They were seated at a desk, with an iPhone 3G S (iOS 6.0.1) and the preinstalled app in front of them, and were asked to perform the tasks defined by our questionnaire. Their actions were captured via a camcorder (Plawa DV-4 SD-Camcorder; image resolution 4.0 MP), which focused only on the iPhone's display so as to ensure anonymity of the test subjects. The video capturing was used to reconstruct the handling of the application "Defi Now!" and to survey the errors made during task execution.

Our usability study was conducted with 74 participants, 35 female and 39 male (for the distribution with respect to age and gender, see Fig. 6). Nine of them have been or still are students of computer science at our campus where we had ran a pre-test in an observation lab. Another eight participants are doctors or qualified medical employees. The other 57 participants have different occupations, such as fitness trainer, banker or steel mill worker. Four participants told us they had experienced a heart attack themselves; one of them even suffered from a sudden cardiac arrest and had to be resuscitated. All but the students were recruited as patients in the waiting room of a doctor's office or as customers of a fitness center where we had reserved a quiet room to perform the experiment.

When witnessing an emergency situation such as cardiac arrest, bystanders and rescuers usually are showing signs of agitation, for example trembling hands. In order to simulate this stress, we applied methods from psychology proposed to *induce*

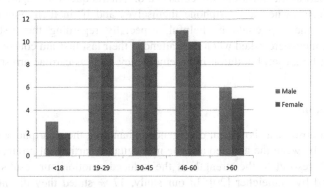

Fig. 6. Distribution with respect to age and gender for the 74 test subjects.

emotions (e.g., [18]). In order to agitate the test participants, showing a movie clip proved to be expedient (e.g., [19] or [20]). Gross and Levenson [21] explain this effect in terms of the high attention and the intensive experience induced by watching a film clip. In our experiment, the film clip was selected from the movie "The Shining" (1980), showing a playing child who heads towards a closed hotel room door. The viewer obtains a feeling that something terrifying is lurking behind the closed door. Hewig et al. [19] rated this film clip as eliciting an emotion of fear as the relevant emotion in the respondent.

In order to examine the effect of agitation, only half of the group of 54 participants was shown the excitement inducing film clip; the other group of 20 participants served as a control group and did not view the film clip before using the app. The distribution regarding age, gender, heritage etc. was equally diverse in both groups.

3.2 Questionnaires

In the initial section of our written questionnaire—where we provided utmost discretion—, the participants were asked about personal factors that might influence accuracy in handling the app (cf. [20]). The participants stated their personal condition in respect of discomforts (e.g., high blood pressure and/or the ingestion of medication). Moreover, they determined their emotional state choosing from: happiness, grief, fear, disgust, or no emotion (if none of the predefined categories matched, they were invited to describe their emotional state in their own terms). In addition, they described their personal physical condition (good, relaxed, nervous, anxious, tired, or bad tempered).

The next part of the questionnaire specified nine tasks covering all features of the application "Defi Now!". After each task, the participants judged the given functions by means of a five-point rating scale, ranging from 1 = "not applicable at all" to 5 = "completely applicable". (The rating scale was developed in reference to Rohrmann [22].) Moreover, they could spontaneously mention what they (dis-)liked about the task. In this phase, the experimenter became active if a test subject was not able to perform a task in a predetermined time. In order to get all tasks performed by the participants, the experimenter gave a (predetermined) hint.

The last part of the questionnaire consisted of general questions regarding whether the test subjects owned a smartphone themselves and if, in their opinion, spoken statements in the app could be helpful, especially regarding the first-aid steps. Furthermore, they were asked when they attended their last first-aid course and if such an app might be a useful addition in an emergency such as cardiac arrest.

3.3 Evaluation

We could not observe a significant divergence in handling the smartphone application "Defi Now!" between the agitated and the non-agitated participant group, despite the fact that with respect to the strength of the induced emotion our results resembled those reported by Schleicher [20]. In our study, 17 % stated they did not feel any emotion while watching the fear inducing video clip. However, the intended emotion was evoked in 70 % of the participants. Moreover, no significant differences emerged between the student group, the medically trained personnel, and the 57 other participants. They all had similar problems with features of the user interface.

Let us first summarize the judgments of personal factors with potential influence on accuracy of handling the app. With respect to their physical condition, 83 % declared they did not experience any health problems. From the 16 % who did experience problems, one participant ingested calmatives, two had a common cold, five were high-blood-pressure patients, and three had problems with their cervical spine. Analysis of the video data and the participants' behavior, suggested the conclusion that some discomforts as well as specific medication could affect a person's performance. The participants who used calmatives, for example, seemed distracted and agitated. Those who suffered from hypertension did not show signs of nervousness. However, the physical condition of the participants had no influence on their subjective feelings.

As regards their current sentiment, 59 % stated they felt good, 13 % were nervous. Five participants declared they were tired, and two felt anxious. None of the participants had a bad temper, and 15 % stated they were relaxed.

Now we sum up the observations recorded during performing specific tasks with the app. Due to space, we focus here on first-aid measures and on locating an AED. When the test participants were asked to open the function "First Aid Measures" and to review the diagram in order to receive first-aid instructions, 57 % stated they knew which step to perform next at all times. Only 12 % felt uncertain about the tasks to be performed; 19 % judged the diagram as not suitable for the task and hoped for more instructions. On the other hand, 63 % judged the diagram to be suitable for learning, since they immediately understood the proper sequence of first-aid measures.

When asked whether they saw the circular symbol in the diagram at the box in the middle of the diagram in Fig. 2, 63 % of the participants denied. 20 % searched for the mentioned symbol on request and found it after an average of 7.6 s. Merely 16 % of the test subjects detected the circular symbol spontaneously. (Correct interpretation of this symbol is required for CPR performance to be effective.) Twelve participants stated here they would appreciate spoken statements or a combination of speech and graphics/text. Eight participants criticized the wording used in the diagram. "Compressions of the thorax" was judged by several participants as too technical a term. Seven test subjects remarked they had rather seen more graphics and less text. One of them asserted that "assembly instructions guide primarily via graphics and not via text; if they would consist mainly of text, people would probably not read it." Two of the study participants—medical doctors—commented that it is not evident from the diagram's graphics whether the movement of the victim's head in preparation of mouse-to-mouse/nose respiration is supposed to be a rotation or a reclination. The intended axis therefore should be depicted more clearly.

The most salient point of criticism concerned the fact that the user has to exit the first-aid guidelines in order to place an emergency call. Six participants voiced the idea that the feature of placing an emergency phone call should be integrated directly into the first-aid measures' diagram, possibly visualized as a button at the beginning of these guidelines. Great advantage of the integrated diagram lies in its suitability for learning. Even when no emergency occurs, the user is able to open the application in order to review the CPR steps in various circumstances. By always being able to refresh their first-aid knowledge, the user will be able to administer first aid more spontaneously when witnessing an emergency, as opposed to only relying on knowledge acquired during a first-aid course attended years ago (cf. the results in [6]).

The app "Defi Now!" contains a metronome for setting the CPR rhythm. The users were prompted to activate the acoustic signal indicating the adequate pace of chest compressions, and then to stop it. This task proved to be error-prone. Only 32 % of the participants recognized the trigger of the metronome immediately while scrolling to the bottom of the diagram (cf. Fig. 3). 40 % had more difficulties and were able to press the button predefining the resuscitation beat after an average of 6.3 s. 5 % initiated the beat after more than 10 s, and 23 % did merely see the trigger after instruction. The implementation did not seem satisfactory to them. Overall 58 % expressed the desire for more directions given by the application itself. 47 % presumed the trigger to be placed at a different location, for example, directly next to the graphics referring to CPR.

If not stopped manually, the metronome sounds repeatedly. When asked to stop the acoustic signal, 47 % were able to fulfill this task within 3.2 s. Nevertheless 41 % required 5 s or longer to pause the metronome. 65 % criticized the button label shown during the interval the metronome is active: While the acoustic signal sounds, the button displays the number of beats per minute and no label referring to stopping the beat.

Participants voiced misgivings regarding controllability, since it obviously takes the user some time to find the trigger setting the resuscitation beat and then to stop it again. Some participants criticized that a user would probably not even expect a metronome. Ten participants suggested highlighting the metronome-trigger, for example by labeling it more clearly, giving it a different color, or adjusting button size.

Moreover, the participants were asked to change the settings regarding the rhythm of CPR: As indicated above, the resuscitation beat can either be adjusted to 100 chest compressions per minute without mouth-to-mouth ventilation (100/minute) or to 30 thorax compressions and two mouth-to-mouth respirations (30:2). 47 % declared they recognized the button referring to the resuscitation beat's setting immediately (Fig. 3). 53 % experienced difficulties fulfilling the task of changing the rhythm of CPR. 26 % of the participants held the opinion that this facility was irrelevant, whereas 74 % acclaimed this option. Six participants criticized that the settings button was not salient enough and desired a more obvious labeling, for example, a written identification of the function of the button.

Three participants (medics) remarked that the duration of time scheduled for mouth-to-mouth ventilation, which is set to three seconds, might not suffice, because a movement by the rescuer is required between ventilation and CPR. Several participants (medical personnel and laymen) remarked that the option of altering settings might be obstructive. They argued that a user might be overchallenged by the options of cardiac-only resuscitation or CPR with mouth-to-mouth ventilation. For them, a precise instruction preinstalled in the application would be preferable. One user criticized the fact that the metronome stops as soon as the user quits the menu section

"First Aid Measures"—for example, in order to go to the map in search of an AED. Unless other users have the same application installed on their smartphones for seeking an AED, the first responder does not have the possibility to adjust his CPR to the pace preset by the metronome. They then might also not be able to keep up the rhythm, which might entail severe consequences, as stated before.

The task of setting the rhythm to perform CPR brought several problems to light concerning the operability. Several participants were not satisfied with the implementation of features such as the labeling of the buttons referring to the starting/stopping of the resuscitation beat and the settings concerning the rhythm for performing CPR. They evaluated these features as being not self-descriptive and expected a clearer labeling for better usability. Moreover they were not satisfied with the controllability since it took them some time to find the trigger starting the metronome and setting the resuscitation beat. They voiced that in an emergency time would be wasted searching for those precise functions and remarked that they should be implemented more eye-catching and distinctly comprehensible.

Testing step 3 "Find an AED" on the top level, where either a table view or an interactive map is provided (see Fig. 7 for the icons in the upper panel to evoke switching), unveiled a mismatch between (heavily inhomogeneous) user expectation and the provided user interface. 40 % of the participants stated they assumed this function within the menu section of adding a new AED location; 54 % expected the table view under "Find an AED". Seven study participants commented on the table view button. In their opinion a written labeling would have marked the function clearer. Three test subjects voiced the idea that the table view might be displayed before revealing the map. This might facilitate the understanding of which AED location is the nearest, legible by the distance value.

With respect to the overall navigation, inhomogeneity (e.g. once the "Back" button occurs in the lower panel whereas it resides usually in the upper left corner)

Fig. 7. Map and list presentation of AEDs. Mode change ensues after pressing the encircled buttons in the top panel.

leads to confusion—as expectable due to learning effects triggering certain user expectations. Unclear icons (cf. list icon ▦ in the left panel of Fig. 7) combined with their positioning cost operating time. Very prominently figures the "Information" button revealing the types of AEDs. Although the icon ⓘ ("i" in a grey circle) is well chosen, its size and position makes it "invisible" (cf. right lower corner in the map). It gets little attention due to the fact that in the same area a considerably bigger panel provides the pair of buttons ⊙ ↻ for getting back to the user's location and for reloading the map, respectively. As another item of smaller size in the same area, icon ⓘ is very likely overlooked.

Selecting a pin provides the selected AED's address. 89 % of the test subjects managed this task right away. However, closing the box again caused unexpected problems. The app expects the user to tap on the box but neither on the encircled blue ⊚ icon within the box nor the just selected AED icon once more nor on the map at any other destination. About 20 % of the test subjects confirmed this as user expectation. Slightly over 80 % indicated the wish for a clear closing symbol provided by the pop-up box.

Adding a new AED also caused more problems than expected—given that this feature is displayed on the app's start screen and described with an extra explanation (cf. start screen in Fig. 1, which shows the ⊞ symbol for adding an AED in the top-left corner). As the study shows, most users searched for the feature under step 3 "Find an AED". Only 11 % noticed its availability in a few seconds. Even when they were pointed to the screen in Fig. 1, they overlooked the explanation text—probably due to its position outside the top panel itself.

As for the final questionnaire, 63 % of the test subjects stated that they own a smartphone. The younger the participants the more likely they possess a smartphone. 25 test subjects visited a first-aid course in the last three years.

In general, 62 % of the participants would welcome spoken hints, rating them as being helpful. Most of them suggested a navigation device with spoken statements. Female participants appreciate spoken statements more than male test subjects, nine of

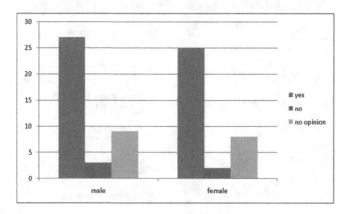

Fig. 8. More or less equal distribution of answers to the question whether or not the app is judged to be helpful in an emergency case for male and female test subjects.

whom stating they would even feel disturbed by spoken statements. Fifteen participants were neutral. When asked specifically whether the app would benefit from
providing spoken statements, 69 % of the participants clearly stated that they assume
it would. Here again more women than men were of this opinion.

Whether or not "Defi Now!" is appropriate when administering first aid in an
emergency, 70 % agreed (see Fig. 8 for the number of "yes"/"no"/"no opinion"
answers; y-axis denotes the number of test subjects). However, 7 % stated that the app
might distract a first responder as long as they are not acquainted with the app itself.
They argued that the user might be irritated by the graphics or not yet fully sophisticated features.

4 Optimizing the User Interface

Based on best practices in other systems and on our user study, we now propose some
easily attainable improvements to the user interface of a first-aid app, and illustrate
them with mock-ups.

In view of German privacy laws, it is advisable to add an installation dialog
requesting permission to localize the smartphone and to place an automatic emergency
call. This feature would also allow drawing the route to the next AED automatically,
such as in "PulsePoint". Mostly desirable is evoking installation without any emergency situation, but recommended by friends, encouraging to join the trained team of
rescuers alarmed in case of nearby emergencies by couching it into social network
environments such as "Arrêt Cardiaque 2.0".

In order to access all available functions easily, we propose a three-part start menu
where the "Emergency Mode" button is preselected as default, to so that no time is
wasted when selecting it under time pressure (cf. Fig. 9, left panel, where the red
color/looking as if already pushed indicates the default choice in Fig. 9). The second
item "Exploration Mode" invites users to try out the app and to learn about CPR and
about nearby AEDs when having spare time. This mode bypasses the emergency call
and directly presents the first-aid guidelines. Moreover, the option of adding AEDs to
the database as an available feature of the app becomes more visible as individual
third item on the screen (cf. the small number of participants who identified the add
button in "Defi Now!" (cf. Fig. 1)). The images[1] provided with each button function
here as eye catchers. They support fast perception of the items' content—following
the test subjects' preference for as little text as possible.

In the initial phase, in the top panel of the screen, a "Quit" button in the left corner
and a help button ⑦ (indicated by an encircled question mark) in the right corner are
permanently visible. Additionally, the top panel provides as headline the name of the
app (cf. left panel of Fig. 9).

After one out of the three items has been selected, its name becomes permanently
visible during the whole session in the top panel of the screen—replacing the app

---

[1] For copy-right of first photo see [23]; the second one stems from a campaign by the German Red
Cross to learn first aid [24]; the third one is an adaptation of a "DefiNow!" map.

Fig. 9. Left panel: Revised top-level screen; right panel: Revised first-aid graph with permanently visible tab-navigation.

name. The "Quit" function of the whole application changes to "Exit" for the currently selected mode. The help button in form of a question mark remains permanently available in the top-right corner where smartphone users nowadays expect help.

Given the observed confusion during navigation, we propose a tab-based surface as used in several other first-aid apps as we outlined in Sect. 2 (cf. second layer of the upper area on the smartphone screen in the right panel of Fig. 9 providing the four tabs "112", "First Aid", "AED Map" and "AED List"). Red color indicates which tab is currently active. Moreover, the emergency call tab (in Germany 112) could become dark grey after having been used once, supporting the rescuer to keep in mind that all necessary steps have already been performed. In case the user returns to that tab, a confirmation of the already made call could appear instead of the initial dialogue suggesting to place an emergency call.

Our user study showed that users have varying expectations about how available AEDs should be best presented to them when they have to find the nearest one. Some prefer a map whereas others find a list more suitable. We could not identify a clearly preferred mode. In order to prevent the user from any additional dialog steps, we suggest that both modes occur in the tabulator list (cf. "AED Map" vs. "AED List").

The application could include more and better graphical support of the first-aid measures—although the participants were fairly satisfied with the presented guidelines. Which graphics and/or videos (cf. examples in Fig. 5) serve the purpose best is an issue to be explored in collaboration with medical experts.

Deciding on the preferred default metronome trigger is a debated issue. Most first-aid courses teach a 30:2 rhythm (see, e.g., [25] for recent recommendations). Thus, we have chosen this mode as default. So far we made the CPR loop more visible (cf. the prominent "Repeat" loop in red compared to the small loop in the right lower corner for that step in Fig. 2). Moreover, the choice options for the metronome function to support CPR became integrated into the graph—as some test subjects suggested. It is now permanently visible. The available audio support is illustrated by a loudspeaker symbol 🔊. It is touch-sensitive—as is a confirmed user expectation—so that the user can switch it on or off as desired. The audio support changes between the two modes by touching the area where the mode is described. In reply, the audio starts in the selected rhythm and the color of the selected mode switches to red whereas the previous option becomes grey and the loudspeaker there goes into off position 🔇 .

In case the realization for CPR mode choice is desired as it is realized now in "Defi NOW!", i.e. a bottom line serves for that purpose, it might be a good idea that both options are directly visible. However, this costs additional space for the additional lines with the disadvantage that it either hides parts of the first-aid graphics or its size has to become smaller. Given the problems we observed during our study, switching the metronome function on and off should become more intuitive by realizing by clear labeling or an obvious loudspeaker symbol.

In order to avoid any loss of time when trying to find the next AED, the dialogues within the maps could be improved. As many test subjects suggested, without loss of space a clear symbol for closing currently displayed information could be provided (see Fig. 10 where the widely applied "x" in the right upper corner closes the window again). Additional information is available by tapping the box once more. This action is elicited more readily by the icon ℹ️ on a blue background than by the ⓘ icon. In order to avoid ambiguous pointing on the small screen, we moved it intentionally away from the closure icon "x".

Fig.10. Left panel: Pop-up box in "Defi Now!". Right panel: Revised pop-up box with a closing icon "x" in the right upper corner and an "i" icon for more information.

5   Conclusions

We have outlined features of different first-aid apps to support rescuing persons suffering from cardiac arrest where immediate help is essential. The participants gave a positive answer to the question of whether or not the "Defi Now!" app is really helpful in an emergency case. We proposed some improvements concluding from best practices in various first-aid apps and from observations during our usability study.

As for future work, more graphical support combined with spoken input/output in such a device will be implemented and tested through prototypes. Beside the audio support for the CPR rhythm, spoken commands supporting graphics and text on the one hand, and managing the whole app on the other, are not provided in any first-aid app so far. Spoken commands have the advantage that hands and eyes of the rescuer are free to administer help—presupposing that background noise is not too disturbing. For instance, a text-to-speech component could be activated when touching a box or image in the first-aid guidelines. The use of spoken commands needs more fine-grained strategies in order not to spoil the support provided by the highly recommended continuous metronome function that guides the correct heart compression rhythm. The design should also pay attention to the objections of users who do not appreciate an oral communication channel. An interesting source to learn how such support texts in an app could look like provides the archive of conducted CPR support via phone by first-aid trained staff [26].

Moreover, we consider integration of first-aid training into an interactive—maybe competitive—*game*.

References

1. Gesundheitsberichterstattung des Bundes. http://www.gbe-bund.de
2. American Heart Association. http://www.heart.org
3. Cummins, R.O., Eisenberg, M.S., Hallstrom, A.P., Litwin, P.E.: Survival of out-of-hospital cardiac arrest with early initiation of cardiopulmonary resuscitation. Am. J. Emerg. Med. **3**(2), 114–119 (1985)
4. Darley, J.M., Latané, J.M.: Bystander intervention in emergencies: diffusion of responsibility. J. Pers. Soc. Psychol. **8**, 377–383 (1968)
5. Jörg, G.: Warum Menschen anderen nicht helfen. http://www.fh-heidelberg.de/?id=5236 (2012)
6. Mata, J., Frank, R., Gigerenzer, G.: Symptom recognition of heart attack and stroke in nine European countries: a representative study. Health Expect. (2014). doi:10.1111/j.1369-7625.2011.00764.x
7. http://www.madison.at
8. http://www.associationrmcbfm.fr
9. http://www.aedlocator.org/
10. http://definow.org
11. http://www.herzsicher.ch
12. http://pulsepoint.org
13. Lange, T.: Entwicklung eines Defibrillator-Verzeichnisses mit zugehöriger Smartphone-Applikation. Diploma Thesis, University of Koblenz-Landau (2011)
14. Hampe, J.F., Stein, S.: "Defi Now!" Entwicklung eines mobilen Clients zur Community-basierten Bereitstellung von Defibrillatorstandorten. In: Multikonferenz der Wirtschaftsinformatik 2012, Braunschweig, Germany, Berlin: GITO, pp. 302–316 (2012)
15. Krause, M., Stein, S., Hampe, J.F.: "Defi Now!" Entwicklung eines inter-organisationalen Defibrillatoren-Registers. In: Erstes Symposium ICT in der Notfall-medizin. Rauischholzhausen. Düsseldorf: German Medical Science Publishing House, pp. 43–48 (2012)

16. http://firedepartment.org
17. Nielsen, J.: Usability Engineering. Academic Press, Cambridge (1994)
18. Otto, J.H.: Methoden der Emotionsforschung: Induktionsverfahren. In: Otto, J.H. (ed.) Emotionspsychologie, pp. 395–408. Beltz, Weinheim (2000)
19. Hewig, J., Hagemann, D., Seifert, J., Gollwitzer, M., Naumann, E., Bartussek, D.: A revised film set for the induction of basic emotions. Cogn. Emot. **19**(7), 1095–1109 (2005)
20. Schleicher, R.: Emotionen & Peripherpherphysiologie. Pabst Science Publishers, Lengerich (2009)
21. Gross, J.J., Levenson, R.W.: Emotion elicitation using films. Cogn. Emot. **9**(1), 87–108 (1995)
22. Rohrmann, B.: Empirische Studien zur Entwicklung von Antwortskalen für die sozialwissenschaftliche Forschung. Sozialpsychologie **9**, 222–245 (1978)
23. http://de.depositphotos.com/
24. http://www.drk-attendorn.de
25. Nolan, J.P., Soar, J., Zideman, D.A., Biarent, D., Bossaert, L.L. Deakin, C., Koster, R.W., Wyllie, J., Böttiger, B.: European Resuscitation Council Guidelines for Resuscitation 2010 Section 1. Executive summary. Resuscitation **81**, 1219–1276 (2010) (see http://dx.doi.org/10.1016/j.resuscitation.2010.08.021)
26. http://www.reanimationsregister.de/aktuelles/91-telefon-reanimation-datenerfassung-im-deutschen-reanimationsregister.html

Self-Service Classroom Capture Generating Interactive Multivideo Objects

Caio César Viel[1], Erick Lazaro Melo[1],
Maria da Graça C. Pimentel[2]([✉]), and Cesar A.C. Teixeira[1]

[1] Universidade Federal de São Carlos, São Carlos, SP, Brazil
[2] Universidade de São Paulo, São Carlos, SP, Brazil
{caio_viel,erick_melo,cesar}@dc.ufscar.br, mgp@icmc.usp.br

Abstract. The capture of lectures for the generation of associated videos is mainstream in several locations. Alternative approaches include the capture of real lectures or studio-produced ones, the latter designed with the only purpose of generating the associated videos. The amount of control offered to instructors during the capture process varies from system to system. In cases in which the lectures are delivered in classrooms while regular classes take place, the capture may occur according to programmed schedules which are unaware of the presence of the instructor in the classroom, and may start before the instructor is in place and may end before the instructor concludes the lecture – the latter occurring when the instructor passes the scheduled time, a situation which is not uncommon in traditional courses. In cases in which the lectures are delivered in studios, the capture is usually directed by professionals that control start and ending times and orient the instructor to look at specific cameras, for instance. We built a prototype system that offers instructors facilities to control the starting and ending times of multiple segments so that the overall exposition is transformed into a corresponding interactive multivideo object, exploiting the multimodal and multi-device nature of the presentation. After a brief overview of our prototype, in this paper we present the document-based workflow which underlies the processes of capture, generation and presentation that offer instructors a self-service alternative to control the generation of a multimedia object composed of synchronized videos, audio, images and context information associated to the lecture. We illustrate the utility of the approach by summarizing data relative to the use of our prototype by a group of instructors.

Keywords: Interactive multimedia · E-learning · Ubiquitous capture · Capture and access · NCL · Interactions

1 Introduction

As demonstrated in the late '90s [1,13], the generation of the web-based lectures achieved by capturing live lectures exploits the fact that the classroom

© Springer International Publishing Switzerland 2014
S. Hammoudi et al. (Eds.): ICEIS 2013, LNBIP 190, pp. 438–456, 2014.
DOI: 10.1007/978-3-319-09492-2_26

can be viewed as a rich multimedia environment where audiovisual information is combined with annotating activities to produce complex multimedia objects. Current platforms that support the capture the capture of lectures include *Matterhorn* [3][1], *virtPresenter* [19], *Video Lectures*[2], *Echo360*[3] and *Eya* [6][4].

Even though there are strong divergences among educators as to the efficiency of the lecture format as a method of instruction, the capture of lectures for the generation of associated videos have become mainstream in several locations, the aim being to offer students the opportunity of review their class lectures after the class[5] using nothing more than a web[6] browser. Moreover, the use of low quality video and high quality images has proven[7] to be very useful.

The amount of control offered to instructors during the capture process varies from system to system. Some systems allow instructors to deliver their lecture in a studio without students, which is a demand for massive online courses such as those deployed in the *coursera*[8] and *edX*[9] platforms. Yet another demand is the generation of lectures via (whiteboard) screencasting, a case in point being the Khan Academy [11]. Given that in many scenarios the lecture material is produced using more than one video source – one video for the instructor and another for the slide or the whiteboard, for instance – recent systems such as Matterhorn and Echo360 allow users to review the contents using more than a single video stream. This is also the case with videoconferencing-based systems which may used in synchronous learning such as BigBlueButton[10] and others [21]. In cases in which the lectures are delivered in classrooms while regular classes take place, the capture may occur according to programmed schedules which are unaware of the presence of the instructor in the classroom, and may start before the instructor is in place and may end before the instructor concludes the lecture – the latter occurring when the instructor passes scheduled time, a situation which is not uncommon in traditional courses. In cases in which the lectures are delivered in studios, the capture is usually directed by professionals that control start and ending times and orient the instructor to look at specific cameras, for instance.

We built a prototype system that offers instructors facilities to control the starting and ending times of multiple segments of lectures so that the overall exposition is transformed into a corresponding interactive multivideo object,

---

[1] http://opencast.org/matterhorn

[2] http://videolectures.net

[3] http://echo360.com

[4] http://sdu.ictp.it/eya

[5] http://sites.la.utexas.edu/lecturecapture

[6] http://caen.engin.umich.edu/lecrecording

[7] http://sdu.ictp.it/eya

[8] www.coursera.org

[9] www.edx.org

[10] http://bigbluebutton.org

exploiting the multimodal and multi-device nature of the presentation. The capture process, pervasive and without human mediation, triggers the automatic generation of an interactive multi-video object associated with the lecture.

Given the several sources of information available in the classroom and that are pervasively captured by our system, students must be given a broad range of interaction alternatives when reviewing the lecture. Our system produces an interactive multivideo object which not only combines the several video streams with contextual and control information but also offers navigation options in the form of *points of interest* such as slides transitions and the position of lecturer in the classroom.

As a result, our approach allows one to interact with the recorded lecture in novel dimensions. The student may be able, for example, to use a multi-window panel to review multiple synchronized audiovisual content that includes the slide presentation, the lecturer's web browsing, the whiteboard content, video streams with focus on the lecturer's face or the lecturer's full body, among others. The student has the option to select, at any time, which video object is more relevant to be exhibited on one larger screen. The student is also able to execute semantic browsing operations using *points of interest* like slide transitions, spoken keywords, lecturer's interactions, etc.

In this paper we present the document-based workflow which underlies the processes of capture, generation and presentation that offer instructors a self-service alternative to control the generation of a multimedia object composed of synchronized videos, audio, images and context information associated to the lecture. We illustrate the utility of the approach by summarizing data relative to the use of our prototype by a group of instructors.

This paper is organized as follows: in Sect. 2 we discuss related works; in Sect. 3 we briefly review our proposed model and corresponding prototype and detail the capture interface; in Sect. 4 we detail our document-based workflow; in Sect. 5 we present results from our the system in use; and in Sect. 6 we present our final remarks.

2   Related Work

The production of video-based educational material can be achieved using a studio-like approach. This approach is very popular and it is used in many platforms of Massive Open Online Courses (MOOC) and other distance education such as coursera[11], edx[12], UAB[13] and videolectures[14]. The instructor enters a TV-like studio and delivers her presentation to cameramen and directors. In this approach, the instructor has few control over the format and recording time, which are in charge of the production crew.

---

[11] www.coursera.org

[12] www.edx.org

[13] www.uab.capes.gov.br

[14] http://videolectures.net

Systems for automatic or semi-automatic recording lectures can be used to remove or reduce the need for a production crew. Some systems, such as Echo360[15], Eya [5] and Matterhorn[16] use a scheduled time to recording the lecture. These systems have the advantage that the instructors do not have to worry about controlling the capture, but they lack flexibility. For instance, if a instructor finishes her presentation earlier, the system will continue the recording. Also, this approach does not allow an instructor to finish her presentation after the scheduled time.

As an alternative to the scheduled approach, the self-service approach allows the instructor to have control over the recording time, but requires that the instructor (or a technical person) operate the system (e.g. [2,4,7–10,12,14,16, 17]).

The model for capturing and recovering lectures we adopt allows more flexibility than the ones above mentioned. The flexibility comes from the ability to specify which context information is captured, how the context information is combined to generate alternative navigation interactions in the resulting multivideo object (as detailed in Sect. 4), and to promote live interventions in the classroom during the capture process — for example, when there is a change in the illumination of the room.

3   Capture and Access Approach

Our proposal works toward a self-service approach, allowing instructors to record lectures themselves.

3.1   Pervasive Capture and Access

Some existing solutions rely on computational vision, tracking techniques and sensors to perform camera orchestrations in a attempt to produce a single video or audio stream output. The approach we propose goes a step further: it aims at capturing the lecture in its entirety by recording much of the content presented in the classroom. The capture process is pervasive, does not rely on human mediation and automatically generates an interactive multivideo object designed to preserve as much of the lecture content and context as possible.

Our approach demands an environment (usually a classroom) which is instrumented with physical devices such as video cameras, microphones, (interactive) whiteboards and projectors (Fig. 1A). The instrumented classroom may also contain sensors, such as temperature and luminosity sensors, and secondary screens, such as notebooks, TVs, tablets, etc. The video cameras should be positioned where it is possible to frame important views of the environment (instructor, students, whiteboard, slides, etc.).

---

[15] http://echo360.com

[16] http://opencast.org/matterhorn

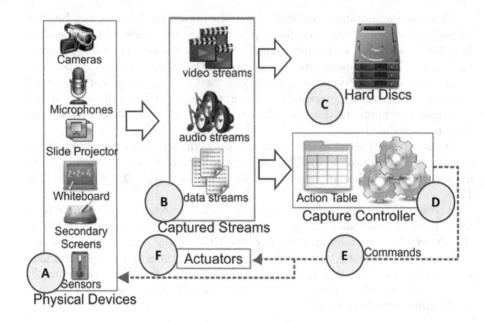

Fig. 1. Pervasive capture and access model.

Computer devices capture the content produced by the physical devices used in the classroom (e.g. whiteboards and slides) and represent them as video, audio and data streams (Fig. 1B). Cameras produce video (and audio) streams, microphones produce audio streams, and sensors produce data streams. By capturing the screen output from the secondary screens or by intercepting the signal sent to the slide projector, we can also produce video streams. The electronic whiteboard can produce both data and video streams: by capturing ink strokes, we can generate a data stream, and by intercepting the output signal sent to the projector, we can generate a video stream.

All captured streams are stored (Fig. 1C) for future use in the multivideo object generation. The streams are also sent to the *capture controller* (Fig. 1D), a component responsible for managing the capture process. The *capture controller* uses signal processing to analyze the captured streams and to send commands (Fig. 1E) back to the physical devices and actuators (Fig. 1F) located in the classroom.

The multivideo object is composed of videos and other captured media — with the association of the appropriate metadata, they would become multivideo learning objects.[17] Although the multivideo object is not able to reproduce the live lecture experience in its totality (which would involve live interactions, odors, temperature, etc.), it offers several interaction alternatives for the students while they are watching the lecture. These may diminish the loss of not having the

---

[17] http://www.ieeeltsc.org/

students present in the classroom, when direct interaction between instructor and students usually bring benefits to the learning process.

3.2 Capture and Access Prototype

As a proof-of-concept of our proposed approach, we developed a prototype tool for capturing lectures and generating multivideo learning objects.

The capture tool prototype was deployed in an instrumented multi-purpose classroom (Fig. 2). In the front of the classroom (Fig. 2(a)) there is a conventional whiteboard, an electronic whiteboard and a notebook in which the presenter can browse the web or use any other software. The interactive whiteboard can be used to present slides (there is a Bluetooth presenter to control the presentation) and it allows drawing and writing over the screen. At the back side (Fig. 2(b)) we placed two AVCHD, each one framing the interactive or the conventional whiteboard. We also placed a webcam as a wide-shot cam, framing the whole front of the room. As the room is a shared space in the university, the equipment is stored in lockers.

(a) Front   (b) Back

Fig. 2. Instrumented room.

Figure 3 illustrates the playback of three multivideo objects generated by the prototype. The multivideo offers some facilities for students. One of these facilities is the synchronization of the captured audio/video. The multivideo object synchronizes the multiple audio/video streams, so students can see what was written in the whiteboard when the lecturer points to the slide presentation. This synchronization is essential to recover the whole audiovisual context of the captured lecture at a given moment. It also offers a more semantic and easier way to navigate in the captured lecture than timeline navigation. For instance, a student can move forward to the next slide transition or backwards to the previous one. When the lecturer begins to write something in the whiteboard, the student can skip all the writing process and see the final result. Similar to in-classroom lecture, wherein the student can pay attention to different spots (the lecturer, whiteboard, slide presentation, the textbook, or another screen),

(a) Multiple Videos   (b) Full-screen

(c) Timeline

Fig. 3. Three views of one multivideo object.

the multivideo object allows the student to choose which video stream he wishes to see and he can even see more than one at the same time.

3.3 Capturing Tool

Figure 4 depicts an overview of the prototype, which was developed mainly in Python. The capturing process is based on video streams, which correspond to video and audio streams produced by AVCHD and outputs produced by computers, such as computer screens and slide presentations. One of the main components is a *capturing tool*, called *classrec*: as indicated in Fig. 4A, specific portions of *classrec* are designed identify and communicate with capture devices (*Device Interface*), to recognize objects in a video stream (*Recognizer*)[18], to carry out audio and video encoding (*A/V Encoding*)[19] to communicate with other components (*Communication*) and to store the capture streams (*Persistence*).

There is one instance of *classrec* for each captured stream (e.g. Figure 4B). The execution of the components is orchestrated via messages exchanged with the support of a message broker (Fig. 4C). All the captured media is stored in a common database (Fig. 4D).

---

[18] Using the *OpenCV* library (http://opencv.org).
[19] Using the *libav* library (https://libav.org).

There is one special instance of *classrec*, called *SessionManager* (Fig. 4E), which corresponds to the *CaptureController* that controls the session as presented earlier in Fig. 1D. The prototype also contains one instance of a *processing tool*, called *classgen* (Fig. 4F), in charge of both analyzing the streams and generating the multivideo object (Fig. 4G).

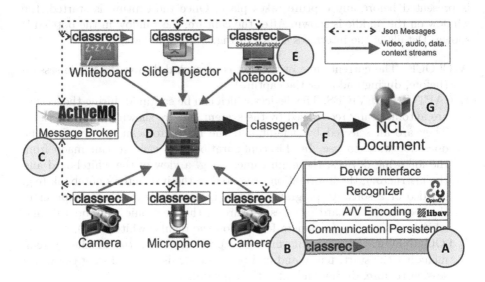

Fig. 4. Prototype overview.

Once the multivideo object is generated, it can be interacted with using a *presentation tool*. Given the importance of the web as a platform for desktop and mobile devices, the *NCL document* (Fig. 4G) can be played back and interacted with in web browsers by an NCL player such the HTML5-based WebNCL [15] as illustrated in Fig. 3. The NCL declarative language is the ITU-T standard declarative language for multimedia IPTV services [20].

It is important to observe that the *NCL document* in Fig. 4G is a declarative XML-based document which was generated by the *classgen* (Fig. 4E) component. This is because our approach is to generate an intermediate XML document which can be transformed into any desired format. This is further discussed Sect. 4.

A more detailed description for the prototype can be found elsewhere [15,23].

3.4 Capturing Interface

In the instrumented classroom, when one instructor wants to record his presentation, all he needs to do is to press one button. Next, he can deliver his lecture as usual. When the lecture is finished, all he needs to do is to press another button. The instructor may plan to divide the capture in small modules, and may choose to discard any module at any time to repeat its recording.

Figure 5 shows the interface offered to an instructor to capture his lecture before he starts the capture (top), during capture (middle) and after the capture (bottom). Upon starting the application, the window on the top is shown, and is presented before any capture takes place. Once the capture is started, the window on the middle is shown. After the capture, the window in the bottom is shown. Details of the interfaces shown in Fig. 5 are as follows:

A CLOCK: The current time of the day is presented during the whole session (before, during and after the capture).

B CAPTURE DEVICES: The devices which can be captured during the lecture are automatically recognized by the system and are shown on the top right. They are all selected by default and the instructor can remove those he does not want to use. In this configuration, the capture can made from the following devices: the main camera (e.g. a view of the whiteboard and the instructor), the information presented in the instructor's notebook (e.g. a video or a software program), slides (presented by another computer in the room), whiteboard (strokes capture in the electronic whiteboard), and whiteboard camera (a camera focused on the regular whiteboard).

C LOG INFORMATION: Information reporting the status of the system, including the start, pause and end of recording, is shown during the whole session (before, during and after the capture).

D MODULE NAME: A lecture may be split into several modules, and the name of each module recording is chosen by the instructor before the start of the session.

E START BUTTON: When the instructor is ready to start the capture, he clicks on the start button. This enables the buttons PAUSE and STOP.

F RED LED and TIMER: The ongoing capture is indicated by a "red led" in the interface: a timer shown on the left-hand side shows the duration of the current captured module.

G PAUSE: At any moment the instructor may pause the recording. When this happens, the START button is enabled, the PAUSE is disabled, the STOP buttons remains enabled.

H STOP: At any moment the instructor may stop the recording. At this moment the options available are RESUME, SAVE and DISCARD.

I MODULES RECORDED: A list of modules recorded for one particular lecture is shown.

J SAVE: if the inscrutor is satisfied with the module he has just captured, he can save it.

K DISCARD: if the inscrutor is not satisfied with the module he has just captured, he can discard it.

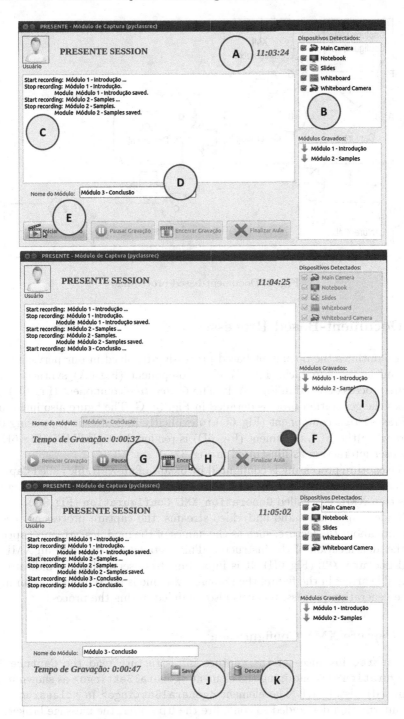

Fig. 5. The self service capture interface: before the capture (top), during capture (middle) and after the capture (bottom).

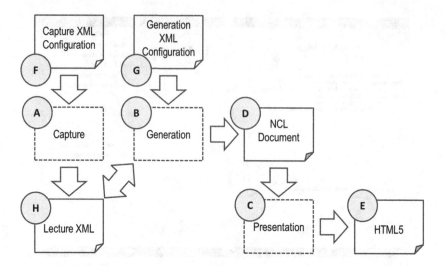

Fig. 6. Document-based processing.

4 Document-Based Processes

Figure 6 outlines the document-based processing involved in our pervasive capture and access approach. The *Capture* component (Fig. 6A) synthesises the capture process detailed in Fig. 4A–E. The *Generation* component (Fig. 6B) synthesises the generation process detailed in Fig. 4F–G. The figure also introduces the *Presentation* component (Fig. 6C) to explicitly indicate the processing that occurs when the NCL document (Fig. 6D) is rendered into HTML5 (Fig. 6E) to allow user interaction as illustrated in Fig. 3.

The capture processing is configured by means of an XML file called `Capture XML Configuration` (Fig. 6F). The generation processing in turn is configured by its own XML file, called `Generation XML Configuration` (Fig. 6G).

Besides capturing audio and video streams, the capture processing records metadata about the lecture, such as the names of the modules, streams captured and the identification of the instructor. This metadata is stored in an XML file called `Lecture XML` (Fig. 6H). It is important to observe that, as indicated by the double arrow in the figure, the `Lecture XML` file is not only used as an input by the generation process, but it is also modified during the process.

4.1 Capture XML Configuration

All `classrec` instances of the capture infrastructure read the `Capture XML Configuration` file containing the element `<generalSettings>` as shown in the (simplified) Listing 1.1. The element `<generalSettings>` in `<classrec>` contains information demanded to configure the ftp server, the message broker and the working directory (the location where the files generated from the captured process will be stored).

Listing 1.1. XML Configuration file: generalSettings.

```
<classrec>
  <generalSettings>
                  <workDirectory type="local">
                  /home/presente</workDirectory>
                  <broker>...</broker>
                  <ftp>...</ftp>
  </generalSettings>
```

Only the session manager contains the `<deviceBase>` element depicted in Listing 1.2. This element specifies the devices used during the capture process, each device represented by a `<device>` element. (Lines 2–12 specifies a device with ID NOTEBOOK and type SCREEN, which indicates the capture of the secondary screen of the device). The element `<video>` specifies how the video will be captured. (Lines 4–10 specifies an X11 terminal (a Unix window manager) at a resolution of 1280×1024 pixels and 24 frames per second). One camera is also specified (BOARD_CAM in line 13). It is possible to define other video cameras or webcams, microphones, screen (PCs), whiteboards and slide presentations.

Listing 1.2. XML Configuration file: deviceBase.

```
<deviceBase>
    <device type="SCREEN" id="NOTEBOOK">
          <name>Instructor's Notebook</name>
      <video source="X11GRAB">
                  <inputName>0:0</inputName>
                  <width>1280</width>
                  <height>1024</height>
          <framerate>24</framerate>
          <transcodingParams>-same_quant -vcodec mpeg2video
          </transcodingParams>
        </video>
    </device>
          <device type="CAMHDV" id="BOARD_CAM">...</device>
  </deviceBase>
</classrec>
```

4.2 Lecture XML

The Lecture XML file specifies metadata about the captured video and audio streams, as in the simplified version shown in Listing 1.3. This file is generated by the capture process (i.e., by the *Capture* component in Fig. 6A which abstracts the several classrec modules in Fig. 4) and used by the generation process (Fig. 6B).

In Listing 1.3, the `<head>` element (Lines 2–8) specifies information about the author, the date and the lecture (e.g. title). The `<body>` element (Lines 9–38) contains one or more <module> elements, each <module> element representing one of the modules captured. The element <module> (lines 10–37) in turn contains <media> elements (Lines 11–18 and 19–28) which represent the audio and video streams captured by the devices. The <media> element holds information about the media itself (size, frame rate, length) and the ID of the device that generated it. Note that the device ID is the same one specified in the <device> element of the Capture XML Configuration document.

When a Lecture XML document is generated by the classrec module, it does not contain <pointofInterest> elements to register, for instance, the time instants of slides transitions and of changes in the position of lecturer in the classroom. These elements are generated by the classgen module when processing the captured data (see below). The <pointofInterest> elements (lines 29–33 and 34–36) inside a <module> element register such context information along with their type, starting and ending times, and the identification of their corresponding recognizers.

Listing 1.3. The Lecture XML:head and module.

```
<session  date="2013−10−09T10:01:53.723381Z"  id="lecture001">
  <head>
    <meta  content="Presente0.1"  name="GeneratorTool"/>
    <meta  content="Introduction  for  Android"  name="Title"/>
    <meta  content="AndroidDev"  name="Course"/>
    <meta  content="Mateus"  name="Author"/>
    <meta  content="Algebra  Linear , Matematica ,"  name="Tags"/>
  </head>
  <body>
    <module  name="Module  1"  id="module1">
      <media  deviceType="SCREEN"
              type="video"  deviceId="NOTEBOOK"  id="video1">
        <video  src="video1 .webm"  type="FILE_WEBM"/>
        <info  name="duration"  value="4391.947"/>
        <info  name="width"  value="1366"/>
        <info  name="fps"  value="24"/>
        <info  name="height"  value="768"/>
      </media>
      <media  deviceType="CAMHDV"
              type="video"  deviceId="SLIDES_CAM"  id="video2">
        <video  src="video2 .webm"  type="FILE_WEBM"/>
        <info  name="height"  value="720"/>
        <info  name="channels"  value="2"/>
        <info  name="width"  value="1280"/>
        <info  name="fps"  value="24"/>
        <info  name="duration"  value="4391.943"/>
        <info  name="samplerate"  value="44000"/>
      </media>
      <pointofInterest  type="FACE"
                        recognizerId="rgzFace2">
        <begin >416.25</begin >
```

```
      <end>422.5</end>
    </pointofInterest>
    <pointofInterest type="SLIDE" recognizerId="rgzSlide">
      ...
    </pointofInterest>
  </module>
  <module name="Module 2" id="module2">...</module>
</body>
</session>
```

4.3   Generation XML Configuration

Listing 1.4 shows a simplified `Generation XML Configuration` file, which is used as input for the generation process (Fig. 6B). It contains an element `<recognitionBase>` which in turn specifies the recognizers components that will analyze the captured data. Each recognizer is represented by a `<recognizer>`. The `<recognizer>` element defines the recognizer type and other parameters. For instance, in lines 2–15 the `<recognizer> rgzFace` processes the videos capture from the device `BOARD_CAM` (lines 4–5).

The `Generation XML Configuration` file can define several elements of the type `<recognizer>` (e.g. lines 2–15 e 16–18 in Listing 1.4). Once the processing corresponding to one `<recognizer>` identifies points of interest, it modifies the file `Lecture XML` by adding the corresponding information in new `<pointOfInterest>` elements (lines 29–36 and 34–36 in Listing 1.3).

Listing 1.4. Generation XML Configuration: recognitionBase.

```
<recognitionBase>
  <recognizer id="rgzFace" type="PATERN" subtype="FACE">
    <inputMapping>
        <inputStream internalName="CAMERA_FACE"
                     deviceId="BOARD_CAM" type="VIDEO"/>
    </inputMapping>
      <xmlCascade>data/haarcascade_frontalface_alt.xml
    </xmlCascade>
      <scaleFactor>1.2</scaleFactor>
      <minimunNeighbors>2</minimunNeighbors>
      <minimunHeight>100</minimunHeight>
      <minimunWidth>100</minimunWidth>
      <leapStep>10</leapStep>
      <minimunSpacing>5</minimunSpacing>
      <minimunDuration>7</minimunDuration>
  </recognizer>
  <recognizer id="rgzSlide"
                   type="TRANSITION" subtype="SLIDE">...
  </recognizer>
<orchestrationSettings>...</orchestrationSettings>
```

<generatorBase >... </ generatorBase>

The `Generation XML Configuration` file may also contain an element `<or-chestrationSettings>` (Listing 1.5) and a `<generatorBase>` (Listing 1.6).

The `<orchestrationSettings>` specifies the orchestration process (Listing 1.5), and defines which streams will be used in the orchestration process (`<inputMapping>` in lines 3–5). Each stream is identified by the device ID from the device that captured it and is associated with a recognizer component. The orchestration process uses the points of interest detected to generate the orchestration stream. For instance, if the recognizer `rgzWhiteBoard` (line 4) detects a point of interest which begins at second 5 and ends at second 12, the correspondent segment from the stream generated by the device `CAMERA_CLOSE` (which is associated with the recognizer `rgzWhiteBoard`) will be used to generate the orchestration stream.

It is also possible to define the order of precedence for the streams, in case two points of interest overlap. The `<orchestrationSettings>` also has the element `<baseStream>` (Line 7) to define the stream that will be used when there are no points of interest. Also, the element `<audioStream>` (line 8) defines which audio stream will be used in the orchestration stream.

Listing 1.5. Generation XML Configuration: orchestrationSettings.

```
<orchestrationSettings>
  <inputMapping>
    <inputStream alias="CAMERA_CLOSE"
        deviceId="BOARD_CAM" recognizerId="rgzWhiteBoard"
                        type="VIDEO" precedence="3"/>
    <inputStream .../>
  <baseStream>CAMERA_GENERAL</baseStream>
  <audioStream>CAMERA_BOARD</audioStream>
  <minimunDuration>5</minimunDuration>
  <faultThreshold>3</faultThreshold>
  <successThreshold>3</successThreshold>
</orchestrationSettings>
```

The `<generatorBase>` element (Listing 1.6) is used to define the output format for the multivideo object. Since the *Generation* component (Fig. 6B) can generate different versions of multimedia objects for the same captured lecture, each version is defined by one `<generator>` element.

Our current implementation generates only NCL documents (line 2), but it can be extended to generate multimedia objects in other formats, such as HTML5 directly. The element `<generator>` in turn contains `<mediaSlot>` and `<pointsOfInterestSlot>` elements, which define which streams and points of interest will be used to generate the multimedia object. The media streams used can be captured from the devices (lines 4–6) or the orchestration stream (line 7).

Listing 1.6. Generation XML Configuration: generatorBase.

```
<generatorBase>
 <generator id="nclGenerator" type="PyNclGenerator">
   <mediaSlot>
     <slot id="0" mediaType="VIDEO" sourceType="DEVICE" source="BOARD_CAM" />
     <slot id="1" mediaType="VIDEO" sourceType="DEVICE" source="CLOSE_CAM"/>
     <slot id="2" mediaType="VIDEO" sourceType="DEVICE" source="SLIDE"/>
     <slot id="3" mediaType="VIDEO" sourceType="ORCHESTRATION" />
   </mediaSlot>
   <pointsOfInterestSlot>
     <pointOfInterest type="FACE" recognizerId="rgzFace" />
     <pointOfInterest type="SLIDE" recognizerId="rgzSlide" />
     <pointOfInterest type="WHITEBOARD" recognizerId="rgzWhiteBoard" />
   </pointsOfInterestSlot>
   <outputName>main.ncl</outputName>
   <nclInterfacePath>
           /home/presente/pyclassrec/ncl_interface
   </nclInterfacePath>
 </generator>
</generatorBase>
```

Note that the elements `<recognitionBase>`, `<orchestrationSettings>` and `<generatorBase>` are all optional in the `Generation XML Configuration` file.

5 Self-Service Capture in Use

Several instructors tried out our prototype, and 9 of them used the system to record lectures. In two opportunities the instructors recorded traditional classes with their groups of students. The instructors were all professors from the Computer Science Department. The recorded lectures were on subjects for the following courses: Computer Organization, Computers Networks, Databases, Distributed Systems; Research Methodology. One instructor also recorded a tutorial on Android Development Tutorial. The prototype was also used to record a term paper presentation, two M.Sc. qualifier exams, one M.Sc. defense, and several demonstrations for workshops.

After a short explanation of how to use the capture tool, all the instructors able to carry out the recording alone, as expected by our self-service proposal. Since the room is a real classroom, the lecturers could perform their presentations naturally, despite the cameras. Some of them did not modularize the presentation and record a single long module. We also observed that most lecturers did not use all the resources available in the environment.

We also carried out three case studies with students of Computer Science and Computer Engineering Majors enrolled in traditional courses, and with students enrolled in an Information Systems Major offered via distance learning. In each case study we invited a professor to capture one lecture. One lecture was for a Computer Organization course. Another lecture was part of an Analysis of Algorithms course. The third lecture was part of a Database course. More details about these case studies can be found elsewhere [22–24].

6 Final Remarks

Extra-class material may be offered to students in the form of multimedia objects that integrates synchronized text, image, audio and video explanations on the studied subject. Context information informing moments of interest such as slide transitions can be included in the multimedia object to provide students with opportunities of semantic navigation.

The model for capturing and recovering lectures we propose uses a fraction of the resources when compared to systems which demand the support of specialized staff — the reason is that the captured is directed by the instructor himself in a self-service approach. Our model also offers more flexibility than systems which use programmed schedules which are unaware of the presence of the instructor in the classroom.

Built according to our pervasive capture-based model, our prototype system offers instructors facilities to control the starting and ending times of multiple segments so that the overall exposition is transformed into a corresponding interactive multivideo object, exploiting the multimodal and multi-device nature of the presentation.

In this paper we detailed the document-based processing involved in our pervasive capture and access approach. We also illustrated the utility of the approach by summarizing data relative to the use of our prototype by a group of 9 instructors.

Regarding future work, we plan to investigate alternatives for: (a) the enrichment of the graphic interface of the multimedia object so as to improve interactivity; (b) the capture of more contextual information during the presentation toward providing novel navigation facilities; (c) the development of visualization tools for the instructor to analyse the information captured while the students interacted with the multimedia object. The aim is to built a general infrastructure that helps building similar capture-based applications [18].

References

1. Abowd, G., Pimentel, M.G., Kerimbaev, B., Ishiguro, Y., Guzdial, M.: Anchoring discussions in lecture: an approach to collaboratively extending classroom digital media. In: Proceedings of Computer support for collaborative learning, CSCL '99. International Society of the Learning Sciences (1999)
2. Bianchi, M.: Automatic video production of lectures using an intelligent and aware environment. In: Proceedings of International Conference on Mobile and Ubiquitous Multimedia (MUM), USA, pp. 117–123. ACM (2004)
3. Brooks, C.A., Ketterl, M., Hochman, A., Holtzman, J., Stern, J., Wunden, T., Amundson, K., Logan, G., Lui, K., McKenzie, A., Meyer, D., Moormann, M., Rihtar, M., Rolf, R., Skofic, N., Sutton, M., Vazquez, R.P., Wulff, B.: Opencast matterhorn 1.1: reaching new heights. In: Proceedings of the 19th ACM International Conference on Multimedia, MM '11, pp. 703–706. ACM (2011)
4. Brotherton, J.A., Abowd, G.D.: Lessons learned from eclass: assessing automated capture and access in the classroom. ACM Trans. Comput. Hum. Interact. 11(2), 121–155 (2004)
5. Canessa, E., Fonda, C., Tenze, L., Zennaro, M.: Apps for synchronized photo-audio recordings to support students. In: Proceedings of WAVe'2013 (2013)
6. Canessa, E., Fonda, C., Zennaro, M.: One year of ictp diploma courses on-line using the automated eya recording system. Comput. Educ. 53(1), 183–188 (2009)

7. Cattelan, R.G., Baldochi, L.A., Pimentel, M.G.: Experiences on building capture and access applications. In: Proceeding of Brazilian Symposium on Multimedia and Hypermedia Systems, pp. 112–127 (2003)
8. Chou, H.-P., Wang, J.-M., Fuh, C.-S., Lin, S.-C., Chen, S.-W.: Automated lecture recording system. In: Proceedings of International Conference on System Science and Engineering, July 2010, pp. 167–172 (2010)
9. Dickson, P.E., Arbour, D.T., Adrion, W.R., Gentzel, A.: Evaluation of automatic classroom capture for computer science education. In: Proceedings of Innovation and Technology in Computer Science Education, ITiCSE '10, pp. 88–92. ACM, New York (2010)
10. Dickson, P.E., Warshow, D.I., Goebel, A.C., Roache, C.C., Adrion, W.R.: Student reactions to classroom lecture capture. In: Proceedings of Innovation and Technology in Computer Science Education, ITiCSE '12, pp. 144–149. ACM, New York (2012)
11. Dijksman, J.A., Khan, S.: Khan academy: the world's free virtual school. Bull. Am. Phys. Soc. **56** (2011)
12. Halawa, S., Pang, D., Cheung, N.-M., Girod, B.: ClassX: an open source interactive lecture streaming system. In: Proceedings of ACM International Conference on Multimedia (MM), pp. 719–722. ACM (2011)
13. Hürst, W., Maass, G., Müller, R., Ottmann, T.: The "authoring on the fly" system for automatic presentation recording. In: ACM CHI'01 Extended Abstracts, pp. 5–6 (2001)
14. Lampi, F., Kopf, S., Effelsberg, W.: Automatic lecture recording. In: Proceedings of ACM International Conference on Multimedia (MM), pp. 1103–1104. ACM (2008)
15. Melo, E.L., Viel, C.C., Teixeira, C.A.C., Rondon, A.C., de Paula Silva, D., Rodrigues, D.G., Silva, E.C.: WebNCL: a web-based presentation machine for multimedia documents. In: Proceedings of the 18th Brazilian Symposium on Multimedia and the Web, WebMedia '12, pp. 403–410. ACM, New York (2012)
16. Nagai, T.: Automated lecture recording system with AVCHD camcorder and microserver. In: Proceedings of ACM SIGUCCS Fall Conference, pp. 47–54. ACM (2009)
17. Pang, D., Halawa, S., Cheung, N.-M., Girod, B.: Classx mobile: region-of-interest video streaming to mobile devices with multi-touch interaction. In: Proceedings of ACM International Conference on Multimedia (MM), pp. 787–788. ACM (2011)
18. Pimentel, M.G., Baldochi Jr, L.A., Cattelan, R.G.: Prototyping applications to document human experiences. IEEE Pervasive Comput. **6**(2), 93–100 (2007)
19. Pospiech, S., Mertens, R., Muller, M.E., Ketterl, M.: TSF-Slider: Combining Time- and Structure-Based Media Navigation in One Navigation Component. In: International Symposium on Multimedia, pp. 333–334 (2011)
20. Soares, L.F.G., Moreno, M.F., De Salles Soares Neto, C.: Ginga-NCL declarative middleware for multimedia IPTV services. Commun. Mag. IEEE **48**(6), 74–81 (2010)
21. Vega-Oliveros, D.A., Martins, D.S., Pimentel, M.G.: This conversation will be recorded: automatically generating interactive documents from captured media. In Proceedings of the 10th ACM Symposium on Document Engineering, DocEng '10, pp. 37–40. ACM (2010)
22. Viel, C.C., Melo, E.L., Pimentel, M.G., Teixeira, C.A.C.: How are they watching me: learning from student interactions with multimedia objects captured from classroom presentations. In: Proceedings of International Conference on Enterprise Information Systems (ICEIS) (2013)

23. Viel, C.C., Melo, E.L., Pimentel, M.G., Teixeira, C.A.C.: Multimedia multi-device educational presentations preserved as interactive multi-video objects. In: Proceedings of the 19th Brazilian Symposium on Multimedia and the Web, WebMedia '13. ACM, New York (2013)

24. Viel, C.C., Melo, E.L., Rodrigues, K.R., Pimentel, M.G., Teixeira, C.A.C.: Interaction with a problem solving multi-video lecture: observing students from distance and traditional learning courses. Int. J. Emerg. Technol. Learn. (iJET) (2013). (Accepted)

Enterprise Architecture

Analysing the M&A Preparedness Building Approach

Nilesh Vaniya[✉], Peter Bernus, and Ovidiu Noran

Centre of Enterprise Architecture Research and Management (CEARM),
Griffith University, 170 Kessels Road, Nathan, Brisbane, QLD 4111, Australia
{n.vaniya, p.bernus, o.noran}@griffith.edu.au

Abstract. One of the complex and dynamic changes on the organisation level
is Mergers and Acquisitions (M&As). M&As have been practiced since several
decades for growth and expansion purposes. Recent developments in the frequency of M&As has drawn attention from researchers resulting in findings that
more than half of the deals fails to achieve the aimed synergies. Solution to this
problem could be to build preparedness to allow organisations to prepare for
future or announced mergers in a way that enable faster pre-merger planning
and smoother post-merger integration (PMI). In this article we will analyse
M&A Preparedness building using a retrospective case study to (a) demonstrate
that the success of such strategic changes depends on several essential and
largely overlooked factors, and (b) outline a possible approach of building
preparedness for M&As.

Keywords: Mergers · Acquisitions · Post-merger integration (PMI) · M&A
preparedness building

1 Introduction

Enterprises as socio-technical systems are subject to continuous evolution. In addition,
enterprises are also required to permanently adapt so as to satisfy the dynamic
requirements of the environment in which they operate. The purpose of the research
reflected in this paper is to demonstrate the principles and use of a Mergers and
Acquisitions (M&A) Preparedness Building Methodology (MAPBM) built on
Enterprise Architecture (EA) concepts in order to create and support strategically
important transformational activities.

In order to demonstrate the use of EA in M&As, firstly we summarise the approaches
suggested in the literature in order to tackle the issues that cause failures in M&As, the
solutions attempted to address those issues and the current gaps in related theory and
practice. Secondly, we summarise the proposed MAPBM which aims to support
enterprises in acquiring the necessary systemic properties before merger/acquisition and
thus build preparedness for the desired type of M&A. Subsequently, we describe a
merger case study and using the MAPBM we demonstrate how, with strategic intent, a
multifaceted transformation of the participating organisations could have been performed so as to achieve a state where the organisation was ready to perform a strategically attractive merger. Finally, we summarise the results and outline future work.

© Springer International Publishing Switzerland 2014
S. Hammoudi et al. (Eds.): ICEIS 2013, LNBIP 190, pp. 459–473, 2014.
DOI: 10.1007/978-3-319-09492-2_27

2   M&A: Problems and Typical Solutions

Kumar [17] categorizes M&As as: horizontal (also known as 'mergers of equals'), vertical (where two or more participants have different position in the supply chain), and conglomerate. In addition to this typology, there are other differentiating aspects when one considers the nature of an M&A – e.g., is the deal forced or voluntary, do the original identities of the participants change as a result of the transaction, etc. Irrespective of the type, M&As can deliver positive outcomes for the participants. Based on the goal and the type of the deal, Walter [31, pp. 62–77] lists some major advantages achievable through M&As: market extension, economies of scale, cost (or revenue) economies of scope, other operating efficiencies, etc.

Unfortunately, according to recent research, while the rate of M&As has increased in the recent past, the probability of achieving the above-mentioned potential benefits has dropped to less than half [23, p. 65]. The precise percentage of the deals that fail to achieve the declared synergies and desired levels of integration varies according to industry, but is generally agreed to be greater than 50 % [1, 21, 23]. M&A problems have been researched from different perspectives and viewpoints, therefore we summarise the findings of current literature, with the intent of categorising and highlighting major M&A issues from an Information Systems (IS) researcher's perspective.

2.1   M&A Issues

We reviewed a wide range of M&A literature to identify typical issue types (or issue categories) that are believed to have significant impact on the outcome of M&As. Major issues having the highest impact on M&A success are claimed to be in the domains of IS and organizational integration [18, 21–23, 25]. Major M&A issues have also been highlighted in [3, 6, 10, 13, 18, 20, 21, 23, 26, 30]. We identified three issue types illustrated in Table 1.

Table 1. Categories of major M&A issues.

Proposed category	Issues/Problems resulting from
Business Management issues/concerns	• Merger motive, expectations and planning, • Level of Coherency of Integration Strategy, • IS/Information Technology (IT) Involvement in M&A planning, • Organisational integration management.
Human Resource (HR) issues	• Lack of strong integration team, executive leadership, • Need to consider not only general HR issues but the individual human side of M&A, • Lack of top-down communication of vision, M&A strategies, and of M&A planning, • Personnel concerns (such as benefits, retention and cut-offs), • Lack of supporting programs, advanced notification, extended benefits, outplacement activities.
IT and IS issues	• IT Attributes, • IT Integration Management, • Information and Communication Technology (ICT) vision • Enterprise Systems / Applications integration such as ERP, SCM, CRM, etc., • Data integration issues, • Technical compatibility

Thus, most issues in strategic transformations (and M&As as a special case thereof) fall in three main categories: Business Management, Human/Organizational and IT/IS). Clearly, solving only one type of issues (e.g. HR) without considering the relationships with the other issue types would be less effective than expected or may be altogether ineffective. Hence for any enterprise-wide transformation methodology we must consider how to jointly solve these three types of issues.

Note that not all of the above issues can be addressed in detail during preparedness building in all circumstances. The ability to address such issues during preparedness building relies on the ability to sense their root causes as well as the ability to respond and control them.

2.2   Existing Solutions

Recent developments in M&A research aimed to study the reasons of M&A failures and improve their success rate. As discussed below, most of the studies focused on a single issue and proposed a solution to it without considering the relationship/effect of that solution on other issue types and sources. In our view, this is due to a lack of a systemic view; hence, the outcomes of these studies could be in fact synthesized to develop a comprehensive solution (Table 2).

Similar to the discussion of M&A issues, M&A solutions can be structured into three categories: Business/Operations, HR/Organisational and IS/IT.

It seems that none of the solutions outlined above are able to address all the issues or to consider the impact on and/or relationships with the other issues. In addition, the models and theories noted above focus on individual aspects of M&A, and results documented in the current literature need to be synthesized in order to adopt a comprehensive approach for solving M&A issues in concert.

2.3   Gaps in Theory and Practice

In their review of the last 30 years of M&A literature, Cartwright and Schoenberg [5] found that M&A research is still incomplete.

Based on our own survey, major gaps in M&As research can be summarised as follows:

- Lack of a multi-disciplinary approach [5, p. 5];
- "the study of M&A desperately needs a new perspective and a new framework for analysis" [11, p. 37];
- Need to consider the emergent nature of M&A [19];
- Lack of agile, flexible, quick-responsive framework suitable to M&As' complexity [22];
- Lack of Systems approach [7; 18; 22, p. 4], whereupon a systems approach would provide a unified framework that able to represent the range of problems that arise from the transformation of two systems into a single system.

Table 2. List of solutions for M&A and post-merger integration (PMI).

Solution/findings	Proposed by	Addressed issue/concern
A model for selection of IT-integration methods for a given type of merger and IT integration objectives	Wijnhoven et al. [32]	Business and IS alignment
A concept of post-merger integration (PMI) as the inheritance of DNAs (process, knowledge, control, data, people and asset)	Mo and Nemes [22]	PMI implementation
A categorization framework to consider the level of integration required based on the targeted level of interoperability	Vernadat [29]	Level of integration
The critical importance of top-down communication and bottom-up participation during M&As	Rodriguez [23]	The anxiety and low degree of bottom-up participation and involvement in the transformation process
A three-stage HR integration model (pre-combination, combination and solidification)	Schuler and Jackson [25]	strategic HR concerns such as cut-offs, retentions, promotions and communication during M&A transformations
The strategic role of HR in enterprise-wide change endeavours	Bhaskar [4]	HR involvement in PMI planning
Ineffectiveness of the view of human resources as a commodity	Dooreward and Benschop [8]	Lack of bottom-up involvement in planning of PMI
Need to consider emergent issues	Lauser [19]	Issues brought about by the dynamicity and complexity of the change process
A model to create an ICT vision for the M&A	Larsen [18]	Negligence of ICT integration during pre-merger planning
An integration planning model for IT intensive M&As	Bannert and Tschirky [2]	PMI planning for IS/IT
A model of post-merger IS integration (total integration, partial integration, no integration and transition)	Giacomazzi et al. [12]	PMI implementation for IT
A methodology to develop an application integration strategy	Eckert et al. [9]	ERP/applications integration planning
An IS Integration decision making framework	Mehta and Hirschheim [21]	Decisions for post-merger integration
A methodology to decide an operating model for the organization	Ross et al. [24]	The level of business process integration & the level of business process standardization

3   The Synthesized Solution: M&A Preparedness Building

From the above discussion it is clear that a systems approach is required to address the high failure rate of M&As. It is unlikely that once an M&A deal is on the horizon there will be sufficient time to perform groundwork and planning for post-merger integration to address relevant problems.

Therefore, the management of an organisation should consider preparing the enterprise for such *types* of transformation before any concrete M&A deal is considered. This is to ensure that the organisation has the right capabilities and systemic properties (such as flexibility, agility, etc.) required to perform post-merger integration tasks. We therefore recommend a preparedness building program for organisations that want to consider such strategic moves as future options.

The discussion below presents the proposed timing of preparedness building (in contrast to the conventional view of the M&A process) and then outlines the actual process of preparedness building.

3.1 The M&A Process

Based on the discussion of M&A problems, it is evident that individual solutions addressing issues independently are not optimal and may not even be feasible. Unfortunately, at the time an actual merger or acquisition is considered, there is typically not enough time to spend on comprehensive planning of post-merger integration. Thus, there seems to be a contradiction between having to make fast decisions to seize the opportunity and the need to perform comprehensive planning.

To solve the above problem (as described in detail in Vaniya [27] and shown in Fig. 1), we could consider desirable life trajectories of an enterprise prior to having actual merger or acquisition plans. Therefore, instead of using the conventional view of a three-stage M&A process (Pre-merger, Merger and Post-merger) we introduce an additional stage, called M&A preparedness building stage. During this stage, some groundwork can be completed to better position the enterprise, so that by the time an opportunity is sighted, the enterprise is in the position to quickly make necessary decisions and finalise comprehensive integration planning. We call these activities 'preparedness building'. They aim to achieve the acquisition of important systemic (system level) properties such as flexibility, agility and interoperability as enablers of future transformations.

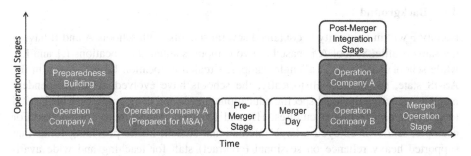

Fig. 1. Preparedness building in M&A process.

3.2 The M&A Preparedness Building Methodology and the Transformation Process

In the following, we shall demonstrate how to conduct the Preparedness Building stage shown in Fig. 1. For this purpose we employ a high-level three-step reference methodology [28], as follows:

- Step 1: Identify Enterprise entities;
- Step 2: Show the role of each entity in the preparedness building transformation;
- Step 3: Demonstrate the relative sequence of transformational activities, using life history diagrams.

Step 1 identifies the participating enterprise entities. They can be existing entities (for example existing Management team, business units, affected business processes, IT infrastructure, etc.) contributing to building preparedness or can be additional entities required in building preparedness (for example Preparedness Building Strategic Program, Gap Analysis Project, Business-, HR- and IS- Preparedness Building Projects, etc., or even strategic partners).

Step 2 shows the role of each entity in the preparedness building transformation. Various graphical models can be used for this particular step; we have chosen the so-called 'dynamic business models' proposed by the IFIP-IFAC Task Force [14] showing the role of each entity in other entities' lifecycle phases.

Step 3 attempts to demonstrate the relative sequence of transformation activities. This step follows the previously identified roles of each of the entities; based on those roles, we first identify activities to match entities' responsibilities and then we establish their relative sequence using so-called 'Life History Diagrams' (see Sect. 5.3).

Note that MAPBM aims to serve as a reference model, with the details and approaches of each step being adapted to meet the specific business needs, management decisions and current business scenarios.

4 Case Study: The Merger of Two Tertiary Study Institutions

4.1 Background

Faculty F within university U contained several schools, with schools A and B having the same profile. School A is based at two campuses situated at locations L1 and L2, while school B is based at a single campus, situated at location L3 (as shown in the AS-IS state, see Fig. 2). Historically, the schools have evolved in an independent manner, reflecting the local specific educational needs and demographics. This has led to different organisational cultures, HR and financial management approaches. For example, school B enjoyed a large international student intake providing funds that supported heavy reliance on sessional (contract) staff for teaching and wide availability of discretionary funds. In contrast, staff in school A had a larger teaching load and had less funds available due to a smaller student intake.

Staff profile level between schools was significantly different (i.e. less high-level positions at school B). Course curriculums also evolved separately in the two schools, with similarly named courses containing significantly different material.

Thus, although of the same profile, and belonging to the same F and U, schools A and B were confronted with a lack of consistency in their profiles, policies, services and resources. This situation caused additional costs in student administration and course/program design/maintenance, unnecessary financial losses as well as staff perceptions of unequal academic and professional standing between campuses, all of which were detrimental to the entire faculty.

Therefore, the management of U and F have mandated that the problems previously described must be resolved and have defined the goals of schools A and B becoming consistent in their products and resources strategy, eliminating internal competition for students and being subject to a unique resource management approach. As a solution, it has been proposed that the schools should merge into a single, multi-campus Merged School (MS in the 'TO-BE' state in Fig. 2). The unified MS management and policies would promote consistency in the strategy regarding the products delivered and the resources allocated to its campuses.

4.2   The Results

The Merged School Project has succeeded, albeit with some difficulties. The decisional, functional, information, resources and organisational models created during the merger have helped significantly to understand the present situation and to select an optimal future state. The use of languages easy to understand and able to manage complexity has resulted in stakeholder buy-in for the project and middle-management consensus on the essential aspect of the future Merged School.

Unfortunately however, most modeling and mappings (including the pre-merger AS-IS situation!) occurred during the merger project rather than before; thus, there was insufficient time to achieve appropriate detail modeling. This has led to the 'devil

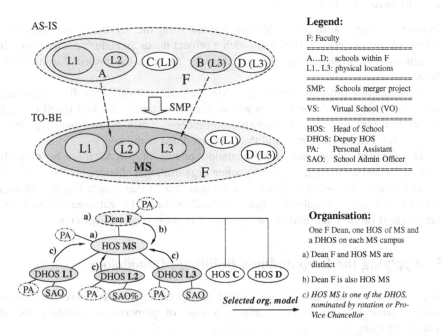

Fig. 2. Rich picture of AS-IS and possible TO-BE states (incl. organisational scenarios).

in the detail' situation: the human resources allocated to accomplish the merger and post-merger integration tasks were unable to do so appropriately due to the lack of proper shared understanding of what needed to be done.

In addition to their inappropriate granularity, the available models were only partially applied. For example, an organisational model showing changes in roles and decisional framework in the transition from the AS-IS to the TO-BE states was implemented only at the top layer due to the lack of time and proper preparation. As a result, the new Head of the Merged School had to spend significant amounts of time 'putting out fires' (finding short term solutions to re-occurring product/resources imbalances). Thus, unfortunately the interventionist and turbulence issues outlined in the pre-merger (AS-IS) organisational and decisional models were not effectively addressed.

Staff consultation has taken place; however, a significant amount of feedback never translated into changes to the proposed organisational model. This has reduced the level of acceptance among staff.

Importantly, the detailed process modeling was never completed and as such the implementation went ahead without detailed models and guidance, in a 'cold turkey' manner (i.e. overnight changeover) resulting in a state of confusion as to 'who does what, now' lasting several months and affecting both staff and clients (students) In other words, there was little attention given to post-merger integration.

On the positive side, the Merged School did achieve a unique image, and in time reached an increased level of integration and consistency across campuses and more efficient resource management.

4.3   Lessons Learned

To sum up, there were a few lessons learned from the successes and short-term failures of this project. To start with, such a project needs an enduring 'champion' in an authoritative management position in order to back the project for its entire duration.

The modeling processes involved in M&As must start early; ideally, a reference model repository should be built in advance and constantly enriched based on each merger post-mortem. Some human-specific processes (such as trust building, negotiations etc.) cannot be rushed and thus, preparedness is the key.

The detailed design and implementation phases of M&As must be properly planned for and performed. Especially when organisational changes involving human aspect are involved, suitable detail must be provided so that people understand their new/changed roles. Feedback from stakeholders must be gathered, refined and incorporated in the final models, being crucial in post-merger integration.

5   Applying the Preparedness Building Methodology

Preparedness can be built for announced and potential M&As. Here the merger partners were known, therefore this is a case of preparedness building for an announced merger.

Out of the three categories of issues (as outlined in Sect. 2.1), major issues presented by the case study are Business and Management and Human Resource issues. In this case IS/IT issues were limited to the challenges in achieving consistency in the way IS and IT are managed for the involved schools. Therefore, the aim of preparedness building could be the following:

- Identify obstacles to the transformation and implement appropriate preventive actions;
- Plan for post-merger integration based on the expected outcomes;
- Prepare a Post-Merger Integration (PMI) Plan and an Integration Strategy
- Involve key stakeholders (both schools' management, administration and academic staff) in the preparedness building activities.

5.1   Step 1: Identify Enterprise Entities

From the discussion of the case study, the entities affected by preparedness building are the Heads of Schools (HOSs), academic and administration Staff, students, services, technical infrastructure and Information Services.

Preparedness building requires a strategic program typically governing several projects covering the proposed organisation-wide change, running for extended periods. A possible list of the program and projects involved is: a Preparedness Building Strategic Program (PBSP), a Business Preparedness Building Project (BPBP) and a HR Preparedness Building Project (HRPBP). In practice, the list of enterprise entities is negotiated between the project/program managers, key stakeholders and the relevant governance body.

5.2   Step 2: Show the Role of Each Entity in Preparedness Building Transformation

The next step is to show how the identified entities will interact with each other to conduct the preparedness building transformation. This can be achieved by developing so-called 'dynamic business models'; the models applicable to the case study are shown in Figs. 3 and 4. It should be noted that, in these models, each 'relationship' is considered a contribution of an entity to another entity's lifecycle activities; According to ISO 15704, for each relationship the acting entities would typically use available reference/partial models to create the design solution for their particular target entity (see Appendix A).

` Figure 3 shows the role of existing entities in establishing the required program and project entities. The management at the University and Faculty levels in consultation with HOSs of schools A and B decide to prepare for upcoming M&As. Therefore they decide, identify, conceptualise and specify the requirements (mandate) of the Preparedness Building Strategic Program (PBSP), structure a strategic management team, and provide the basis for a master plan of the program (Relationship 1). Potentially, PBSP management can be made up of both HOSs, with one of them being the Program Manager, and key staff of all two schools in addition to members from University and Faculty. From here on, PBSP management is responsible for the design

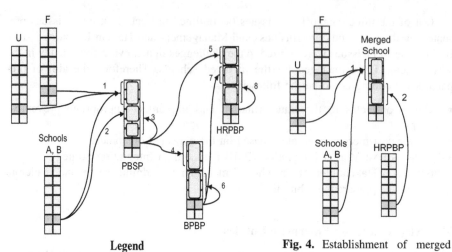

Legend

U: University

F: Faculty   A,B: Two schools

PBSP: Preparedness Building Strategic Program

BPBP: Business Preparedness Building Project

HRPBP: HR Preparedness Building Project

Fig. 3. Establishment of preparedness building program & projects.

Fig. 4. Establishment of merged school.

and implementation of PBSP. In the detailed design, program management designs the program team, and plans their tasks. This planning follows a project-based design to develop the detailed design of the program (i.e. to identify projects, their tasks and prepare a mandate for each project) (Relationship 3); in doing so, the Program Management Team also seeks the guidance of all staff of two schools (Relationship 2).

For the identified change activities, the PBSP defines two separate projects which can be called BPBP (Business-) and HRPBP (HR-) Preparedness Building Projects with BPBP being the governing project to maintain the strategic alignment during the transformation. The PBSP program team identifies conceptualises and specifies the mandate of BPBP (Relationship 4) but only identifies and conceptualises HRPBP (Relationships 5). This is because HRPBP's mandate will have to be defined by the BPBP (Relationships 7). Relationships 6 and 8 represent the self-designing and re-engineering capabilities of BPBP and HRPBP respectively.

Figure 4 shows the establishment of merged school. Management at the university, faculty and school level identifies conceptulise and specifies requirements for the merged school (Relationship 1). The operation of PBSP (see Fig. 5) will help HRPBP to structure the merged school (Relationship 2).

Figure 5 shows the preparedness building changes initiated by PBSP, BPBP and HRPBP. The role of PBSP is to govern and monitor the progress of M&A preparedness building, and the operations of BPBP as well as HRPBP. BPBP is responsible for planning and implementing preparedness building (key tasks: Gap Analysis, Requirement Specifications, preparing mandates for HRPBP, plan for

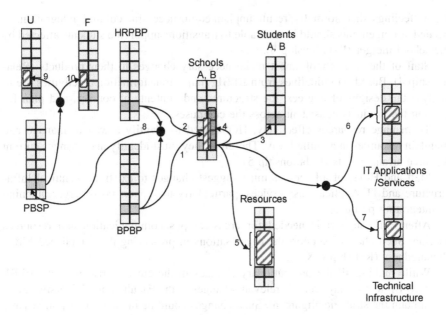

Fig. 5. Transformational initiatives in building preparedness.

business processes & product integration, improve consistency in current operation). The role of HRPBP is critical for our case, as HRPBP would be responsible for preparing staff for the merger, achieving consistent organisational structure and HR management practices across the campuses.

Starting with the operation of BPBP, the BPBP identifies necessary changes at the HOS level to achieve consistency in managing schools, their staff and products (Relationship 1). HOSs are the leaders for their respective schools and they are also part of the PBSP team, therefore it is necessary to first implement changes at their level. Such initiatives reflect that preparedness building has executive management's commitment and support.

Similarly, the HRPBP, with the help of BPBP, suggest equivalent changes for the staff such as preparing staff for future organisational structure (Relationship 2). Key transformational activities may involve identifying and categorising roles that would become redundant, remain unchanged and any new roles required after the merger. This would also require changes into the staff structure and organisational processes. For example, for a course offered at multiple campuses we might need a new role such as Primary Course Convener supervising (existing) Campus Conveners. In addition these smaller teams must plan for possible changes into designs and structures of their respective courses and should come up with an integration plan for their respective courses/programs.

To reflect such major changes into organisational structure, the schools also need to identify changes in current reporting mechanisms, communication methods, promotion arrangements. Another major task for HRPBP would be to plan, initiate and continuously foster the culture change. Cultural change would be critical for transforming two competitive teams into a collaborating one and prevent residual 'us and them' feelings that normally result unplanned/unsuccessful cultural integration. If needed, arrangements should be available to transition/support the students affected by the school merger (Relationship 3).

Staff of the two schools must make necessary changes to their products (Relationship 4). Based on guidelines from BPBP, major transformational activities are to analyse the designs of degrees, the structures and contents of courses, and plan for making the products consistent across the campuses.

To manage resources effectively, HOSs need to identify a way to manage and maintain resources in a unified way. Therefore they must identify and changes current resource arrangements (Relationship 5).

Staff and HOSs of all schools must suggest changes to existing Technical Infrastructure and IT Applications/Services, particularly to support post-merger planning of integrating products.

After PMI, support is needed for cross-campus communication and resources sharing. Such changes support the organisations in preserving the established M&A Preparedness (Rel'ship 6 & 7).

While making all the precautionary changes in the current arrangements, BPBP and HRPBP teams may identify relevant changes at the Faculty and University levels to maintain the strategic alignment. Such changes could be in the current policies and principles, reporting systems, management and controlling procedures. As noted by Mcdonald, Coulthard and Lange [20] such changes in existing strategy are required for an effective M&A implementation. Therefore BPBP and HRPBP can inform the PBSP team about such changes (Relationship 8). In turn PBSP team recommends those changes to the Faculty and University Management (Relationships 9 & 10).

Changes will then be proposed to U&F, which may approve (or not); nevertheless, they must reach consensus that can maintain strategic alignment between M&A strategy and corporate goals, and that of the Business, HR and IS strategy for M&A Preparedness building.

In this discussion we have argued that a possible Preparedness Building Exercise can be planned to achieve basic systemic properties/design properties, so that change can become a natural and dynamic exercise rather than the occasional forceful imposition on the organisation. In this case study, there were no explicit shared representations of processes (in a formal enough manner), which would have allowed to define the new processes needed by the merged organisation. Preparedness building would have entailed the development of explicit and shared process models. As no resources were allocated to perform the necessary modelling even after the merger, the distributed operation of MS was affected by process inefficiencies.

5.3 Step 3: Demonstrate Relative Sequence of Transformational Activities

Finally, once the mandate of preparedness building transformation is finalised, it is important to identify the detailed activities that must be performed as well as by whom and when.

For this particular step we have used so-called 'life history' diagrams (c.f. ISO 15704), that show entities and their lifecycle phases on a vertical axis and time on the horizontal axis. Such diagrams show major milestones and then may become the basis for project management charts (such as Gantt). As explained in Vaniya and Bernus [28], MAPBM is developed based on EA concepts using GERAM [14, 15].

6 Conclusions and Future Research

The paper has reviewed three categories of issues that are commonly considered the reason for high failure rates for M&As. Using a systems view of enterprise transformation (based on an EA approach), we have identified a contradiction between the need to address post-merger integration planning in detail and the usual time pressure when an M&A deal is considered.

Our main contribution is that we proposed a solution called 'preparedness building', that allows enterprises to consider M&As as strategic possibility (even if not actual yet), and determine what systemic changes are necessary in the three categories (business, IS/IT and HR), so that the organisation can develop flexibility in these areas. To achieve such preparedness building requires strategic initiative and organisational change. Given the complexity of this transformation we used an Enterprise Architecture approach to demonstrate how a simultaneous transformation of business, HR and IS/IT aspects can be orchestrated to achieve M&A preparedness as a systemic property of the enterprise. We have also discussed a case study, and what areas could have been addressed by the proposed preparedness building methodology, so as to improve the speed and efficiency of the Merger that was eventually completed.

The proposed M&A Preparedness Building Methodology could be evolved into a Preparedness Building package aiming to improve M&A success rate by addressing the root causes of issues, so that an enterprise is ready for M&As and similar enterprise-wide change endeavours. It is also important to have a mechanism to determine whether the organisation is ready for the desired type of M&A. Based on such a determination, a prescriptive list of activities can be provided as a roadmap towards building preparedness for the desired type of M&A. Therefore, research is in progress to develop the checklist of key M&A issues and their solutions, define the state of M&A Preparedness in terms of systemic properties and develop an optimal list of M&A Preparedness Building Activities for different types of M&As.

For the above goals, a mixed-method research will involve an international survey and follow-up semi-formal interviews to consider industry response to the M&A Preparedness Building Methodology development. The results of this research will also be verified by an expert panel consisting of M&A practitioners and researchers.

Appendix A

Generalised Enterprise Reference Architecture (Gera) Modelling Framework

See Fig. 6.

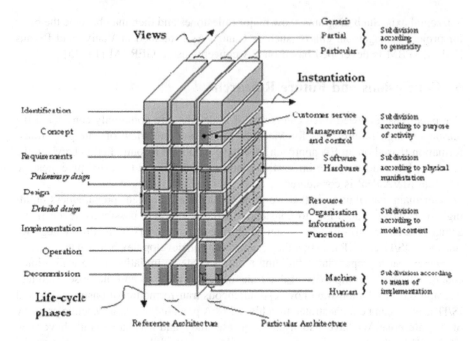

Fig. 6. GERA modelling framework with lifecycle phases, viewpoints. Source: (IFIP-IFAC Task Force (1999) and ISO 15704).

References

1. Alaranta, M., Henningsson, S.: An approach to analyzing and planning post-merger IS integration: insights from two field studies. Inf. Syst. Front. **10**(3), 307–319 (2008)
2. Bannert, V., Tschirky, H.: Integration planning for technology intensive acquisitions. R&D Manag. **34**(5), 481–494 (2004)
3. Baro, G.A., Chakrabarti, A., Deek, F.: Organizational and informational system factors in post-merger technology integration. In: AMCIS 2008 Proceedings, Paper 359 (2008). http://aisel.aisnet.org/amcis2008/359
4. Bhaskar, A.U.: HR as business partner during mergers and acquisitions: the key to success is to get involved early. Hum. Resour. Manag. Int. Dig. **20**(2), 22–23 (2012)
5. Cartwright, S., Schoenberg, R.: Thirty years of mergers and acquisitions research: recent advances and future opportunities. Brit. J. Manag. **17**(S1–S5), 1–5 (2006)
6. Chatterjee, S.: The keys to successful acquisition programmes. Long Range Plan. **42**(2), 137–163 (2009)
7. DiGeorgio, R.: Making mergers and acquisitions work: what we know and don't know – part I. J. Chang. Manag. **3**(2), 134–148 (2002)
8. Doorewaard, H., Benschop, Y.: HRM and organizational change: an emotional endeavor. J. Organ. Chang. Manag. **16**(3), 272–286 (2003)
9. Eckert, M., Freitag, A., Matthes, F., Roth, S., Schilz, C.: Decision support for selecting an application landscape integration strategy in mergers and acquisition. In: ECIS 2012 Proceedings, Paper 88 (2012). http://aisel.aisnet.org/ecis2012/88

10. Epstein, M.J.: The drivers of success in post-merger integration. Organ. Dyn. **33**(2), 174–189 (2004). doi:10.1016/j.orgdyn.2004.01.005
11. Epstein, M.J.: The determinants and evaluation of merger success. Bus. Horiz. **48**, 37–46 (2005)
12. Giacomazzi, F., Panella, C., Pernici, B., Sansoi, M.: Information systems integration in mergers and acquisitions: a normative model. Inf. Manag. **32**, 289–302 (1997)
13. Hwang, M.: Integrating enterprise systems in mergers and acquisitions. In: AMCIS 2004 Proceedings, Paper 12 (2004). http://aisel.aisnet.org/amcis2004/12
14. IFIP-IFAC Task Force: The generalised enterprise reference architecture and methodology (GERAM) (1999). http://www.ict.griffith.edu.au/~bernus. Accessed 1 May 2010
15. ISO/IEC: 'Annex A: GERAM'. In: ISO/IS 15704:2000/Amd1:2005: Industrial Automation Systems - Requirements for Enterprise-Reference Architectures and Methodologies (2005)
16. ISO/IEC: ISO/IEC 42010:2007: Recommended Practice for Architecture Description of Software-Intensive Systems (2007)
17. Kumar, R.: Post-merger corporate performance: an Indian perspective. Manag. Res. News **32**(2), 145–157 (2009)
18. Larsen, M.H.: ICT integration in an M&A process. In: PACIS 2005 Proceedings, Paper 95 (2005). http://aisel.aisnet.org/pacis2005/95
19. Lauser, B.: Post-merger integration and change processes from a complexity perspective. Baltic J. Manag. **5**(1), 6–27 (2009)
20. Mcdonald, J., Coulthard, M., Lange, P.D.: Planning for a successful merger or acquisition: lessons from an Australian study. J. Glob. Bus. Technol. **1**(2), 1–11 (2005)
21. Mehta, M., Hirschheim, R.: Strategic alignment in mergers and acquisitions: theorizing IS integration decision making. J. Assoc. Inf. Syst. **8**(3), 143–174 (2007)
22. Mo, J.P.T., Nemes, L.: Issues in using enterprise architecture for mergers and acquisitions. In: Doucet, G., Gotze, J., Saha, P., Bernard, S. (eds.) Coherency Management, pp. 235–262. Author House, Bloomington (2009)
23. Rodriguez, A.: Mergers and acquisitions in the banking industry: the human factor. Organ. Dev. J. **26**(2), 63–74 (2008)
24. Ross, J.W., Weill, P., Robertson, D.C.: Enterprise Architecture as Strategy: Creating a Foundation for Business Execution. Harvard Business School Press, Boston (2006)
25. Schuler, R., Jackson, S.: HR issues and activities in mergers and acquisitions. Eur. Manag. J. **19**(3), 239–253 (2001)
26. Stylianou, A.C., Jeffries, C.J., Robbins, S.S.: Corporate mergers and the problems of IS integration. Inf. Manag. **31**, 203–213 (1996)
27. Vaniya, N.: Building preparedness for M&As: the role of EA practice (2011). http://www.ict.griffith.edu.au/cearm/docs/pubs/vaniya-2011a.pdf
28. Vaniya, N., Bernus, P.: Strategic planning to build transformational preparedness: an application of enterprise architecture practice. In: ACIS 2012 Proceedings (2012). http://dro.deakin.edu.au/view/DU:30049142
29. Vernadat, F.B.: Interoperable enterprise systems: principles, concepts, and methods. Ann. Rev. Control **31**, 137–145 (2007)
30. Walsh, J.P.: Doing a deal: merger and acquisition negotiations and their impact upon target company top management turnover. Strateg. Manag. J. **10**, 307–322 (1989)
31. Walter, I.: Mergers and Acquisitions in Banking and Finance. Oxford University Press, New York (2004)
32. Wijnhoven, F., Spil, T., Stegwee, R., Fa, R.T.A.: Post-merger IT integration strategies: an IT alignment perspective. J. Strateg. Inf. Syst. **15**, 5–28 (2006)

From Gaps to Transformation Paths in Enterprise Architecture Planning

Philipp Diefenthaler[1,2]([✉]) and Bernhard Bauer[2]

[1] Softplant GmbH, Munich, Germany
[2] Institute for Software & Systems Engineering, University of Augsburg,
Augsburg, Germany
philipp.diefenthaler@softplant.de,
Bernhard.Bauer@informatik.uni-augsburg.de

Abstract. Planning changes in an enterprise and its supporting IT can be supported by enterprise architecture (EA) models. The planned changes result in gaps which can be derived by a gap analysis. But, knowing the gaps is not enough. Also important is to know in which sequence gaps are to be closed for transformation path planning. In this paper we show how gaps are identified and reused for detailing a model of the target architecture. Based on this refinement further gaps become visible. Furthermore, we describe how it is possible to create with a transformation model and an action repository transformation paths towards a desired and detailed target architecture. Afterwards, we give a use case example and propose a technical realization of the solution.

Keywords: Enterprise architecture planning · Gap analysis · Transformation model · Graph transformation

1 Introduction

Enterprises nowadays face challenges like changing markets, security threats, evolving technologies and new regulations that drive the need to adapt the enterprise. Enterprise architecture management (EAM) supports this change in a structured manner. An enterprise architecture (EA) is the "fundamental organization of a system [the enterprise] embodied in its components, their relationships to each other, and to the environment, and the principles guiding its design and evolution" [1].

Models of this architecture can support decision making for planning purposes. Such EA models cover aspects from business, processes, integration, software and technology [2]. To cope with the complexity of an EA it is crucial for enterprises to use a managed approach to steer and control the redesign of the enterprise. The complexity arises from the level of abstraction, the number of stakeholders involved, and the change of internal and external conditions inherent to EAs.

© Springer International Publishing Switzerland 2014
S. Hammoudi et al. (Eds.): ICEIS 2013, LNBIP 190, pp. 474–489, 2014.
DOI: 10.1007/978-3-319-09492-2_28

To plan the change it is necessary to have a plan basis, i.e. the current architecture, and to know the goal of planning activities, i.e. the target architecture. According to [3,4] the planning activities take place at different decision levels. Each of them varies in detail and levels of abstraction seem to be inevitable [4]. The need to change and the resulting moving target are challenges for EA planning, as part of the EAM, has to meet [5,6]. EAM and particularly EA planning is supported by tools which allow the creation of visualizations, automated documentation and analysis of EA models.

In this paper we describe how gaps can be derived from two EA models for different points in time. Furthermore, we introduce the transformation model by Aier and Gleichauf [7] to connect architectural building blocks from the models of the current and target EA. With the results from gap analysis and the information contained in the transformation model we introduce an action repository for the creation of different transformation paths. We exemplify the solution to get from gaps to transformation paths based on a model of a current and target architecture of an application architecture within a use case for a master data consolidation challenge. Furthermore, we propose a technical realization based on semantic web technologies and graph transformations.

2 Foundations

This section gives an introduction to the foundations of EA models and their usage for planning purposes. Furthermore, we introduce semantic web technologies and graph transformations for planning purposes, as they are of relevance for our proposed technical realization of the solution.

2.1 Enterprise Architecture Models

According to Buckl and Schweda [8] EAM follows a typical management cycle that consists of the phases plan, do, check and act. The plan phase is concerned with developing change proposals that are implemented in the do phase. Within the check phase differences between intended and actually achieved results are controlled. Based upon the results from the check phase the act phase provides input to the plan phase by supplying information for the next plan phase. Models, as an abstraction mechanism, of an enterprise, can support the plan phase as part of an EAM approach [9,10].

EA models can be used to describe an EA for different points in time [8]. The model of the current architecture of the enterprise is a documented architecture at the present point in time and serves as a starting point for defining a model of a target architecture. In contrast the model of the target architecture represents a desired architecture in the future which can be used to guide the development of an EA from the current towards a target architecture. The development of a target architecture depends on the enterprises' EA goals. It is influenced by business requirements, strategic goals and IT objectives like master data consolidation, improving the flexibility of IT and drive the coverage of standard platforms [11].

Which factors and how exactly they influence the target architecture depends on the architecture method applied and how it is integrated into the enterprise's governance processes.

A gap analysis, sometimes also referred to as delta analysis, is the comparison between two models of an EA that is used to clarify the differences between those two architectures. Different models of architectures that can be compared are current to target, current to planned, planned to target and planned to planned [8].

2.2   Semantic Web Technologies in a Nutshell

Semantic web technologies are used to integrate heterogeneous data sets and formalize the underlying structure of the information to allow a machine to understand the semantics of it [12]. The World Wide Web Consortium (W3C) provides a set of standards to describe an ontology and to query it. An ontology "is a set of precise descriptive statements about some part of the world (usually referred to as the domain of interest or the subject matter of the ontology)" [13].

Two standards are of relevance for a proposed technical realization: firstly, the Web Ontology Language (OWL) [13] for making descriptive statements and secondly, the SPARQL Query Language for RDF (SPARQL) [14], which allows querying these statements.

The Resource Description Framework (RDF) [15] is a basis for both standards, as OWL ontologies can be serialized as RDF graphs and can be accessed via SPARQL. An RDF graph consists of triples of the form 'subject, predicate, object', whereas subjects and objects are nodes and predicates are relations. Every resource in an ontology is identified by a resource identifier which allows for example distinguishing between a bank in a financial context and a bank of a river. Information from the ontology is queried via SPARQL, which provides the resources that match patterns specified within the query.

Semantic web technologies have already been applied to domains of interest that range from semantic business process modeling [16] to diagnosis of embedded systems [17]. First implementations based upon semantic web technologies for EAM already exist from TopQuadrant with its TopBraid Composer[1] and Essential Project[2].

2.3   Graph Transformations for Planning Purposes

Several different approaches, techniques and representations to planning problems have been developed over the last decades [18,19]. These approaches range from state space model based planning to task networks, where tasks for reaching a goal are decomposed and sequenced. A state space based approach is preferable, because models of the current and target architecture are used in many EAM approaches [5,11,20,21] and are present in tools used in practice [22].

---

[1] www.topquadrant.com/docs/whitepapers/WP-BuildingSemanticEASolutions
-withTopBraid.pdf

[2] www.enterprise-architecture.org/

Graph transformations for AI planning purposes solve a planning problem by applying graph transformations to a model until a solution for the planning problem is found. The result of such a planning process is a sequence of actions changing a model into another model.

However, graph transformations have the disadvantage that they provide a huge state space regarding the states, which have to be examined when all states in the graph are computed. As a consequence this influences the computation time of all possible worlds created through the transformations. With graph transformations a planning problem can be solved by searching for graph patterns in a state represented by a graph and applying graph transformations to change the state [23]. Graph transformations have the benefit that they have a sound theoretical foundation [24].

3 From Gaps to Transformation Paths as Sequences of Actions

The goal of the proposed approach is to deliver a more detailed model of the target architecture by making suggestions to a domain expert how a detailed target architecture could look like. Afterwards, we describe how these gaps are related to each other to generate a transformation path which allows to structure change activities, which close gaps, in sequence of actions.

3.1 Modeling Current and Target Architecture

First, a current architecture is modeled and afterwards, a target architecture is modeled, at the same level of detail. We reuse the model of the current architecture and change it to the desired target architecture. The same level of detail is necessary to ensure the comparability of the models.

The current architecture may be more detailed, but can be aggregated in a way which restores the comparability [25]. Business support maps, which relate applications to supported processes and organization units, are an example for such a model with the same level of detail [11].

Results of the Modeling. The result of this phase are the two sets:

$currentArchitecture$ = model of the current architecture of the EA
$targetArchitecture$ = model of the target architecture of the EA

In our solution the core of an EA model is a set which consists of three different types of elements. The EA model contains the architecture building blocks (B) of the EA, relations between architecture building blocks (R) and attributes of architecture building blocks (A). In this sense an EA model can be defined as:

$M := \{B \cup R \cup A\}$
$B := \{x \mid x$ is an architecture building block$\}$
$R := \{x \mid x \in B \times B\}$ and $A := \{x \mid x \in B \times V\}$

Architecture building blocks stand for the elements of the EA, for instance a Customer Relationship Management application within the application architecture. Relations hold between these architecture building blocks, for example when an application depends on another application the respective building blocks are connected by a dependency relation. Attributes are values associated with architecture building blocks that characterize measurable and observable characteristics of the architecture building block, e.g. the release number of an application or the uptime of an service.

3.2   Performing Gap Analysis

Gap analysis is performed to compare the modeled current and target architecture. It compares the differences between *currentArchitecture* and *targetArchitecture*. In terms of a set operation this comparison corresponds to a intersection of the two compared sets. As a result three subsets are identified: *onlyCurrentArchitecture*, *onlyTargetArchitecture* and *stable*.

Results of Gap Analysis. *onlyCurrentArchitecture* is the set of building blocks, relations and attributes which only exist in the model of the current architecture.

$$onlyCurrentArchitecture := \{x \mid x \in currentArchitecture$$
$$\land \ x \notin targetArchitecture\}$$

In contrast, *onlyTargetArchitecture* is the set of building blocks, relations and attributes which only exist in the target architecture.

$$onlyTargetArchitecture := \{x \mid x \notin currentArchitecture$$
$$\land \ x \in targetArchitecture\}$$

The third set *stable* is the set of building blocks, relations and attributes which the current and target architecture have in common.

$$stable := \{x \mid x \in currentArchitecture \land x \in targetArchitecture\}$$

3.3   Setting the Successor Relationships for Building Blocks

The successor relationships are modelled within a transformation model [7]. The transformation model is defined as follows: $transformationModel := \{x \mid x \in currentArchitecture \times targetArchitecture\}$

With the successor relationships at hand it is possible to identify the successor type for building blocks which can be divided into *noSuccessor*, *noPredecessor*, *oneToOne*, *oneToMany*, *manyToOne*, and *manyToMany*. The inverse of the successor relation is the predecessor relation.

All building blocks in *onlyCurrentArchitecture* that do not have a successor belong to the set *noSuccessor*. All building blocks that belong to *onlyTargetArchitecture* and do not have a predecessor belong to the set *noPredecessor*. The set *oneToOne* consists of the pairs of building blocks that have exactly one successor and this successor has only one predecessor.

oneToMany is the set of building blocks that have several successors in the target architecture whereas the set *manyToOne* is the set of building blocks which have the same successor in the target architecture. *manyToMany* is the set of building blocks which have common successors, which in turn have several predecessors. By querying the models we can determine to which set a building block belongs.

A successor relationship is part of exactly one of the above subsets. Within the six different sets disjoint subsets exist. For the *noSuccessor* and *noPredecessor* set each building block represents a disjoint subset and are planned independently in contrast to the other successor sets. This is an implicit information of the transformation model, as we do not model self-directed relations for this information.

3.4   Creating Suggestions for a Detailed Target Architecture

In order to make suggestions the model of the current architecture considers applications, services and business building blocks. Business Building Blocks are in a tight relationship with the business activities of an enterprise but implementation independent. With the detailed information of the current architecture and the successor relationships at hand for applications it is possible to generate suggestions how a model of a detailed target architecture could look like.

Each application belongs to exactly one subset of the transformation model. Different suggestions are made for the subsets how to detail the target architecture. By following a suggestion the target is stepwise getting more detailed, as all sets of successor relationships are getting processed. A suggestion may be inappropriate for a domain expert she can overrule it by modeling different details. The result is a model of a detailed target architecture. At first all services are transferred to the model of a detailed target architecture. Then the dependencies can be added to the model of the detailed target architecture.

Suggestions for Provided Services.

1. *noSuccessor* set: for each provided service in the current architecture check if it is used by an application that is part of the target architecture or the consuming application has a successor relationship.
   (a) If there are any applications it is necessary to check if they still can work properly without consuming the service.
   (b) Otherwise, no information from the current architecture is added to the target architecture.
2. *noPredecessor* set: it is not possible to suggest a detail for the target architecture as there exists no detail in the current architecture. A manual addition of provided services and their business building blocks in the target architecture is necessary.

3. *oneToMany* set:
   (a) If the predecessor is part of *onlyCurrentArchitecture* all provided services of the predecessor, including their business building blocks, are suggested to be provided by one of the successor applications.
   (b) Otherwise, all provided services and business building blocks of the predecessor are suggested to be provided by one of the successor applications or the remaining part of the predecessor in the target architecture.
4. *manyToOne* set:
   (a) If the successor is part of *onlyTargetArchitecture* it is suggested to provide each service of its successors, but only one per business building block.
   (b) Otherwise, it is suggested that the successor provides the services already provided in the current architecture, i.e. by itself, and provide all services of the other predecessors, but only one per business building block.
5. *manyToMany* set: All provided services are suggested to be provided by one of the successors. If more than one predecessor provides a service with the same business building block the suggestion is to provide only one service in the target architecture with such a business building block. Further suggestions were not identified as this type represents a complex type of restructuring. Nevertheless, the domain expert should be supported with information about applications changing business support and assigned customer groups. Furthermore, information which applications belong to *onlyCurrentArchitecture* and *onlyTargetArchitecture* needs to be presented to the domain expert.
6. *oneToOne* set: all services, including their business building blocks, provided by the predecessor are suggested to be provided by the successor.
7. Furthermore, the domain expert can model additional services or let suggested services be provided by an application that is not a successor of the application that provided it in the current architecture.
8. For each service information is stored if it is the successor of one or more services in the current architecture. This is necessary to allow a sound transformation planning [9].

As a result all provided services have been modeled in the target architecture including their business building blocks. Furthermore, the information about successor relationships of the services is available.

Suggestions for Used Services.

1. *manyToMany* set: all used services of predecessors are suggested to be used by at least one successor. The domain expert can choose if more than one successor uses the service of a predecessor.
2. *oneToOne* set: all services used by the predecessor are suggested to be used by the successor.
3. *manyToOne* set: used services of the predecessors are suggested to be also used in the target architecture.

4. *oneToMany* set:
   (a) If the predecessor is part of *onlyCurrentArchitecture* all used services of the predecessor are suggested to be used by one of the successor applications.
   (b) Otherwise, all used services of the predecessor are suggested to be used by one of the successor applications or the remaining part of the predecessor in the target architecture.
5. *noPredecessor* set: which services are used by the application need to be modeled manually as no information from the model of the current architecture is available.
6. *noSuccessor* set: as the application does not exist in the model of the target architecture no information about used services needs to be added to the target architecture.
7. Furthermore, the domain expert can model additionally used services for every application.

Results of the Guided Refinement. The result is a model of a detailed target architecture including provided and used services with related business building blocks. Consistency checks can be performed on the model to check whether services exist which are provided but no longer used by any application. Gap analysis can be performed again and the detailed gaps between the models of the current and target architecture are available.

With the results of gap analysis and a detailed current architecture it is possible to assist a domain expert in modeling a detailed target architecture by making suggestions how to detail it based on the current architecture. The variety of suggestions that can be provided is limited to the information available in the EA model. For example, technical information about the services can be added to allow more sophisticated suggestions, like to prefer web service technology for services of applications that have to be build.

3.5 Creating an Action Repository

Before the transformation path from the current to the target architecture can be created, it is necessary to describe possible changes in a way which allows the sequencing of actions. This is realized with an action repository where abstract actions are modeled. An abstract action consists of two parts. One part specifies the preconditions for an action to be applicable. The other part is the effect part, which specifies the changes to an architecture model if an (abstract) action is applied to it.

The creation of the action repository is only done once as the actions are described on an abstract level. However, if the meta-model of the EA changes the actions in the action repository need to be checked if they are impacted by these changes.

In a technical sense the abstract action matches via a graph pattern into the concrete model of the different states. Concrete actions relate to concrete entities and relationships in an architecture model and concrete changes to the state of architecture models. The application of a concrete action to an architecture model, may enable the application of several other concrete actions.

Abstract actions are either atomic or composed. An atomic action changes exactly one element of either *currentArchitecture* or *targetArchitecture*. Composed actions are a composition of other actions, regardless if atomic or composed. To create a transformation path it is necessary to model at least abstract actions for shutting down and developing building blocks and abstract actions that take care of the relationships between the building blocks and the attributes of the building blocks.

Logical Order of Abstract Actions. The abstract actions are modeled in a logical order, which means that it is only possible to apply the action if the preceding actions were already applied. For example, it is not possible to change the dependencies from a service to its successor service if it has not yet been built. Furthermore, it may be necessary to build the application first to allow the creation of a new service. After the dependencies of a service have been changed to a successor it is possible to shutdown the service.

If all services of an application have been shutdown it is possible to shutdown the application. The logical order prevents the creation of loops in the transformation path, i.e. to shutdown and create the same application several times. It may be the case that it is not necessary to enact the *develop application* action. For example, if a service which has to be developed for an application that already exists. In this case it is not necessary to develop that application again since it already exists in the current architecture. The logical order prevents the shutdown of the predecessor services, until the successor service is developed.

3.6   Creating the Transformation Path

With the action repository, the transformation model, the models of current architecture and target architecture at hand it is possible to start the creation of possible transformation paths.

We derive all applicable concrete actions by checking which preconditions of abstract actions match in

$$planningKnowledgeBase := \{transformationModel \cup currentArchitecture \cup targetArchitecture\}$$

This corresponds to a breadth search of applicable actions for a possible change from the current towards the target architecture. If a concrete action is applied to *planningKnowledgeBase* it changes the state of the *planningKnowledgeBase*. In contrast if we apply a depth search we receive a transformation path changing the EA in a sequence of concrete actions from the current to the target architecture. If no such transformation path exists the more exhaustive breadth search can be omitted and we are informed that no transformation path was found. By applying the breadth search on each state recursively and we get the whole state space.

With the state space it is possible to determine all possible transformation paths from the current to the target architecture. By selecting concrete actions we create the transformation path, change the *planningKnowledgeBase* and get each time a list of concrete actions which we now can apply. When the transformation path is complete, i.e. all necessary changes have been applied, no further actions are applicable and the transformation path is saved. If gaps are not to be closed it is possible to stop the creation of the transformation path.

The selection process for choosing concrete actions can be enhanced by providing development costs for proposed applications and services, and maintenance costs for applications and services which are to be retired. Furthermore, the consideration of desired benefits, anticipated risks and resource constraints could be considered if available to allow for a weighting of favorable sequences of actions.

4 Use Case - Development Master Data Management

In the past, applications were often developed to address the specific business needs that a part of the organization had at a certain moment. However, considering the whole enterprise it is not effective to store redundant data in several applications as this increases the risk of outdated and inconsistent data. This is the basis for the master data management (MDM) challenge [26]. In our use case we show a typical (and simplified) example for the introduction of master data management in the research and development division of an organization. Figure 1 shows a part of the model of the current architecture of the organization's IT landscape. There has already been placed a development master data management (DMDM) system in the organization which provides services (MasterData_v1 and _v2) to other applications. However, not all existing applications use the master data provided by DMDM: the application DevManager provides similar data that is still used by existing applications such as the product planning tool and the quality tests planning tool. Other applications such as the virtual quality test result database store the master data themselves and are not connected to DMDM. For the modification of products (from one test to another) there exist two applications for the different product classes the organization provides to their customers. Additionally, applications to plan the product, the quality tests and store the results that have been gathered during the (physical or virtual) quality tests, exist. In the model of the target architecture the functionality in the different applications shall be united and all other tools will use the data provided by DMDM. There will be only one planning tool that includes planning for the product as well as the quality tests. All quality tests (including the results) will be managed by one quality test assistance and result management tool (cf. Figure 2).

Please note that Figs. 1 and 2 already contain the services, which may not be considered in the first place for planning purposes.

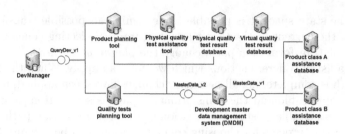

Fig. 1. Master data management: current architecture.

Fig. 2. Master data management: target architecture.

Solution Applied to the Use Case

At first *currentArchitecture* and *targetArchitecture* are created by modelling both architectures. Applying gap analysis it is possible to derive that *onlyCurrentArchitecture* contains: DevManager, Product Planning Tool, Quality tests planning tool, Physical quality test assistance tool, Physical quality test result database, Virtual quality test result database, Product class A assistance database, Product class B assistance database, QueryDev_v1, MasterData_v1 and _v2.

The set *stable* contains only Development master data management system (DMDM) whereas *onlyTargetArchitecture* contains Product and Quality test planning tool, Quality test assistance and result management tool, Product modification assistance database, MasterData_v3 and PlanningData_v1.

Within the transformation model information on the successor relationships is kept: Product planning tool and Quality tests planning tool have the same successor (Product and Quality test planning tool). Physical quality test assistance tool, Physical quality test result database and Virtual quality test result database have the Quality test assistance and result management tool as a common successor. DMDM is a successor of itself, which is in accordance with [7], and DevManager has no successor. Product modification assistance database is the successor of Product class A assistance database and product class B assistance database.

Regarding the services the following successor relationships are contained in the transformation model: MasterData_v3 is a successor of MasterData_v1 and _v2. The QueryDev_v1 has no successor and PlanningData_v1 has no predecessor. Based upon this information the action repository can show that it is possible to develop MasterData_v3 in the first place or one of the successor applications.

If for example as the first action the development of MasterData_v3 is selected it is possible to take care of the dependencies of applications to the predecessors of the service. After removing the dependencies and creating the new ones to the successor service it is possible to shutdown the predecessors. The development of the new applications are to be selected as the next steps in the transformation path. The remaining actions are not described in detail, however their sequence is constrained by the logical order of the abstract actions.

5 Discussion

The discussion is divided into two parts. At first we discuss the results of solution and its application to the use case. After that, the limitations of the solution are presented.

The solution describes how it is possible to derive gaps between the models of a current and target architecture for planning purposes using a set theoretic description. With the gaps at hand and information regarding the successor relationships of elements the solution reuses existing information to aid in the detailing the model of the target architecture. Afterwards, an action repository aids in the creation of possible transformation paths, which are sequences of actions. Overall, the solution considers a domain expert as an important part of the activities and assists her in the decision making process.

Creating suggestions for detailing the model of a target architecture is only possible if business building blocks are available. However, the mechanism of gap analysis, the transformation model and the creation of transformation paths using the action repository are not impacted by this limitation.

Furthermore, requirements regarding the meta-model are posed by the solution. If the EAM approach does not concern application architectures, and as a consequence the models of applications and their dependencies to services, the solution would in its current shape not be suitable. However, the mechanisms as described in the solution can be adapted to aid in the modelling and creation of transformation paths which address the concerns of the stakeholders. From our point of view, applications and their provided services are an important part of an EA.

Currently, we create the connection of the models of the current and target architecture manually, which is prone to errors and time consuming. The model of the target architecture does currently not consider information which transformation paths, taking technology architecture aspects into account, are possible.

6 Proposed Technical Realization

Using semantic web technologies for formalizing information sources yields a number of advantages, starting with having a formal, unambiguous model to the possibilities of reasoning and consistency checking. The knowledge base containing, the current and target EA models, as well as the transformation model, can be consulted at run time by humans as well as by applications.

Identifying gaps can be realized using standard tools like Protégé[3] for modeling and OWLDiff[4] for comparing the modeled EAs. For detailing the model of the target architecture we suggest the usage of SPARQL as it allows querying and adding information in a semi-automated manner.

Regarding the creation of transformation paths we suggest to use a more sophisticated graph transformation approach, as it provides the expressiveness necessary for the creation of transformation paths. This requirement exceeds the current capabilities of SPARQL. A promising World Wide Web Consortium standard is the Rule Interchange Format[5] (RIF), which initial purpose was the exchange of rules. The second edition of RIF provides an action language which can be used to express the actions necessary for transformation path planning. However, we were not able to test the proposed solution as no free implementations are available yet. Therefore, we propose to use a mature graph transformation tool like GROOVE[6].

However, this proposed technical realization requires a model to model (M2M) transformation of the ontologies to a model which is interpretable for a graph transformation approach.

7   Related Work

In this section related work is introduced. As a starting point the technical report 'On the state of the Art in Enterprise Architecture Management Literature' [8] was taken, as they consider gap (delta) analysis as part of the different EAM approaches. Besides the listed approaches in the technical report an approach from the University of Oldenburg and a technical standard from The Open Group was identified as relate work.

7.1   University of Oldenburg

The Institute for Information Technology of the University of Oldenburg presents a tool supported approach for performing a gap analysis on a current and ideal landscape [27]. The approach is tightly coupled to the Quasar Enterprise approach, which can be used to develop service-oriented application landscapes.

In order to be able to perform their gap analysis it is necessary to model the current application landscape consisting of current components, current services, current operations and business objects. The ideal landscape is modeled with ideal components, ideal services, ideal operations and domains. Based on these two models the tool is capable to generate a list of actions that would, if all were applied, result in the ideal landscape. Within the paper the suggested procedure

---

[3] http://protege.stanford.edu/
[4] http://krizik.felk.cvut.cz/km/owldiff/
[5] http://www.w3.org/TR/2013/NOTE-rif-overview-20130205/
[6] http://groove.cs.utwente.nl/

for selecting actions is to allow an architect to select certain actions that result in a target. Furthermore, the tool is capable to provide metrics for quantitative analysis of the application landscape.

Gringel and Postina state that gap analysis needs a "detailed level of description when it comes to modeling both landscapes" ([27], p. 283) and as a result the "data necessary to perform gap analysis on the entire application landscape on a detailed level considering operations is overwhelming" ([27], p. 291). How the different actions interfere with each other is not considered and actions can only be provided if an ideal landscape with all details has been modeled.

7.2 Strategic IT Managment by Hanschke

The 'Strategic IT Management' [11] approach is intended to serve as a toolkit for EAM by providing best-practices derived from work experience. After a target architecture has been modeled and agreed upon gap analysis is used to detect differences between the current and target architecture. Gap analysis is performed on the basis of process support maps visualizing which applications support which business processes (x-axis) and which customer group (y-axis) the applications are assigned to. For a more fine grained gap analysis Hanschke suggests to additionally add information about services and information objects of the applications. Afterwards, for each gap possible actions to close the gap are considered.

The actions range from introducing a new application, adding or reducing functionality of an existing application, changing or adding services to the shut down of applications and services. Based upon the results of gap analysis and derivation of appropriate actions it is necessary to clarify dependencies between the actions, bundle the actions and create planned architectures as recommendations for change. As far as we were able to verify the limitations of the tool and approach it is not possible to create suggestions for a detailed target architecture.

7.3 ArchiMate

ArchiMate ([21], Chap. 11) introduces an Implementation and Migration Extension including a Gap element. A gap can be associated with any core element of the ArchiMate meta-models, except for the Value and Meaning element. In general, a gap links several elements of two EA models and contains elements to be removed (retired) and to be added (developed). The linkage of the differences between the EA models and the resulting gap is not described.

8 Future Work

Creating transition architectures as plateaus (see [21]) between the current and target architecture should be supported by actions. A plateau is a stable state of the EA. The current and target architecture are also plateaus according to ArchiMate. However, we need to identify at first in which situations actions are of relevance for transition architecture creation and if it is possible to provide meaningful support for a domain expert.

A value based weighting for different transformation paths is currently elaborated to support a domain expert with information which paths seem to be more promising than others. This ranking will take into account different factors relevant for transformation planning.

The methodology how to create, use and maintain the action repository is currently extended to cope with different EA models and different concerns which need to be addressed during transformation planning.

9   Conclusions

We have shown how it is possible to get from identified gaps to transformation paths by creating a transformation model, detailing a target architecture and using an action repository to create possible sequences of actions for transformation paths.

An use case for parts of an application architecture was presented and the solution was applied to it. Furthermore, we presented a proposition for a technical realisation to allow for tool support.

We discussed the results and limitations of the solution and clarified its connection to related work. Future work to be addressed was also presented.

References

1. International Organization for Standardization. ISO/IEC 42010:2007 Standard for systems and software engineering - recommended practice for architectural description of software-intensive systems (2007)
2. Winter, R., Fischer, R.: Essential layers, artifacts, and dependencies of enterprise architecture. In: 2006 10th IEEE International Enterprise Distributed Object Computing Conference Workshops (EDOCW'06), IEEE, p. 30 (2006)
3. Pulkkinen, M., Hirvonen, A.: Ea planning, development and management process for agile enterprise development. In: Proceedings of the 38th Annual Hawaii International Conference on System Sciences, IEEE, p. 223c (2005)
4. Pulkkinen, M.: Systemic management of architectural decisions in enterprise architecture planning, four dimensions and three abstraction levels. In: Proceedings of the 39th Annual Hawaii International Conference on System Sciences (HICSS'06), IEEE, p. 179a (2006)
5. Niemann, K.D.: From Enterprise Architecture to IT Governance: Elements of Effective IT Management. Vieweg, Wiesbaden (2006)
6. Aier, S., Gleichauf, B., Saat, J., Winter, R.: Complexity levels of representing dynamics in EA planning. In: Albani, A., Barjis, J., Dietz, J.L.G. (eds.) Advances in Enterprise Engineering III. LNBIP, vol. 34, pp. 55–69. Springer, Heidelberg (2009)
7. Aier, S., Gleichauf, B.: Towards a systematic approach for capturing dynamic transformation in enterprise models. In: Sprague, R.H. (ed.) Proceedings of the 43rd Hawaii International Conference on System Sciences 2010 (HICSS-43). Los Alamitos, IEEE Computer Society (2010)

8. Buckl, S., Schweda, C.M.: On the State-of-the-Art in Enterprise Architecture Management Literature (2011)
9. Aier, S., Gleichauf, B.: Application of enterprise models for engineering enterprise transformation. Enterp. Model. Inf. Syst. Archit. **5**, 56–72 (2010)
10. Buckl, S., Ernst, A.M., Matthes, F., Schweda, C.M.: An information model capturing the managed evolution of application landscapes. J. Enterp. Archit. **5**, 12–26 (2009)
11. Hanschke, I.: Strategisches Management der IT-Landschaft: Ein praktischer Leitfaden für das Enterprise Architecture Management, 1st edn. Hanser, München (2009)
12. Shadbolt, N., Hall, W., Berners-Lee, T.: The semantic web revisited. IEEE Intell. Syst. **21**(3), 96–101 (2006). (IEEE Computer Society)
13. Motik, B., Patel-Schneider, P.F., Horrocks, I.: Owl 2 web ontology language: Structural specification and functional-style syntax (2009)
14. Prud'hommeaux, E., Seaborne, A.: SPARQL Query Language for RDF. World Wide Web Consortium (2008)
15. Manola, F., Miller, E., McBride, B.: RDF Primer. World Wide Web Consortium (2004)
16. Lautenbacher, F.: Semantic Business Process Modeling: Principles, Design Support and Realization. Shaker, Aachen (2010)
17. Grimm, S., Watzke, M., Hubauer, T., Cescolini, F.: Embedded $\mathcal{EL}^{+}$ reasoning on programmable logic controllers. In: Cudré-Mauroux, P., Heflin, J., Sirin, E., Tudorache, T., Euzenat, J., Hauswirth, M., Parreira, J.X., Hendler, J., Schreiber, G., Bernstein, A., Blomqvist, E. (eds.) ISWC 2012, Part II. LNCS, vol. 7650, pp. 66–81. Springer, Heidelberg (2012)
18. Russell, S.J., Norvig, P.: Artificial Intelligence: A Modern Approach, 3rd edn. Prentice Hall, Upper Saddle River (2010)
19. Ghallab, M., Nau, D.S., Traverso, P.: Automated Planning: Theory & Practice. Morgan Kaufmann/Elsevier Science, San Francisco/Oxford (2004)
20. The Open Group: TOGAF Version 9.1. TOGAF Series, 1st edn. Van Haren Publishing, Zaltbommel (2011)
21. The Open Group: Archimate 2.0 Specification. Van Haren Publishing, Zaltbommel (2012)
22. Matthes, F., Buckl, S., Leitel, J., Schweda, C.M.: Enterprise Architecture Management Tool Survey 2008. Technische Universität München, München (2008)
23. Edelkamp, S., Rensink, A.: Graph transformation and AI Planning. In: Edelkamp, S., Frank, J. (eds.) Knowledge Engineering Competition (ICKEPS), Rhode Island, USA (2007)
24. Rozenberg, G.: Handbook of Graph Grammars and Computing by Graph Transformation, vol. 1. World Scientific River Edge, NJ, USA (1997)
25. Binz, T., Leymann, F., Nowak, A., Schumm, D.: Improving the manageability of enterprise topologies through segmentation, graph transformation, and analysis strategies. In: 2012 16th IEEE International Enterprise Distributed Object Computing Conference (EDOC 2012), pp. 61–70 (2012)
26. Loshin, D.: Master Data Management. Elsevier/Morgan Kaufmann, Amsterdam/Boston (2009)
27. Gringel, P., Postina, M.: I-pattern for gap analysis. In: Engels, G., Luckey, M., Pretschner, A., Reussner, R. (eds.) Software Engineering 2010. Lecture Notes in Informatics, pp. 281–292. Gesellschaft für Informatik, Bonn (2010)

An Automated Architectural Evaluation Approach Based on Metadata and Code Analysis

Felipe Pinto[1,2(✉)], Uirá Kulesza[1], and Eduardo Guerra[3]

[1] Federal University of Rio Grande do Norte (UFRN), Natal, Brazil
felipe.pinto@ifrn.edu.br, uira@dimap.ufrn.br
[2] Federal Institute of Education, Science and Technology of Rio Grande do Norte (IFRN), Natal, Brazil
[3] National Institute for Space Research (INPE), São José dos Campos, Brazil
guerraem@gmail.com

Abstract. Traditional methods of scenario-based software architecture evaluation rely on manual review and advanced skills from architects and developers. They are used when the system architecture has been specified, but before its implementation has begun. When the system implementation evolves, code analysis can enable the automation of this process and the reuse of architectural information. We propose an approach that introduces metadata about use case scenarios and quality attributes in the source code of the system in order to support automated architectural evaluation through of static and dynamic code analysis and produce reports about scenarios, quality attributes, code assets, and potential tradeoff points among quality attributes. Our work also describes the implementation of a code analysis tool that provides support to the approach. In addition, the paper also presents the preliminary results of its application for the architectural analysis of an enterprise web system and an e-commerce web system.

Keywords: Architectural evaluation · Source code analysis

1 Introduction

Over the last decade, several software architecture evaluation methods based on scenarios and quality attributes have been proposed [1, 2]. These methods use scenarios in order to exercise and evaluate the architecture of software systems. A scenario represents the way in which the stakeholders expect the system to be used [1]. The methods allow the gain of architectural-level understanding and of predictive insight to achieve desired quality attributes [3].

Traditional scenario-based methods produce a report as output of the process that contains information about risk analysis regarding architecture decisions. Existing methods, such as ATAM (Architecture Tradeoff Analysis Method) [1], produce information about sensitivity and tradeoff points. Risks [1, 4] are architecturally important decisions that have not been made, for example, when the development team has not decided which scheduling algorithm will be used, or if they are going to

S. Hammoudi et al. (Eds.): ICEIS 2013, LNBIP 190, pp. 490–505, 2014.
DOI: 10.1007/978-3-319-09492-2_29

use a relational or object-oriented database. Risks can also happen when decisions have been made, but their consequences are not completely understood. One example of such case is when the architecture team has decided to include an operating system portability layer, but they are not sure which functions will part of it or how it will affect the system performance [1].

Sensitivity points [1, 4] are architectural decisions involving one or more architectural elements that are critical for achieving a particular quality attribute. In that case, the response measure is sensitive to changing the architectural decision. For example, the level of confidentiality in a virtual private network might be sensitive to the number of bits of encryption. Sensitivity points indicate to software architects and developers where they should focus attention when trying to understand the achievement of some quality attribute. They have to be careful when changing those properties of the architecture because particular values of sensitivity points might become risks. Finally, a tradeoff point [1, 4] is a sensitivity point for more than one quality attribute. For example, changing the level of encryption could have impact on both security and performance. If the time of processing a message has hard real-time requirements, the level of encryption could be a tradeoff point because it improves the security, but it requires more processing time affecting the system performance.

Existing architecture evaluation methods are applied manually and rely on manual review-based evaluation that requires advanced skills from architects and developers. They are applied when the system architecture has already been specified, but before its implementation has begun. The system implementation is one additional element that can be useful when suitably analyzed, for example, when a software evolves causing critical architectural erosion [5] implying on the need of executing the process of evaluation again because the architecture design has several differences to the architecture implemented [6]. In this case, the implementation can provide information to help the automation of the architectural evaluation, enabling information reuse from previous manual evaluations.

In this context, this paper proposes an approach that introduces metadata about use case scenarios and quality attributes in the source code of the system, which ideally should come from traditional architecture evaluation methods. The main aim is to allow automated static and dynamic code analysis in order to produce reports with information, such as: (i) the scenarios affected by particular quality attributes; (ii) the scenarios that potentially contain tradeoff points and should have more attention from the development team; (iii) the execution time of a particular scenario; and (iv) if the scenario was successfully executed or not. In our approach, when the system implementation evolves, it is possible to keep or adjust the metadata information and automatically generate a new updated evaluation report. The approach does not aim to replace traditional architecture evaluation methods, but it complements them by promoting the continuous architecture evaluation during the implementation and evolution of software systems.

The rest of this paper is organized as follows: Sect. 2 introduces the approach; Sect. 3 presents the tool developed; Sect. 4 shows two case studies where we have applied our approach; Sect. 5 discusses some related works and, finally, Sect. 6 concludes the paper.

2 Approach Overview

This section presents an overview of our approach. The main goal is to automate the architecture evaluation by adding extra information with metadata to the application source code. The approach presented here is independent of programming language or platform. Figure 1 presents an overview of the approach showing input and output artifacts of each step.

Next subsections detail the steps shown in Fig. 1 to prepare information systems to be analyzed using our approach, which are: (i) choosing scenarios from the target architecture to be evaluated; (ii) identifying starting methods from evaluation scenarios; (iii) identifying and annotating quality attributes in the source code of the target system; and (iv) executing our analysis tool that uses all the provided information to perform automated scenario-based software architecture evaluation.

The approach is not limited to particular quality attributes, although the developed tool is currently addressing only the performance and robustness quality attributes. It is important to realize that the dynamic analysis is feasible only for quality attributes that can be quantified during the system execution. On the other hand, the static analysis can be used to perform traceability of any quality attribute that has associated source code.

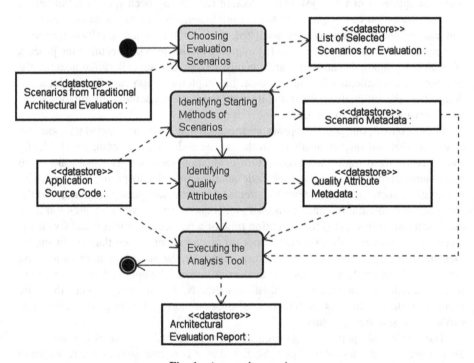

Fig. 1. Approach overview.

2.1   Choosing Evaluation Scenarios

The first step of the approach is to choose the scenarios from the target architecture to be evaluated. In order to perform this step, we can reuse information produced by previous activities from the development process. In particular, the elicited relevant scenarios gathered during the application of traditional architecture evaluation methods, such as ATAM or others [7], might be reused during this step.

2.2   Identifying Starting Methods of Scenarios

In this step, we identify the starting points of the execution of the chosen scenarios in the application source code under evaluation. A scenario execution defines paths of execution which can be abstracted to a call graph, where each node represents a method and each edge represents possible invocations.

Our challenge in this step is to define how identifying scenarios or paths of execution in the application source code. A simple solution to associate scenarios to the source code is to identify the methods that begin the use case scenarios execution, considering them as the call graph root nodes. In order to allow the introduction of this information in the source code, our approach defines the `Scenario` metadata, which defines a name attribute to identify it uniquely.

2.3   Identifying Quality Attributes

The identification of quality attributes in the application source code is similar to the identification of scenario starting methods. We have to add the metadata to the code element that we are interested. The approach is not limited to particular quality attributes, but the tool currently defines metadata considering performance, security, reliability and robustness.

Figure 2 shows the metadata definition with their respective attributes. `Performance` metadata has two attributes: name and limit time. Name is a string that uniquely identifies it, and limit time is a long integer that specifies a maximum time expected in milliseconds. The related method must complete its execution in a shorter time compared to the limit time value. Consequently, we can monitor if particular methods related to this metadata are executing according to the expected time or if they have improved or decreased their performance in the context of an evolution between two different releases of the system.

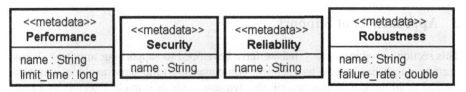

Fig. 2. Approach metadata for quality attributes.

`Robustness` metadata has a string name attribute that is unique and a double attribute that specifies the failure rate. It represents the maximum failure rate expected for a particular method from zero to one. Zero means that it never fails and one that fails in all the cases, in the same way, a value of 0.9 means it fails in 90 % of cases. Similarly to performance, we can monitor if the method fails more times than the value specified in the attribute. In this case, a warning should alert the developer team.

`Security` and `Reliability` metadata have currently one attribute, a string that uniquely identifies each one. The main aim is to annotate source code elements where these quality attributes are critical. This is useful because it enables traceability providing the possibility of determining statically, which use case scenarios are affected by quality attributes or which ones have potential to contain tradeoff points. For example, increasing the level of encryption could improve the security of the system, but it requires more processing time. That is, if a path of scenario execution is associated to more than one quality attribute, we need to observe and monitor it carefully because it has potential to contain tradeoff points.

2.4   Executing the Analysis Tool

The last step of the approach involves the execution of static and dynamic analysis implemented in a tool. This tool parses the metadata from the source code and performs analysis in order to proceed with the automated architecture evaluation based on the chosen scenarios and specified quality attributes.

During the static analysis, the tool parses the source code and metadata and builds a call graph of the methods. The root nodes of the call graph are those methods indicated by the `Scenario` metadata as scenarios starting points. After that, the tool uses the call graph: (i) to discover the quality attributes associated to a particular scenario or which scenarios have potential to have tradeoff points; (ii) to find out which methods, classes or scenarios could be affected due to a particular quality attribute; and (iii) to perform source code traceability of scenarios and quality attributes.

The dynamic analysis also benefits from the metadata information in order to perform the architecture evaluation during the system execution. It allows monitoring the performance and robustness quality attributes. In addition, dynamic reflective calls are captured only by dynamic analysis. The analysis currently accomplished by the tool allows: (i) calculating the performance time or failure rate from a scenario or a particular method; (ii) verifying if the constraints defined by quality attribute metadata are respected during the system execution; (iii) logging several information captured during the runtime; and (iv) adding more useful information to detect and analyze tradeoff points.

3   Approach Tool Support

This section introduces a tool that we have developed to support our approach. It has been accomplished as two independent components: (i) the static analysis is implemented as an Eclipse plugin; and (ii) the dynamic analysis is made available as a JAR file. The tool implements the metadata by using Java annotations.

3.1 Tool Support for Static Analysis

The static analysis tool allows executing the architecture evaluation over Eclipse projects. It currently parses source code from Java projects. Figure 3 shows a partial class diagram of the tool.

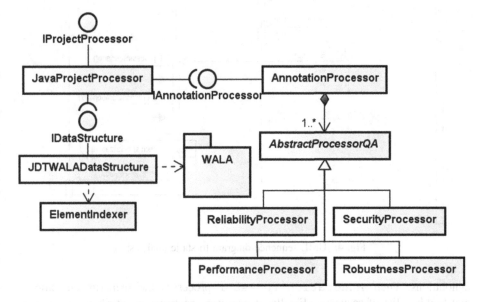

Fig. 3. UML class diagram showing tool processors.

The JavaProjectProcessor class calls other classes in order to build the call graph of the system under architectural evaluation. We have used the CAST (Common Abstract Syntax Tree) front-end of WALA (Watson Libraries for Analysis) static analysis framework [8] to build the call graph of the scenarios of interest. AnnotationProcessor class aggregates a set of different concrete strategy classes to process the different quality attribute annotations. Each one of them is responsible for the processing of a particular kind of annotation. During the annotation parsing, the AnnotationProcessor class also builds the list of scenarios annotated to complement the data structures built previously.

JavaProjectProcessor class also uses the JDTWALADataStructure to access and manipulate the application call graph and the indexes. The JDTWALA-DataStructure class uses ElementIndexer to build indexes of methods, classes and annotations to be used during the analysis. Actually, the annotation index is created by the AnnotationVisitor class that reads the source code looking for annotations.

Figure 4 summarizes the static analysis process. JavaProjectProcessor uses JDTWALADataStructure to build the call graph and the indexes. ElementIndexer is used to build the method index and the annotation index, but it creates an AnnotationVisitor object that parsers the source code looking for

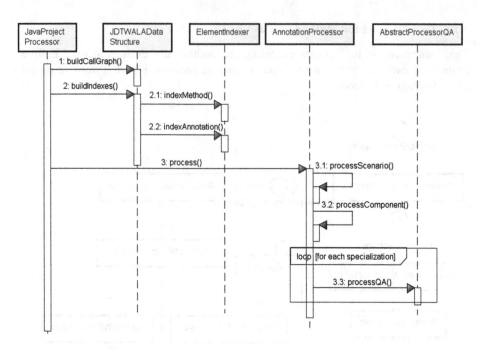

Fig. 4. UML sequence diagram to static analysis.

annotations. Then, `AnnotationProcessor` processes the scenario annotations and builds a list of scenarios. Finally, it processes each quality attribute annotation calling every `AbstractProcessorQA` subclasses.

The static analysis tool uses a model to represent the relationships among the system assets, such as classes, methods, scenarios and quality attributes. Figure 5 shows a partial class diagram of this model. The `ScenarioData` class has a starting root method, and `MethodData` has a declaring class. Each quality attribute is a specialization of the `AbstractQAData` class that keeps a reference to its related method. Finally, every `MethodData` instance has also an attribute signature that references the method node in the WALA call graph.

3.2 Tool Support for Dynamic Analysis

The dynamic analysis tool has been implemented using the AspectJ language. It defines aspects to monitor the execution of annotated methods. Essentially, the tool builds a dynamic call graph during application execution by using aspects to intercepting the approach annotations. The dynamic analysis should ideally be executed during the tests of the system. The quality of the analysis is directly related to the tests used to monitor the system execution because if they do not stress the system enough, the system failures will never happen, and the aspects will not be able to detect them.

In this way, the tool intercepts and monitors the scenarios execution by using the aspects, in other words, methods annotated with the scenario annotation.

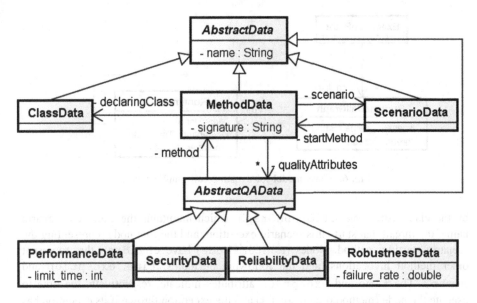

Fig. 5. UML class diagram of the static analysis model.

The execution flow is followed from the annotated method while the tool builds a dynamic call graph that accurately reflects the path executed in a particular scenario. In this graph, each node represents a method or constructor and keeps information of the quality attributes of interest, such as the execution time and if it ran successfully or not.

The current version of our tool has implemented aspects to intercept scenarios and quality attributes annotations for performance, security, robustness and reliability. In addition, the aspects can quantify values for the performance and robustness quality attributes. For performance, the tool calculates the time to execute a particular method or a full scenario depending on the analysis focus. For robustness, the tool indicates if the method or the full scenario was successfully executed or not. In this case, the tool considers that the method failed when it throws some exception. Similarly, the scenario fails when one or more of its methods fail. For security and reliability, our approach cannot provide any mechanism to quantify them. Thus, they are used to the traceability of important points in the application source code helping in the analysis and detection of tradeoff points among quality attributes.

The main aspect implemented in our approach is the `Scenario` aspect. It intercepts method invocations annotated with the scenario annotation from a particular point in order to determine the path of the scenario execution. The aspect follows the execution from the scenario starting method and builds a call graph that represents a particular execution of the scenario. Figure 6 shows the class structure for the dynamic call graph support built by scenario aspect.

A dynamic call graph (`RuntimeCallGraph`) is created for each new scenario execution and stored inside a list of execution paths (`ExecutionPaths`). Essentially, the `ExecutionPaths` class contains a list of dynamic call graphs represented

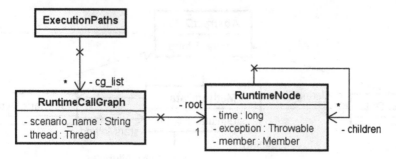

Fig. 6. Class model for dynamic call graph support.

by the class `RuntimeCallGraphGraph`, which maintains the executed scenario name, the thread that starts this scenario execution, and the root node representing the scenario starting method. Nodes (`RuntimeNode`) have `children` that represent other method invocations, and the following attributes: `time`, `exception` and `member`. The `time` and `exception` attributes indicate, respectively, the time to execute the node (method or constructor) and the exception thrown if its execution has failed (it will be null otherwise). The `member` attribute represents the node element, in other words, the method or constructor executed. The time of the full scenario execution is equal to its root node execution time.

The tool also implements default strategies to gather and store information about the execution of the relevant architecture scenarios. In addition, we have also implemented specific strategies for our case studies, which will be presented in the next section (Sect. 4).

4   Approach Evaluation

The approach has been applied to two different systems. In the first one, we have explored the static analysis in an academic enterprise large-scale web system developed by our institution. In addition, we have also applied the dynamic and static analysis to an e-commerce web system. Our main goal was to conduct an initial evaluation of the approach in order to verify its feasibility and how the developed tool behaves in practice.

4.1   Academic Enterprise Web System

We have applied the static analysis tool of our approach to enterprise web systems from SINFO/UFRN. SINFO is the Informatics Superintendence at Federal University of Rio Grande do Norte (UFRN), Brazil. It has developed several enterprise large-scale information systems [9], which perform full automation of university management activities. Due to the quality of these systems, several Brazilian government and education institutions have licensed and extended them to address their needs.

Our main goal was to verify the approach feasibility of static analysis in practice when used to a large-scale software system. In this sense, the tool should extract useful information in order to help developers answering some questions, such as: (i) what scenarios does a specific method belong to? (ii) what kinds of quality attributes can affect a specific scenario? (iii) what are the scenarios that contain potential tradeoff points among quality attributes? Next subsections describe the results of applying the approach to the academic management web system developed by SIN-FO/UFRN.

4.1.1 Choosing Evaluation Scenarios
In the first step, we have chosen some specific scenarios from the chosen analyzed system: (i) sending message – scenario used for sending messages (e-mails); (ii) authenticated document generation – scenario used to generate authenticated documents; (iii) user authentication – scenario used to authenticate users in the web application; and (iv) mobile user authentication – scenario used to authenticate users from a mobile device.

4.1.2 Identifying Scenarios
In this step, the starting execution methods for each chosen scenario were identified. They are, respectively, in the same order of the scenarios:

(i) `Mail.sendMessage()`: the class Mail contains some methods for sending messages;

(ii) `ProcessorDocumentGeneration.execute()`: the class `ProcessorDocumentGeneration` is a processor responsible for generating authenticated documents;

(iii) `DatabaseAuthentication.userAuthentication()`: the class `DatabaseAuthentication` implements user authentication strategy by using database;

(iv) `DatabaseAuthentication.mobileUserAuthentication()`: the class `DatabaseAuthentication` also supports mobile user authentication by using database strategy.

4.1.3 Identifying Quality Attributes
In the third step, we need to identify the quality attributes of interest in the application source code. The following methods and quality attributes were identified:

(i) `DatabaseAuthentication.getJdbcTemplate()` with `@Performance` – it was considered to be relevant for performance requirements because it is accessed by several database operations;

(ii) `Mail.enqueue()` with `@Security` – it is used by the system to enqueue messages that will be sent over the network;

(iii) `ProcessorDocumentGeneration.createRegistry()` with `@Security` – it is used to create the registry of an authenticated document to ensure its legitimacy;

(iv) `UFRNUtils.toMD5()` with `@Security` – it is used to create an MD5 hashing of strings, for example, passwords;

(v) `Database.initDataSourceJndi()` with `@Reliability` – it is used to initialize the access to the database and was considered critical for reliability because if the database initialization fails, the system is not going to work adequately.

4.1.4   Executing the Static Analysis Tool: Preliminary Results

The tool execution has extracted useful and interesting information in order to help us answering the questions highlighted in Sect. 4.1. Considering the first question – (i) what scenarios does a specific method belong to? – the tool can determine that the `get-JdbcTemplate()` method, for example, belongs to the following scenarios: user authentication, mobile user authentication, and authenticated document generation. This is possible because the tool builds a static call graph of each scenario and calculates if a call to a particular method exists in some of the possible paths of execution.

Regarding the second question – (ii) what kinds of quality attributes can affect a specific scenario? – the tool verifies all the paths for a specific scenario checking which ones have any quality attribute. The tool has identified, for example, all the quality attributes related to the User Authentication scenario: (i) performance quality attribute – because the `getJdbcTemplate()` method belongs to a possible path; (ii) the reliability quality attribute because the method `initDataSourceJndi()` also belongs to a possible path; and (iii) finally, the security quality attribute for the same reason, the method `toMD5()` is used to encrypt the user password.

Finally, for answering the third question – (iii) what are the scenarios that contain potential tradeoff points among quality attributes? – the tool looks for scenarios affected by more than one quality attribute because they potentially contain tradeoff points. The tool has identified: (i) user authentication and mobile user authentication are potential scenarios to have tradeoff because they are affected by performance, security and reliability; (ii) authenticated document generation scenario is another potential tradeoff point because it addresses the reliability and security quality attributes; and, on the other hand, (iii) the sending message scenario does not represent a tradeoff point because it is only affected by the security quality attribute. Table 1 summarizes these results.

The information automatically identified by our tool is useful to indicate to the architects and developers which specific scenarios and code assets they need to give more attention when evaluating or evolving the software architecture through the conduction of code inspections, or during the execution of manual and automated testing. In that way, our preliminary evaluation in a large-scale enterprise system has allowed us to answer the expected questions previously highlighted showing the feasibility of our static analysis approach.

4.2   e-Commerce Web System

The evaluation of the dynamic analysis was performed by applying our tool to the EasyCommerce web system [10, 11], which is an e-commerce system that has been

Table 1. Some information about tradeoffs in scenarios.

User Authentication		Mobile User Authentication	
Performance:	getJdbcTemplate()	Performance:	getJdbcTemplate()
Security:	toMD5()	Security:	toMD5()
Reliability:	initDataSourceJndi()	Reliability:	initDataSourceJndi()
Tradeoff:	Potential	Tradeoff:	Potential
Authenticated Document Generation		Sending Message	
Performance:	–	Performance:	–
Security:	createRegistry()	Security:	enqueue()
Reliability:	initDataSourceJndi()	Reliability:	–
Tradeoff:	Potential	Tradeoff:	No

developed by graduate students from our research group. It implements a concrete product of an e-commerce software product line described in [12]. During the evaluation process, we also have applied the static analysis to this system. This section shows both results.

This evaluation has two main aims: (i) finding out if there is potential scenarios that contain tradeoff points between their quality attribute; and (ii) understanding how quality attributes affect each scenario, for example, analyzing the execution time of scenarios and if they have failed or not. The static analysis has been used to explore the first aim. On the other hand, to the second aim, we need to use the dynamic analysis. Next subsections describe the steps followed.

4.2.1   Choosing Evaluation Scenarios
We have chosen some of the scenarios that represent the main features of Easy-Commerce: (i) registration of login information – it records the user information about login, such as user name and password; (ii) registration of personal information – it records personal information about the user, such as name, address, birthday, document identification; (iii) registration of credit card information – it records information about users credit card, such as card number and expiration date; (iv) searching for products – it allows searching for products by its name, type or features; and (v) inserting product item to cart – it allows users adding a product item to their shopping cart.

4.2.2   Identifying Scenarios
In this step, the starting execution methods for each chosen scenario were identified. They are, respectively, in the same order of the scenarios: (i) registerLogin(), (ii) registerUser() and (iii) registerCreditCard() from RegistrationMBean class that contains methods responsible for registering of user information; (iv) searchProducts() from SearchMBean class that includes methods for basic and advanced search of products; and (v) includeItemToCart() from CartMBean class that manages the virtual user-shopping cart.

4.2.3   Identifying Quality Attributes

We have chosen some methods belonging to the scenarios that appear to have potential to be relevant to specific quality attributes. The selected ones were:

(i) `GenericDAOImpl.save()` with `@Performance`, `@Reliability` and `@Robustness` – it is used by the system to save all its objects, because of that it should run as fast as possible and it also represents a critical action;

(ii) `RegistrationMBean.registerLogin()`, `RegistrationMBean.registerUser()`, and `RegistrationMBean.registerCreditCard()` with `@Security` – these methods manipulate user confidential information and they are in some way related to security.

4.2.4   Executing Static and Dynamic Analysis: Preliminary Results

First, we have executed the static analysis. Table 1 presents an overview of the generated report. The tool has detected for each scenario the relevant quality attributes. For example, all scenarios of registration of information are related to security because their starting method was annotated with @Security. The registration of credit card scenario also has reliability, performance and robustness quality attributes because some of the methods inside this scenario has specific annotations, in this case, the `save()` method. Looking at Table 1, we can identify potential trade-off points between quality attributes. The registration of credit card scenario, for example, is associated to four quality attributes, where security and performance are classical examples of quality attribute conflict. Because of that, this scenario was identified as a potential tradeoff point.

In order to evaluate the behavior of the performance and reliability quality attributes, we have used the dynamic analysis to quantify them. The system was executed to exercise the chosen scenarios thus enabling the monitoring by the aspects.

Table 2 shows some information collected by the aspect, which were extracted during the execution of the following scenarios: register of login, register of personal information, and register of credit card information. By executing these scenarios, we have one occurrence of performance, reliability and robustness in `save()` method and three occurrences of security in `registerLogin()`, `registerUser()` and `registerCreditCard()`. For each scenario, the tool also calculated the execution time and the failure rate. Table 3 shows some examples.

Table 2. Scenarios and quality attributes which affect them.

Scenario	Quality Attribute
Registration of login information	Security
Registration of personal information	Security
Registration of credit card	Reliability Security Performance Robustness
Search for products	–
Include product item to cart	–

Table 3. Sample of data collected by dynamic analysis.

Register of login	Register of personal information	Register of credit card information
Execution time: 4 ms	Execution time: 3 ms	Execution time: 152 ms
Failure rate: 0 %	Failure rate: 0 %	Failure rate: 0 %
@Performance: -	@Performance: -	@Performance: save()
@Security: registerLogin()	@Security: registerUser()	@Security: registerCreditCard()
@Reliability: -	@Reliability: -	@Reliability: save()
@Robustness: -	@Robustness: -	@Robustness: save()

The dynamic analysis process in this study has met our expectations because it has allowed us extracting useful information of the execution context, such as, monitoring of scenarios and quality attributes, calculating the execution time and failure rate of scenarios and last, but not least, helping the detection of executed paths with potential tradeoff points.

5 Related Work

To the best of our knowledge, there is no existing proposal that looks for the automation of architecture evaluation methods using annotation and code analysis as we have proposed in this paper. In this section, we summarize some research work that address architectural evaluation or propose analysis strategies similar to ours.

Over the last years, several architecture evaluation methods, such as ATAM, SAAM, ARID [1] and ALMA [2] have been proposed. They rely on manual reviews before the architecture implementation. Our approach complements these existing methods by providing automated support to static and dynamic analysis over the source code of the software system. It contributes to the continuous evaluation of the software architecture during the system implementation and evolution.

Some recent research work have proposed adding extra architectural information to the source code with the purpose of applying automated analysis or document the software architecture. In that way, Christensen et al. [13] use annotations to add information about components and design patterns with the purpose of documenting the architecture. On the other hand, Mirakhorli et al. [14] present an approach for tracing architecturally significant concerns, specifically related to architectural tactics which are solutions for a wide range of quality concerns. These recent research work, however, do not explore the integrated usage of adding information related to scenarios or quality attributes with dynamic and static code analysis.

The approach presented in [15] proposes to identify when the developer changes to the program source code, tests, or environment affect the system behavior. That approach does not address scenarios or quality attributes in order to provide any kind of architectural evaluation, but parts of the technique that has been applied is similar with ours. In the same way of our approach, it builds the static graph through the source code analysis and the dynamic graph with AspectJ during the tests execution.

It can be used, for example, to confront the graphs and determine if changes in the system (static graph) affect the system behavior (dynamic graph), or vice versa.

6 Conclusions

We presented an approach to automating the software architecture evaluation using the source code as input of this process. The approach proposes: (i) to add metadata to the source code in order to identify relevant scenarios and quality attributes for the architectural evaluation; and (ii) to execute static and dynamic code analysis that supports the automated architectural evaluation based on the annotated scenarios and quality attributes. The paper has also presented an implementation of a tool that supports the static and dynamic analysis of the approach for the architectural evaluation of systems implemented in the Java language. Finally, we have also described the application of the approach in two existing systems: a large-scale enterprise information system and an e-commerce web system. The preliminary obtained results of the approach usage have allowed us to provide and quantifying several and useful information about architecture evaluation based on scenarios and quality attributes.

The presented approach is still under development and we are currently evolving it in order to apply to other large-scale enterprise information systems. The tool might be used to check missing paths [16], which happens when a path exists in the static call graph and it does not exist in the dynamic call graph meaning a not tested path or dead code.

In addition, we are also evolving the approach in order to analyze the architecture erosion of existing software systems by allowing the execution of the static and dynamic code analysis over different versions of the same software system. The main aim is to observe how quality attributes evolve when the scenarios implementation are changed and evolved. In this new implementation, our tool is used: (i) to persist the information extracted and quantified from each version of the system; and (ii) to compare the obtained results for the different versions of the system in order to verify if the code changes have caused degradation of the system quality attributes. Finally, the tool is also been extended to mine the source code repository of the system (e.g. subversion repository system), to find out the tasks that are responsible to introduce these changes, and to indicate which kind of tasks are more likely to cause degradation to specific quality attributes.

Acknowledgements. This work was partially supported by the National Institute of Science and Technology for Software Engineering (INES) - CNPq under grants 573964/2008-4 and CNPq 560256/2010-8, and the Informatics Superintendence (SINFO) from Federal University of Rio Grande do Norte (UFRN), Brazil.

References

1. Clements, P., Kazman, R., Klein, M.: Evaluating Software Architectures: Methods and Case Studies. Addison-Wesley, MA (2002)
2. Bengtsson, P., Lassing, N., Bosch, J., Vliet, H.: Architecture-level modifiability analysis (ALMA). J. Syst. Softw. **69**, 1–2 (2004)

3. Kazman, R., Abowd, G., Bass, L., Clements, P.: Scenario-based analysis of software architecture. IEEE Softw. **13**(6), 47–55 (1996)
4. Kazman, R., Klein, M., Clements, P.: ATAM: Method for Architecture Evaluation. Technical report, CMU/SEI-2000-TR-004, ESC-TR-2000-004, Software Engineering Institute, August 2000
5. Silva, L., Balasubramaniam, D.: Controlling software architecture erosion: a survey. J. Syst. Softw. **85**(1), 132–151 (2012)
6. Abi-Antoun, M., Aldrich, J.: Static extraction and conformance analysis of hierarchical runtime architectural structure using annotations. SIGPLAN Not. **44**, 321–340 (2009)
7. Babar, M.A., Gorton, I.: Comparison of scenario-based software architecture evaluation methods. In: Proceedings of the 11th Asia-Pacific Software Engineering Conference (APSEC '04), pp. 600–607. IEEE Computer Society, Washington, DC (2004)
8. Wala, T.J.: Watson Libraries for Analysis, September 2013. http://wala.sourceforge.net
9. SINFO/UFRN (Informatics Superintendence), September 2013. http://www.info.ufrn.br/wikisistemas
10. Torres, M.: Systematic Assessment of Product Derivation Approaches. MSc Dissertation, Federal University of Rio Grande do Norte (UFRN), Natal, Brazil (2011) (in Portuguese)
11. Aquino, H.M.: A Systematic Approach to Software Product Lines Testing. MSc Dissertation, Federal University of Rio Grande do Norte (UFRN), Natal, Brazil (2011) (in Portuguese)
12. Lau, S.Q.: Domain Analysis of E-Commerce Systems Using Feature-Based Model Templates, MSc Dissertation, University of Waterloo (2006)
13. Christensen, H.B., Hansen, K.M.: Towards architectural information in implementation (NIER track). In: Proceedings of the 33rd International Conference on Software Engineering, (ICSE '11), pp. 928–931. ACM, New York (2011)
14. Mirakhorli, M., Shin, Y., Cleland-Huang, J., Cinar, M.: A tactic-centric approach for automating traceability of quality concerns. In: Proceedings of the 2012 International Conference on Software Engineering (ICSE 2012), pp. 639–649. IEEE Press, Piscataway (2012)
15. Holmes, R., Notkin, D.: Identifying program, test, and environmental changes that affect behaviour. In: Proceedings of the 33rd International Conference on Software Engineering (ICSE '11), pp. 371–380. ACM, New York (2011)
16. Liu, S. Zhang, J.: Program analysis: from qualitative analysis to quantitative analysis (NIER track). In: Proceedings of the 33rd International Conference on Software Engineering (ICSE '11), pp. 956–959. ACM, New York (2011)

Joining Data and Maps in the Government Enterprise Architecture by a Semantic Approach: Methodology, Ontology and Case Study

Daniela Giordano, Alfredo Torre, Carmelo Samperi,
Salvatore Alessi, and Alberto Faro[✉]

Department of Electrical, Electronics and Computer Engineering,
University of Catania, viale A. Doria 6, 95125 Catania, Italy
{danigiordan, alfredo.torre, carmelo.samperi,
salvatore.alessi, afaro}@dieei.unict.it

Abstract. The problem of managing data and maps within an ontological approach is little studied in the Government Enterprise Architecture. Aim of this paper is to present a methodology to solve this problem in case we would join municipal and cadastral data bases. In particular, we aim at linking the information contained in the local taxation registry to the urban territory to allow the Public Administration managers to check if the taxes have been paid, and the citizens to compute the correct amount to pay. The paper presents in detail the adopted ontology and the technological architecture, whereas a case study clarifies how the methodology works in practice. We plan to extend this methodology to manage e-gov services needing to interconnect data stores of city interest to vector layers derived from the Cadastre or other CAD systems.

Keywords: E-Government · Government Enterprise Architecture · Geographic information systems · Ontology engineering

1 Introduction

The Semantic Web is a mesh of information linked up in such a way to be processed easily by machines on a global scale [1]. The Semantic Web is built generally on syntaxes which use *International Resource Identifiers* (IRIs) to represent resources, i.e., subjects and objects, linked by properties. Subject-predicate-object relations are represented by triples, also called semantic web statements. Let us recall that IRI is an extension of the *Uniform Resource Identifier* (URI) that provides an encoding for Unicode character sets.

The semantic web statements are usually formalized by the Resource Description Framework (RDF), i.e., a directed multi-graph consisting of subjects, predicates and objects [2]. The RDF graph can be queried by means of the SPARQL query language to retrieve and manipulate the stored data [3]. The RDF Scheme (RDFS) is a collection of RDF resources that behaves as a vocabulary of terms and properties related to application-specific domain. Such vocabularies may range from controlled lists of

© Springer International Publishing Switzerland 2014
S. Hammoudi et al. (Eds.): ICEIS 2013, LNBIP 190, pp. 506–519, 2014.
DOI: 10.1007/978-3-319-09492-2_30

terms to taxonomies and thesauri depending on the type of terms and relationships that can be expressed (e.g. parent-child relationships in a taxonomy).

Ontology refers to a formal specification of a shared vocabulary and allows us to define formally a set of terms, interconnections, constraints and rules of inference on a particular domain [4, 5]. A logical formalism is needed to represent an ontology such as Description Logic (DL) [6].

Ontology, with rule definition language and description logic, can also provide a new kind of data retrieving and mash up with the "backward chaining" concept to make possible the inference of data structures not present in the knowledge base at the moment of the query.

The use of an ontology with the intention of describing a particular aspect of reality, provides information reusable for all parties in the given domain. Regarding the *e-government* activities, the Linked Data group at the W3C and the Government Linked Data (GLD) are publishing data sets and knowledge bases (often in the form of light-weight ontologies and vocabularies) to support e-government services involving different organizations. These ontologies are under test and will be refined in the next future by incorporating novel global and local vocabularies.

The problem of managing data and maps within the mentioned ontological approach is little studied because it is necessary to study more complex problems that involve location based information, and because unifying terms of proprietary vocabularies such as road and street in view of a shared vocabulary implies only an equivalence between symbols, whereas equivalent drawings even if they are labeled by the same name, e.g. building, needs to be processed by complex conversion procedures when passing from the adopted Geographic Information System (GIS) to the one used by another organization to be sure that they deal with the same physical entity.

Therefore, in problems starting from personal and cadastral data based on maps, as well as for identifying the escape routes in case earthquake, we have to adopt not only a standard vocabulary that behaves as a bridge between equivalent terms used in the proprietary systems, but also conversion procedures to ensure that a physical vector in a GIS is the same in another one.

Of course, such problem would disappear if one adopts the same vocabulary and the same GIS in all the computing systems, however this is not only unrealistic but also not useful since proprietary codification of data and drawings may be more effective than the standard ones to carry out some basic operations such as storing and updating.

Aim of this paper is to present an ontology based methodology to solve this problem by illustrating how it works in practice by a case study dealing with the computation of local taxes from municipal and cadastral data. In particular, we discuss how linking the information contained in the local taxation registry to the urban territory by geographic points (*Points Of Interest* - POI) to allow the Public Administration (PA) to check if the taxes have been paid, and the citizens to determine the correct amount to pay.

At more general level, by this work, we also aim at supporting the transition of the PA information systems from their current structure, often consisting of separated silos of data, towards a *Government Enterprise Architecture* (GEA) following the principles of the *Connected Government* Model that enables "the governments to connect seamlessly across functions, agencies, and jurisdictions to deliver effective and efficient services to citizens and businesses" [7].

In particular we take into account the dimensions of the *Connected Government* Model that may be improved by adopting a better data organization, i.e., the first three dimensions of ones featuring an effective Government Enterprise Architecture:

1. Common infrastructure and interoperability,
2. Collaborative services and business operations,
3. Citizen centricity,
4. Social inclusion,
5. Networked organizational model,
6. Public sector governance.

Consequently, aspects such as public sector governance, networked organizational model and social inclusion mainly depending on the PA organization model are outside the scope of the paper and will discussed in further studies.

More specifically, with reference to the GEA model, the paper is focused on presenting a methodology to integrate data and processes residing at the lower layers of the GEA layered model consisting of the following four main layers:

1. the technological infrastructure where all the application processes and data are implemented.
2. the data layer where we have the data required to study and define the strategies of the general business processes,
3. the specific management processes dealing with a well defined application domain, and
4. the business processes and related outcomes to carry out the strategies of the organization enabling the services required by citizens and enterprises.

This will be obtained by using the *semantic web* technologies that facilitate better than the ones available on the market the data and processes integration over the web [8]. To avoid of illustrating the proposed methodology at a too theoretical level, in the paper we discuss a specific case, i.e., the computation of local taxes that requires integration of municipal and cadastral data stored at different PA offices following the requirements of a project, named K-Metropolis, supported by the Regional Government of Sicily, whose principal aim is collecting data originating from databases of different organizations to offer suitable e-services to citizens and enterprises [9]. However, the proposed methodology may be followed to manage other problems involving data and maps integration.

Let us note that another relevant part of the K-Metropolis project, called Wi-City, aiming at supporting mobile people activities following a semantic approach will not be discussed in the paper. The interested reader may find detailed information on the methodology adopted in Wi-City and its implementation structure in [10–12].

Section 2 illustrates the ontology and technologies that allow the taxation registry and the land registry to be interconnected in a single RDF framework.

Section 3 points out, by a case study, the main steps to convert the proprietary SQL codification of the original data bases into standard RDF statements, as well as the map conversion to allow the physical entities associated to the terms of the ontology to be represented by the same physical entity in almost all the available open source GISs.

Section 4 presents an example of the SPARQL queries that allow the citizens to extract the geo-referenced reports on how much they should pay to PA for their estates and support the PA employers to check if the citizens are in arrears.

2 Joining Municipal Data and Cadastral MAPS: Ontologies and Technologies

As pointed out in the introduction, the final purpose of this work is to develop a new kind of distributed system architecture capable of aggregating heterogeneous data from multiple data sources that have their own storage and representation format. In particular, the paper aims at integrating municipal and cadastral data bases by using a specific ontology and suitable technologies, as illustrated in the following sections.

2.1 K-Metropolis Ontology: KMET

To identify the relevant ontology of an e-government problem, the first step is the one of classifying the entities involved in the specific domain of interest. With reference to the mentioned local taxation problem discussed in detail in the case study, the main conceptual elements are: the *taxpayer* and her/his *personal data*; the *property tax data* referred to a specific period of time; and the *waste fee tax data*.

The element enabling the right connections among the various entities in the database is the taxpayer identification number subdivided in people and organization identification number. Therefore, the main taxation concepts are as follows:

- County
  - **City**
- Taxpayer
  - **Citizen**
  - **Organization**
- Tax Return
  - **real estate property tax**
  - **waste fee tax**

Although the above classification has been used to manage the entities of a specific city, the entity *City* has been taken into account in our ontology as a concept, i.e., the class *taxpayer* consists of citizens and organizations of a city that is viewed as an autonomous entity rather one of citizens and organizations attributes.

For what concerns the *Tax Return* class, it is connected to the cadastral geographic entities to compute the local taxes, thus depending on the specific cadastral data organization adopted at the national level. Therefore, our ontology depends on how the Cadastre is organized in Italy and may differ for another country.

In Italy, the Cadastre consists of two main sections: the Cadastre of Land Properties and the one of Real Estates. The data deal with owners and holders of the estates or the lands whose relevant attributes are geographical location, size, intended use, earning capacity and consistency.

Since in the paper we are interested in the Real Estates Cadastre (REC), we have deepened only its structure and found that it is divided into sections and *"pages"*, each of which includes *parcels* associated to the basic entities, i.e., the Urban Real Estate Unit (UREU), defined as a portion of a building, an entire building or set of buildings that is capable of producing an independent income and has functional autonomy (access independence, self-sufficiency and autonomy in terms of use classification).

It should be emphasized that the UREU is no constrained to belong to a single owner. Consequently, a Real Estate Unit belonging to more owners will be reported with a single contextual registration and multiple identification. The identification of an UREU is made by the following identifiers:

- *Cadastral municipality*, i.e., the municipality where the property is located;
- *Administrative Section*, i.e., a portion of the municipality;
- *Page*, i.e., a section of the municipality that is represented in the cartographic maps of the Cadastre Registry;
- *Parcel*, i.e., a piece of land or building and any area of relevance within the Page;
- *Subordinate:*, i.e., the actual element identifier of the UREU

Generally, each UREU is identified by its own subordinate, but, if the building is made up of a single UREU, then the subordinate may be missing. Considering the case of our interest and the above cadastral data structure, we attached the cadastral main entities (*section, page, parcel, subordinate*) to the fundamental geometrical ontology, as shown in Fig. 1.

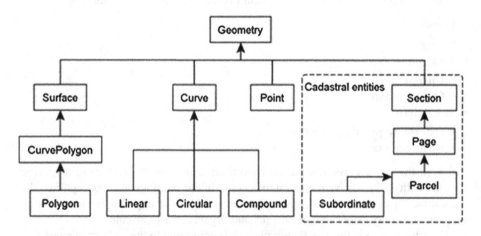

Fig. 1. Geographic and cadastral entities.

Also, two more identifiers can be found in addition to those above listed: *Development* and *Attachment*, denoted respectively in the national cadastre as "sviluppo" and "allegato"; the values of these identifiers indicate printings that represent on a larger scale some particular portion of the territory of a Page drawn on a smaller scale.

All the above concepts have been implemented using the Ontology Web Language (OWL) defined by the World Wide Web Consortium (W3C) in http://www.w3.org/2004/OWL/. Figure 2 shows this ontology named KMET since it has been adopted by the mentioned K-Metropolis project.

Such ontology is available at http://purl.org/net/kmet. On the left we have the entities related to *taxpayer*, whereas on right we have the ones related to *tax returns* and *cadastral units*.

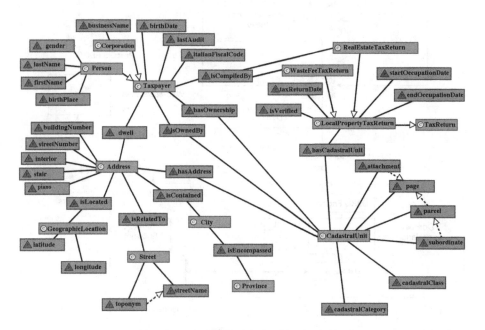

Fig. 2. K-METropolis (KMET) ontology.

2.2   Technologies

Figure 3 presents how the users may query the RDF triple store and the technologies involved in the deployment of the proposed distributed architecture. Each technology is a free and open source software to allow the Public Administration to reduce running expenses and maintenance costs.

Also, this choice allows us to follow the cornerstone philosophy of the Open Data movement, whose description is given at http://opendefinition.org.

As shown on the right of Fig. 3, our model suggests that the data sources from the cadastral domain are converted from CXF format to *shapefiles, i.e.,* ESRI SHP files;

512   D. Giordano et al.

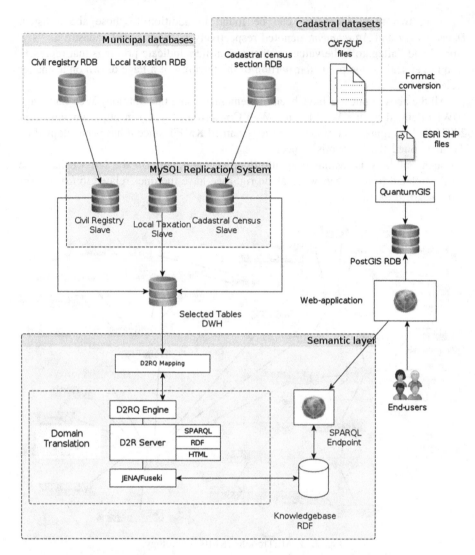

Fig. 3. Overview of the multi-tier system architecture and of the technologies adopted.

then they are imported into Quantum GIS to be exposed as vector layers provided with geo-referenced data.

These latter data are then imported to a PostGIS relational database to be available, together with the public administration data, to the end users through SQL queries (with automatic GeoJSON marshalling) via a RESTful Webservice.

Since our aim is to expose these data as RDF data structures through a SPARQL endpoint, in our model the relational databases at the center of Fig. 3, derived from the original municipal and cadastral databases drawn at the top of Fig. 3, are mapped in RDF triples using the D2RQ Platform (http://d2rq.org), that is an Open Source system that offers RDF based access to the contents of the relational databases.

A Jena/Fuseki framework contained into the domain translation, drawn at the bottom of Fig. 3, allows the end user to receive RDF formatted responses to the queries issued through external SPARQL endpoints. Such responses are also stored in a knowledge base to be reused to speed up the future queries.

Figure 4a shows the result of a query to visualize the UREUs of an area using a web GIS application as a layer superimposed to the OpenStreetMap raster layer. Such response has been obtained by using the GIS capabilities of our system, i.e., by using the right part of the model drawn in Fig. 3 devoted to manage the queries issued by the users to visualize a specific portion of the urban cadastral map. In particular, the queries of this type are directed to Quantum GIS to extract the shape files related to the specific cadastral map of user interest that will be superimposed to the raster background chosen by the user.

Figure 4b, shows how the public administration data mapped through the D2RQ Platform into RDF schemas may be visualized by another type of user query issued through the semantic layer i.e., the query managed by the mentioned multi-tier querying by RESTful Web Services, RDF marshalling and HTML/XHTML visualization. In particular, after received the *shapefiles* of her/his interest (e.g., urban blocks or districts) superimposed to the chosen raster background following the first type of query, the users may issue the other type of query to extract data coming from the different data stores to know detailed administrative information about a specific graphical element (e.g., a building or an apartment) located in the selected area, as shown in Fig.4b.

Fig. 4. Responses to two typical user queries: a) cadastral map of user interest superimposed to a raster background (i.e., OpenStreetMap), and b) detailed administrative information about the specific graphical element selected by the user that is located at the center of the figure.

3 Case Study

In this section we point out the main problems that arise when one tries to implement the previous architecture to provide in practice a specific e-government service, i.e., the local estate taxation depending on both personal data of the owners and cadastral data of the real estate units.

3.1 Municipal Databases

The datasets about citizen and taxation were provided by the local administration in the form of IBM DB2 Databases. Therefore, before using the D2RQ Platform these databases were converted into MySQL databases to work on an open source format.

Then, after selecting the relevant data bases, e.g., the relational data base (RDB) at the top of Fig. 3, we have exported them as normalized tables into an additional MySQL database. Finally, the last step of the process was the one of mapping the contents of the databases into RDF triples through the on-the-fly translation obtained by the above mentioned D2RQ Platform.

Although the above procedure seems easy, several problems were encountered such as the large number of tables in the original databases and the lack of semantics in the table definition.

In particular, we have cut off the tables to a large extent since such RDBs were made up of 58 tables and 19,170,374 records containing many repetitions. Also, only a subset of the data that would be useful for the problem at hands were selected. In fact, since the taxation process has to be applied to citizens who own a property, only the table rows corresponding to estate owners were selected, whereas only the columns of these tables relevant for the taxation process were imported in the mentioned MySQL database, with the intent of mapping them in RDF triples to be used for supporting the taxation payment and checking using SPARQL queries.

To this aim, we have carried out a connection of the resulting municipal triple stores to the information stored in the cadastral database, using a multi-tier distributed system that gives the ability to expose cartographic representation (stored on a PostGIS database) and makes it responsive to the end user inputs treating the GIS data bases not as MySQL or PostGIS data bases, but as a RDF graph obtained using a custom D2R mapping system, such as G2R [13]. Thanks to these structured semantic connections we obtained a unique SPARQL endpoint where it is possible to attach many kinds of end-user application logic.

3.2 Cadastral Databases and GIS

Let us note that the cadastral datasets were provided by the provincial Land Administration as an extraction of the national cadastral map database from WEGIS, that is a licensed closed source powered by SOGEI (http://www.sogei.it) and used by the Italian Land Administration. In this extraction each Page is represented by a pair of ASCII files: a CXF file (*Cadastral eXchange Format*) containing all the graphical elements that compose the cadastral map, and a homonymous SUP file containing statistical data and parcel surfaces. Thus, a suitable conversion of the CXF and SUP files has been done to store the cadastral information within relational GISs that can be interconnected to the municipal data, as suggested in the previous section.

For this reason, the format of these two files was converted to ESRI *shapefile*, i.e., a geospatial vector data format for geographic information system software developed by ESRI using *CXFToShape,* i.e., a free CXF to *ESRI shapefile* converter. Then, the *shapefile* formatted files was imported into Quantum GIS, i.e., a cross-platform free and open source GIS application that provides capabilities of data visualization, editing, and analysis and may be viewed as a set of graphical elements linkable to the virtual RDF store obtained through the mentioned D2R Platform.

Let us note that in this way we may use the textual information contained in the Cadastre as RDF triples, but for using the related drawings in any GIS it is necessary to represent them into a reference system known by all the GISs available on the market. Thus, we have geo-referenced the *shapefile* imported into Quantum GIS by means of the *Cassini-Soldner* geo-coordinate system through the definition of a custom projection algorithm.

In this way the cadastral data may be processed as triples and the related vector drawings can be overlapped to any raster data layers (e.g., *Google Street Maps satellite*, *Bing Map Aerial* layers and cartographic regional data provided by the Province Bureau) or added to existing vector data layers (such as *OpenStreetMap*, *Google Streets* and *Bing Road*).

Figure 5 shows the almost perfect overlapping obtained in Quantum GIS of the Cassini-Soldner layer dealing with the coast area and of some buildings close to the sea derived from the Cadastre over the OpenStreetMap raster data layer.

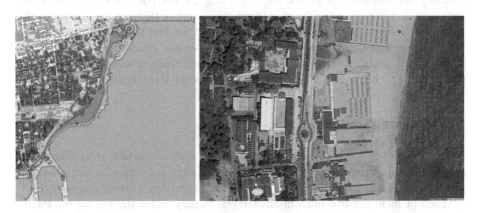

Fig. 5. Almost perfect overlapping of the Cassini-Soldner layer of a coast area (on the left), and of a resort area (on the right) to the OpenStreetMap raster layer.

This means that not only a SPARQL query allow us to join the municipal and cadastral data using the relevant shared fields, e.g., the fiscal codes of the owner or the UREU codes of the estates, but also that the vector layers of the cadastral entities involved in the problem at hands (e.g., buildings, roads, zones) may be represented in any GIS as entities colored depending on the map theme.

Fig. 6. Thematic map displaying tax payments and waste collection services for an urban area chosen by the user.

In this way, we may visualize on OpenStreetMaps in red the buildings registered in the cadastre data base that contain commercial activities that are in arrears if one is checking tax evasions, in yellow the roads that are not covered by regular waste collection and in orange the downsized schools if one is studying the quality of the services offered to the citizens. For example, from the fact that all the buildings in Fig. 6 are in green and some streets in yellow we can easily deduce that all the administrative taxes related to the buildings of the area under consideration were paid, but that some problems about the regular waste collection were signaled by the citizens.

4 Querying Data and Maps

The semantic web gives to a developer two major choices when using distributed databases for querying in a semantic manner: the former is to copy the entire amount of data in a unique knowledge base, the latter is to perform a distributed query.

Each of them has two main disadvantages: latency and scale, but for the Public Administrations that have usually to manage large databases and big amount of data, copying an entire data store is hardly feasible.

Thus, in our approach we adopted the distributed model already shown in Fig. 3 to allow the users to query two or more RDF knowledge bases using a formula expressed in SPARQL, or to combine relational databases to be queried with a D2RQ mapping language that translates the SPARQL query to SQL on the fly.

As said before, the user interface allows the user to select a single Parcel showed on a multi layered map through a mouse click on a single polygon that represents a building as shown in Fig. 7. These polygons are recreated by processing the GeoJSON vector layers obtained from a SQL query against PostGIS database and produced by a PHP Web Service.

Fig. 7. Building chosen by the end user using the interface of the web GIS application.

The mouse click is detected on the client-side via Leaflet JavaScript library (available at http://leafletjs.com/) and then the following SPARQL query is produced to know the payment situation of each apartment of the selected building:

```
prefix kmet:<http://purl.org/net/kmet#>
SELECT DISTINCT ?CadastralUnit ?Page ?Parcel
?Subordinate ?LocalPropertyTaxReturn
WHERE {
?CadastralUnit a kmet:CadastralUnit;
kmet:page ?Page;
kmet:parcel ?Parcel;
kmet:subordinate ?Subordinate.
FILTER(str(?Page)='0069').
FILTER(str(?Parcel)='20317').
?LocalPropertyTaxReturn kmet:hasCadastralUnit ?CadastralUnit.
}
```

The following table shows the results of the previous SPARQL query to be appended to the map shown previously.

Cadastral unit	Page	Parcel	Subordinate	LocalPropertyTaxReturn
<cadastralunit/16076>	"0069"	"20317"	"0029"	< WasteFeeTaxReturn /9213>
<cadastralunit/36713>	"0069"	"20317"	"0028"	<WasteFeeTaxReturn/29215>
<cadastralunit/36710>	"0069"	"20317"	"0019"	<WasteFeeTaxReturn/29310>
<cadastralunit/230222>	"0069"	"20317"	"0073"	<RealEstateTaxReturn/96445>
<cadastralunit/230227>	"0069"	"20317"	"0055"	<RealEstateTaxReturn/98014>
<cadastralunit/230228>	"0069"	"20317"	"0047"	<RealEstateTaxReturn/98019>
<cadastralunit/36720>	"0069"	"20317"	"0110"	<RealEstateTaxReturn/119214>

Let us note that the same result may be obtained by executing the above query in either the centralized or distributed scenario. A performance analysis to compare these two scenarios is outside the scope of the paper and will be discussed in future works, even if better performance may be achieved certainly if the queries may reuse previous results stored on a RDF knowledge base such as the one shown at the bottom of Fig. 3.

5 Conclusions

Related works to the subject of the paper deal mainly with cadastral system interconnection and introducing spatial dimensions to RDF schemas.

An ontology architecture for the land administration domain, targeted to achieve semantic interoperability between cadastral systems is proposed in [14]. The architecture complies with both Geospatial and Land Administration standards. An example of extension dealing with the specificities of their national cadastre is also provided. In [15], a Semantic Web approach is proposed to customize the applications of the Land Administration Domain. Also, an OWL layered architecture adaptable across jurisdictions is outlined. Both these works differ from our proposal in the conversion from relational data models to ontology and in the presence of an explicit ontology alignment step that has been illustrated in detail in Sect. 2.

The work of introducing spatial dimensions to the semantic web is described in [16] where it is demonstrated how crowd sourced geographical data transformed into RDF can be interlinked (mapped) with other (spatial data) sets to enable spatial data web applications.

A similar work, i.e., [13] focuses explicitly on some computational issues influencing the use of GIS from the semantic web standpoint, and proposes to treat GIS as virtual RDF graphs instead of re-implementing GIS functionalities in semantic web frameworks. This is achieved through an extension of the D2RQ mapping language to include spatial data types.

Therefore, the application scenario addressed in this work and clarified by many examples and a suitable case study, i.e., integration of cadastral systems with citizen data, has not been tackled before.

Let us note that the proposed ontology based methodology to manage data and maps using RDF schemas is being experimented in the project promoted by the Sicily Region, named K-metropolis, to support the municipal Governments not only in defining the local taxation policy but also in the transition from the current not interoperable GIS platforms to the implementation of a spatial data infrastructure to integrate data and maps of different municipalities.

For example, we are studying how the proposed methodology may support the municipal Governments to define city master plans and civil protection policies by interconnecting both public and private data stores to the drawings derived not only from the Cadastre but also from any relevant institutional CAD system.

This will allow the municipal Government not only to draw the intended land use and the emergency plans over any raster background, such as aerial photogrammetry or satellite images, but also to represent these plans by a standard graphical notation immediately understandable by any other involved organization.

References

1. Sheth, A.: Enterprise applications of semantic web. In: IFIP International Conference on Industrial Applications of Semantic Web (IASW2005), Jyväskylä, Finland (2005)
2. Hayes, P.: RDF Semantics. W3C Recommendation 10 (2004). http://www.w3.org/TR/rdf-mt
3. Prud'hommeaux, E., Seaborne, A.: SPARQL Query Language for RDF, W3C Rec. 15.1.2. (2008). http://www.w3.org/TR/rdf-sparql-query/
4. Zhai, J., Jiang, J., Yu, Y., Li, J.: Ontology-based integrated information platform for digital city. In: IEEE Proceedings of Wireless Communications, Networking and Mobile Computing, WiCOM '08 (2008)
5. Faro A., Giordano D., Musarra A.: Ontology based mobility information systems. In: Proceedings of Systems, Men and Cybernetics Conference, SMC'03, vol. 3, pp. 4288–4293. IEEE (2003)
6. Baader, F., Calvanese, D., McGuinness, D.L., Nardi, D., Patel-Schneider, P.F.: The Description Logic Handbook: Theory, Implementation, Applications. Cambridge University Press, Cambridge (2003)
7. Saha, P.: Government Enterprise Architecture Research Project, NUS Systems Science Institute (2010). http://unpan1.un.org/intradoc/groups/public/documents/unpan/unpan039390.pdf
8. Langegger, A., Wöß, W., Blöchl, M.: A semantic web middleware for virtual data integration on the web. In: Bechhofer, S., Hauswirth, M., Hoffmann, J., Koubarakis, M. (eds.) ESWC 2008. LNCS, vol. 5021, pp. 493–507. Springer, Heidelberg (2008)
9. Costanzo, A., Faro, A., Giordano, D., Venticinque, M.: Wi-City: a federated architecture of metropolitan databases to support mobile users in real time. In: International Conference on Computer and Information Science, ICCIS, A Conference of World Engineering, Science and Technology Congress, ESTCON (2012)
10. Nebot, V., Berlanga, R.: Building data warehouses with semantic data. Decis. Support Syst. 52(4) (2012). http://sparql-wrapper.sourceforge.net/
11. Costanzo, A., Faro, A., Giordano, D.: WI-CITY: living, deciding and planning using mobiles in Intelligent Cities. In: 3rd International Conference on Pervasive and Embedded Computing and Communication Systems, PECCS, Barcelona, INSTICC (2013)
12. Faro, A., Giordano, D., Spampinato, C.: Integrating location tracking, traffic monitoring and semantics in a layered ITS architecture. Intell. Transport Syst. IET 5(3), 197–206 (2011)
13. Della Valle E., Qasim, H.M., Celino, I.: Towards treating GIS as virtual RDF graphs. In: Proceedings of the 1st International Workshop on Pervasive Web Mapping, Geo-processing and Services, WebMGS (2010)
14. Boškovic, D., Ristic, A., Govedarica, M., Przulj, D.: Ontology development for land administration. In: IEEE 8th International Symposium on Intelligent Systems and Informatics, SISY, (2010)
15. Hay, G.C, Hall, G.B.: A semantic web approach to application configuration in the land administration domain. FIG Congress 2010 Facing the Challenges - Building the Capacity Sydney, (2010)
16. Auer, S., Lehmann, J., Hellmann, S.: LinkedGeoData: adding a spatial dimension to the web of data. In: Bernstein, A., Karger, D.R., Heath, T., Feigenbaum, L., Maynard, D., Motta, E., Thirunarayan, K. (eds.) ISWC 2009. LNCS, vol. 5823, pp. 731–746. Springer, Heidelberg (2009)

Blueprint of a Semantic Business Process-Aware Enterprise Information Architecture: The EIAOnt Ontology

Mahmood Ahmad[(✉)] and Mohammed Odeh

Software Engineering Research Group, Faculty of Environment and Technology,
University of the West of England, Coldharbour Lane, Bristol BS16 1QY, UK
Mahmood2.Ahmad@live.uwe.ac.uk, Mohammed.Odeh@uwe.ac.uk

Abstract. A robust design of enterprise information resources and their optimal usage can significantly enhance the information management (IM) capability of an enterprise. Enterprise Information Architecture (EIA) is a critical success factor for this objective and needs to be business process-aware in order to add value to the firm's IM capability and to obtain dynamic views of information through extended knowledge of business processes. We present the generic Enterprise Information Architecture Ontology (EIAOnt) that lays the foundation for the EIA design activity to use additional business information by incorporating the business process knowledge. We also present an approach that semantically derives EIA from Enterprise business process architecture (BPA) using Riva BPA methodology. A semantic representation of EIA through EIAOnt Ontology suggests a step forward to bridge the gap between business process architecture and enterprise information architecture.

Keywords: Enterprise information architecture · Semantic information architecture · Semantic information integration

1   Introduction

1.1   Enterprise Information Architecture (EIA)

The design of Information architecture (IA) is an established activity that has been recognised to have a central importance for information system development community since 1980s. Brancheau and Wetherbe defined in [1] that information architecture '... *is a high level map of the information requirements of an organisation. It is a personnel-, organisation- and technology-independent profile of major information categories used within the enterprise.*' Among more recent definitions, Godinez et al. [2] define Information Architecture as '*[The description of] principles and guidelines that enable consistent implementation of information technology solutions, how data and information are both governed*

© Springer International Publishing Switzerland 2014
S. Hammoudi et al. (Eds.): ICEIS 2013, LNBIP 190, pp. 520–539, 2014.
DOI: 10.1007/978-3-319-09492-2_31

and shared across the enterprise, and what needs to be done to gain business-relevant trusted information insight.' (p. 28). The Enterprise Information Architecture (EIA), is *'the framework that defines the information-centric principles, architecture models, standards, and processes that form the basis for making information technology decisions across the enterprise'.* [2].

Enterprise Information Architecture is an integral part of Enterprise Architecture of modern enterprise. Enterprise Architecture is regarded as *'... a comprehensive description of all of the key elements and relationships that make up an organisation.'* [3]. Enterprise architecture (EA) attempts to provide structure to the whole organisation where information is found from strategic level to business to information resources, hence a structured EA approach (for example, see Fig. 1) is essential to architect enterprise-wide information for a successful information system (IS) and a sound technology infrastructure. Enterprise information resources are structured in EIA that is in close proximity with business architecture (including business process architecture) and business strategy (Fig. 1). EIA is relevant to EA so much so that some EIA researchers have found it easy to design the whole enterprise architecture (EA), such as [4].

1.2   Components of EIA

The Enterprise Information Architecture (EIA) has following components [2,5]:

– Information Entities, attributes and relationships
– Enterprise Data Models, Entity-Relationship diagrams

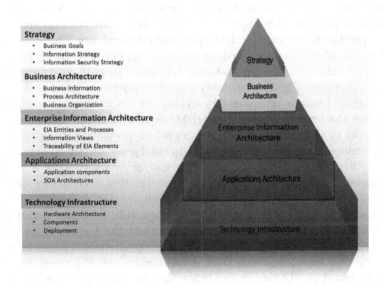

Fig. 1. Enterprise architecture. Note that the EIA elements contain entities as well as processes in this slightly modified view.

- Models of Information value chain, such as Information flow diagrams
- Information views for stakeholders
- Traceability of EIA Components
- Business domain knowledge (Ontologies, taxonomies and metadata etc.)

Critical issues relating to the design of EIA include requirements for information quality, storage and retrieval, searchability, findability and accessibility, information security [6]. While these issues are related to EIA from within Information Management domain (Fig. 1), the knowledge of these issues has a positive impact on the design of EIA components itself and provides credibility to the EIA design process.

1.3   Motivation for this Research

Classically, the EIA design activity consisted of building a map of a firm's information resources and business functions based on time-consuming managerial interviews. The subsequent time requirements led to an increasing lack of interest from the strategic management in this vital design effort. However, a consistent emphasis on the vitality of IA (Information Architecture) design in relation to a firm's business processes and information resources has remained the case [7–10] in the business information management research community. Recent research has identified that the information management capability of an enterprise has a significant contribution towards development of its capabilities in customer management, process management and performance management, [11,12]. The Information Management (IM) Capability may be defined as the ability to provide data and information within the desired accuracy and time scale for a given enterprise business process. This implies that the design of information architecture (IA) is of pivotal importance for developing the IM capability. The enhancement implied by this ability develops customer management (CM) capability that generates opportunities to develop customer relationships both as consumers and innovation partners. The IM capability can also contribute towards developing and redesigning business processes for carrying out the activities of an enterprise, reflecting on the Process Management (PM) capability of the enterprise, [11].

A number of factors motivate this work which provides ontological foundation of a business process-oriented EIA of an enterprise. Firstly, in organisations that deal with information as a commodity and/or as a service, it is suggested that organizations that use their business information successfully can be as much as 27 % more effective. This requires a fresh look into information strategy with a goal to achieve optimal information usage [13]. Secondly, a vast majority of contemporary IA design practice has lacked the knowledge of business process information due to: (a) the lack of appropriate technologies to capture business process knowledge, and (b) the continuing lack of interest from management to invest in EIA design and hence the absence of a comprehensive EIA design that can support not only any business process reengineering (redesign) effort but this EIA could also support the design of new business processes. Thirdly, recent research in two independent areas has provided impetus for this research. One is in the areas of Business process architecture (BPA) methodologies and business process modeling technologies such as Business Process Modeling Notation (BPMN), [14], which has facilitated the structured definition and representation of business processes. The other is the advancement of research in knowledge representation (KR) mechanisms and the advancement of Semantic Web (SW) technologies [15,16]. The use Ontologies (Sect. 2.1) as KR mechanisms in Enterprise Information Systems (EIS) can be instrumental in representation of information resources and other areas related to information management. And finally, classical IA design approaches identified information categories and processes with the help of long manager interviews. This resulted in lack of management interest in IA design approaches [1,8,9,17,18] and comprehensive methodologies like Information Engineering (IE) [7] and its derived forms like IBM's Business Systems Planning (BSP) and Strategic Data Planning (SDP), [19].

This paper presents a blueprint of such an approach that bridges this gap between business architecture and enterprise information architecture using semantic technologies. Section 2 discusses the related work in classical and contemporary attempts to BPA-oriented EIA. Section 3 details the concepts and relationships of the EIAOnt ontology for the EIA elements and discusses rationale behind chosing these concepts. Section 4 discusses the proposed approach that semantically derives EIA entities and processes of the enterprise from BPA ontological artefacts. Section 5 demonstrates the current work through a case-study in cancer-care domain while identifying some adjustments for the parent framework that conceptualises the BPA methodology. Section 6 discusses issues in this approach that we currently face with some possible remedies, and Section 7 concludes this paper with directions for further work.

2   Related Work

2.1   Non-semantic Approaches to IA Design

Non-Semantic approaches to IA design include enterprise data model approach by [18], long-range information architecture and ends/means analysis approaches [17], critical success factors approach [20], Information Engineering (IE) based approaches [7] such as IBM's Business System Planning (BSP) and strategic data modeling (SDM). These approaches relied upon long time-consuming interviews which heavily contributed to a lack of interest in IA design activity by the strategic enterprise managers. Among these approaches, the enterprise data model approach and the IE-based approaches were business process-centric; however, the IE-based approaches lacked appeal due to the absence of technological advances of today [8,9], which could reduce the astronomical time requirements for EIA design.

More recently, the EIA is seen as a part of the overall enterprise architecture (EA) of an enterprise and is also mentioned as data architecture. Examples of these approaches include Zachman's Information Systems Architecture (ISA)

[21,22], the Architecture Development Model (ADM) by TOGAF [23], the four-layer Process-Driven Architecture (PDA) model [24] and the CiESAR model [25].

The TOGAF's data architecture is based on business entities (list of things important to the business), Entity-Relationship Diagrams, logical data model and data flow diagrams, which constitute four out of 30 cells within Zachman's ISA [21] as identified in Figure. With the advent of knowledge-based techniques such as conceptual modelling and meta-data techniques like ontologies, data transforms into Enterprise Information Architecture (EIA) using information vocabularies such that the information model describes the information item (or information entity as we name it) that represents a data item (or entity). However, the EIA is still not completely informed by the business process architecture as it lacks a complete knowledge of business elements such as that of business processes and the knowledge of interdependence within these elements. In a critical investigation, TOGAF has also been found to have failed to provide a sound and appropriate basis for its designs for enterprise engineering [26].

2.2 Ontologies and Ontology Engineering Methodologies

Ontology is 'a formal explicit specification of a shared conceptualization', [27]. It is a knowledge representation (KR) mechanism that represents knowledge of a domain that is consensual (shared and agreed between stakeholders) and machine-understandable (has a formal basis), [28]. It is different from a knowledge-base (KB) in that a knowledge-base provides some concrete knowledge of the domain whereas ontology presents the vocabulary of the domain and the concepts and their inter-relationships. The Web Ontology Language OWL [29] is the current standard for development of Ontologies, and has three sub-categories, OWL Lite, (for designers of classification and simple constraints) OWL-DL (for maximum expressiveness using description logics) and OWL Full (for maximum expressiveness and syntactic freedom of the Resource Description Framework language RDF).

Some of state-of-the-art methodologies in Ontology Engineering are METHONOTOLOGY [30], CYC Method [31], DILIGENT (Pinto, Tempich et al. 2010), TOVE [32], FOIS [33], Ontology Development 101 [34], Ontology based on Lexicon [35] and BORO [36] among others.

2.3 Semantic EIA Design Methodologies

Semantic approaches to EIA design include the use of Resource-Event-Action (REA) Ontology in TOGAF [23], however, its EIA is based only business data and not on a thorough business information analysis. Genre and Ontologies Based Information Architecture Framework (GOBIAF, [37]) is based on information need interviews and this approach is also not based on knowledge of business entities and processes. The Field-Actions approach by [38] uses field actions for incorporating business process information and uses HL7 ontology but it lacks derivation of fully derived information model of an organization.

The Design and Engineering Methodology for Organizations (DEMO) Methodology (Dietz 2006) was developed to bridge the gap between business processes and information systems using Language/Action (or L/A) Perspective, which 'assumes that communication is a kind of action in that it creates commitments between the communicating parties', (Dietz 1999). The DEMO methodology is rooted in χ-theory and provides an integration of three aspects of organisations, namely: B-organisation (business), I-organization (information) and D-organization (document). However, this methodology also limits itself to translate information entities, attributes and relationships from χ-theory to Enterprise Information Architecture (Gomes 2011).

The Toronto Virtual Enterprise (TOVE) Ontology project has developed a set of integrated ontologies for the modelling of both commercial and public enterprises [32]. The Ontologies suite of TOVE is divided into three groups: Core, Derivative and Enterprise Ontologies. These Ontologies are designed in Knowledge Interchange Format (KIF) and use Resource Ontology as the core level and use Information Resource Ontology as the derivative ontology [39]. These ontologies have been designed in line with requirements of product manufacturing organizations and cannot be converted into OWL-DL format because the KIF uses First-Order logic (FOL) as compared to Description Logics (DL) in OWL-Description Logics which uses only a part of FOL.

3   The Enterprise Information Architecture (EIAOnt) Ontology

We present an Ontology, namely the EIAOnt Ontology, for Enterprise Information Architecture (EIA) on the theoretical basis set by [40] using Bunge-Wand-Weber (BWW) Ontology. The artefacts of the EIAOnt Ontology consist of concepts that represent information entities (IEs), information- and EIA-related processes, their sub-concepts and the relationships that exist within and between these concepts.

3.1   Need and Scope

In order to deal with the issues of semantic heterogeneity of information that originates from diverse resources, ontologies can provide a structured approach to represent knowledge of basic concepts that are common across a variety of domains [41]. These ontologies are extensible and for particular domains, these act as metadata vocabularies. The EIAOnt ontology is considered as a generic ontology for EIA design within the Enterprise Architecture domain and is designed to construct a sharable knowledge of EIA design terms and concepts within the enterprise, hence it forms a much needed component within the Enterprise Architecture to ensure a business process-aware EIA.

The scope of the EIAOnt Ontology is defined by its use within various Enterprise Architecture domains. As EIA is only one of the four architectures within the EA domain, the EIAOnt Ontology is limited in its scope to conceptualise

EIA elements. On one hand, this Ontology is based on the knowledge of vital place of Information within the enterprise and hence it is aware of EIA's role within Information Management department as well as Business Strategy enterprise. On the other hand, the EIAOnt is generic and can provide easy interface with domains of business process knowledge, knowledge of business strategy and goals, knowledge of Information Management requirement such as data quality, availability and information security to construct a semantic structure for Enterprise with sound theoretical base. We have used the methodology by [34] to development EIAOnt ontology for a generic Enterprise Information Architecture identifying concepts and relationships for a business process-oriented EIA.

3.2   Conceptualisation of EIA Entities

In order to establish a clear understanding of what qualifies to become an EIA entity (hereinafter called an 'information entity'), we delve into philosophies that define entities and classify them.

Entities in Bunge-Wand-Weber Ontology. Bunge, in his philosophical study of the world systems, Mario Bunge [42, 43] presented ontological foundation of real world systems that was adopted by [44] to present a formal model of objects (things that physically exist in the real world). According to Bunge's philosophy [42], the world is made up of two kinds of things, namely concrete things - also called entities or substantial individuals - and conceptual things, which do not have a physical existence. Because Bunge's model of objects deals only with real world systems, it presents the ontological representation for only concrete things (or substantial individuals) and not for conceptual things. According to the representation mapping rules defined by [45], this implies that every BWW-Thing or entity can be modelled as an object in an object-oriented modelling language like UML. However, in software design, not every object is substantial, or in other words, not every information system object physically exists nor it is always a BWW-Thing. This view is also shared by [27] that "For AI systems, what 'exists' is that which can be represented" [46].

Critics of Bunge's ontology and Weber's model of objects, such as [47], have the view that BWW model provides an inappropriate foundation for conceptual model of business information systems. However, in their ontological model of information systems, Wand and Weber [40] have argued that 'all objects are things, but only some types of things are objects', which establishes (with examples) that conceptual entities can also be modeled using the BWW ontology. In their discussion, they have referred to BWW-Thing as their 'object' and by 'things' they mean concrete as well as conceptual things, and have selected INVENTORY ITEM, CUSTOMER ORDER, CUSTOMER ACCOUNT, CUSTOMER REPAYMENT and INVENTORY REPLENISHMENT as illustrative examples of 'things' from a Customer Order and Payment System whereby none can be regarded as a BWW-Thing as none has a physical existence. Therefore, this ontological model can facilitate the analysis of things and other artifacts of a business information system.

Entities in Top-Level Classification by John F. Sowa. John F. Sowa [48] represented the top-level classification of things by an Ontology lattice. This Ontology lattice classifies entities with primitive categorisation of Independent, Relative, Physical, Mediating, Abstract, Continuant (entities that endure in time) and Occurrent (that never fully exist at any instant; instead they unfold with time; for example processes or events). Objects or physical entities (BWW-Things) are represented as independent physical continuants (IPCs). Although this classification elaborates abstract sub-categories such as situation, structure, reason and purpose (or goals), yet it lacks classification of conceptual entities like PAYMENT, which belongs to none of these abstract sub-categories. The entity PAYMENT is, in Sowa's ontological lattice terms, a conceptual (or Abstract) continuant and does not belong to any of the above sub-categories. For enterprise information modeling purposes, this ontology needs to add the notion of Abstract Continuant (AC) for conceptual entities.

Abstract Derived Entities (ADEs). The concept of Abstract Derived Entities (ADEs) within the data abstraction model is different from derived data types (sometimes referred to as derived entities) in the object-oriented design and programming paradigm. Instead, an ADE refers to 'a data object present in an abstract data model that may be referenced by other entities in the abstract data model as though it were a relational table present in a physical data source.', [49]. An example of an ADE is AGE which is an ADE corresponding to the DATE_OF_BIRTH conceptual entity. The ADEs are conceptual entities that are derived from the primitive (or non-derived) conceptual or concrete entities.

3.3   Conclusion - What are Entities in EIAOnt Ontology?

The BWW model in [40] facilitates the formal base for both concrete and conceptual entities which exist side by side in enterprise information models. In order to suggest the derivation of EIA information entities from business process architecture, we firstly propose that all business entities should be conceptualized using the InformationEntity concept. Conceptual and concrete things are modeled in EIAOnt Ontology as ConceptualEntity and ConcreteEntity sub-categories respectively (Fig. 2). As an ADE is always a conceptual entity, the AbstractDerivedEntity, as subconcept of the ConceptualEntity concept conceptualizes ADEs in the EIAOnt ontology with the help of boolean properties isConcreteEntity and isADE set to suitable values.

3.4   Categorization of EIA Processes

Processes in the EIAOnt ontology represent EIA processes, generally described by the EIAProcess concept. This concept is sub-categorised into six sub-concepts: IEProcess, IECRUDProcess, IEMP and IESP, depicted in Fig. 3. The IECRUDProcess concept is further sub-categorised into IECreateProcess,

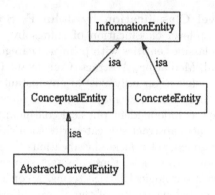

Fig. 2. Concept hierarchy for the `InformationEntity` concept in the EIAOnt ontology.

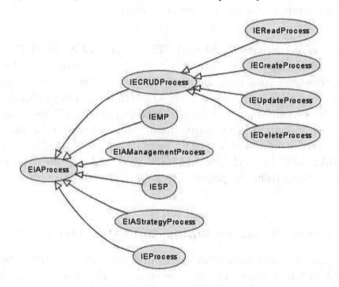

Fig. 3. Process concept and sub-concepts in the EIAOnt ontology.

IEReadProcess, IEUpdateProcess and IEDeleteProcess sub-concepts, individuals
of which represent respectively the Create, Read, Update and Delete processes for
an `InformationEntity` individual. Figure 3 elaborates how `InformationEntity`
concept is linked to EIA processes.

Once the enterprise information system has the knowledge of business entities
and business processes, corresponding to every `InformationEntity` individual
which was originally a business entity, there can be assigned one individual
of each of the three process subConcepts of the `EIAProcess` concept, namely
`IEProcess`, `IEMP` and `IESP` concepts. The `IEMP` process is used to manage the
corresponding `InformationEntity` instance such that it supervises the comple-
tion of `IEProcess` instances of the corresponding `InformationEntity` instance.

The IESP process concept is used to maintain a strategic view of both IEProcess and IEMP instances that correspond to a particular InformationEntity instance. This strategic view can be in the form of producing entity analytics to assess the use of IEs in information system of the enterprise. When an InformationEntity directly corresponds to a business entity, its corresponding IESP instance can contribute to compilation of business analytics if and when required. Some of the individuals of each of the IEProcess, IEMP and IESP concepts corresponding to this particular InformationEntity individual may be directly derived from their relevant counterparts in the business process architecture. The instances of these EIA process concepts can trace back to the corresponding InformationEntity instances in instantiated EIAOnt ontology with the help of properties that are defined in the complete meta-model of entities and processes. The EIAOnt ontology also provides conceptualisation of separate processual links with the enterprise management and enterprise strategy through EIAManagementProcess and EIAStrategyProcess concepts.

3.5   Traceability of EIA Concepts

The TraceabilityMatrix concept of EIAOnt ontology is used to establish traceability among EIA elements. Traceability determines whether and to what extent EIA information elements such as entities and processes can be traced back within information value chain of the enterprise. Traceability can provide information for:

- InformationEntity individual that was originally a business entity
- Business entities correspond to a InformationEntity individual
- InformationEntity individuals corresponding to a particular business entity
- IEProcess individuals corresponding to an InformationEntity individual
- IECRUDProcess individuals corresponding to an InformationEntity individual
- IEMP individuals corresponding to a given InformationEntity individual
- IESP individuals corresponding to a given InformationEntity individual
- IEMP individuals corresponding to a EIAManagementProcess individual
- IESP individuals corresponding to a given EIAStrategyProcess individual

This information is collected by individuals of TraceabilityMatrix concept which represent various traceability matrices, e.g. traceability matrix for business entity vs InformationEntity individuals and traceability matrix for InformationEntity vs IEProcess individuals etc.

3.6   Information Views

The Enterprise Information Architecture is expected to contain both static and dynamic views for information. Static views include structures of information elements such as logical data models, data standards, metadata and taxonomies. Dynamic views include a business process model, an information work flow model and a data flow model that describes the transitions and states of information during its lifecycle [50]. In EIAOnt Ontology, information views are conceptualised as the EIADiagram concept. The instances of this concept may be diagrams that are useful in depicting data and information flow from one location in the information system (or enterprise) to the other. Traditionally, data flow diagrams (DFDs) and entity-relationship (ER) diagrams, originate from system analysis (SA) activity when designing the enterprise information models. UML Diagrams also provide both high and low-level diagrams for information modelling. Information Flow Diagrams (IFDs) provide high level view of information flow from one point to the other.

Business process models (BPMs) provide representation of business processes and their associations that an enterprise performs. BPMs belong to Business Process Architecture (BPA) of the enterprise. However, these should be accessible to EIA architects, particularly for a business process-aware EIA design suggested in this research.

4   Semantic Derivation of Enterprise IA from Business Process Architecture

4.1   Business Process Architecture and the BAOnt Ontology

The approach presented in this paper derives the EIA elements from the fundamental elements of business process architecture of an enterprise modelled using the Riva BPA methodology [51]. The Riva methodology concentrates on the business of the enterprise and collects essential business entities (EBEs) without which the enterprise will cease to perform its function. It extracts from these business entities a set of units of work (UoWs), each of which leads to a business process at the operational (case processes - CPs), managerial (case management processes - CMPs) and strategic (case strategy processes - CSPs) levels respectively. Their names indicate the very nature of the tasks they carry out for a particular EBE of UoW. The CMP and CSP, however, can be used by business managers and/or CIOs to induce changes in BPA for the corresponding entities corresponding to any new decisions made at the enterprise level. This needs to be carried out using enterprise information systems which rely on the EIA, hence highlighting the need for the EIA elements to be directly derivable from the BPA.

The BPAOnt ontology [52] in their BPAOntoSOA Framework capture this ontological representation of BPA as semantically enriched BPA. The BPAOnt ontology was developed in OWL [29] and contains all the above concepts and relationships among these concepts, which makes a good starting point for the design of the EIA. The BPAOntoSOA Framework starts with crude BP models of an enterprise modelled using Role-Activity Diagrams (RADs) or more recent BP modelling languages like BPMN [53]. The business information that causes the development of BPA of an enterprise can originate from some other sources such as business documents etc, but this does not affect the EIA derivation process.

4.2   EIA Semantic Derivation from BPA

As the effort of developing the semantically enriched BPA is a one-off activity for an enterprise corresponding to the developed business process architecture, and needs only minor adjustment corresponding to business change, an Enterprise Information Architecture that holds direct additional knowledge of business processes helps improving the automation of the EIA design process. Thus, it reduces the time requirements for interviews and questionnaires in the sense that the knowledge of business entities and processes is already captured through a semantically enriched BPA. However, this time-saving is more relaizable once the process of semantically enriched BPA development is automated by either accessing machine-readable business process models and workflows or by using natural language processing techniques to analyse business documents and extract business process architectural elements. The EIAOnt ontology has been designed in OWL [29] using the approach by [34] and is based on IA concepts by [5,50] and [4,18], and forms a major component of semantic EIA derivation approach presented in this work. Fundamental EIA elements are EIA entities and EIA processes which are conceptualised as `InformationEntity` and `EIAProcess` concepts respectively in the EIAOnt Ontology. The EIA derivation methodology (shown in Fig. 4) consists of a three-step approach for EIA derivation:

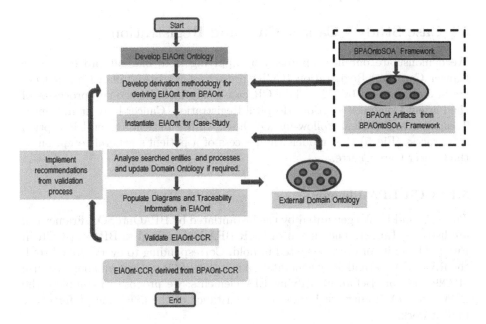

Fig. 4. Proposed approach for semantic derivation of EIA from BPA using the EIAOnt ontology.

1. The first step of this approach derives initial set of EIA entities and processes from the EBE and process instances of the BPAOnt ontology by instantiating the BPAOntoSOA Framework for a particular enterprise. The semantic derivation of the EIA entities includes which EBEs qualify to become EIA entities and classifies each of them into concrete and conceptual entities. The semantic derivation also includes derivation of EIA processes from process concepts of BPA, and also captures the associated relationships among process instances, which are taxonomic (whole-part) and/or non-taxonomic.
2. The second step of this derivation uses the instances of the EIA information entity and process concepts of the EIAOnt ontology to search for related concepts in external domain ontologies. This also includes identifying the taxonomic and non-taxonomic relationships among new and existing case-study entities and processes. The search for related entities and processes may also result in formation of new external domain ontologies or updating enriching external ontologies through a structured process of searching and cataloguing EIA information entities and processes.
3. Finally, more complex EIA elements such as EIA traceability matrices, EIA diagrams (such as Information flow diagrams and/or Entity-Relationship diagrams) and EIA information views are to be derived. As the name suggests, the EIA traceability matrices provide traceability information for information entities (IEs) corresponding to EBEs in BPA, IEs vs EIA Processes.

5   Case Study - Cancer Care and Registration

We demonstrate our new approach by applying it to one sub-process of the Cancer Care and Registration (CCR) process of King Abdullah Cancer Centre in Jordan, used by [52]. The CCR case-study includes the sub-processes of the Patient General Reception, Hospital Registration, Cancer Detection, Cancer Treatment and Patient Follow-up. Of these, we use Patient General Reception sub-process (Fig. 5) that models the process of a patient's general reception at the Cancer Care Centre.

5.1   CCR BPA Elements

The EBEs and UoWs generated by the instantiated by BPAOntoSOA Framework are listed in Table 1. The output of CCR BPA is described as BPAOnt-CCR in Fig. 4. The units of work are listed in bold. Corresponding to every UoW listed, the Riva BPA methodology generates an instance of CP concept and one instance of CMP concept. Before identifying EIA elements, we propose to complete the BPAOntoSOA framework by adding an instance of the CSP concept for every unit of work.

5.2   CCR EIA Elements

The BPA elements generated by BPA (Table 1) form the basis for the EIA entities and processes in this derivation approach. Use of SWRL rules [54] can

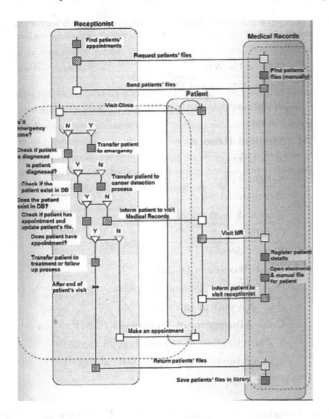

Fig. 5. Patient general reception sub-process in CCR case-study.

identify which EBEs qualify to become EIA entities. The EBEs, which are semantically derived as EIA entities, are classified as concrete or conceptual entities. This basic classification is useful because it can facilitate the decision-making processes within business information system, e.g. supply chain and delivery of a printed book or an electronic book (ebook) version and decide upon cost of delivery accordingly. In the CCR context, EMERGENCY UNIT is a physical entity and has a location, whereas DATABASE is a conceptual entity.

The EIA derivation function generates the CRUD (Create, Read, Update and Delete) processes for every EIA entity and are sub-concepts of EIAProcess concept in EIAOnt Ontology. The CPs and CMPs also form an initial set of EIA (non-CRUD) processes. Once relationships between these concepts are established and traceability among these elements is determined, the EIA design function then moves on to search in external domain and process ontologies, using automated ontology search processes to look for related entities and processes. This is possible only when domain specific knowledge for a particular business exists, e.g. cancer care domain knowledge for CCR case-study. Otherwise, the EIA design process can then develop new domain specific knowledge as its by-product. This search may result in significant increase in the number of EIA entities and

Table 1. BPA elements for the patient general reception sub-process in the CCR case-study.

EBEs or UoWs
Patient General Reception
Receptionist (General)
Patient
Medical Records
Appointment
Patient File
Emergency Unit
Cancer detection unit
Database
Patient details
Case Processes (CPs)
Handle Patient general reception
Handle a patient medical record
Case Management Processes (CMPs)
Manage the flow of patient general reception
Manage the flow of patient medical record

processes. The traceability for these newly found EIA elements should establish many-to-many relationships between EIA entities and the initial set of EIA entities which were originally EBEs in BPA. Many-to-many relationships also exist between EIA processes and the EIA entities they access, use and/or modify. Table 2 lists the set of EIA entities and processes in the case-study sub-process after searching for related entity and process concepts in the NCI Thesaurus [55] and the Medical Ontology by Advance Genome Clinical Trials (ACGT) project [56]. The IEMP processes are the processes for CMPs in the BPA that manage CPs, and the IESP processes correspond to CSPs. We have noted that entities in these ontologies are not classified into concrete and conceptual entities and we therefore recommend constructing a new ontology using this classification for EIA entities. The complete EIA for CCR is referred to an EIAOnt-CCR in Fig. 4.

6 Discussion

A number of issues can be significant for a complete and correct derivation of an EIA. Firstly, we note that this approach significantly depends upon the correctness and completeness of the Riva BPA elements identified by instantiating [52]'s BPAontoSOA framework. The starting point of the BPAOntoSOA framework is, however, the business process models of the case-study enterprise

Table 2. Count of EIA elements derived from BPA for patient general reception sub-process in CCR case-study after look-up in ACGT medical ontology for entities.

EIA Element	Count
EIA Entities	**10**
Entities derived from BPA	8
Entities searched from domain ontologies	2
Concrete entities	5
Conceptual entities	5
EIA Processes	**41**
EIA Processes	3
CRUD Processes	32
IE Management Processes - IEMPs	3
IE Strategy Processes - IESP	3
EIA Traceability Matrices	4

that were originally developed through on-site interviews in a previous research [57]. We suggest that the input for BPA development needs to be business documents and business use cases and not necessarily BP models. This, however, should not affect the correctness and validity of EIA as the needed BPA elements are instances of the BPAOnt concepts, and hence it will generate an EIA corresponding to these BPA elements.

Secondly, although this approach causes EIA design to be heavily dependent upon the business process architecture, yet this becomes a strength and not a weakness of the approach because our proposed EIA is more business process-aware and it is more responsive to business process change if it includes a change management mechanism that tracks any changes in BPA and makes corresponding adjustments to EIA architectural elements. Changes in BPA translate into changes in Riva BPA business entities, processes or relations between its units of work. The change management mechanism of the EIA should capture these changes and initiate EIA 'change processes' to assess the impact of these changes and implement them. Thus, future information requirements, that are not yet expressed in process models will need to emerge from a review of BPA models (driven by strategic management), followed by change in EIA. This limitation or dependence should be seen as an opportunity to review business process architecture. Future information requirements that do not need change in process models may be met through change management processes acting independently of BPA.

Thirdly, the EIA derivation process needs to identify whole-part relationships among the EIA entities derived from BPA and also for the entities searched from external domain ontologies. We may call this refactoring of EIA entities. For instance, there are 10 RECEPTIONIST EBE instances in the BPA. This leads the information architect to define one RECEPTIONIST instance with a variable place of deployment. Furthermore, the RECEPTIONIST entity may be a sub-entity of a PERSON entity of which PATIENT is another sub-entity. The whole-part relationship may be added to the information about EIA entities using OWL properties and SWRL rules (SWRL 2004).

Fourthly, in order to ensure the correctness of EIA derivation approach, human input from information architect (IA) may be essential at certain stages of EIA derivation. For example, the IA's input may be required when refactoring of EIA entities and processes is carried out. This may be carried out through special-purpose dialogue boxes, which may render the above derivation process semi-automated rather than being fully automated, hence further work for further evolution of the current work.

Finally, limitations of such an approach to derive EIA from BPA emerge from those of BPA methodology. This approach is critically dependent upon the Riva methodology as the underlying BPA methodology. This is because the Riva BPA methodology is systematic and focuses on business entities and process in a way that brainstorms all entities and units of work that lead to processes, thus identifying the business components along its natural fault-lines and hence providing a comprehensive (initial) set of EIA entities and processes.

7   Conclusion and Future Work

We have presented a new generic approach for semantically deriving the Enterprise Information Architecture of an enterprise from its Business Process Architecture. We have also demonstrated results of this derivation using a real and validated case study based on Cancer Care and Registration in Jordan, namely the CCR case-study. Moreover, we have identified some shortcomings in the current BPAOntoSOA framework algorithm with respect to the extraction of EBEs from business processes and hence the reflection on the inclusion of case strategy process (CSP) in the BPAOnt ontology for a given BPA case. Currently, this approach is limited to the derivation of the fundamental EIA elements such as EIA entities and processes, and the traceability matrices that ensure forward/backward traceability from/to these elements. This approach is to be extended to generate more advanced EIA elements such as information views and information flow diagrams while exploiting the dynamic relations within the BPA's units of work and the traceability of EIA entities and EIA processes that access these entities. Further research includes the generalisation of this approach to a validated Semantic Framework, with maximum automaticity, for deriving the design of an enterprise information architecture from the given business process architecture of that enterprise.

References

1. Brancheau, J.C., Wetherbe, J.C.: Information architectures: methods and practice. Inform. Process. Manag. **22**(6), 453–463 (1986)
2. Godinez, M., Hechler, E., Koenig, K., Lockwood, S., Oberhofer, M., Schroeck, M.: The Art of Enterprise Information Architecture: A Systems-Based Approach for Unlocking Business Insight. IBM Press, Boston (2010)
3. Hermon, P.: Developing an Enterprise Architecture. White Paper, Business Process Trends (2003)
4. Evernden, R., Evernden, E.: Information First: Integrating Knowledge and Information Architecture for Business Advantage. Elsevier Butterworth Heinemann, Oxford (2003)
5. Mosley, M.: Challenging EIM issues ahead. www.eiminstitute.com/library/eimi-archives, April 2010
6. Martin, A., Dmitriev, D., Akeroyd, J.: A resurgence of interest in information architecture. Int. J. Inf. Manag. **30**(1), 6–12 (2010)
7. Martin, J.: Information Engineering - Book I: Introduction. Prentice-Hall, Englewood Cliffs (1989)
8. Teng, J.T.C., Kettinger, W.J.: Business process redesign and information architecture: exploring relationships. DATABASE Adv. **26**(1), 30–42 (1995)
9. Kettinger, W.J., Teng, J.T.C., Guha, S.: Information architectural design in business process reengineering. Int. J. Inf. Technol. **11**, 27–37 (1996)
10. Chaffey, D., White, G.: Business Information Management, 2nd edn. Pearson Education Limited, Harlow (2011)
11. Mithas, S., Ramasubbu, N., Sambamurthy, V.: How information management capability influences firm performance. MIS Q. **35**(1), 237–256 (2011)
12. Sauer, C., Willcocks, L.: Establishing the business of the future: the role of organisational architecture and informational technologies. Eur. Manag. J. **21**(4), 497–508 (2003)
13. Capegemini: How to make your business information count: generate a performance improvement of 27 percent by becoming an intelligent enterprise. http://www.uk.capgemini.com/sites/default/files/resource/pdf/-How_to_Make_Your_Business_Information_Count.pdf (2010). Accessed 14 April 2013
14. OMG: Business process model and notation. http://www.bpmn.org/ (2012). Accessed 27 Sept 2013
15. Berners-Lee, T., Hendler, J., Lassila, O.: The semantic web. Sci. Am. **284**(5), 28–34 (2001)
16. Hendler, J.: Agents and the semantic web. IEEE Intell. Syst. **16**(2), 30–37 (2001)
17. Wetherbe, J.C., Davis, G.B.: Developing a long-range information architecture. In: Proceedings of National Computer Conference, Anaheim, Calefornia, pp. 261–269. ACM, New York, 16–19 May 1983
18. Brancheau, J.C., Schuster, L., March, S.T.: Building and implementing an information architecture. SIGMIS Database **20**(2), 9–17 (1989)
19. Goodhue, D.L., Kirsch, L.J., Quillard, J.A., Wybo, M.D.: Strategic data planning: lessons from the field. MIS Q. **16**(1), 11–34 (1992)
20. Rockart, J.F.: Chief executives define their own data needs. Harvard Bus. Rev. **57**(2), 81–89 (1979)
21. Zachman, J.A.: A framework for information systems architecture. IBM Syst. J. **26**(3), 276–292 (1987)

22. Sowa, J.F., Zachman, J.A.: Extending and formalizing the framework for information systems architecture. IBM Syst. J. **31**(4), 590–616 (1992)
23. TOGAF: Phase C. information systems architecture - data architecture. http://pubs.opengroup.org/architecture/togaf8-doc/arch/ (2012). Accessed 1 Feb 2012 at 17:47 Hrs
24. Strnadl, C.F.: Aligning business and IT: the process-driven architecture model. Inf. Syst. Manag. **23**(4), 67–77 (2006)
25. CEiSAR: Enterprise modelling. White Paper. http://www.ceisar.com/ (2008). Accessed 6 July 2011
26. Dietz, J.L.G., Hoogervorst, J.A.P.: A critical investigation of TOGAF - based on the enterprise engineering theory and practice. In: Albani, A., Dietz, J.L.G., Verelst, J. (eds.) EEWC 2011. LNBIP, vol. 79, pp. 76–90. Springer, Heidelberg (2011)
27. Gruber, T.R.: A translation approach to portable ontology specifications. Knowl. Acquis. **5**(2), 199–220 (1993)
28. Gasevic, D., Djuric, D., Devedzic, V.: Model Driven Architecture and Ontology Development. Springer, Heidelberg (2006)
29. Smith, M.K., Welty, C., McGuinness, D.L. (eds.): OWL web ontology language guide. http://www.w3.org/TR/owl-guide/ (2004). Accessed 29 Sept 2009
30. Fernandez-Lopez, M., Gomez-Perez, A., Juristo, N.: Methontology: from ontological art towards ontological engineering. In: Proceedings of AAAI Spring Symposium, Menlo Park, California, pp. 33–40. AAAI Press (1997)
31. Lenat, D.B.: CYC: a large-scale investment in knowledge infrastructure. Commun. ACM **38**(11), 33–38 (1995)
32. Fox, M.S., Barbeceanu, M., Gruninger, M.: An organisation ontology for enterprise modelling: preliminary concepts for linking structure and behaviour. Comput. Ind. **29**, 123–134 (1995)
33. Guarino, N.: Formal ontology, conceptual analysis and knowledge representation. Int. J. Hum.-Comput. Stud. **43**(5/6), 625–640 (1995)
34. Noy, N., McGuiness, D.L.: Ontology development 101: a guide to creating your first ontology. Technical report SMI-2001-0880 (2001)
35. Breitman, K.K., Leite, J.C.S.P.: Ontology as a requirements engineering product. In: Proceedings of 11th IEEE International Requirements Engineering Conference. IEEE Computer Society (2003)
36. Partridge, C.: The role of ontology in semantic integration. In: 2nd Workshop on the Semantics of Enterprise Integration, OOPSLA, pp. 1–10 (2002)
37. Kilpelainen, T.: Genre and ontologies based business information architecture framework (GOBIAF). Master's thesis, University of Jyvaskyla, Finland (2007)
38. Pascot, D., Bouslama, F., Mellouli, S.: Architecturing large integrated complex information systems: an application to healthcare. Knowl. Inf. Syst. **27**(1), 115–140 (2011)
39. Grunninger, M.: Enterprise modelling. In: Bernus, P., Nemes, L., Schmidt, G. (eds.) Handbook on Enterprise Architecture. International Handbooks on Information Systems, pp. 515–541. Springer, Heidelberg (2003)
40. Wand, Y., Weber, R.: An ontological model of an information system. IEEE Trans. Softw. Eng. **16**(11), 1282–1292 (1990)
41. Doerr, M., Hunter, J., Lagoze, C.: Towards a core ontology for information integration. J. Digit. Inf. **4**(1), 1–22 (2003)
42. Bunge, M.: Treatise on Basic Philosophy: Ontology I: The Furniture of the World. Springer, D. Reidel, Netherlands (1977)

43. Bunge, M.: Treatise on Basic Philosophy: Ontology II A World of Systems. D. Reidel, Dordrecht (1979)

44. Wand, Y.: 21. In: A Proposal for a Model of Objects, pp. 537–559. Addison-Wesley, Reading (1989)

45. Evermann, J., Wand, Y.: Ontology based object-oriented domain modelling: fundamental concepts. Requir. Eng. **10**, 146–160 (2005)

46. Guarino, N., Oberle, D., Staab, S.: 1. In: What is an Ontology?, 2nd edn. Springer, Heidelberg (2009)

47. Allen, G.A., March, S.T.: A critical assessment of the bunge-wand-weber ontology for conceptual modeling. In: Workshop on Information Technologies and Systems, Milwaukee, WI, 9–10 December 2006, pp. 1–6

48. Sowa, J.F.: Knowledge Representation: Logical, Philosophical and Computational Foundations. Brooks/Cole, Pacific Grove (2000)

49. Dettinger, R.D., Stevens, R.J., Tenner, J.W.: Method and system for processing abstract derived entities defined in a data abstraction model. US Patent US2006/0020582 A1, 26 January 2006

50. Fisher, M.: 1. In: Developing an Information Model for Information- and Knowledge-based Organisations. Facet Publishing, London (2004)

51. Ould, M.A.: Business Process Management: A Rigorous Approach. British Computer Society, Swindon (2005)

52. Yousef, R., Odeh, M., Coward, D., Sharieh, A.: BPAOntoSOA: a generic framework to derive software service oriented models from business process architectures. In: Second International Conference on Applications of Digital Information and Web Technologies, 2009. ICADIWT '09, London, UK, pp. 50–55 (2009)

53. Yousef, R., Odeh, M., Coward, D., Sharieh, A.: Translating RAD business process models into BPMN models: a semi-formal approach. Int. J. Web Appl. **3**(4), 187–196 (2011)

54. Horrocks, I., Patel-Schneider, P., Boley, H., Tabet, S., Grosof, B. N., Dean, M.: SWRL: a semantic web rule language combining OWL and RuleML. http://www.w3.org/Submission/SWRL/, May 2004

55. Ceusters, W., Smith, B., Goldberg, L.: A terminological and ontological analysis of the NCI thesaurus. Methods Inf. Med. **44**, 498–507 (2005)

56. Cocos, C., Brochhausen, M., Bonsma, E., Martin, L.: Design principles of the ACGT master ontology: examples and discussion. Technical report Deliverable 7. 7, UPM, Madrid, Spain (2008)

57. Aburub, F.A., Odeh, M., Beeson, I., Pheby, D., Codling, D.: Modeling healthcare processes using role activity diagramming. Int. J. Model. Simul. **28**(2), 147–155 (2008)

Author Index